The faith EXPLAINED TODAY

Nihil obstat	Reverend Father Pelin T. D'Souza Censor
Imprimatur	His Grace + Raphael Ndingi Mwana 'a Nzeki Archbishop of Nairobi October 28, 2006, Feast of Sts. Simon & Jude

Published by Scepter Publishers, Inc.

www.scepterpublishers.org

Cover and text design by Rose Design

Printed in the United States of America

ISBN: 978-1-59417-215-1

The faith EXPLAINED TODAY

Joe Babendreier

From the sixth hour there was darkness over all the land until the ninth hour. And about the ninth hour, Jesus cried out in a loud voice. "Eli, Eli, lama sabachthani"; that is "My God, My God, why have you deserted me?" When some of those who stood there heard this, they said, "The man is calling on Elijah," and one of them quickly ran to get a sponge which he dipped in vinegar and, putting it on a reed, gave it to him to drink. "Wait!" said the rest of them, "and see whether Elijah will come to save him." But Jesus, again crying out in a loud voice, yielded up his spirit. At that, the veil of the temple was torn in two from top to bottom; the earth quaked; the rocks were split; the tombs opened and the bodies of holy men rose from the dead, and these, after his resurrection, came out of the tombs, entered the Holy City and appeared to a number of people. Meanwhile the centurion, together with the others guarding Jesus, had seen the earthquake and all that was taking place, and they were terrified and said, "In truth this was a son of God."

MATTHEW 27:45–54

Contents

Part Four: The Way Christians Worship

Part Five: The Human Person

Part Six: The Way Christians Pray

Introduction

God wants to reveal himself to you. God has a plan for you. You were born for a purpose.

When you study religion, you discover the way God chose to reveal himself. You study God's plan for mankind. As you come to understand God's plan for creation, you come to understand your place in that plan. As you learn how God began to reveal himself long ago, you come to understand how God wants to reveal himself to you now.

This book will help you study what God revealed through Jesus Christ, as the Church has believed it, preserved it, and treasured it from the beginning. It is an attempt to explain what the Church has been teaching for the last two thousand years. The Church began to teach first through St. Peter and the Apostles. She has continued to teach through their successors, namely St. Peter's successor and the successors of the other Apostles—the men we call the Pope and the bishops.

The message

If the message of this book could be summarized in one sentence, it would be this: We come to know everything there is to know about God by coming to know Jesus personally. This book summarizes the Church's teaching. But learning about God's revelation goes far beyond knowing what the Church teaches. More than knowing facts, you need to know Jesus. You need to know him the same way you know your parents, your brothers and sisters, or your best friend.

One of the greatest saints said:

> I have been crucified with Christ; it is no longer I who live, but Christ who lives in me.
>
> Galatians 2:20

St. Paul wrote this. This is the way he lived. This is the way God wants everyone to live. This is the goal—to have Jesus living within you.

Two worlds

There are two worlds. There is this world and there is the next world. In this world, good and evil are mixed together. In the next world, God will separate good and evil. In this world, it is difficult for us to distinguish between good and evil—at least it is hard to do it accurately all the time. And it is hard to figure out where all the evil comes from. It is also hard to figure out where all the good comes from. Both the good and the evil are mysteries. Both this world and the next world are mysteries. The mixture of good and evil that you experience every day makes this world mysterious, that is, hard to understand.

The first step towards understanding good and evil in this world is to start with yourself. You have lots of good inside of you. You have lots of evil inside of you. You were born that way. This makes your life a mystery.

Jesus is your Savior. This means many things. Above all else, it means that he—and he alone—has the power to get rid of the evil inside you. Only he can make you completely good once and for all.

SACRED SCRIPTURE

Since you have been brought back to true life with Christ, you must look for the things that are in heaven, where Christ is, sitting at God's right hand. Let your thoughts be on heavenly things, not on the things that are on the earth, because you have died, and now the life you have is hidden with Christ in God. But when Christ is revealed—and he is your life—you too will be revealed in all your glory with him.

Colossians 3:1–4

One of the ways in which Jesus does this involves showing you what's inside you. Once you see it, he asks you to work together with him to build up all that is good and eliminate all that is evil. If you do this, you will be ready when the time comes for him to separate good and evil in the next world. You will stay with Jesus forever. Everything you experience will be good, forever and ever. If you deliberately and willingly allow evil a place in your heart, you are in deep trouble, unless you change. If you don't change, then, in the next world, you will know nothing but evil, forever and ever.

Part One

What Christians Believe

1.

God

God is the Creator. He created all things out of nothing. He alone needs no one to make him exist.

God is Lord. He rules over all creation. He has a plan for creation. His plan will be completed at the end of time.

Looking at the beauty and the order of the world, people of all times and places have concluded that the Creator of all this must be wise and powerful. Because God appeared to Abraham, to Moses, and to the prophets, the Jews knew more about the Creator than any other nation. When God sent his only Son, our Lord Jesus Christ, we came to know much more. When Jesus returns the second time, he will complete God's plan and God's revelation.

Divine nature

God is free. He does whatever he wants. He does it the way he wants. When we rebel, even our rebellion fits into his plan. He does not want us to rebel, but he foresees it. In his plan, we are also free; we choose to obey or rebel.

God is wise. He alone sees the whole of creation in one glance from beginning to end. No one can judge his actions.

God is infinite. He has no limitations. No one can comprehend all his perfection. God is immutable. He never changes. No one can do anything to change him. God is immense. He is greater than all possible universes combined. Nothing can be used to measure his greatness.

God is simple. God is one. He is a single, perfect being. He has no parts. He has no competition. God is eternal. He is the beginning and the end. He has no history. He has no future. He lives outside of time. The past is always present to him. The future is always present to him.

God is all-knowing. He alone knows himself perfectly. He alone knows every detail of the past, the present, and the future with infallible precision.

God is all-present. He is everywhere. He reaches every creature not only from outside but also from the inside. God is all-powerful. The most powerful creature is a small and helpless being that cannot breathe a single breath without depending completely on God.

God is holy. Nothing evil can touch him, influence him, or tempt him. God is good. Everything is good because he made it good. Our rebellion against God is the only reason evil exists. God is light. There is no darkness in him at all. God is life. Death has no power over him.

God is merciful. He forgives sinners. No sin is too great for him to forgive as long as we are sorry. God is just. Although we suffer in this life to purify ourselves from sin, he will not allow us to be overcome by evil if we place our hope in him.

God is supreme majesty. We are less than dust in his presence. God is absolute. He does not need his creatures. He would still be infinitely perfect even if he had never created anything. He has no point of reference. No comparison can explain all that he is. I AM is God's most perfect name. He is pure being. His very essence is *to be*.

God is beyond our notions of God

These are some of God's characteristics. We use them to define what God is like. No matter how thorough we are when listing the wonders that describe God, we say little. He is so far above us that we cannot begin to imagine the distance between God and creation. It is truly an infinite distance. To express this reality, we use the word "transcendence."

Sacred Scripture

See what love the Father has given us, that we should be called children of God; and so we are. The reason why the world does not know us is that it did not know him. Beloved, we are God's children now; it does not yet appear what we shall be, but we know that when he appears we shall be like him, for we shall see him as he is.

1 John 3:1–2

God transcends time and space. God transcends the whole of creation. No matter how much everything changes, it never affects him. This does not mean he remains aloof. He loves us. He loves us so much that he sent his Son to be our Savior.

> Do not be deceived, my beloved brethren. Every good endowment and every perfect gift is from above, coming down from the Father of lights with whom there is no variation or shadow due to change. Of his own will he brought us forth by the word of truth that we should be a kind of first fruits of his creatures.
>
> James 1:16–18

Mistaken notions about God

Many different notions have been used to describe God. Not all are correct. The following notions are the errors. Since these notions can be dressed up in different disguises, it is important to recognize them when you hear them. Because they are false and yet widespread, they have done great harm to many people.

- ***Polytheism or paganism:*** There are many gods and goddesses. They are immortal but look like human beings or animals or other creatures. Each one of these gods rules over that portion of the universe he or she created.
- ***Deism:*** God lives far away in his own perfect world. He pays no attention to what happens to us. Like a rich man in a palace who never cares what happens to the poor, God is happy in heaven even though we are suffering on earth. God is like a watchmaker who made a clock, set it running, and then forgot about it.
- ***Pantheism:*** Everything is God. We are God. God is the final result, the total combination, of all things existing together in harmony.
- ***Atheism:*** There is no God. No higher being created the universe. Everything simply is. The universe has no cause. The universe has no purpose. Life has whatever meaning we choose to give it. Believing in God is a waste of time. Religion often causes harm because all faith is a lie.

- ***Agnosticism:*** We are incapable of knowing anything about God. It is fine for someone to believe in God. For all we know, God may exist. But faith must remain private because we have no way of knowing whether any of our beliefs are true.
- ***Naturalism:*** Nature is the beginning and the end of all things. The laws that govern the order of the universe explain everything there is to know about the universe. No higher being made these laws. They simply exist as they always have existed and always will exist. Atheism, agnosticism, and naturalism tend to go together.
- ***Indifferentism:*** All religions are the same. They all worship the Creator but none of them can tell us the whole truth about God. They all have an element of truth, but it is impossible to know which parts are true and which parts are false. The best approach is to pick and choose from different religions and come up with a way of life that suits your personal needs.

All these errors share one thing in common. They contradict the mysteries God has revealed through Jesus Christ. It is not difficult to know the truth about God. He has revealed himself to us. If you seek this revelation, if you listen to it, study it, and accept it, then you will come closer to knowing everything about God.

God and the Word of God

"In the beginning . . ." These are the first words of the Bible. When the Bible talks about the beginning, it talks about the eternity where God lived before he created the universe. "In the beginning . . ." These are also the first words in St. John's Gospel. St. John asks us to go back to the beginning. That is the only way to understand God.

St. John tells us about the way God lived before he created the universe. ("Before" is a manner of speaking. With God there is no before; there is no after.) St. John talks about that unimaginable moment of eternity "before" there was a heaven and earth. He is talking about a "time" before God created time.

> In the beginning was the Word, and the Word was with God, and the Word was God.
>
> John 1:1

In the beginning, there was a person called the "Word." He existed before creation. This person—this Word—is mysterious. He has several names in the Bible. The Word is also called "Son" because he is the Son of God. When he became a man, we started calling him "Jesus."

St. John talks about the beginning because he wants us to understand something about this person *as he existed before the creation of the universe*. What was the Word like before we started calling him "Jesus"? What was he like in the beginning?

The Word was "with God" in the beginning. Here "God" refers to God the Father. The Word is his Son. Before creating anything, God the Father lived together with his Son. From the beginning, God's plan was to send his Son into the world and call him "Jesus."

Fathers of the Church

We shall see God. Now, this will be so great—yes, so great a thing will it be—that in comparison to it, all the rest is nothing.

St. Augustine, *Sermon* 127, 8

The Gospel tells us what God was like before he created anything. It describes God as he always was, always is, and always will be. It tells us that God is Father and Son.

St. John's text transmits to us a revelation from God. We know that God is Father and Son only because God decided to reveal it. In other words, it is a mystery. We know all this about God because God revealed it. Otherwise, we would not know that he is Father and Son.

In God there is one person who generates life, called "Father." There is another person who receives this life, called "Son." The Son really and truly *comes from* the Father. In God there is one person who knows (Father) and one person who is known (Son). Because the Father knows the Son, the Son is called the "Word of God."

The Father is God and the Son is God. They are not two different gods. There is only one God. The Son is equal to the Father. If you understand this, then you are beginning to understand the most mysterious truth about God. God the Father and God the Son have always been together—even before the world was created. They will always be together. They cannot be separated.

The Holy Spirit

The Bible speaks about a third person who is God. His name is the Holy Spirit.

The Father is God. The Son is God. The Holy Spirit is God. And yet there is only one God. The Father and the Son are united together in the Holy Spirit as one single being.

The *Catechism of the Catholic Church* teaches:

> God's very being is love. By sending his only Son and the Spirit of Love in the fullness of time, God has revealed his innermost secret: God himself is an exchange of love, Father, Son, and Holy Spirit; and he has destined us to share in that exchange.
>
> *CCC*, n. 221

The Holy Spirit is like a river of love flowing back and forth between the Father and Son. As St. John says: "God is love" (1 Jn 4:8). This infinitely powerful being wants you to be immersed in that river of love. That is what the *Catechism* means when it says you are destined to *share* in the *exchange* of love between Father and Son.

> **MAGISTERIUM**
>
> The Father sent his Son, the eternal Word who enlightens all people, to dwell among us and to tell us about the inner life of God.
>
> Vatican II, *Dogmatic Constitution on Divine Revelation*, n. 4

God wants to pour love into your heart. Jesus said:

> "If any one thirst, let him come to me and drink. He who believes in me, as the scripture has said, 'Out of his heart shall flow rivers of living water.'"
>
> John 7:37–38

Any man or woman who turns to Jesus and believes in him can receive this gift. God will pour out the Holy Spirit like a fountain of fresh water. When the Father and Son send the Holy Spirit into your heart, they are allowing you to share in their love.

God created everything through the Word and the Spirit

God the Father Almighty created heaven and earth. But the Father never does anything without the Son and the Spirit. The Father created *through* his Son and his Spirit. The Father used the Son and the Spirit in order to create the universe. Quoting St. Irenaeus, the *Catechism* puts it this way:

> The Father made all things by himself, that is, by his Word and by his Wisdom, by the Son and the Spirit, who, so to speak, are his hands.
>
> St. Irenaeus, cf. *CCC*, n. 292

What we mean by "mystery"

The life of the Father, Son, and Holy Spirit is a mystery. We will never come to understand it completely. It is beyond our imagination and beyond our intelligence. God decided to reveal this mystery to man. Revelation is the only reason we know about it. If God had not revealed this mystery, we would never know it.

The most amazing fact of all human history is that God revealed himself to us. One of the Old Testament psalms asks: "What is man that thou art mindful of him, and the son of man that thou dost care for him?" (Ps 8:4) It is extraordinary that God has decided to tell us everything about himself. We don't have any right to know about God's intimate life. There's more. Not only did God decide to tell us about his life as Father, Son, and Holy Spirit. He decided to reveal this mystery by doing two amazing things. First he sent his Son to become one of us. Then he sent the Holy Spirit to make us sons and daughters of God.

The Father reveals everything through his Son and his Spirit

God began to reveal himself first to Adam and Eve and then through other men and women in later ages.

> In many and various ways God spoke of old to our fathers by the prophets, but in these last days he has spoken to us by a Son, whom he appointed the heir of all things, through whom also he created the world.
>
> Hebrews 1:1–2

The Father sent first his Son and then his Spirit to reveal himself to us.

When it came time for God to send the Savior who would crush the head of Satan, God the Father sent his Son. St. John's Gospel says:

> And the Word became flesh and dwelt among us, full of grace and truth; we have beheld his glory, glory as of the only Son from the Father.
>
> John 1:14

Jesus is the Word made flesh. Jesus is God's only-begotten Son. Jesus is God made man.

The Son came down from heaven by becoming a man. He became a man in an event the Church calls the "Incarnation." In-*car*-nation comes from *caro*, the Latin word for "flesh." To "incarnate" means to become flesh. God's Son became incarnate—i.e., he became flesh.

The Father sent his Son to save us. He also sent his Son to tell us about God. Jesus came to tell us that he is God's only Son. He came to tell us that the Father loves us and wants us to become sons and daughters of God. Only those who open their minds and hearts to the Holy Spirit can accept this mystery.

Wisdom of the Saints

O immeasurably tender love! Who would not be set on fire with such love? What heart could keep from melting? . . . It seems you are so madly in love with your creatures that you could not live without us! Yet you are our God, and have no need of us.

St. Catherine of Siena, *The Dialogue*, n. 25

Just as God *created* everything through the Son and the Spirit, God *reveals* everything through the Son and the Spirit. It is only through the Son and the Holy Spirit that you can be saved.

Father and Son sending the Spirit

When Jesus was on earth, he spoke to his closest friends about the Holy Spirit. He made it clear that the Spirit is equal to the Father and Son. Then he told them about the coming of the Holy Spirit.

Jesus said he was going to send the Holy Spirit to his disciples and that the Spirit would remain with them forever.

> And I will pray the Father, and he will give you another Counselor, to be with you for ever, even the Spirit of truth, whom the world cannot receive, because it neither sees him nor knows him; you know him, for he dwells with you, and will be in you.
>
> But when the Counselor comes, whom I shall send to you from the Father, even the Spirit of truth, who proceeds from the Father, he will bear witness to me . . .
>
> John 14:16–17; 15:26

The Holy Spirit is called the "Advocate" or "Paraclete" (which means Consoler). He begins to live within us once we are baptized.

First God sent his Son. He asked his Son to sacrifice himself on the cross to save us from our sins. After Jesus rose from the dead, he ascended into heaven. He was seated at the right hand of the Father. Then the Father and Son sent the Holy Spirit.

Becoming children of God

We can be freed from slavery to sin by welcoming Jesus into our heart. We are free to accept him. We are also free not to accept him. St. John explains:

> He came to his own home, and his own people received him not. But to all who received him, who believed in his name, he gave power to become children of God;
>
> John 1:11–12

Once we believe in Jesus and dedicate our lives to him, he gives us power. It is a gentle power—a power to be children. We receive this power as soon as we are baptized.

This is not power in any earthly sense. It is God's power, not man's power. It is a power to love God and to love one another. We get this power when the Holy Spirit changes us into God's children.

What does it mean to be God's children? It means becoming like him and God is love. We become like God—we become like this infinite, loving being—when he gives us grace. Jesus asks us to believe this. St. Paul says:

> Therefore, since we are justified by faith, we have peace with God through our Lord Jesus Christ. Through him we have obtained access to this grace in which we stand, and we rejoice in our hope of sharing the glory of God. . . . And hope does not disappoint us, because God's love has been poured into our hearts through the Holy Spirit which has been given to us.
>
> Romans 5:1–2, 5

God does not reveal mysteries for the sake of mystery. He wants to share his love with us. It is good to study about God. But getting to know him requires more than just reading. If you want to get to know God and love him, you have to talk to him. Still, clarifying these ideas may help you avoid the mistakes that have kept others from getting to know God and being one of his children.

Review Questions

1. Explain the common errors about God.
2. Explain what we mean by mystery.
3. Where can you get the power to be like God? What does that power do to you?
4. How can you be filled with the Holy Spirit and live as a child of God?

2.

God Creates the World

From the beginning of recorded history, people have been looking at the world and asking: Where does it all come from?

The very first words of the Bible state:

> In the beginning God created the heavens and the earth.
>
> Genesis 1:1

God created all things—all the things we see and all the things that we cannot see.

The text then goes on to talk about the "six days" of creation. Each day is dedicated to one of God's acts of creation. On the first day, God says, "Let there be light!" On the sixth day, God creates man. On the seventh day, he rests. Why did the holy writer choose to divide creation into seven days? He wanted to emphasize how all things exist only because God brought them into existence.

Ancient man could see seven heavenly lights forever changing their position against a background of fixed stars. Men came up with the idea of naming a day for each one. They thought they were gods. We have stuck to a seven-day week ever since, using more or less the same names: Sunday for the sun and Monday for the moon. Saturday is for Saturn. In English speaking countries, we use the Anglo-Saxon names of the other visible planets. The Old English equivalents for Mars, Mercury, Jupiter, and Venus are Tiw, Oden, Thor, and Freya. Add the possessive "s" and you get Tiwsday (Tuesday), Odensday (Wednesday), Thorsday (Thursday), and Freyasday (Friday).

Instead of using the pagan names for the days of the week, the Jews used numbers. Sabbath, for instance, is simply the Hebrew word for the number seven. It corresponds to our Saturday, the last day of the week. God rested on the Sabbath, that is, the seventh day.

The Holy Spirit inspired the holy writer when he wrote. He reversed the custom of dedicating each day to a pagan god and instead dedicated each day of the week to an act of the one true God. He showed how God created all things—even the lights in the sky that other nations worshipped as gods.

God creates angels

Besides creating things visible to us, God created spiritual beings we cannot see. The Israelites knew about these spirits and called them "angels." The word "angel" means messenger. Many biblical texts describe them as messengers that God uses to reveal his plans to man.

Angels appear frequently throughout the Bible, especially in the New Testament. Jesus himself referred to the guardian angels (Mt 18:10). Angels announce the birth of St. John the Baptist and then the birth of Jesus (Mt 1:20; Lk 1:11, 26, 2:13). At every major moment in the history of salvation, angels appear. Describing the end of time, the Book of Revelation explains how angels work together with God. Repeating a text from the Book of Daniel, it says that "ten thousand times

Sacred Scripture

For it is always in thy power to show great strength, and who can withstand the might of thy arm? Because the whole world before thee is like a speck that tips the scales, and like a drop of morning dew that falls upon the ground. But thou art merciful to all, for thou canst do all things, and thou dost overlook men's sins, that they may repent. For thou lovest all things that exist, and hast loathing for none of the things which thou hast made, for thou wouldst not have made anything if thou hadst hated it. How would anything have endured if thou hadst not willed it? Or how would anything not called forth by thee have been preserved? Thou sparest all things, for they are thine, O Lord who lovest the living.

Wisdom 11:21–26

ten thousand angels" are gathered around God's throne in heaven (cf. Rev 5:11).

The Bible speaks about the physical appearances of angels. These references describe the way angels can appear to us. An angel has power to use matter in different ways. He can appear to us using a human figure or in some other way. But sacred Scripture calls them "spirits": God "makes his angels winds and his servants flames of fire" (Heb 1:7). The holy writers use these terms—wind and flame—to convey the idea that angels have no bodies.

At some point in the beginning, one of the angels rebelled against God. Many other angels followed him. This evil one has many names in the Bible: Devil, or the divider (Rev 20:2); Abaddon, or Perdition (Job 26:6); tempter (Mt 4:3 / 1 Thess 3:5); Asmodeus, or worst of demons (Tob 3:8); angel of the abyss and Apollyon, or exterminator (Rev 9:11); prince of demons (Mt 9:34); ruler of this world (Jn 16:11); ruler of world darkness (Eph 6:12); father of lies (Jn 8:44); Beelzebul, or Lord of the flies (Mt 12:24); Beliar, or useless one (2 Cor 6:15). The name that seems to fit this angel best is "Satan," the adversary who accuses (Job 1:6 / Rev 20:2).

Satan has often accused man of being evil. This is deeply mysterious to us. Why would an angel, created to work together with God to make us happy, turn against both God and man? While we cannot answer this question, Satan's rebellion confirms that angels are free. The Church teaches:

> As creatures of a spiritual nature, the angels are endowed with intellect and free will, like human beings, but in a degree superior to us . . . The angels are therefore personal beings and, as such, are also "in the image and likeness" of God. Sacred Scripture refers to the angels by using terms that are not only personal (like the proper names of Raphael, Gabriel, and Michael) but also collective (like the titles seraphim, cherubim, thrones, powers, dominations, principalities), just as it distinguishes between angels and archangels.
>
> St. John Paul II, *Catechesis on the Creed*, Vol I, p. 302

Based on the witness of the Gospel, the Church believes that God assigns everyone a guardian angel. St. Basil the Great, one of the Church Fathers, wrote:

> Every one of the faithful has beside him an angel as tutor and pastor, to guide him to life.
>
> St. Basil, cf. *Catechesis on the Creed,* Vol I, p. 305

You can talk to your guardian angel and ask him to help you. His mission is to help you to become a holy person. He can do many things for you—even simple things like reminding you to pray at your usual time for prayer.

How did God create?

At times we talk about artists being "creative." They have a special talent to put together a work of art. Artists do this with sculptures, paintings, music, dance, poetry, drama—sometimes mixing media electronically to produce amazing combinations. When God creates, he does something even more spectacular.

God is outside of creation. He is not a creature. No one made him. Nor did he have to create himself. He simply *is.* He needs no cause to explain how he came to be. He is being itself. No artist in this world can say that about himself. Not even angels can say such a thing. They are also creatures. Without God, they would not exist.

> **FATHERS OF THE CHURCH**
>
> Living man is the glory of God, but man's life consists in vision of God.
>
> St. Irenaeus, *Against Heresies,* IV, 20, 7

There is another reason why God's act of creation is different from that of artists. To create, God did not take things that already existed and put them together in some new form. Instead, he created all things out of nothing. He did not start with something rough and make it look better. He started with nothing and made everything. The Church teaches:

> We read in the Letter to the Romans Abraham believed in God, "who gives life to the dead and calls into existence the things that do not exist." (Rom 4:17). "Creation" therefore means: to make from nothing, to call into existence, that is, to form a being from nothing.
>
> St. John Paul II, *Catechesis on the Creed,* Vol I, p. 201

There is an infinite "distance" between something and nothing. It requires infinite power to create something out of nothing. Only God has this infinite power.

Some people have the mistaken notion that God somehow appeared in the middle of empty space at the beginning of time and created everything. When God created, he created everything—literally everything—out of nothing. He created time and space out of nothing. Without God's act of creation, there would be nothing—no things at all. There would be no time. There would be no space. There would be no laws of nature. There would be no nature. Only God would exist.

When we say "universe," we do not limit ourselves to what scientists call the universe, that is, the cosmos with its billions of galaxies. There are other worlds that we cannot see. For instance, God has revealed that there is a heaven and hell—what Jesus often called the "next world." All of this forms part of the "universe" that God created.

Creation reveals God's glory

"The heavens are telling the glory of God" (Ps 19:1). We get some idea of how great God is when we look at the beauty of creation. Creation is God's first revelation. We see the beauty of creatures. We see the order in the universe. We see the grades of perfection leading from the lowest to the highest—from rocks to stars, from plants to animals, from men to angels. All this gives us an idea of how much more beautiful and perfect God must be.

The prophets often spoke of giving glory to God: "Give glory to the LORD your God" (Jer 13:16). God created us to give him glory. This does not mean that he needs us so that he would have someone to praise him. He does not need our praise. Why do we have to give him glory? Perhaps the best answer was the one Jesus gave the Pharisees, when they got upset at the way his disciples were praising him. "I tell you, if these were silent, the very stones would cry out," he said (Lk 19:40). Once we see how great God is, praise bursts out of our hearts spontaneously.

We only realize how great Michelangelo was when we see one of his works of art, e.g., the painting of the Last Judgment in the Sistine

Magisterium

Together with all that sacred Scripture says in different places about the work of creation and about God the Creator, this description enables us to set out certain elements in relief:

1. God created the world by himself. His creative power cannot be transmitted to others.
2. God freely created the world, without any exterior compulsion or interior obligation. He could create or not create. He could create this world or another one.
3. The world was created by God with a beginning; therefore, it is not eternal. It has a beginning in time.
4. The world created by God is constantly maintained in existence by the Creator. This "maintenance" is, in a certain sense, a continual creation.

St. John Paul II, *Catechesis on the Creed*, Vol I, p. 205

Chapel. Something similar happens in God's work of creation. We cannot see how great God is by looking at him. He is invisible. We begin to grasp how great he is when we see his works. More than looking at how beautiful the stars and flowers are, we have to look at how wonderful we are. St. Paul wrote:

> For we are his workmanship, created in Christ Jesus for good works, which God prepared beforehand, that we should walk in them.
>
> Ephesians 2:10

We are God's masterpiece. And yet, we only give glory to God if we do his will. When we rebel against God, instead of looking like a masterpiece, we look like a mistake. To give glory to God, we need to work together with him, doing everything he asks us to do.

God creates with love

There is a scene in the Gospel where Jesus has a long conversation with a rich young man.

> And as he was setting out on his journey, a man ran up and knelt before him, and asked him, "Good Teacher, what must I do to inherit eternal

> life?" And Jesus said to him, "Why do you call me good? No one is good but God alone.
>
> Mark 10:17–18

The young man did not know that Jesus was the Son of God. Jesus did not want anyone to call him "good" because he was a nice man who did lots of nice things. He would only allow others to call him "good" if they recognized that he was God. This is a reminder that all good things come from God. The Church teaches:

> Christ replies to the young man in the Gospel. He says: "No one is good but God alone." . . . Why is God alone good? Because he is love. Christ gives this answer in the words of the Gospel, and above all by the witness of his own life and death: "For God so loved the world that he gave his only Son." God is good precisely because he "is love."
>
> St. John Paul II, *To the Youth of the World*, n. 4

God is infinite being. God is infinite love. He creates not because he has to but because he wants to. He creates us so we can share in his infinite being. He creates us so we can share in his infinite love. We were created by love. We were created for love.

God had a choice to create or not to create. His act of creation did not come from any need to create. Love is the only reason that can explain why God created the universe. The Church has always insisted on this fact to explain that our very being is a gift from God. God did not have to give you life. God did not have to give you all the good things you have. He gave them to you because he loves you.

When you love someone, you tend to do so because you need the other person. The other person has something that is good for you. Even the noblest human love works this way. Speaking of man, in general, the Church teaches:

> He cannot always give, he must also receive. Anyone who wishes to give love must also receive love as a gift.
>
> Benedict XVI, *God Is Love*, n. 7

When a man and woman fall in love, they look at each other with eyes that say: "You are good for me. I need you." The relationship should never be reduced to the satisfaction of personal needs—where the man *uses* the woman to satisfy his needs or the woman *uses* the man to satisfy her needs—because that destroys love. And yet the man and woman really do need each other. They love when each one becomes consumed with satisfying the needs of the other. But even then they must be open to receiving love because each one needs the other.

Like God, we love by giving. As we will see in more detail later, love consists in giving one's very self completely. God's way of giving is infinitely perfect.

The diagram below is a simplified representation of the Holy Trinity. The Father "begets" because he knows. The Son is the Word (cf. Jn 1:1). He is "begotten" because he is known. The Father is lover and the Son is the beloved: "This is my beloved Son," the Father says when Jesus is baptized (Mt 3:17).

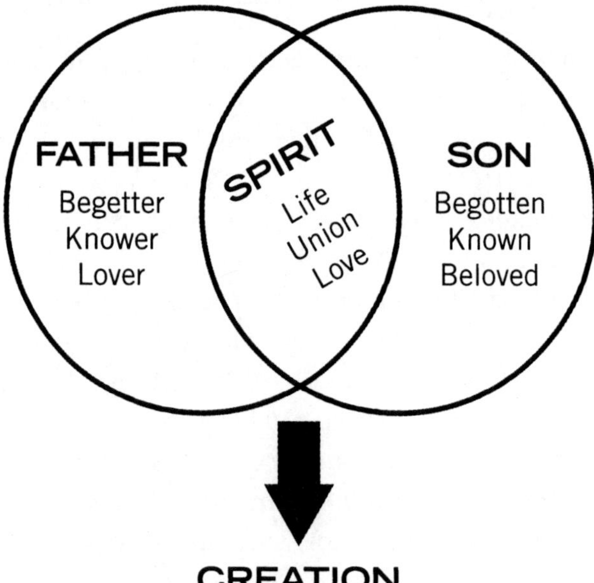

This representation also shows the Holy Spirit. He is the third person of the Trinity. The Father lives in the Son and the Son lives in the Father. The two are one with each other. The Holy Spirit is the union of Father and Son. He is the infinite love between Father and Son. Creation comes from this love of Father for Son and Son for Father.

> God alone is the most perfectly liberal giver, because he does not act for his own profit, but only for his own goodness.
>
> St. Thomas Aquinas, *Summa Theologiae*, I, 44, 4

God is so liberal—so utterly free—that he gives without needing anything in return. Nothing in creation will ever satisfy any of God's "needs." God is infinitely perfect. He has no needs of any kind whatsoever.

This raises a question. In what sense does creation come from God's love? To answer this, we have to go back to the mystery of the Trinity and remember how God the Father creates the universe through his Son, the two acting in total union with one another in the Holy Spirit.

The Father and Son love each other. Their love for each other is the Holy Spirit. Creation springs forth from this divine person who is life-giving Love. Creation is a gift made possible by this divine person who is Uncreated Gift. Based on the Scriptures that narrate God's act of creation, the Church teaches:

> In the beginning God created heaven and earth—the universe—and "the Spirit of God was moving over the face of the waters" (Gen 1:2). Evocative though vague, this reference to the action of the Spirit . . . appears significant. . . . The world is created in that Love, which is the Spirit of the Father and of the Son. Embraced by eternal Love, this universe begins to exist in the instant chosen by the Trinity as the beginning of time.
>
> In this way the creation of the world is the work of Love. The universe is a created gift that springs forth from the Uncreated Gift—from the reciprocal Love of the Father and Son, from the Most Holy Trinity.
>
> St. John Paul II, *Catechesis on the Creed*, Vol I, p. 211

The Holy Spirit is Love because he is the union of the Father and Son. This Love is the "reason" why the Father and Son create. This Love is the "place" where they carry out their act of creation. This Is Love is the "power" they use to create all things out of nothing.

Some people doubt this mystery when they look at all the evil in the world. They say, "Look at all the bad things happening to good people. Look at all the babies who suffer. Look at all the poor who live in misery.

How can so much evil come from love?" If you have experienced any of that evil yourself, you may find it hard to believe that creation springs forth from God's love.

Oddly enough, our power to love and to give life is the answer to this objection. It is the answer because this freedom includes the opposite ability, that is, the power to hate and to destroy.

The problem of evil

Let's go back to the analogy between God and the artist. A perfect painter could paint a painting of a maggot eating the flesh of a rotten corpse. If it was an exact representation, it would convey horror and disgust. But only a pervert would find it attractive. The perfect painter shows the most talent by choosing to portray beauty. This is exactly what God chose to do. First he chose his own beauty as the model. Then he created a creature that was an image and likeness of himself. Man reflects God's infinite beauty.

Man shows us how perfect God is on two accounts. First, we glimpse God's perfection by looking at man. Secondly, we glimpse God's "artistic talent." Who else could make visible what is inherently invisible?

Since God is love, we can only reflect his beauty by loving him and loving one another. But to love, we have to be free. So God made us free. This meant taking a risk. If he wanted to make us free, he had to leave creation in our hands and give us the power to do whatever we wanted to do with it.

Wisdom of the Saints

St. Paul tells us that the hidden things of God can be "clearly perceived in the things that have been made" (Rom 1:20). If what he says is true, then it must be possible to use human reason to prove that God exists.

St. Thomas Aquinas,
Summa Theologiae, I, 2, 2

God created creatures who were free to choose. He created angels—spirits who are free to choose. He created us—creatures of body and soul that are also free to choose. Among both men and angels, some choose to love and to give life. Among both men and angels, some choose to hate and to destroy life.

In the beginning, there was no evil. To convey the perfection of all God's creatures, Genesis describes how God judged creation once it was finished:

> And God saw everything that he had made, and behold, it was very good.
>
> Genesis 1:31

When God created, he made everything good—and not only good but *very good.* Even Satan himself was good in the beginning. He became evil later only because he deliberately chose to rebel against God. He became so evil that he is the evil one. He became evil because he refused to love anyone else except himself. He became hopelessly selfish.

All the evil present in the world today begins with Satan's rebellion against God. At the end of the world, God will solve the problem of evil once and for all. He will separate those who want to love and to give life from those who prefer to be selfish and destroy life. He will take those who love life into his kingdom. He will send the others off to hell forever to live with the evil one.

Review Questions

1. Explain God's act of creating.
2. What do we know about angels?
3. How can we give glory to God?
4. How do we explain the existence of evil?

3.

God Creates Man

The Bible offers two different accounts on how God created the universe. Both focus on God creating man.*

The first chapter of *Genesis* divides God's action into six days. After describing the creation of light and darkness, sun and moon, earth and sea, birds and fish, cattle and wild beasts, God looks at everything and sees how good it is. He is pleased, but he wants something better—something special. He wants to create man. He pauses, or rather, *they* pause. There is a hint of Father, Son, and Holy Spirit having a conversation. God speaks with the plural "we," saying: "Let us make man in our own image, in the likeness of ourselves." Having made this awesome decision, God carries it out. The text says:

> So God created man in his own image, in the image of God he created him; male and female he created them.
>
> Genesis 1:27

"Man" is the name God chose to describe this new creature.

> When God created man, he made him in the likeness of God. Male and female he created them, and he blessed them and named them Man when they were created.
>
> Genesis 5:1–2

Here the Bible calls man the union of male and female. It also tells us that this creature is the image and likeness of God.

* Besides referring to a single male, "man" can also be used as a collective noun. The Book of Genesis uses it both ways.

Adam and Eve

First God created Adam's body "man of dust from the ground" (Gen 2:7). Then he "breathed" into this body "a breath of life." This is a metaphor. God does not have a mouth and he does not breathe. He is pure spirit. The metaphor means that the human soul—symbolized by God's breath—comes from God.

Just as the "breath of God" is a metaphor, the "dust of the earth" could also be a metaphor. Maybe Adam's body came directly from dust—the leftovers of some rocks, or something more like mud. Or maybe the "dust" is a symbol for something more complex. In either case, the point is the same. The first human body came from *something that already existed* before God put Adam's soul into it. The Bible makes a contrast between the human soul and the human body. Whereas the body (dust) comes from something God had already created, the soul (breath) is created out of nothing, coming directly from God.

The Book of Genesis also describes Eve's creation. Though surrounded by many living creatures, Adam cannot find a "companion fit for him." He is alone. God declares that it is not good for him to be alone. He puts Adam into a deep sleep and takes a rib from his side. "the rib . . . he made into a woman and brought her to the man (Gen 2:22).

The first chapter of Genesis concludes by saying that God rested after creating man. In other words, once he had created Man in his own image and likeness, God had finished creating everything he wanted to create.

God's image and likeness

The sun and the moon, the plants and the animals all have their own special beauty. Man is greater. Man is the image and likeness of the Creator. When we look at man, we are looking at a creature that shows how great God is.

We are the image and likeness of our Creator for three reasons:

1. Every man and every woman is the image and likeness of God.

Every human person conceived in the history of the world will exist for all eternity.

> For God created man for incorruption, and made him in the image of his own eternity . . .
>
> Wisdom 2:23

You are body and soul. Your soul is spiritual. Because of your soul, you continue to exist even if you die. Because of your soul, you can know truth with your intellect. Because of your soul, you can make decisions freely. This spiritual element—your soul—makes you the image and likeness of God. God knows all truth with his divine intellect; having a perfectly free will, he chooses whatever he wants. God's intellect and free will are infinitely powerful. Your intellect and free will are limited. Even so, having intellect and free will makes you God's image and likeness.

Mind and will constitute an essential difference between human beings and animals.

2. Being created male and female makes man the image and likeness of God.

The purpose of making man male and female was to create two persons who would exist *for* each other. The Church teaches that being male and female makes man similar to God:

> Man is "male and female" right from the beginning . . . Man became the image and likeness of God not only through his own humanity, but also through the communion of persons which man and woman form right from the beginning. The function of the image is to reflect the one who is the model, to

Sacred Scripture

Therefore a man leaves his father and his mother and cleaves to his wife, and they become one flesh.

Genesis 2:24

• • •

And Pharisees came up to him and tested him by asking, "Is it lawful to divorce one's wife for any cause?" He answered, "Have you not read that he who made them from the beginning made them male and female, and said, 'For this reason a man shall leave his father and mother and be joined to his wife, and the two shall become one'? So they are no longer two but one. What therefore God has joined together, let not man put asunder."

Matthew 19:3–6

reproduce its own prototype. Man becomes the image of God not so much in the moment of solitude as in the moment of communion. He is, in fact, right "from the beginning" . . . essentially an image of an inscrutable divine communion of persons.

St. John Paul II, *Theology of the Body*, p. 46

The moment of *solitude* was the moment when Adam was alone. The moment of *communion* defines the experience of Adam and Eve becoming husband and wife. Being created male and female did not make man like the animals. On the contrary, being created male and female made man the image and likeness of God. Human sexuality is different from the sexuality of the animals.

Adam and Eve are a communion of persons because they are husband and wife. The same logic applies to the marriage of any other man and woman. Every spousal union is a *communion of persons*; in other words, the man and woman exist *for each other*. Husband and wife become a communion of persons by committing themselves totally to each other. Their total belonging to each other reflects the total belonging of Father to Son and Son to Father, in the unity of the Holy Spirit.

Fathers of the Church

Through love many souls become one soul as they approach God. Through love many hearts become one heart. What about the very fountain of love in the Father and Son? Is it not still more so here that the Trinity is one God? Love comes to us from that Holy Spirit, as the Apostle says: "God's love has been poured into our hearts through the Holy Spirit which has been given to us" (Rom 5:5). If then the love of God, poured into our hearts by the Holy Spirit, makes many souls one soul and many hearts one heart, how much more are Father, Son and Holy Spirit, one God, one light and one beginning?

St. Augustine, *Treatise on John*, 35, 5

We can think of the Father, Son, and Holy Spirit as Lover, Beloved, and Love. We can also think of husband and wife as lover, beloved, and love. The two are lover and beloved, joined together by the God who is love.

Despite the enormous differences, spousal union reflects the Trinitarian union because both unions are a communion of love.

The fact that man "created as man and woman" is the image of God means not only that each of them individually is like God, as a rational

MAGISTERIUM

The ancient narrative speaks of a divine breath which is breathed into man so that he may come to life: "the LORD God formed man of dust from the ground, and breathed into his nostrils the breath of life; and man became a living being" (Gen 2:7).

The divine origin of this spirit of life explains the perennial dissatisfaction that man feels throughout his days on earth. Because he is made by God and bears within himself an indelible imprint of God, man is naturally drawn to God. When he heeds the deepest yearnings of the heart, every man must make his own the words of truth expressed by St. Augustine: "You have made us for yourself, O Lord, and our hearts are restless until they rest in you."

How very significant is the dissatisfaction which marks man's life in Eden as long as his sole point of reference is the world of plants and animals (cf. Gen 2:20). Only the appearance of the woman, a being who is flesh of his flesh and bone of his bones (cf. Gen 2:23), and in whom the spirit of God the Creator is also alive, can satisfy the need for interpersonal dialogue, so vital for human existence. In the other, whether man or woman, there is a reflection of God himself, the definitive goal and fulfilment of every person.

St. John Paul II, *The Gospel of Life*, n. 35

> and free being. It also means that man and woman, created as a "unity of the two" in their common humanity, are called to live in a communion of love, and in this way to mirror in the world the communion of love that is in God, through which the Three Persons love each other in the intimate mystery of the one divine life. The Father, Son, and Holy Spirit—one God through the unity of the divinity—exist as persons through the inscrutable divine relationship. Only in this way can we understand the truth that God in himself is love (cf. 1 Jn 4:16).
>
> St. John Paul II, *The Dignity of Women*, n. 7

Husband and wife become a communion of love by becoming one flesh. This union of bodies is meant to lead to spiritual union. It is meant to lead to an awareness of "being in love" that prompts each spouse to say to the other: "I belong to you and you belong to me" (cf. Sgs 2:16). The "I" and the "you" become simply "us." This spousal union is the essence of human love. Because the man and woman's communion with each other is love, it is an image of the infinite Love that created it. The mystery of human love helps us understand what the Bible means when it says that God is love.

3. God created us to work.

God works when he creates. He calls us to do something similar. When we work, this activity reflects something about God. Human work reveals another essential difference between human beings and animals.

The Book of Genesis says that God took Adam and "put him in the garden of Eden to till it and keep it" (Gen 2:15). God told Adam and Eve: "Be fruitful and multiply, and fill the earth and subdue it" (Gen 1:28). The Church teaches that God did this because work forms part of being God's image and likeness:

> From the beginning, therefore, man is called to work. Work is one of the characteristics that distinguishes man from the rest of creatures. . . . Only man is capable of work, and only man works. . . . Thus work bears a particular mark of man and of humanity, the mark of a person operating within a community of persons.
>
> St. John Paul II, *On Human Work*, n. 1

Like animals, we do things, at times, just to survive: we breathe, we eat, we drink, etc. But unlike animals, we also spend time doing things that have no immediate benefit. Sometimes we do something even though we will never benefit from it. We do it knowing that others will benefit. We plant trees to provide shade that we will never see, hoping our children will see it. We do this gladly, thinking of the way others will enjoy the fruits of our labor.

God is the first one to work. He is the first one to do things that do not benefit him, benefiting others instead. He creates not because it will make him happy. He was already infinitely happy before creating and would have been infinitely happy without creating anything. He creates only to make us happy. When we work, when we serve others, it makes us like God. We imitate the Creator by working as he works, focusing on others instead of focusing on self.

Christian materialism

God uses ordinary things to give us a glimpse of his infinite love—the Trinitarian love we will see more clearly in heaven. When Christians look at the world this way, they no longer see the world as an obstacle to being close to God. This means learning how to "materialize" our spiritual lives:

> There is only one life, made of flesh and spirit. And it is this life, which has to become, in both body and soul, holy and filled with God: we discover the invisible God in the most visible and material things. . . . Either we learn to find our Lord in ordinary, everyday life, or we shall never find him. That is why I tell you that our age needs to give back to matter and to the apparently trivial events of life their noble, original meaning.
>
> St. Josemaría, *Passionately Loving the World*, nn. 2–3

God asks us to work so that we can find him through our work.

Working together with God

One of the ways God wanted Adam and Eve to cooperate with him was to have children—lots of children to "fill the earth." Though there are many people populating our planet, it would be a mistake to think that God is satisfied. He gave us the ingenuity to figure out how to be more fruitful and, at the same time, improve the standard of living for everyone in the world. This aspect of human work remains the same today as it was in the days of Adam and Eve.

God is the Creator. He loves to create. He has entrusted the human race with the potential for the birth of new human life. He will judge us

Wisdom of the Saints

You said, "Let us make man in our own image and likeness." And this you did, eternal Trinity, willing that we should share in all that you are. . . . Why did you give us such great dignity? With unimaginable love, you looked upon your creatures within your very self, and you fell in love with us. So it was love that made you create us and give us being, just so that we might taste your supreme eternal good . . .

O depth of love! What heart could keep from breaking at the sight of your greatness descending to the lowliness of our humanity? We are your image, and now, by making yourself one with us, you have become our image. . . . And why? For love! You, God, became human, and we have been made divine!

St. Catherine of Siena, *The Dialogue*, n. 13

on how we administered this awesome capability and whether we used it to carry out his plans.

Every father and mother should stand before God and recognize the greatness of the vocation God has entrusted to them. The *Catechism* explains:

> In marriage God unites them in such a way that, by forming "one flesh," they can transmit human life: "Be fruitful and multiply, and fill the earth." By transmitting human life to their descendants, man and woman as spouses and parents cooperate in a unique way in the Creator's work.
>
> CCC, n. 372

Having children takes lots of work. Though all human work can be an act of cooperating with God, bearing children—and teaching them to believe in Jesus—is one of the most important ways in which Christians cooperate in the work of creation. Not only do couples bring new life into this world, they bring children into existence who can live with God forever in Paradise.

REVIEW QUESTIONS

1. How did God create Adam and Eve?
2. How is man God's image and likeness?
3. Why does God want us to work?
4. What is "Christian materialism"?

4.

Man Rebels Against God

After creating Adam and Eve and joining them together as husband and wife, God asked them to take care of the garden where they were living. This work was delightful. There was no death, no pain, no tiredness, no disease, and no suffering. For Adam and Eve, life together was full of peace and joy and was meant to stay that way.

Divine grace was the greatest of all the gifts God gave Adam and Eve. He lifted them up above the limits of human nature. He lifted them far above all natural perfection to the heights of a *supernatural* perfection. By giving them divine grace, Adam and Eve became "children of God." This grace was a share in God's own life. The *Catechism* teaches:

> Our first parents, Adam and Eve, were constituted in an original "state of holiness and justice" . . . As long as he remained in the divine intimacy, man would not have to suffer or die. The inner harmony of the human person, the harmony between man and woman, and, finally, the harmony between the first couple and all creation, comprised the state called "original justice."
>
> This entire harmony of original justice, foreseen for man in God's plan, will be lost by the sin of our first parents.
>
> CCC, nn. 375, 376, 379

The first man and woman were close to God. The Book of Genesis talks about them: "And they heard the sound of the LORD God walking in the garden" (Gen 3:8). They could talk with him directly. After Adam and

Eve sinned, they were thrown out of the garden. They no longer enjoyed the same familiarity with God.

We have no direct experience of what Adam and Eve's life was like in the state of original justice. Our world is full of pain and suffering. We get tired. At times the routine of life weighs heavy on us. Even those who are filled with faith, hope, and love—precisely those with such virtues—know that we have no hope of ever being perfectly happy in this life. We have to pick up our cross and follow Jesus. He felt fear before his cross and asked his Father to remove it if possible. But it was not possible. We, too, feel fear before our cross.

Even our best moments are tinged with unpleasant memories from the past and prospects of future disaster, the worst being the possibility of losing our way and letting our love grow cold. Our best days carry some reminder of death. The most potent pleasures and earthly delights become tiring after a while. Our only lasting joy lies in finding God. Sometimes, though, even that joy escapes us. God allows us to be tested—at times with severe trials and temptations.

The Book of Genesis speaks about yet another difference between our experience and that of Adam and Eve in the garden: "And the man and his wife were both naked, and were not ashamed" (Gen 2:25). Though nakedness is shameful in the present age, their nakedness was something good. As the Bible says about everything in the beginning, before Adam and Eve sinned, God looked at the world he had created and saw that "it was very good" (Gen 1:31). This means that the first man and woman were free from lust.

All these facts taken together—the freedom from death, pain, tiredness, and lust—describe a different state from ours. We call their state the "state of original innocence." We call ours the "historical state."

God gives and God commands

The Garden of Eden was full of trees. Two were special. One was the Tree of Life. By eating its fruit, Adam and Eve would live forever. Then there was the Tree of the Knowledge of Good and Evil. God commanded the man and woman not to eat the fruit of this tree. He told them, "For in the day that you eat of it you shall die" (Gen 2:17). This did not mean that the tree was evil. It meant that eating its fruit would do serious harm.

This story is so strange that some find it hard to believe. It describes something we have never experienced and cannot experience. The strangest part is that it *did* happen. Certainly some of the language is poetic, especially the names of the two trees. Perhaps even the trees are only metaphors for another reality so foreign to us that it cannot be described. In either case, Adam and Eve lived in a beautiful garden where life was perfect.

Satan appears

One day Satan appeared in the garden. The Book of Genesis portrays him as a serpent, whereas, in reality, he is an angel. Satan used his great intelligence to tempt Adam and Eve and draw them away from God. We do not know the exact details. Perhaps he took some visible form and appeared before Adam and Eve. Perhaps he tempted them more subtly, as he does with us, using spiritual powers to plant suggestions within our mind. In either case, pursuing some evil purpose, Satan tempted our first parents. The Bible says:

Sacred Scripture

Now the serpent was more subtle than any other wild creature that the LORD God had made. He said to the woman, "Did God say, 'You shall not eat of any tree of the garden'?" And the woman said to the serpent, "We may eat of the fruit of the trees of the garden; but God said, 'You shall not eat of the fruit of the tree which is in the midst of the garden, neither shall you touch it, lest you die.'" But the serpent said to the woman, "You will not die. For God knows that when you eat of it your eyes will be opened, and you will be like God, knowing good and evil." So when the woman saw that the tree was good for food, and that it was a delight to the eyes, and that the tree was to be desired to make one wise, she took of its fruit and ate; and she also gave some to her husband, and he ate. Then the eyes of both were opened, and they knew that they were naked; and they sewed fig leaves together and made themselves aprons.

Genesis 3:1–7

> God created man for incorruption, and made him in the image of his own eternity, but through the devil's envy death entered the world, and those who belong to his party experience it.
>
> Wisdom 2:23–24

Satan was proud enough to think he was greater than God. And yet, with all his pride, he envied Adam and Eve. We do not know why. Maybe it was because God made the man and woman masters over the whole world. Maybe Satan, being God's most powerful creature, thought he was master over the whole of creation.

Satan draws man into sin

We do not know why God allowed Satan to enter the Garden of Eden and tempt Eve. We only know that God must have allowed it. We can only assume that, like us, Satan was free to choose between good and evil, and he chose evil. Knowing how much harm it would do, he tempted Eve to eat the forbidden fruit. She ate it and gave some to Adam. He ate it, too.

You may wonder why Adam and Eve ate the fruit. There were many other fruits to eat on many other trees. Besides, God clearly commanded them not to eat the fruit. If they ate it, they would die. So why did they eat it? If your friend told you that eating the fruit was going to kill you, would you eat it?

Satan tricked Adam and Eve by lying to them. This is what happens in every temptation. Satan lies, and we believe the lie. Adam and Eve knew God's command without any doubt. But they did not have any experience. Besides, the fruit looked good. In the end, they listened to Satan instead of trusting God.

The nature of temptation

We are no different from Adam and Eve. Many of God's warnings can seem exaggerated at times. In a moment of temptation, people ask: "What could be so bad about getting drunk or watching pornography or stealing money?" It is hard for us to take heaven and hell seriously.

We cannot see heaven or hell. The temptation always looks good at the moment. Satan often tricks us into disobeying God as easily as he tricked Adam and Eve.

Instead of believing God, our first parents believed Satan. Satan told them the fruit would make them equal to God. He said, "You will not die. For God knows that when you eat of it your eyes will be opened, and you will be like God, knowing good and evil" (Gen 3:4–5). Satan was telling Adam and Eve not to worry about dying. He said that instead of causing death, the fruit would make them as powerful as God.

After eating the forbidden fruit, Adam and Eve did not die immediately—at least not a physical death. Instead, a different kind of death entered into them. It was spiritual death—the kind of death we call "sin." Their bodies continued to live. But they lost the spark of divine life in their soul—the life we call "sanctifying grace."

Spiritual death is the loss of grace

Adam and Eve died a spiritual death. After committing sin, Adam and Eve noticed this spiritual death, and they noticed it in a peculiar way. They felt ashamed. They could no longer look at each other. They felt naked. They pulled leaves off a tree and covered themselves. Even with the fig leaves, they still felt ashamed, so they hid from each other.

Later in the day, towards evening, God came to talk to Adam and Eve, the way a father comes to see how his children are doing. They were so filled with shame that they tried to hide from him.

If you ever commit a serious sin, you, too, will feel this kind of shame. It is the unmistakable sign of spiritual death. You know you did something wrong. It was not just an accident. You chose evil, knowing it was against God's law, and you did it deliberately.

Your soul dies when you lose the life of grace given to you at baptism. You have thrown God out of your soul. You feel alone. This kind of sin is called "mortal sin" because it causes spiritual death. Spiritual death means losing God's grace. Spiritual death means entering into the state of sin—the opposite of the state of grace. You remain in the state of sin until God forgives you and gives back the grace you lost through sin.

Original sin

Adam and Eve's sin affected all their descendants. We are born without God's grace. This lack of grace is called "original sin"—*original* because it was the sin of the first man and woman. It does *not* mean that a baby has committed a sin. We do not *commit* original sin; we *contract* it. Original sin is not a presence of sin but rather a *lack of grace* we were meant to have.

St. Paul describes the reality of original sin by calling it "death." God warned Adam and Eve that death would enter the world if they disobeyed. The Apostle contrasts the spiritual death due to original sin with the spiritual life Jesus gives us:

> Therefore as sin came into the world through one man and death through sin, and so death spread to all men because all men sinned. . . . Then as one man's trespass led to condemnation for all men, so one man's act of righteousness leads to acquittal and life for all men.
>
> Romans 5:12, 18

In some mysterious way we cannot comprehend, the whole human race sinned in Adam. Adam and Eve could not pass on the grace of original holiness to us because they lost it when they sinned. If they had not sinned, God's grace would have been passed on to each person at the

Fathers of the Church

Let us turn our gaze towards Mary again. When Gabriel entered into her chamber and began to speak with her, she asked, "How can this be?" The Holy Spirit's servant replied to her saying, "For nothing will be impossible with God." Firmly believing what she has just heard, she said, "Behold the handmaid of the Lord."

At that instant the Lord descended upon her and entered into her, and made his resting place in her, without anyone being aware of it. Without any loss of virginity, Mary conceived. The Lord became a baby within her womb.

This day is not like the beginning of creation. . . . Through sin, Adam and Eve had brought death to the world. But the Lord of the world has given us new life in Mary. . . . O happy Adam! In the birth of Christ, you have discovered the glory you had lost.

St. Ephrem the Syrian, *Hymn for the Birth of Christ*

moment of conception. Instead, at the moment of conception, God creates the soul without giving that person his gift of grace. God does this because of the unity of the human race.

The unity works both ways. It explains why all men and women are born into the world with a kind of spiritual death in their soul. It also explains how all men and women can be saved by the "good act of one man"—the act of Jesus offering a perfect sacrifice for our sins. The first Adam causes spiritual death for all. The "last Adam"—Jesus—is the cause of salvation for all who accept him.

The *Catechism* reminds us that this mystery is part of revelation. We believe the mystery not because we were smart enough to figure it out, but because God tells us that it is true.

> The transmission of original sin is a mystery that we cannot fully understand. But we do know by revelation that Adam had received original holiness and justice not for himself alone, but for all human nature. By yielding to the tempter, Adam and Eve committed a personal sin, but this sin affected the human nature that they would then transmit in a fallen state. It is a sin which will be transmitted by propagation to all mankind, that is, by the transmission of a human nature deprived of original holiness and justice.
>
> *CCC*, n. 404

This teaching is one of the dogmas of the Church: Original sin is transmitted by propagation. Original sin is passed on from generation to generation by the very fact that a child receives human nature, deprived of grace, through the parents.

We cannot understand all the implications of this mystery. We can neither prove it nor disprove it by human reason alone. Even so, this particular fact of revelation is one of the truths that is mostly easily confirmed by personal

Magisterium

By our first parents' sin, the devil has acquired a certain domination over man, even though man remains free. Original sin entails captivity under the power of him who thenceforth had the power of death, that is, the devil. Ignorance of the fact that man has a wounded nature inclined to evil gives rise to serious errors in the areas of education, politics, social action, and morals.

Catechism of the Catholic Church, n. 407

experience. We only have to ask why, from the beginning of recorded history, men and women have strayed far from God. There is something wrong with the human race. We are all oppressed by misery. We all feel a strong inclination towards evil and death. The *Catechism* states that these realities only make sense if we connect them to "Adam's sin and the fact that he has transmitted to us a sin with which we are all born afflicted, a sin which is the death of the soul" (*CCC*, n. 403).

You only have to look at your own soul and you, too, will begin to suspect that some evil has lodged itself deep inside. You begin to realize that without Jesus to save you, you will never make it. You will only become more entangled in the perverse tendencies within you.

Because God chose Mary to be the Mother of our Redeemer, he gave her the privilege of being preserved from original sin. Anticipating the way he would apply the power of Christ's redemptive death and resurrection to all those who are saved, God applied it to the Virgin Mary at the very moment of her conception. She was conceived without sin.

Errors about original sin

In the past some Christians made the mistake of thinking that we are born into this world without any spiritual defect. They did not see original sin as a lack of grace. They thought Adam and Eve's sin was nothing more than a bad example. The Church condemned this error, stating that anyone who wants to lead a morally good life must have God's grace (cf. *CCC*, n. 406). Anyone who deliberately neglects the means to obtain God's grace will eventually fall into temptation and commit serious sin.

Some Christians went to the opposite extreme, claiming that original sin did so much damage that it destroyed any possibility of recovery. They said original sin not only weakened the human will but corrupted it so much that we can no longer choose freely between good and evil. They made the mistake of thinking that original sin (which baptism takes away) is the same as our tendency towards evil (which baptism does not take away). The Church also condemned this error, stating that all people have a free will. She further teaches that Christians can struggle against their evil tendencies, and, through the sacraments, live habitually in the state of grace.

State of Original Innocence

GARDEN OF EDEN

Before the Fall

This was the first state of man's existence. Adam and Eve were "just"—holy before God—because they had sanctifying grace. They were immortal. They were free from all suffering and concupiscence.

Historical State

THIS WORLD

After the Fall / Before Christ

At the Fall, death entered into the world through sin. Sin was everywhere. Everyone was subject to the effects of original sin. The best anyone could do was to anticipate the first coming of the Savior—Jesus Christ, the Son of God made man. God prepared the world for his coming through Abraham and his descendants.

THIS WORLD

With Christ / Before the End

Jesus freed us from sin by dying and rising from the dead. But even those whose sins are forgiven remain subject to death, pain, concupiscence, and other effects of original sin. God asks us to anticipate Christ's return. He prepares the world for the Second Coming through the Church.

Eschatological State

THE NEXT WORLD

After the Last Judgement

The *eschaton* is the final state of man's existence. The damned will suffer in hell for all eternity. The saints will live together with God in Paradise, where there will be no war, no death, no concupiscence, no tension—no suffering of any kind. All will be love, peace, and joy.

Effects of original sin

Besides the fact that Adam and Eve's disobedience causes us to be born in a state of sin, we have internal defects caused by original sin. Though baptism frees us from original sin, these defects remain even after being baptized. These defects are usually called "wounds" in human nature. These wounds do not make it impossible to enjoy the presence of God in our lives, but they do make it more difficult.

> **WISDOM OF THE SAINTS**
>
> The loss of God is death to the soul.
>
> St. John of the Cross, *Spiritual Canticle*, 2, 7

Our minds are clouded with ignorance. This makes it hard to grasp truths of the spiritual world. We tend to focus our attention almost entirely on material things. The mysteries God has revealed often seem boring to us. We might spend hours watching television, talking with friends, or reading a novel and then feel that Mass is too long just because it takes a few minutes longer than we were expecting.

We suffer from concupiscence. This is an inborn lack of mastery over our desire for pleasure. Even the saints spoke of the need to struggle against temptations of lust, not only in their youth but also in old age. We often feel an urge to satisfy carnal desires that are completely senseless, like drinking more and eating more after having feasted on the best food and drink.

Our will is also affected. It is bent on evil things—not entirely, but just enough to make us feel a craving for them. Even when we see the evil of certain sinful actions (e.g., dreaming of ways to seek revenge), we will often feel attracted to that evil, as if it were good. We know that we should forgive others. It is the only way God will forgive our sins. Something malicious inside us leads not towards forgiveness but towards satisfying a desire for vengeance.

Original sin affects courage. We may feel attracted to something good, like doing our work well. We may admire friends who seem to be close to God. But the effort to do these things overwhelms us and we give up almost as soon as we begin to work or pray. We are easily overcome by laziness and cowardice.

These personal defects are all inside of us. Adam and Eve's sin is also the reason for many evils we see in the world around us. In the beginning, our work was meant to be an enjoyable experience. It can be at times. But now it often becomes monotonous and tiring. God pointed out this effect of original sin when he told Adam: "Cursed is the ground because of you; in toil you shall eat of it all the days of your life" (Gen 3:17). God told Eve that she too would have to endure a special punishment because of her sin: "I will greatly multiply your pain in childbearing; in pain you shall bring forth children" (Gen 3:16).

Originally life on earth was meant to be pleasant and free from physical pain. It still can be at times, but sometimes everything goes horribly wrong. Famine, floods, and earthquakes kill enormous numbers of people. We feel as if the world has become a "valley of tears." All this is the result of original sin. Finally, there is death. God told Adam and Eve: "For out of it you were taken; you are dust, and to dust you shall return" (Gen 3:19).

God promises a savior

After Adam and Eve sinned, God felt compassion for them. He was full of mercy from the very beginning. He promised to send a savior. Besides being a promise to our first parents and the whole human race, it was Satan's punishment for lying to Eve. God said to the serpent:

> "Because you have done this, cursed are you above all cattle, and above all wild animals; upon your belly you shall go, and dust you shall eat all the days of your life. I will put enmity between you and the woman, and between your seed and her seed; he shall bruise your head, and you shall bruise his heel."
>
> Genesis 3:14–15

Who was this woman who will give birth to a son that is destined to crush the head of the serpent? Because Eve had just rebelled against God, the woman could not be Eve. Her firstborn son was Cain, the first man to commit murder. The Virgin Mary is the woman who gives birth to a son who crushes the head of Satan. God makes Satan and Mary "enemies of each other" when he preserves her from sin. She is the only woman conceived without original sin.

The prophecy contains a further mystery. Satan will "strike at his heel." Satan does this when he orchestrates the actions of those who crucify Jesus. Paradoxically, this is how Jesus crushes Satan's head. He destroys sin by "becoming sin." He destroys death by dying.

When they sinned, Adam and Eve did so much harm to themselves that God had to force them to leave the garden. For their own good, he had to allow them to experience physical death. Instead of a life full of joy and peace, they had to suffer. They were no longer protected from disease. Instead of living off the fruit in the garden, they had to toil to get food. Their work was mostly unpleasant, monotonous, and exhausting. The woman had to suffer pain when giving birth. Her husband would mistreat her: "And he shall rule over you," God said to Eve (Gen 3:16). After a life of toil and hardship, Adam and Eve had to die. God said, "And to dust you shall return" (Gen 3:19). Upon dying, their bodies were buried to rot in the earth. Then Adam and Eve had to wait in the world of the dead—Hades—until the mysterious "son born of a woman" appeared to redeem them.

Pain and the suffering, ending in death, show us how evil sin is. Because we are slow to learn, God continues to allow all men and women to experience this just as Adam and Eve experienced it.

God did not abandon Adam and Eve. To help the man and woman handle their shame more easily, he made clothes out of animal skins. Adam and Eve put them on.

REVIEW QUESTIONS

1. What is original sin?
2. How does Satan tempt us?
3. What are the mistakes some have made when trying to explain original sin?
4. What are the effects of original sin?

5.

God Becomes Man

Four basic realities define what happened in the beginning.

- **Grace.** God created Adam and Eve. He made them holy with sanctifying grace. God promised to care for them forever. God expected them to be faithful to him but left them free to choose. Being holy, they could communicate with God with ease. Being holy, they could easily live a life of virtue. By becoming one with each other, the first man and woman were meant to pass on God's grace to all their children.
- **Temptation.** Satan tempted the man and woman to rebel against God. He convinced them to doubt God's love. He wanted them to break their covenant with God.
- **Sin.** The man and woman disobeyed God's command. By doing so, they lost sanctifying grace. Not only did they lose this gift for themselves; they were unable to pass it on to their children. They suffered many other consequences as well: death, pain, ignorance, concupiscence, fear, etc.
- **Salvation.** God promised the man and woman that he would send a savior. The Savior would be a man born of a woman. He would destroy the power of Satan and undo the damage caused by sin.

After Adam and Eve left the garden, the story of the human race can be summarized as one long preparation for the coming of the Savior. To prepare the world for redemption, God appeared to Abraham. The Savior would be a descendant of this great man of faith. God made a covenant with Abraham and then renewed it with Isaac and Jacob. These men were the patriarchs of God's Chosen People. The *Catechism* teaches:

> After the patriarchs, God formed Israel as his people by freeing them from slavery in Egypt. He established with them the covenant of Mount Sinai and, through Moses, gave them his law so that they would recognize him and serve him as the one living and true God, the provident Father and just judge, and so that they would look for the promised Savior.
>
> *CCC*, n. 62

Looking forward to the coming of the Savior explains all the other events in the Old Testament—indeed, all events in the history of mankind.

God comes down from heaven

The Father, Son, and Holy Spirit, acting as one, created the world. Because of the sin of Adam and Eve, the Trinity decided that the Son would become a man. Before becoming a man, the Son of God lived in heaven with his Father. After centuries of preparation, God sent his Son.

The Son came down from heaven by becoming a man. The Church calls this event the "Incarnation." In-*car*-nation comes from *caro*, the Latin word for flesh. To "incarnate" means to become flesh. God's Son became incarnate; i.e., he became a man.

Before becoming a man, the Son of God had no flesh. He was divine, and God is pure spirit. He had no body because he was not yet human. When the Trinity decided that the Son would become man, the Son did not lose his divinity. The Son of God became a man without ceasing to be God. Still, it meant humbling himself. Until his baptism in

Sacred Scripture

In the beginning was the Word, and the Word was with God, and the Word was God. He was in the beginning with God; all things were made through him, and without him was not anything made that was made.

And the Word became flesh and dwelt among us, full of grace and truth; we have beheld his glory, glory as of the only Son from the Father.

John 1:1–3;14

the Jordan River, Jesus lived without any display of his power and majesty. As he grew up in Nazareth, no one knew that he was the Son of God. Though the Virgin Mary and St. Joseph knew he was God's Son and lived with him for thirty years, even they could not see his divine glory.

Jesus' humility is an invitation to be humble. St. Paul wrote:

> Do nothing from selfishness or conceit, but in humility count others better than yourselves. Let each of you look not only to his own interests, but also to the interests of others. Have this mind among yourselves, which is yours in Christ Jesus, who, though he was in the form of God, did not count equality with God a thing to be grasped, but emptied himself, taking the form of a servant, being born in the likeness of men. And being found in human form he humbled himself and became obedient unto death, even death on a cross.
>
> Philippians 2:3–8

When the Son of God became flesh, he did it with total humility. He became a man by being conceived in the womb of the Virgin Mary. He was a baby—totally helpless and totally dependent on Mary and Joseph.

To announce the Incarnation, God sent the Angel Gabriel to Nazareth. The angel told Mary that God had chosen her to be the mother of his Son. Gabriel said the child was going to be a descendant of King David (cf. Lk 1:32). He spoke of another deep mystery. Instead of being conceived in the usual way, the child was going to be conceived by the power of the Holy Spirit. For this reason, the angel concluded, the child was going to be called the "Son of God" (Lk 1:35).

Pope Leo the Great, one of the Fathers of the Church, explained that this decision was both an act of humility and an act of power. Humility, because the Son of God became exactly like us in all things but sin. Power, because it was a miracle:

> For a virgin to conceive, for a virgin to give birth and remain a virgin, is humanly unique. It reveals the power of God.
>
> St. Leo the Great, *Second Homily on the Nativity*

The Incarnation took place when the Holy Spirit "overshadowed" the Virgin Mary and created the human body and the human soul of Jesus Christ. Mary conceived the child in her womb by the power of the Holy Spirit.

Jesus saves

After the Virgin Mary became pregnant, Joseph began wondering how she had conceived a child. Though they were "betrothed" (Mt 1:18)—legally they were already husband and wife—they were not yet living together. According to Jewish custom, betrothal was a period of preparation. The parents would seal a marriage contract with the husband and then plan the wedding feast. As the day of the wedding feast was approaching, Joseph had to decide what to do. An angel appeared to explain that his wife had conceived by the power of the Holy Spirit.

The Word became flesh in the womb of the Virgin Mary when she conceived by the power of the Holy Spirit. Being God, Jesus is truly the Son of God. Being man, Jesus is truly the Son of the Blessed Virgin Mary. He is perfect God and perfect man. Because he is God, Jesus is infinitely powerful. Because he is man, Jesus experiences all our limitations. He is just like us in all things but sin.

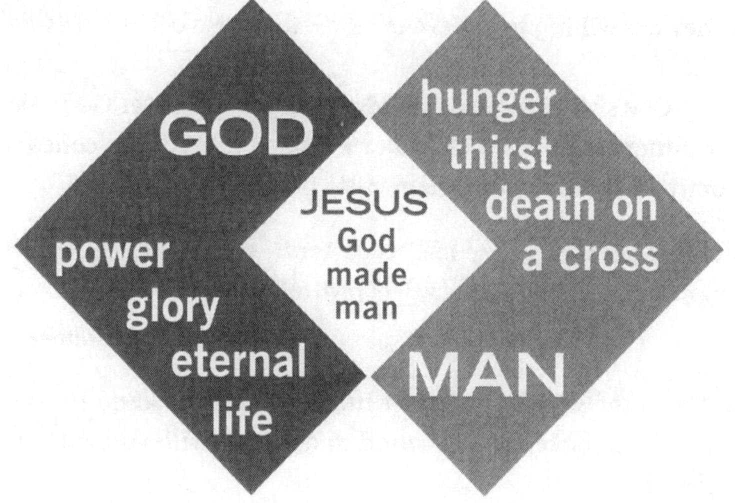

The angel told him: "Do not fear to take Mary your wife" (Mt 1:20). He also commanded Joseph to give the Child a name, something that the father had a right to do in Jewish tradition. According to the angel, the Child was to be named Jesus, because he was destined to save his people from their sins. Jesus (or Yeshua) is a Hebrew name that means "Yahweh saves."

Jesus was born into the world to save us from our sins and free us from the power of Satan. He is the only one who can save us. He came to save everybody—literally everybody, from Adam and Eve up to the last child ever to be born.

Although God wants all people of all times and places to be saved, salvation is not automatic. It is personal. Salvation is a gift from God. No one is forced to accept it. Each person makes his or her own decision.

God sent his Son to save you. God wants you to believe in his Son. You have to make your own decision.

> . . . if you confess with your lips that Jesus is Lord and believe in your heart that God raised him from the dead, you will be saved.
>
> Romans 10:9

Besides believing, God wants you to obey. Just because you are a Christian does not mean you will be saved. Just as people decide whether or not they are willing to believe in Jesus, they also decide whether to do God's will.

Doing God's will requires a readiness to do whatever God asks—but *first*, a willingness to find out what he wants. Everyone is called to find out exactly what God wants them to do in this life. Jesus said:

> Not every one who says to me, "Lord, Lord," shall enter the kingdom of heaven, but he who does the will of my Father who is in heaven.
>
> Matthew 7:21

Jesus fulfilled the will of his Father in heaven by shedding his blood on the cross. If you make up your mind to do God's will, you will enter the kingdom of heaven.

Who is Jesus?

Jesus did many things any man would do. Jesus got tired and had to sleep. He got hungry and had to eat. He got thirsty and had to drink. He was known as "the carpenter's son" (Mt 13:55) and worked as a carpenter himself (cf. Mk 6:3). He used to laugh, tell stories, and visit his friends. He corrected others to help them overcome their ignorance and mistakes. He became indignant when his disciples unwittingly made others suffer. He got angry when people rejected the evidence of truth obvious in his many miracles (cf. Mt 11:20–24). He showed a sense of wonder and amazement, especially when he noticed how much faith someone had (cf. Lk 7:9)—or didn't have (cf. Mk 6:6).

Jesus felt intense emotions. A few weeks before his crucifixion, Jesus went to Bethany because Lazarus had just died. This incident, among others, led St. John to declare: "Jesus loved Martha and her sister and Lazarus" (Jn 11:5). Even though Jesus was going to bring his friend back to life, he was undone—so filled with sorrow that he began to weep. Moving as that was, Peter, James, and John saw something even more striking the night before Jesus died. The Master no longer appeared self-assured: "And [he] began to be greatly distressed and troubled" (Mk 14:33).

> **Fathers of the Church**
>
> Christ Jesus our Lord, the Son of God . . . became the Son of Man so that man could become the son of God. Rejoicing because of this, Mary cried out, prophesying on behalf of the Church, "My soul magnifies the Lord, and my spirit rejoices in God my Savior" (Lk 1:46–47).
>
> St. Irenaeus, *Against Heresies*, III, 10, 2

Jesus was a man. This was evident to the Apostles and anyone else who saw him. If they needed further convincing, they got the ultimate proof when they saw Jesus die on the cross. Many doubted that Jesus was God. Nobody doubted that he was a man.

At first Jesus seemed to be nothing more than human. Only gradually did he reveal to his disciples that he was "from above." He often said that his Father in heaven "sent" him (Jn 8:42). People began to realize what this implied. Speaking of Jesus' enemies among the Jewish elders, St. John wrote:

> This was why the Jews sought all the more to kill him, because . . . [he] called God his Father, making himself equal with God.
>
> John 5:18

Jesus was clear about being equal to God. He said he was "one" with his Father (Jn 10:30).

This is why Caiaphas, acting officially as high priest, condemned Jesus to death before the Sanhedrin. They thought he was guilty of blasphemy—guilty of claiming to be God's equal even though he was a man. To emphasize his equality with us, Jesus often called himself "Son of Man." But when Caiaphas asked him if he claimed to be equal to God, Jesus did not hesitate to reveal his identity. He called himself the "Son of God." He also said they would see him seated at the right hand of the Father. In other words, they would see his divine power when he came to judge the world at the end of time.

> Again the high priest asked him, "Are you the Christ, the Son of the Blessed?" And Jesus said, "I am; and you will see the Son of man seated at the right hand of Power, and coming with the clouds of heaven." And the high priest tore his garments, and said, "Why do we still need witnesses? You have heard his blasphemy. What is your decision?" And they all condemned him as deserving death.
>
> Mark 14:61–64

Although Jesus knew the Sanhedrin would condemn him to death for saying he was the Son of God, he stated it as clearly as he could. Throughout the whole New Testament—indeed, throughout the entire history of the Church—you will discover the many ways Christians have suffered for proclaiming that Jesus is God's Son.

However, a question remains. How can we be sure that Jesus was telling the truth? Anyone can claim to be the Son of God. Many emperors and kings of the ancient past were so deluded by their power and majesty that they fancied themselves to be equal to God. Some called themselves "Son of God" and then insisted that the people worship them. What makes Jesus different from them?

Jesus' death and resurrection

Jesus did not look like the Son of God while he was dying. Even Christians have to admit that it makes little sense for God to let his Son die. It is more preposterous to imagine God's Son being stripped naked and nailed to a cross while his Father in heaven remained silent. Why did God let Jesus' enemies humiliate him and mock him? If Jesus really was the Son of God, why didn't God do something?

You can only begin to make sense of that disaster when you realize that Jesus died this way in order to redeem the world. It is also a personal thing—something between you and Jesus. It's so personal that St. Paul expressed it by exclaiming: "Who loved me and gave himself for me" (Gal 2:20). Jesus was ready to die on the cross if only to save one soul. He died for everybody; and yet, what he really did was die for each one of us. But this only makes Jesus' death more mysterious. How could the death of one man take away your sins or my sins or the sins of anyone else?

We will cover this question in the next chapter. First, we have to look at Jesus' resurrection. If Jesus did not rise from the dead, then he was not the Son of God. And if he was not the Son of God, his death on the cross was useless.

All four accounts of the Gospel include a series of historical facts that are meant to explain to all people what happened two thousand years ago. All four accounts describe the same basic facts about Jesus' death and resurrection. Some of them are listed below. As you can see, while reading through them, the facts all converge on one conclusion. Jesus rose from the dead on the third day and appeared to his Apostles.

Facts about Jesus' Resurrection

1. The resurrection was prophesied for the third day. This is one of the few instances in history for which the day was specified beforehand, stating exactly when a prophecy would be fulfilled. Long before he died, Jesus told his disciples that he would rise from the dead on the third day after he died. Related prophecies in the Old Testament, like the sign of Jonah being in the belly of the whale for three days, indicated the same idea.

Mt 12:38–40; Mk 8:31; Lk 18:31–34; Jn 2:18–22

2. Pilate handed over the body of Jesus for burial. Being the Roman governor, Pilate had to make sure Jesus was dead before releasing the body. There is no question that Jesus was truly dead when taken down from the cross.

Mt 27:58; Mk 15:44–45; Lk 23:52; Jn 19:38

3. The body was buried in a tomb hewn in the bedrock. On Friday evening, before sunset, the same day as his death, the disciples placed the dead body in a tomb that no one could break into. No one could dig their way into the tomb from behind and steal the body.

Mt 27:60; Mk 15:46; Lk 23:53

4. The entrance of the tomb was sealed. A stone was placed in front of the tomb to close it. Then soldiers were stationed day and night to guard the entrance. There was no way any of Jesus' disciples could enter the tomb and steal the body.

Mt 27:60–66; Mk 15:47; Lk 24:2; Jn 20:1

5. The tomb was new. No other body had ever been buried in that tomb. When the disciples buried Jesus, no other body was present that might be confused with his.

Mt 27:60; Lk 23:53; Jn 19:41

6. The women found the tomb empty. On the third day, before sunrise, St. Mary Magdalene and the other holy women went to the tomb to finish the burial rites they had been unable to complete on Friday. The stone had been rolled away. They entered the tomb expecting to find Jesus' dead body. The tomb was empty. The empty tomb does not prove that Jesus resurrected. But if the tomb was *not* empty—if a dead body was still in the tomb—it would make no sense to say Jesus had risen. St. John narrates a further detail. Jesus' body was missing from the tomb, but the burial cloths had been left behind. Why would anybody remove the burial cloths before stealing the body?

Mt 28:1–8; Mk 16:1–6; Lk 24:3, 12; Jn 20:3–7

7. The disciples were not expecting Jesus to rise from the dead. Some disciples refused to believe that Jesus had risen even after other disciples told them they had seen him alive. Despite the clear prophecy Jesus had made, the disciples assumed they would never see Jesus again. They had lost all hope. Jesus' death had been too humiliating for them to expect a resurrection. While his enemies were enjoying the success of their triumph, the Apostles were so terrified that they locked themselves inside the Upper Room.

Mt 28:17; Mk 16:11; Lk 24:9–11; Jn 20:19

8. Jesus appeared to several disciples before appearing to the Apostles. These disciples told the Apostles they had seen Jesus and that he had risen from the dead. Even before Jesus appeared, angels told the holy women: "He has risen, as he said he would!" The angels' words emphasized the fulfilment of Jesus' prophecy and the need to announce this to the Apostles.

Mt 28:1–8; Mk 16:10–13; Lk 24:13–35; Jn 20:11–18

9. Jesus appeared to the Apostles. To fulfill the promise he had made to them before dying, the Risen Lord showed himself to the Apostles. He asked them to touch the wounds in his hands and feet. There was no question about who had been nailed to the cross. Everyone saw Jesus get crucified. The wounds in the risen body were proof that the man nailed to the cross was the same man who was now alive.

Mt 28:16–20; Mk 16:14; Lk 24:36–43; Jn 20:19–21

What do these facts about the resurrection show? The miracles Jesus worked are signs that God is with him and that his words are true. Jesus' resurrection is the greatest of all his miracles. None of the patriarchs or judges ever rose from the dead. None of the prophets or kings ever rose from the dead. Jesus not only rose from the dead, he prophesied the exact day when he would do it.

Some pagan myths portray a hero who rises from the

Magisterium

Jesus Christ is perfect God and perfect man, with a rational soul and human flesh.

Equal to Father because of his divinity, he is lower than the Father because of his humanity. Although he is both God and man, Christ is not two persons but only one person.

The Athanasian Creed, n. 30–32

dead. These, however, were just that—*myths* that no one ever believed—stories that poets invented about deeds that never really happened. Anyone who compares Jesus' resurrection to the pagan myths is forgetting this essential element. Nobody ever believed the myths were true. The Apostles stated again and again for everyone to hear that they saw Jesus die with their own eyes and then saw him risen from the dead with their own eyes. Jesus rose from the dead, never to die again.

Jesus' resurrection is a historical fact. We know it happened because Jesus' disciples saw the Risen Lord. This historical fact is essential to our faith. It means we can believe—we can accept as fact—that Jesus was speaking the truth when he claimed to be the Son of God. It also means he was speaking the truth when he promised to raise us from the dead at the end of the world.

Two natures in one person

A week after Jesus rose from the dead, he appeared again to the Apostles. Not present the first time, St. Thomas was present on this occasion. After seeing the holes made by the nails in our Lord's hands and feet, he made an act of faith. He said, "My Lord and my God!" (Jn 20:28). He believed that Jesus was the Lord, Creator of the Universe. He was calling Jesus "God."

The Apostles' Creed states several facts about Jesus: He is the Son of God. He was born of the Virgin Mary after being conceived in her womb by the Holy Spirit. He rose from the dead and ascended into heaven to be seated at the right hand of his Father. He will come again to judge the living and the dead.

This is what Christians believed in the times of the Apostles. This can never change. If you want to call yourself a Christian, you must be ready to make the same act of faith.

As the centuries passed, a controversy arose. What do we mean when we say that the Son of God became a man? When trying to understand Jesus, it was no longer sufficient to repeat the simple statements of the Apostles' Creed. Some Christians started saying that Jesus was a mixture of God and man. They said the mixing of natures resulted in a creature that was neither divine nor human. They thought Jesus was something less than God but more than man.

The Church condemned this error, stating that Jesus was true God and true man. The Church was not inventing a new teaching, but only clarifying what we know from God's revelation. It is clear in Scripture and Tradition that Jesus was truly a man. It is equally clear that he claimed to be the Son of God in the strictest sense of the word, being equal to his Father. Therefore, the Church asks all Christians to make this act of faith in Jesus:

> We believe in one Lord, Jesus Christ, the only Son of God, eternally begotten of the Father, God from God, Light from Light, true God from true God, begotten, not made, of one being with the Father. Through him all things were made. For us men and for our salvation he came down from heaven; by the power of the Holy Spirit he became incarnate from the Virgin Mary and was made man.
>
> Council of Nicea, *The Nicene Creed*

When the Word became flesh, he did not cease in any way whatsoever to be God. For this reason, the Church teaches that Jesus is "perfect God and perfect man."

After the Church clarified this matter at the Council of Nicea (AD 325), some Christians started saying that the Christ we read about in the Gospel was really two different persons. One person was the man named Jesus of Nazareth, who was born of the Virgin Mary. The other person was the Son of God who descended from heaven when Jesus was baptized so he could live inside Jesus. The Christians who made this

Wisdom of the Saints

The Church says, "Tomorrow you shall see in yourselves the majesty of God." After he makes you holy, he will let you see his majesty . . . and that vision will consist in nothing less than becoming like the majesty you see. We will become like him because we will see him as he really is.

So we do not say: "You shall see the majesty of God." Instead, we say that you shall see the majesty of God *in yourselves.*

St. Bernard, *Homilies for Christmas Eve*, V, 3

mistake started saying that the Virgin Mary was not the Mother of God, but only the Mother of Jesus.

The Church condemned this teaching about two persons at the Council of Ephesus (AD 431). The Church stated that there was only one person—the Word of God. This divine person assumed a human nature. The Word assumed a human nature at the very moment when the Word was conceived as a baby in the womb of the Virgin Mary. Mary's baby was the Son of God at the same time being her own Son.

This union of two natures in one person is called the "hypostatic union." The union of Jesus' divine nature with his human nature is a union taking place in his *hypostasis*, that is, in his person. The dogma of the hypostatic union explains why we say that God died to save us from our sins. If Jesus was only some "mixture" of human and divine—not truly divine—then Jesus' death on the cross did not redeem us from sin. If there are two persons, one called Jesus who died on the cross and another called the Word who did not die, then Jesus' death did not redeem us from sin. Precisely because the one offering his life was truly a man, he could shed blood and die. Precisely because the one shedding blood was truly the Son of God, the Father accepted his sacrifice.

At the Council of Ephesus, the Church also stated that Christians must call Mary the *Theotokos*, that is, the Mother of God. Precisely at the moment when St. Elizabeth was filled with the Holy Spirit, she called Mary the "mother of my Lord" (Lk 1:41–43). Mary is the Mother God because she conceived Jesus in her womb, and Jesus is God.

It is this phrase, perhaps more than any other, that sends our minds reeling in wonder. How can a woman become God's mother? She cannot be the one who brings God into existence. But, somehow, through the action of the Holy Spirit, she was the one who conceived a baby who was the Son of God. How was that possible? This question is part of a bigger mystery. How could the Creator become a creature? How could someone who is eternal—and necessarily outside of time—enter into time? How could someone who is incapable of changing in any way whatsoever become a man who changes with every breath he takes? How could someone who is infinitely powerful die on a cross?

Since these questions are difficult to answer, some Christians were tempted to say that Jesus was not *fully* divine or that he was human *only in appearance*. The Church rejected these explanations as heresies and declared that the two natures—the human and the divine—remain complete in Jesus. The Church declared this dogma of Catholic teaching in the Council of Chalcedon (AD 451):

> We confess that one and the same Christ, Lord and only begotten Son, is to be acknowledged in two natures without confusion, change, division or separation. The distinction between the natures was never abolished by their union, but rather the character proper to each of the two natures was preserved as they came together in one person and one hypostasis.
>
> Council of Chalcedon, DS 302; cf. *CCC*, n. 467

The two natures cannot be *confused*: Jesus' divinity and humanity do not mix to become some intermediate nature, half human and half divine. The two natures cannot be *changed*: As God, Jesus will always be infinitely powerful; as man, Jesus suffered and died the same way we suffer and die, while in the resurrection he now enjoys all that the saints will enjoy in their resurrection. The two natures cannot be *divided*: Because Jesus died, the Son of God died. The two natures cannot be *separated*: Because the Word became flesh, he will always be both God and man.

Jesus has both divine intelligence and human intelligence. The two minds work together, each working with its own proper way of knowing truth. Jesus has both a divine will and an entirely free human will. The two wills work together, each working with its own proper way of making decisions, of choosing a course of action, and of loving others.

In summary, the Incarnation means that Jesus Christ is perfect God and perfect man. He is perfect God because he is "of one being with his Father." He and his Father are not only similar to each other; they are the exact same substance—one single Supreme Being, in the unity of the Holy Spirit. Jesus is perfect man because he became a baby in the womb of the Virgin Mary, was born, and grew up to be just like any other man. The Church teaches:

> The Son of God . . . worked with human hands; he thought with a human mind. He acted with a human will, and with a human heart he loved. Born of the Virgin Mary, he has truly been made one of us, like to us in all things except sin.
>
> Vatican II, *The Church in the Modern World,* n. 22

REVIEW QUESTIONS

1. The Word existed "in the beginning." Explain what this means.
2. What does "incarnation" mean?
3. How did the Incarnation take place?
4. Jesus is perfect God and perfect man. Explain what this means.

6.

God Redeems Man

Satan is the thief—the one who brings sorrow and death. Jesus is the Good Shepherd—the one who brings joy and life.

> The thief comes only to steal and kill and destroy; I came that they may have life, and have it abundantly. I am the good shepherd. The good shepherd lays down his life for the sheep. . . . I am the good shepherd; I know my own and my own know me, as the Father knows me and I know the Father; and I lay down my life for the sheep.
>
> John 10:10–11, 14–15

Of all the images Jesus used to describe why his Father sent him, this one probably expresses it best. You understand why God created you when you can finally say that he knows you and that you know him.

Jesus is God's mercy

Since God never told us, we do not know what would have happened if Adam and Eve had obeyed him instead of listening to Satan. Paradoxically, we are better off because Adam and Eve rebelled against God. To redeem us from sin, the Son of God became a man. Every year to celebrate Easter, the Church sings:

> To ransom a slave you gave away your Son! *O felix culpa!* O happy fault! O necessary sin of Adam, that gained for us so great a redeemer.
>
> *The Easter Proclamation*

The new creation is better than the first creation. Before the Fall, God was not one of us. Now he is.

After the Fall of Adam, sin flooded the world. And yet, this abundance of sin is being swallowed up in a superabundance of grace: "but where sin increased, grace abounded all the more" (Rom 5:20). God is a Father full of mercy. His mercy is truly infinite.

God knows our weaknesses. He knows all the different ways we are enslaved to sin. He sent his Son to set us free. The Church teaches:

> Not only does Christ speak of God's mercy and explain it by the use of comparisons and parables, but above all he himself makes it incarnate and personifies it. Jesus himself, in a certain sense, is mercy. God becomes particularly "visible" as the Father who is "rich in mercy" whenever we see that mercy in Christ, whenever we find it in him.
>
> St. John Paul II, *Rich in Mercy*, n. 2

The closest the human race has ever come to seeing the full force of God's power was when everyone thought—perhaps Satan himself thought—that God was unable to save Jesus. When the world was covered in darkness and Jesus was hanging on the cross—that is the day when we saw what God is really like.

The cross is where we see the Father loving the world so much that he sent his Son to redeem it. The cross is where we see the Son of God dying in order to give us life. The cross is where we see how willing God is to forgive all sins. The cross is where we see good overcoming evil. God uses the cross to show us that his humility is more powerful than Satan's pride.

Redemption is not a wrestling match where the strongest man wins. God asked his Son to become weak. The Son became weak by accepting death—"as a sheep led to the slaughter" (Acts 8:32). The Son became weak because he loaded himself with the guilt of all the sins of mankind—past, present, and future.

The action of the divine Father was foreshadowed when Abraham put Isaac on the altar—a human father ready to sacrifice his son. God asked his Son to accept the cross.

> "For our sake he made him to be sin who knew no sin" (2 Cor 5:21), St. Paul will write, summing up in a few words the whole depth of the

> cross. . . . Indeed this Redemption is the ultimate and definitive revelation of the holiness of God . . .
>
> St. John Paul II, *Rich in Mercy*, n. 7

> Christ—without any fault of his own—took on himself "the total evil of sin."
>
> St. John Paul II, *On the Christian Meaning of Human Suffering*, n. 19

Jesus took our guilt upon himself and then died with it. By dying with it, he destroyed it. God suffered unspeakable agony in order to redeem us. To redeem a slave, God asked his Son to pay the price. We can only conclude that the Father is indeed "rich in mercy" (Eph 2:4).

Jesus is God's justice

The cross is where we see how evil sin is and how final death was meant to be. God's mercy was also an act of justice.

God pardoned sin and solved the problem of death. But he did not dismiss sin and death as trifles. On the contrary, sin was so damaging and death was so final that God arranged for the sacrifice of his Son. This sacrifice—and nothing else—cleanses us from sin and rescues us from death. The guilt was lifted from our shoulders only after God burdened his Son with it. Death was conquered by nothing less than the death of God. Sin was cleansed by nothing less than God's blood. Sin and death did not vanish into thin air. Jesus buried them with him when he went to his grave.

This is the paradox; Jesus reveals the power of God by becoming weak. Jesus reveals the holiness of God by "becoming sin." Jesus reveals God's mercy by revealing God's justice. The cross reveals justice, because by dying, Jesus *re*-deemed us, which literally means that he paid *back* the debt due to sin.

Sacred Scripture

While we were still weak, at the right time Christ died for the ungodly. Why, one will hardly die for a righteous man—though perhaps for a good man one will dare even to die. But God shows his love for us in that while we were yet sinners Christ died for us. Since, therefore, we are now justified by his blood, much more shall we be saved by him from the wrath of God.

Romans 5:6–9

But even when revealing justice, God is revealing mercy. God's love for us "is so great that it turns God against himself, his love against his justice. . . . [S]o great is God's love for man that by becoming man he follows him even into death, and so reconciles justice and love" (Benedict XVI, *God Is Love*, n. 10). The Father allowed us to crucify his Son so that we could be his children.

This is the mystery of God's love. He not only forgives us. He wants each of us to be "another Christ, Christ himself." Jesus both revealed this and made it possible by shedding his blood.

Jesus pays the ransom

All men and women, without exception, were doomed to an eternity of suffering because of Adam and Eve's sin.

> And you, who were dead in trespasses . . . God made alive together with him, having forgiven us all our trespasses, having canceled the bond which stood against us with its legal demands; this he set aside, nailing it to the cross.
>
> Colossians 2:13–14

God the Father saved us from eternal condemnation by asking his Son to suffer in our place.

St. Peter explains the same idea with a different image. He talks about a "ransom." In ancient times, a ransom was the price paid to set a slave free.

> You know that you were ransomed from the futile ways inherited from your fathers, not with perishable things such as silver or gold, but with the precious blood of Christ, like that of a lamb without blemish or spot.
>
> 1 Peter 1:18–19

God "paid a ransom" in the sense that it cost him dearly to free us from slavery. The "price" God paid was to allow his Son to offer his blood as a sacrifice for our sins.

Let's examine the texts of sacred Scripture further so we can understand why shedding blood on a cross had the power to wash away our sins.

Blood redeems us

After centuries of following the Law God gave to Moses, it was clear to the Jews that "without the shedding of blood there is no forgiveness of sins" (Heb 9:22). To understand why this was so and to understand what happened on the cross, go back to the Old Testament. The Book of Leviticus explains the value of blood. God commanded his people not to drink blood because all blood—all life—belonged to him.

> For the life of the flesh is in the blood; and I have given it for you upon the altar to make atonement for your souls; for it is the blood that makes atonement, by reason of the life. Therefore I have said to the people of Israel, No person among you shall eat blood, neither shall any stranger who sojourns among you eat blood.
>
> Leviticus 17:11–12

The Israelites had to atone for their sins—make up for their sins—by shedding the blood of an animal and then pouring it on the altar. Since an animal was food, burning it as a holocaust instead of eating it was meant to establish a sense of *paying back*, thus undoing the damage caused by

Fathers of the Church

Nobody is an outsider to this happiness. The same cause for joy is common to all. Since our Lord found nobody free from guilt when he came to bring an end to death and to sin, he came with redemption for all.

O Christian, be aware of your nobility—it is God's own nature that you share: do not then, by an ignoble life, fall back into your former baseness. Think of the Head, think of the Body of which you are a member. Recall that you have been rescued from the power of darkness, and have been transferred to the light of God, the kingdom of God.

Through the sacrament of baptism, you have been made a temple of the Holy Spirit; do not, by evil deeds, drive so great a guest away from you, submitting yourself once more to the slavery of the devil. For you were bought at the price of Christ's blood.

St. Leo the Great, *Homilies on the Nativity*, I, 1, 3

sin. It was the justice of giving "life for life, eye for eye, tooth for tooth, hand for hand, foot for foot, burn for burn, wound for wound, stripe for stripe" (Ex 21:23–25). To offer blood was to offer life. The blood and ashes of the sacrificed animal were sprinkled on the person who had committed the offense. Having been in contact with the altar, the blood and ashes were holy and transferred that holiness to the person they touched.

Having only an external value, these rites could not cleanse the soul. Only a sacrifice of infinite value could make up for the damage done by Adam and Eve's sin—and all our own sins. God sent his Son to offer such a sacrifice.

> For if the sprinkling of defiled persons with the blood of goats and bulls and with the ashes of a heifer sanctifies for the purification of the flesh, how much more shall the blood of Christ, who through the eternal Spirit offered himself without blemish to God, purify your conscience from dead works to serve the living God.
>
> Hebrews 9:13–14

Jesus' blood did not become holy because it was poured over an altar. It was holy because it was the blood of the God made man. By being baptized, we "wash our robes"—our souls—"and make them white in the blood of the Lamb" (Rev 7:14).

Jesus had to shed his blood twice. The first time, to keep the covenant between God and Abraham, St. Joseph shed Jesus' blood when circumcising the child on the eighth day (cf. Mt 1:25; Lk 2:21). By shedding blood at the very beginning of life, Jesus shows us that his life was an act of redemption from beginning to end. Circumcision was the "a sign or seal of the righteousness" (Rom 4:11). Given the nature of the sign, this ritual was also a vivid reminder to the sons of Israel that God alone has power to give life. Christ's circumcision reminds us that he came to make us righteous and to give us life.

The second time he shed blood, Jesus became the lamb of sacrifice for the new Passover. On the same day, at the same hour when each Jewish family was sacrificing a lamb to recall the events that ended Israel's slavery in Egypt, Jesus was nailed to the cross. Blood from the paschal lamb in the times of Moses saved Israel from physical death.

Jesus' blood saves anyone who believes in him from everlasting spiritual death. Jesus' blood saves us from spending eternity in hell.

Obedience redeems us

Sacred Scripture emphasizes the power of Christ's blood to cleanse us from sin. It also says that this power comes from Jesus' willingness to obey. The night before he was crucified, Jesus asked his Father to "take away the cup," that is, to escape from the suffering of the crucifixion and find some other way of redeeming us.

> Father, if thou art willing, remove this cup from me; nevertheless not my will, but thine, be done.
>
> Luke 22:42

The Son obeyed, overcoming his fear of the cross. St. Paul contrasts Adam's refusal to obey with Jesus' submission to his Father's will.

> Then as one man's trespass led to condemnation for all men, so one man's act of righteousness leads to acquittal and life for all men. For as by one man's disobedience many were made sinners, so by one man's obedience many will be made righteous.
>
> Romans 5:18–19

To redeem us, Jesus had to obey his Father. What exactly was it that the Father wanted?

To understand this, we have to go back to the notion of Jesus taking our place. Like the scapegoat in the Old Testament offered on the Day of Atonement (Yom Kippur), Jesus is the substitute: "The goat shall bear all their iniquities upon him to a solitary land" (Lev 16:22). Jesus talked about being the substitute when stating that he had to "give his life as a ransom for many" (Mk 10:45).

In the "Song of the Suffering Servant of Yahweh," Isaiah prophesied that the Messiah would be a kind of substitute. This servant would be totally innocent. He would be a "man of sorrows," not because he had any reason to be sorry for sin but because he came to bear the burden of our sins—as if he were the one who had sinned.

> Behold, my servant shall prosper, he shall be exalted and lifted up. . . . Surely he has borne our griefs and carried our sorrows; yet we esteemed him stricken, smitten by God, and afflicted. But he was wounded for our transgressions, he was bruised for our iniquities; upon him was the chastisement that made us whole, and with his stripes we are healed.
>
> Isaiah 52:13, 53:4–5

Jesus is a substitute or ransom because he endured the punishment that we were supposed to endure. He suffered so that we would not have to suffer. At a level beyond our imagining, his hour upon the cross forced him to experience deep within his soul the loneliness of sin. In his heart he felt the horror of being separated from God, of being rejected by God. It was so intense, that Isaiah portrayed Christ as appearing to be "struck down by God"—even though he was the Son of God and totally incapable of offending his Father in any way.

The sacrifice of the Bridegroom

To substitute for us, Jesus had to become one with us. He did it willingly: "I lay down my life. . . . No one takes it from me, but I lay it down of my own accord" (Jn 10:17–18). He loved us with a total love. He loved us as a bridegroom loves the bride. The Church teaches:

> Love induced Christ to give his life, by accepting death on a cross . . . Thus this "substitution" signified the superabundance of love.
>
> St. John Paul II, *Catechesis on the Creed,* Vol II, p. 446

Jesus called himself the "Bridegroom" (cf. Mt 9:15, Jn 3:29). By dying on the cross, Jesus became the Bridegroom for the Church and the Church became his bride.

The Book of Genesis speaks of a man "leaving father and mother" to become "one flesh" with his wife (Gen 2:24). To understand the relationship between Christ and the Church, we have to think of Christ, as a man, making a sacrifice for the woman who will be his bride. St. Paul wrote:

Magisterium

Many episodes, many discourses during Christ's public teaching bear witness to the way in which from the beginning he accepts this suffering which is the will of the Father for the salvation of the world. However, the prayer in Gethsemane becomes a definitive point here. The words: "My Father, if it be possible, let this cup pass from me; nevertheless, not as I will, but as thou wilt" (Mt 26:39) . . . prove the truth of that love which the only-begotten Son gives to the Father in his obedience. At the same time, they attest to the truth of his suffering.

After the words in Gethsemane come the words uttered on Golgotha, words which bear witness to this depth—unique in the history of the world—of the evil of the suffering experienced. When Christ says: "My God, my God, why hast thou forsaken me?," his words are not only an expression of that abandonment which many times found expression in the Old Testament, especially in the Psalms (Ps 22:2). . . . One can say that these words on abandonment are born at the level of that inseparable union of the Son with the Father, and are born because the Father "laid on him the iniquity of us all" (Is 53:6). They also foreshadow the words of Saint Paul: "For our sake he made him to be sin who knew no sin" (2 Cor 5:21). Together with this horrible weight, encompassing the "entire" evil of the turning away from God which is contained in sin, Christ, through the divine depth of his filial union with the Father, perceives in a humanly inexpressible way this suffering which is the separation, the rejection by the Father, the estrangement from God. But precisely through this suffering he accomplishes the Redemption, and can say as he breathes his last: "It is finished" (Jn 19:30).

St. John Paul II, *On the Christian Meaning of Human Suffering*, n. 18

> For no man ever hates his own flesh, but nourishes and cherishes it, as Christ does the church, because we are members of his body. "For this reason a man shall leave his father and mother and be joined to his wife, and the two shall become one flesh." This mystery is a profound one, and I am saying that it refers to Christ and the church . . .
>
> Ephesians 5:29–32

Jesus sacrificed himself for the Church. Like any husband, he had to "leave father and mother." He did this by emptying himself out, not clinging to his divinity but humbling himself to become a man (cf. Phil 2:6–8). He "left father and mother" by accepting death on a cross. He did it to make his bride holy (cf. Eph 5:25).

St. Paul equates being a bridegroom with making a sacrifice for the bride. This fact of revelation is key to understanding the priesthood, as we shall see later when studying the sacrament of holy orders.

Jesus is the "new man" and the Church is the "new woman." To explain this "great mystery," the Church Fathers compared God creating Eve to God forming the Church. To form Eve, God put Adam into a deep sleep. To form the Church, the Father asked his Son to experience the "deep sleep" of death on a cross. To form Eve, God took a rib from Adam's side. To form the Church, Jesus had to be pierced by a lance; causing blood and water to flow from the wound in his side (cf. Jn 19:34).

> As happened when God took a rib from Adam's side and formed woman, so Christ gave us blood and water from his side and formed the Church. Just as when he took the rib while Adam was in a deep sleep, so now he gave blood and water after his death.
>
> St. John Chrysostom, *Catechesis*, 3, 18

The Church is the new Eve, the Bride of the Lamb. She came from the side of Christ after he died on the cross.

The reason a man leaves father and mother is that he wants to become one body with the woman. The "great mystery" begins with Jesus making his sacrifice and concludes with Communion. Jesus becomes one with his bride by rising from the dead, going away to receive his kingdom (cf. Mt 19:12) and returning at the end of time for the "marriage supper of the Lamb" (Rev 19:9).

After allowing him to be humiliated on the cross, the Father has to glorify his Son. He is preparing a wedding feast for his Son (cf. Mt 22:2).

The whole Christ

St. Paul wrote:

> For just as the body is one and has many members, and all the members of the body, though many, are one body, so it is with Christ.
>
> 1 Corinthians 12:12

The text is surprising. Because St. Paul is describing how Christians form a unity, you would expect him to call this unity the "Church." Instead, he calls it "Christ." By saying, "So it is with Christ," he states that the unity of all Christians is Christ. The whole Christ is the head plus the body.

Jesus Christ is the Word made flesh. Once he has redeemed us and united us to himself, Christ and the Church can neither be confused nor separated and constitute a single whole Christ. The *Catechism* teaches:

> Christ and his Church thus together make up the "whole Christ" (*Christus totus*). The Church is one with Christ. The saints are acutely aware of this unity. . . . A reply of St. Joan of Arc to her judges sums up the faith of the holy doctors and the good sense of the believer: "About Jesus Christ and the Church, I simply know they're just one thing, and we shouldn't complicate the matter."
>
> *CCC*, n. 795

St. Augustine said that the whole Christ is the Bridegroom united to his Bride.

> This is the whole Christ, head and body, one formed from many . . . Whether the head or members speak, it is Christ who speaks. He speaks in his role as the head (*ex persona capitis*) and in his role as body (*ex persona corporis*). What does this mean? "The two will become one flesh. This is a great mystery, and I am applying it to Christ and the Church." And the Lord himself says in the Gospel: "So they are no longer two, but one flesh." There are in fact two different persons, yet they are one in the conjugal union. . . . As head, he calls himself the "bridegroom"; as body, he calls himself "bride."
>
> St. Augustine, cf. *CCC*, n. 796

In the first creation, God created the union of Adam and Eve to be his image and likeness. In the new creation, the union of Christ and his Church constitutes the perfect image of the Creator. This will only become evident when Christ returns to share his glory with the Church at the end of the world.

Wisdom of the Saints

Jesus prayed to the Father with these words: "Father, if you are willing, take this cup away from me." Even so, he placed his own will at the service of his Father's will. . . . We should never desire to be above others. Instead, we should be servants, subject to every kind of human authority. The Spirit of the Lord will rest upon all who do these things and persevere to the end. He will make his dwelling-place, his home, within them. And because they do his will, they will be children of their heavenly Father. They are the spouses and brothers and mothers of our Lord Jesus Christ.

St. Francis of Assisi, *Letter to All the Faithful*

Anticipating this event, God made a special plan for the Virgin Mary. Just as she shared in her Son's grace by being conceived without original sin and shared in the agony of his death, God wanted her to share in her Son's resurrection. After her life ended on earth, she was taken up into heaven, body and soul. The Church teaches:

> Mary is the beginning and the image of the Church as bride of the new covenant.
>
> St. John Paul II, *Catechesis on the Creed,* Vol IV, p. 111

An ancient Christian prayer calls the Virgin Mary "our life, our sweetness, and our hope." She already enjoys the glory of the resurrection. She has already received the reward we hope to receive on that day when Jesus comes to raise us from the dead.

The Church is the new Eve. Being the Mother of the Church, the Virgin Mary is also the new Eve:

> Mary became the Woman, the new Eve—"mother of the living"—the mother of the "whole Christ."
>
> *CCC,* n. 726

She gives life to the whole Christ because God chose her to be the Mother of Jesus and then chose her to be our Mother, too. She cooperated with her Son in the work of redemption by being ready to accept God's will always and everywhere.

REVIEW QUESTIONS

1. What does "redemption" mean?
2. How does Christ's blood redeem us?
3. What did Jesus mean by saying he was the "ransom for many"?
4. What does the Church mean when it speaks of the "whole Christ"?

7.

The Holy Spirit

Imagine being one of Christ's disciples two thousand years ago. You would hear St. John the Baptist talk about Jesus baptizing you with "the Holy Spirit" (Jn 1:33). You would hear Jesus tell you not worry about what to say when put on trial for your faith because it will not be you speaking, "but the Holy Spirit" (Mk 13:11). Finally, at the Last Supper, you would hear Jesus promise that he was getting ready to send the Holy Spirit:

> And I will pray the Father, and he will give you another Counselor, to be with you for ever, even the Spirit of truth, whom the world cannot receive, because it neither sees him nor knows him; you know him, for he dwells with you, and will be in you.
>
> John 14:16–17

If you are a Christian, you know something about the Holy Spirit. He is "with you." He is "in you."

When trying to understand who this third person of the Holy Trinity is, remember that he is there in your soul to enlighten you. He wants you to know who he is.

What is a spirit?

The union of Father and Son is a great mystery. Still, their names are familiar names. We know what a father is. We know what a son is. When Jesus speaks about the Holy Spirit, that name is not familiar—at least not as familiar to us as "father" and "son."

The Bible speaks about spirits called angels. It also mentions demons, who are also spirits—angels that were cast out of heaven after rebelling against God. Even so, you may not understand the term "spirit" exactly. You have never seen a spirit, and you *cannot* see a spirit. Not knowing much about spirits, you probably find it hard to grasp what the Holy Spirit is like. Before you can understand the Holy Spirit—the *uncreated* Spirit—you need to understand the spirits God created. The Holy Spirit was not created. He is God. But he is a spirit. It will help to understand spirits when trying to understand him.

There is an entire world beyond this world that you cannot see. This invisible world is home to billions of angels, plus an unknown number of evil spirits called "devils" or "demons." Both angels and devils are spirits.

Being spirit means that angels and devils have no body at all. They can appear in human form. They can appear in other forms, too. The Bible narrates many examples of such apparitions. But any physical shape they *seem* to have merely allows them to speak in human language or do things in a human way. They are not human. They are pure spirits with no bodies.

The world of angels is just as invisible as they are. This world is not somewhere far away. This world is very close to us. Even though it is close to us, we cannot see it and, normally, we cannot see the angels who live there. But our two worlds are intermingled. You have a guardian angel who goes with you everywhere you go. There are demons who can (and do) approach you to tempt you. You cannot see either angels or demons, but they see you.

The Bible describes how angels help us. Angels appeared on the night Jesus was born to announce the Good News to the shepherds. Angels also helped Jesus. For instance, when he was praying in the Garden of Gethsemane the night before his crucifixion, "there appeared to him an angel from heaven, strengthening him" (Lk 22:43).

The Bible explains how evil spirits can do harm. When you read the story about the devils that destroyed a herd of two thousand pigs (cf. Mk 5), you begin to get an idea of just how much damage they can do—both physically and spiritually. Satan and the other demons are bent on enticing all men and women away from God.

All these spirits, both good and evil, are creatures created by God. They are all very real—just as real as the men and women around you.

Who is the Holy Spirit?

Like the angels, the Holy Spirit is also a spirit; but he is much different. The other spirits are creatures, whereas he is God. At the First Council of Constantinople (AD 381), the Church declared as a dogma of faith that the Holy Spirit deserves to be worshipped the same way Christians worship the Father and the Son:

> We believe in the Holy Spirit, the Lord, the Giver of life, who proceeds from the Father and the Son. He is worshipped and glorified. He has spoken through the prophets.
>
> Constantinople I, *Niceno-Constantinopolitan Creed*

We adore the Holy Spirit because he is God. He is equal to the Father and the Son.

To understand how the Holy Spirit differs from created spirits like angels, consider the way angels love. Angels are intelligent creatures with a free will. They can love one another, just as we are called to love one another. The Holy Spirit is different. Angels love. The Holy Spirit *is* love.

It is like the difference between fire and heat. The Holy Spirit is like fire. Fire gives heat. The love the angels have for one another—or the love we have for one another—is like the heat that comes from fire. Demons cannot love because they have been completely cut off from the Holy Spirit. We have the power to love one another only when we have "the Lord, the Giver of life" within us.

Sacred Scripture

If the Spirit of him who raised Jesus from the dead dwells in you, he who raised Christ Jesus from the dead will give life to your mortal bodies also through his Spirit which dwells in you.

For all who are led by the Spirit of God are sons of God. For you did not receive the spirit of slavery to fall back into fear, but you have received the spirit of sonship. When we cry, "Abba! Father!" it is the Spirit himself bearing witness with our spirit that we are children of God, and if children, then heirs, heirs of God and fellow heirs with Christ, provided we suffer with him in order that we may also be glorified with him.

Romans 8:11,14–17

The only real love is the love that comes from the Holy Spirit. St. John speaks of this mystery when he says in his first letter:

> Beloved, let us love one another; for love is of God, and he who loves is born of God. . . . He who does not love does not know God; for God is love. . . . By this we know that we abide in him and he in us, because he has given us of his own Spirit.
>
> 1 John 4:7, 8, 13

If you want to love others, ask the Father and Son to fill your heart with the Holy Spirit.

FATHERS OF THE CHURCH

You went down into the water to be baptized. Remember how you replied to the questions. You said that you believe in the Father, that you believe in the Son, that you believe in the Holy Spirit. You were not supposed to say, "I believe in one who is greater and one who is less and another who is least." You are bound by the very promise you made with your own voice to believe in the Son exactly as you believe in the Father, and to believe in the Holy Spirit exactly as you believe in the Son.

St. Ambrose, *On the Mysteries*, 28

The Holy Spirit is love, union, and gift

When St. Paul speaks of God sending the Holy Spirit, he implies that God sends us his love:

> . . . and hope does not disappoint us, because God's love has been poured into our hearts through the Holy Spirit which has been given to us.
>
> Romans 5:5

The Holy Spirit is the third person of the Holy Trinity. The Creed says that he proceeds from the Father and the Son. The Son comes from the Father. The Holy Spirit comes from both the Father and the Son. The best way to understand the Holy Spirit is to look again at the mystery of the Father and Son.

Jesus often spoke to his disciples about his Father. The word "father" was probably one of the first words you ever learned. Your father is someone you lived with when you were a child. Your father took care of you. He provided for you. He helped you. He protected you. But your father is much more than all that. Even if you never had these wonderful experiences, one fact still defines your father. You came from him. He gave you life. You are his child.

Jesus is the Son of the Father. This is the person who gave him life. This is the person he came from. The story gets complicated because Jesus, as man, also has a mother, and Jesus, as man, started off his earthly life calling Joseph his "father." (The Virgin Mary called Joseph his "father," so we assume the Child Jesus would have done the same) cf. Lk 2:48). After dying on the cross and rising from the dead, he started calling us his brothers and sisters. And to add to the mystery of all this, Jesus becomes the Bridegroom of his Bride, "leaving his father and mother to become one body with her." (St. Paul uses these words from Genesis to describe the mystery of Christ's union with the Church: cf. Eph 5:31–32). Despite these many complexities that come to define Jesus' existence as a man, one reality continues to define him above all others: He comes from the Father. He is one with the Father. He is the Son.

Once you fully understand Father and Son this way, you understand the Holy Spirit. The Holy Spirit is the *union* of this Father and this Son. You can even imagine the Holy Spirit as the "embrace" of Father and Son—a description used by the Church Fathers. You could even think of the Holy Spirit as the glue between Father and Son. This is what the early Christians writers meant when they talked about the Holy Spirit as the "bond" of love between Father and Son. The Spirit is the bond that ties the Father and Son together—a bond of pure love. He is the love the Father has for his Son. He is the love the Son

MAGISTERIUM

The Old Testament on several occasions speaks of "fire from heaven" which burnt the oblations presented by men. By analogy one can say that the Holy Spirit is the "fire from heaven" that works in the depth of the mystery of the cross.

The Holy Spirit as Love and Gift comes down, in a certain sense, into the very heart of the sacrifice offered on the cross. Referring here to the biblical tradition, we can say: He consumes this sacrifice with the fire of the love that unites the Son with the Father in the Trinitarian communion.

St. John Paul II, *The Holy Spirit*, n. 41

has for his Father—not two separate loves meeting in the middle, but a single love that is like the embrace of two who love each other.

Besides describing the Holy Spirit as the union of Father and Son, the Church also calls him "Gift."

> The Holy Spirit as the Spirit of the Father and the Son . . . "searches even the depths of God." . . . In the Holy Spirit the intimate life of the Triune God becomes totally gift, an exchange of mutual love between the divine Persons. . . . Through the Holy Spirit God exists in the mode of gift. It is the Holy Spirit who is the personal expression of this self-giving, of this being-love. He is Person-Love. He is Person-Gift.
>
> St. John Paul II, *The Holy Spirit*, n. 10

Jesus talked about the Father "giving"—giving him life, giving him glory, giving him love. When we look at the Father, we see God "giving." When we look at the Son, we see God "receiving." The Church teaches that "through the Holy Spirit, God exists in the mode of gift." When we look at the Spirit, we see God being the "gift" between Father and Son.

The Father gives us the life he gave his Son. The Father gives us the glory he gave his Son. The Father gives us the love he gave his Son. All this can be summarized by saying that the Father gives us the Holy Spirit. This Spirit makes us "sons in the Son." The Father gives us life and glory and love—he gives us the Spirit—through Jesus.

Because the Holy Spirit is union and gift, we become one with each other when the Father and Son send him to us. This is why Jesus says, "The glory which thou hast given me I have given to them, that they may be one even as we are one" (Jn 17:22).

The Holy Spirit appears

The Holy Spirit has appeared to us in many different forms. For instance, he appeared as a dove when Jesus was baptized. He appeared as a cloud overshadowing Peter, James, and John during Christ's transfiguration. He appeared as fire when he descended upon the disciples at Pentecost. Jesus also described the Holy Spirit as a fountain of living water springing up within us.

The Holy Spirit is not a dove or fire or water. These appearances are symbols of the great power he has. By appearing as a dove, he reveals himself giving us purity and peace. By appearing as fire, he reveals himself giving us a burning desire for union with God. By appearing as water, he reveals himself giving life and quenching our thirst for love.

The Holy Spirit is a person—not a thing or an action. Jesus never talked about the Holy Spirit using the pronoun "it." He always spoke of the Holy Spirit using the pronoun "he": "For he dwells with you, and will be in you. . . . He will bear witness to me" (Jn 14:17;15:26). St. Paul speaks of the Father and Son pouring love into our hearts by sending us the Holy Spirit. This does not mean sharing an idea or a desire or a feeling. The Father and Son send us a *person.* And this person shows us the secret of the Father and Son's love for each other because he *is* their love.

Pentecost

The Father sent his Son when the Holy Spirit overshadowed the Virgin Mary and the Word was made flesh. The Father and Son sent the Holy Spirit at Pentecost. When the Father sent the Son, God was uniting the divine nature with human nature in only one person—Jesus. When the Father and Son sent the Holy Spirit, God was—in some sense—uniting divine nature with human nature in many persons. In other words, by being baptized with the Holy Spirit at Pentecost, all Jesus' disciples became "other Christs."

To become so like Christ that we can say we are another Christ—*this* is why God sends us the Holy Spirit. The Church invites us to marvel at this mystery:

> All the baptized are invited to hear once again the words of St. Augustine: "Let us rejoice and give thanks; we have not only become Christians, but Christ himself. . . . Stand in awe and rejoice, we have become Christ."
>
> St. John Paul II, *The Vocation and Mission of the Lay Faithful,* n. 17

Each person somehow becomes "another Christ, Christ himself." This does not mean that every Christian is already perfect and has no further need of grace to advance in holiness. If you want to be a saint, you have

Wisdom of the Saints

No one knows the "mystery hidden from all ages" except the one who has received it. No one receives it except the one who has desired it. No one desires it except the one who has been deeply penetrated by the fire of the Holy Spirit—the fire Christ came to cast upon the earth. This is why the Apostle says that this mystical wisdom is revealed through the Holy Spirit.

If you want to understand how this happens, seek the answer in grace, not study; in desire, not understanding; in earnest prayer, not in reading books. Seek it from the betrothed, not a teacher. Ask God, not man. Look for it in darkness, not in brilliance. Do not seek it from a light, but from a fire that completely inflames you and transports you to God with extreme sweetness and burning affection. This fire is God himself; the furnace is in Jerusalem; and Christ sets it ablaze with all the burning fervor of his passion.

St. Bonaventure, *Journey of the Mind to God*, 7

to allow the Holy Spirit to work inside you, making you a little more like Christ every day. The Holy Spirit is like a sculptor chiseling a block of stone until the perfect image of Christ is formed in you.

St. Paul complained to the Christians living in Galatia. They needed "more sculpting" before they were ready to enter God's kingdom:

> And because you are sons, God has sent the Spirit of his Son into our hearts, crying, "Abba! Father!" So through God you are no longer a slave but a son, and if a son then an heir. . . . How can you turn back again to the weak and beggarly elemental spirits, whose slaves you want to be once more? . . . I am afraid I have labored over you in vain. . . . My little children, with whom I am again in travail until Christ be formed in you!
>
> Galatians 4:6–7, 9, 11, 19

Christ is "formed" in each Christian as the Holy Spirit acts. The Spirit works through the ministry of people like St. Paul who teach, correct, guide, and encourage others to be faithful.

When you are filled with the Holy Spirit, you cry out, "Abba, Father!" You call God your Father with the same word Jesus used to call his Father in heaven (Mk 14:36). When you are filled with the Spirit, you realize that God is your Father. You know that God looks at you the same way he looks at Jesus. When God looks at you, he sees his Son.

A Christian becomes "another Christ, Christ himself." But this does not mean they all end up with the same personality. Each man, each woman, acquires the personality God wants them to have. Look at the great variety of personalities among the saints! Nevertheless, the Holy Spirit does something to each man and woman that brings about unity. He unites all Christians together in one body—the Church.

> . . . until we all attain to the unity of the faith and of the knowledge of the Son of God, to mature manhood, to the measure of the stature of the fullness of Christ.
>
> Ephesians 4:13

As the Holy Spirit perfects each person, he draws all of us together into perfect unity. The Holy Spirit is like the "soul" of this "body" that is the Church.

Gifts of the Holy Spirit

To help you live as a true child of God, the Holy Spirit gives you certain spiritual powers. These are the seven gifts of the Holy Spirit.

The seven gifts were first prophesied by Isaiah (cf. Is 11:1–2). He said the Messiah—Jesus—would be the first to have all these gifts. Jesus wants to share them with us. This is why he said to the Apostles, "The Spirit will take what is mine and give it to you" (cf. Jn 16:14–15).

These are the names of the seven gifts of the Holy Spirit, with an example to describe each gift:

Wisdom: This gift leads you to experience God's love. It also opens your mind so that you gradually begin to grasp the true meaning of all the mysteries God has revealed.

Ephesians 3:16–19; Ecclesiasticus 24:16–22

Understanding: All creatures lead you to understand more about God. When you look at the sky, understanding leads you to think: "The One who created that beautiful star must be more beautiful than all the stars put together!" When you see human love, you think, "The One who created something so wonderful must love with greater passion than all the lovers that ever lived." Without this gift, you will be confused by the arguments of those who explain all existence as nothing more than an accident of nature having no rhyme or reason.

Ephesians 1:17–18

Counsel: You grasp the details of God's plan so that you can help others do God's will. When others seem to have no sense of purpose and ask for advice, you will know how to direct them towards God. When disaster strikes, you will know how to resist the temptation of being overwhelmed by sadness and, instead, look for the way God plans to turn this disaster to your advantage.

Romans 8:28

Fortitude: You have strength to serve God even when you don't feel like it. You can overcome tiredness when you need to serve others. You can overcome hardness of heart when you need to forgive.

Philippians 4:13

Knowledge: You know how to use things to serve God. If you have money, instead of dreaming of ways to use it for your own comfort and amusement, you will think of ways of using it to help others.

2 Corinthians 9:6–15

Piety: You are ready to pray at any time of the day. Instead of feeling indifferent towards the things of God, you will feel attracted to them. This does not mean that prayer will always be a joy. Even Jesus suffered his agony in the garden. Rather it means that you will know almost instinctively that you cannot get through life without prayer anymore than you can survive without food.

1 Thessalonians 5:16–18

Fear of the Lord: Trusting God with total abandonment, your only fear is sin, that is, offending the One you love. This gift allows you to endure anything—loneliness, poverty, ridicule, pain—even when you might easily avoid such suffering by giving into temptation. In the most literal sense of the word, you would rather die than commit a sin.

2 Maccabees 7:26–29

Are you wondering how you might be blessed with all these gifts? Seek God's will. Perhaps you have made up your mind to do God's will. That is not enough. Have you ever asked yourself *what* he wants you to do?

By studying everything God has revealed, you learn more about his plan for you. Still, you need more. God does not give the gifts of the Holy Spirit to those who have studied the most. He gives them to the humble person. Jesus said that our heavenly Father gives the Holy Spirit to "those who ask him" (Lk 11:13). Have you ever asked the Father to give you the Spirit?

REVIEW QUESTIONS

1. What did Jesus say about the Holy Spirit?
2. What is the difference between an angel and the Holy Spirit?
3. In what ways has the Holy Spirit appeared? What does each one of these appearances tell us about him?
4. How is the Holy Spirit both a Person and a Gift?

8.

The Church

You cannot become a Christian without the Church. You cannot be saved without the Church. You cannot preach the gospel to yourself. You cannot baptize yourself. You cannot fill yourself with the Holy Spirit. For all these, you need the Church.

When writing his first letter to the early Christians, St. John announced:

> . . . that which we have seen and heard we proclaim also to you, so that you may have fellowship with us; and our fellowship is with the Father and with his Son Jesus Christ.
>
> 1 John 1:3

You join the Church by accepting the gospel and being baptized. This makes you one with Christ and a member of his Church. The Church is our unity with each other. The Church is the communion of all the saints. God calls us to be one with each other so that we can be one with the Father, Son, and Holy Spirit.

When Jesus used the word "Church," he was talking about gathering his disciples together (cf. Mt 16:18). He wanted to make his disciples one with each other:

> . . . that they may all be one; even as thou, Father, art in me, and I in thee, that they also may be in us, so that the world may believe that thou hast sent me.
>
> John 17:21

The union of Father and Son is the *model* for our union with one another. (We become one *the way* they are one.) Their union is the *place* for our union. (We become one *in* them.) Their union is the *cause* of our union. (We become one *because* they make us one.)

The Father and Son create the Church by sending us the Spirit who, being the union of Father and Son, is the only person who can make us one as they are one.

The kingdom of Christ, the Church of Christ

Jesus spoke frequently about the kingdom of God. He told us to ask the Father: "Thy kingdom come" (Mt 6:10). The kingdom is God bringing his plan to completion at the end of this world. At that time, all destined to be saved—that is, the whole Church—will enter the kingdom of God. It is God's kingdom. It is the kingdom the Father gives to his Son. It will be Christ reigning over all.

The Church makes the kingdom of Christ present in this world.

> Christ calls the Church into existence so that this kingdom may last and develop in her and through her during the course of human history on earth.
>
> St. John Paul II, *Catechesis on the Creed,* Vol IV, p. 58

The Church is the beginning of the kingdom. The Church is also the goal of the kingdom. Christ reigns by drawing us together.

As recorded in sacred Scripture, Jesus used the word "Church" on two occasions (Mt 16:18, 18:17). The first time, Jesus made one of the Apostles the "Rock" on which he wanted to "build" his Church. He was speaking to Simon, son of John, who afterward was called "Simon Peter," meaning Simon the Rock. Jesus promised that the "gates of hell would not prevail against it" (Mt 16:18). He meant that the Church would be a gathering of disciples collectively capable of resisting the power of hell and capable of growing in holiness despite the weaknesses of its individual members.

Other books of the New Testament speak of the Church dozens of times. It always means the gathering of Christians into one body. The Acts of the Apostles portrays the Church as being born when the Holy Spirit came down on the disciples at Pentecost. The First Letter to the

Corinthians describes the Church as a human body. St. Paul compares the Church united to Christ as a body united to the head. Christ is part of his Church because he is the "head." Christians form part of the Church because they are "members of the body." Just as a body has lots of different parts, the Church has lots of different members:

> Now you are the body of Christ and individually members of it. And God has appointed in the church first apostles, second prophets, third teachers, then workers of miracles, then healers, helpers, administrators, speakers in various kinds of tongues. Are all apostles? Are all prophets? Are all teachers? Do all work miracles? Do all possess gifts of healing? Do all speak with tongues? Do all interpret?
>
> 1 Corinthians 12:27–30

The diversity of members does not harm the unity of this body any more than the diversity of members in a human body prevents a person from being truly human.

The head-united-to-body analogy implies both diversity and order. A body is not a jumble of parts randomly attached to each other. A foot attached to an elbow would make the body a monstrosity. Being the head of the Church, Jesus establishes order: "first apostles, second prophets, third teachers," etc.

Other texts of the New Testament speak of the Church as the bride of Christ and the New Jerusalem (cf. Eph 5:25–33 and Rev 21:9–14). As his bride, the Church is the one Jesus loves. As the holy city, the Church is the union of all saints coming together to worship God.

Following the logic of covenant used throughout the Bible, the Church has come to see herself as God's Chosen People. The Church fulfils the

Sacred Scripture

I do not pray for these only, but also for those who believe in me through their word, that they may all be one; even as thou, Father, art in me, and I in thee, that they also may be in us, so that the world may believe that thou hast sent me. The glory which thou hast given me I have given to them, that they may be one even as we are one, I in them and thou in me, that they may become perfectly one, so that the world may know that thou hast sent me and hast loved them even as thou hast loved me.

John 17:20–23

ultimate purpose of the covenant God made with Abraham, Isaac, and Jacob. The Church is the whole reason for creation. The Church is the final result of that action Jesus prophesied when he told his disciples: "And when I am lifted up from the earth, I shall draw all men to myself" (Jn 12:32). By making a new heaven and a new earth, Jesus prepares the final dwelling place for his Church.

One, holy, catholic, apostolic

Though there are many buildings called churches and many Christian communities calling themselves churches, Jesus founded only one Church. When summarizing their beliefs, the very first Christians—still living in the times of the Apostles—called this unity of all Christians the "holy, catholic Church." For centuries, while gathered together for the Eucharist on Sundays, Christians all over the world have recited the Creed, saying they "believe in one, holy, catholic, and apostolic Church."

In order to be fully Christian, you have to be one with Christ. To be fully Christian, the Christian community you belong to has to be fully connected to Christ through the Apostles. For this to make sense, you need to look at each of the characteristics of the Church and what it means to be one, holy, catholic, and apostolic. These characteristics are sometimes called the four "marks" of the Church: unity, sanctity, catholicity, and apostolicity.

The Church is one

St. Paul expressed the mystery of Christian unity when he said that Christians are united by "one Lord, one faith, one baptism" (Eph 4:5). The Church is a mystery of communion—not just a global organization.

> The Church is . . . sent to the world to announce and witness, to make present and spread the mystery of communion which is essential to her, and to gather all people and all things into Christ.
>
> St. John Paul II, *Call for Christian Unity*, n. 5

Fathers of the Church

Do not separate yourself from the Church. Nothing is stronger than the Church. The Church is your hope. The Church is your salvation. The Church is your refuge. It is higher than the heavens and broader than the earth. It never grows old. Its vigor is eternal.

St. John Chrysostom, *The Fall of Eutropius*, 6

Jesus founded his Church to draw all his disciples—indeed all things in heaven and on earth—into one single whole. He wants his Church to be a *unity*—not just a gathering.

The way a human person is one being made of body and soul, the Church is a single creation that is both as visible as the human body and as invisible as the human soul. Church unity, besides being spiritual, must necessarily manifest itself visibly. St. Paul expressed this mystery by calling the Church a unity of body and spirit: "There is one Body, one Spirit" (Eph 4:4).

One of the problems facing Christians today is the lack of visible unity. If your body is covered with sores and rashes, you know there is an invisible problem inside, like a virus. So too with the Church. When Christians are not visibly united, this lack of unity becomes obvious to the whole world and scandalizes non-Christians. When we as Christians are not united, something is lacking in our faith and in our practice of the faith. This lack of visible unity is the fault of all Christians. Neither Catholics, nor Orthodox, nor Anglicans, nor Evangelicals, nor Protestants are excused from blame for this insult to God.

After many centuries of disagreement among Christians, no one knows how to bring all Christians together into visible unity. As we Christians need to ask God to show us how to heal the wounds. God must show us how to achieve perfect unity.

Despite the many wounds to unity among all Christians, the Church is one, even now, both visibly and invisibly. The Second Vatican Council declared:

> Christ bestowed unity on his Church from the beginning. This unity, we believe, subsists in the Catholic Church as something she can never lose, and we hope that it will continue to increase until the end of time.
>
> Vatican II, *Decree on Ecumenism*, n. 4

To achieve unity, Christians do not need to invent something new. The perfect unity we seek already exists in the Catholic Church. By saying that this unity "*subsists* in the Catholic Church," we mean not only that it is there now but also that it has always been there and will always be there.

Problems of disunity arise even among Catholics whenever someone refuses to accept the official teachings of the Church. (For more on this topic, see chapters 17 and 18). But the problems are never so great that they nullify the unity Christ wants for his Church. Though problems may make it difficult for some people to perceive the Church's unity, that unity exists.

Knowing of the many obstacles to unity, the Vatican Council concluded:

> Human powers and capacities cannot achieve this holy objective—the reconciling of all Christians in the unity of the one and only Church of Christ. It is because of this that the Council rests all its hope on the prayer of Christ for the Church, on our Father's love for us, and on the power of the Holy Spirit.
>
> Vatican II, *Decree on Ecumenism*, n. 24

Although perfect unity cannot be achieved by following some ingenious plan we might invent, Christians are supposed to struggle for unity as much as they are supposed to struggle to be holy. Even in the very beginning, shortly after Pentecost, factions arose within the Church and St. Paul gave Christians the command: Do all you can "to maintain the unity of the Spirit in the bond of peace" (Eph 4:3).

The Church is holy

Christ wants his Church to be one. He also wants his bride to be holy. For the Church to be holy, each and every one of the members of the Church must strive to be holy. St. Peter said: "Be holy in all you do, since it is the Holy One who has called you, and scripture says: 'You shall be holy, for I am holy' " (1 Pt 1:15). If you want to call yourself a Christian, you cannot be satisfied with striving for anything less than heroic sanctity. If you are not ready to sacrifice everything for Christ, you are not ready to be a Christian.

Jesus told his disciples, "You, therefore, must be perfect, as your heavenly Father is perfect" (Mt 5:48). He knows that we are sinners. All members of the Church—including the bishops, priests, and deacons—see some sins and defects if they examine themselves honestly. If we "fight the good fight," God forgives us and rewards our efforts with his gift of grace in order to make us holier (cf. 1 Tim 6:12).

God wants you to be a saint. Sanctity is not a privilege reserved for a few Christians who are good at making sacrifices. God calls everyone, including you, to live a holy life.

The holiness of the Church, like the unity of the Church, is already mysteriously present within the Church despite our sins and defects. The Church's holiness does not come from our progress in holiness. Just the reverse: we can become holy in the Church because God made her holy from the beginning. The *Catechism* explains it as an action of the Father, Son, and Holy Spirit.

> The Church is holy: the Most Holy God is her author; Christ, her bridegroom, gave himself up to make her holy; the Spirit of holiness gives her life. Since she still includes sinners, she is "the sinless one made up of sinners." Her holiness shines in the saints; in Mary she is already all-holy.
>
> CCC, n. 867

The holiness of all Christians, like the unity among all Christians, is a goal God calls us to pursue. By a special gift of grace, the Blessed Virgin Mary was the first Christian to achieve perfect holiness. God created her "full of grace" at the moment of her conception (cf. Lk 1:28).

The Church is catholic

The Creed calls the Church "catholic." This is a Greek word meaning "universal." Being catholic means that the Church exists for the salvation of all people of all times and all places. The *Catechism* explains:

> The Church is catholic: she proclaims the fullness of the faith. She bears in herself and administers the totality of the means of salvation. She is sent out to all peoples. She speaks to all people. She encompasses all times.
>
> CCC, n. 868

The Church proclaims the fullness of faith because she teaches everything that God revealed through Jesus and his Apostles. She offers the totality of the means of salvation, among other reasons, because she administers all the sacraments. She cares for all people—the rich and the poor, the young and the old, the healthy and the sick.

Because the Church is catholic, she has a mission to offer the means of salvation to everybody, everywhere in the world. Just as the Church is catholic, every Christian needs to be catholic, that is, to have a universal outlook. Every Christian has to feel the urgency of spreading the gospel.

Being catholic means giving no importance to tribes, races, nationalities, or languages. Seek that which unites and overcome that which divides. St. Josemaría describes this universal outlook:

> There is only one race, the race of the children of God. There is only one color, the color of the children of God. And there is only one language, the language that speaks to the heart and to the mind, without the noise of words, making us know God and making us love one another.
>
> St. Josemaría, *Christ Is Passing By*, n. 106

Magisterium

[T]he Church's unity is not only a future hope; it already exists. Jesus Christ did not pray for it in vain. Nevertheless, unity has not yet reached its visible achievement among Christians and indeed, as is well known, down the centuries it has been subject to various difficulties and trials.

Similarly, it should be said that the Church is holy, but her holiness requires a constant process of conversion and renewal by the faithful as individuals and by communities. This also includes the humble request for the forgiveness of sins committed. Moreover, the Church is catholic, but her universal dimension must increasingly be expressed in missionary activity, inculturation of the faith and ecumenical effort guided by the Holy Spirit, until the divine call to faith in Christ is fully achieved.

Thus the problem of ecumenism is not to bring about from nothing a unity that does not yet exist, but to live fully and faithfully, under the action of the Holy Spirit, that unity in which Christ constituted the Church.

. . . And should we ask if all this is possible, the answer will always be Yes. It is the same answer which Mary of Nazareth heard: "For with God nothing will be impossible" (Lk 1:37).

St. John Paul II, *Catechesis on the Creed*, Vol IV, pp. 690–693

To acquire a catholic mentality, begin by finding out why you need to spread the Gospel to all those who do not know Christ.

A Catholic is any Christian who submits not only to the authority of the local church but also to the authority of the Bishop of Rome (also called the "Roman Pontiff" or the "Pope"). As a label, the term "Catholic" (with a capital "C") is often misunderstood—as if being a Catholic were just one more way of being a Christian, and the Catholic Church were just one more Christian denomination. Being *catholic* is for all Christians. Being *Catholic* is for all Christians. Jesus is the one who wants all Christians in the world today to submit to the authority of the Pope.

If you are fully united to the Catholic Church, you are fully united to the Church Christ established. If you are not in full communion with the Catholic Church, then you are not in full communion with the Church Christ established. To be in full communion with the Catholic Church, you have to accept the authority of the Pope. Jesus is the one who established this authority.

The Church is apostolic

The Church is apostolic for three reasons: because she is founded on the Apostles, because she hands on the teaching of the Apostles, and because she continues to be taught, sanctified, and guided by the bishops, who are the successors of the Apostles. Today's bishops have the power to teach, sanctify, and govern the Church because they received it from the Apostles. This makes the Church apostolic.

How does a man become a bishop—that is, a successor of the Apostles? He receives spiritual power from the bishops who came before him and they received it from the bishops who came before them—in a line of *succession* going all the way back to the Apostles. This line of succession, that began when the Apostles gave their spiritual powers to their first successors, is called "apostolic succession." Without it, there would be no Church.

There is only one reason a bishop today has any spiritual power to teach, to sanctify, and to govern—he received it from the bishops who came before him. Without this handing on of the powers, there would be no one capable of preserving God's revelation free from error, no one capable of sanctifying men and women by administering the sacraments, and no one capable of governing the Church according to God's will.

St. Irenaeus summarized this belief around the year 180, a mere eighty years after the death of St. John the Apostle:

> Those who wish to discern the truth may observe the apostolic Tradition manifest in every church throughout the world. We can enumerate in the churches, down to our day, both those who were appointed bishops by the Apostles and those who were successors [to these bishops]. . . . For they [the Apostles] were desirous that these men should be perfect and blameless in all things, since they were leaving them behind as their successors, delivering up their own place of government to these men.
>
> St. Irenaeus, *Against Heresies*, III, 3, 1

St. Irenaeus was a bishop. He knew how the Apostles appointed the bishops before him. St. Polycarp had made him a bishop, and St. Polycarp had become a bishop when St. John the Apostle laid hands on him.

The New Testament calls the Apostles "foundations" upon which the Church has been built (cf. Rev 21:14). Of course, the Church is not a building. The metaphor explains how the Church has its origin in Christ's choice of twelve men. It explains how the Church received God's revelation and God's power from Jesus through these men.

We trace the practice of our faith back to the Apostles. No matter how much we venerate the Bible, we are missing something vital if we forget that Christ's teaching came to us through the Apostles *before* it came to us through sacred Scripture. Jesus did not build his Church on the Bible. Instead, he made the Apostles the foundation of his Church. And among those twelve, he singled out one—Simon—and said: "You are Peter and on this rock I will build my Church" (Mt 16:18). All Christians should show special respect for the Pope and obey him as they would obey Christ. The Pope is the successor of St. Peter. He is the Vicar of Christ, that is—he takes Christ's place on earth. He is the one God has chosen to be the visible head of the Church here in this world.

Wisdom of the Saints

Before all else—fidelity to the Church: one, holy, catholic and apostolic. Jesus did not found several churches, but one single Church . . . which is not a French or a Greek or a Slavic Church, according to the names of different nations, but an apostolic and universal Church.

And this is the Church of Rome: the true Mother of all peoples, splendid in the variety of her rites, in the use of the different languages according to the liturgical development of different periods and different nations, but always with the same flame of belief and discipline, of order and sacred organization. The formula comes from St. Ambrose: *Ubi Petrus, ibi Ecclesia*—Where you find Peter, there you find the Church.

St. Pope John XXIII, Venice, March 15, 1959

How are Christians today connected to the Apostles? The Acts of the Apostles states how the first Christians understood it:

> And they devoted themselves to the apostles' teaching and fellowship, to the breaking of bread and the prayers.
>
> Acts 2:42

Being faithful to the teaching of the apostles ensured "the brotherhood," that is, the unity of the Church. Being faithful to the apostles also guaranteed the proper celebration of the "breaking of the bread," the Eucharist. How do Christians today enjoy the same guarantee?

Knowing that they were going "to depart and be with Christ" (Phil 1:23), the Apostles appointed successors to govern and care for the Church. These successors were called "bishops." In other words, if Christians today want to be connected to the Apostles—if they want to remain faithful to the teaching of the Apostles—they must be connected to their successors, the bishops of the Church. Being connected to the Apostles is not a vague notion. It means that Christians obey their bishops and the bishops obey the Pope.

If you want to know the correct interpretation of sacred Scripture, turn to the bishops who are in communion with the Pope. If you want forgiveness for sins committed after baptism, turn to the bishops. If you want the body and blood of Christ in the breaking of the bread, turn to the bishops. If you do not do this, you will not get what you are looking for. The power needed to preserve God's revelation free from error, the power needed to forgive sins, and the power needed to celebrate the Eucharist was not given to all Christians but only to the Apostles and to their successors. This is why the Church will always be apostolic.

Divisions in the Church

Shortly after the end of the first millennium, the Church was split apart, between East and West. At that time "East" referred to that region of the world dominated by the Byzantine Empire and regions to the east of its capital, Constantinople. "West" referred to Rome and the lands comprising western Europe. By that time, Jerusalem and all of northern Africa—Ethiopia being the notable exception—were under Muslim domination. The bishops in the East began to claim that they had no need to submit to the authority of the Bishop of Rome. They called themselves "Orthodox," implying that they were the ones who were teaching the "orthodoxy," that is, the correct teaching.

Christians in the West remained faithful to the Pope. These Christians used the term "Roman Catholic" to define the Church. They emphasized "Roman" to show their loyalty to the Bishop of Rome. They believed—as all Christians should believe—that this bishop and only this bishop is the rightful successor of Peter the Apostle. They believed that the Pope had the "power of the keys"—the keys to the kingdom of heaven given to St. Peter. This power gives him authority over the whole Church.

Jesus gave this authority to Peter when he told him: "I will give you the keys of the kingdom of heaven" (Mt 16:19). By God's will, St. Peter passed this power to his successor, St. Linus (the second pope), who in turn passed it on to St. Cletus (the third pope)—and so on, up until the present day. Catholics are those Christians that claim the Bishop of Rome has authority over the Church of Jesus Christ throughout the whole world. Other Christians belong to communities which, at least in practice, have been operating as if no one person has authority over the whole Church.

The split between East and West took place in AD 1054. This split is usually referred to as the "Eastern Schism." About 500 years after that, another division among Christians developed in the West. Under the influence of Martin Luther, a Catholic priest in Germany, some Christians broke away from the Roman Catholic Church.

For centuries, Catholics have referred to these Christians as "Protestants" because the break began with Martin Luther's *protest* on October 31, 1517. The Protestants said they wanted to *reform* the Church, going back to the original plan that Jesus had for his Church. For this reason, Martin Luther's split with Rome was called the "Reformation."

After Martin Luther's split with Rome, some Protestants continued to call the Church "one, holy, catholic, and apostolic." Others stopped using these words. In both cases, Protestants claimed that the Catholic Church was not the visible institution where Christians might find the true Church established by Jesus. They were convinced that the Catholic Church had betrayed Christ and the gospel. They not only broke away from the authority of the Bishop of Rome, but they also came to believe that no bishop anywhere had the authority to tell them what to believe.

Thousands of books have been written to describe exactly what happened during the Reformation and why it happened. It would be difficult to summarize here. Many different events took place all at once. Describing just one aspect of the whole story requires a lengthy treatise. However, after many centuries and many misunderstandings on all sides, a few conclusions can be stated.

- "Baptism makes us members of the body of Christ. Baptism incorporates us into the Christ's Church" (*CCC*, no. 1267). Anyone validly baptized is a Christian. Anyone validly baptized is by definition a member of Christ's Church. When someone is validly baptized—no matter where the baptism takes place and no matter who does the baptism—that person receives God's gift of grace.
- Though they do not accept the authority of the Bishop of Rome, the Orthodox churches have kept all the other essential elements of Christian practice, including the valid celebration of the seven sacraments.
- The members of other Christian communities not in communion with Rome (Anglicans, Lutherans, Methodists, Baptists, etc.) truly

believe in Jesus Christ. They seek salvation in Christ's death and resurrection, sometimes making heroic efforts to spread the gospel. They accept the Bible as the Word of God. However, they do not agree with each other on how to interpret specific texts in the Bible. For this reason, these Christians are split among themselves into many different denominations.

- Christ founded only one Church. He wants all Christians to be visibly united here on earth in that one Church. As Jesus prayed to his Father at the Last Supper: "May they all be one, so that *the world may see* that it was you who sent me" (cf. Jn 17:21). *Spiritual* unity among Christians is not enough. We have to work towards *visible* unity. Jesus wants the world to *see* the unity of all Christians in one Church.
- Unity requires one faith. All Christians should believe the same thing. For instance, if some say God has revealed that Jesus' mother remained a virgin, while others say this is not true, Christians are not united.
- The constant teaching of the bishops of Rome has maintained that Christians are faithful to God's will only when they hold fast to the Pope's authority. It is not clear when the Orthodox churches and other Christian communities will come to accept this teaching. There can be no visible unity among Christians unless they accept the authority of the Bishop of Rome, as it was established by Jesus when giving St. Peter the "power of the keys."
- All Christians have an obligation to re-examine the past.

> Besides the doctrinal differences needing to be resolved, Christians cannot underestimate the burden of long-standing misgivings inherited from the past, and of mutual misunderstandings and prejudices. Complacency, indifference, and insufficient knowledge of one another often make this situation worse. Consequently, the commitment to ecumenism must be based upon the conversion of hearts and upon prayer, which will also lead to the necessary purification of past memories.
>
> St. John Paul II, *Call for Christian Unity*, n. 2

Ecumenism is the goal of bringing all Christian communities into visible unity. It requires that Catholics, Orthodox, Anglicans, Evangelicals, and Protestants* examine the past together to see what mistakes were made. Then, counting on God's grace, they can try to correct them.

All can be saved

God wants all people to be saved. He saves not only those who are visibly members of Christ's Church but also other men and women. The Church teaches:

> The salvific action of Jesus Christ, with and through his Spirit, extends beyond the visible boundaries of the Church to all humanity.
>
> *The Lord Jesus*, n. 12

Anyone who has been baptized receives the gift of salvation (sanctifying grace) and can truly be called a Christian and a member of the Church. The Church says that salvation is also possible for those "beyond the visible boundaries of the Church," that is, for those who have not been baptized.

The *Catechism* explains how God makes salvation possible for those who are not baptized with water:

> All those who, without knowing of the Church but acting under the inspiration of grace, seek God sincerely and strive to fulfil his will, are saved even if they have not been baptized.
>
> CCC, n. 1281

This does not mean that a person will find salvation no matter what religion he or she follows. Everyone has an obligation to seek God's will and fulfill it.

No one can be satisfied with merely keeping the faith their parents taught them. We find the full truth only by seeking God's will. Even

* The term *Protestant* normally refers to Christian communities that originated in the Reformation. Many of these communities prefer to describe themselves using the term *Evangelical* instead.

Catholics are called to discover what more God wants from them, rather than being content with what they learned as children.

This quest for truth is the main reason why the Church has made great efforts over the centuries to explain God's revelation in ever more precise terms. Because God wants us to find the whole truth, he has given his Church a special grace. It is guidance from the Holy Spirit to pass on God's revelation and develop teachings, totally free of any error, that define this revelation.

Seeking God's will means many things, but first and foremost it means seeking the whole truth that God revealed through Jesus Christ. Do not reduce salvation to a question of being cleansed from sin. God not only takes away your sins but lifts up your mind and heart to know mysteries that lie beyond human wisdom. Your salvation—your entrance into the kingdom of God—demands that you possess a deep knowledge of these truths. That is why St. Paul, besides telling us that God "wants everyone to be saved," also says that God wants everyone "to come to the knowledge of the truth" (1 Tim 2:4). St. Paul insisted on this many times in his letters:

> . . . that the God of our Lord Jesus Christ, the Father of glory, may give you a spirit of wisdom and of revelation in the knowledge of him, having the eyes of your hearts enlightened, that you may know what is the hope to which he has called you, what are the riches of his glorious inheritance in the saints, and what is the immeasurable greatness of his power in us who believe according to the working of his great might . . .
>
> Ephesians 1:17–19

Each person has an obligation in conscience to seek this full knowledge of the truth.

Faith in Jesus, faith in the Church

One, holy, catholic, and apostolic: These four qualities will always define the Church. The *Catechism* sums it up this way:

> The Church is ultimately one, holy, catholic, and apostolic in her deepest and ultimate identity, because it is in her that "the kingdom of heaven,"

> the "reign of God," already exists and will be fulfilled at the end of time. The kingdom has come in the person of Christ and grows mysteriously in the hearts of those incorporated into him, until its full eschatological manifestation. Then all those he has redeemed and made "holy and blameless before him in love" will be gathered together as the one People of God, the "Bride of the Lamb," "the holy city Jerusalem coming down out of heaven from God, having the glory of God."
>
> *CCC*, n. 865

The "full eschatological manifestation" of the Church means that, at the end of time, everyone will see the full beauty of the Church. When Christ returns in glory, everyone will know that the Church's beauty consists in being one, holy, catholic, and apostolic. Until then, it will always require faith to believe that Jesus is the Son of God and faith to believe the Church is one, holy, catholic, and apostolic.

The communion of Saints

The communion of saints is the union of all Christians. It also refers to the way that all Christians share spiritual goods (cf. *CCC*, n. 948). It is a mysterious sharing that we can neither see nor measure. The sharing of spiritual goods means that any good work performed by one Christian adds to the spiritual gifts enjoyed by the others. If you spend time in prayer or make some sacrifice, it helps all the other members of the Church.

The Church is a communion of saints. All the faithful form one body. We call this the "mystical Body of Christ." It is mystical because we cannot see it physically, and yet it is very real. It is Christ's body: "Now you are the body of Christ and individually members of it" (1 Cor 12:27).

The good of each member is communicated to the others. "If one member suffers, all suffer together; if one member is honored, all rejoice together" (1 Cor 12:26). The least act done with love increases the spiritual good of all members of the Church. Any sin we commit harms this communion.

Some members of this communion are pilgrims on earth. Traditionally, we call this the "Church militant," because we must fight "the good fight" (2 Tim 4:7), struggling to be holy. Some members of this communion are souls in purgatory. They are the Church suffering, because God is purifying them to prepare them for heaven. Other members of this communion already enjoy seeing God face-to-face. This is the Church triumphant, because these are the saints who have conquered (cf. Rev 2:7). All three are united to each other and form a single communion of saints.

REVIEW QUESTIONS

1. What words did Jesus use during the Last Supper to pray for the unity of all Christians? Why does the Church need visible unity?
2. What do we mean when we say that the Church is one? What do we mean when we say that the Church is holy? What do we mean when we say that the Church is catholic? What do we mean when we say that the Church is apostolic?
3. Who belongs to the Church?
4. What is the communion of saints?

9.

The Virgin Mary

No other disciple was as close to Jesus as the Blessed Virgin Mary. She was close to him not only physically but, more importantly, spiritually. She was the "handmaid of the Lord" (Lk 1:38), ready to do whatever God wanted her to do.

Mary dedicated herself completely to God by remaining a virgin. She remained a virgin for her whole life, and so we call her the "ever virgin Mary." She became the mother of Jesus miraculously, through the power of the Holy Spirit. She willingly accepted the sacrifice of giving birth to Jesus in a stable. She was again ready to sacrifice everything when it came time for Jesus to die.

She fulfilled the prophecy of Simeon who said to her in the Temple that Jesus "was destined to be a sign that is rejected—and a sword will pierce through your own soul also" (Lk 2:35). This prophecy meant not only that Mary would suffer, as any mother would, seeing her son die, it also meant that she would offer a pleasing sacrifice to God because she would offer her Son to the Father by accepting his death willingly.

Mary's faith was like Abraham's, only greater. To grasp how great her faith was, recall what the angel Gabriel promised Mary and then compare that to what she saw when Jesus died. The Church teaches:

> Mary . . . had received the angel's revelation at the Annunciation. At that moment she had also heard the words: "He will be great . . . and the Lord God will give to him the throne of his father David, and he will reign over the house of Jacob for ever; and of his kingdom there will be no end."

> And now, standing at the foot of the cross, Mary is the witness, humanly speaking, of the complete negation of these words. On that wood of the cross her Son hangs in agony as one condemned. "He was despised and rejected by men; a man of sorrows . . . he was despised, and we esteemed him not": as one destroyed. How great, how heroic then is the obedience of faith shown by Mary in the face of God's "unsearchable judgments"! How completely she "abandons herself to God" without reserve, offering the full assent of the intellect and the will to him whose "ways are inscrutable"!
>
> St. John Paul II, *Mother of the Redeemer*, n. 18
> (cf. Lk 1:32–33, Is 53:3–5, Rom 11:33)

Mary kept faith when darkness covered the earth. She believed that Gabriel's prophecy would be fulfilled.

Abraham believed that God would fulfil his promise despite the demand that he should sacrifice his son, Isaac. As Mary stood at the foot of the cross suffering together with her Son, she believed Jesus would rise from the dead. Abraham became our father in faith. Mary became the mother of all who believe.

The Marian privileges

Mary is the Mother of God. The Church defined this dogma in the Council of Ephesus, one of the earliest ecumenical councils. The Church praises and honors Mary because God chose her to be the Mother of Jesus and gave her more grace than he will ever give all the angels and saints put together. She is truly *full* of grace.

The Virgin Mary is the Immaculate Conception. Mary was conceived without sin because God granted her an extraordinary privilege when

Sacred Scripture

On the third day there was a marriage at Cana in Galilee, and the mother of Jesus was there; Jesus also was invited to the marriage, with his disciples. When the wine failed, the mother of Jesus said to him, "They have no wine." And Jesus said to her, "O woman, what have you to do with me? My hour has not yet come." His mother said to the servants, "Do whatever he tells you."

John 2:1–5

creating her. When defining this dogma, the Church clarified that God preserved her from all stain of sin. From the first moment of her existence, in anticipation of the merits of Christ's death and resurrection, Mary was "full of grace" (Lk 1:28). This anticipation of effect preceding cause does not match our normal understanding of time. Still, God, who lives outside of time, had the power to grant whatever privilege he wanted when he created Mary.

> We face here a mystery of love. Human reason barely begins to comprehend. Only faith can shed some light on how a creature can be raised to such great heights, becoming a loving target for the delights of the Trinity. We know this is a divine secret. Yet because our Mother is involved, we feel we can understand it more—if we are entitled to speak this way—than other truths of our faith.
>
> How would we have acted, if we could have chosen our own mother? I'm sure we would have chosen the one we have, adorning her with every possible grace. That is what Christ did. Being all-powerful, all-wise, Love itself, his power carried out his will.
>
> St. Josemaría, *Christ Is Passing By*, n. 171

All of Mary's privileges come from the fact that God chose her to be Jesus' mother.

Besides being Mother of God and being the Immaculate Conception, Mary has many other privileges. The Church celebrates many feasts for our Lady throughout the year to remind us. Of the many Marian privileges we could mention, two more ought to be highlighted since they form part of Church dogma—Mary's perpetual virginity and her assumption into heaven.

By conceiving the child through the power of the Holy Spirit, Mary remained a virgin while at the same time becoming the mother of the baby Jesus. Having chosen to work this great miracle, God wanted her to remain a virgin forever. Quoting St. Augustine, the *Catechism* describes this in detail:

> Mary "remained a virgin in conceiving her Son, a virgin in giving birth to him, a virgin in carrying him, a virgin in nursing him at her breast,

> always a virgin": with her whole being she is "the handmaid of the Lord" (Lk 1:38).
>
> *CCC*, n. 510

Mary's perpetual virginity is a prophetic sign of the Church. United to Christ, the Church will be the ever-virgin bride in that age where the saints are "are like angels in heaven" (Mk 12:25).

Our Lady's assumption also constitutes a prophetic sign of future glory. Mary already enjoys not only the beatific vision, as all the other saints enjoy it; she has also been blessed with the total effect of the final resurrection. When we contemplate her beauty next to the Risen Lord in Paradise, we see the perfection of the Church.

Mary, Mother of the Church

Filled with the Holy Spirit two thousand years ago, the Virgin Mary made God's Son present in the world as a man. Glorified in heaven, she fulfils a similar mission. She continues to make Jesus specially present in our lives today. The Spirit works through her to make each man and woman another Christ. Mary is the Mother of Jesus and our Mother.

The Virgin Mary was the one who interceded for the newly married couple when, having no more wine, their wedding feast was about to be cut short. She was the one who spoke to Jesus and moved him to work the miracle of changing water into wine. Just as she was able to intercede for the bridegroom and the bride before, she can intercede for us today. At that time she was not yet glorified. Now that Jesus has taken her, body and soul, into heaven, she has more power than ever to help us when we have no more wine—when we lack whatever it is we need to be happy and serve God. She really loves us. She really cares for us the way a mother cares for her child.

> Thus, in her new motherhood in the Spirit, Mary embraces each and every one in the Church, and embraces each and every one through the Church.
>
> St. John Paul II, *Mother of the Redeemer*, n. 47

The Church calls Mary the "Mediatrix of all graces." All of God's blessings come to us through her.

Fathers of the Church

It was fitting that she who had preserved her virginity unspotted in giving birth should keep her body incorrupt even after death. It was fitting that she who had borne the Creator as a child in her bosom should have a dwelling place with God. It was fitting that the bride espoused by the Father should dwell in the bridal chambers of heaven. It was fitting that she who had gazed at her Son on the cross, receiving then in her breast the sword of sorrow she had been spared at his birth, should behold him seated with the Father. It was fitting that the Mother of God should enjoy the privileges of the Son and should be honored by all creation as the Mother and the Handmaid of God.

St. John Damascene, cf. Pius XII, *Constitution on the Assumption*

When all the bishops of the world were gathered together for the Second Vatican Council, Pope Paul VI declared that Mary is the Mother of the Church. She is the Mother of the Church because she is the Mother of Jesus and the Mother of all members of the Church.

When Jesus was dying on the cross, he wanted to reveal this mystery to us. St. John narrates how it happened:

> But standing by the cross of Jesus were his mother, and his mother's sister, Mary the wife of Clopas, and Mary Magdalene. When Jesus saw his mother, and the disciple whom he loved standing near, he said to his mother, "Woman, behold, your son!" Then he said to the disciple, "Behold, your mother!" And from that hour the disciple took her to his own home.
>
> John 19:25–27

St. John was the disciple who took Mary into his home. If we want to be like the disciple Jesus loved, we should also make a place for the Blessed Virgin Mary in our lives. We can do this in many ways.

Some people put a picture of Mary in their sitting room, along with other family pictures. Some pray the Rosary. This prayer is especially pleasing to her, since we repeat the words that the archangel Gabriel used to greet her: "Hail, Mary, full of grace, the Lord is with you" (cf. Lk 1:28).

When St. John made a place for her in his home, he was not merely asking her to live with him. He looked at her the way Jesus told him to look at her. When he saw the Virgin Mary, he saw the woman who

Magisterium

At Cana, thanks to the intercession of Mary and the obedience of the servants, Jesus begins "his hour." At Cana Mary appears as believing in Jesus. Her faith evokes his first "sign" and helps to kindle the faith of the disciples.

We can therefore say that, in this passage of John's Gospel, we find, as it were, a first manifestation of the truth concerning Mary's maternal care. . . . The Second Vatican Council . . . illustrates Mary's maternal role as it relates to the mediation of Christ. Thus we read: "Mary's maternal function towards mankind in no way obscures or diminishes the unique mediation of Christ, but rather shows its efficacy," because "there is one God, and there is one mediator between God and men, the man Christ Jesus" (1 Tim. 2:5). This maternal role of Mary flows . . . "from the superabundance of the merits of Christ; it is founded on his mediation, absolutely depends on it, and draws all its efficacy from it." It is precisely in this sense that the episode at Cana in Galilee offers us a sort of first announcement of Mary's mediation, wholly oriented towards Christ and tending to the revelation of his salvific power.

From the text of John it is evident that it is a mediation which is maternal. As the [Second Vatican] Council proclaims: Mary became "a mother to us in the order of grace." This motherhood in the order of grace flows from her divine motherhood. . . . "This maternity . . . will last without interruption until the eternal fulfillment of all the elect."

St. John Paul II, *Mother of the Redeemer*, nn. 21–22

was both Jesus' mother and his own mother. He knew that Jesus was so intent on making us his brothers and sisters that he wanted us to have the same mother.

Because she is our Mother, we must honor her. As the fourth commandment says: "Honor your father and mother." The *Catechism* teaches:

> We believe that the Holy Mother of God, the new Eve, Mother of the Church, continues in heaven to exercise her motherly role on behalf of the members of Christ.
>
> CCC, n. 975

Devotion to the Virgin Mary lies at the heart of the Gospel message. When we praise and honor Mary, we fulfil the biblical prophecy that she made in the house of Zechariah: ". . . All generations will call me blessed; for he who is mighty has done great things for me" (Lk 1:48–49).

The Holy Family

To understand Jesus as perfect man, Christians need to understand the mystery of the Holy Family. God chose a carpenter named Joseph to be Mary's husband. The Virgin Mary was both perfect mother and perfect spouse. Since she remained a virgin, her husband had to have the same vocation. "The virginal mystery of Joseph corresponds to this virginal maternity of Mary" (St. John Paul II, *Theology of the Body,* p. 268). St. Josemaría explains:

> **MAGISTERIUM**
>
> Holy Mary, Mother of God, you have given the world its true light, Jesus, your Son—the Son of God. . . . Show us Jesus. Lead us to him. Teach us to know and love him, so that we too can become capable of true love and be fountains of living water in the midst of a thirsting world.
>
> Benedict XVI, *God Is Love,* n. 42

> I don't agree with the traditional picture of St. Joseph as an old man, even though it may have been prompted by a desire to emphasize the perpetual virginity of Mary. I see him as a strong young man, perhaps a few years older than our Lady, but in the prime of his life and work.
>
> You don't have to wait to be old or lifeless to practice the virtue of chastity. Purity comes from love; and the strength and gaiety of youth are no obstacle for noble love. Joseph had a young heart and a young body when he married Mary, when he learned of the mystery of her divine motherhood, when he lived in her company, respecting the integrity God wished to give the world as one more sign that he had come to share the life of his creatures. Anyone who cannot understand a love like that knows very little of true love and is a complete stranger to the Christian meaning of chastity.
>
> St. Josemaría, *Christ Is Passing By,* n. 40

While respecting God's desire that Mary remain a virgin forever, Joseph truly loved his wife. According to the liturgy used to celebrate his feast on March 19th, he "cherished her with a husband's love."

Joseph and Mary were married. They were also committed to virginity within marriage. Their mutual commitment to virginity did not lead them to love each other less; on the contrary, it was the source of deeper affection.

Similar logic applies to St. Joseph's love for the child Jesus. Far from being a distant presence in the life of Jesus, Joseph cared for him more affectionately than any man has ever cared for his son.

Feasts of the Virgin Mary and St. Joseph

January 1 – Mary, Mother of God

The Church celebrates the greatest privilege ever shown to a creature—that of being chosen to be Christ's Mother. Mary is the Mother of God because she is truly Jesus' mother and Jesus is truly God.

February 2 – The Presentation

Forty days after Christmas. Simeon tells Mary that a sword will pierce her heart. She will suffer together with her Son while he sheds his blood for us on the cross.

February 11 – Our Lady of Lourdes

This date commemorates our Lady's promise to St. Bernadette Soubirous.

March 19 – St. Joseph, Husband of Mary

God chose the carpenter to be the head of the Holy Family, making him the husband of the Virgin Mary and a father to the divine Child.

March 25 – The Annunciation

Nine months before Christmas, this feast celebrates that moment in our Lady's life when St. Gabriel announced to her that God had chosen her to be the Mother of Jesus.

May 1 – St. Joseph the Worker

All men and women who carry out their work with a spirit of service can, like St. Joseph and Our Lady, become great saints without having to accomplish extraordinary feats.

May 31 – The Visitation

The Virgin Mary visits her cousin St. Elizabeth.

May–June – Immaculate Heart of Mary

This feast is celebrated on the Saturday after the feast of the Sacred Heart of Jesus.

continued

Feasts of the Virgin Mary and St. Joseph *continued*

July 16 – Our Lady of Mount Carmel
This date commemorates our Lady's promise to St. Simon Stock.

August 5 – Our Lady of the Snows
This date commemorates the dedication of the basilica in Rome built in honor of the Virgin Mary.

August 15 – The Assumption
After her life on earth, Mary was taken up into heaven, body and soul, to enjoy the blessing of the resurrection together with her Son, Jesus.

August 22 – The Queenship of Mary
The Virgin Mary is crowned by Father, Son, and Holy Spirit as Queen of heaven and earth.

September 8 – Birth of the Virgin Mary
Nine months after the feast of the Immaculate Conception, we celebrate Mary's birthday.

September 12 – Holy Name of Mary
We remember the holy name of Jesus' mother.

September 15 – Our Lady of Sorrows
The day after the Feast of the Holy Cross (September 14), the Church remembers how Our Lady suffered when Jesus was crucified.

October 7 – Our Lady of the Rosary
The Church dedicates this feast to promoting the Holy Rosary, the most traditional of all Marian devotions.

November 21 – Presentation of Our Lady
This feast recalls the tradition of Mary being taken as a child to the Temple in Jerusalem.

December 8 – The Immaculate Conception
The Virgin Mary, "full of grace," was conceived without sin. God preserved her from all stain of sin to prepare her to be the Mother of Jesus.

Sunday after Christmas – The Holy Family
Jesus, Mary, and Joseph's union as the Holy Family is the model for all Christian families.

> [T]he Family of Nazareth has its own special mystery. And in this mystery, as in the Incarnation, one finds a true fatherhood: the human form of the family of the Son of God, a true human family, formed by the divine mystery. In this family, Joseph is the father: his fatherhood is not one that derives from begetting offspring; but neither is it an "apparent" or merely "substitute" fatherhood. Rather, it is one that fully shares in authentic human fatherhood and the mission of a father in the family.
>
> St. John Paul II, *Guardian of the Redeemer*, n. 21

Jesus is perfect man because God created his humanity perfectly. However, it would be a mistake to think that Jesus became perfect man "out of the blue."

Could the Son of God have become perfect man without being born of a woman? Could he have become perfect man without growing up under the loving gaze of a man he called "father"? We only know this: God chose to have Jesus grow up in a family the same way any other child grows up. Jesus experienced true motherly love from Mary and true fatherly love from Joseph. In this man and woman, the Child Jesus witnessed the mutual affection of a husband and wife—and more, because he witnessed in his parents a humanly perfect love forged by the action of the Holy Spirit. For this reason, the Church deeply venerates the Holy Family, and proposes the life of Jesus, Mary, and Joseph together in Nazareth as the model for all families.

Wisdom of the Saints

The Mother of God has fallen asleep. Around her bed are the twelve Apostles—Matthias in the place of Judas.

And we, through a grace respected by all, are also at her side.

But Jesus wants to have his Mother, body and soul, in heaven. And the heavenly court, arrayed in all its splendour, greets our Lady. You and I—children, after all—take the train of Mary's magnificent blue cloak, and so we can watch the marvellous scene.

The most blessed Trinity receives and showers honors on the Daughter, Mother, and Spouse of God. . . . And so great is the Lady's majesty that the angels exclaim: Who is she?

St. Josemaría, *Holy Rosary*, Fourth Glorious Mystery

REVIEW QUESTIONS

1. Name the privileges of the Blessed Virgin Mary.
2. Why do we call Mary "Mother of the Church"?
3. In what way is Mary's assumption a prophetic sign for the Church?
4. Why does the Church propose the Holy Family as a model for all families?

10.

God's Plan

Before going deeper into the mysteries revealed by God, let's summarize what we have seen so far. The following are the central mysteries of Christian belief:

- **The Holy Trinity:** The Father is God. The Son is God. The Holy Spirit is God. There is only one God. The Father, Son, and Holy Spirit are three persons in one being.
- **Man is created in God's image:** By creating man as male and female and giving them dominion over the whole of the visible world, God created an image and likeness of the Trinitarian communion.
- **Man sins:** Adam and Eve rebelled against God by disobeying his command.
- **The Incarnation:** The Father sent his Son into the world when the Virgin Mary conceived Jesus by the power of the Holy Spirit. Because he is the Word made flesh, Jesus is perfect God and perfect man.
- **Redemption:** By shedding his blood on the cross and rising from the dead, Jesus redeemed the whole of creation.
- **The Church:** The Father and Son sent the Holy Spirit into the world to create the Church. All those who are baptized become children of God and members of Christ's body. The Spirit raises Christians high above the limits of human nature. He "divinizes" them; that is, he gives each person a share in God's own way of living and being. He unites all Christians into one body—the mystical Body of Christ.

God did not reveal these mysteries by handing us a document with a list of Christian beliefs. Instead, God revealed himself gradually, not only through words but also through actions. This chapter is meant to give you an overview of the whole plan, from the beginning of human history until the end. It is an attempt to provide you with the big picture—the context for all the beliefs that Christians accept as revelation coming from God.

God's plan

The following scheme summarizes the major events of human history from beginning to end. This scheme has nothing to do with the usual categories of nation building and human civilization. Instead it looks at history as a series of events foreseen by God to bring man to his final destiny, namely, the kingdom of God. This scheme is designed as a progression from one stage to the next, focusing on events narrated in sacred Scripture.

GOD CREATES MAN

God creates Adam and Eve in his own image and likeness. As husband and wife, the man and woman are called to be a visible sign of the Trinitarian communion of persons. As creatures working together with God, they are called to multiply and fill the earth. As children of God, they are called to give him glory by caring for his creation.

MAN REBELS

Adam and Eve allow themselves to be deceived by Satan. They disobey God. In his great mercy, God promises Adam and Eve that he will send a man born of a woman who will crush the head of Satan. This man is the Savior and Redeemer.

GOD CHOOSES ABRAHAM

By appearing to Abraham and making a covenant with him and his descendants, God prepares the world for the coming of the Messiah. The promised Savior will be an Israelite and, more specifically, a son of King David.

GOD'S SON REDEEMS MAN

By dying for our sins and rising from the dead, Jesus establishes a new and everlasting covenant between God and man. He begins to draw all things to himself in order to restore the whole of creation to its original purpose.

JESUS RETURNS AS KING

Once the time for evangelizing the world comes to an end, Jesus will come again in glory on a day God has fixed according to his plan. He will triumph over all evil—both spiritual and physical—and banish Satan forever.

JESUS JUDGES ALL PEOPLE

All the dead will rise. All men and women of all times and places will be gathered together for a final judgment. The saints will enter Christ's kingdom. The damned will be cast into hell with Satan.

JESUS REIGNS FOREVER

The world will be transformed into a new heaven and a new earth. All the angels and saints will live together in perfect harmony and peace, made as perfectly one with each other as the Father and Son are one in the Holy Spirit. Once we have achieved union with God and with one another, we are perfect. We have no other goal to achieve. We will spend eternity enjoying this union in a kingdom where God is "all in all" (1 Cor 15:28).

God's plan at the present time

In the overview shown above, each one of the stages marks a dramatic change in man's history. We are now in the stage of evangelization, the stage of spreading the gospel. The next major event will be the Parousia, i.e., the Second Coming of Christ at the end of time.

Ever since the day of Pentecost, about two thousand years ago, we have been in the stage of evangelization. Christians continue to spread the Good News. The Church continues to grow as the number of those to be saved increases. As human history develops and as we advance in knowledge and culture, we come to understand God's revelation more clearly.

This defines the big picture and the present moment of human history. The next question concerns your place in these events.

Why did God create you?

The first thing a person worries about is survival. You need food and shelter. You need a way to earn a living. Once you have the essentials, then what? Where do you fit into the big picture of human history? Does your life have any meaning beyond survival for another day? You begin to ask yourself, "Why am I here? Why did God create me? What does he want me to do?"

Perhaps as a child you memorized the answer to one of the most important questions in the *Baltimore Catechism* where it asks, "Why did God make us?" We say that God made us—God made you—to know love and serve him here on earth and to be happy with him forever in heaven.

This is the whole purpose of your existence. God wants you to live with him and all the angels and saints in a place where you will be perfectly happy forever. To get there you need to learn to know him and love him.

Sacred Scripture

And he called to him his twelve disciples and gave them authority over unclean spirits, to cast them out, and to heal every disease and every infirmity. . . . These twelve Jesus sent out, charging them . . . And preach as you go, saying, "The kingdom of heaven is at hand."

Matthew 10:1, 5, 7

Knowing him and loving him means serving him—and learning to love others by serving them.

If you want to be happy, you have to learn to give yourself to others. This is a law like the law of gravity. In other words, it defines the way things necessarily happen. If you drop a rock, it falls. If you want to be happy, you have to give yourself to others.

Justice requires giving. A just person is someone who gives others what belongs to them. Love also requires giving—*lots* of giving—giving beyond the requirements of justice. If you want to be happy, you have to learn to sacrifice yourself for others—to give and give and never stop giving.

Jesus set the standard very high. Not only does he want us to love others. He said that we should love them as he has loved us.

> A new commandment I give to you, that you love one another; even as I have loved you, that you also love one another. By this all men will know that you are my disciples, if you have love for one another.
>
> John 13:34–35

The purpose of your existence is learning how to love, how to give yourself to others.

How will others recognize Christ in you? When they see you loving others as he loves you. When they see you willing to forgive others the way that God forgives you. If you learn to do this here on earth, you will be ready to do it forever in the next world.

The idea is not simply to be a nice person who is nice to other nice people. Our Lord had something much more radical in mind. He wants us to love absolutely everybody, even our enemies. He said to his disciples:

> But I say to you that hear, Love your enemies, do good to those who hate you, bless those who curse you, pray for those who abuse you. To him who strikes you on the cheek, offer the other also; and from him who takes away your coat do not withhold even your shirt.
>
> Luke 6:27–29

Turning the other cheek means forgiving instead of seeking revenge.

> Your reward will be great, and you will be sons of the Most High; for he is kind to the ungrateful and the selfish. Be merciful, even as your Father is merciful. Judge not, and you will not be judged; condemn not, and you will not be condemned; forgive, and you will be forgiven; give, and it will be given to you; good measure, pressed down, shaken together, running over . . .
>
> Luke 6:35–38

One day God will judge you by measuring one thing—love. How did you love God? How did you love those you lived with? As the *Catechism* says, quoting the great mystic, St. John of the Cross: "At the evening of life, we shall be judged on our love" (CCC, n. 1022).

If you are found worthy of entering into God's kingdom, your life is a success. If you are excluded from that kingdom because of your selfish habits, your life is a disaster.

Make a firm commitment to Jesus Christ. Ask him to fill you with his Spirit so that you learn what it means to love others and sacrifice yourself for them.

Enter by the narrow gate

Following Jesus demands sacrifice. He told his disciples:

> Enter by the narrow gate; for the gate is wide and the way is easy, that leads to destruction, and those who enter by it are many. For the gate is narrow and the way is hard, that leads to life, and those who find it are few.
>
> Matthew 7:13–14

You cannot find your place in God's plan by living a life of luxury and laziness. You do not need to do extraordinary deeds. Instead, you need to do the ordinary things of everyday life with extraordinary love.

Your struggle to live this way consists in learning how to serve others with your work. Look at Jesus' own life. Before setting out to preach and work miracles, Jesus worked in an ordinary job. He expects you to work. Only a handful of saints were ever given the ability to perform miracles. Every man and woman can reach sanctity by faithfully fulfilling his or her ordinary obligations.

ECCLESIASTICAL WRITERS

There are two ways: one of life and one of death. And there is a great difference between these two ways. Now the way of life is this: First, love the God who made you. Second, love your neighbor as yourself.

The Teaching of the Twelve Apostles, I, 1–2

The father who does his work well and takes good care of his family can be a great saint. The mother who devotes herself to making her home cheerful and pleasant for her husband and children is also walking the road to sanctity. As the Church teaches, all people—even those who spend their lives doing routine jobs in the middle of the world—are called to be saints. Jesus was speaking to the men and women of all times when he said, "You, therefore, must be perfect, as your heavenly Father is perfect" (Mt 5:48).

Supernatural life

Holiness would remain beyond reach except for one fact. God will give you the grace you need to be a saint. Take the hard road that leads to the narrow gate. But remember: your efforts will be useless without God's grace. The goal of sanctity lies beyond virtue. Being holy means seeking human perfection, but it something much greater than that.

The scheme given above outlines human history. Like all stories, history has a beginning, a middle, and an end. In this case, the story begins with God planning to send Jesus. It climaxes when Jesus comes the first time. It ends when Jesus comes the second time. In order to describe how you personally become holy, one more box should be included in that scheme. It would mention what St. Bernard said about a "third coming" of Jesus Christ.

The first coming took place when Jesus was born in Bethlehem. The second coming will take place when Jesus appears at the end of the world with all his angels. The third coming takes place in secret. It takes place inside of you, now, during your life on earth.

> The third coming takes place between the other two. . . . In brief, his first coming was in flesh and in weakness, this intermediary coming is in spirit and in power, the last coming will be in glory and majesty. . . . Do

Magisterium

Earthly progress must be carefully distinguished from the growth of Christ's kingdom. Even so, such progress is vital to the kingdom of God to the extent that it contributes to the better ordering of human society.

After we have obeyed the Lord, and in his Spirit nurtured on earth the values of human dignity, brotherhood and freedom—indeed, all the good fruits of our nature and enterprise—we will find them again, but freed of all stain of sin, illuminated and transfigured, when Christ presents to his Father an eternal and universal kingdom: "a kingdom of truth and life; a kingdom of holiness and grace; a kingdom of justice, love and peace." That kingdom is already mysteriously present in this world. When the Lord returns, it will enter into its perfection.

Vatican II, *The Church in the Modern World*, n. 39

> not imagine that what we are saying about the intermediary coming is simply our own fabrication. Listen to Christ himself: "If a man loves me, he will keep my word, and my Father will love him, and we will come to him and make our home with him" (Jn 14:23).
>
> St. Bernard of Clairvaux, *Sermons for Advent*, V, 1–2

Jesus comes with his Father to live inside of you. They pour the gift of Holy Spirit into your heart to make you holy. When God does this to you—when you allow him to do it to you—it is a *supernatural* act. It is *super*natural because it is *above* human nature.

Having the Father, Son, and Spirit living within you changes the deepest depths of your being. St. Peter did not hesitate to tell the first Christians that they were being immersed in God's inner life:

> His divine power has granted to us all things that pertain to life and godliness, through the knowledge of him who called us to his own glory and excellence, by which he has granted to us his precious and very great promises, that through these you may escape from the corruption that is in the world because of passion, and become partakers of the divine nature.
>
> 2 Peter 1:3–4

God calls you to "share the divine nature." You become one with God and live his life. Though you live in a world "sunk" in vices like pride, greed, and lust, you "escape corruption." You leave your former sinful life behind and live as a child of the light. This is what sanctity is all about. This is the kind of life that God is calling you to live.

You are free to choose. God will not force you to be a saint. He gives you whatever you want. If you want good, he will give you good. If you want evil, it is there for you to take, and God will not stop you. You are free to choose either path. However, only one thing will make you happy—finding out why God created you and then dedicating your life to that.

Finding your vocation

There are many ways of learning to love as Jesus loved. Find the particular way that God has planned for you. This means finding your vocation or calling.

Only God can tell you why he created you. Only he knows what he put you here on earth to accomplish. On one hand, he has given you certain talents and leaves you free to decide how you will use them to serve others. On the other hand, he has something very specific he wants you to do for him. He has been preparing you for it from the very first day of your existence.

It is up to you to spend time in prayer. Listen attentively to inspirations that he stirs in your heart. By dedicating time to quiet conversation with our Lord, you open your mind and heart to his plan for you.

You may look at your life and be tempted to think that nothing you do could possibly be important. You would be making a great mistake. It is true that you are just one among billions of people. It is almost impossible to see the consequences. What can you do to prepare the world for the coming of the kingdom of heaven? Probably very little. And yet, for as small as your life is, it is worth sacrificing yourself to do God's will.

The Virgin Mary and St. Joseph are the two greatest saints the Church has ever had or ever will have. Even they did not comprehend how their lives were crucial to God's plan. You should not expect to see how crucial your decisions are, either. The time will come, however, when the whole world will see how great your life was, because you did

God's will, or how pathetic is was, because, like Satan, you said: "I will not serve!" (cf. Jer 2:20).

God wants you to be a saint. Holiness is not something for the privileged few. God calls everyone to be a saint. The history of the Church is full of examples of men and women who took this challenge seriously. St. Louis was the king of France. He became a saint by ruling his country well. Edith Stein was a Jew who converted to faith in Christ. She became a saint by dying a martyr's death in a Nazi's prison camp during World War II. St. Thomas Aquinas was a monk. He became a saint by dedicating his life to teaching and writing about God. Blessed Mother Teresa was a nun who lived in Calcutta. She became a saint by taking care of the poorest of the poor. St. Mukasa was a young man serving the Kabaka of Uganda. He became a saint by dying a martyr's death after refusing to deny his faith in Christ. St. Zita was a young woman who gave up the possibility of getting married and having her own family so that she could cook and clean in someone else's home. She became a saint by remaining a virgin and dedicating her life to serving others by doing domestic work. St. Francis Xavier was a missionary. He became a saint by leaving his country and traveling to Asia to spread the Gospel. Blessed Luigi and Maria Beltrame were married. They became saints together by loving each other and taking care of their four children.

Each saint is different, but they all have one thing in common. They struggled to live a holy life. They did penance for their sins. They loved God and neighbor. They dedicated themselves to prayer and work. They gave us concrete examples of how to put the gospel into practice. Now it's your turn.

Each person has a distinct path to follow. You have to follow yours. Why did God create you? What did he put you on earth to accomplish? No book can tell you the answer to this question. It is something between you and God. Reading good books may help you discover it. Getting good advice may help even more. But in the end, only God can show you. You need to talk to him about it.

No matter who you are, one thing is certain. God wants you to be a saint. He wants all men and women everywhere to be saints. That is what

Jesus declared in the Sermon on the Mount. He said, "You, therefore, must be perfect, as your heavenly Father is perfect" (Mt 5:48). He was not speaking just to priests and nuns when he talked about being perfect. He was speaking to a huge crowd of people. He was talking to the world.

Our Lord often asks for more. Perhaps you will have to make a sacrifice that strikes you as impossible the first time you think about it, like remaining celibate for the sake of the kingdom of God or being the father or mother of a large family. Many people pursue other difficult goals—to pursue a career or win a gold medal—and do it gladly. Some are motivated by nothing more than a desire to hear the crowds applaud.

God does us an enormous favor when he calls us to serve him. Vocation requires sacrifice, and yet every vocation is a gift and a blessing from God.

> What zeal people put into their earthly affairs: dreaming of honors, striving for riches, bent on sensuality. Men and women, rich and poor, old and middle-aged and young and even children: all of them the same. When you and I put the same zeal into the affairs of our souls, we will have a living and operative faith: and there will be no obstacle that we cannot overcome in our apostolic undertakings.
>
> St. Josemaría, *The Way,* n. 317

Do not be surprised when God asks for more. Do not be afraid, either. It is natural to fear. Even the Virgin Mary felt fear when the angel Gabriel appeared to her and told her that God had chosen her to be Jesus' mother. "Do not be afraid, Mary, for you have found favor with God" (Lk 1:30).

If you feel fear, you can master it by remembering our Lord's promise:

> And every one who has left houses or brothers or sisters or father or mother or children or lands, for my name's sake, will receive a hundredfold, and inherit eternal life. But many that are first will be last, and the last first.
>
> Matthew 19:29–30

Some "leave behind" father and mother, spouse and children by remaining celibate instead of getting married. Others "leave behind" land by declining to take up a comfortable social position and dedicating themselves to other work that will give greater glory to God. For instance, instead of being the head of a wealthy business in the city, someone might start a hospital in a poor rural area. Those who make these sacrifices for the sake of serving God will receive a great reward.

What is the reward? God makes us like Christ. That was God's plan from the beginning. "The Son of God became man so that we might become God," says St. Athanasius (cf. *CCC*, n. 460). No small reward! Can you think of anything better than "becoming God"?

Vocations in the Church

Being baptized is just the beginning. More is necessary, because baptism does not completely cure us. It takes away all our sins but does not take away our inclination to sin. When the Church teaches that all men and women are called to be holy, she is also pointing to a goal far beyond baptism.

God wants all men and women to fight a battle against evil—starting with the evil that is inside of them. Speaking to those who thought they had done enough for God by being baptized, the Letter to the Hebrews recalls the example of Jesus enduring shame and suffering on the cross. To anyone who equates the quest for holiness to a search for peace and comfort, the Holy Spirit says: "In your struggle against sin you have not yet resisted to the point of shedding your blood" (Heb 12:4).

When describing the various ways of following Christ within the Church, this is the first point to make. No matter what the specifics of a particular vocation, all paths reduce to the one Jesus told the Apostles: "If any man would come after me, let him deny himself and take up his cross daily and follow me" (Lk 9:23). If you want to share in Christ's glory, you must first share in his suffering. Carrying your daily cross is the only way to become "another Christ, Christ himself."

The *Catechism* explains the various ways Christians can live out the call to sanctity (cf. *CCC*, nn. 871–945)

- Vocation to the priesthood: becoming a deacon, priest, or bishop by receiving the sacrament of holy orders. Any man who receives this sacrament enters into the clerical state.

- Vocation to consecrated life: this means joining one of the religious orders, congregations, or institutes, or dedicating oneself as a hermit or a consecrated virgin. Those entering religious life take vows of poverty, chastity, and obedience. A man or woman accepting this vocation enters into the religious state and becomes a public witness, reminding all people that this world is passing away.
- Vocation of the lay faithful: a true vocation—a calling from God to use all one's energies in the quest for holiness. A layperson is an ordinary Christian who seeks sanctity by working for Christ in the affairs of this world. Laypeople are called by God to spread the gospel through their daily contact with their friends, relatives, and colleagues.

Universal call to holiness

God wants you to be holy. This is the "universal call to holiness." It is universal because God wants all men and women to be saints. It is a call because God invites each person to make this the whole reason of life on earth. After spending many years repeating this teaching of the Church, St. Josemaría once wrote:

> I dream—and the dream has come true—of multitudes of God's children, sanctifying themselves as ordinary citizens, sharing the ambitions and endeavours of their colleagues and friends. I want to shout to them about this divine truth: if you are there in the middle of ordinary life, it doesn't mean Christ has forgotten about you or hasn't called you. He has invited you to stay among the activities and concerns of the world. He wants you to know that your human vocation, your profession, your talents, are not omitted from his divine plans. He has sanctified them and made them a most acceptable offering to his Father.
>
> St. Josemaría, *Christ Is Passing By*, n. 20

Sanctity is not for experts. God calls everyone—you, your friends, your relatives—literally everyone to be a saint.

This is not just a theory. Already, many ordinary Christians have taken their call to sanctity seriously. By doing their daily work, by fulfilling their obligations toward society and towards the Church and by offering all this to God, they are becoming saints. By living this way, not only do these men and women become holy, they also make others holy through their work.

How can you offer your work to God? First, do it with human perfection, as well as you can. When the moment of failure or success or routine comes, remember that your work now belongs to God. It is not yours any more. It belongs to God.

This has a practical consequence. If you succeed, you have no right to brag. That work belongs to God. He deserves the applause, not you. Instead of seeking applause, you want to make sure that God gets *all* the glory. So if applause comes, offer that to God as well. Then the applause will be for him and not for you.

When things go wrong, despite your effort to do a good job, you have no right to be sad. Your work was pleasing to God. Perhaps you failed in the eyes of the world. In God's eyes, your work was a success.

When monotony sets in and you feel weighed down, repeating the same tasks over and over again, that too is for God. Wasn't the life of Jesus in Nazareth routine? Day after day, he worked as a carpenter. For almost thirty years, before going out to *preach* the gospel, he was *living* the gospel. He lived an ordinary life with the Virgin Mary and St. Joseph. It was a life full of routine. But it was the life of God's only-begotten Son—a life full of love.

Wisdom of the Saints

In our poor present life, let us drink to the last drop from the chalice of pain. What does it matter to suffer for ten, twenty, fifty years, if afterwards there is heaven forever, forever . . . forever! And, above all—even better than for the sake of the reward, *propter retributionem*—what does suffering matter if we accept it to console, to please God our Lord, with a spirit of reparation, united to him on his cross—in a word: if we suffer for Love?

St. Josemaría, *The Way*, n. 182

By offering your work to God, you, too, can turn your life into a never-ending act of love. Your Father in heaven will look at you and see what he saw when Jesus was busy in the workshop making chairs and tables. Being a child of God, you will become another Christ, Christ himself. You will be like the king who changed the world around him just by touching it:

> You have the power to transform everything human into something divine, just as King Midas turned everything he touched into gold!
>
> St. Josemaría, *Friends of God,* n. 205

REVIEW QUESTIONS

1. Give a brief summary of God's plan for the world.
2. What did Jesus mean when he talked about entering a "narrow gate"?
3. How can ordinary people in the middle of the world become saints?
4. What do we mean by "vocation"? What does the Church teach about the universal call to holiness?

11.

Heaven and Hell

When Jesus was crucified, two thieves were crucified with him. One of the two thieves said, "Jesus, remember me when you come into your kingdom." Because he made this act of faith, we call him the "Good Thief." The words "when you come into your kingdom" express faith. Jesus did not look like a king about to enter a kingdom; he looked like a criminal condemned to death. He told the Good Thief, "Truly, I say to you, today you will be with me in Paradise" (Lk 23:43).

Jesus had different ways of referring to the place where the saints will rejoice with him forever. He called it the "kingdom of God," "paradise," "heaven" and the "house of his Father." Whatever the name, it is a place. Jesus is physically present there already, having risen from the dead and ascended to his Father. So is the Virgin Mary, having been assumed body and soul into heaven. The other saints are spiritually present; at the end of the world, they will rise from the dead and live with God in paradise.

All those who live in God's grace and persevere to the end of their lives will go to heaven. Among these holy souls, anyone not entirely purified of all defects has to be purified first. Those who need no purification are taken by angels immediately into God's presence where they can see God.

What heaven is like

No one has ever seen God. In heaven we will see him. We will see the Holy Trinity. We will see how the Father, Son, and Spirit are one single being. It will be obvious to us that they are totally one with each other. This mystery, which is baffling to us in this life, will be revealed to us in all its splendor. St. Paul said, "For now we see in a mirror dimly, but then face-to-face" (1 Cor 13:12).

The Church calls this experience the "beatific vision." It is a way of seeing that is more powerful than the most perfect physical eyesight. It is a way of seeing God directly, not with your eyes but with your soul—as if the divine life of Father, Son, and Spirit were a movie that you can watch being shown inside your soul. The beatific vision will be the greatest of all your joys in heaven.

Besides seeing God, the saints will see Jesus Christ risen from the dead, together with the Blessed Virgin Mary and St. Joseph, her husband. They will also see the archangels Sts. Michael, Gabriel, and Raphael; the Twelve Apostles and the holy women of the Gospel, together with all the other angels and saints.

Since Jesus is the Son of God—and therefore part of the Trinity—it may seem confusing to you when the Church speaks of seeing both the Holy Trinity *and Jesus*. Because Jesus Christ is both God and man, you will see him in two different ways. You will see him as he has existed forever with his Father in the unity of the Holy Spirit. In other words, you will see him in the Holy Trinity—in the beatific vision, as mentioned above. You will also see Jesus as the Risen Lord. This means seeing Jesus with your own physical eyes, because you, too, will have risen from the dead.

This is what we know about heaven. There is much more we do not know. St. Paul saw heaven while still alive. Very few people have ever had this privilege. He said it was impossible to describe what he saw:

> I know a man in Christ who fourteen years ago was caught up to the third heaven—whether in the body or out of the body I do not know, God knows. And I know that this man was caught up into Paradise—whether in the body or out of the body I do not know, God knows—and he heard things that cannot be told, which man may not utter.
>
> 2 Corinthians 12:2–4

Writing in the third person, as if this man were simply a friend, St. Paul is speaking about his own personal experience. The "third heaven" he refers to is the highest heaven, that is, the place where God dwells with the angels and saints. In ancient times, the first heaven was the place of the sun and the moon, while the second heaven was a place farther away, where the angels live. People thought the stars were angels. St. Paul was trying to tell us that the place where God lives—the third heaven—is so beautiful that no words can describe it.

Sacred Scripture

Again, the kingdom of heaven is like a net which was thrown into the sea and gathered fish of every kind; when it was full, men drew it ashore and sat down and sorted the good into vessels but threw away the bad. So it will be at the close of the age. The angels will come out and separate the evil from the righteous, and throw them into the furnace of fire; there men will weep and gnash their teeth.

Matthew 13:47–50

We will never grasp the splendor of heaven until we see it for ourselves. But we do have some idea of what it will be like because the Holy Spirit has been given to us. St. Paul hinted at this when explaining the wisdom we receive from God through revelation:

> But we impart a secret and hidden wisdom of God, which God decreed before the ages for our glorification. None of the rulers of this age understood this; for if they had, they would not have crucified the Lord of glory. But, as it is written, "What no eye has seen, nor ear heard, nor the heart of man conceived, what God has prepared for those who love him," God has revealed to us through the Spirit. For the Spirit searches everything, even the depths of God.
>
> 1 Corinthians 2:7–10

Scripture calls the Holy Spirit a "token," "pledge," or "guarantee" of future glory (cf. Eph 1:13–14). A token or pledge is a special kind of coin or note that entitles a person to full payment later. In other words, the Spirit's action within us gives us a foretaste of the way he will make us completely happy in heaven. He is the love that the Father and Son pour into our hearts.

By knowing a little of this divine love here on earth, we have some idea of what love will be like in heaven. As St. Josemaría said:

> If Love, even human love, gives so many consolations here, what will Love be like in heaven?
>
> St. Josemaría, *The Way*, n. 428

Any experience we have of love now in this world is a sign of an even greater love waiting for us in heaven.

Even when filled with the Holy Spirit, we experience pain and suffering. As long as we live in this world, they are our traveling companions. The pledge of future happiness, though, means that no pain or sorrow can dampen our hope. St. Paul said:

> What then shall we say to this? If God is for us, who is against us? He who did not spare his own Son but gave him up for us all, will he not also give us all things with him?
>
> Romans 8:31–32

When you are surrounded by problems or tormented by your own sins, never despair. Though God does not always solve your problems here in this world, he always forgives. Look forward to the reward he offers you for being faithful to him in the midst of your trials and tribulations.

What hell is like

Jesus spoke frequently about hell. He called it "Gehenna," which was the name of the rubbish dump near Jerusalem where all the trash was burned. Expanding on this image, he described hell as a place where the damned are tormented by an "unquenchable fire" (Mk 9:43). Hell will be physically painful.

Jesus explained hell in parables by describing someone being thrown "into the outer darkness; there men will weep and gnash their teeth" (Mt 22:13). This symbolizes the way the damned will feel: lonely, angry and empty. Our hearts were created for love. Instead of being filled with love, the damned will be filled with hatred. They will hate God. They will hate themselves. They will hate one another. The "grinding of teeth" expresses this hatred and bitterness.

When speaking about fire and darkness, Jesus speaks about realities much worse than anything here on earth. Fire normally destroys bodies very quickly. The fire in hell is different. It will burn without consuming, and so the damned will burn in the fire forever.

In contrast to the kingdom of light, where the saints will shine like the sun, hell will be a kingdom of darkness. As with the fire, so also the darkness. It is not an earthly darkness. The damned will see horrible things in hell: human beings suffering in agony and ugly forms assumed by demons. The damned will live in spiritual darkness since they will never be able to see God. This will cause them more suffering than all the rest of their woes. Being created for love means we were created to see God, who is love. Being cut off from this possibility forever—and knowing how cut off they are—the damned will despair with the deepest despair man has ever known.

Our Lord uses yet another graphic image to describe the pain of hell—"where their worm does not die" (Mk 9:48). This metaphor suggests guilt, like a worm eating away inside the flesh. It will be a kind of shame for sin. The damned will realize how they performed evil deeds deliberately. The guilt will never die because the damned will remember their sins and realize how these sins brought them to this state of total disgrace.

Though the damned will remind each other of their past mistakes, this will not lead anyone to repentance. They will feel guilty for their sins, but without feeling any sorrow for sin. Just like guilty people here in this world who try to bury their guilt by accusing everyone else, the damned in hell will spend eternity accusing each other. Satan will be the master of this game.

When thinking of hell, do not make the mistake of imagining lots of nice people hoping God will eventually forgive them. Anyone in hell is there for one and only one reason. People in hell are damned forever because they refuse to be sorry for the evil they have done.

The abyss between heaven and hell

The parable of the rich man and Lazarus describes many things about life after death. The main lesson of the parable is to warn the rich that they have a serious obligation to care for the poor. Some people busy themselves with consuming their wealth while neglecting the needs of those who are starving to death. Since they refuse to show mercy—a mercy they have an obligation in justice to show toward the destitute—they cut themselves off from God's mercy. Unless they repent, they will be condemned to hell for all eternity.

Besides using the parable to explain why the greedy go to hell, Jesus also used it to describe how God has separated heaven and hell. In the parable, Abraham says to the rich man:

> And besides all this, between us and you a great chasm has been fixed, in order that those who would pass from here to you may not be able, and none may cross from there to us.
>
> Luke 16:26

Before you can understand *why* heaven and hell are separated, try to understand what this separation means.

Saints cannot visit hell even for a brief moment. Neither can any of the damned sneak out of hell for a holiday in heaven. In other words, the saints will live in heaven for all eternity. They will never have to worry about losing their reward. The damned will be stuck in hell forever. They have no hope whatsoever of going to heaven.

The Book of Revelation says that heaven is a place of rest; and hell, a place of torment:

> And the devil who had deceived them was thrown into the lake of fire and sulphur where the beast and the false prophet were, and they will be tormented day and night for ever and ever. . . . And he said to me, "It is done! I am the Alpha and the Omega, the beginning and the end. To the thirsty I will give from the fountain of the water of life without payment. He who conquers shall have this heritage, and I will be his God and he shall be my son. But as for the cowardly, the faithless, the polluted, as for murderers, fornicators, sorcerers, idolaters, and all liars, their lot shall be in the lake that burns with fire and sulphur, which is the second death."
>
> Revelation 20:10; 21:6–8

Hell is a punishment for sin. God keeps the damned in hell against their will. This would seem to be the only way of explaining why St. Michael had to cast Satan out of heaven and why, once again, Satan has to be chained in hell (cf. Rev 12:7–9, 20:1–3, 10). Presumably, the rest of those damned to hell would rather escape their torments if they could.

Some parables suggest that the damned would like to enter into heaven. They will "knock" on heaven's door, saying, "Lord, Lord, open the door for us." After explaining this, Jesus said:

> And then will I declare to them, "I never knew you; depart from me, you evildoers."
>
> Matthew 7:23

Jesus has no desire to "even the score." He wants to forgive everybody. But his infinite justice moves him to separate those who are saved from those who are damned. If God did not separate them, the people intent on doing evil would wreak havoc on those who love God.

Anyone who persists in pride, greed, lust, or any other vice must be locked out of heaven. Otherwise, in the next life, the saints would continue to suffer. The damned do not want to stop doing evil deeds. If God allowed them to enter heaven, they would do lots of harm the same way they caused lots of harm while living in this world. That is why God's justice is also a sign of love—love protecting the saints from pain and suffering.

Why eternity?

Some people ask how a merciful God could condemn a soul to hell forever. The *eternity* of hell seems to contradict our notion of mercy. What if someone in hell finally decides to repent? Will God inflict punishment forever just because that person took more time to repent than the sinners who got to heaven by repenting earlier?

The answer starts with remembering why the damned go to hell. No one ends up in hell by accident. The damned are not there because they begged God for mercy and were ignored. God is not the one who refused to forgive. The person in hell is the one who refused to be sorry.

> And this is the judgment, that the light has come into the world, and men loved darkness rather than light, because their deeds were evil.
>
> John 3:19

Fathers of the Church

"There is one glory of the sun, and another glory of the moon, and another glory of the stars; for star differs from star in glory. So is it with the resurrection of the dead. . . ." (1 Cor 15:41–42). Consider this teaching and ask: What are we to learn from it? Even though all the saints will enjoy living in God's kingdom, they will not enjoy the same reward. Even though all the damned will suffer in hell, they will not endure the same punishment.

St. John Chrysostom, *Commentary on First Corinthians*, 41, 4

God sent his Son—the Light of the world—to save absolutely everyone and forgive all sins. The damned refused to be sorry even though God made it as easy as possible for everyone to seek forgiveness. They preferred darkness to light.

Think of it in personal terms. You are the one who will end up in either heaven or hell. If you end up in heaven, it will be through God's infinite mercy and your willingness to embrace that mercy. If you end up in hell, it will be for one and only one reason—your refusal to do what God was asking you to do to seek forgiveness. If you have committed all the worst sins imaginable but later repent and receive the sacraments instituted by Jesus Christ for the forgiveness of sins, then God will forgive you. If you stubbornly refuse to repent, there is no forgiveness. The Letter to the Hebrews states:

> If we sin deliberately after receiving knowledge of the truth, there no longer remains sacrifice for sins but a fearful prospect of judgment, and a fury of fire which will consume the adversaries.
>
> Hebrews 10:26–27

Even after considering God's justice, some do not understand why a soul in hell cannot somehow be "cured" of his or her sinful past and eventually be allowed to go to heaven. In the end, we are faced with a mystery.

By telling us about the abyss that separates heaven and hell and the inability to cross from one side to the other, God is revealing something about the human will.

For reasons we cannot fully understand, the will is fixed at the moment of death. A person who perseveres in God's grace to the end will be forever fixed in God's love. It will be a sense of infinite freedom, the kind of freedom that comes from being madly in love with someone.

A person who dies in the state of mortal sin will be forever fixed in a habit of selfishness, being utterly incapable of loving others and utterly incapable of being sorry.

Death is a mystery. The fixing of your will at the moment death is also hard to understand. It is, however, real. That is why it is so important to cling to God *now*. Don't wait for tomorrow to be sorry for your sins. There may be no tomorrow for you. When you accept your guilt and humble yourself before God, when you repent and seek his forgiveness, God turns your sorrow into joy. So eagerly does God forgive that Jesus exclaimed: "Just so, I tell you, there will be more joy in heaven over one sinner who repents than over ninety-nine righteous persons who need no repentance" (Lk 15:7).

Death and judgement

When you die, your soul separates from your body. At that moment, God tells you whether you are going to heaven or to hell. How does he decide? He judges you according to your deeds.

Sacred Scripture has many passages describing this. God will reward you for good works performed with good intention. If you are destined to heaven, Jesus will say, like the master in the parable of the talents, "Well done, good and faithful servant; you have been faithful over a little, I will set you over much; enter into the joy of your master" (Mt 25:21). If you refused to follow God's will and then rejected his mercy, you will be cast out. Like the king who separates the sheep from the goats, Jesus will say to you, "Depart from me, you cursed, into the eternal fire prepared for the devil and his angels" (Mt 25:41).

Purification before heaven

Once you have died and Jesus has judged you, you will know clearly whether you are going to heaven or to hell. Some souls going to heaven need to be purified before they can see God in beatific vision. We call this act of purification after death "purgatory."

God's purifying action means getting rid of all impurities. You may find yourself after death still burdened with bad tendencies, e.g., a tendency to get angry or a tendency to be lazy. You will be glad to be cured of these tendencies once and for all. You will be grateful that God prepares you before you enter into heaven. After all, would you want to enter heaven and have everyone see your defects? Obviously not. That is why purgatory is a great blessing. It frees you completely from the slightest defects. It burns away all your evil tendencies.

The need for purification

Imagine that you are a garden, with weeds growing among the flowers. Before you go to heaven, all the weeds have to be purged—pulled out by the roots. If this has not been done before you die, then the purging takes place in "*purg*atory." You need to be cleansed once and for all. You cannot go to heaven until all the weeds have been destroyed and your soul is all flowers. God's love cannot fill your soul until it is totally free of evil tendencies.

Hell is an eternal punishment for sin. Purgatory is different from hell for three reasons. First, purgatory is only for those who are going to heaven. Second, purgatory is temporary. Third, souls passing through this purification are filled with hope, knowing that the joys of heaven will follow their purification.

If, despite being a Christian, you watch ten pornographic movies, God will forgive all those sins when you go to confession. But after confession, you may still have a cesspool of evil tendencies in your soul

Magisterium

Heaven is the ultimate end and fulfilment of the deepest human longings, the state of supreme, definitive happiness. To live in heaven is "to be with Christ." The elect live "in Christ," but they retain—or rather find—their true identity, their own name: "He who has an ear, let him hear what the Spirit says to the churches. To him who conquers I will give some of the hidden manna, and I will give him a white stone, with a new name written on the stone which no one knows except him who receives it" (Rev 2:17).

Catechism of the Catholic Church, nn. 1024–1025

created by all the trash that entered through your eyes. You need to be purified. You need to regain control over your sexual desires. You need to correct your attitude towards the opposite sex after having allowed your mind to be perverted. If you die before being purified, you will need to pass through purgatory. You will need to be purified before you are ready to enter heaven.

If, despite being a Christian, you have a habit of getting drunk or using drugs, God will forgive you when you go to confession. But you will still feel attracted towards that same sin. You will still feel like wallowing in self-pity and depression. Confession forgives your sins, allowing you to escape the eternal punishment of hell. But it does not heal your bad habits. For instance, it does not take away the craving for drugs or alcohol created by getting addicted. You need to be purified of the addiction. Hopefully you will be purified before you die. If not, then you will have to be purified after you die.

The logic used in these examples applies to other sins: pride, greed, anger, envy, laziness, etc.

Doing penance for sins

The Church speaks about *temporal* punishment due to sin in order to distinguish it from *eternal* punishment. A person guilty of mortal sin who dies without repenting will suffer in hell forever. This is the eternal punishment due to sin. Temporal punishment is different. A person whose sins have been forgiven in confession still needs to do penance. The penitent carries a burden of temporal punishment due to sin. Temporal punishment defines our need for penance, that is, the need to break habits that leave our will inclined to evil.

Acts of penance like fasting teach us to overcome our craving for evil pleasures. They help us increase mastery of self. Acts of penance like almsgiving teach us to overcome greed. They help us to be poor in spirit. Acts of penance like prayer teach us to overcome hatred. They help us long for God's love. This is what the Church means when speaking about canceling the debt of sin called "temporal punishment." If we do not do penance for our sins in this life, we will need purification in the next life.

Penance purifies your soul if you do it with humility. Jesus condemned the Pharisees for putting on a show while fasting. When you do acts of penance, make sure never to brag about it. Then God will reward you. You will have much greater self-control. Evil things that used to attract you—like fornication, getting drunk, watching pornography, being violent—will cease to attract you. You will find that it is easier to spend time in silent prayer.

What gets purified after death?

Mortal sins must be forgiven before death. Anyone dying in the state of mortal sin will suffer in hell forever. If we refuse to be sorry for our sins, we have no hope of obtaining pardon for our sins after we die.

Venial sins—like lying to your friend to avoid being embarrassed—can be cleansed after death. It would be better to be sorry for venial sins before you die. But venial sins can be cleansed after you die if you neglect to be sorry while still alive. Some people say, "But telling a little lie is such a small sin. What difference does it make?" It makes a lot of difference. You cannot go to heaven without first being sorry for all your sins, even venial sins.

Some Christians make little or no effort to be sorry for their minor offences: using bad language, getting impatient when interrupted, lying to avoid trouble, sulking when others fail to notice their success, holding a grudge instead of forgiving, etc. God is not going to condemn a person to hell because of these minor acts of selfishness. But he will not overlook them, either.

God loves us with perfect love. He does not treat us like spoiled children. "Those whom I love, I reprove and chasten; so be zealous and repent" (Rev 3:19). God is a loving Father who loves so much that he wants to correct our smallest faults. He wants us to be as perfect as he is.

> For the Lord disciplines him whom he loves, and chastises every son whom he receives." It is for discipline that you have to endure. God is treating you as sons; for what son is there whom his father does not discipline?
>
> Hebrews 12:6–7

Some men and women live a truly holy life and need no purification. Others repent only late in life and retain traces of deeply ingrained habits of serious sin. Even Christians habitually living in the state of grace may retain minor defects they were never able to overcome. Until all venial sins and the remains of sin—all the leftovers of sinful tendencies—have been completely purged from their souls, they are not ready for heaven.

More examples

A man used to go to Mass every Sunday but usually forgot about God the rest of the week. He kept telling himself he should spend some time in daily prayer. But year after year passed, and he always put his own projects ahead of his love for God. He managed, by God's mercy, to avoid serious sins—or at least go to confession after a serious fall. He was generous with the poor. But he avoided prayer, saying he was too busy. This man must be purified before he is ready to enter into God's presence. By passing through purgatory, he will be ready to love God with his whole heart and mind and will.

A woman had a habit of gossiping about a friend. She knew it was wrong. But since it was not a mortal sin, she assumed it didn't matter. By passing through purgatory after death, she can be purified.

The idea with these examples is to stress the importance of purifying what the world considers minor defects. Perhaps the most frequently overlooked of these minor defects is the tendency we have to compare ourselves with others.

> In heaven, there will be no looks of indifference, because all the saints owe so much to one another. No envious glances will be cast, because the happiness of each is the happiness of all. With the doctors of the Church, we shall be like doctors; with the martyrs, like martyrs; with the virgins, like virgins. . . . When we see the glory of the great saints, and know that through the secret workings of Providence, we have helped them to attain it, our joy and happiness will perhaps be as intense as theirs. A shepherd boy may be the familiar friend of an Apostle or a doctor of the Church; a little child may be in close intimacy with a patriarch.
>
> St. Thérèse of Lisieux, *Counsels and Reminiscences*

In heaven, there can be no envy or jealousy whatsoever. The point here, though, goes deeper. In heaven, no one has the slightest tendency to be jealous. Anyone destined for heaven who has this tendency must first be purified.

Purgatory in the Bible

Some people find it hard to believe purgatory exists. They doubt because they cannot find it in the Bible. It is true that the word "purgatory" does not appear anywhere in the Bible. Then again, the word "Bible" never appears anywhere in the Bible either.

Forget the word and look for the concept. Even though the word "purgatory" never appears, the concept appears many times. Purgatory means purification after death.

St. John wrote in the Book of Revelation, the New Jerusalem is as holy as God is holy: "Nothing unclean shall enter it" (Rev 21:27).

St. Paul refers to purification at the end of one's life when he speaks about some of the saved being purified by fire. This concept—holy souls needing purification in the next world—is the very definition of purgatory:

> According to the grace of God given to me, like a skilled master builder I laid a foundation, and another man is building upon it. Let each man take care how he builds upon it. For no other foundation can any one lay than that which is laid, which is Jesus Christ. Now if any one builds on the foundation with gold, silver, precious stones, wood, hay, straw. . . . If any man's work is burned up, he will suffer loss, though he himself will be saved, but only as through fire.
>
> 1 Corinthians 3:10–12, 15

To explain purification, St. Paul talks about a building. After serving God in this world, some of those destined to be saved will suffer *because of defects in their work for God.* The Apostle says they were built on the right foundation—faith in Jesus Christ—but their works were poor. Their works were like wood, grass, and straw. They will be saved, but they must "go through fire." It will purge the defects—the wood, the grass, the straw—and then they will be ready to enjoy heaven.

When describing this purging process, St. Paul says it will take place when "the Day will disclose it" (1 Cor 3:13). He is speaking about Christians alive at the end of the world who will be purified when Jesus comes to judge the living and the dead. However, the logic of purification described here applies not only to them but also to those who die before the Second Coming of our Lord. If you die and you need purification, you do not have to wait until the Day of Judgement for purification. Purgatory allows you to be purified immediately after death, if you need it, so you can enter heaven as soon as possible.

This does not mean Christians can relax and wait for purification after they die. Never delay the hour of repentance. Any deliberate rebellion against God's commandments—murder, fornication, theft, and adultery—is a serious sin that must be forgiven in this life or it will never be forgiven. Anyone who is not sorry for such sins is guilty of the worst sin of all—the rejection of God's mercy. Anyone who rejects God's mercy in this life will never be purified. This is what Jesus meant when referring to sins that cannot be forgiven "in the age to come" (cf. Mt 12:32).

Suffering in purgatory

The amount of suffering souls experience in purgatory depends on how much they need to be purified. Someone who manages only a weak act of contrition, moved mainly by fear of hell, while making his or her confession, after wasting a lifetime in debauchery, will require a lot of purification. God always forgives, but he also insists on purifying.

Some people ask how a soul in purgatory can suffer. To get a rough idea, look at what purifies you in this life. If you find prayer so tedious that you habitually avoid it, you will suffer in purgatory. There won't be anything else to do. If you find it so hard to endure a moment of discomfort that you tend to pamper yourself, you will suffer in purgatory. There won't be any "cushions" there to comfort you.

There is a big difference between accepting purification voluntarily now and being forced to suffer in purgatory. While alive, seeking purification for our bad habits results from a personal decision. This increases our love for God. In purgatory, we can no longer increase our love for

God. Purgatory means losing something we could have had if we had been more diligent while alive.

In the midst of their suffering, the holy souls in purgatory rejoice. They know that as soon as their purification has been completed, they will enter into heaven and see God. The more they are purified from their attachment to sinful habits, the more they long for the joys of heaven. As they come to desire God above all things, their longing for heaven becomes part of their purification. Their yearning makes them suffer because it can only be satisfied by seeing the God they long to see.

Praying for the souls in purgatory

The Old Testament offers a beautiful example of praying for the dead. Judas Maccabeus, the leader of the Jewish army fighting to free Israel from the domination of pagan kings, sent an offering to the Temple in Jerusalem for some soldiers who died in battle.

> Therefore he made atonement for the dead, that they might be delivered from their sin.
>
> 2 Maccabees 12:45

The context of this pious act makes it clear that the sins of these soldiers were minor sins committed while they were sacrificing their lives for God's glory. The Holy Spirit praises Judas Maccabeus for his good deed.

It was common among the Jews to pray for the dead. The early Christians preserved this custom. We call it "praying for the holy souls in purgatory."

When a Christian dies, the priest from the local church normally organizes a funeral. During the funeral liturgy, we pray for the soul of the departed man or woman about to be buried. We do this in case the person who died needs purification in order to enter into heaven. The prayer in the funeral rite reads:

> May God give him (her) a merciful judgement and forgive all his (her) sins. May Christ the Good Shepherd lead him (her) safely home to be at

> peace with God our Father. And may he (she) be happy forever with all the saints in the presence of the eternal King.
>
> *Rites of the Catholic Church*, Funerals, n. 46

Besides praying for the faithful departed during their funeral, the Church recommends that we pray for *all* the holy souls in purgatory. To remind us to pray for the dead, the Church celebrates a special Mass every year on All Souls Day, November 2nd. The holy sacrifice of the Mass is the best prayer we can offer for the souls in purgatory.

Indulgences

Drawing on the infinite merits of Jesus Christ and those of the saints, the Church grants indulgences. Christians can gain indulgences every day.

> An indulgence is a remission before God of the temporal punishment due to sins whose guilt has already been forgiven. The faithful Christian who is duly disposed gains the indulgence under certain prescribed conditions . . .
>
> *CCC*, n. 1471

It may be hard to understand this. The word "indulgence," as normally used in English, is often associated with lack of moderation—for example, when parents *indulge* a spoiled child. The indulgences granted by the Church have nothing to do with this. Nor does an indulgence forgive sins. Indulgences take away the temporal punishment due to sin *after* the sin has been forgiven. Indulgences require us to be sorry

Wisdom of the Saints

I will only say that if there were nothing else in heaven to delight the eyes but the extreme beauty of the glorified bodies of the saints, that alone would be the greatest bliss. A most special bliss, then, it will be for us when we see the humanity of Jesus Christ. If it is so beautiful even on earth, when his Majesty reveals himself in the limited way our wretchedness can bear, what will it be like once we can enjoy it completely?

St. Teresa of Avila, *Life*, ch. 28

for our sins—especially our lack of moderation—since this always offend God.

Gaining an indulgence is essentially a way of purifying the soul by doing some pious deed. These deeds generally involve the traditional acts of penance: prayer, almsgiving, and fasting. These are deeds that would ordinarily purify the soul; because the Church grants an indulgence, a specific deed acquires an extraordinary power to purify, if carried out according to the conditions set by the Church.

A *partial* indulgence removes part of the temporal punishment due to sin. A *plenary* indulgence removes all of the temporal punishment due to sin. The faithful can gain indulgences for themselves or apply them to the dead.

When the Church grants indulgences, it is as if she were scooping out a handful of treasure from an enormous treasure chest, full of spiritual wealth earned by Jesus when he sacrificed himself, and by the saints when they offered their lives to God. The Church dips into this treasure chest and lavishes these spiritual riches on God's children.

The following conditions must be fulfilled whenever Christians seek to gain a partial indulgence. These general conditions are in addition to the specific conditions of the indulgenced work (e.g., a pilgrimage to a shrine, a visit to the sick, a gift of alms to the poor). The person must be baptized and not excommunicated from the Catholic Church. The person must be in the state of grace, at least at the end of doing the indulgenced work. The person must have at least a general intention of gaining the indulgence. (This can be fulfilled by making a general intention at the beginning of the day to gain the indulgences for which one is eligible that day, or by making a specific intention at the time of doing the indulgenced work). The person must do the prescribed work as the Church has indicated, fulfilling any special conditions particular to the indulgenced work in question.

Besides the conditions for a partial indulgence, the following additional conditions must be fulfilled whenever Christians seek to gain a plenary indulgence. The person must receive the sacrament of penance within a period of several days before or after the indulgenced work. (The period of time here is usually understood to be within an octave—that is, eight days—before or after doing the work). One confession suffices for several plenary indulgences. The person must receive Holy Communion within a period of several days before or after; it is most fittingly received on the day that the work is done. One reception of Holy Communion does *not* suffice for several plenary indulgences; the person must receive Holy Communion in each instance of seeking a plenary indulgence. The person must pray for the intentions of the Pope (e.g., by saying an Our Father and a Hail Mary); these prayers may be made several days before or after, but are most fittingly made on the day the work is done. The person must be detached from all sin, even venial sin. Incomplete detachment from sin would result in gaining only a partial indulgence. It is this disposition to renounce all attachment to our sins that opens our heart to the receipt of the full remission of the temporal punishment of sin, which God grants us through the Church.

Christians can gain only one plenary indulgence per day. There is no limit to gaining partial indulgences. Among the many acts for which the Church grants a plenary indulgence, the three most common ones are: praying the Rosary together with others, making the Stations of the Cross, and spending thirty minutes of prayer before the Blessed Sacrament.

REVIEW QUESTIONS

1. List the ways the saints will experience joy in heaven. List the ways the damned will experience suffering in hell.
2. What do we mean when we say that our will is "fixed" at the moment of death?
3. What do we mean by purification in the next life?
4. Why do we pray for the dead?

12.

God Judges Man

Speaking about himself, Jesus said:

> For the Son of man is to come with his angels in the glory of his Father, and then he will repay every man for what he has done.
>
> Matthew 16:27

At the end of time, Jesus will come to judge the living and the dead. He will come in power and glory, accompanied by all the angels. He will judge all men and women, from Adam and Eve to the very last person ever born. Some will still be alive. Those who are dead will resurrect. The angels will gather everyone together. St. Paul says:

> For we must all appear before the judgment seat of Christ, so that each one may receive good or evil, according to what he has done in the body.
>
> 2 Corinthians 5:10

One day you will stand before Jesus Christ, and he will judge you—and everyone else—in public.

When will you die?

Death often comes when people least expect it. Perhaps someone among your own relatives or friends has already died. One day the same will happen to you. It could be today or tomorrow or years from now. You just never know. No matter what age you are, it is a matter of common sense to look at yourself and ask: "Am I ready to die?"

Following the averages, you will probably live for years to come. But that is just an average. Death could surprise you at any moment because of an accident, a contagious disease, or a freak disaster like a fire or an earthquake.

It is not a matter of being afraid of death. Just the opposite: Welcome death. Prepare for it, so that when it comes you are ready.

It would be unhealthy to think about death all the time. It would be foolish if you never thought about it. You will die sooner or later. And when you die, God will judge you. Jesus said: "Therefore you also must be ready; for the Son of man is coming at an hour you do not expect" (Mt 24:44).

The mystery of death

We believe that Jesus will appear again on earth as the King of kings and the Lord of lords. We believe that he will judge the living and the dead. These are mysteries. Death is also a mystery. It requires no special faith to believe that people die. That part is obvious. Still, death remains a mystery because, when you die, something happens that others cannot see.

When you die, you leave your body. Death is the separation of body and soul. No one can see your soul leave the body. The only visible reality is that you stop breathing and your heart stops beating. Within a few hours, decay sets in with a vengeance. Your body starts rotting.

After you die, your family and friends will bury the dead body. Eventually the body will decay completely. Nothing will be left but the bones. Given enough time, even those will turn to dust. But you will continue to be you. You will continue to exist in another world.

After dying, you will exist in a state of death. Being in a state of death means that the soul is separated from the body. You will continue to know with your intellect and desire with your will. In fact, the only thing you will be able to do is understand with the intellect and desire with the will. Having no body, you will not be able to do anything else.

The rich man and Lazarus

Jesus told a parable about the rich man and Lazarus. The parable gives us a glimpse at what happens when someone dies:

> The poor man died and was carried by the angels to Abraham's bosom. The rich man also died and was buried; and in Hades, being in torment, he lifted up his eyes, and saw Abraham far off and Lazarus in his bosom. And he called out, "Father Abraham, have mercy upon me, and send Lazarus to dip the end of his finger in water and cool my tongue; for I am in anguish in this flame."
>
> Luke 16:22–24

This parable explains what happens at death. Lazarus goes immediately to a place of comfort, while the rich man goes straight to hell. At the moment of death, you know whether you are going to heaven forever or to hell forever. You do not have to wait until the Last Judgment.

This requires something the Church calls a "particular judgment." You will see Jesus Christ, and he will show you where you are going to spend eternity. The *Catechism* says:

> Each man receives his eternal retribution in his immortal soul at the very moment of his death, in a particular judgment that refers his life to Christ: either entrance into the blessedness of heaven—through a purification or immediately—or immediate and everlasting damnation.
>
> CCC, n. 1022

Sacred Scripture

When the Son of man comes in his glory, and all the angels with him, then he will sit on his glorious throne. Before him will be gathered all the nations, and he will separate them one from another as a shepherd separates the sheep from the goats, and he will place the sheep at his right hand, but the goats at the left. Then the King will say to those at his right hand, "Come, O blessed of my Father, inherit the kingdom prepared for you from the foundation of the world." . . . Then he will say to those at his left hand, "Depart from me, you cursed, into the eternal fire prepared for the devil and his angels." . . . And they will go away into eternal punishment, but the righteous into eternal life.

Matthew 25:31–34, 41, 46

At the moment of death, some souls will enter heaven immediately. Others will enter heaven after passing through purgatory. Others will go straight to hell.

Looking forward to death

Set your goal high. Try to live a perfect Christian life. Then you will be able to say, as St. Paul said, "We are full of confidence, I say, and actually want to be exiled from the body and make our home with the Lord" (2 Cor 5:8). Like the saints, you will look forward to death. You will be ready for it whenever it comes. You will be eager to embrace Jesus and be taken to heaven. At the moment of your particular judgment, standing before Christ, you will hear the words he spoke to the Good Thief on the cross, "Truly, I say to you, today you will be with me in Paradise" (Lk 23:43).

Parables about judgment

How does Jesus judge people at the moment of their death? Our Lord told so many parables about it that it is hard to summarize. Two will give you an initial idea.

In the parable of the talents, Jesus praises the first and second servants. They did their work well, increasing the talents the master had entrusted to them. Do your work well by serving the people around you. Then Jesus will say to you as he said to them: "Well done, good and faithful servant; you have been faithful over a little, I will set you over much; enter into the joy of your master" (Mt 25:21).

In the same parable, the third servant wasted the talents the master had entrusted to him. He was lazy. If you are lazy, God will reject you, and say to you as the master said to that man, "You wicked and slothful servant!" (Mt 25:26).

In another parable, Jesus talks about judging us according to what we know about God's will for us. He says:

> And that servant who knew his master's will, but did not make ready or act according to his will, shall receive a severe beating. But he who did

Ecclesiastical Writers

By divine power all our hidden affairs will become public. Everything that is covered will be revealed. . . . We may think that this will require a long period of time. . . . But it will not. When God wishes to show all people, all at once, everything done by each person throughout the whole of history. . . . he will do it using a power beyond words. God does not do things the way we do them. . . . The "day" of judgment will come, but it will not require time. Instead, I think the Last Judgment will be like the resurrection, which will take place "in a moment, in the twinkling of an eye" (1 Cor 15:52).

Origen, *Commentary on Matthew*, 14, 9

> not know, and did what deserved a beating, shall receive a light beating. Every one to whom much is given, of him will much be required; and of him to whom men commit much they will demand the more.
>
> Luke 12:47–48

Since you have a chance to learn about Jesus, you can receive a greater reward. You are learning how to love God and how to love others. Through the practice of frequent confession and Communion, you can lead a holy life. If you lead a sinful life, you will suffer more than those who also led a sinful life but never knew about Jesus.

Everyone knows that it is wrong to steal, to fornicate, and to get drunk. People who do these things deserve to be punished. They will be punished unless they repent. If you know these things are wrong and you *also* know that God forgives sins through baptism and penance but reject the opportunity to receive these sacraments, your punishment will be greater.

What happens once you die

The person who dies in God's grace will go to heaven. The person who dies in a state of mortal sin will go to hell. The *Catechism* explains:

> Those who die in God's grace and friendship, and are perfectly purified, live forever with Christ. They are like God forever, for they see him as he is, face-to-face . . .

> To die in mortal sin without repenting and accepting God's love means remaining separated from him forever by our own free choice. This state of definitive self-exclusion from communion with God and the blessed is called "hell."
>
> CCC, nn. 1023, 1033

When you die, you go to meet Jesus Christ. He will judge you. He will decide whether you have been faithful to him, being sorry for your sins, or whether you turned your back on him, ignoring him and his mercy. If you have been faithful, he will share his glory with you. If you have not been faithful, it will be too late to repent.

The Holy Spirit reminds us of the example of Esau, the one who sold his birthright to Jacob:

> For you know that afterward, when he desired to inherit the blessing, he was rejected, for he found no chance to repent, though he sought it with tears.
>
> Hebrews 12:17

Now is the time to choose between good and evil. Make your choice wisely now. There will be no chance to change your mind after you die. Death means that the time has come for God to judge you. Once you die, you can no longer choose.

Magisterium

It is a certitude of faith that "the Father . . . has assigned all judgment to the Son" (Jn 5:22). Now then, if the divine power to judge belongs to Christ, it is a sign that he—the Son of Man—is true God, because judgement belongs to God alone. Since this power of judgement is deeply united to the will to save . . . it is a new revelation. . . . It is the Christian revelation of the God who is Love. This corrects the too human way of viewing God's judgement as a cold act of justice or some kind of revenge. In actual fact, judgement . . . is the last link in the chain of God's love for all of us. God judges because he loves and in view of love.

St. John Paul II, *Catechesis on the Creed*, Vol II, pp. 223–225

The Last Judgment

In the Nicene Creed, we say:

> We believe in one Lord, Jesus Christ . . . He will come again to judge the living and the dead.
>
> *The Nicene Creed*

When Jesus returns as king, he will judge all men and women. We call this the "Last Judgment."

Since everyone has to appear in the Last Judgment, does that mean you will be judged twice? Yes, once immediately after you die and again at the end of the world. You will be judged on two occasions, but the particular judgment is much different from the Last Judgment.

Immediately after you die, you will know whether you are going to heaven or to hell. It will be something private between you and God. At the Last Judgment, all men and women from the whole history of the world will see and know how you are being judged. And you will see how they are being judged. You and everyone else will see your good deeds and your bad deeds. You will also see how those deeds caused great benefit—or great harm—to many people, generation after generation.

> **SAINTLY WISDOM**
>
> Without familiarity with God, there is, in the end, no consolation in death. For that is exactly what God intends with death—that at least in this one sublime hour of our life, we allow ourselves to fall into his love without any other security than the love he offers us.
>
> St. John Paul II, *Address to the Elderly,* Munich, November 19, 1980

A man or woman who refused to answer God's call will understand how that refusal became an obstacle to the holiness of many others. The person who was faithful till the end will see how that sacrifice made salvation possible for many people.

A father or mother who took care of a child will see how that care resulted in many beautiful events even after centuries had gone by. Think of Abraham taking care of Isaac. At the Last Judgment, he will see the fruit of the sacrifices he made. Think of Jesus' first disciples. They will see how their faith bore fruit, leading to the conversion of billions of men and women throughout the history of the Church.

At the Last Judgment, the results of all the good you ever did—and all the evil you ever did—will suddenly become evident. God will judge you by showing this to the whole world. Then all will see why each person gets the reward or punishment he or she deserves.

The Last Judgment will also be the moment when we will see the meaning of all the events that have ever taken place. The *Catechism* explains:

> The Last Judgment will come when Christ returns in glory. Only the Father knows the day and the hour; only he determines the moment of its coming. Then through his Son, Jesus Christ, he will pronounce the final word on all history. We shall know the ultimate meaning of the whole work of creation and of the entire economy of salvation and understand the marvelous ways by which his Providence led everything toward its final end. The Last Judgment will reveal that God's justice triumphs over all the injustices committed by his creatures and that God's love is stronger than death.
>
> *CCC*, n. 1040

When you do not understand why those doing evil seem to triumph while those serving God seem to cry out to him in vain, remember this: Christ will come to judge all people. Everyone will see how evil did not really triumph at all. Everyone will see how God awards the final victory to those who were faithful to him in the midst of their trials.

The Church says that Christ's act of judgment will be an act of love, not an act of revenge. Jesus does not want to condemn anybody. Nevertheless, he will be forced to condemn those who refuse to be sorry for their sins. Why? Anyone who refuses to repent of evil deeds is, by definition, someone who intends to continue causing harm to others. Jesus has to send away those who refuse to stop causing harm. If he did not do that, they would continue to make life miserable for those who seek God's mercy.

People often want to accomplish now what only God can do at the end of the world—to separate good and evil once and for all by banishing those who do evil. Separating "good people" from "evil people" in this world can never be final and absolute for the simple reason that we are all sinners. Even saints have their defects. The worst among us may eventually repent and become holy.

Any time we rely on human judgment to distinguish between "good people" and "evil people," we make mistakes. Since all are sinners, the only good people are the ones who repent. How are we supposed to judge the conversion that takes place deep within the human soul? We have no ability to determine whether a person has truly repented. We can be deceived both ways. We too easily welcome gracious idlers who have mastered the ability to appear innocent and charming while harboring all manner of hatred, envy, and pride. We too easily condemn rough characters who sincerely desire to change their evil ways even though externally they seem to be hardened criminals. God alone knows what is in the heart of each person.

No one knows their ultimate fate. Never judge the people around you—neither for good nor for evil. Perhaps the person everyone praises today will end up being disgraced forever. Perhaps the one everybody despises in this world will be a great saint in the next world. Someone described it this way:

> It is a serious thing to live in a society of possible gods and goddesses, to remember that the dullest and most uninteresting person you can talk to may one day be a creature which, if you saw it now, you would be strongly tempted to worship, or else a horror and a corruption such as you now meet, if at all, only in a nightmare. All day long we are, in some degree, helping each other to one or the other of these destinations.
>
> There are no ordinary people. You have never talked to a mere mortal. Nations, cultures, arts, civilizations—these are mortal, and their life is to ours as the life of a gnat. But it is immortals whom we joke with, work with, marry, snub, and exploit—immortal horrors or everlasting splendors.
>
> C.S. Lewis, *The Weight of Glory*

Take care what you say. You know very little about what is going on inside the people you meet. Even when all the saints are gathered in glory, there is much that is so personal to each one that only God really knows what name he or she deserves.

REVIEW QUESTIONS

1. What will the Last Judgment be like?
2. What is death? When does it come for you?
3. What happens immediately after we die?
4. How should a Christian prepare for death?

13.

God Ends Time

The day is coming when God will change the world by separating good and evil once and for all. History will come to an end. All men and women will enter into eternity. Until that day, God wants Christians to spread the gospel. The Church will continue to grow as the number of those to be saved increases.

This era of human history is the last. St. John wrote:

> Children, it is the last hour; and as you have heard that antichrist is coming, so now many antichrists have come; therefore we know that it is the last hour.
>
> 1 John 2:18

God has revealed that this world is coming to an end. He first revealed this through the prophet Daniel. Jesus confirmed Daniel's prophecy, describing a few details of what the end will be like.

Completing the number

What will happen before the end comes? Sacred Scripture speaks of completing the number of those chosen by God to reign with Christ in glory. For instance, the Book of Revelation describes the saints who have been martyred for their faith. They eagerly anticipate Christ's return in glory because only then will they rise from the dead. God tells them they have to wait "a little longer":

> When he opened the fifth seal, I saw under the altar the souls of those who had been slain for the word of God and for the witness they had borne; they cried out with a loud voice, "O Sovereign Lord, holy and

Sacred Scripture

Then God's temple in heaven was opened, and the ark of his covenant was seen within his temple; and there were flashes of lightning, voices, peals of thunder, an earthquake, and heavy hail.

And a great portent appeared in heaven, a woman clothed with the sun, with the moon under her feet, and on her head a crown of twelve stars; she was with child and she cried out in her pangs of birth, in anguish for delivery. And another portent appeared in heaven; behold, a great red dragon . . . that ancient serpent, who is called the Devil and Satan . . .

Revelation 11:19–12:3, 12:9

> true, how long before thou wilt judge and avenge our blood on those who dwell upon the earth?" Then they were each given a white robe and told to rest a little longer, until the number of their fellow servants and their brethren should be complete, who were to be killed as they themselves had been.
>
> Revelation 6:9–11

Together with the saints in heaven, we await the time of our Lord's Parousia, that is, his Second Coming. But we cannot be content with merely waiting.

God is counting on us to work for him in this world—to win the hearts of those far away and lead them into the Church. He has many places in heaven. He wants to fill them. We fill them by spreading the gospel to everyone, by baptizing more and more people, and by living holy lives in the middle of the world.

Conversion of the Jews

The Church must preach the gospel to all people in all parts of the world before Jesus comes to judge the world. Evangelization will climax when the Jews accept the gospel. Based on the prophecy made by St. Paul in the Letter to the Romans, the *Catechism* teaches:

> The glorious Messiah's coming is suspended at every moment of history until his recognition by "all Israel," for "a hardening has come upon part of Israel" in their "unbelief" toward Jesus.
>
> *CCC*, n. 674; cf. Rom 11:16–32

Jesus will not return until God gives a special grace to the Jews. This grace will enable them to recognize that Jesus is the Messiah they have been waiting for. Before God gives them this grace, the full number of Gentiles—those who are not Jews—must be complete.

Shortly after Pentecost, St. Peter told the Jews in Jerusalem how Jesus was going to return.

> Repent therefore, and turn again, that your sins may be blotted out, that times of refreshing may come from the presence of the Lord, and that he may send the Christ appointed for you, Jesus, whom heaven must receive until the time for establishing all that God spoke by the mouth of his holy prophets from of old.
>
> Acts 3:19–21

The "universal restoration" refers to the prophecies made in the Old Testament about God coming to rid the world of all evil. Isaiah called it the "Day of the LORD of hosts" (cf. Is 2:12), when God will establish an everlasting reign of peace and justice (cf. Is 11:1–16). When speaking about the "universal restoration," St. Peter would have had in mind the day he saw Elijah—Jesus' Transfiguration—and how our Lord promised that Elijah was going to come "to restore all things" (Mt 17:11).

It may seem odd that, from the very beginning, St. Peter started preaching about the "universal restoration" set for the end of time. However, it shows how crucial the conversion of the Jews is to God's plan. According to the Fathers of the Church, God will send the prophet Elijah for the special purpose of converting the Jews.

St. Paul contrasted the Jews and the Gentiles to remind us that God's covenant with the Jews has not yet been fulfilled. He argued that their present rejection of the gospel is part of a mystery that has enabled the Gentiles to enter into Christ's kingdom. Finally, he connected the conversion of the Jews with other events that will take place at the end of the world:

> Now if their trespass means riches for the world, and if their failure means riches for the Gentiles, how much more will their full inclusion mean! . . . For if their rejection means the reconciliation of the world, what will their acceptance mean but life from the dead?
>
> Romans 11:12, 15

God's plan for the end of the world depends on these two aspects of evangelization. One is spreading the gospel to all peoples. The other is the conversion of the Jews. The *Catechism* teaches:

> The "full inclusion" of the Jews in the Messiah's salvation, in the wake of "the full number of the Gentiles," will enable the People of God to achieve "the measure of the stature of the fullness of Christ," in which "God may be all in all."
>
> *CCC*, n. 674

Once the conversion of the Jews takes place, Jesus will return—but exactly when we do not know. The end times is shrouded in mystery. It will involve a great upheaval because, among other reasons, the Antichrist will appear.

The end times

From various texts in the New Testament, we can put together a sequence of events that will take place leading up to the end of the world. Here it is impossible to give a full account of what the Scriptures prophesy. However, you should be familiar with the major events.

We cannot be sure of the order in which the events will occur. The list below is not meant to specify the exact sequence. It is a collection of scriptural quotes on the end times, with brief comments. Besides the texts included here, there are many others not included. For instance, St. John speaks about the battle of Armageddon (Rev 16:16). However, it is not clear whether this is a real military battle (as some interpret it) or a metaphor to describe spiritual combat. The following list draws mostly from our Lord's own words and prophecies written by the Apostles in their letters.

1. The Antichrist appears. The Antichrist will establish his reign on earth. He will claim to be the true Messiah, the savior of the world. Having diabolic power to work miracles, he will deceive many, enticing them to worship both him and Satan.

> The coming of the lawless one by the activity of Satan will be with all power and with pretended signs and wonders, and with all wicked

> deception for those who are to perish, because they refused to love the truth and so be saved.
>
> 2 Thessalonians 2:9–10

St. Paul speaks of the Rebel—literally the "man of lawlessness"—while St. John uses the name "Antichrist." St. Paul warns Christians to prepare for the hardships they will have to endure. St. John gives similar warnings throughout the Book of Revelation.

Pope St. Gregory the Great wrote: "The Antichrist will unleash so much evil against the just that even the hearts of the chosen ones will be overwhelmed with fear. Consequently, Scripture says it will be so great that it will 'be enough to deceive even the chosen, if that were possible' (Mt 24:24)—which does not mean that the chosen will fall into sin, but only that they will be terrified" (*Moralia*, 14, 23). Like St. Gregory, the other Church Fathers described the Antichrist as a man who would have power to rule over the whole world.

2. Final trial of the Church. Jesus once asked, "Nevertheless, when the Son of man comes, will he find faith on earth?" (Luke 18:8). To explain this text, the *Catechism* says, "The Church will pass through a final trial that will shake the faith of many believers" (*CCC*, n. 675). Many Christians will be martyred during this period of intense persecution.

> Then they will deliver you up to tribulation, and put you to death; and you will be hated by all nations for my name's sake. And then many will fall away, and betray one another, and hate one another. And many false prophets will arise and lead many astray. And because wickedness is multiplied, most men's love will grow cold. But he who endures to the end will be saved. And this gospel of the kingdom will be preached throughout the whole world, as a testimony to all nations; and then the end will come.
>
> Matthew 24:9–14

3. Cosmic disaster. A cosmic disaster, followed by the appearance of a mysterious sign in the sky, will be the signal to all people that Jesus is about to return. It is not clear what our Lord means by the "sign of the Son of Man," but it will have to be something people will associate with the one who was crucified and then rose from the dead. Jesus words imply that the cosmic disaster will follow the persecution instigated by the Antichrist.

> Immediately after the tribulation of those days the sun will be darkened, and the moon will not give its light, and the stars will fall from heaven, and the powers of the heavens will be shaken; then will appear the sign of the Son of man in heaven, and then all the tribes of the earth will mourn, and they will see the Son of man coming on the clouds of heaven with power and great glory; and he will send out his angels with a loud trumpet call, and they will gather his elect from the four winds, from one end of heaven to the other.
>
> Matthew 24:29–31

Both Jesus and St. Paul mention the trumpet and connect it with the appearance of angels. Jesus also said:

> And there will be signs in sun and moon and stars, and upon the earth distress of nations in perplexity at the roaring of the sea and the waves, men fainting with fear and with foreboding of what is coming on the world; for the powers of the heavens will be shaken. And then they will see the Son of man coming in a cloud with power and great glory.
>
> Luke 21:25–27

Here Jesus emphasizes cosmic disaster. An event involving the sun, moon, and stars will appear to threaten our planet with total destruction.

Fathers of the Church

In the last days before the Judgment, the Jews shall believe in the true Messiah, that is, our Christ, by means of the great and admirable prophet Elijah, who will expound the Law to them. For not without reason do we hope that, before the coming of our Judge and Savior, Elijah will come. We have good reason to believe that he is alive now. As Scripture most distinctly informs us (2 Kgs 2:11), he was taken up from this life in a chariot of fire.

St. Augustine, *The City of God*, XX, 29

4. The Parousia. Jesus will come in glory with all the angels and saints. Everyone on earth will see him in his risen flesh. This is the Second Coming of Christ. St. Jude wrote:

> It was of these also that Enoch in the seventh generation from Adam prophesied, saying, "Behold, the Lord came with his holy myriads, to execute judgment on all, and to convict all the ungodly of all their deeds of ungodliness which they have committed in such an ungodly way, and of all the harsh things which ungodly sinners have spoken against him."
>
> Jude 14–15

Other texts also equate Christ's return with his final victory. Our Lord had to humble himself by dying on a cross at his first coming. The Second Coming will be a show of divine power that will banish all evil forever:

> And just as it is appointed for men to die once, and after that comes judgment, so Christ, having been offered once to bear the sins of many, will appear a second time, not to deal with sin but to save those who are eagerly waiting for him.
>
> Hebrews 9:27–28

Jesus compared his Second Coming with lightning lighting up the whole sky (Lk 17:24), implying that his appearance will be both sudden and visible. Because there will be no special warning—other than the perennial message of the Gospels—he urged us to be vigilant, prepared to meet him at any moment:

> And then they will see the Son of man coming in a cloud with power and great glory. Now when these things begin to take place, look up and raise your heads, because your redemption is drawing near. . . . But watch at all times, praying that you may have strength to escape all these things that will take place, and to stand before the Son of man.
>
> Luke 21:27–28, 36

Jesus also compared the Parousia with a thief coming in the night (cf. Mt 24:42–44), again implying that the event will catch people unawares. He stated that no one can foretell when his glorious return will take place:

> But of that day and hour no one knows, not even the angels of heaven, nor the Son, but the Father only.
>
> Matthew 24:36

5. The resurrection of the just. The saints will physically resurrect and join the faithful that are living on earth at the time of the Parousia. (It is possible that the dead destined for eternal damnation will also resurrect at the same time, or they may only rise from the dead after the Retribution.) St. Paul refers to this event in a letter where he urges the Thessalonians to be confident that Christians who have already died will one day see Christ return in glory.

> But we would not have you ignorant, brethren, concerning those who are asleep, that you may not grieve as others do who have no hope. For since we believe that Jesus died and rose again, even so, through Jesus, God will bring with him those who have fallen asleep. For this we declare to you by the word of the Lord, that we who are alive, who are left until the coming of the Lord, shall not precede those who have fallen asleep. For the Lord himself will descend from heaven with a cry of command, with the archangel's call, and with the sound of the trumpet of God. And the dead in Christ will rise first; then we who are alive, who are left, shall be caught up together with them in the clouds to meet the Lord in the air; and so we shall always be with the Lord. Therefore comfort one another with these words.
>
> 1 Thessalonians 4:13–17

Being a public event that others will see, the resurrection of the saints and the rapture will make Christ's Second Coming all the more glorious.

6. The rapture. When Jesus returns, his disciples will meet him first. He will send his angels to gather together both the resurrected saints and all those living who are worthy of his kingdom. All the angels and saints will accompany him—physically—as he descends from heaven. Several texts refer to the role of the angels: "So it will be at the close of the age. The angels will come out and separate the evil from the righteous . . ." (Mt 13:49). Our Lord insists once again that this moment will catch everyone by surprise:

> And he said to the disciples, "The days are coming when you will desire to see one of the days of the Son of man, and you will not see it. And they will say to you, 'Lo, there!' or 'Lo, here!' Do not go, do not follow them. For as the lightning flashes and lights up the sky from one side to the other, so will the Son of man be in his day. But first he must suffer many things and be rejected by this generation. As it was in the days of Noah, so will it be in the days of the Son of man. They ate, they drank, they married, they were given in marriage, until the day when Noah entered the ark, and the flood came and destroyed them all. Likewise as it was in the days of Lot—they ate, they drank, they bought, they sold, they planted, they built, but on the day when Lot went out from Sodom fire and sulphur rained from heaven and destroyed them all—so will it be on the day when the Son of man is revealed. On that day, let him who is on the housetop, with his goods in the house, not come down to take them away; and likewise let him who is in the field not turn back. Remember Lot's wife. Whoever seeks to gain his life will lose it, but whoever loses his life will preserve it. I tell you, in that night there will be two in one bed; one will be taken and the other left. There will be two women grinding together; one will be taken and the other left." And they said to him, "Where, Lord?" He said to them, "Where the body is, there the eagles will be gathered together."
>
> Luke 17:22–37

MAGISTERIUM

Established in this last age of the world, and made manifest in the outpouring of the Spirit, the Church will be brought to glorious completion at the end of time. At that moment, as the Fathers put it, all the just from the time of Adam, "from Abel, the just one, to the last of the elect" will be gathered together with the Father in the universal Church.

Vatican II, *Dogmatic Constitution on the Church*, n. 2

According to St. Paul, we will be gathered around the Lord (cf. 2 Th 2:1). We call this the "rapture" because the Apostle talked about being *lifted up* into the clouds—into a manifestation of divine glory. We will meet Jesus "in the air." Our bodies will be glorified with the glory of the resurrection as we are lifted up. The glory of the saints will make Jesus' return all the more spectacular. Everybody else on earth will be watching.

St. Paul adds one more detail to this scenario. Just as the saints who resurrect will have glorious bodies, those still alive who are worthy of the rapture will be *physically glorified*—they will be the same as the resurrected saints. He states:

> Lo! I tell you a mystery. We shall not all sleep, but we shall all be changed, in a moment, in the twinkling of an eye, at the last trumpet. For the trumpet will sound, and the dead will be raised imperishable, and we shall be changed.
>
> 1 Corinthians 15:51–52

The repeated mention of the "last trumpet" is the thread that links several events together. It gives the impression that certain events will happen at about the same time: the appearance of many angels gathering the just, the resurrection of the just who were dead, the glorification of those who are still alive, the Parousia and the rapture.

7. The retribution. Jesus will conquer the Antichrist. This will be an awesome and terrifying event far exceeding the force of any natural disaster. Whatever the nature of this event, one thing is clear: it will take place *after* Jesus appears in glory.

> For they themselves report concerning us what a welcome we had among you, and how you turned to God from idols, to serve a living and true God, and to wait for his Son from heaven, whom he raised from the dead, Jesus who delivers us from the wrath to come.
>
> 1 Thessalonians 1:9–10

Anyone gathered by the angels to be with Jesus will not suffer the retribution.

Some time before the end of the word, the Rebel will establish an earthly power defying God so brazenly that St. Paul calls it the "Great Revolt." This implies that the Antichrist will lead large numbers of Christians into apostasy. St. Paul says that the Antichrist will convince many people to worship him.

> Now concerning the coming of our Lord Jesus Christ and our assembling to meet him, we beg you, brethren, not to be quickly shaken in mind or

> excited, either by spirit or by word, or by letter purporting to be from us, to the effect that the day of the Lord has come. Let no one deceive you in any way; for that day will not come, unless the rebellion comes first, and the man of lawlessness is revealed, the son of perdition, who opposes and exalts himself against every so-called god or object of worship, so that he takes his seat in the temple of God, proclaiming himself to be God. Do you not remember that when I was still with you I told you this? And you know what is restraining him now so that he may be revealed in his time. For the mystery of lawlessness is already at work; only he who now restrains it will do so until he is out of the way. And then the lawless one will be revealed, and the Lord Jesus will slay him with the breath of his mouth and destroy him by his appearing and his coming.
>
> 2 Thessalonians 2:1–8

Though the early Christians knew, we no longer know what St. Paul meant when referring to an obstacle that was preventing the Antichrist from appearing. What is clear is that Christ will not come until the Antichrist begins the Great Revolt—a worldwide rebellion against God and against the Church. There have been many minor rebellions throughout history in various nations. The distinctive sign of the Antichrist will be his ability to convince large numbers of people all over the world to worship him and to persecute Christians.

The retribution consists in Jesus' act of destroying the power of the Antichrist. This event may also include the consummation of the world by fire that St. Peter mentions in his second letter, quoted below.

8. The Last Judgment. After Jesus conquers the Antichrist, all men and women who have ever lived will be assembled for the Last Judgment.

> Then I saw a great white throne and him who sat upon it; from his presence earth and sky fled away, and no place was found for them. And I saw the dead, great and small, standing before the throne, and books were opened. Also another book was opened, which is the book of life. And the dead were judged by what was written in the books, by what they had done. And the sea gave up the dead in it, Death and Hades gave up the dead in them, and all were judged by what they had done. Then Death and Hades were thrown into the lake of fire. This is

Wisdom of the Saints

[A] persecution awaits the Church, before the end. . . . This persecution is to be attended with the cessation of all religious worship: "They shall take away the Daily Sacrifice"*—words which the early Fathers interpret to mean, that Antichrist will suppress for three years and a half all religious worship. St. Augustine questions whether baptism even will be administered to infants during that season. . . . Moreover the reign of Antichrist will be supported, it would appear, with a display of miracles, such as those the magicians of Egypt effected against Moses.

Bl. John Henry Newman, *Tracts for the Times*, 83, 3

> the second death, the lake of fire; and if any one's name was not found written in the book of life, he was thrown into the lake of fire.
>
> Revelation 20:11–15

Jesus will send the damned away to hell and welcome the saints into his kingdom. When speaking about this event, our Lord implied that all the dead would rise to be physically present before him:

> For as the Father has life in himself, so he has granted the Son also to have life in himself, and has given him authority to execute judgment, because he is the Son of man. Do not marvel at this; for the hour is coming when all who are in the tombs will hear his voice and come forth, those who have done good, to the resurrection of life, and those who have done evil, to the resurrection of judgment.
>
> John 5:26–29

Jesus will be the judge. The Acts of the Apostles quotes St. Peter stating: "God appointed him to judge the living and the dead" (Acts 10:42). It then quotes St. Paul saying: "There will be a resurrection of both the just and the unjust" (Acts 24:15). We do not know exactly when those destined for damnation will rise from the dead. But, at some point, all people will appear before Jesus for the Last Judgment.

9. The final restoration. Jesus will establish the new heavens and the new earth.

(*cf. Dan 9:27)

> But do not ignore this one fact, beloved, that with the Lord one day is as a thousand years, and a thousand years as one day. The Lord is not slow about his promise as some count slowness, but is forbearing toward you, not wishing that any should perish, but that all should reach repentance. But the day of the Lord will come like a thief, and then the heavens will pass away with a loud noise, and the elements will be dissolved with fire, and the earth and the works that are upon it will be burned up.
>
> Since all these things are thus to be dissolved, what sort of persons ought you to be in lives of holiness and godliness, waiting for and hastening the coming of the day of God, because of which the heavens will be kindled and dissolved, and the elements will melt with fire! But according to his promise we wait for new heavens and a new earth in which righteousness dwells.
>
> 2 Peter 3:8–13

We must be patient, without worrying that God seems to delay the day of the Parousia.

St. Peter's words remind us that the biblical reckoning of time is metaphorical, not literal. A day can be a thousand years. According to St. Augustine in *The City of God* (bk. XX, 1), this applies to the end of the world. The "Day of the Lord," with all its apocalyptic events, should not be thought of as a period of twenty-four hours. It is a period of time—we have no idea how long—when the whole world will see Jesus and witness the way he uses divine power to conquer evil. The last day refers to an unknown stretch of time when the events associated with the Parousia will take place.

We also don't know what means Jesus will use to conquer the Antichrist, nor how long it will take. We know even less about the timing of events following that victory, as can be seen from the perennial debate, even among the Church Fathers, over the meaning of St. John's words about the thousand years: "The rest of the dead did not come to life until the thousand years were ended. This is the first resurrection" (Rev 20:5).

What is clear is that the Church's final trial will last for an extended period of time, coinciding with the reign of the Antichrist. At some point during this persecution, the just will rise from the dead. This is the great hope of all those who believe in Jesus Christ.

St. John's Apocalypse

Some authors have produced detailed lists of events prophesied for the end times by adding references to Old Testament prophets (especially Daniel and Ezekiel) and St. John's Book of Revelation. However, both St. John's prophecies and those of the Old Testament rely heavily on metaphor. Besides this difficulty, commentators take different approaches to interpretation. These approaches vary so widely that one author equates certain metaphors with events that occurred in times of the Roman empire, while another author equates the same metaphors with recent events.

The Church has no definitive teaching on how the Book of Revelation, as a whole, should be interpreted. She teaches that we must accept it as the divinely inspired word of God, equal in dignity to all other books of the Bible. Even though specific images are hard to interpret, the general message is crystal clear. One day the world will end. Jesus will return in glory to judge all people. Before that happens, the whole world will experience a time of great tribulation.

The final Passover

Jesus offered himself as a sacrifice and that sacrifice was the true Passover. The Church will imitate her Lord by passing through a period of extreme suffering at the end of the world. This is the main idea that every Christian should have of the end times.

God wants us to work. We try to make the world better. We try to make life more pleasant for others. We should love life and all that God has given us. Even so, God calls us to do something greater than make this a better world. He wants us to prepare for another world. We prepare for it by imitating Christ's willingness to obey his Father even to the extreme of dying on a cross.

> The Church will enter the glory of the kingdom only through this final Passover, when she will follow her Lord in his death and resurrection. The kingdom will be fulfilled, then, not by a historic triumph of the Church through a progressive ascendancy, but only by God's victory over the final unleashing of evil, which will cause his Bride to come down

> from heaven. God's triumph over the revolt of evil will take the form of the Last Judgement after the final cosmic upheaval of this passing world.
>
> *CCC*, n. 677

We must be on guard and not make comfort our main goal in life. Our ultimate victory over evil consists in embracing suffering and death. Jesus warned us of this on several occasions: "For whoever would save his life will lose it, and whoever loses his life for my sake will find it" (Mt 16:25).

Patience untill he comes

"Be patient, therefore, brethren, until the coming of the Lord" (Jas 5:7). There are several levels of patience.

- **Resignation.** You learn that you have to suffer no matter who you are, no matter how rich you are, and no matter how famous you are. You resign yourself to suffering and accept it without complaining.
- **Serenity.** You reach the second level of patience when you can smile and remain calm, even when your whole life falls apart and everything goes wrong.
- **Joy.** You discover that picking up your cross willingly, to embrace it and follow in the footsteps of Christ, leads to some happiness here on earth.
- **Total identification with Christ.** The final level of patience goes beyond anything you are capable of. It is a gift. St. Paul calls it "being nailed with Christ to the cross." The Christian goes beyond being a Christian and becomes Christ himself: "It is no longer I who live, but Christ who lives in me," St. Paul said (Gal 2:19–20).

REVIEW QUESTIONS

1. What is the Parousia?
2. What did Jesus say about the end times?
3. What is the rapture?
4. What is the final Passover?

Part Two

The Way God Reveals

14.

God Talks to Man

God is Father, Son, and Holy Spirit. Jesus is the Word made flesh. He died and rose again to redeem us. Along with these three mysteries—the Trinity, the Incarnation, and the Redemption—Christians believe many others that cannot be demonstrated by human reason. When someone asks how we know these things are true, a Christian can say, "It's in the Bible." He can also say, "This is what the Church teaches." Both are good answers. However, these answers raise further questions: Where do the teachings come from? Where did the Bible come from? These questions point back in time, leading to a more basic question: How does God reveal?

God has revealed himself through words and actions. God appeared to certain individuals and spoke to them. For instance, he appeared to Isaiah. The Old Testament prophet described his experience with these words:

> In the year that King Uzziah died I saw the Lord sitting upon a throne, high and lifted up; and his train filled the temple. Above him stood the seraphim; each had six wings: with two he covered his face, and with two he covered his feet, and with two he flew. And one called to another and said: "Holy, holy, holy is the LORD of hosts; the whole earth is full of his glory."
>
> And I heard the voice of the Lord saying, "Whom shall I send, and who will go for us?" Then I said, "Here am I! Send me."
>
> Isaiah 6:1–3;8

This happened at the Temple in Jerusalem about 2,800 years ago.

Can you imagine seeing God appear to you and talking to him the way Isaiah did? Probably not. It happened to Isaiah, but that was a rare and extraordinary event. God wants to reveal himself to you and everyone else. One day you will see him. But for now, he does not reveal himself directly to everybody.

God appeared to Isaiah and spoke to him. The vast majority of people have never had this experience. Throughout history, God has chosen a few and appeared to them. They heard him speak in human language. The Old Testament tells us of several—most notably the three patriarchs: Abraham, Isaac, and Jacob. There were several others, including Moses and the other prophets. God appeared to these people to reveal his plan for the world's salvation.

God selects a few, reveals certain mysteries to them, and then relies on them to tell others. He has the power to reveal himself to each person individually. But he has chosen not to do so. The vast majority of people living in the world today believe what God has revealed only because they heard it from someone else.

Sharing in God's glory

Why has God chosen to reveal himself through others? Wouldn't it better for God to appear to each person and make sure that everyone gets the message directly from the source? Only God can answer. Many of us will understand this only when we see God in heaven. But even in heaven, God's mysterious ways will remain a mystery. St. Paul wrote:

> O the depth of the riches and wisdom and knowledge of God! How unsearchable are his judgments and how inscrutable his ways!
>
> Romans 11:33

Though we cannot fully explain why God wants the majority of us to discover his revelation through others, we can say this much. By choosing certain individuals to pass on the truths of revelation to everyone else, he lets them share his glory. It is similar to the way God allows a husband and wife to work together with him

SACRED SCRIPTURE

In many and various ways God spoke of old to our fathers by the prophets, but in these last days he has spoken to us by a Son, whom he appointed the heir of all things, through whom also he created the world.

Hebrews 1:1–2

to create new human life. God could create each human being without any cooperation from anyone. By allowing our parents a role in our creation, God shares his glory with our father and mother.

Because of their role in our creation, we show respect to our parents. Similarly, we honor the people God chose to pass on to us the mysteries of revelation. We venerate Abraham and call him our "father in faith" because his faith made it possible for the world to believe in the one true God. We venerate all the other men and women of the Old Testament who served God by being faithful to his covenant. With even greater reason we venerate the Apostles. These twelve men were the ones Jesus chose to hand on to us the mysteries of the new covenant. Something similar applies to those who saw the Risen Lord and worked together with the Apostles.

We venerate all these men and women because without them we would know nothing of God's revelation. Indeed, we should count ourselves fortunate. After two thousand years of Church history, the majority of the world's population has yet to hear the gospel preached to them effectively. Billions of men and women do not know Jesus Christ. They have never heard anyone tell them how Jesus came to save us from sin and make us children of God. All who know these mysteries recognize God's blessing.

Perhaps we do not fully appreciate just how much God wants to share his glory with us. Jesus promised that God would exalt anyone willing to encourage others to believe in his revelation. This is what Jesus meant when he spoke to his disciples, sending them out to tell everyone that the kingdom of God is close at hand:

> So every one who acknowledges me before men, I also will acknowledge before my Father who is in heaven; but whoever denies me before men, I also will deny before my Father who is in heaven.
>
> Matthew 10:32–33

If you believe in Jesus, tell others about him. God rewards those who spread the gospel and punishes those who are ashamed of it.

Jesus used a parable to explain the honor God will shower on us for working to spread the gospel. The Master will welcome his servant into God's kingdom, saying:

> Well done, good and faithful servant; you have been faithful over a little, I will set you over much; enter into the joy of your master.
>
> Matthew 25:21

Jesus equates "being faithful in small things" with telling others how they, too are, called to believe God's revelation. This means telling them that God is ready to forgive their sins. It means telling them that they can become God's children by being baptized.

By spreading the gospel, we become like Christ himself. This may sound like an exaggeration. It isn't. If you spread the gospel, you are another Christ. That's why Jesus said:

> He who receives you receives me, and he who receives me receives him who sent me.
>
> Matthew 10:40

God wants to reveal himself. But he wants to do it through a long chain of individual believers. One person hands on the revelation to another, and this to the next, and so on.

You understand this better when you become personally involved. You grasp more fully what God is revealing when you try to speak to others about it. St. Paul said that our salvation depends on spreading the gospel:

> . . . If you confess with your lips that Jesus is Lord and believe in your heart that God raised him from the dead, you will be saved. For man believes with his heart and so is justified, and he confesses with his lips and so is saved.
>
> Romans 10:9–10

Do you want to be saved? Then spread the gospel.

Prophets speak for God

In the Creed we say the Holy Spirit spoke through the prophets. The prophets were not merely saying nice things about God. The Holy Spirit was in them, speaking through them. God was revealing mysteries through them.

In the strictest sense of the word, a mystery is a truth that we would never have known unless God revealed it to us. The main mystery God revealed through the Old Testament prophets was the truth about the coming of Christ. There is no way that even the wisest man in the world could have figured out that God wanted to send a savior to take away the sins of the world. When the prophets told us that the Messiah would have to suffer great humiliation and agony, it was the Holy Spirit revealing God's plan for our salvation.

We often think of prophets as people who tell the future. The prophets did foretell future events. But this is only one aspect of what they had to say to us. A prophet is someone who speaks for God. He tells us what God wants to reveal. Moses is one of the greatest prophets because God gave the Israelites the Law through Moses.

The Law was everything to the Chosen People. Just before dying, as Moses was preparing the Israelites to submit to his successor, Joshua, and cross the Jordan River into the Promised Land, he told them:

> Lay to heart all the words which I enjoin upon you this day, that you may command them to your children, that they may be careful to do all the words of this law. For it is no trifle for you, but it is your life, and thereby you shall live long in the land which you are going over the Jordan to possess.
>
> Deuteronomy 32:46–47

Moses promised that in the future God would give his people another prophet: "The LORD your God will raise up for you a prophet like me from among you, from your brethren—him you shall heed" (Dt 18:15). God sent many great prophets in the times of the Old Testament: Elijah, Isaiah, Jeremiah, and others. But the Israelites expected someone even greater than these. With the passing of centuries, the Jews came to think of this prophet as *the* Prophet. This prophet would be the Messiah—literally meaning the Anointed One, the Christ—the one who would save Israel. Not only would the Messiah be a savior and redeemer but also a prophet: someone who would speak in God's name.

John the Baptist appeared, preaching a baptism of repentance. The Pharisees asked him if he was Elijah, since Elijah was supposed to return at the end of the world to prepare the Jews for God's glorious appearance. John said no. They asked him if he was "the Prophet"—the one promised by Moses. John said no. He insisted that he had been sent to prepare the way for the coming of the "Son of God" (Jn 1:34). St. John the Baptist was the last of the Old Testament prophets. He was sent to prepare the people of Israel for the coming of the one who would "baptize you with the Holy Spirit and with fire" (Lk 3:16).

Jesus reveals God's mystery

Jesus is the Prophet Moses told the Israelites to wait for. Jesus was a prophet in the most perfect sense. He did not come to speak in God's name. Being the Son of God, he spoke as only God can speak. The Old Testament prophets introduced their pronouncements by saying: "These are the words of Yahweh your God." Jesus did not use this phrase.

Jesus does not speak *for* God. He is God. So he speaks in the first person. For instance, he says:

> You have heard that it was said to the men of old, "You shall not kill; and whoever kills shall be liable to judgment." *But I say to you* that every one who is angry with his brother shall be liable to judgment . . .
>
> Matthew 5:21–22

First Jesus quotes the fifth commandment: "You shall not kill," noting that God gave us this commandment through the prophets. Then he speaks in the first person: "*I* say this to you . . ." He is not speaking as someone who represents God. He is God speaking to us.

Jesus not only reveals truths about God. He *is* the truth God wants to reveal. He not only reconciles us with God, he *is* our reconciliation. ". . . In Christ God was reconciling the world to himself." (2 Cor 5:19). Jesus is God forgiving all our sins.

Fathers of the Church

In his eagerness to arrive at the truth, the wise listener reminds me of swift hunting dogs. With their wonderful sense of smell, they run back and forth around the hiding places of the game they are seeking. . . . The seeker must seek diligently. . . . The greater the difficulty he encounters [in understanding some mystery of faith], the greater the effort and enthusiasm he must put in to laying bare the hidden truth.

St. Cyril of Alexandria, *Commentary on John*, IV, 2

When Jesus reveals, he does so with more clarity and power than all the prophets put together. Jesus not only *reveals*; he *is* God's revelation. "For in him the whole fulness of deity dwells bodily, and you have come to fulness of life in him" (Col 2:9–10). You experience God when you become one with Jesus.

Believing mystery

Jesus' life is a mystery. Why? In one sense there is nothing mysterious about it. Many people saw him grow up in Nazareth. Many saw him die on the cross. Many saw him after he rose from the dead. These are historical facts. But even if you had lived in the times of Christ, it would take a lot of faith to believe in Jesus. Many people who knew Jesus did not believe. Some did, but many did not.

Many rejected Christ's revelation. Even after he rose from the dead, it took faith to believe in Jesus. He hinted at this in one of his parables, putting these words into the mouth of Abraham: ". . . Neither will they be convinced if some one should rise from the dead" (Lk 16:31). It was hard to believe in Jesus two thousand years ago. It is doubly hard for you to believe today.

If you are like the rest of us, you have not seen Jesus. You have not heard him speak. You have not witnessed the miracles he worked long ago. You believe only because others heard him preach the gospel and then passed on their faith to the next generation. Before you can believe anything about Jesus, you first have to believe that these witnesses have given an accurate account about what really happened. Then you need faith to believe that everything Jesus said is true.

Faith is a gift from God. You can only believe what Christ came to reveal—you can only believe what the Church teaches today—if you open your soul to God's grace. You cannot make an act of faith simply by being intelligent. Highly educated people are capable of faith, but so are those who never went to school. More than intelligence, what is needed is humility. Jesus once said in prayer to God:

> I thank thee, Father, Lord of heaven and earth, that thou hast hidden these things from the wise and understanding and revealed them to babes; yea, Father, for such was thy gracious will.
>
> Luke 10:21

Faith is a virtue that leads us to accept what God has revealed. We accept it not on the basis of how well we understand it, but simply because God is the One revealing. By faith we accept all that God has revealed and handed on to us by Christ's Church. We accept it even if at times the revelation does not make sense to us. If God has revealed something, it has to be true. God is Truth. He can neither deceive nor be deceived.

To doubt God's revelation because something does not make sense would be a lack of faith.

We must remember that God is revealing himself to us. God and everything about God is a mystery beyond our understanding. When God reveals to us that he is three persons in one being, we can only stand in awe. It is beyond our comprehension. When God shows us that his Son became a man in order to die for our sins, we can only stand in awe. These are not truths that one can prove or explain with human reason. These are mysteries revealed by God.

The difficulty of believing

When Jesus raised Lazarus from the dead, many refused to accept the miracle. Jesus' enemies hated him so much that they would not admit the evidence they had seen with their own eyes. This is what is known as being willfully blind.

Lazarus died many days before Jesus arrived in Bethany. His body was already buried and rotting. When Jesus told Martha to open the

Magisterium

In his goodness and wisdom, God chose to reveal himself and to make known to us the hidden purpose of his will. It is his will that through Christ, the Word made flesh, man might have access to the Father in the Holy Spirit and come to share in the divine nature.

This plan of revelation is realized by deeds and words. . . . By this revelation then, the deepest truth about God and the salvation of man shines out for our sake in Christ. Jesus is both the mediator and the fullness of all revelation.

Vatican II, *Dogmatic Constitution on Divine Revelation*, n. 2

tomb, she objected. The stench would be overpowering. But Jesus wanted to work a great miracle. He wanted to give a sign of what he would one day do for all those who believe in him, raising the dead back to life. Martha had the tomb opened. Jesus called Lazarus to come out of the tomb. To everyone's amazement, Lazarus appeared, walking on his own two feet. Rather than accept the miracle and believe in Jesus, the Pharisees wanted to kill both Jesus and Lazarus. St. John narrates:

> When the great crowd of the Jews learned that he was there, they came, not only on account of Jesus but also to see Lazarus, whom he had raised from the dead. So the chief priests planned to put Lazarus also to death, because on account of him many of the Jews were going away and believing in Jesus.
>
> John 12:9–11

Believing requires an act of the will. No matter how many miracles you witness, you are free to believe or not believe.

If you had been there to see Jesus raise Lazarus from the dead, you would have seen something that nobody could explain. Only God could raise a dead man back to life. This is just common sense. Common sense is necessary for faith, but it is not yet faith. To jump from recognizing the miraculous nature of Lazarus' resurrection to believing that Jesus is God's Son requires a decision. Besides an act of the intellect, you must also make an act of the will in order to believe.

God is pure spirit. He is totally beyond our senses. None of the people living with Jesus could see his divine nature. No one could see that he was the Son of God. They heard Jesus call God his "Father." They saw him work miracles. They heard him promise that they would enter God's kingdom if they believed in him. But they could not see that Jesus was God. Believing always requires you to accept as true something you cannot see and cannot prove. This makes it difficult to believe in Jesus—even if you had seen him and lived with him.

When Jesus was hanging on the cross, it was difficult for his disciples to believe that the man being crucified was the Son of God. Jesus wanted them to believe it. Because he rose from the dead, they had good reason to believe. Even so, faith was difficult for people two thousand years ago. Just because they could see the Risen Lord did not mean they automatically believed in him. Seeing does not necessarily lead to believing.

Do not be surprised if you or your friends also find it difficult to believe. Today, you cannot see Christ's divinity—you cannot see that he is the Son of God. To make it *more* difficult, you cannot see Jesus at all. His divinity is hidden from us. His humanity is also hidden from us.

Through the Church

After dying on the cross and rising from the dead, Jesus entered into his glory to be seated at the right hand of his Father. He ascended into heaven, promising to return at the end of time. Until Jesus returns in glory, we have no way of seeing him. He wants us to believe in him because of the preaching of the gospel. That preaching comes to us through the Church.

That is why, when praying the Creed, we say, "We believe in the one, holy, catholic, apostolic Church." To believe that Jesus is the Son of God, we need the Church. We need the Church, because the Church is the way God has chosen to let us know his revelation. We cannot see Jesus' miracles with our own eyes. We cannot listen to his preaching with our own ears. We have to believe the testimony of others, handed on from generation to generation, since the time of the Apostles until our own day.

Jesus said that this kind of faith—faith without seeing—is worthy of special merit. He said this when speaking to Thomas after his resurrection. Seeing the wounds in Jesus' hands and feet, Thomas made an act of faith, calling Jesus "my Lord and my God." Jesus replied:

> Have you believed because you have seen me? Blessed are those who have not seen and yet believe.
>
> John 20:29

We are the ones who have not seen Jesus and yet believe in him. Believing in him demands accepting all that he taught.

Believing the Church

To believe in Jesus, we have to listen to others who have come before us. This is God's plan for spreading the gospel. Jesus put it bluntly to the Apostles:

> He who hears you hears me, and he who rejects you rejects me, and he who rejects me rejects him who sent me.
>
> Luke 10:16

Since we cannot listen to Jesus speak the way people listened to him two thousand years ago, faith demands listening to those who relay the message to us. Faith demands believing the teachings of the Bible that the Church passes on to us.

The Father and Son gave the Holy Spirit to the Church to ensure that later generations would receive the Bible without any errors mixed in. People have introduced errors and, unfortunately, errors abound. However, by listening to the one, holy, catholic, apostolic Church, a Christian can avoid all these errors.

The ones who invent errors usually attack the Catholic Church. They may sincerely believe that they are right. Precisely because they think the Church is wrong, they can shake your faith. They may suggest, "What you believe is absurd." They may claim that your faith does not agree with science or that it contradicts common sense. They may even say that some of the Church's teachings contradict the Bible. They can make their arguments sound so reasonable that it makes you doubt.

In this situation, keep in mind the basic idea explained in this chapter. God reveals mysteries. Mysteries go beyond what human reason is capable of proving. They go beyond what human reason is capable of comprehending. The words of the prophet Isaiah, speaking on behalf of God, are testimony to this fact of revelation:

> For my thoughts are not your thoughts, neither are your ways my ways, says the LORD. For as the heavens are higher than the earth, so are my ways higher than your ways and my thoughts than your thoughts.
>
> Isaiah 55:8–9

God far surpasses us in wisdom and power. When God reveals, never be surprised to discover things so wonderful that they are beyond your understanding.

Also remember that after centuries of answering thousands of objections to her teachings, the Church has an answer for each and every one of them. Perhaps when someone challenges you to respond to an objection, you do not have an answer immediately ready. In those situations, remember that the Church does have an answer. Then take the trouble to find out exactly what the Church teaches.

Put faith into practice

In the practice of Christian faith, the most difficult questions concern behavior. Accepting the divinity of Jesus Christ requires faith. But it is often more difficult to accept the Church's teachings on morals. A person used to watching pornographic movies finds it hard to stop. A person used to getting drunk finds it hard to change. A couple living together without being married finds it hard to make a decision. A couple using contraceptives will often look for all kinds of excuses to continue using them. In all these cases, people might refuse to change an evil habit and yet continue to think they are good Christians because they believe that Jesus is the Son of God. They will say something to the effect that they believe in Jesus but not the Church. Or they will "shop around" till they find a church that avoids those topics.

Why should people accept the Church's teaching on matters of moral life? Why can't they simply "believe in Jesus" and prefer their own view on controversial moral questions? For instance, why can't a divorced person who has married again ignore the Church's teaching on divorce and keep a strong faith in Jesus?

Faith goes beyond believing that Jesus saves. I am not saved if I deliberately engage in behavior that contradicts, Christian life. St. Paul wrote:

> Do you not know that the unrighteous will not inherit the kingdom of God? Do not be deceived; neither the immoral, nor idolaters, nor adulterers, nor homosexuals, nor thieves, nor the greedy, nor drunkards, nor revilers, nor robbers will inherit the kingdom of God. And such were some of you. But you were washed, you were sanctified, you were justified in the name of the Lord Jesus Christ and in the Spirit of our God.
>
> 1 Corinthians 6:9–11

Faith alone is not enough to save us. God expects us to repent from sin, and that includes a firm purpose of amendment, a decision to stop committing sins—a decision to leave our sinful life behind.

God wants to forgive our sins and welcome us into his kingdom. No matter how great our sins are, he will forgive us. But if we continue to live in sin without repenting, deliberately engaging in immoral behavior, God will not save us no matter how much we say we believe in Jesus Christ. A Christian man who remarries after divorce is not going to enter the kingdom of heaven unless he recognizes the fact that he is offending God and repents. His faith is not useless. Hopefully that faith will lead him to be sorry, for his sins. But, in the end, God is calling him to listen to the teaching of the Catholic Church. Once he accepts it, he can be sorry, and God will forgive him.

The Church's teachings on moral issues are part of the gospel. However, it is easy to get confused. People make all kinds of contradictory statements. Despite the clarity of Jesus' words in the Gospels, some Christians think there is nothing wrong with divorce and remarriage. They are confused, and they confuse others.

The teachings of the Catholic Church remain the solid rock of certainty in the midst of all the confusion. Christians are called to listen to the Church not only when she announces the sublime mysteries of Christ's divinity. They are also called to listen when the Church speaks on matters related to moral life. When it comes to divorce and remarriage, the Catholic Church has always taught that this is seriously wrong. Jesus said:

> Every one who divorces his wife and marries another commits adultery, and he who marries a woman divorced from her husband commits adultery.
>
> Luke 16:18

Believing in Jesus means that we accept him as our Lord and Savior. It also means that we accept his moral teaching. No one solves his problem of faith by looking for a Christian community where it is "easier to believe" because that community conveniently omits some of Jesus' teachings or misinterprets them.

Because of all the confusion about what is right and wrong, especially in matters of human sexuality and family life, we need to hold fast to Catholic teaching. It is relatively easy to begin with a strong faith. Many people do. But persevering to the end is the hard part. We must endure many temptations against faith. We must escape the confusion that engulfs people when they refuse to listen to the Church. We must give no importance to the fact that others think we are fools for believing what we believe, even if we feel utterly alone at times.

Speaking to Timothy, St. Paul warned all Christians:

> But understand this, that in the last days there will come times of stress. For men will be lovers of self, lovers of money, proud, arrogant, abusive, disobedient to their parents, ungrateful, unholy, inhuman, implacable, slanderers, profligates, fierce, haters of good, treacherous, reckless, swollen with conceit, lovers of pleasure rather than lovers of God, holding the form of religion but denying the power of it. Avoid such people. . . . Indeed all who desire to live a godly life in Christ Jesus will be persecuted, while evil men and impostors will go on from bad to worse, deceivers and deceived.
>
> 2 Timothy 3:1–5;12–13

These difficulties are bound to afflict anyone who tries to keep faith. The worst attacks do not come from pagans, but from those who keep up the "outward appearance of faith." The "impostors" would be hard to distinguish from other believers except for one fact: They live immoral lives and recommend the same for others. They talk about faith in Jesus, but they reject Christian morality.

Never let yourself be deceived by the impostors. Christ asks us to keep a clear conscience, always distinguishing between good and evil. The *Catechism* states:

> Faith is an entirely free gift that God makes to man. We can lose this priceless gift, as St. Paul indicated to St. Timothy: "Wage the good warfare, holding faith and a good conscience. By rejecting conscience, certain persons have made shipwreck of their faith" (1 Tim 1:18–19). To live, grow, and persevere in the faith until the end, we must nourish it with the word of God; we must beg the Lord to increase our faith; it must be "working through charity," abounding in hope, and rooted in the faith of the Church.
>
> *CCC*, n. 162

You "reject conscience"—to use St. Paul's phrase—whenever you reject the Church's teaching. Faith demands that you accept not only those aspects of Christ's teaching that appeal to you but also the moral precepts you find hard to put into practice.

This does not mean you will never sin. Jesus knew that all his disciples would be weak. For this reason, he provided the sacrament of penance to forgive sins committed after baptism. To accept Christ's teaching means that when you sin, you have to call it a sin and be sorry for it. Committing a sin and calling it a "good deed" means rejecting God's revelation.

Personal experience

Having studied the rational arguments, let's look at the need for personal experience. God wants to reveal himself to you. Revelation cannot be limited to God speaking. Somebody has to be listening. To put it more personally, you have to listen.

You might want—or even expect—God to appear to you the way he did to Abraham or Isaiah. Then you wouldn't have any doubts, right? Maybe. As mentioned above, everybody is capable of rejecting overwhelming evidence. And even if you are more than willing to embrace whatever God reveals, revealing his existence is the easy part. There is a reason why God chooses a more subtle approach. He has a reason for asking you to accept his revelation as it is passed on to you by others.

God wants to reveal himself to you. But before he can do that, he has to prepare you for it. In order to reveal himself, he has to show you

Wisdom of the Saints

You may think that in these Canticles [the Song of Songs], there are some things that might have been said in a different way. We are so stupid that I should not be surprised if you did think this way. . . . O God, what miserable creatures we are! . . . I conclude by advising you, whenever there is anything that you do not understand, either in sacred Scripture or in the mysteries of our faith . . . not to be surprised at the tender words which you may read of in Scripture as passing between God and the soul. . . . Think of the love God has shown us and of all that he has done for us. Once you realize that his love was so strong and powerful that it made him suffer so much, how can we be amazed by any words that he may use to express it?

St. Teresa of Avila, *Conceptions of the Love of God*, ch. 1

who you are—or, rather, who you are supposed to be. You are called to share his divine nature. You are called to be his child. When the Father sent his divine Son into this world, God showed how a divine person can become human. Now he wants to show you that a human person—like you—can be divine. God wants to show you how he intends to lift you up and make you holy beyond your wildest dreams. He wants to show how you can be as perfect and as holy as he is.

This is the hard part. You are wretched and miserable. You are covered with sin and soaked through to the bone with perversity. Therefore, it makes sense to wonder whether you are really capable of becoming a child of God. God has to convince you that, with his grace, you can change. This is what revelation is really all about. God reveals his plan, and he waits to see if you will accept it by doing what he wants.

One day God will reveal his glory. Even the angels will gaze in silent admiration. But that revelation will not help anyone to repent. The revelation that helps us repent is the sight of Jesus on the cross pleading with his Father, "Forgive them . . ." St. Paul counted this as the greatest discovery of his life:

> Christ Jesus came into the world to save sinners. And I am the foremost of sinners; but I received mercy for this reason, that in me, as the foremost, Jesus Christ might display his perfect patience for an example to those who were to believe in him for eternal life.
>
> 1 Timothy 1:15–16

You understand who God is and who you are by contemplating the Son of God accepting death to forgive your sins.

Looking for God

The first step in becoming a Christian is not your step. It is the step God takes when giving you his grace. He may have done that through baptism when you were a child. Or perhaps you have yet to be baptized and God is now awakening in your soul the desire for salvation. In either case, God takes the initiative. He is the one who comes looking for you. Long before you make any move towards him, he is the one who gives grace.

God's revelation usually comes to us through Christians who have come before us. But the grace to accept that revelation comes directly from God. When that grace comes, it is up to you to open your heart to it. No one can do that for you. Others can pass along the wonderful news of the Gospel. But only you can answer God's call and believe in Jesus Christ. Each one of us stands alone before God. Each one of us is responsible for the way we accept or reject his invitation to faith.

If you have a hard time believing, turn to God. Ask him to open your eyes. He *will* help you. He is the one who wants to reveal himself. He is the one who insisted, "Seek, and you will find" (Lk 11:9). All those who seek God find him.

REVIEW QUESTIONS

1. Why is it difficult to believe?
2. What is faith?
3. How do we know what God wants us to believe?
4. How do Christians resolve questions about their faith?

15.

Sacred Tradition

Tradition is the process of handing down from one generation to the next all the beliefs, institutions, customs, and attitudes that constitute the culture of that society. Each new generation learns their traditions in a multitude of ways, mostly by observing and listening to their elders.

Tradition from the Apostles

Jesus did not write the word of God. He *is* the Word of God. He did not write the gospel. He *is* the gospel. The Good News entered the world when the Word became flesh. The gospel did not begin with either Tradition or Scripture. It began with Jesus. It began with an act of God revealing himself through the Word made flesh. Revelation comes before Scripture and Tradition.

After his baptism, Jesus began telling everyone, "The time is fulfilled, and the kingdom of God is at hand" (Mk 1:15). Then he gathered disciples around him. He dedicated special effort to a few chosen men—the Twelve Apostles—and a group of women who also accompanied him on his travels (cf. Lk 8:2–3).

The Apostles did not commit to writing everything they saw Jesus say and do. That would have been impossible. When concluding his account of the Gospel, St. John wrote:

> But there are also many other things which Jesus did; were every one of them to be written, I suppose that the world itself could not contain the books that would be written.
>
> John 21:25

Most of what Jesus did and said was never written down.

This is why sacred Tradition is essential to the Church. We call it "sacred" because it comes from God. God uses Tradition to pass on his revelation. Sacred Scripture and sacred Tradition are the two sources of revelation. If we want to know what God has revealed to us, we need both.

Sacred Tradition works the same way any tradition works, with one crucial exception. The Holy Spirit guides the whole process. God provides this special guidance because Tradition is one of the ways he has chosen to hand on his revelation from generation to generation.

What is sacred Tradition?

Like Scripture, sacred Tradition contains the word of God. It contains the divine revelation God made first through the patriarchs and prophets and finally through Jesus Christ and the Apostles. Sacred Tradition is sometimes called "Apostolic Tradition" because it transmits all that Jesus Christ taught his Apostles.

While Scripture contains God's revelation in writing, Tradition transmits it in various ways—various because Tradition does not reduce to words. There are certain ways of doing things that form part of Tradition. For instance, the essential elements for how to baptize or how to celebrate the Eucharist were handed on from the Apostles to their successors. The second generation of Christians saw how the first generation celebrated baptism and the other sacraments and preserved that way of doing things for the third generation and so on. The Bible specifies Jesus' command to baptize. But some aspects of baptism are not spelled out in Scripture. These had to be handed on to us through Tradition. For example, even though Scripture does not specifically mention the need to baptize infants, the early Christians baptized infants whenever the parents were baptized.

> **Sacred Scripture**
>
> And beginning with Moses and all the prophets, he interpreted to them in all the scriptures the things concerning himself.
>
> Luke 24:27

St. Paul tells us how important sacred Tradition is for the Church. When telling the Corinthians how the Eucharist was established and how Christ wanted them to celebrate the Eucharist, he emphasized sacred Tradition:

> For I received from the Lord what I also delivered to you, that the Lord Jesus on the night when he was betrayed took bread, and when he had given thanks, he broke it, and said, "This is my body which is for you. Do this in remembrance of me." In the same way also the cup, after supper, saying, "This cup is the new covenant in my blood. Do this, as often as you drink it, in remembrance of me." For as often as you eat this bread and drink the cup, you proclaim the Lord's death until he comes. Whoever, therefore, eats the bread or drinks the cup of the Lord in an unworthy manner will be guilty of profaning the body and blood of the Lord.
>
> 1 Corinthians 11:23–27

The Apostle's words speak of consecrating bread and wine so that Christians could receive the body and blood of Christ. This text describes the way the Apostle *passed on* not only the words Christ spoke but also his actions—actions that had to be imitated and kept alive by successive generations. Being one of the Apostles, St. Paul was part of this act of receiving revelation from Christ and passing it on. This "passing on" is the essence of sacred Tradition.

In the early Church, Christians came to know about God's revelation through Tradition. The same remains true today. The Bible speaks of sacred Tradition as a source of God's revelation, the same as sacred Scripture. St. Paul wrote:

> So then, brethren, stand firm and hold to the traditions which you were taught by us, either by word of mouth or by letter.
>
> 2 Thess 2:15

By insisting that Christians "keep the traditions . . . taught by word of mouth" and equating them with those taught "by letter," St. Paul indicated that sacred Tradition was essential for passing on God's revelation. Like the written word, Tradition is God's word to all people. Therefore, it deserves to be called the "word of God" the same way that Scripture is called the "Word of God."

Tradition came before Scripture

Most of the teaching that the Apostles passed on was passed on orally. The same was true in the time of the prophets of the Old Testament. Much of the content of sacred Scripture was passed on orally for years before it was written down.

Jesus did not write any of the Scriptures. Nor did his disciples take dictation from him. It was only several years after Jesus ascended into heaven that his disciples began to compose the texts now included in the New Testament. Many years before a single book of the New Testament was written, the Apostles were preaching. The *oral* word of God came before the *written* word of God.

Arguing that the Bible is the only source of revelation contradicts history. When the Apostles started preaching at Pentecost, they did not have copies of the Bible to pass around to the people listening to them. All the texts now collected in the New Testament were written many years later.

Some people do not know that God wants the Church to rely on Tradition as well as Scripture. Therefore, it must be emphasized that the Bible is not the only source of revelation. Sacred Tradition is also the word of God. To know all that God has revealed, we rely on Tradition as much as we rely on Scripture.

Role of the Apostles' successors

Scripture was not the only source of revelation in the beginning of the Church. Nor is it now. To understand how this works in practice, you must understand the role of the men who were appointed by the Apostles to be their successors.

The apostles knew that Jesus had given them a responsibility to preserve God's revelation. St. Peter realized that preserving revelation and passing it on to others would be crucial for the Church after he died. He knew someone had to take his place. He wrote:

> Therefore I intend always to remind you of these things, though you know them and are established in the truth that you have. I think it right, as long as I am in this body, to arouse you by way of reminder, since I know that the putting off of my body will be soon, as our Lord Jesus Christ showed me. And I will see to it that after my departure you may be able at any time to recall these things.
>
> 2 Peter 1:12–15

One of the ways the Apostles used to preserve God's revelation was to put it in writing. They also wanted to preserve it by appointing successors who would hand on God's revelation by example and by teaching. These successors of the Apostles are called "bishops." Just as Peter had a special role among the other Apostles, the Bishop of Rome has a special role among the other bishops. He has this special role because he is St. Peter's successor.

In the early Church, St. Timothy was a successor to St. Paul, one of the apostles. St. Paul used the laying on of hands to make Timothy a bishop. He later warned the young man to be sure to safeguard sacred Tradition:

> Follow the pattern of the sound words which you have heard from me, in the faith and love which are in Christ Jesus . . .
>
> 2 Timothy 1:13

The Apostles appointed successors in order to preserve sound teaching. St. Paul told Timothy to be faithful to the "sound teaching you have *heard* from me." First St. Paul passed on revelation to Timothy by word of mouth. Later he wrote to Timothy to remind him of this oral teaching. The oral word is a source of teaching that has to be "kept as a pattern."

This defines a critical role for the successors of the Apostles. Bishops can only do this—they can only "keep" the Apostles' teaching "as their pattern"—by being faithful to sacred Tradition.

We need Tradition to understand Scripture

The Acts of the Apostles tells the story of a man, a eunuch from Ethiopia, who was reading a text from one of the Old Testament prophets. He believed in God. He had just been on a pilgrimage to Jerusalem. But he could not understand the text he was reading. St. Philip was one of the first deacons.

> So Philip ran to him, and heard him reading Isaiah the prophet, and asked, "Do you understand what you are reading?" And he said, "How can I, unless some one guides me?"
>
> Acts 8:30–31

The Ethiopian eunuch was reading a passage that said,

> He was oppressed, and he was afflicted, yet he opened not his mouth; like a lamb that is led to the slaughter, and like a sheep that before its shearers is dumb, so he opened not his mouth.
>
> Isaiah 53:7

Fathers of the Church

Jesus once exclaimed: "Beware of false prophets, who come to you in sheep's clothing but inwardly are ravenous wolves" (Mt 7:15).

These were the men that the Apostle Paul attacked in the Second Letter to the Corinthians, when he said, "For such men are false apostles, deceitful workmen, disguising themselves as apostles of Christ. And no wonder, for even Satan disguises himself as an angel of light. So it is not strange if his servants also disguise themselves as servants of righteousness" (2 Cor 11:13–15).

According to the teaching of the Apostle Paul, whenever false prophets, false apostles or false doctors quote passages from the Bible—in an attempt to support their errors with the aid of false interpretations—they are imitating the cunning machinations of their master. It is clear why Satan has invented this tactic. He knows that it is the easiest way to deceive people. He makes them think the errors he wants to introduce are truths coming straight from the Bible.

. . . But someone may ask, "If it is true that Satan and his disciples . . . make use of the promises, passages and texts of Scripture, what should Catholics do?"

They will devote all their care and attention to interpreting the texts of God's word according to the traditions of the Catholic Church and the rules of Catholic dogma. Within the Catholic and Apostolic Church, they must follow the principles of universality, antiquity and consent. . . . They should place traditional religion before profane novelty. Likewise, within tradition . . . they should place, first the general decrees of an ecumenical council . . . and follow the concordant opinions of great and outstanding teachers.

St. Vincent of Lerins, *Commonitorium*, 25, 27

The Ethiopian did not know how to interpret this text. Because of Tradition, Philip knew what it meant.

Philip knew that the text was a prophecy describing the way Jesus would be condemned to death. Despite his good intentions, the Ethiopian was not able to figure this out from the text itself. In order to understand it correctly, he needed someone who knew sacred Tradition, as it was handed down from the Apostles. Philip knew and explained it to the Ethiopian. This is a clear example—in the Bible—showing how we rely on sacred Tradition to understand the written word. The *Catechism* teaches:

> Sacred Tradition and sacred Scripture, then, are bound closely together, and communicate one with the other. For both of them, flowing out from the same divine well-spring, come together in some fashion to form one thing, and move towards the same goal. Each of them makes present and fruitful in the Church the mystery of Christ, who promised to remain with his own "always, to the close of the age."
>
> *CCC*, n. 80

Scripture and Tradition go together. Christians need both to understand what God has revealed.

We need Tradition to interpret Scripture

Tradition is especially important when it comes to interpreting the Bible. When the Ethiopian did not know how to interpret a text written by Isaiah, Philip was there to give him the correct interpretation. Something similar happens whenever people argue about the meaning of a specific text. Whenever that happens, we realize that we need something that goes beyond the Bible. Without sacred Tradition some passages would not make any sense. Even the ones that do make sense require interpretation. Without Tradition we would all be like the Ethiopian. We would be unable to understand God's revelation in sacred Scripture. Or what would be worse, we might think we understand when, in fact, we are giving the wrong interpretation.

Tradition and Scripture are not two different revelations. In fact, neither one is revelation. They are two different *sources* of one single revelation. To take just one example of the way these two sources complement each other, look at the biblical texts that speak of the Virgin Mary. Many different interpretations have been given. Some argue that the Mother of Jesus did not remain a virgin after getting married to St. Joseph. Since Mary asked the angel Gabriel *how* she was to conceive a child, others conclude she asked only because she knew that God wanted her to remain a virgin for her whole life (cf. Lk 1:34). Both groups claim to offer the correct interpretation of the texts in the Bible. They cannot both be right. Either Mary remained a virgin or she didn't. Sacred Tradition is clear. The early Christians believed that Mary was a virgin before Jesus was born and that she remained a virgin after he was born. This is obvious to anyone who reads the writings of the Church Fathers and examines prayers used in the liturgy of the early centuries.

Christians often come up with new interpretations to biblical texts. When this happens we need to go back to Tradition. Before accepting new interpretations, we must remember how the early Church interpreted the text. We cannot accept an interpretation that explicitly contradicts sacred Tradition. One of the ways we know how the early Church interpreted a specific text is to study the way it was understood by the Fathers of the Church.

Church fathers, ecclesiastical writers and church doctors

The Church fathers are saints from the early centuries of Church history who left behind extensive writings. Most of them were bishops. Many writings of the Church fathers are commentaries on Scripture, collections of sermons and catechetical treatises, that is, works explaining what God revealed.

We call these men "fathers" because, like the Apostles, they had enormous influence on the Church in the very early stages of the Church's development. The earliest of the Church fathers knew some of the Apostles personally. Speaking about one of them, St. Irenaeus wrote:

MAGISTERIUM

By their oral preaching, by example, and by observances . . . the Apostles handed on what they had received from the lips of Christ—from living with him and from what he did—or what they had learned through the prompting of the Holy Spirit. . . . In order to keep the Gospel forever whole and alive within the Church, the Apostles left bishops as their successors, "handing over" to them the authority to teach in their own place. . . . And so the apostolic preaching, which is expressed in a special way in the inspired books, was to be preserved by an unending succession of preachers until the end of time.

. . . This Tradition, as it comes from the Apostles, developed in the Church with the help of the Holy Spirit. For there is a growth in the understanding of both the realities and the words handed down to us. This happens through the contemplation and study made by believers. . . . As the centuries succeed one another, the Church constantly moves forward toward the fullness of divine truth . . .

The words of the Holy Fathers witness to the presence of this living Tradition. . . . Through the same Tradition the Church's full canon of the sacred books is known, and the sacred writings themselves are more profoundly understood and unceasingly made active in her . . .

Vatican II, *Dogmatic Constitution on Divine Revelation*, nn. 7–8

> Polycarp was trained by the Apostles and conversed with many [disciples] who had seen Christ. He was appointed bishop of the Church in Smyrna by the Apostles in Asia. I knew him in my early youth.
>
> St. Irenaeus, *Against Heresies*, III, 3, 4

St. Polycarp learned the gospel from St. John the Apostle. As a young man, St. Irenaeus listened to St. Polycarp preach the gospel. This continuity—John to Polycarp to Irenaeus—defines the irreplaceable value of the teachings of the Church fathers.

St. Justin is another one of the Church fathers. He converted to Christianity around the year 150—a few decades after the death of St. John the Apostle. Before being martyred, he wrote a letter to Antonius Pius, the Roman emperor. By doing so, he provided something we cannot find in sacred Scripture. That letter provides a description of the liturgy the early Christians used when celebrating the Eucharist. The following quote is taken from the letter. St. Justin describes the main parts of the Mass. It is amazing to note that the main parts of the Mass have remained the same throughout the history of the Church.

> On the day we call the day of the sun, all who dwell in the city or country gather in the same place. The memoirs of the apostles and the writings of the prophets are read, as much as time permits. When the reader has finished, he who presides over those gathered admonishes and challenges them to imitate these beautiful things. Then we all rise together and offer prayers for ourselves . . . and for all others, wherever they may be, so that we may be found righteous by our life and actions, and faithful to the commandments, so as to obtain eternal salvation. When the prayers are concluded we exchange the kiss.
>
> Then someone brings bread and a cup of water and wine mixed together to him who presides over the brethren. He takes them and offers praise and glory to the Father of the universe, through the name of the Son and of the Holy Spirit and for a considerable time he gives thanks that we have been judged worthy of these gifts. When he has concluded the prayers and thanksgivings, all present give voice to an acclamation by saying: "Amen."
>
> When he who presides has given thanks and the people have responded, those whom we call deacons give to those present the "eucharisted" bread, wine, and water and take them to those who are absent.
>
> St. Justin, cf. *CCC*, n. 1345

The text describes the basic outline of the Mass as we celebrate it today: readings followed by a sermon and the prayer of the faithful; offering of the gifts followed by the consecration, that is, the changing of bread and wine into the body and blood of Christ (here referred to as *eucharisted* bread and wine); reception of Holy Communion. The final paragraph describes the deacons taking Holy Communion to the sick who were not able to attend Sunday Mass.

Saintly Wisdom

Placing oneself in the school of the Fathers of the Church means learning to know Christ better and to know the human person better.

St. John Paul II, *Address to Augustinian Patristics Institute*, May 8, 1982

The quote included above is one brief text of one Church father. There are thousands upon thousands of other texts from other Fathers of the Church like Sts. Augustine, John Chrysostom, Basil the Great, etc. (Perhaps you have noticed that every chapter in this book highlights some of those texts.)

If you read the books written by the Church fathers, you will find that some explain the Trinity and the Incarnation. Some explain baptism and confirmation. Some explain Christian morals. Some explain marriage and celibacy. Some describe the way people confessed to a priest if they committed sins after baptism. Some explain Christian devotion to the Virgin Mary. Some explain heaven and hell. Some explain the end of the world and the Antichrist. In short, these works cover the whole range of topics explaining what the early Christians believed.

In addition to the writings of the Church fathers, other writings are crucial to sacred Tradition. Some are anonymous; for instance, the *Letter to Diognetus*. Others were written by Christians who were never canonized as saints but who left priceless testimony on how the early Church interpreted sacred Scripture. These men are called "ecclesiastical writers." The most important ones are Origen and Tertullian. Both were born in the second century, i.e., less than one hundred years after the death of St. John the Apostle.

Another official title given to some men and women is "doctor of the Church." By giving this title, the Church claims that the writings of these saints have contributed most towards helping others understand God's revelation. The greatest of all the doctors of the Church is St. Thomas Aquinas.

The Bible depends on Tradition

There are many passages of sacred Scripture which, before being written down, were part of sacred Tradition. Strictly speaking, though, sacred Scripture does not depend on sacred Tradition. They are *two different sources of revelation*. Even so, the Bible—as a whole—depends on Tradition.

All the books in the Bible are the inspired Word of God. That makes them different from all other human writings. Christians need to know which writings belong in the Bible. But no biblical text provides a list of books. No biblical text mentions the idea that there is a list defining which books were divinely inspired. This raises a question. On what basis did the early Church decide which books to include in the Bible?

One of the most important truths of our faith comes to us through sacred Tradition—a truth not explicitly stated anywhere in the Bible. It is the truth defining which writings were inspired by God and which ones were not. The *Catechism* states:

> It was by the Apostolic Tradition that the Church discerned which writings are to be included in the list of the sacred books. This complete list is called the "canon of Scripture."
>
> *CCC*, n. 120

Because of Tradition, Christians know that no book in the Bible was included by mistake and that no book is missing. Without Tradition, we would have doubts about particular texts—or entire books—wondering if they are truly the inspired word of God. Without Tradition, we would wonder if some texts really belonged in the Bible.

REVIEW QUESTIONS

1. What is sacred Tradition?
2. Why do we need sacred Tradition?
3. Explain the meaning of the terms: "father of the Church," "ecclesiastical writer," and "doctor of the Church."
4. What is the canon of Scripture and where does it come from? How does the Bible depend on sacred Tradition?

16.

Sacred Scripture

All Christians need to read sacred Scripture. Writing to one of the early Christians, St. Paul said:

> . . . from childhood you have been acquainted with the sacred writings which are able to instruct you for salvation through faith in Christ Jesus. All scripture is inspired by God and profitable for teaching, for reproof, for correction, and for training in righteousness . . .
>
> 2 Timothy 3:15–16

If you are a Christian, you believe that the Bible is the Word of God. Before I explain what that means, I want to encourage you to read it on your own. If you read it every day—even just for a few minutes—God's holy Word acts on you. It opens your mind and heart to his revelation.

Although it contains a story—a true story—with a beginning and an end, the Bible was not meant to be read like a novel. Every line is a precious jewel. Read a little every day. One verse alone is sometimes enough to inspire greater faith and love. If you've never read any book of the Bible, begin with one of the four Gospels. The Gospels are easier to understand than most of the other books. Besides, they take you right to the heart of the Bible, namely, the life of Jesus Christ.

What is the Bible?

First came revelation, then came the Bible. The prophets prepared Israel for the coming of the Messiah. When the Son of God came, he revealed all that his Father wanted to reveal. After each stage of revelation—first through the prophets and then through Jesus Christ—God decided to transmit his revelation by selecting and inspiring certain men to put it in writing. These sacred writings have been collected into one volume called the Bible.

The Bible is divided into two parts: the Old Testament and the New Testament. The first corresponds to the covenant preparing the people of Israel for the coming of the Messiah; the second corresponds to the new covenant Jesus established when fulfilling the promises made in the first covenant.

The Catholic Church recognizes seventy-three books as sacred Scriptures: forty-six in the Old Testament and twenty-seven in the New Testament. The Church teaches that all these books and all their parts are the inspired word of God. If a text is in the Bible, it means that it is the inspired Word of God. If the Church has not included a particular book or text, it means that this text is not one of the Scriptures inspired by God, even if some people in earlier times thought it was.

The Bible is called the "Word of God." God is the author of all the texts collected together in this book. All the texts were written by someone working under the influence of God's inspiration. The *Catechism* explains:

> The sacred Scriptures contain the word of God and, because they are inspired, they are truly the word of God. God is the author of sacred Scripture because he inspired its human authors; he acts in them and by means of them. He thus gives assurance that their writings teach his saving truth without error.
>
> *CCC*, nn. 135–136

The Bible is truth without error. But a book consisting of many pages repeating the statement "God is good" would also be truth without error. Sacred Scripture offers much more than freedom from error. It communicates much more than nice ideas on how to live a good life. It gives us a new way of looking at God, at ourselves and at the world. It contains divine mysteries—truths we would never know unless God had revealed them.

We must treat God's revelation with utmost reverence. St. Paul says, "You accepted it not as the word of men but as what it really is, the word of God" (1 Thess 2:13). The Apostle goes on to say that the message is "the word of God, which is at work in you believers" (1 Thess 2:13). Sacred Scripture was written in such a way that it captures God's message perfectly. Those who read the Bible with faith are opening their minds and hearts to God's "living power." This is why the Catholic Church has made Scripture the foundation of her liturgy. This is why she encourages everyone to study the Bible.

Divine inspiration

The only phrases ever written directly by God were the Ten Commandments. He wrote them on stone tablets (cf. Ex 31:18, 34:1). Everything else in the Bible was written by a holy writer based on the living experience of men and women telling us how God revealed himself to them.

The living experience of the patriarchs, the prophets, and the disciples of Jesus Christ came first. It was only later that the sacred writers wrote the Scriptures. The sacred writers used their own words to capture what God had revealed. While doing so, they were inspired. The Holy Spirit was guiding them from within their minds and hearts. Therefore, their words are divine words while also being human.

Because all the texts in sacred Scripture are the inspired Word of God, they are free from error. This is the principle of biblical inerrancy. God is the main author; he used the human authors as instruments. The texts are free from error because God used his almighty power to make sure the human writers would write the truth.

> **SACRED SCRIPTURE**
>
> Moses came and told the people all the words of the LORD and all the ordinances; and all the people answered with one voice, and said, "All the words which the LORD has spoken we will do." And Moses wrote all the words of the LORD. And he rose early in the morning, and built an altar at the foot of the mountain, and twelve pillars, according to the twelve tribes of Israel. . . . Then he took the book of the covenant, and read it in the hearing of the people; and they said, "All that the LORD has spoken we will do, and we will be obedient."
>
> Exodus 24:3–4, 7

The Bible not only contains God's revelation but contains it exactly as God wanted it written. When we say that a text was inspired by God, we mean that God gave the sacred writer a special grace. This grace of inspiration enabled the holy writer to put into words *everything* that God wanted and *only* what God wanted him to write.

A sacred text, by definition, is a text written by someone inspired by the Holy Spirit. Referring to the sacred writings, St. Paul said, that "All scripture is inspired by God" (2 Tim 3:16). Divine inspiration is the only criterion for including a book in the Bible. Only inspired books can be included in the Bible.

Apart from the texts in the Bible, the Church does not recognize any other writings as the inspired Word of God. Other revelations are possible. God can reveal whatever he wants to anyone he wants whenever he wants. However, other revelations or scriptures, no matter how useful they are, only serve to help us understand more accurately what is already written by divine inspiration in the Bible. Later revelations—even if they are truly and authentically revelations from God recorded without distortion—differ from the revelation contained in the Bible. Later revelations are useful only if they direct us back to God's act of revealing himself to us by sending his Son, Jesus Christ.

The Word of God

The Bible is the only book that Christians call the "Word of God." The greatest works of literature cannot be placed side by side with biblical texts. Nor can other books used by other religions. Many non-biblical writings can help us understand something about God. But even the best of these do not constitute the holy Word of God. All biblical texts, even those that appear to have little significance, are holy texts from God that he uses to transmit to us the truths of his revelation. All biblical texts are revealed truth and reveal it without error. We cannot remove any texts from sacred Scripture without offending God, nor can we add any. The Scriptures are not words written from one human being to another, but words from God to all people of all times.

The Bible is the Word of God. Sacred Tradition is the word of God. We also use this name for Jesus. The reason for doing this is explained in sacred Scripture. St. John says Jesus is "the Word became flesh" (Jn 1:14). The Word of God took human flesh.

Jesus is God speaking to us. The Bible is God speaking to us. Sacred Tradition is God speaking to us. Jesus Christ, Scripture, and Tradition are all the "word" of God because in them we find God's revelation.

We venerate the Bible because it is the Word of God. But the Bible and Jesus are not two different revelations. Quoting from St. Augustine, the *Catechism* says:

> Through all the words of sacred Scripture, God speaks only one single Word—his one Utterance in whom he expresses himself completely. . . . "One and the same Word of God extends throughout Scripture. . . . One and the same Utterance resounds in the mouths of all the sacred writers . . ."
>
> For this reason, the Church has always venerated the Scriptures as she venerates the Lord's body.
>
> *CCC*, nn. 102–103

Jesus is the one single Word that God speaks. The Bible is composed of many words, but all pointing to this one single Word who is the Son of God.

The Scriptures are precious to us because God uses them to tell us about Jesus. God's plan was to take his Son back to heaven until the end of time. The Bible is God's way of allowing us to go back in time and understand what it was like when the disciples could see Jesus. It is God's way of preparing us for the day when Jesus will come again.

By becoming flesh, the Word made the invisible God visible. Similarly, sacred Scripture makes the inaccessible mystery of God accessible to the human mind. The Bible is composed exclusively of words taken from ordinary speech. Even so, it tells us the secret of God's life as Father, Son, and Holy Spirit. And it tells us the secret of how we can become like God.

The purpose of the Bible

The vast majority of Christians have lived and died without ever seeing Jesus. He lived on earth for only a short time. After his resurrection he appeared only to certain select individuals, the Apostles and the holy women. To those who became members of the Church a few years after Jesus' resurrection, St. Paul said:

> . . . even though we once regarded Christ from a human point of view, we regard him thus no longer.
>
> 2 Corinthians 5:16

God's plan demands that we learn about Jesus through the Bible. The Bible leads to a deep knowledge of Christ. It leads to the one Word who is the total revelation of all that God can possibly reveal. Without Scripture, we would know very little about Jesus.

The need for Scripture must be understood properly. There are some who call Christians the "people of the book," along with Jews and Muslims. They are making a mistake. It is true that Christians need the Bible because God uses it to transmit his revelation. Even so, Christian faith cannot be reduced to belief in writings or belief in doctrine.

> **FATHERS OF THE CHURCH**
>
> The Scriptures are perfect, having been spoken by the Word of God and with his Spirit. We are lesser beings and, in comparison with the Word of God and his Spirit, we are indeed the least of all. This is the measure of how far we fall short of understanding God's mysteries.
>
> St. Irenaeus, *Against Heresies*, II, 41, 1

The Bible is not revelation. Jesus is the revelation. The Bible tells us all about him. Real faith means getting to know a person. To know everything God has revealed, we need the Bible. But we need more than the Bible. We get to know what God has revealed only when we achieve intimate union with Jesus through the work of the Holy Spirit.

> The Christian faith is not a "religion of the book." Christianity is the religion of the Word of God—a word that is not a written and mute word, but the Word that is incarnate and living. If the Scriptures are not to remain a dead letter, Christ, the eternal Word of the living God, must, through the Holy Spirit, "open our minds to understand the Scriptures."
>
> *CCC*, n. 108

Jesus opens our minds by giving us the light of the Holy Spirit. The Spirit shows us how all that has been written leads to Jesus.

The purpose of the Bible is to lead us to a total commitment to Jesus. What St. John says at the end of his Gospel applies to the rest of sacred Scripture. These things have been written down so "that you may believe that Jesus is the Christ, the Son of God, and that believing you may have life in his name" (Jn 20:31).

The Role of the Church

To safeguard revelation, God has entrusted the Church with three responsibilities:

1. To decree the canon of Scripture—the list of books inspired by the Holy Spirit.
2. To care for all translations from the original languages (Hebrew, Greek, and Aramaic) into modern languages.
3. To interpret the texts of sacred Scripture correctly.

Over the past two thousand years, the Church has encountered many difficulties accomplishing these three tasks. To understand why, first let's look at where the Bible came from.

Where the Bible came from

The Catholic Church teaches that all the books in the Bible and all their parts are the inspired word of God. But the Bible did not drop down out of heaven, ready-made. Nor is there a book in heaven that was used as a model. God did not invite the sacred writers to copy from something already written. Nor did God dictate the texts to them. Instead, they had to write from their own experience, recording what they knew about God's revelation.

They were able to write exactly what God wanted them to write because the Holy Spirit was working through them. Still, the human authors had to sit down and figure out what to write about and how to put their ideas into words. Many texts, in both the Old and New Testaments, were written by men who did not see the original events.

For instance, St. Luke never met Jesus. He was baptized after Pentecost. When beginning his account of the Gospel, he mentions the work he had to do before putting anything into writing:

> Inasmuch as many have undertaken to compile a narrative of the things which have been accomplished among us, just as they were delivered to us by those who from the beginning were eyewitnesses and ministers of the word, it seemed good to me also, having followed all things closely for some time past, to write an orderly account for you . . .
>
> Luke 1:1–3

St. Luke relied on the "eyewitnesses and ministers of the word" to find out what Jesus did and said. Then he had to decide how to put it together in a written account.

Genesis, the first book in the Bible, was written many centuries before Revelation, the last book. We know the human authors of some books, e.g., the letters of St. Paul. We have no idea who God inspired for others, e.g., the Book of Job. The most ancient texts included in the Bible were written at least three thousand years ago. The most recent texts date from about the year 100, when St. John composed his account of the Gospel. The Bible puts them all together.

In the year 392, a council of bishops made a list of the books that belong in the Bible. It is the same list the Catholic Church uses today: seventy-three books, with forty-six in the Old Testament and twenty-seven in the New Testament.

Today people can buy a Bible from a bookstore. Because it comes ready-made and neatly printed, they may not realize how this single volume came into existence. Some people are shocked to discover that, for almost three centuries, Christians had no Bible—certainly not the single volume we are used to seeing today. This is such a surprise for most people that it is worth repeating the fact: for three centuries after Jesus died, Christians had no Bibles because the Bible, as we know it today, did not yet exist.

There were several reasons why it took the Church centuries to produce the book we now call the Bible. Up until the end of the first century, the Apostles and Evangelists were still writing texts. Even after all

Books of the Bible

OLD TESTAMENT

Genesis, Exodus, Leviticus, Numbers, Deuteronomy, Joshua, Judges, Ruth, 1 and 2 Samuel, 1 and 2 Kings, 1 and 2 Chronicles, Ezra and Nehemiah, Tobit, Judith, Esther, 1 and 2 Maccabees, Job, Psalms, Proverbs, Ecclesiastes, the Song of Songs, the Wisdom of Solomon, Ecclesiasticus (Sirach), Isaiah, Jeremiah, Lamentations, Baruch, Ezekiel, Daniel, Hosea, Joel, Amos, Obadiah, Jonah, Micah, Nahum, Habakkuk, Zephaniah, Haggai, Zechariah, Malachi.

NEW TESTAMENT

Gospels according to: Matthew, Mark, Luke and John; Acts of the Apostles; Letters of St. Paul to: the Romans, 1 and 2 Corinthians, Galatians, Ephesians, Philippians, Colossians, 1 and 2 Thessalonians, 1 and 2 Timothy, Titus, Philemon; Letter to the Hebrews; Letters of: James; 1 and 2 Peter; 1, 2, and 3 John; Jude; Book of Revelation (Apocalypse).

the texts had been written, persecution often prevented Christians from circulating them freely. Until the year 311—with a few brief respites—it was a crime for anyone in the Roman empire to be a Christian. Being caught with a scroll of one of the sacred writings could lead to imprisonment or death.

There were other problems. As simple as it seems today, bringing all the various texts together required resources not yet available. Copies were difficult to make. Printing presses and photocopiers did not exist. To copy a text, a trained copyist had to write out each word by hand. Compared to the abundance of paper in today's society, writing materials in those days were scarce. The words had to be written in large print, for the sake of clarity, and many pages were needed. This made the writing process both tedious and expensive. There were few copies of any written text. All this made it difficult to produce a book with all the texts together in a single volume.

The oldest copies we have of the entire Bible date back to about the year 350—more than three hundred years after Christ lived on earth. When the Emperor Constantine came to power in the beginning of the fourth century, he put an end to persecution and ordered fifty copies of the Bible to be made at his expense. It was a daunting task to gather together several dozen scrolls, copy them one by one, and arrange them in one volume. If you want to know the whole story, you would have to read the history of Origen's monumental effort in the early third century to produce the *Hexapla*—and he was only trying to gather together all the writings of the Old Testament.

Printing fifty copies seems like a paltry number by modern standards. But in those days it meant spending vast sums of money. Every letter on every page of every copy had to be printed by hand. To get an idea how hard it was, try copying just one page of the Bible by hand. Then remember that a copyist had to transcribe about 1,700 pages.

The organizational difficulty was only part of the story. You begin to understand where the Bible came from when you realize how many other texts—besides the ones now included in the Bible—were also circulating among the early Christians. Many pious texts about God and the coming of the Messiah were written before the birth of Jesus. Many "gospels"—besides the four we have now—were written after Jesus ascended into heaven.

The *Book of Henoch*, the *Testament of the Twelve Patriarchs*, the *Description of the Heavenly Jerusalem*, the *Book of the Final War* and the *Book of Jubilees* were titles popular among the Jews before Christ began preaching the gospel. Besides these books, there were dozens more. Many of the early Christians treasured these writings, but the Church did not include them in the Old Testament.

Similarly, many texts written about Jesus were never included in the New Testament. The *Apocalypse of Peter*, the *Gospel of Thomas*, the *Acts of Paul* and the *Letter of Barnabas*—to name a few examples—were all left out of the Bible.

When it came time to put all the sacred writings together, the Church had to answer complicated questions: Which texts belong in the Bible and which ones don't? Which books were inspired by God and which ones were merely the work of human genius? These questions continue to be important. One further question, though, was even more crucial. It determined the answer to all others and it was this: Who had the authority to decide which texts should be included in the Bible?

When all is said and done, it is the Church, guided by the Holy Spirit, that tells us which books are inspired. When we ask where the Bible came from, we should say that it came from God, but we have to add that it came to us *through the Church*. This is why St. Augustine said:

> I would not believe in the Gospel, had not the authority of the Catholic Church already moved me.
>
> St. Augustine, cf. *CCC*, n. 119

This father of the Church lived precisely during the time when the Church was fixing the canon of sacred Scripture, that is, the official list of books. Anyone who rejects the authority of the Catholic Church rejects the authority that God used in order to determine which books he wanted to include in the Bible.

Which books belong in the Bible and how does the Church decide this question in practice? It all comes down to the bishops. The Bible was put together under the authority of the bishops acting as successors of the Apostles. The Bible we have today exists because about sixteen hundred years ago, the bishops, basing their decision on sacred Tradition, selected the texts that now comprise sacred Scripture. Until that selection was made, the Bible, as we know it today, did not yet exist. That is why we say that for three hundred years after Jesus' death and resurrection, Christians had no Bibles.

Let's look at some of the problems the bishops faced when selecting texts.

Problems with selecting texts

There is no list anywhere in sacred Scripture stating which books belong in the Bible. The list of books printed in any of today's versions of the Bible is not part of sacred Scripture.

In the early centuries of the Church, many Christians wondered whether the Old Testament Scriptures were worth preserving. The controversy was not about which books belonged in the Old Testament. They were worried about the value of the Old Testament *as a whole*. This controversy arose mainly because of Gnosticism, a false teaching propagated by Marcion and others. Marcion said Christians should get rid of the Old Testament. He believed in two gods: one good and one bad. He said the Old Testament was the work of the evil god, while the New Testament was the work of the good god.

Condemning Marcion's doctrine, the Church stated that there is only one God, who is infinitely good, and that the Old Testament was the inspired word of the one, true God. The *Catechism* teaches:

> The Old Testament is an indispensable part of sacred Scripture. Its books are divinely inspired and retain a permanent value, since the Old Covenant has never been revoked. Indeed, the economy of the Old Testament was deliberately so oriented that it should prepare for and declare in prophecy the coming of Christ, redeemer of all men. Even though they contain matters imperfect and provisional, the books of the Old Testament bear witness to the whole divine pedagogy of God's saving love: these writings are a storehouse of sublime teaching on God and of sound wisdom on human life, as well as a wonderful treasury of prayers; in them, too, the mystery of our salvation is present in a hidden way.
>
> *CCC*, nn. 121–122

Another major doubt arose when trying to determine the list of books to be included in the Bible. Besides a dispute over books in the Old Testament, there was a dispute about two books in the New Testament. Many Christians in the East had their doubts about the Book of Revelation (also called Apocalypse). Many Christians in the West had doubts about the Letter to the Hebrews. It was not until the end of the fourth century that these doubts were resolved and both books were recognized to be the inspired Word of God. It was also at this time—around the year 400—that Pope St. Damasus asked St. Jerome, one of the most learned men of his time, to translate the entire Bible into Latin. (Latin was the most common language at that time.) St. Jerome's Latin version of the Bible is known as the Vulgate. From that time on, the list of books for both the Old Testament and the New Testament was set.

When the Protestant reformers broke away from the Catholic Church in the sixteenth century, they rejected this ancient tradition.

Before the split between Catholics and Protestants, Christians had no serious doubts about which books belonged in the Bible.

Martin Luther, one of the Protestant reformers, published a German translation of the Bible. In this new version, seven of the Old Testament books were listed under the title "Apocrypha." These seven are: Tobit, Judith, First Book of Maccabees, Second Book of Maccabees, Book of Wisdom, Ecclesiasticus (also called Sirach), and Baruch, plus parts of Daniel and parts of Esther. Luther did not consider these seven books to be the inspired word of God.

Because of Luther's decision, some Christians find this issue confusing. Has anybody been given the special guidance of the Holy Spirit to know which books should be included in the Bible, and if so, who received that grace? Before Martin Luther cast doubts, all Christians believed that the Church had this special grace and manifested it through the authority of the Pope and the bishops in communion with him. The Protestant reformers claimed that this belief was false. When asked who had the authority, they claimed that no authority was needed since it was obvious to all Christians which books belonged in the Bible. Ever since then, this dispute has been one of the points of disagreement between Catholics and Protestants.

It is *not* obvious which books belong in the Bible. If it were obvious, disputes in the early Church would never have taken place. In the end, someone who has God's authority—or acts as if he did—ends up telling other Christians which books to include in the Bible. For all practical purposes, the Protestant reformers were claiming they had the authority to decide which texts were inspired and which were not.

About thirty years after Luther published his version of the Bible, the bishops of the Church gathered together in the city of Trent for an ecumenical council. It was the year 1546. There, under the authority of Pope Paul III, the Church repeated the traditional list—the one from the Vulgate—and declared as a dogma of faith that *all* the books and *only* the books on this list were part of sacred Scripture. The Church stated that we know for sure which books are included in the Bible based on revelation as it has come down to us through sacred Tradition.

What difference does it make whether those seven books rejected by Luther are included in the Bible? First, it is a matter of principle. When making the Bible, the Church only accepts texts or rejects texts based on a clear criterion: What was the tradition of the early Christians and how has that tradition been maintained over the centuries? There is another reason why the Church must safeguard the list of books comprising the Bible and prevent anyone from changing it. Every text in the Bible has something to teach us. Every text in the Bible contains God's revelation. If we reject a text, we are rejecting God's revelation.

Take the example of a text in the Second Book of Maccabees (one of the books Luther no longer considered to be inspired). It portrays the Jewish war hero Judas Maccabeus sending money to the Temple in Jerusalem to have a sacrifice offered for some soldiers who died in battle. The Scriptures praise him for doing so (cf. 2 Maccabees 12:43–45). Christians also offer sacrifices for the dead when they ask a priest to offer Mass for someone who has died. Even though most Christians still pray for the dead, some claim this is wrong. It is not wrong. It is good to pray for the dead, as the passage in the Second Book of Maccabees makes clear.

Translation of texts

The story of the way Catholics and Protestants ended up with different versions of the Old Testament highlights something about the Bible that we cannot take for granted. The Bible's authority ultimately depends on the authority of the Church, and the Church's authority depends on God.

The Church's authority is also crucial when it comes to translating the Bible. The texts of Scripture were all written in either Hebrew or Greek, with some phrases in Aramaic. Before you can read the Bible in your own language, someone has to translate it. Some translations are faithful to the original; some distort what was written in the original text.

For instance, some translations use the feminine instead of the masculine pronoun for God, talking about God the Mother instead of God the Father. God has no gender, because he has no body. Still, according to the original Greek texts, when Jesus spoke about God, he always spoke about his "Father." The Greek word for "mother" never appears in this context. This is merely one example among thousands explaining why the Church tells Christians which translations are trustworthy and which ones are not.

MAGISTERIUM

Since God speaks in sacred Scripture through men in human fashion, the interpreter of sacred Scripture, in order to see clearly what God wanted to communicate to us, should carefully investigate what meaning the sacred writers really intended, and what God wanted to manifest by means of their words.

To search out the intention of the sacred writers, attention should be given, among other things, to literary forms. Truth is set forth and expressed differently in texts which are variously historical, prophetic, poetic, or modeled on other forms of discourse.

Vatican II, *Dogmatic Constitution on Divine Revelation*, n. 12

Interpreting the Scriptures

The Church has the ultimate responsibility for teaching us how to interpret texts of sacred Scripture. The first task of interpreting Scripture is to figure out what the writer was trying to say. The *Catechism* states:

> In order to discover the sacred authors' intention, the reader must take into account the conditions of their time and culture, the literary genres in use at that time, and the modes of feeling, speaking, and narrating then current. For the fact is that truth is differently presented and expressed in the various types of historical writing, in prophetical and poetical texts, and in other forms of literary expression.
>
> CCC, n. 108

Before trying to interpret a biblical text, the reader must ask: Was the writer speaking factually, metaphorically, or allegorically?

With this in mind, read the following four texts from the Bible. You will see how difficult it can be to determine exactly what the sacred writer wanted to communicate with his words:

1. From the first chapter of Genesis, describing creation:

> And there was evening and there was morning, a third day.
>
> And God made the two great lights, the greater light to rule the day, and the lesser light to rule the night; he made the stars also. And God set them in the firmament of the heavens to give light upon the earth,

> to rule over the day and over the night, and to separate the light from the darkness. And God saw that it was good. And there was evening and there was morning, a fourth day.
>
> Genesis 1:13, 16–19

Is the six-day creation account strictly factual? Could evening and morning come on the third day before God created the sun on the fourth day? Is the text metaphorical? If so, what do the six days represent? Is each "day" a stage in creation, along the lines of another text that says for God "a day is like a thousand years"?

2. From the Book of Isaiah, describing how King Hezekiah asked for a sign to be sure God was going to help him:

> "This is the sign to you from the Lord, that the Lord will do this thing that he has promised: Behold, I will make the shadow cast by the declining sun on the dial of Ahaz turn back ten steps." So the sun turned back on the dial the ten steps by which it had declined.
>
> Isaiah 38:7–8

Does this text describe a historical fact—a real event when the sun's shadow moved "backward"? Did the shadow cast by the setting sun shift so radically that people could see it move in the opposite direction, as if the whole planet were shifting on its axis? Or is the text an allegory? Is the "shifting of the sun" a metaphor indicating a radical change in the fortunes of the kingdom of Israel?

3. From the Gospel of Luke, when Jesus concluded his explanation on why his disciples do not fast as long as he remains with them:

> "And no one puts new wine into old wineskins; if he does, the new wine will burst the skins and it will be spilled, and the skins will be destroyed. But new wine must be put into fresh wineskins And no one after drinking old wine desires new; for he says, 'The old is good.'"
>
> Luke 5:37–39

This passage is obviously metaphorical. But what is the lesson? Jesus wants us to make sure we preserve the "new wine" so that it does not get ruined. But what does new wine symbolize? Does it symbolize Jesus' presence in the world? Does it symbolize his miracle at Cana? The Holy Spirit? A new revelation? What do the new wineskins symbolize? Do they symbolize his disciples? Their hearts? A new set of Scriptures containing the Word of God?

4. From the *Gospel according to John*, when Jesus speaks to the Apostles at the Last Supper:

> "If you loved me, you would have rejoiced, because I go to the Father; for the Father is greater than I."
>
> John 14:28

This text is often quoted by non-Christians. They claim it contradicts the texts which state that Jesus is the Son of God. They argue that Jesus was no more than a man and that he knew it. The text is difficult to interpret. This difficulty led to a dispute in the early Church. However, this text is a good example of how Christians should approach interpretation of the Scriptures. Rather than using one obscure text to interpret the meaning of many obvious texts, we always use the many obvious texts to interpret the one that is obscure. In this case, the Church teaches: "Jesus Christ is equal to the Father in his divinity but lower than the Father in his humanity" (*Athanasian Creed*, n. 31). Jesus said he was the Son of God because his divine nature makes him equal to the Father. He called himself the "Son of Man" because his human nature makes him equal to us—and, in that sense, he is lower than the Father.

These four examples offer only a glimpse at the difficulty of interpreting Scripture properly. In the *Catechism* (cf. CCC, nn. 112–114), the Church provides criteria for interpreting the Bible. By following these criteria, we interpret the texts in the light of the same Spirit who inspired them.

- **Be especially attentive to the content and unity of the whole Bible.** There are seventy-three different books, written by many different human authors. Even so, sacred Scripture is a unity. It is a unity because God is the main author of all the texts. We respect that unity when we look for the connection between passages, instead of isolating them. For instance, some texts speak about Jesus having brothers and sisters, e.g., "James and Joses and Judas and Simon" (Mk 6:3). Since there is no word for "cousin" in Aramaic—Jesus' mother tongue—his cousins were called "brothers and sisters." This becomes evident when examining other Gospel texts. One states that two of these "brothers"—James and Joses—were sons of the Virgin Mary's sister-in-law, who was also named Mary (cf. Mk 15:40 and Jn 19:25). The Virgin Mary was the mother of one and only one child: Jesus Christ.

- **Read sacred Scripture within the living Tradition of the Church.**

Just as no text of Scripture should be isolated from other texts, no text should be isolated from sacred Tradition. For instance, in the Book of Revelation, St. John speaks of the saints rising from the dead and "reigning with Christ for one thousand years." Of all the many different ways this text might be interpreted, the Church fathers ruled out a political interpretation. For this reason, the Church condemned the teaching of millenarianism, which holds that Jesus will return to establish an earthly kingdom full of earthly pleasures for one thousand years before the Last Judgment.

- **Be attentive to the analogy of faith.**

When interpreting the Bible, we have to see how different truths of revelation fit together to form a single revelation, a coherent whole. God has revealed many mysteries. He said there is only one God. But he also revealed that the Father is God, the Son is God, and the Holy Spirit is God. Somehow these two truths must fit together. The Church does this by teaching that God is one being in three persons. Analogy is all about comparing one thing with another. The analogy of faith means comparing one truth of revelation with another mystery also revealed by God. The Bible does not explicitly state that there are three persons in one God, but this conclusion is the only way to make any sense out of the various texts.

Wisdom of the Saints

Those things that flow from the will of God alone, beyond all that is due to creatures, can come to us only to the extent that they are handed down in sacred Scripture, which makes God's will known.

St. Thomas Aquinas,
Summa Theologiae, III, 1, 3

- **Accept the teaching of the Church whenever she gives a specific interpretation to a biblical text.**

On various occasions, the Church has declared the official interpretation of a specific text. For example, the Church has declared as definitive teaching—to be held as an article of faith by all Christians—that the text on the Eucharist in St. John's account must be interpreted literally. When Jesus told his disciples to eat his flesh and drink his blood (cf. Jn 6:54–56), he meant this in the literal sense of eating and drinking.

REVIEW QUESTIONS

1. Why do we call God the "author" of sacred Scripture?
2. Where did the Bible come from?
3. How can you be sure that the translation of a text in Scripture matches the Hebrew or Greek in the original text?
4. What do Christians need to keep in mind when interpreting a text in sacred Scripture?

17.

The Magisterium

"The church of the living God [is] the pillar and bulwark of the truth" (1 Tim 3:15). God gave authority to the Church to teach the truth. This authority to teach is called the "Magisterium of the Church."

The Church is the People of God. Every people—every nation or society—has leaders. The Magisterium is the teaching that comes from the Church's leaders. The *Catechism* explains:

> The Pope and the bishops are authentic teachers, that is, teachers endowed with the authority of Christ, who preach the faith to the people entrusted to them—the faith to be believed and put into practice. The ordinary and universal Magisterium of the Pope and the bishops in communion with him teach the faithful the truth to believe, the charity to practice, the beatitude to hope for.
>
> CCC, n. 2034

When teaching, the Pope and the bishops pass on to all Christians not only the doctrine summarized in the Creed but also a whole way of life. We live this way of life by loving God and loving others as Jesus loves us.

You may think loving others is easy. Learning to love is harder than learning to be a doctor who can cure cancer or learning to be an engineer who can build electronic circuits. You do not learn medicine or science on your own. You need someone to show you. As with medicine and engineering, so it is with learning to love others the way God created us to love them.

Controversy over authority

The Church teaches us about the Trinity and all the other mysteries we need to know in order to be saved. The Church also teaches us how to distinguish between right and wrong on moral issues ranging from the right to life (You shall not kill) to the right to truth (You shall not bear false witness). These issues raise controversies.

Some people think they need to kill. This happens, for instance, when doctors think they are justified in killing unborn babies by performing abortions. The Church has proclaimed her teaching on the right to life to explain how abortion, euthanasia, experimentation on human embryos, and other practices kill innocent human beings and do enormous harm to the whole of society.

Through her moral teaching, the Church tries to help in other ways. She helps couples using contraceptives to see why this practice is intrinsically evil. Because some political leaders are convinced that reducing birth rates reduces poverty, they want to mandate programs of population control; the Church tries to help them find morally acceptable ways of dealing with the problems caused by widespread destitution. The Church has developed extensive teaching on many similar questions of social order—for example, guiding international efforts to resolve conflicts through dialogue instead of violence.

People can be blinded by social customs and public support for immoral behavior. To make matters worse, some Christians do not accept the Church's authority to teach on moral issues. Consequently, the world is faced with a crisis of love and a crisis of authority. Some Christians do not realize that God wants them to accept the Church's authority. They think the Church's teaching will lead them away from love. They think her teaching will make it more difficult to establish peace and justice. They do not appreciate the role of the Church's authority in the affairs of this world. They do not understand how such attitudes endanger the eternal salvation of their own souls. To overcome these crises, we need to examine the way Jesus established authority in his Church.

Authority in the Church

Jesus did not give all Christians equal authority. He gave certain chosen men authority to lead other Christians. This fact appears quite clearly in the New Testament. First he chose the Twelve and gave them authority to cast out demons, cure the sick, and announce: "The kingdom of heaven is at hand." Then he picked another seventy-two men from among his disciples and gave them similar authority (cf. Lk 9:1, 10:1).

After Jesus ascended into heaven, the same pattern was followed in the early Church. Not all Christians had equal authority. Instead, the Twelve had authority over the entire Church. These men led others in prayer. These men explained the Scriptures. These men spoke and others listened. The Acts of the Apostles gives clear testimony to this fact. After telling us that three thousand people were baptized on the day of Pentecost, St. Luke states:

> And they devoted themselves to the apostles' teaching and fellowship, to the breaking of bread and the prayers.
>
> Acts 2:42

Why was the teaching of the Twelve so important? The early Christians accepted the authority of the Apostles because it came from Jesus. It was this way in the beginning. It is meant to remain that way until Jesus comes at the end of time. As the Holy Spirit says in the Letter to the Hebrews:

Sacred Scripture

Jesus said to Simon Peter, "Simon, son of John, do you love me more than these?" He said to him, "Yes, Lord; you know that I love you." He said to him, "Feed my lambs." A second time he said to him, "Simon, son of John, do you love me?" He said to him, "Yes, Lord; you know that I love you." He said to him, "Tend my sheep." He said to him the third time, "Simon, son of John, do you love me?" Peter was grieved because he said to him the third time, "Do you love me?" And he said to him, "Lord, you know everything; you know that I love you." Jesus said to him, "Feed my sheep."

John 21:15–17

> Remember your leaders, those who spoke to you the word of God; consider the outcome of their life, and imitate their faith. Jesus Christ is the same yesterday and today and for ever.
>
> Obey your leaders and submit to them; for they are keeping watch over your souls, as men who will have to give account. Let them do this joyfully, and not sadly, for that would be of no advantage to you.
>
> Hebrews 13:7–8, 17

Jesus established leaders in his Church. When we disobey them, we are the first to suffer. We suffer because confusion and conflict divide the Church. The rest of the world also suffers. Being divided, Christians become a stumbling block to faith instead of being a sign of God's salvation.

Imitating the early Christians means learning to respect the authority Jesus established in his Church. We show that respect to the bishops, remembering that they are the successors of the Apostles. The bishops must show the respect to their head, the Bishop of Rome—the "Pope." Because the Pope is St. Peter's successor, he has the same authority St. Peter had among the other Apostles. The Pope is the visible head of the Church. He is the Vicar of Christ, that is, the one who takes the place of Christ as the head of the Church on earth.

The Pope's authority

Among the Apostles, one had more authority than the others. His name was Simon Peter. St. Matthew—one of the Twelve—narrates the event that led Jesus to single out Simon the fisherman and make him the "Rock." Jesus asked the Apostles, "Who do you say that I am?" Simon replied, "You are the Christ, the Son of the living God." Because of Simon's answer, Jesus declared:

> Blessed are you, Simon Bar-Jona! For flesh and blood has not revealed this to you, but my Father who is in heaven. And I tell you, you are Peter, and on this rock I will build my church, and the powers of death shall not prevail against it. I will give you the keys of the kingdom of

> heaven, and whatever you bind on earth shall be bound in heaven, and whatever you loose on earth shall be loosed in heaven.
>
> Matthew 16:17–19

What did Jesus mean when he gave Simon the fisherman this new name—Peter? Why was Jesus giving him the "keys to the kingdom"?

Keys are a symbol of authority. Just think of someone giving you the keys to his house or his car. He is giving you the right to use it. When Jesus told Peter, "I give you the keys to the kingdom of heaven," he was saying in effect, "Peter, I give you authority over my Church."

"Peter" means rock. Jesus called this man the "Rock" using the Aramaic word *kephas*. In nine passages of the New Testament—originally written in Greek—the Aramaic word *kephas* is used as a proper name to designate St. Peter (cf. Jn 1:42, Gal 2:11, etc). More than just a stone, *kephas* refers to bedrock, the rock that makes up the earth we stand on. This is the kind of rock builders look for when they want a foundation that will last forever.

Jesus wanted his disciples to remember this new name whenever they thought of Simon Peter. He is the Rock that no power on earth can shake. He is the bedrock that will remain in place after everything else is washed away. The name indicates permanence.

Because of this permanence, the early Christians believed that St. Peter's authority did not disappear when St. Peter died. They believed that St. Peter's successors shared in the unique task Jesus had assigned to St. Peter. They believed that the man chosen to be the Bishop of Rome would be St. Peter's successor. St. Peter was chosen to be the Prince of the Apostles and had greater authority than the other Apostles. In the same way, St. Peter's successor rules over the whole Church.

Any bishop that recognizes the unique authority that Jesus has given to the Pope is called a "bishop in communion with the Pope." Some bishops do not recognize the Pope's authority. If they are successors of the Apostles, then they are truly bishops—just as much as those who are in communion with the Pope. But until they recognize the Pope's authority, they are not *fully* united to the one true Church of Christ.

Some Christians have assumed the title "bishop" but are not really bishops because they did not receive episcopal power from the Apostles.

Hierarchy in the Church

If we look at the early Church, we see a hierarchy. Hierarchy comes from the Greek words *hieros* (meaning "sacred") and *archein* (meaning "to rule"). The hierarchy of the Church is a sacred rule or sacred order. God chooses men from among the multitude of Christian faithful and gives them authority when they receive the sacrament of holy orders. The men who receive this sacrament become sacred persons—persons specially dedicated God. These are the bishops, priests, and deacons of the Church.

Only bishops, priests, and deacons belong to the clergy. Some Christians are called "Brother" or "Sister" because they belong to a religious order or a religious congregation. Some of those belonging to religious communities join the clergy by being ordained priests. Ordinary Christians are not part of religious orders or congregations; they are not part of the clergy, either. Ordinary Christians are called "laypeople" or the "laity."

Holy orders is not meant to establish a ranking among Christians. Ordinary Christians are called to be just as holy as bishops, priests, and deacons. While the clergy dedicate themselves to sacred ministry, ordinary Christians dedicate themselves to their work in the middle of the world. Holy orders does not exist in the Church to make some people more important than others. Everyone in the Church is equal. Everyone is a child of God the Father, a brother or sister of Jesus Christ, and a temple of the Holy Spirit.

Equality and hierarchy go together. We are all equal, but not everyone has the same authority. We have an obligation to obey the person who has authority. In matters of faith and morals, the Apostles and their successors have authority from God to tell other Christians what to believe and what to do. Jesus gave them this authority. He also gave them a special fullness of the Holy Spirit.

Working from within the minds and hearts of the Apostles and their successors, the Holy Spirit showed them what they were supposed

> **Fathers of the Church**
>
> Let all follow the bishop, as Jesus Christ follows his Father, and the college of presbyters as the Apostles; respect the deacons as you do God's law. Let no one do anything concerning the Church in separation from the bishop.
>
> St. Ignatius of Antioch, cf. *CCC*, n. 896

to teach. At the Last Supper, Jesus promised the Apostles that he would send them the Spirit of his Father and that the Spirit of truth would guide them "into all the truth" (Jn 16:13). St. John narrates how Jesus appeared to them on the day of his resurrection and "he breathed on them, and said to them, 'Receive the Holy Spirit'" (Jn 20:22). Jesus' breath was a symbol of the invisible power—a gentle power—that he was giving the Apostles so that they would know how to exercise their authority.

Christians obey the Pope and the bishops in communion with him *in matters of faith and morals*. Matters of faith include all matters directly connected to any truth God has revealed. Moral matters are those that determine whether an act is good or evil.

Christians do not have any obligation to obey the Pope and the bishops in matters of opinion. For instance, it would be an abuse of their authority if the Pope or the bishops told Christians how to organize a bank or a hospital or a political party—or any similar aspect of life that we call "temporal affairs" or "matters of opinion." The Church intervenes in temporal affairs only when she needs to clarify a specific issue related to faith or morals. She intervenes precisely because matters of faith and morals are not matters of opinion but issues of revelation where there can be no difference of opinion. The Pope and the bishops teach truths of faith and morals and leave ordinary Christians the responsibility of making decisions in worldly affairs.

Why is the authority of the bishops limited to declaring what to believe and what to do in matters of faith and morals? There are several reasons. God has established three authorities in this world: the Church, the State, and the family. The Church has authority over all matters concerning our eternal salvation. The State has authority over all matters concerning our temporal welfare. The family is the most basic authority of all. Parents have authority over their children; and the husband and wife have to "be subject to one another out of reverence for Christ" (Eph 5:21).

Every nation has its own government. God gives the leaders of each government authority over the rest of the citizens. St. Paul's describes this authority saying:

> Let every person be subject to the governing authorities. For there is no authority except from God, and those that exist have been instituted by God. Therefore he who resists the authorities resists what God has appointed, and those who resist will incur judgment. . . . For the same reason you also pay taxes, for the authorities are ministers of God, attending to this very thing.
>
> Romans 13:1–2, 6

Because of the way God created man as male and female, he has established a hierarchy within marriage. The husband has to accept his wife's authority over him. This means that every husband has a sacred obligation to love his wife and be faithful to her the same way Jesus sacrificed himself for the Church. The wife has an obligation to accept her husband's authority. She accepts his authority the same way the Church submits to the authority of Christ. St. Paul describes this family hierarchy:

> Be subject to one another out of reverence for Christ. Wives, be subject to your husbands, as to the Lord. For the husband is the head of the wife as Christ is the head of the Church, his body, and is himself its Savior. As the Church is subject to Christ, so let wives also be subject in everything to their husbands. Husbands, love your wives, as Christ loved the Church and gave himself up for her . . .
>
> Ephesians 5:21–25

In family hierarchy, the husband has to subject himself to his wife in one way, while the wife has to subject herself to her husband in another way.

> Wives, be subject to your husbands, as is fitting in the Lord. Husbands, love your wives, and do not be harsh with them.
>
> Colossians 3:18–19

The wife subjects herself to her husband by accepting the authority he has to make decisions. A husband subjects himself to his wife by sacrificing *all* his plans—especially in matters of sex, use of time, and professional ambition—in order to put her needs first and make her happy.

Just as God established one kind of authority for the government of nations and another kind for families, Jesus established a specific kind of authority for the Church. He put all authority in the hands of the hierarchy, that is, in the hands of the Pope and the bishops. No Christian has the authority to change this—not even the Pope or the bishops.

Errors regarding Church hierarchy

Some people misunderstand the hierarchy of the Church because of four errors.

The first error assumes that the bishops are free to impose their own will on others, demanding that other Christians to serve them. Jesus warned his apostles, "You know that those who are supposed to rule over the Gentiles lord it over them, and their great men exercise authority over them. But it shall not be so among you. . . . the Son of man also came not to be served but to serve, and to give his life as a ransom for many" (Mk 10:42–43, 45). God did not give bishops authority so they could do whatever they want. They have to obey God just as Jesus obeyed his Father.

Magisterium

In order to preserve the Church in the purity of the faith handed on by the Apostles, Christ who is the Truth willed to confer on her a share in his own infallibility.

The Roman Pontiff, head of the college of bishops, enjoys this infallibility in virtue of his office, when, as supreme pastor and teacher of all the faithful—who confirms his brethren in the faith—he proclaims by a definitive act a doctrine pertaining to faith or morals. . . . The infallibility promised to the Church is also present in the body of bishops when, together with Peter's successor, they exercise the supreme Magisterium, above all in an Ecumenical Council. When the Church through its supreme Magisterium proposes a doctrine for belief as being divinely revealed and as the teaching of Christ, the definitions must be adhered to with the obedience of faith.

Catechism of the Catholic Church, nn. 889, 891

The second error says that a few power-hungry Christians invented the notion of authority, contrary to Jesus' original intention of founding a church where everyone was equal. This is an error because Jesus wants both equality and hierarchy. The two concepts are not opposed but complementary. Ordinary Christians have the same dignity as the bishops, priests, and deacons. "For as many of you as were baptized into Christ have put on Christ. There is neither Jew nor Greek, there is neither slave nor free, there is neither male nor female; for you are all one in Christ Jesus" (Gal 3:27–28). But the same man who wrote these words—St. Paul—insisted that Jesus Christ gave him an authority that was not given to other Christians (cf. Gal 1:11—2:10). He also insisted that he could choose a successor and pass on this authority by making Timothy a bishop (cf. 1 Tim 6:11–14).

The third error says nobody has a right to tell others what to believe. Jesus told his Apostles, "Go into all the world and preach the gospel to the whole creation. He who believes and is baptized will be saved; but he who does not believe will be condemned" (Mk 16:15–16). "[Teach] them to observe all that I have commanded you" (Mt 28:20). Jesus entrusted the Apostles and their successors with the duty of preserving the purity of God's revelation. Bishops have both a right and a duty to exercise their authority. When they fail to tell others what to believe, they disobey God.

The fourth error assumes that fervent believers serve God best by reaching positions of authority. This error has done so much harm that a special explanation is needed.

The goal of every Christian is not to have authority but to be holy. Having authority did not make the Apostles holier than the other disciples. Having authority does not make the bishops holier than other Christians today. Jesus never praised anyone for the fact of having authority. He praised the ones who were willing to obey:

> Not every one who says to me, "Lord, Lord," shall enter the kingdom of heaven, but he who does the will of my Father who is in heaven. On that day many will say to me, "Lord, Lord, did we not prophesy in your name, and cast out demons in your name, and do many mighty works in your

> name?" And then will I declare to them, "I never knew you; depart from me, you evildoers."
>
> Matthew 7:21–23

Jesus will reject some of those who had authority within the Church. People who have authority can do a lot of good. They can prophesy, cast out demons, and work miracles. But none of this makes them holy. We are holy only if we obey. Only those who do God's will can enter his kingdom.

The Blessed Virgin Mary is the holiest creature God ever created. Even so, Jesus did not include her among the Twelve Apostles. She never held a position of authority. Only once does the Gospel describe her giving a command. She asked the servants at the wedding feast to help Jesus so he could change water into wine. The only time she gave a command, she did not ask anyone to obey her. She said, "Do whatever he tells you" (Jn 2:5). She was asking them to obey Jesus. The servants obeyed, and Jesus worked the miracle. The Virgin Mary is the ultimate proof that Christians can be very holy—full of grace!—even though they have no authority.

The deposit of faith

When we want to know what God revealed, we turn to sacred Tradition and sacred Scripture. These form one sacred deposit of the Word of God. It is a "deposit" roughly similar to a deposit we put in a bank. Somebody makes a deposit of cash, and the bank has an obligation to keep it safe. The Word of God, contained in sacred Tradition and sacred Scripture, is the deposit of faith because God entrusted it to the Church. The Church has an obligation to keep it safe.

Keeping the deposit of faith safe means making sure that all preaching in all local churches and in all groups within the Church accurately reflects the Word of God contained in sacred Tradition and sacred Scripture. One aspect of keeping it safe is to make sure to interpret sacred Scripture correctly, avoiding any errors that contradict God's revelation.

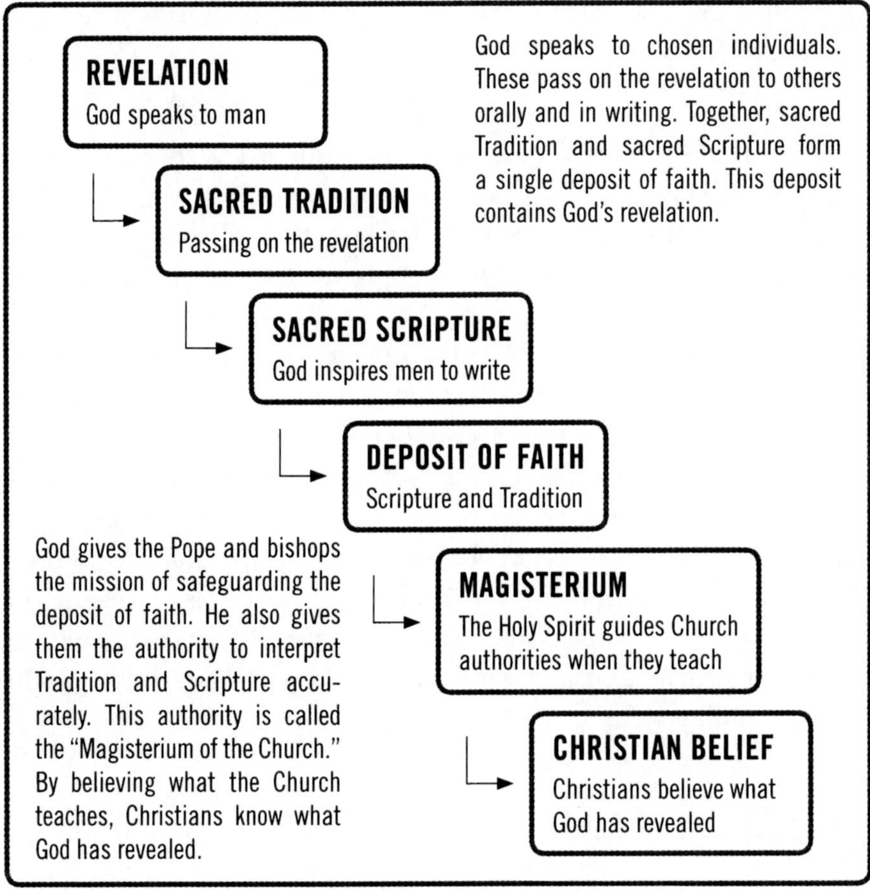

God established an authority to interpret sacred Scripture

Christians should read the Scriptures. But interpreting sacred Scripture requires more than personal effort. Individuals can make mistakes. To deny this is to deny a fact of history. In every century of Church history, different Christians have offered contradictory interpretations. For instance, in the fourth century some Christians claimed that Jesus was not really God but only a man, while others insisted that Jesus was truly God. These two interpretations cannot both be correct.

The problem of contradictory interpretations has repeated itself many times throughout the history of the Church. St. Peter explained the basic principle for the correct interpretation of sacred Scripture:

> First of all you must understand this, that no prophecy of Scripture is a matter of one's own interpretation, because no prophecy ever came by the impulse of man, but men moved by the Holy Spirit spoke from God.
>
> 2 Peter 1:20–21

Individuals do not have God's authority to give the definitive interpretation for biblical texts. Only the Church has this authority. How does the Church do it? Over the centuries we have developed a term to describe it. We call it "the Magisterium." It is the teaching office of the Church—*office* not in the sense of a room in a building, but *office* in the sense a position of authority.

The prophets were speaking for God when they prophesied. The holy writers were speaking—writing—for God when they wrote the texts of sacred Scripture. Without a God-given authority to interpret the Scriptures correctly, we would not understand what God inspired men to prophesy and what God inspired men to put in writing. Without a God-given authority to interpret the Scriptures correctly, it would be impossible to possess Scriptures that are free from error. Despite all the effort God made to provide accurate accounts of all that was handed on to us by the prophets and Apostles, we would not only remain ignorant if we made the wrong interpretation. It would be much worse than ignorance. We would think we believed what God had revealed, while in fact we believe something *contrary* to God's revelation—and encouraging others to believe it. Instead of spreading the gospel, we would be spreading error and confusion, leading people *away from God*. Our conviction that we were leading them closer to God would only make things worse. It would be like a doctor who thinks he is curing patients by giving them medicine when he is giving them poison.

A practical example will help. Some preachers tell everyone: "Believe in Jesus and he will make you rich. Believe in Jesus and he will make you successful. Believe in Jesus and he is going to take away all your pain. Believe in Jesus and he will rescue you from tribulation when persecution comes." The preachers who present the gospel this way may be very sincere. They may think they are speaking the truth. They have their reasons for interpreting the Scriptures the way they do.

But they are wrong. They are telling people to believe something that God does not want anybody to believe.

The Apostles died poor. They were persecuted. They were ridiculed so much that one of them wrote:

> For I think that God has exhibited us apostles as last of all, like men sentenced to death; because we have become a spectacle to the world, to angels and to men. We are fools for Christ's sake . . .
>
> 1 Corinthians 4:9–10

No matter how much Christians believe in Jesus, they may have to suffer for their entire lives. It is precisely in suffering that they will find Christ and be happy—even if they continue to be poor, feel pain, and suffer persecution.

The problem just described is only one example of the way an individual Christian can make mistakes when interpreting sacred Scripture. The problem arises every time two Christians contradict each other trying to interpret the Bible. God foresaw this problem and provided a solution. He placed an authority in his Church, giving Peter and the Apostles—and later the bishops as their successors—a special grace to interpret Scripture correctly.

Individual interpretation can provide wonderful insights. However, individual interpretation will never be sufficient and can sometimes cause harm. The only interpretation Christians should believe with wholehearted faith is the interpretation that comes to us from the men to whom God has given authority.

The Holy Spirit guides the Pope and the other bishops so that they can teach what God wants everyone to believe. This authority is called the "Magisterium of the Church." The word comes from the Latin *magister*, meaning "teacher." The Church can teach with authority—not merely guessing—because of the special guidance the Holy Spirit gives to the Pope and the bishops in communion with him.

The role of the Pope and the other bishops is not to reveal God's mysteries. God is the only one who can reveal. The Pope and the bishops have the responsibility of safeguarding the deposit of faith. The Church teaches:

> The task of authentically interpreting the word of God, whether written or handed on, has been entrusted exclusively to the living Magisterium of the Church, whose authority is exercised in the name of Jesus Christ. This Magisterium is not above the Word of God, but serves it, teaching only what has been handed on, listening to it devoutly, guarding it scrupulously, and explaining it faithfully in accord with a divine commission. And with the help of the Holy Spirit, it draws from this one deposit of faith everything which it presents for belief as divinely revealed.
>
> It is clear, therefore, that sacred Tradition, sacred Scripture, and the Magisterium of the Church, in accord with God's most wise design, are so linked and joined together that one cannot stand without the others, and that all together and each in its own way under the action of the one Holy Spirit contribute effectively to the salvation of souls.
>
> Vatican II, *Dogmatic Constitution on Divine Revelation*, n. 10

Christians accept the Magisterium because this is the authority God established to preserve revelation free from error.

Church Dogma

The text just quoted comes from the Second Vatican Council. In the history of the Church, this council of bishops was the twenty-third *ecumenical* council. An ecumenical council is itself an exercise of the Church's Magisterium. It consists of a meeting of all the bishops in union with the Holy See. The Holy See refers to the "See of Rome" or that place where the Pope exercises his authority. A bishop is in "union with the Holy See" if he recognizes the supreme authority of the Pope over all Christians.

During an ecumenical council, the Pope and the bishops issue a document (or several documents) stating the official teaching of the Church on particular issues. These documents, taken together with all the documents from previous councils and papal decrees, constitute the Church's Magisterium, that is, her official teaching.

The Pope and the bishops are not merely dedicated Christians who do their best to tell us what they think is right. On the day of his

Wisdom of the Saints

Kingdoms and empires have crumbled. Peoples famous for their name and their civilization have disappeared. . . . The Church remains young and vigorous. . . . The powerful ones of this earth have risen up against her. They have vanished but she remains. The learned ones in their pride have devised an infinite variety of systems which, they thought, would make a breach in the teaching of the Church, destroy the dogmas of her faith and demonstrate the absurdity of her teaching authority.

But history shows us how all these systems have been abandoned and forgotten, utterly destroyed. And all this time, from the heights of the citadel of Peter, the true light has shone out in all the brilliance which Christ communicated to it in the very beginning and which he nourishes with this divine sentence: "Heaven and earth will pass away, but my words will not pass away" (Mt 24:35).

Pope St. Pius X, *Jucunda Sane*, March 12, 1904

resurrection, Jesus breathed on the Apostles and said, "Receive the Holy Spirit" (Jn 20:22). Just as the Apostles had a special power to carry out their mission two thousand years ago, the Holy Spirit gives special guidance to the Pope and the bishops today. The Pope and the bishops do not teach with authority because they are more intelligent than other Christians. Instead, as stated by the Second Vatican Council, "they have been constituted true and authentic teachers of the faith . . . by virtue of the Holy Spirit who has been given to them" (Vatican II, *Decree on Bishops*, n. 3).

Some statements made either directly by the Pope or by the Pope together with the bishops in an ecumenical council have special importance because they are *definitive* formulations of belief. When the Pope declares a definitive teaching infallibly, we call this definitive formulation a "dogma" of the Church. For example, in the year 431, the Council of Ephesus decreed a dogma concerning the Blessed Virgin Mary. It stated that we know through divine revelation that she is the Mother of God.

A teaching is called a "dogma" when the Pope and the bishops, guided by a special grace of the Holy Spirit, make a definitive statement that a specific teaching of the Church is the correct interpretation of God's revelation as it comes to us through Tradition and Scripture. By declaring a dogma, they are not inventing a new revelation. They are using their authority to define what God had revealed. Whenever the Church defines a teaching on some mystery revealed by God, we call this teaching a "dogmatic definition." A dogma is a definition that can never be changed. It can never be changed because it is a truth that God revealed and God's truth cannot change.

Papal infallibility

When Jesus met St. Peter after the resurrection, he asked him three times, "Simon, son of John, do you love me?" Having stated three times, just before the crucifixion, that he had nothing to do with Jesus, it was hard for Peter to hear Jesus ask him three times, "Do you love me?" The Apostle answered three times, finally insisting, "Lord, you know everything; you know that I love you." Three times, Jesus told him, "Feed my sheep" (Jn 21:16–17). Jesus was still counting on Peter—despite his weaknesses—to be the Rock. Jesus wanted him to "feed" the world with the truth of God's revelation.

St. Peter and his successors have a special grace to teach the truth infallibly—that is, to teach without error. Some people make the mistake of thinking that papal infallibility means that the Pope cannot commit sins. The Bishop of Rome is just as capable of sinning as any other Christian. Many popes have been saints, but even these were, like St. Peter, capable of betraying Christ at some moment in their lives and had to be sorry for their sins.

There have been some incidents, rare but unfortunately real, when the Bishop of Rome deliberately engaged in behavior that was so evil that he scandalized other Christians. The Church regrets this deeply. However, this is a different issue. Infallibility does not negate the special protection God gives the Pope. Infallibility means being incapable of error *when teaching*. The Pope is infallible *only* when he officially declares a teaching of the Church and proposes it for Christians all over the world to believe as God's revelation.

To the men who wrote the sacred texts in the Bible, God gave a special grace called "inspiration." He gives the Church a special grace called "infallibility" to remain free from error when declaring and believing dogmas. The Pope and the bishops in union with him can declare dogmas free from error only because God gives them this special grace. When ordinary Christians believe the Church's dogmas, they believe without error the truth revealed by God.

If the Church cannot teach the truth, Christians cannot believe the truth. St. Paul put it clearly when speaking about the mystery of Christ's resurrection, "if Christ has not been raised, then our preaching is in vain and your faith is in vain" (1 Cor 15:14). The preaching has to be true; otherwise believing is useless. Either God gives the Church the power to speak the truth without error or the Church is teaching a lie and leading everyone astray. Papal infallibility—a power given to St. Peter and his successors to avoid error—is God's guarantee that the Church teaches the truth.

The Pope enjoys universal power over the whole Church. He has authority over all bishops and over all the other members of the Church. His authority extends not only to matters of declaring the official teaching of the Church but also to matters of determining the laws by which the Church is governed and in making judgments about particular cases.

Spreading Church teachings

Ordinary Christians also have a role to play in the Magisterium. It would not do any good for the Pope and the bishops to give the correct teaching if only a few hear it. By being faithful to the teaching of the Church and spreading these teachings, ordinary Christians help others discover the truth.

Disseminating the teachings of the Church is part of spreading the gospel. People will always need to go back to the original sources and read the Bible themselves. But they also need someone who can offer them the correct interpretation of what they read. By helping others discover what the Magisterium teaches, Christians help them understand the true sense of many texts in the Bible that would otherwise remain obscure or even confusing.

Ordinary Christians can also advise the bishops on matters that require professional competence in worldly affairs. The Church's teaching must give light to understand the spiritual and moral aspects of medicine, business, politics, education, family life, and dozens of other fields of human endeavor. By speaking with the bishops, laypeople can help them explain the Church's teaching with greater precision and clarity.

REVIEW QUESTIONS

1. What is the hierarchy of the Church?
2. What is the Magisterium of the Church?
3. Why does God want us to accept the authority he has established in the Church?
4. How does the Magisterium fit together with sacred Tradition and sacred Scripture?

(1) sacred order giving men whom are called by God authority. ~~ove~~

(2) The Magisterium is the teaching that comes from the church leaders.

(3)

18.

The Creed

The Creed is the most basic of all the Church's teachings. The Creed summarizes the most important mysteries that God has revealed to us. When we recite the Creed, we remind ourselves of the mysteries Jesus revealed two thousand years ago. The Creed is a statement of facts about God and facts about the world. But it is much more. It is a prayer. When we say the words of the Creed, we are making an act of faith. That is why the Creed begins with the words: "We believe . . ."

Every Sunday, in churches all over the world, Christians stand to recite or sing the Creed. The words of the Creed are outlined later in this chapter (see pp. 243–246) so that you can study them carefully. The better you understand what you are saying, the stronger your faith will be.

What exactly do we mean by having a stronger faith? Let's take an example. Suppose you have a friend who thinks the teachings of the Catholic Church are wrong. Perhaps he has read some books that attack the Church. He may present all kinds of arguments to convince you to stop believing what the Church teaches and accept some theory he thinks is better. If you have never studied the Creed and the other teachings of the Church, how will you defend your faith?

Defending your faith is one reason why you need to study the Creed carefully, line by line. Growing in your love for God and for the Church is another reason. You love more when you know what God has revealed. You can only love God with your whole heart when you also love him "with your whole mind" (cf. Mt 22:37).

Before looking at the meaning of each phrase in the Creed, you may want to know where this prayer comes from. So first we will look at the origin of the Creed.

The Apostles' Creed

The first formula summarizing Christian beliefs appeared a few decades after Jesus founded the Church. The first word of this prayer in Latin is *credo*, meaning "I believe." Because of the Latin word "*credo*," we call this prayer a "creed." The Apostles' Creed gets its name from the Apostles since it was formulated while they were preaching the gospel.

The Nicene Creed

Several hundred years passed. Then the Apostles' Creed was expanded at a meeting of bishops in the city of Nicea. The meeting was called an "ecumenical council." It was the first ever held. An *ecumenical* council means a council of bishops from all over the world. In this case, at Nicea, there were a total of 318 bishops. These bishops, in union with the Pope, wrote a longer version of the Creed. This new formulation was called the Nicene Creed, since it was adopted by the Church at the Council of Nicea in 325 AD.

The main reason for expanding the Apostles' Creed into a longer formula was to clarify a doubt some Christians had about Jesus Christ. Some people were saying Jesus was the Son of God only in the sense that he was *similar* to God. Being similar to God meant that Jesus was like God in power, but ultimately different from God since he was merely a creature—not eternal as only God can be eternal. Others were saying Jesus was really and truly the Son of God. They said he was much more than *similar* to God. They said Jesus was *really and truly* God.

> **Sacred Scripture**
>
> Jesus . . . lifted up his eyes to heaven and said, "Father, the hour has come; glorify thy Son that the Son may glorify thee, since thou hast given him power over all flesh, to give eternal life to all whom thou hast given him. And this is eternal life, that they know thee the only true God, and Jesus Christ whom thou hast sent."
>
> John 17:1–3

Why was there so much confusion about what Christians were supposed to believe? It was a difficulty with interpreting Scripture. Both sides were producing quotes from the New Testament in order to prove their point. Each side came up with a different conclusion. To put an end to all doubt, the Church declared in the Nicene Creed that:

> Jesus Christ, the Only Begotten Son of God, born of the Father before all ages. God from God, Light from Light, true God from true God, begotten, not made, consubstantial with the Father . . .
>
> Nicene Creed

The Son is equal to the Father. He is begotten, that is, he comes from the Father. He is "*eternally* begotten." There was no time when the Father was alone, as if planning for the day when he would bring his Son into existence. The Father has always existed and, so too, the Son has always existed. The Son is "consubstantial with the Father." This means that the Father and Son are both God, *forever united in one being*, together with the Holy Spirit.

The Council of Constantinople

Not long after the Council of Nicea, another doubt arose. This was a doubt about whether the Holy Spirit was God.

Some people argued that the Holy Spirit was truly a spirit and truly holy but not truly divine. They refused to worship the Holy Spirit as God. Others said the Holy Spirit was equal to the Father and Son and that Christians were obliged to worship him.

Once again, both sides were producing quotes from Scripture to prove their point. To clarify this new doubt, another ecumenical council was called, this time in the city of Constantinople. It was the year AD 381. In this council the Church expanded the Creed by adding a paragraph about the Holy Spirit. The added words explicitly stated that the Holy Spirit is "Lord" and that he should be "worshipped and glorified."

As you can see, the Church has decided to make additions to the Creed. This does not mean the Church changed what God revealed through Jesus Christ. Rather it means that, when disputes arise, the Church recognizes the need to specify exactly what Jesus revealed.

The formula that we pray together at Mass on Sundays is the Creed that was approved by Pope St. Damasus and the bishops of the Council of Constantinople in 381—plus one extra addition added by another

pope many centuries later, and the most recent changes implemented by Pope Benedict XVI. It is officially called the "Niceno-Constantinopolitan Creed," often abbreviated simply as the Nicene Creed.

Whenever you pray this prayer, you are using the same words that Christians have used every Sunday for more than a thousand years all over the world. The Creed states the basic truths of our faith. We believe these truths because they express what God revealed.

How the Creed relates to the Bible

The Nicene Creed mentions the Bible explicitly. It states that Jesus' death and resurrection were prophesied in "the Scriptures." This does not mean that you can find the Creed printed in the Bible.

The Creed gives only a brief summary of what we believe. It does not contain everything God wanted to reveal. Jesus himself, in his living flesh, is everything God wants to reveal. Jesus cannot be reduced to words on paper. When revealing himself, Jesus asked us to believe in him. The Creed is not a substitute for Jesus. The Creed is not a substitute for the Bible. Even so, we need the Creed in order to know Jesus better. It keeps us from making mistakes when trying to understand God. It is a prayer that expresses our belief in the Father, Son, and Holy Spirit.

Since we cannot see the truths of our faith, it is sometimes difficult to state exactly what we believe. We need a brief summary defining what we believe about Jesus, about his Father, about his Spirit, about his Church. The Creed defines these truths. When it comes to believing everything that God revealed, it is easy to get confused. Some people saw Jesus and did not believe anything he said. Others saw Jesus and believed the wrong thing. The point of the Creed is to state what Christians are supposed to believe.

An outline of the Nicene Creed

The following is a step-by-step explanation of every line in the Nicene Creed. It will help you understand the meaning of each phrase. The words of the Creed appear in bold italics.

> *I believe in one God, the Father almighty, maker of heaven and earth, of all things visible and invisible.*

God the Father, working through his Son, in the unity of the Holy Spirit, decided to create. Everything that exists was created by God. God is not part of creation. Therefore, we say that he lives "above" his creation or "outside" of it. We can see many creatures, like the plants and animals. Other creatures are invisible, like the angels. God created them all, using his infinite power.

> *I believe in one Lord Jesus Christ, the Only Begotten Son of God, born of the Father before all ages. God from God, Light from Light, true God from true God, begotten, not made, consubstantial with the Father; Through him all things were made.*

Jesus Christ is perfect God and perfect man. He is perfect God because he is the Son of God and lived with his Father in eternity "before" the beginning of creation. He is perfect man because he took upon himself real human flesh and became a man. God is light because he is pure spirit. Being the Son of God, Jesus is equal to his Father in all things—equally eternal and equally powerful.

> *For us men and for our salvation he came down from heaven, and by the Holy Spirit was incarnate of the Virgin Mary, and became man. For our sake he was crucified under Pontius Pilate, he suffered death and was buried, . . .*

The Son of God humbled himself, becoming a man like us. As man, Jesus is completely equal to us in all things but sin. He is equal to us in his intellect and free will, equal in his use of sight and touch, equal in his way of eating, drinking, sleeping, etc. The only difference is sin. He could never be touched by sin because, being the Son of God, he is

Fathers of the Church

If one yields ground on any single point of Catholic doctrine, one will later have to yield in another, and again in another, and so on, until such surrenders come to be something normal and acceptable. And when one gets used to rejecting dogma bit by bit, ultimately one ends up rejecting the Church's authority to teaching anything at all.

St. Vincent of Lerins, *Commonitorium*, 23

perfectly holy. Even so, he took our sins upon himself in the moment of his crucifixion. By dying with the guilt of our sins laid upon him, he destroyed the power of Satan and won forgiveness for our sins. Since he really and truly died, his dead body was laid in a tomb.

. . . and rose again on the third day in accordance with the Scriptures. He ascended into heaven and is seated at the right hand of the Father. He will come again in glory to judge the living and the dead and his kingdom will have no end.

Jesus' soul separated from his body on the day he was crucified. Because of this, Jesus entered in the world of the dead—which, in ancient times was called "Hades" or "hell." Being as physically limited as any man, he died on the cross. Being as all-powerful as his Father in heaven, he rose from the dead on the third day. Prophecies are recorded in sacred Scripture pointing to the resurrection. For instance, just as Jonah was in the whale for three days, Jesus was in the earth and rose from the dead on the third day. Forty days after his resurrection, he went to heaven to be glorified by his Father. He will return at the end of the world and show his glory to all people. He will judge all men and women. Then he will reign forever over the saints in a kingdom of peace and love.

I believe in the Holy Spirit, the Lord, the giver of life, who proceeds from the Father and the Son, who with the Father and the Son is adored and glorified, who has spoken through the prophets.

The Holy Spirit is God. He is equal to the Father and the Son. The Son comes from the Father alone. The Holy Spirit comes from the Father and Son together. He inspired the writings of both the Old and the New Testaments.

I believe in one, holy, catholic, and apostolic Church.

Before ascending into heaven, Jesus founded his Church. He did not found many churches just one Church. That Church is holy—all its members are called to be saints. It is catholic—it is meant for all people throughout the entire world. It is apostolic—it is founded on the Apostles.

I confess one baptism for the forgiveness of sins and I look forward to the resurrection of the dead and the life of the world to come. Amen.

The Church administers the sacraments, the first being baptism. This sacrament forgives all sins. Christians do not put their hope in anything this world offers. Instead we look forward to a new heaven and a new earth—the next world—where we will all rise from the dead and live with God forever.

Making an act of faith

Merely repeating the words of the Creed does not mean you believe. You need to make an act of faith. When you recite the Creed, don't just repeat words. Say what you believe and believe what you say.

Do you believe that God the Father Almighty created heaven and earth? If you do, you can use the words of the Creed to state your belief. If you believe God created heaven and earth, you can say, "I believe in God the Father Almighty . . ."

Do you believe that Jesus Christ is the Son of God? If you do, you can use the words of the Creed to state your belief. You can say, "I believe in Jesus Christ, his only Son, our Lord . . ."

Do you believe that the Holy Spirit gives you a share in the life of God? If you do, you can use the words of the Creed to state your belief. You can say, "I believe in the Holy Spirit, the Lord, the Giver of life . . ."

By reciting the Creed, you declare your faith in the One who created you, the One who saved you and the One who makes you holy. Address God and tell him you believe in him. Speak with conviction. Speak intelligently. Speak with love and gratitude. Use your heart, your mind, and your soul to say, "This is what I believe. I believe it because this is what God has revealed."

Development of doctrine

When going through your study of the Creed, did you notice how it developed? The Creed started off in a simple version called the Apostles' Creed. The next step took place at the First Council of Nicea when

Magisterium

Revelation remains charged with mystery. It is true that Jesus, with his entire life, revealed the face of the Father, for he came to teach the secret things of God. But our vision of God's face is always fragmentary and impaired by the limits of our understanding. Faith alone makes it possible to penetrate the mystery in a way that allows us to understand it coherently . . .

By faith, men and women give their assent to this divine testimony. This means that they acknowledge fully and integrally the truth of what is revealed because it is God himself who is the guarantor of that truth. . . . This is why the Church has always considered the act of entrusting oneself to God to be a moment of fundamental decision which engages the whole person. In that act, the intellect and the will display their spiritual nature, enabling the subject to act in a way which realizes personal freedom to the full. It is not just that freedom is part of the act of faith: it is absolutely required. . . . Men and women can accomplish no more important act in their lives than the act of faith; it is here that freedom reaches the certainty of truth and chooses to live in that truth.

St. John Paul II, *Faith and Reason*, n. 13

words about Jesus Christ were added. The next step took place at the First Council of Constantinople when words about the Holy Spirit were added. This process took several centuries. We call it the "development of doctrine."

Ever since the day of Pentecost, the Apostles and their successors have faced challenges to Church teaching. For instance, some Christian may come along saying, "I think God's revelation implies that only Jews can become Christians." Now it is true that Jesus sometimes gave the impression that he was only interested in telling Jews about the coming of God's kingdom. So if someone wanted to isolate those incidents, he could argue that only Jews can become Christians and that any pagan who wants to be a Christian has to become a Jew first by being circumcised. In the early Church, some Christians actually started insisting on this idea. Therefore, the Apostles had to clarify what Jesus really wanted. They had to clarify the true doctrine of the Church. Did pagans who wanted to be baptized also have to be circumcised?

The Apostles met together in Jerusalem. This was the first council of the Church. They discussed the matter among themselves. St. Luke describes the event in the Acts of the Apostles. He concludes by noting the decision taken by the Apostles. They sent a letter to the non-Jewish Christians, issuing the first decree ever officially made by the Church. This letter stated:

> The brethren, both the apostles and the elders, to the brethren who are of the Gentiles in Antioch and Syria and Cilicia, greeting. Since we have heard that some persons from us have troubled you with words, unsettling your minds, although we gave them no instructions. . . . For it has seemed good to the Holy Spirit and to us to lay upon you no greater burden than these necessary things: that you abstain from what has been sacrificed to idols and from blood and from what is strangled and from unchastity. If you keep yourselves from these, you will do well. Farewell.
>
> Acts 15:23–24;28–29

The Apostles knew they had both the authority to interpret God's revelation and the authority to state that another interpretation was wrong. They knew the Holy Spirit gave them the power to interpret accurately. These two facts imply that God expected them to develop the teaching of the Church.

The most important truths of faith have been summarized in the Creed. There are many others besides. You will never find a single teaching believed by Christians today that started out clear and complete on the day of Pentecost. Take the most basic doctrine of all—the Church's doctrine on the Trinity. This teaching states that the Father is God, the Son is God, the Holy Spirit is God. It also states that, instead of three gods, there are three distinct *persons* in one divine *being*. Even though this doctrine comes from revelation, it had to be developed.

Some people ask, "Why bother developing doctrine? Why not stick to sacred Scripture?"

Sacred Scripture is not enough to define what we believe. Christians always end up arguing about what the texts mean, even on a basic question about whether or not Jesus is truly the Son of God. If we cannot formulate a clear statement declaring that the Son is equal to the Father, then we do not know what God revealed. Our faith depends on how specific texts are interpreted. As centuries of disputes demonstrate, the Church had to develop clear statements on the Trinity and on a whole range of mysteries contained in Scripture. If these doctrines were crystal clear from the beginning—if the texts did not need any interpretation—then why did the very first Christians argue about it?

The wording used to express what we believe about Jesus Christ had to be developed. The wording used to express what we believe about the Holy Spirit had to be developed. The same is true for all the other truths of revelation. They had to be developed. Church teaching for some aspects of revelation still needs to be developed. An issue remains open to discussion as long as the Church continues to develop her definitive teaching on that issue. For instance, the Church needs to develop further her teaching on the papal ministry. (What powers can the Bishop of Rome share with other bishops and which powers are reserved to him alone? How does this affect the task of renewing unity between the Catholic Church and Christian communities not in full communion with the Church?)

Dogmas and heresies

From the beginning, the Church has taken great care to spell out for all men and women exactly what they should believe and what God wants them to do. The development of the Church's teachings proceeds by three stages.

1. Ordinary Magisterium: The Church teaches primarily by spreading the gospel. The clergy preach publicly to proclaim all that God has revealed and to explain the teachings of the Church. The lay

Wisdom of the Saints

Besides using reason to investigate the truths of science and philosophy, human happiness requires us to study all that God has revealed. Why? Above all because God has planned us for an end beyond the grasp of reason. According to Isaiah, "From of old no one has heard or perceived by the ear, no eye has seen a God besides thee, who works for those who wait for him" (Is 64:4).

St. Thomas Aquinas, *Summa Theologiae*, I, 1, 1

faithful speak privately to friends and relatives about their own personal encounter with Christ. The Church also teaches by making official decrees, using carefully chosen words to state truths of faith and morals as precisely as possible. In such cases, the Pope issues an official document (an encyclical, exhortation, address, letter, constitution, audience, etc.) that states the Church's teaching on a specific issue or a range of related issues. Because some truths of the natural order—for instance, truths about human nature—directly affect our understanding of revealed mysteries and Christian morality, the Church also makes official statements to clarify these.

There are thousands of papal documents that form part of the Church's ordinary Magisterium. For example, Pope Leo XIII issued an encyclical in 1891 titled *Rerum Novarum*. This is a typical example of the Church's ordinary Magisterium. The document defines the social doctrine of the Church—the Church's teaching on the responsibility that all people have, especially leaders of government and business, to organize social structures that foster prosperity for all citizens and all nations, as opposed to ones that benefit the rich while depleting the resources of the poor. This teaching has been further refined and expanded by subsequent popes, most notably St. John Paul II, who issued the encyclical *Centesimus Annus* in 1991 (the 100th anniversary of Leo XIII's encyclical). When issuing this kind of document, the Pope expresses the Church's ordinary Magisterium.

The Second Vatican Council declared that Christians should accept all the teachings of the ordinary Magisterium:

> This loyal submission of the will and intellect must be given, in a special way, to the authentic teaching authority of the Roman Pontiff, even when he does not speak *ex cathedra* . . .
>
> Vatican II, *Dogmatic Constitution on the Church*, n. 25

You give "loyal submission of will and intellect" when you believe in your own heart what the Church teaches. (The meaning of *ex cathedra* will be explained below.)

Before explaining what we mean by definitive teachings and dogmatic definitions, keep one thing in mind. Do not judge people when you hear them contradict or deny one of the Church's teachings. Only God can judge whether it is their fault because they lack faith or whether they are simply confused about what they are supposed to believe.

It is very easy to get confused. Many people believe something that is utterly false and yet remain convinced that they should believe it. Do not make the mistake of letting them confuse you. But do not judge them. When you have to discuss some issue where they refuse to accept what the Church teaches, do not get angry with them. Instead, encourage them to study what the Church teaches.

If you yourself do not accept some teaching of the ordinary Magisterium, then, by definition, you do not accept the Church's authority to teach. It is one thing to have questions; it is another to doubt. Ask as many questions as you need to ask. Seek guidance from someone who understands the Church's teaching and can explain it to you.

A Catholic who stubbornly refuses to accept some teaching of the ordinary Magisterium and who is aware of the need to accept the Church's authority is guilty of serious sin and should repent and seek forgiveness of sins in the sacrament of penance by confessing this lack of faith.

Other Christians, not in full communion with the Catholic Church, should study both the specific teaching that they do not accept and also the general need they have to accept the teaching authority of the Pope and the bishops in communion with him.

2. Definitive Teaching: Either acting on his own authority or acting together with the other bishops, the Pope can declare a particular teaching on faith and morals as *definitive teaching* of the Church.

A definitive teaching may eventually be declared a dogma. In other words, the Church may declare explicitly what we already believe implicitly; namely, that we believe the mystery because God revealed it. For example, the Church teaches that only men can be ordained priests. Because it is a definitive teaching, all Christians should believe it. However, the Church has not yet explicitly declared that this teaching expresses a truth that God has revealed.

Some definitive teachings will never become dogmas of the Church because they do not form part of God's revelation. For instance, there are historical facts which, if denied, cast doubt on the teachings of the Church. We know which men have been elected Bishop of Rome. We know when and where the Church has held ecumenical councils. We know the exact words that these popes and councils used to declare the dogmas of the Church. Anyone who casts doubt on the historical facts implicitly denies the value of the teachings formulated by the popes and councils.

All definitive teachings are infallible teachings. Therefore, the Church has declared that all Catholics have a strict obligation to accept them:

> Each and everything set forth definitively by the Magisterium of the Church regarding teaching on faith and morals must be firmly accepted and held; namely, those things required for the holy keeping and faithful exposition of the deposit of faith. Therefore, anyone who rejects propositions which are to be held definitively sets himself against the teaching of the Catholic Church.
>
> St. John Paul II, *Ad Tuendam Fidem*, n. 4

Whoever denies a definitive teaching of the Church rejects a truth of Catholic doctrine and would therefore no longer be in full communion with the Catholic Church. A Catholic who rejects such teachings—after being warned of the seriousness of the matter—cannot be allowed to receive Holy Communion until he or she has manifested true repentance.

3. Dogmatic Definition: These are the teachings that the Church has declared to be revealed by God. Either acting on his own authority or acting together with the other bishops gathered in an ecumenical council, the Pope can declare a dogma. Such a teaching is called *ex cathedra*, a Latin phrase meaning that the Pope speaks from his chair, that is, from the chair of Peter with the authority of St. Peter the Apostle.

A dogma is any truth that the Church has formally declared that everyone everywhere should believe *because it forms part of the revelation God has made through Jesus Christ and the Apostles*. In other words, a dogma is always a statement declaring to the world that God has revealed this truth, and therefore all men and women should believe it. When the Church defines a dogma, she is stating that there is absolutely no doubt whatsoever that this teaching expresses a truth revealed by God. Therefore, the teaching is irreformable, that is, it can never change. The Nicene Creed is the most important of all the Church's dogmas.

The Church is careful to distinguish between definitive teachings and non-definitive teachings. At times in the past, very holy men and women, now numbered among the saints, disputed the interpretation of specific texts in sacred Scripture where the meaning was not clear. Some of them made statements which, if repeated today, would contradict what the Church now teaches. Before the Pope and the bishops in communion with him found the exact words that appropriately express the mystery revealed by God, these disputes form part of development of the Church's doctrine.

Going into the details of the controversies in ages past would require a lengthy exposition. The point here is to explain that there have been disputes in which even the saints did not immediately understand the correct way of interpreting sacred Scripture. By relying on the grace God gives the Church, these controversies have been resolved and the Church has developed the definitive teaching for questions that arose when trying to understand exactly what God wants us to believe.

Another further point needs to be clarified. It is one thing to offer an opinion before the Church has declared the definitive teaching on a particular issue. It is entirely different to speak out against a definitive teaching. Any Christian who publicly denies one of the dogmas of the Church is called a "heretic." A heretic refuses to believe a truth that has been revealed by God and handed down to us through the Church. A heresy is any opinion that directly contradicts one of the dogmas of the Church. Spreading a heresy does enormous harm.

Even though they are false, heresies have often been the occasion for some greater good. After all, most heresies began their existence simply as a dispute among Christians before the Church made a definitive declaration on the issue. For instance, at one point, some Christians got the idea that it was wrong to make statues or paintings of Jesus and the saints. It took almost a hundred years of heated dispute for the Church to develop her teaching on sacred art. This all happened about six centuries after Pentecost. In the early Church, the issue was never critical to people's faith. It was only when some people started destroying precious works of Christian art that the Church had to study the issue in depth. An ecumenical council was held to declare a definitive teaching. This happened in 787 at the Second Council of Nicea. Following the dogmas declared at this council, the Church teaches that "Christian iconography [e.g., statues and paintings] expresses in images the same Gospel message that Scripture communicates by words" (*CCC*, n. 1160).

Heresies—before they are formally declared to be false teachings—are part of the development of doctrine. The problem comes when Christians spread a heresy *after* the Church has declared the definitive teaching. Heretics lead people away from God because they are leading them away from the truth. Heresies are especially damaging whenever heretics use sacred Scripture in order to promote false teachings. According to Church law, the damage done is considered so serious that the Church automatically excommunicates any Catholic guilty of heresy.

The Church has always had to confront heresy. Even after the Apostles made their decree at the Council of Jerusalem, some Christians—called "Judaizers"—insisted that non-Jewish Christians had to be circumcised. We get a glimpse of how serious the problem was when reading St. Paul's words, "Certain persons . . . have wandered away into vain discussion, desiring to be teachers of the law, without understanding either what they are saying or the things about which they make assertions" (1 Tim 1:6–7). These problems will always exist. Never be surprised by this. Whenever a doubt arises about what God wants us to believe, Christians can turn to the Church and study her doctrine.

Study, though, is not enough. It is necessary to make an explicit act of faith. This is the whole point of a having the Creed. More than simply summarizing what God has revealed, it is an invitation to face the world and say: "I believe all that the holy catholic Church teaches."

Private revelations

You should believe all that God has revealed. Throughout this discussion we have been careful to talk about *public revelation*, that is, revelation made first through the patriarchs and prophets of the Old Testament and then through Jesus Christ and his Apostles. The Church teaches that the Roman Pontiff and the other bishops have an obligation "not to admit any new public revelation" into the deposit of faith (cf. Vatican II, *Constitution on the Church*, n. 25). Therefore, the Church does not ask us to believe in *private revelations*, that is, any revelation made after the time of the Apostles. There are several reasons for this.

After centuries of experience, the Church knows that some private revelations—for example, prophecies about the end of the world—have turned out to be utterly false. This does not mean that we should reject all private revelations. On the contrary, many have benefited the Church. It would be impossible to list here even the most famous and beneficial private revelations. Two examples will suffice. On the feast of St. John the Apostle, December 27, 1673, Jesus appeared to a humble woman named Mary Margaret Alacoque. She later wrote: "He made me repose for a long time upon his Sacred Breast, where he made me discover the marvels of his love and the inexplicable secrets of his Sacred Heart." For several days the saint remained inflamed with an interior fire of divine Love. In the middle of World War I, between May 13 and October 13, 1917, the Blessed Virgin Mary appeared several times to three children near the Portuguese town of Fatima. She told them that great evil would come from Russia. According to Lucia, the oldest of the three children, Our Lady said: "The good will be martyred. The Holy Father will have much to suffer, and various nations will be annihilated. In the end my Immaculate Heart will triumph. The Holy Father will consecrate Russia to me; it will be converted, and a certain period of peace will be granted to the world."

Both of these incidents have been officially approved by the Church; they have been judged by the bishops to be in accord with Church teaching and worthy of belief. Even when a bishop—or the Pope himself—judges that a private revelation is trustworthy, the Church does not ask us to believe it. All Christians should have devotion to the Sacred Heart of Jesus and the Immaculate Heart of Mary. Our knowledge of the infinite, divine love that Jesus bears for us within his human heart comes from public revelation. He has even commanded us: "Even as I have loved you, that you also love one another" (Jn 13:34).

However, no one has to believe that Jesus appeared to St. Margaret Mary or that his Mother appeared in Fatima. We can accept it as true history, the same as we would trust advice given by a close friend.

The Church never puts private revelations in the same category with public revelation, the revelation God made through Jesus Christ and his Apostles. The Church assumes that if a revelation is necessary for our salvation, then it was already revealed through Jesus Christ. The *Catechism* teaches that "no new public revelation is to be expected before the glorious manifestation of our Lord Jesus Christ" (*CCC*, n. 66).

REVIEW QUESTIONS

1. What is the Nicene Creed? Where did it come from?
2. What is the purpose of having a creed? Why do Christians recite the Creed?
3. Why is it important for Christians to make explicit acts of faith?
4. What is a dogma? What is heresy? Why does heresy cause harm?

Part Three

Christian Morality

19.

Freedom and Law

Ever since you were a child, your family has demanded good behavior. Your elders taught you what is right and what is wrong. They rewarded you when you behaved and punished you when you misbehaved. As you grew older you learned more about good and evil. You discovered that countries have laws and that people are supposed to obey them. At some point, you also discovered God's law.

Having discovered all these realities while still a child, perhaps you began to wonder why some laws change while others cannot change. Some laws are like the rules made by your parents about what time to come home. Such rules are arbitrary. They are based not on a reality fixed by God but on convention. Such rules, like the ones regulating traffic, are flexible. Driving on the right versus driving on the left is one example. Traffic laws are arbitrary and yet necessary. People need to agree on what to expect when driving. So everybody agrees to either left or right. It could be either one, but it cannot be both. This is a law based on convention. It is arbitrary and can change.

Some laws are not arbitrary. They are based on nature. We call this set of laws "natural law." These are the laws that forbid murder, rape, and robbery. They are different from traffic laws—or any other set of rules based on convention. Natural law remains fixed. It is not flexible. If a government wants to protect its citizens, it must have laws that forbid murder, rape, and theft. If a government gives murderers a right to murder and thieves a right to steal, that government is a disaster. It is doing harm to its citizens by making laws that contradict natural law.

A government decides which side of the road will be used for traffic. It does not decide whether people have a right to life or a right to own property. God has given all people these basic rights. As long as you respect life and respect the property of others, no one can legitimately deny you your basic rights.

No one has the right to kill an innocent person. There is something written into the very nature of man's existence that gives every human being the right to life. Because of the way God creates us in his image and likeness, all people, even the weakest, have a right to life. No earthly authority can take it away—no government, no church, and no individual—not even a father or mother, a brother or sister.

The Ten Commandments

When God gave us the Ten Commandments, he was not setting rules, like a code of traffic laws. The Ten Commandments define what will make us eternally happy and what will make us eternally unhappy. They teach us to distinguish between acts leading to love and acts leading to hatred. They tell us what we have to do in order to protect the rights of all men and women. They tell us how to treat God, ourselves, and others. They define the bedrock of what is good and evil.

God wrote the Ten Commandments on two tablets of stone. Sacred Scripture lists two slightly different versions (cf. Exodus 20 and Deuteronomy 6). When the Jews talked about "the Law," they meant the entire revelation given to Moses on Mount Sinai. It included the Ten Commandments—those written on the stone tablets—and all the other precepts.

In different times and places, the Church has used two ways of numbering the commandments. One was based on the Jewish numbering,

Sacred Scripture

And one of them, a lawyer, asked him a question, to test him. "Teacher, which is the great commandment in the law?" And he said to him, "You shall love the Lord your God with all your heart, and with all your soul, and with all your mind. This is the great and first commandment. And a second is like it, You shall love your neighbor as yourself. On these two commandments depend all the law and the prophets."

Matthew 22:35–40

The Ten Commandments

1. You shall worship the Lord your God and him only shall you serve.
2. You shall not take the name of the Lord your God in vain.
3. Remember the sabbath day, to keep it holy.
4. Honor your father and your mother.
5. You shall not kill.
6. You shall not commit adultery.
7. You shall not steal.
8. You shall not bear false witness against your neighbor.
9. You shall not covet your neighbor's wife.
10. You shall not covet your neighbor's goods.

Matthew 4:10; Exodus 20:2–17; Deuteronomy 5:6–21

made popular by Origen, one of the most influential theologians of the early Church. The other, which is used in this book, was devised by St. Augustine.

The numbering of God's commandments depends on convention. The contents do not. The contents are fixed by human nature. Some people have made the mistake of thinking God picked the commandments at random. They think that instead of saying, "You shall not steal," God could have said that stealing is good. They argue that being free and all-powerful, God could have issued any commandments he wanted.

This is a misconception of the nature of freedom. To be consistent, they would have to say that God could have commanded us to worship Satan. As absurd as it may seem, it is worth asking why God cannot ask us to worship Satan even though he is free to do whatever he wants.

What is freedom?

Adoring Satan would mean calling the devil our Creator. Satan did not create anything. God cannot command us to adore Satan because God always tells the truth. Satan is the one who deceives us. God cannot deceive us. Does that mean that God is not free? Is he somehow "forced" to tell the truth?

The essence of freedom goes beyond doing whatever a person wants to do. True freedom consists in being filled with nothing but the desire to do good and avoid evil. God is totally free because all his desires are good and he never has any desire to do evil. He is never "forced" to tell the truth. He *is* the truth. He is never "forced" to be good. He *is* the very essence of goodness. He is never "forced" to obey the law. He *is* the law. He is not "forced" to exist. He is being. He simply *is*. His very essence is to be.

God cannot tell us to adore Satan. He would be lying to us if he told us it was good to adore Satan. He would also be lying if he told us it was good to murder or steal. By telling us to adore him and him alone, God tells us the truth about himself. By telling us it is wrong to murder and steal, he tells us the truth about man.

Nature is fixed. We cannot change nature by taking a vote. We are not free to decide that the force of gravity will stop working. We are not free to declare that from now on adultery is good. We cannot decide these issues by voting. Some think they are free to decide that from now on pride, greed, and lust will be virtues instead of vices. They do not understand freedom because they fail to connect freedom with truth.

Freedom depends on truth. Freedom depends on the way things are in reality. This means that our freedom has limits. We cannot make a law that cancels the force of gravity. We cannot make a law that turns murder from being evil into being good. We cannot change gravity because we did not create the world. We cannot change the right to life because we did not create man.

You are free to jump off a building. But you are not free to decide where you will go once you have jumped. If you jump, you will drop like a stone and become a pool of blood when you hit the ground. You are not free to decide how gravity will act. The same logic applies to good and evil. You are free to steal your friend's life savings. But once you have stolen the money, you are not free to decide whether he will be happy or sad. Your friend will be angry and demand that you give back the money. No matter how much you smile, your friend will cease to be your friend, and he will no longer trust you.

Natural law

God created all things. He made each thing to act in a certain way. Nothing we say will ever change this fact. We are not the ones who create. We are not the ones who decide what is real and unreal. Reality is a given. Reality defines nature. Thus Christians speak about natural law. Natural law is law based on nature. It is law based on the way things are. It is law based on the way God created us.

The Ten Commandments reveal to us the precepts of natural law. In other words, these commandments tell us what is good and evil for man. They define good and evil for the men and women who lived with Moses thousands of years ago. They define good and evil for all men and women from Adam and Eve until the end of the world.

Jesus told us: "The truth will make you free" (Jn 8:32). We become free when we accept the truth. God is the truth. Finding God makes us free. Obeying God's law makes us free. By the same logic—the logic of truth—some deeds are good because they make us happy and some deeds are evil because they make us miserable. God has done us a great service by telling us which deeds are good and which ones are evil. By giving us the Ten Commandments, he has told us how to be happy here on earth and also how to be happy with him forever in heaven.

God's law and human law

Some find it hard to see the difference between human law and God's law. They assume that both are basically the same. Human law forbids murder and theft, and so do the Ten Commandments. Human law calls for rewards and punishments, and God's revelation tells us about

Fathers of the Church

The law can no longer say, "You shall not commit adultery" to the one who has no desire for another man's wife. . . . The law can no longer say, "You shall not covet your neighbor's field or his ox or his donkey" to the one who no longer yearns for earthly possessions and, instead, is building up a treasure in heaven.

St. Irenaeus, *Proof of the Apostolic Preaching*, 96

heaven and hell. These similarities are real, but most people eventually notice one striking difference between human law and God's law.

Human law has to be written into a code of law, published and then imposed by a government. Natural law—God's law for man—is written on our hearts. Referring to the way many people in ancient times obeyed the Ten Commandments without knowing about Moses, St. Paul wrote:

> When Gentiles who have not the law do by nature what the law requires, they are a law to themselves, even though they do not have the law. They show that what the law requires is written on their hearts, while their conscience also bears witness and their conflicting thoughts accuse or perhaps excuse them . . .
>
> Romans 2:14–15

Each person, whether pagan or Jew, Christian or non-Christian, can use reason to distinguish between good and evil. God's law is not a code of conduct written in a rulebook. His law is built into creation—"wired" into the way we were created. The better we understand creation, the more clearly we see what is good for us and what is harmful. This is what we call "morality."

Morals tell us about virtue and vice, about good and evil. Making accurate moral judgments means distinguishing between right and wrong. Christian morality begins with the Ten Commandments and has been perfected by the beatitudes. The beatitudes come from the Sermon on the Mount.

Before looking at the details of the commandments and the beatitudes, try to grasp more fully what we mean by saying that God's law is built into creation—"wired" into the way we were created.

The Ten Commandments do not depend on conventions. Nor do the beatitudes. Nor do Christian morals. You will only begin to distinguish between right and wrong once you see the connection between your actions and the purpose for which you were created. If something helps you to achieve the purpose for which you were created, then it is good for you. If something leads you away from the purpose for which you were created, then it is evil. So the immediate goal is to look at the reason why you were created.

Connecting law and creation

Natural law depends on creation. God fixed it in the very act of creating us. To understand freedom and law better, take a closer look at the notion of creation. Your ability to distinguish between good and evil depends on what you think about God's act of creation.

All nations of every time and place have concluded that some invisible, intelligent being—or beings—created the universe and everything in it. However, their understanding of God was overshadowed by several confusing ideas—mostly because they made mistakes when trying to explain where evil comes from.

Before the coming of Christ, there were four different ways of looking at the origin of the universe. After looking at these pre-Christian views, we will look at the Christian view. Keep in mind, that this exercise is necessary if you want to understand the difference between good and evil.

Pre-Christian views of creation and morality

Monotheism. The first pre-Christian view of creation was belief in one God, a God who was pure spirit. Some ancient civilizations incorporated this view of creation into their culture. In the case of Israel, it was more than a view; it was faith based on revelation. According to the Bible, God began with absolutely nothing. He spoke the word—he made a decision to create—and that alone was enough to create the entire universe. In revealing himself to the patriarchs of the Old Testament, Yahweh God showed the Israelites that he alone is the Lord of heaven and earth. The pagan gods do not exist. All things, whether visible or invisible, are his creatures—even the invisible beings of the spirit world. Some spirits are faithful to God and adore him in the heavens. Some spirits rebelled against God; they are destined for eternal damnation. Along with these angels, we have a special place in God's creation because we are free to make our own decisions. Some people choose evil, and some choose good. Following this view of creation, morality was defined by following the law God revealed through Moses. However, in this view, it was hard to explain why many good people suffered while many evil people prospered. It was difficult to explain why God would allow an innocent child to suffer unspeakable pain and die young. And it was not clear what man's ultimate destiny would be. Even the Jews disputed these mysteries among themselves. Why did God create us? What are we here on earth to accomplish? What is the fate of all the men and women born into this world?

Polytheism. The second pre-Christian view of creation was belief in many gods. People influenced by this view assumed that various gods created different parts of the universe—one god creating the heavens, one creating the earth, one creating the seas, etc. Each god was determined to dominate the others, so they fought among themselves. Conflicts among creatures reflected battles among the gods. In this view of creation, the gods were sexually promiscuous. Their sexual activities were supposed to explain different aspects of the created world. Many civilizations instituted pagan rites of worship, honoring these false gods and their habits of promiscuity. The notion of good and evil in society depended on the particular god that society chose to adore as the most powerful. Polytheistic cultures also developed elaborate fertility cults. Many degenerated into worshiping animals, especially bulls. Some descended into even more barbaric habits, offering human sacrifices to their gods. Some, like the Canaanites of the Old Testament, combined all these elements, offering newborn babies as a sacrifice to statues of bulls while the people indulged in an orgy. Other societies tried to be more reasonable. They based their morality on imitating the divine attributes of wisdom, order, and justice. However, even these nations, e.g., the Romans and Greeks, engaged in practices of polytheism, fertility cults and emperor worship. St. Paul spoke of the morality typical among them:

> Claiming to be wise, they became fools, and exchanged the glory of the immortal God for images resembling mortal man or birds or animals or reptiles. Therefore God gave them up in the lusts of their hearts to impurity, to the dishonoring of their bodies among themselves, because they exchanged the truth about God for a lie and worshiped and served the creature rather than the Creator, who is blessed for ever! Amen.
>
> Romans 1:22–25

Dualism. The third pre-Christian view about the origin of the universe held that there are two gods: one good and one evil. The two gods are equally powerful. The good god created all the spirits, and the evil god created all matter. Though pre-Christian in origin, this view became widespread even among some Christians in the early Church. The Church condemned this heresy, usually known as dualism. Dualism—belief in two equally powerful gods—rejects the goodness of matter. For the Manicheans, the gnostics, and all other heretics accepting dualistic beliefs, man used to be pure spirit. Due to Adam and Eve's sin, the man and woman were punished by being forced to have a body. Salvation meant being freed from the body, freed from sexual desire and freed from everything that is flesh. In dualist systems, the ultimate sin was sexual intercourse—even between husband and wife—since this led to the creation of more flesh. Resurrection was considered evil because returning to the body would mean returning to a state of punishment. This view of creation is totally incompatible with Christian faith. We believe that God created Adam and Eve as male and female and that sex between husband and wife is both noble and sacred because God created us this way. We believe that the Word was made flesh not only

Magisterium

Once all reference to God has been removed, it is not surprising that the meaning of everything else becomes profoundly distorted. Nature itself, from being "mater" (mother), is now reduced to being "matter," and is subjected to every kind of manipulation. This is the direction in which a certain technical and scientific way of thinking, prevalent in present-day culture, appears to be leading when it rejects the very idea that there is a truth of creation which must be acknowledged, or a plan of God for life which must be respected.

Something similar happens when concern about the consequences of such a "freedom without law" leads some people to the opposite position of a "law without freedom," as for example in ideologies which consider it unlawful to interfere in any way with nature, practically "divinizing" it. Again, this is a misunderstanding of nature's dependence on the plan of the Creator. Thus it is clear that the loss of contact with God's wise design is the deepest root of modern man's confusion, both when this loss leads to a freedom without rules and when it leaves man in "fear" of his freedom.

St. John Paul II, *The Gospel of Life*, n. 22

to save us from sin but also to raise us from the dead. At the resurrection, every man will be a man in his own male body and every woman will be a woman in her own female body. Anyone who rejects this truth ends up with twisted notions of good and evil. St. Paul spoke of this problem:

> Now the Spirit expressly says that in later times some will depart from the faith by giving heed to deceitful spirits and doctrines of demons . . . who forbid marriage and enjoin abstinence from foods which God created to be received with thanksgiving by those who believe and know the truth.
>
> 1 Timothy 4:1, 3

Deism/Atheism. This is the fourth pre-Christian view about the origin of the universe. It holds that there is no evidence of a Creator. Everything is matter. Matter needs no explanation. It needs no creator. It exists simply because it exists. The laws of the universe follow the same logic. These laws need no explanation. They exist simply because they exist. All order and beauty in the universe is merely an illusion. Beauty and order come from the random collisions of tiny particles of matter. There is no God. There are no spirits. There is no spiritual world. Such notions, according to the atheist, are myths. These myths are the invention of ignorant people who look for spiritual causes instead of using scientific investigation to identify purely material causes. According to this view of creation, people have to invent their own morality. Since they invented it, they can change it whenever they want.

Those stuck in an atheistic view of the world have no ability to distinguish between good and evil. Any attempt to define good and evil depends on the likes and dislikes of the individual person. Since there are billions of people—each one deciding what is right or wrong—there is no fixed right or wrong. Those in power decide what is right and wrong.

The Church calls this an "individualistic concept of freedom." It is a false freedom. It is the freedom of the strong against the weak. Wherever this concept of freedom takes hold in the minds of a majority of people, those who are weak lose their freedom. Those who are weak lose all rights—especially their right to life and their right to own property. Those in power abuse them, exploit them, or simply eliminate them.

Though often associated with the rise of modern science, atheism was first proposed in ancient times. It is the most blind of all views. It has become quite widespread in the world today. Therefore, you should be on your guard against it. It rejects God either in theory or in practice. It makes the existence of the human person meaningless.

Creation has a purpose

Of these four pre-Christian views, the first view remains the only one that is true. Monotheism was the view of creation given by the prophets in the Old Testament. It is the belief that God is Lord and Creator of all that exists. However, among those who believed in the one, true God, there was something missing. Their notion of creation was incomplete.

When Jesus came, he completed the Old Testament view of creation. He revealed the reason why God created us. He told us that God has a plan for us. He told us that God's plan is to raise us from the dead and take us into his kingdom. This revelation from Jesus gives a full answer to the mystery of good and evil. Only Christ explains why we exist.

How does Christ explain our existence? Why did God create us? The Church teaches:

> Man cannot live without love. He remains a being that is incomprehensible for himself, his life is senseless, if love is not revealed to him, if he does not encounter love, if he does not experience it and make it his own, if he does not participate intimately in it. This is why Christ the Redeemer fully reveals man to himself.
>
> St. John Paul II, *The Redeemer of Man*, n. 10

There are three ideas contained in this teaching. These ideas are key to distinguishing between good and evil:

1. You and all other human beings have been created for love. You exist in order to experience love. Your life will be a waste if in the end you do not discover this truth.

2. God loves you and all other human beings with infinite love. God's decision to send his Son and make him one of us reveals how great we are in his eyes, how much he loves us.
3. Only Jesus has the power to make you experience God's love.

To explain these three ideas more explicitly, the Church teaches:

> The man who wishes to understand himself thoroughly—and not just in accordance with immediate, partial, often superficial, and even illusory standards and measures of his being—must with his unrest, uncertainty and even his weakness and sinfulness, with his life and death, draw near to Christ. He must, so to speak, enter into him with all his own self. He must "appropriate" and assimilate the whole of the reality of the Incarnation and Redemption in order to find himself. If this profound process takes place within him, he then bears fruit not only of adoration of God but also of deep wonder at himself.
>
> How precious must man be in the eyes of the Creator, if he "gained so great a Redeemer," and if God "gave his only Son" in order that man "should not perish but have eternal life."
>
> St. John Paul II, *The Redeemer of Man*, n. 10

Do you want to understand what makes you special? You must draw near to Christ with your defects, your sins, your doubts, and your yearning for love. You must learn to talk to Jesus about your problems. This is what the Church means when saying that you must "enter into him with your whole self."

You must find yourself in Jesus—somehow. You probably do not know how. That does not matter. Jesus will show you how if you trust in him. He will show you if you spend time in prayer. Ask him to show you how "enter into him with your whole self."

Even though you have many sins, God loves you. He loves you so much that he sent Jesus to be your brother, your savior, your king. He sent Jesus to lift you out of your misery by forgiving your sins and making you a child of God. That is why God created you. God is love, and he created you to experience his infinite love. God is Father, Son, and Holy Spirit, and he created you to be a child of God. All definitions of good and evil are based on this.

Christian freedom

All men and women are called to be sons and daughters of God. This revelation is the new basis for defining what is right and what is wrong.

You are free if you find the love God created you to experience. You become a slave when you cling to anything else, no matter how good it seems at the moment. Being greedy, getting drunk, being promiscuous, or indulging in violence leads you down into a pit of slavery. Pursuing a style of life that contradicts God's plan makes it impossible to love others.

Christian freedom consists in dominion. But it is not worldly dominion, giving you power over others. Instead, it is spiritual dominion, giving you the willpower to embrace God's plan. This spiritual dominion of self allows you to escape the slavery of sin. This spiritual dominion makes it possible to love others.

Jesus describes the slavery of living in sin when he tells the parable of the Prodigal Son (cf. Lk 15:11). There were two sons. The younger took his father's money and wasted it, getting drunk and sleeping with prostitutes. After running out of money, he got a job feeding pigs. He was so poor that the pigs were eating better food than he was. The pathetic state of this young man is a symbol of the slavery of sin. We fall into it when we turn our back on God.

Jesus also describes the slavery of sin when talking about the lack of mercy in the heart of the older son. This son obeyed his father but refused to forgive his brother. Some people abandon God by embracing sins of the flesh. Others, like the older son, live very sad lives because they are filled with desires for revenge. They, too, lose sight of God. They are overcome by anger towards others who have insulted them or done them harm.

Christian freedom means freedom from all forms of sin and selfishness. It is freedom from sins of the flesh, like gluttony, drunkenness, laziness, and lust. It is also freedom from more subtle evils like pride, anger, envy, and greed.

Slavery to sin makes us feel spiritually dead. Christian freedom makes us feel spiritually alive. St. Paul connects this sense of freedom with being a child of God.

> For all who are led by the Spirit of God are sons of God. For you did not receive the spirit of slavery to fall back into fear, but you have received the spirit of sonship. When we cry, "Abba! Father!" it is the Spirit himself bearing witness with our spirit that we are children of God, and if children, then heirs, heirs of God and fellow heirs with Christ, provided we suffer with him in order that we may also be glorified with him.
>
> Romans 8:14–17

God wants us to know that he is our Father and we are his children. This awareness is the greatest freedom any man or woman can experience.

We will have to suffer in this life. No one escapes suffering. Even Jesus suffered. But no one can take our freedom away from us. Again, St. Paul is the one who describes it best:

> For I am sure that neither death, nor life, nor angels, nor principalities, nor things present, nor things to come, nor powers, nor height, nor depth, nor anything else in all creation, will be able to separate us from the love of God in Christ Jesus our Lord.
>
> Romans 8:38–39

Christian freedom is freedom we feel even when the whole world is against us. Not even our sins will take away our sense of peace if we turn immediately to God, seeking forgiveness through the sacrament of penance.

Church precepts

A precept is a law established by those who have authority. In the Church the Pope and the bishops in communion with him are the ones who have authority over God's people. They have established certain precepts to help us to obey the laws of God. The main precepts of the Church are the following (cf. *Compendium of the Catechism of the Catholic Church*, n. 432):

1. *Attending Mass on Sundays and other holy days of obligation. Refraining from work and activities that impede the sanctification of those days.*

Jesus becomes present during the celebration of the Eucharist, hidden under the appearances of bread and wine. We go to Mass to be with Jesus. The Church asks us to spend this time with him as a practical way of obeying the commandment that obliges us to keep the Lord's Day holy. If, out of neglect or laziness, you deliberately skip Mass on a Sunday or a holy day of obligation, it is a mortal sin.

Besides attending Mass, Catholics are obliged to observe a day of rest on holy days. That means finding time to spend with your family instead of spending the day at work or doing business. The bishops in each country determine which days are holy days of obligation.

2. *Confessing your sins, receiving the sacrament of reconciliation at least once a year.*

Going to confession once a year is a minimum. We tend to grow lukewarm. Knowing our weakness, the Church asks for this minimum. It is better to go to confession often, even when we have no mortal sins to confess.

3. *Receiving the sacrament of the Eucharist at least during the Easter season.*

This precept of the Church is sometimes called the "Easter duty." To fulfil the Easter duty, you receive Holy Communion sometime between the First Sunday of Lent and the Feast of Pentecost. Once a year is the minimum. It is better to receive Jesus in Communion frequently. You should only receive if you are properly prepared, though.

4. *Abstaining from eating meat on days of abstinence. Observing the days of fasting prescribed by the Church.*

On Ash Wednesday and Good Friday, those ages fourteen and above are obliged to abstain from meat. On Ash Wednesday and Good Friday, those from eighteen to fifty-nine years of age are obliged to fast.

On Fridays all Christians should practice penance in memory of the Friday when Jesus died on the cross. In some countries, to fulfill the precept of doing penance on Friday, all Fridays of the year are prescribed as days of abstinence. In other countries, to fulfill the precept of doing penance on Friday, only the Fridays of Lent are prescribed as days of abstinence while, on other Fridays, each person chooses some form of penance—that is, making some act of self-denial to be sorry for sins committed and imitating the suffering of Jesus on the cross. This act of self-denial can be made either by skipping food, drink, or entertainment normally enjoyed on other days or by giving alms—i.e., making a generous gift to someone in need.

5. ***Helping to provide for the material needs of the Church, according to your ability.***

There are several ways of doing this. The easiest is to make a contribution to the church you attend for Mass on Sundays.

The beatitudes

The Ten Commandments do not define the essence of Christianity. The precepts established by the Church are not the essence of Christianity. Commandments and precepts are laws and the essence of being a disciple of Jesus Christ goes far beyond law. God expects more. He wants us to love. Loving God and loving others for his sake is the essence of Christian faith.

When Jesus explained the way we prepare to enter God's kingdom, he told his disciples that they had to go beyond laws. To give them a guide of what he meant, he announced the beatitudes. More than laws, they are promises.

The beatitudes tell us that God wants us to be detached from all earthly goods, to be ready to forgive those who harm us. God wants us to be pure, not only in deeds but also in the way we think. God wants us to be ready to die in order to spread the gospel to others. This new way of life is based on a new commandment:

> A new commandment I give to you, that you love one another; even as I have loved you, that you also love one another. By this all men will know that you are my disciples, if you have love for one another.
>
> John 13:34–35

Not only is this a new commandment, this is a new *kind* of commandment. It covers your whole life and absolutely everything you do from birth to death.

The Beatitudes

Blessed are the poor in spirit,
for theirs is the kingdom of heaven.

Blessed are those who mourn,
for they shall be comforted.

Blessed are the meek,
for they shall inherit the earth.

Blessed are those who hunger and thirst for righteousness,
for they shall be satisfied.

Blessed are the merciful,
for they shall obtain mercy.

Blessed are the pure in heart,
for they shall see God.

Blessed are the peacemakers,
for they shall be called sons of God.

Blessed are those who are persecuted
for the sake of righteousness,
for theirs is the kingdom of heaven.

Blessed are you when men revile you and persecute you and utter all kinds of evil against you on my account. Rejoice and be glad, for your reward is great in heaven.

Matthew 5:3–12

Jesus told the Apostles he would give them the power to love others. He said, "You shall be baptized with the Holy Spirit" (Acts 1:5). He meant that he was going to give the Holy Spirit to all those dedicated to him.

This is the New Law. It is new because the world still needs to hear it. It is law, but in a different way. It is a law that sets people free. It comes with the promise of being filled with the Spirit. St. Paul said that anyone who experiences this gift feels free:

> Now the Lord is the Spirit, and where the Spirit of the Lord is, there is freedom.
>
> 2 Corinthians 3:17

Saintly Wisdom

The Apostle Paul adds, "Where the Spirit of the Lord is, there is freedom" (2 Cor 3:17). To be set free from injustice, fear, constraint, and suffering would be useless if we were to remain slaves in the depths of our hearts, slaves of sin. To be truly free, man must be liberated from this slavery and transformed into a new creature. The radical freedom of man thus lies at the deepest level—the level of openness to God by conversion of heart. For it is in man's heart that the roots of every form of subjection [and] every violation of freedom are found.

St. John Paul II, *Message for World Peace Day*, 1980, n. 11

From the beginning of the Church, during the time of the Apostles, some people twisted the meaning of Christian freedom. They thought it meant that Christians were free to sin. St. Paul warned them that this was a perversion of the truth. Christian freedom is not a license from God to act like infidels. The Holy Spirit makes us free by giving us the strength to fight against our defects, to be sorry for our sins, and to love others.

> For you were called to freedom, brethren; only do not use your freedom as an opportunity for the flesh, but through love be servants of one another. For the whole law is fulfilled in one word, "You shall love your neighbor as yourself." But if you bite and devour one another take heed that you are not consumed by one another. But I say, walk by the Spirit, and do not gratify the desires of the flesh.
>
> Galatians 5:13–16

You are free when you learn to detect the hidden ways in which you tend to be selfish. You are free when you enjoy doing good. You are free when you hate evil—when you feel repulsion for anything that would get in the way of your love for God. You are free when serving others becomes second nature to you.

REVIEW QUESTIONS

1. Some people say the only way we can be free is to get rid of all laws. Explain why this does not make sense.
2. How does error about God and creation affect a person's ability to distinguish between good and evil?
3. What did Jesus reveal about man that gave us a better understanding of human freedom?
4. Explain the freedom that comes from the Holy Spirit.

20.

Sin

There are many evils: hunger, disease, pain, and death. They last only for as long as we live in this world. They do not offend God. In addition to these evils, there is sin. Sin is worse than all other evils because it is an offense against God.

King David committed adultery with Bathsheba, the wife of Uriah (cf. 2 Sam 11:1). Uriah was a soldier in the Israelite army. While Uriah was away at war, Bathsheba conceived David's child. After the adultery, David committed another sin. He ordered Joab to make sure Uriah got killed in battle. Then David took Bathsheba as his wife. Later David repented of his sins. One of David's psalms expresses his guilt and sorrow: "Against thee, thee only, have I sinned, and done that which is evil in thy sight" (Ps 51:4). The king knew that his deeds offended God.

No one ever goes to hell because of hunger. No one ever goes to hell because of disease. No one ever goes to hell because of pain. But you will go to hell forever if you commit a mortal sin and refuse to be sorry. One sin is worse than all hunger, all disease, and all pain.

What is sin?

You commit a sin every time you deliberately choose to do something wrong. If you know God's commandments and disobey them, you commit a sin. Every sin is an offense against God. Every sin is an act of disobedience. Sin is any word, deed, desire, or omission that goes against God's law.

People commit a sin by doing some evil action. People also commit sins by failing to do what they are supposed to do. If you fail to fulfill an obligation, you are guilty of a sin of omission. Failing to do something can be seriously wrong. Many serious sins are sins omission. If you refuse to go to church on Sunday out of laziness, you are seriously offending God. If you are married and fail to take care of your spouse or your children, you are doing something seriously wrong.

It is difficult to measure how much harm sin does. But when committing a sin, you are always aware, at least in some vague way, that you are choosing something wrong. If you were not aware of it, you would not be guilty of sin. The real mystery of a sin lies here. Sin is never an accident. You *know* you are doing something evil, and yet you do it anyway.

Sin does not pass away like a shadow flitting across the wall. If you kill somebody, the act lasts only for a minute. The dead body falls to the ground. People mourn and have a funeral. Life goes on for everyone else. The murder fades into the past. But the sin called murder remains deep in your soul. You can bury a dead body, but you cannot bury your sin. Even if no one saw you do it, God saw it. Even if no one else knows about your sin, God knows. You can hide from other people; you cannot hide from God.

Guilt is the lasting effect of sin. The guilt remains long after the sin has been committed. After you have done something wrong—murder, adultery, theft—the guilt of sin stays inside of you. You carry it with you wherever you go. You wake up with it. You eat with it. You leave home with it. You walk with it. You work with it. You go home with it. You sleep with it. You live with your sin—all day and all night, every day, week after week. You may eventually put it out of your mind, especially if you commit more sins. But sin never goes away until you repent and God forgives you.

Mortal sin and venial sin

Stealing a pencil is not the same as stealing someone's wedding ring. Getting impatient with someone who bothers you is different from smashing his skull to pieces. Lying to hide a defect from your friends is not as serious as lying to a judge under oath.

Sacred Scripture

But Peter said to him, "Explain the parable to us." And he said, "Are you also still without understanding? Do you not see that whatever goes into the mouth passes into the stomach, and so passes on? But what comes out of the mouth proceeds from the heart, and this defiles a man. For out of the heart come evil thoughts, murder, adultery, fornication, theft, false witness, slander."

Matthew 15:15–19

Sins like murder and adultery are serious sins that take away sanctifying grace and destroy your friendship with God. These sins are called "mortal sins"—mortal meaning deadly. St. Paul made it clear that those who are guilty of mortal sin cannot go to heaven:

> Now the works of the flesh are plain: fornication, impurity, licentiousness, idolatry, sorcery, enmity, strife, jealousy, anger, selfishness, dissension, party spirit, envy, drunkenness, carousing, and the like. I warn you, as I warned you before, that those who do such things shall not inherit the kingdom of God.
>
> Galatians 5:19–21

St. Paul does not say that people who commit these sins can never be forgiven. Heaven is full of sinners who repented. He means that people guilty of sin must repent. If they refuse to repent, they will not enter God's kingdom.

Some sins, like telling a small lie, weaken our love for God but do not deprive us of sanctifying grace. These minor sins are called "venial sins." Venial sin is the choice of something wrong in a less serious matter or the choice of something seriously wrong without full knowledge or complete consent.

Mortal sin is a deliberate choice of something seriously wrong, carried out with full knowledge. A person commits mortal sin only when acting with both complete consent and full awareness.

Consent

You consent when you make a deliberate choice. You are not being forced. You decide what you want to do.

Take the case of a man who drinks too much alcohol because he wants to get drunk. This man *consents* by making a deliberate choice to get drunk. He may have no intention of offending God. However, he knows that getting drunk is wrong. Therefore, his consent is complete any time he deliberately chooses to get drunk.

Take the case of a man suddenly overcome by anger while playing football. After knocking a player to the ground, he is immediately sorry for having done so. His act was not the result of a willful decision. Instead, caught up in the intensity of the match, he acted on the spur of the moment, without full control of himself. He is sorry. He has done something wrong. There was *some* element of consent. Therefore, he should apologize to the other player. And he should also learn to control his emotions better. But he did not give complete consent; he did not make a deliberate choice.

Awareness

You are aware when you know what you are doing. Your awareness is limited when you do something while half asleep or while being in some similar condition of semiconsciousness. When lacking full awareness, you are not guilty of mortal sin because you are not in full control of your ability to reason. You do not know exactly what you are doing but have only a shadowy impression of the event. However, if you deliberately induce this state of blurred reasoning to make it easier to commit a crime—e.g., drinking heavily before committing murder—you are guilty of serious sin and must repent.

You are aware when you know the good or evil of what you are doing. When you are not aware that a particular act offends God seriously, you are not guilty of mortal sin. If you refuse to seek the truth about the good or evil of your actions, you may not be acting with full awareness; however, you are offending God seriously by deliberately choosing ignorance. You cannot claim innocence after choosing to remain ignorant of God's law. Jesus said:

> And this is the judgment, that the light has come into the world, and men loved darkness rather than light, because their deeds were evil.
>
> John 3:19

If you have any doubt about the morality of your actions, seek guidance.

Take the case of a married couple that does not know using contraceptives to avoid childbirth is seriously wrong. Perhaps others have assured them that using contraceptives is normal. They are not guilty of mortal sin, even though they are causing harm by doing something that is objectively evil. As the years go by, the couple's own experience will raise doubts. For instance, the wife may feel that something is not right because of the way her husband behaves. She will begin to wonder whether their decision to use contraceptives was right. Whether it is the man or the woman, the person in doubt has a serious obligation to seek moral guidance.

Consequences of sin

Mortal sin kills the life of God in your soul. Mortal sin takes away charity and sanctifying grace. If you commit a mortal sin, then you deserve eternal punishment. In other words, if you commit a mortal sin, it means you will go to hell unless you repent and seek God's forgiveness. If you ever commit a mortal sin, pray to God for mercy. If you are a Christian, go to confession as soon as possible.

Do not let God's eagerness to forgive blind you to how much harm sin does. Looking at Jesus on the cross is the best way of seeing how evil sin is. He suffered all that pain in order to take away your sins.

When you disobey God's law, you sin. The decision to do something evil makes you evil. Sin is the only evil that separates you from God. Other evils can bring you closer to God. Sin never brings you closer to God. Instead, it puts an obstacle between you and God.

Look at the evil things that happen to you because of sin. If you commit a mortal sin, these are the consequences:

- You are cut off from God.
- You lose sanctifying grace.

- You lose the gift of God's love.
- You are no longer worthy to receive Holy Communion.
- You have damaged your friendship with other members of the Church.
- You must live with a guilty conscience, knowing you deserve to go to hell forever.
- After you repent, you will have to endure some kind of suffering temporarily to be purified. (This is the temporal punishment due to sin.)
- If you refuse to repent, you will suffer in hell forever. (This is eternal punishment.)

The consequences of venial sin are less drastic. Perhaps for this reason, after committing venial sins, some people never bother to be sorry. They give no importance to venial sins—for example, telling a lie to avoid being embarrassed. This is a great mistake. Even though venial sins do not separate us from God, they keep us from being filled with his love; they make it difficult to enjoy his presence in our lives. These are the consequences of venial sin:

- You feel more attracted to evil.
- You lose your eagerness for the things of God.
- You will have to endure some kind of suffering temporarily to be purified.

Deliberate venial sin is any venial sin committed *knowing* that God wants you to reject it. It is a sin in some small matter that you commit with full consent—for example, carefully planning a lie in order to avoid work. You may say to yourself: "It won't send me to hell. It's not a mortal sin. It doesn't matter." This is false logic. It *does* matter. Deliberate venial sins lead you to commit mortal sins.

Sins of weakness and sins of malice

When speaking about mortal sins, it helps to distinguish between sins of weakness versus sins of malice. Both are serious, but sins of malice cause more harm.

Sins of weakness are sins committed when people feel weak at the moment of temptation. For instance, a man gets drunk because he goes out with some friends who are drinking. He does something seriously evil by getting drunk. He is guilty of a mortal sin if he does it with full knowledge and complete consent. Even if he was not thinking about God when he got drunk, he has offended God seriously. Sins of weakness arise from the weakness caused by original sin—that tendency to sin which we feel almost physically in our bodies.

A sin of malice is much worse than a sin of weakness. It means deliberately stirring up evil desire—stirring up desires of the flesh or stirring up pride, hatred, envy, and greed. It is one thing to murder someone in a moment of anger. That is a sin of weakness. It is different to torture and murder a man because you want to make him suffer. It is one thing to watch pornography because it popped up by chance on television and you were too weak to turn it off. It is much worse to go out looking for a nasty movie because you want to immerse yourself in lust.

> **FATHERS OF THE CHURCH**
>
> While he is in the flesh, man cannot help but have at least some light sins. But do not ignore these sins that we call "light." If you take them for light when you weigh them, tremble when you count them. A number of light objects makes a great mass. A number of drops fills a river; a number of grains makes a heap.
>
> What then is our hope? Above all, confession.
>
> St. Augustine, cf. *CCC*, n. 1863

If you commit many sins of weakness—for example, skipping Mass on Sundays because you're too tired to get out of bed—and make no attempt to be sorry, you gradually slide into sins of malice. You begin to skip Mass on Sunday because you begin to despise a life of prayer. You soon find yourself deliberately rebelling against God. Unrepented sins of weakness lead to sins of malice.

If you ever have the misfortune to commit a mortal sin, try to be sorry as soon as possible. Ask God to forgive you. Go to confession. And then begin again. If you make no attempt to repent, you become more and more evil. You begin to desire *many* evil things. Never give up hope in the mercy of God. But don't fool yourself, thinking you can repent later. Don't think you can wallow in drunkenness, lust, pride, or greed and then, when you're older, be sorry before it's too late.

It is more difficult to be sorry for sins of malice. By putting off the moment of repentance, you are refusing God's mercy. If you continue to refuse his mercy, your heart becomes harder and harder. The more you refuse his mercy, the more difficult it will be for you to repent later. "If today you hear his voice, harden not your hearts" (cf. Ps 95:7).

If you do not repent now, how can you be sure you will repent later? This is true for mortal or venial sin. Some people commit lots of deliberate venial sins, like telling lies, and never bother to be sorry. They think they are in no great danger as long as they avoid mortal sin. Deliberate venial sin does a lot of harm because it opens the way to mortal sin. Some people commit lots of mortal sins and get used to it—so used to it that they begin to think these sins are not really so serious. They may even think these sins are acts of virtue. They begin to think that adultery, contraception, and abortion are natural expressions of a person's right to choose.

The idea that you can have fun by doing evil is wrong. If you allow yourself to become accustomed to promiscuity, violence, pornography, or drug and alcohol abuse, you'll end up living a miserable life. Deliberately choosing evil will make your life hell on earth.

A person who starts with sins of weakness can become hardened. A man who began committing adultery out of weakness—he was away from his wife on a business trip—can become malicious. By failing to repent after committing sins of weakness, he becomes hard of heart, deliberately staying away from home and beginning to feel hatred towards his wife.

Sins against the Holy Spirit

Jesus warns us that we are capable of turning away from God so completely that he cannot forgive us. This is what he meant by speaking about sins against the Holy Spirit:

> He who is not with me is against me, and he who does not gather with me scatters. Therefore I tell you, every sin and blasphemy will be forgiven

> men, but the blasphemy against the Spirit will not be forgiven. And whoever says a word against the Son of man will be forgiven; but whoever speaks against the Holy Spirit will not be forgiven, either in this age or in the age to come.
>
> Matthew 12:30–32

Jesus spoke these words to condemn the way the Pharisees were telling everyone that his miracles were acts of Beelzebul, acts of Satanic power. It was one thing to say that they could not believe in Jesus. Though it was a serious lack of faith, Jesus was ready to forgive. It was another matter altogether for the Pharisees to claim that Jesus' miracles were evil deeds performed by Satan.

The sin against the Holy Spirit consists in refusing to repent even after God uses miracles to move us to repentance. God uses his infinite power to show us how much he loves us. If, after seeing God's mercy with our own eyes, we refuse to repent, there is nothing more he can do to save us. If we refuse to repent, he will not forgive. He will not force us to repent. To explain the sin against the Holy Spirit, the *Catechism* teaches:

> There are no limits to the mercy of God, but anyone who deliberately refuses to accept his mercy by repenting rejects the forgiveness of his sins and the salvation offered by the Holy Spirit. Such hardness of heart can lead to final impenitence and eternal loss.
>
> *CCC*, n. 1864

If a person is conscious of sin but refuses to repent even at the end of his or her life, it is called "final impenitence." The person who dies without being sorry for a mortal sin goes to hell forever.

If this sounds exaggerated to you, pay careful attention to what follows. If you think it is impossible for any human being to suffer forever, listen carefully to God's revelation. Hell is real because evil is real. We are free to choose evil instead of good.

Some Christians shut themselves off from God's grace deliberately. They know they need to be sorry for their sins, but they put it off for later. They are in serious danger. To help us understand just how far they can distance themselves from God, the Letter to the Hebrews reveals the evil inside Christians who are not sorry for their sins:

Magisterium

Sin, in the proper sense, is always a personal act, since it is an act of freedom on the part of an individual person and not properly of a group or community. This individual may be conditioned, incited, and influenced by numerous and powerful external factors. He may also be subjected to tendencies, defects, and habits linked with his personal condition. In not a few cases such external and internal factors may attenuate, to a greater or lesser degree, the person's freedom and therefore his responsibility and guilt. But it is a truth of faith, also confirmed by experience and reason, that the human person is free. This truth cannot be disregarded in order to place the blame for individuals' sins on external factors such as structures, systems, or other people. Above all, this would deny the person's dignity and freedom, which are manifested—even though in a negative and disastrous way—also in this responsibility for sin committed. Hence there is nothing so personal and untransferable in each individual as merit for virtue or responsibility for sin.

St. John Paul II, *Reconciliation and Penance*, n. 16

> For if we sin deliberately after receiving the knowledge of the truth, there no longer remains a sacrifice for sins, but a fearful prospect of judgment, and a fury of fire which will consume the adversaries. A man who has violated the law of Moses dies without mercy at the testimony of two or three witnesses. How much worse punishment do you think will be deserved by the man who has spurned the Son of God, and profaned the blood of the covenant by which he was sanctified, and outraged the Spirit of grace?
>
> Hebrews 10:26–29

No matter how far you have fallen by choosing evil, you should never despair. As long as you are alive, God is ready to forgive all your sins. However, a moment can come when, in addition to committing sins, you choose not to be sorry. If you become obstinate—hardening your heart in order to revel in evil deeds—you end up, as the Scriptures put it, "trampling on the Son of God." You end up scorning the blood that washed away your sins. You are insulting the Holy Spirit.

Once you choose not to be sorry for your sins, you easily fall into a state of confusion. Good and evil get mixed up. You begin to think that peace, joy, and love are merely masks of hypocrisy for weaklings with nothing better to do than worship God. Bloodshed, anger, and hatred

The Seven Capital Sins

PRIDE leads you to chase after honors and fame, obsessed with getting others to praise you and making enemies out of anyone who criticizes you.

ANGER, as a vice, means overreacting to a situation you dislike when it would be in everyone's best interest to remain calm. Also called "wrath."

LAZINESS makes you slow to do anything that you find hard to do. Also called "sloth."

LUST drives you to use others as objects to gratify sexual urges.

ENVY makes you sad when you see the happiness, success, or good fortune of your neighbor.

GLUTTONY means eating and drinking more than you need or being fussy about your food and drink.

GREED leads you to desire material possessions without any limit, always craving more wealth and more money no matter how much you already have. Also called "avarice."

become the only realities worthy of your time and effort. You despise purity, and you ridicule those who are honest.

Once you have drifted into this cloud of confusion, you find yourself doing things you once thought you would never do. You become insensitive to the suffering of those around you. You even begin to laugh at it, as if their pain were entertaining. Worst of all, you do not notice this happening. You become blind to your own state of confusion. If someone tries to explain it to you, you become furious. You look at the one trying to help you as your enemy. You begin to despise people dedicated to God, since they remind you of the truth that you have rejected.

All this is possible. All this has been the sad story of some men and women who at one time earlier in their lives were enthusiastically dedicated to God. For this reason, St. Peter warned the early Christians not to be scandalized when they see a Christian begin to act in strange ways, encouraging sinful behavior:

> They are blots and blemishes, reveling in their dissipation, carousing with you. They have eyes full of adultery, insatiable for sin. They entice unsteady souls. They have hearts trained in greed. Accursed children! Forsaking the right way they have gone astray; they have followed the

> way of Balaam, the son of Beor, who loved gain from wrongdoing, but was rebuked for his own transgression; a dumb ass spoke with human voice and restrained the prophet's madness.
>
> 2 Peter 2:13–16

If you are leading a life of sin, remember that even in such a sorry state God offers you the grace to go to confession, be forgiven, and start over again. When St. Peter describes the tragedy of a Christian who abandons the way and returns to pagan habits, he includes the example of an Old Testament prophet (cf. Num 22:1–35). Though he did not deserve it, Balaam was blessed by a miracle after betraying God's trust. God sent an angel to help him repent from his evil ways. As long as we are alive, God continues to pour out his graces. He calls us to accept the gospel and be cleansed from our sins.

Some people refuse to repent. St. Peter describes them:

> These are waterless springs and mists driven by a storm; for them the nether gloom of darkness has been reserved. For, uttering loud boasts of folly, they entice with licentious passions of the flesh men who have barely escaped from those who live in error. They promise them freedom, but they themselves are slaves of corruption; for whatever overcomes a man, to that he is enslaved. For if, after they have escaped the defilements of the world through the knowledge of our Lord and Savior Jesus Christ, they are again entangled in them and overpowered, the last state has become worse for them than the first. For it would have been better for them never to have known the way of righteousness than after knowing it to turn back from the holy commandment delivered to them. It has happened to them according to the true proverb, The dog turns back to his own vomit, and the sow is washed only to wallow in the mire.
>
> 2 Peter 2:17–22

You should never judge anyone. However, when you see another Christian refuse to accept correction and begin to live the way described here, have the prudence to treat that person with caution. Be respectful; do not condemn; but remember that this person is living a lie and cannot be trusted to speak the truth.

God wants to forgive

The Pharisees accused Jesus of being an evil person because he made friends with sinners. "This man welcomes sinners!" they protested. "And he eats with them." According to the Pharisees, a holy person was supposed to avoid any contact with people who had a reputation for doing evil things.

> **Wisdom of the Saints**
>
> Consider how long it is since you first began to commit sin; how since that first beginning, sin has multiplied in your heart; how every day has added to the number of your sins. . . . Consider your evil tendencies and how far you have followed them. . . . Consider your ingratitude towards God.
>
> Humble yourself. Ask pardon. Resolve to make every effort to tear up the roots of sins from your heart, especially that particular sin which troubles you most.
>
> St. Francis de Sales, *Introduction to the Devout Life*, ch. 12

To explain to the Pharisees why they were wrong, Jesus told them a parable about a shepherd going out to find a lost sheep. He described the scene by picturing a flock of a hundred sheep. One of them goes astray. This "lost sheep" represents the sinner who wanders away from God. Jesus then asked the Pharisees: "Wouldn't you leave the ninety-nine and go after the one you lost and keep searching until you found it?" Jesus then described what any shepherd would do:

> And when he has found it, he lays it on his shoulders, rejoicing. And when he comes home, he calls together his friends and his neighbors, saying to them, "Rejoice with me, for I have found my sheep which was lost."
>
> Luke 15:5–6

The gospel is the revelation of God's mercy to sinners. God wants to forgive our sins—all our sins. "For God sent the Son into the world, not to condemn the world, but that the world might be saved through him" (Jn 3:17).

During his public life, Jesus forgave many sinners. He gave the Apostles and their successors the power to forgive sins. The sacraments of baptism and penance bring us back to God. They restore the friendship destroyed by sin. To describe how eager God is to forgive our sins, Jesus concluded the parable of the lost sheep by saying:

> Just so, I tell you, there will be more joy in heaven over one sinner who repents than over ninety-nine righteous persons who need no repentance.
>
> Luke 15:7

If you have fallen into a habit of sin, do not despair. God will forgive you if you repent.

REVIEW QUESTIONS

1. Why is sin the worst evil?
2. Explain the difference between mortal sin and venial sin.
3. What are the consequences of committing a mortal sin?
4. What are the consequences of deliberate venial sin?

21.

Righteousness

In the Letter to the Romans, St. Paul laments that his people, the Jews, turned away from God by refusing to accept Jesus as the Messiah. He describes it by saying:

> I bear them witness that they have a zeal for God, but it is not enlightened. For, being ignorant of the righteousness that comes from God, and seeking to establish their own, they did not submit to God's righteousness.
>
> Romans 10:2–3

Virtue is not the same as righteousness. A person can have lots of religious fervor and yet fail to be righteous before God.

On the day Jesus appeared to him, St. Paul was shocked to discover that he was not righteous. It was a lesson he never forgot.

> . . . as to the law a Pharisee, as to zeal a persecutor of the church, as to righteousness under the law blameless. But whatever gain I had, I counted as loss for the sake of Christ.
>
> Philippians 3:5–7

St. Paul claimed that before meeting Jesus he was "blameless." And yet he was so deeply shaken after the experience that he began to call himself "the foremost of sinners" (1 Tim 1:15). God chose someone who had never disobeyed the Law and gave him grace in order to prove to the rest of us that it is grace—not obedience to the Law—that makes us righteous.

Even if you had never committed any sins, you would still need salvation. Once Adam and Eve sinned, the whole human race was cut off from God. All men and women were destined to remain separated from him forever.

God wanted the Virgin Mary to be free from all sin. He preserved her from original sin. But even she needed salvation. She never committed any sins. But that is not what made her righteous. She was righteous because of Christ's death on the cross. She was righteous because God filled her with grace. This is the grace Jesus obtained for her—and for everyone else. He obtained it by dying on the cross.

The terms "righteous" and "righteousness" are not used often in daily conversation. But they are used 150 times in the New Testament. Since you may not be familiar with this term, let's begin with a simple explanation. Righteousness is the opposite of sin. A righteous person is someone who is completely free from sin. In positive terms, it means holiness.

One of the first persons described in the Gospel as being "righteous" was St. Joseph, the husband of the Virgin Mary. Many English translations say that St. Joseph was a "just man" or a "man of honor." A literal translation (from the Greek) would say that he was a "righteous man" (Mt 1:19).

Grace and justification

How can you become righteous? First, you must remember that being righteous has nothing to do with being self-righteous. You cannot make yourself righteous. You cannot free yourself from sin. Only God can do that. He will do it if you believe in the gospel, repent, and get baptized.

Sin is something real inside you. Sin is a spiritual reality. You cannot reach inside of your soul and rub away your sins. Fortunately, God can. He uses his all-powerful gift of sanctifying grace to cleanse your soul from sin. By doing so, God makes you righteous.

Sin is mysterious. God's grace is more mysterious. We do not know exactly how it works. But we do know that

Sacred Scripture

Unless the Lord builds the house,
those who build it labor in vain.
Unless the Lord watches over the city,
the watchman stays awake in vain.

Psalm 127:1

For just as you once yielded your members to impurity and to greater and greater iniquity, so now yield your members to righteousness for sanctification.

Romans 6:19

grace takes away sin. We know that grace is a gift from God. Grace is a gift of holiness that we do not deserve. God gives his grace to those who seek forgiveness in the sacrament of baptism—and also in the sacrament of penance for sins committed after baptism. The wonder of God's grace is that it really works. Even if you have lots of sins, grace can take them all away in an instant.

Baptism justifies you. This justification makes you righteous. But there is more to justification than simply being free from sin. The Church teaches:

> Justification is not merely remission of sins, but also the sanctification and renewal of the interior man through the voluntary reception of the grace and gifts, whereby an unjust man becomes a just man, and an enemy becomes a friend . . .
>
> Council of Trent, *Decree on Justification*, ch. 6

Grace makes you righteous before God. Grace also sanctifies you, that is, it makes you holy.

The Pharisee and the tax collector

Jesus told a parable about two men going up to the Temple to pray. He concluded the parable by telling his disciples that God did not justify the Pharisee and instead justified the tax collector. The parable explains why God justifies some and not others.

Imagine yourself dying today and going to stand before God. He looks at you and asks, "Do you want to go to heaven?" Hopefully you will say, "Yes!" But imagine he asks you a further question. Imagine that he asks: "Why should I let you enter into my kingdom?"

When Jesus told the parable of the Pharisee and the tax collector, he was, in essence, saying that there are two answers to this question—the proud answer and the humble answer. Like the Pharisee, the proud person tells God he deserves to go heaven because he prayed every day, fasted a lot, and gave money to the poor. Like the tax collector, the humble person does not dare lift up his eyes, but beats his breast and asks for mercy.

"If you want to know why you should let me go to heaven," the humble man says to God, "I can think of only one reason. Your Son died

Magisterium

Called by God not in virtue of their works but by his design and grace, and justified in the Lord Jesus, the followers of Christ have been made sons of God in the baptism of faith and partakers of the divine nature, and so are truly sanctified. They must therefore hold on to and perfect in their lives that sanctification which they have received from God. They are told by the Apostle to live "as is fitting among saints," and—as God's chosen ones, holy, and beloved—to "put on compassion, kindness, humility, meekness, and patience," to have the fruits of the Spirit for their sanctification. But since we all offend in many ways, we constantly need God's mercy, and must pray every day: "Forgive us our trespasses."

Vatican II, *Dogmatic Constitution on the Church*, n. 40
(cf. Eph 5:3, Col 3:12, Gal 5:22; Rom 6:22, Jas 3:2, Mt 6:12)

on the cross to save me from my sins. He cleansed me with his blood. He made me your child by rising from the dead."

The concluding words of the parable about the Pharisee and the tax collector are the key to understanding God's idea of holiness. Jesus said:

> I tell you, this man [the tax collector] went down to his house justified rather than the other [the Pharisee]; for every one who exalts himself will be humbled, but he who humbles himself will be exalted.
>
> Luke 18:14

You are not justified because of the good works you do. God alone can justify you, that is, forgive your sins and give you sanctifying grace. You cannot save yourself. Only Jesus can save you from your sins. You cannot make yourself holy. Only God can make you holy by washing you in the blood of Christ.

From the very beginning, the Church has always taught that no one deserves the grace of conversion. This teaching is based on St. Paul's declaration that all men and women need salvation from Jesus:

> Since all have sinned and fall short of the glory of God, they are justified by his grace as a gift, through the redemption which is in Christ Jesus.
>
> Romans 3:23–24

Grace is a gift. God has no obligation to give it to you.

The events of both the Old Testament and New Testament prove beyond all doubt that we are sinners. Holy people like Abraham, Moses, and David had serious defects. With the exception of the Virgin Mary, Jesus' disciples also had serious defects. St. Peter's triple denial the night before Jesus died—he swore he was not one of Jesus' disciples—and Judas Iscariot's decision to hand Jesus over to the chief priests are sad reminders of the many times we, too, have betrayed our Lord.

God sent his Son to save us from our sins. "Jesus our Lord . . . was put to death for our trespasses and raised for our justification" (Rom 4:24–25). This is the Good News. God wants to forgive our sins. God wants to make us holy. God lifts us up so we can be his children, so we can be like him. Jesus once told his Apostles:

> Blessed are the eyes which see what you see! For I tell you that many prophets and kings desired to see what you see, and did not see it, and to hear what you hear, and did not hear it.
>
> Luke 10:23–24

The Gospel repeats these words for all those who receive God's gift of sanctifying grace.

Three kinds of grace

Grace is a spiritual gift that God pours into your soul. There are three kinds of grace:

- **Sanctifying grace:** This is the grace God gives you when you get baptized. 'Sanctifying' means making something holy. Sanctifying grace is the grace that makes you holy. It is a share in God's life. It stays in your soul making you holy. You lose it only if you commit a mortal sin. You can get it back by being sorry for the sin and going to confession.
- **Actual graces:** These are graces that last momentarily to help you—here and now—to do something God wants. For instance, God gives actual grace to help you pay attention while attending Mass.

He can give you actual grace to help you work when you don't feel like it. He can give you actual grace to help you repent and go to confession after you have sinned.

- **Charisms:** These are graces given to particular people for a special purpose. The gift of healing is an example of a charism. The person who has this charism has a special power to heal others, either physically by working a miracle to cure a disease, or spiritually, as all priests have in order to forgive sins. God gives charisms to some people so they can help others. He uses charisms to build up the Church. A charism does not make you holy. A charism gives you power to do something to help others. It is meant to lead others to discover God's mercy and help them become holy.

Living a virtuous life

Baptism forgives all sins and makes us holy. It is what Jesus called being "born of water and the Spirit" (Jn 3:5). Like physical birth, spiritual birth leaves you ready to grow into the mature adult God wants you to become. Christian life means growing in holiness.

The Blessed Virgin Mary was conceived without sin and was "full of grace" before becoming the Mother of Jesus. Even she increased in holiness by working in close union with her Son to bring about our

The Three Theological Virtues

FAITH enables you to believe in God and accept everything he has revealed.

HOPE enables you to desire heaven, to trust in God, and to rely on his mercy.

CHARITY gives you the power to love God above all things and to love others for his sake.

The Four Cardinal Virtues

PRUDENCE leads you to see what you should do and the best means to do it.

JUSTICE makes you willing to give God and others what belongs to them.

FORTITUDE makes you strong in the moment of difficulty and constant in the pursuit of good.

TEMPERANCE moderates your attraction to pleasure and your attachment to creatures.

salvation. We learn from Our Lady and all the other saints that holiness is not some squishy sentiment for soft people who happen to like saying prayers. Growing in holiness requires sacrifice. The Virgin Mary gave all Christians an example of heroic faith. She believed the message of the Archangel Gabriel even in the hour of darkness when Jesus was hanging on the cross.

Your growth in holiness depends on receiving more grace from God. It also depends on your effort to do God's will. You become righteous by being virtuous. At the Sermon on the Mount, Jesus said to his disciples:

> For I tell you, unless your righteousness exceeds that of the scribes and Pharisees, you will never enter the kingdom of heaven.
>
> Matthew 5:20

It is not enough to *talk* about being a good person—as the Pharisees used to do. God wants you to root out all bad habits from your life and put the virtues into practice. If you want to be holy—if you want to be the saint God created you to be—you cannot sit around waiting for it to happen. You have to struggle.

Struggling to be a saint means praying when you feel too cold or too empty or too busy to bother with it. Struggling to be a saint means serving others with your work when you feel tired. Struggling to be a saint means learning to forget about yourself so you can do God's will all day, every day, for as long as you live.

Faith, hope, and love

To live a virtuous life, begin by asking God for more faith, more hope, more love. More faith, so that you can dedicate your entire existence to knowing everything there is to know about God. More hope, so that you look forward to union with God above any other expectation, longing to see him face-to-face. More love, so that you yearn to be consumed in the fire of the Holy Spirit—the fire that Jesus came to cast upon the earth.

Faith, hope, and love are the theological virtues—that is, virtues that you cannot acquire by your own effort. They are the virtues only God can give you. Going to confession often and receiving Holy Communion frequently show God your desire to grow in these virtues. Receiving the sacraments increases these virtues in our soul.

St. Paul says, "So faith, hope, love abide, these three; but the greatest of these is love" (1 Cor 13:13). God's gift of love is so great and so effective that St. Augustine felt compelled to say, "Love, and do what you will."

Human virtues

Besides the theological virtues, you need the cardinal virtues: prudence, justice, fortitude, and temperance. We will look at practical ways of living these virtues when we study the Ten Commandments.

Being prudent, just, courageous, and even-tempered is not enough. You need to acquire other human virtues as well: like humility, courtesy, and order.

Be humble as Jesus was humble. If you empty yourself, God can fill you with his grace. This makes it easier for others to love you.

Be courteous. Be gracious. Be refined. If you rub people the wrong way by being vulgar and rude, you become repulsive. A virtuous person makes life more pleasant for others.

Be orderly. If you habitually arrive late and are chaotic when making plans, then, instead of serving others, you will make their life harder. When you lack order—failing to fulfill promises—you leave behind a trail of problems someone else has to resolve. By doing things on time, you begin to be more orderly.

The *Catechism* explains how we acquire human virtues (cf. *CCC*, n. 1810):

- **Education:** We usually rely on someone to teach us virtue. Few people learn to be virtuous on their own.
- **Deliberate acts:** Some acts of virtue come naturally, while others do not. For some people being cheerful is easy whereas overcoming laziness seems difficult. To acquire a virtue, you may have to "force" yourself to do things you do not feel like doing. By performing *deliberate* acts, you begin to acquire a virtue.

- **Perseverance, making repeated efforts:** Like learning a sport, we acquire virtue by repeating actions many times until it becomes second nature. Virtues are habits. The more you practice a particular human virtue, the easier it becomes. If you have a habit of being punctual, you come to enjoy being punctual—and, of course, others benefit as well.

Christian life means living like Jesus. He said, "The Son of man came not to be served but to serve" (Mt 20:28). All Christians must ask themselves: "Do I serve others?" You can ask yourself: "What have I done to serve others?"

Serving others applies everywhere: at home, at school, with your friends—even when greeting strangers. Instead of taking the best for yourself at meals, serve others by letting them choose first. Instead of complaining, make life more pleasant by overlooking things that annoy you. Be positive and cheerful. Sacrifice yourself for others in these little ways, and you will learn something very big as the years go by. You'll learn what it is to be happy. You'll learn how to love others and to make yourself lovable to them.

To become a saint, struggle to live a life of virtue. However, do not think that you need to do dazzling deeds that millions can admire. Remember what Jesus said about becoming like a little child:

> At that time the disciples came to Jesus, saying, "Who is the greatest in the kingdom of heaven?" And calling to him a child, he put him in the midst of them, and said, "Truly, I say to you, unless you turn and become like children, you will never enter the kingdom of heaven. Whoever humbles himself like this child, he is the greatest in the kingdom of heaven.
>
> Matthew 18:1–4

You can become a great saint by making small sacrifices. Sanctity does not consist in doing lots of great things. It consists in taking care of your daily duties with great love.

Merit

God forgives not because he has to but because he is full of compassion and mercy. When you were in the state of sin before being baptized, there was nothing you could do to merit the grace God was planning to give you. You did not deserve to be baptized. The *Catechism* states: "No one can merit the initial grace of forgiveness and justification, at the beginning of conversion" (*CCC*, n. 2010).

Similar logic applies after baptism. If you commit a mortal sin after baptism, you cannot merit the grace needed to reconcile with God. It is necessary to state this since some Christians foolishly think: "After I commit this sin, I'll patch everything up later by going to confession." This makes as much sense as saying, "I'll jump into this well and, after I reach the bottom, I'll pull myself out." You cannot pull yourself out of a well. You cannot decide whether you will have the grace needed to be sorry for your sins.

God's grace is not a pill you can pop when you have a headache. It is a mercy that Jesus won for you by shedding his blood. God will forgive you as often as necessary, but only if you humble yourself. If you reject the grace he gives you to avoid sin, how can you be sure you will accept the grace needed to repent? The grace of conversion does not depend on your good works. So how can conversion depend on a plan to repent when that plan includes rebelling against God? Never take God's grace for granted.

Just as no one can merit the grace of conversion, no one can merit the grace needed to persevere in faith to the end. To die and enter God's kingdom, you need a special grace, even if you have been living a very holy life. This is the grace of final perseverance. No one can merit this grace. And yet, you should believe that God wants to give it to you. Humbly ask him for this grace often throughout your life.

Does this mean that Christians never merit anything? No. Merit means that anything they deserve for making an effort to do God's will depends on God's promise to reward them. No one can stand before God and claim equality. No one can stand before God and claim justice. Jesus talked about our heavenly Father giving us a reward. But all his rewards are gifts.

To understand better the Christian notion of merit and the reward God gives for being the "good and faithful servant," remember Jesus' words at the Last Supper: "Apart from me you can do nothing" (Jn 15:5). He expected them to go out and "bear much fruit." But he made it clear that any success in spreading the gospel was due to God's grace working in them—not to any power or eloquence of their own. He told them they had to be like branches united to the vine.

Jesus' warning on the correct way of giving alms, praying, and fasting provides another key to understanding Christian merit. He said:

> Beware of practicing your piety before men in order to be seen by them; for then you will have no reward from your Father who is in heaven. "Thus, when you give alms, sound no trumpet before you, as the hypocrites do in the synagogues and in the streets, that they may be praised by men. Truly, I say to you, they have received their reward. But when you give alms, do not let your left hand know what your right hand is doing, so that your alms may be in secret; and your Father who sees in secret will reward you.
>
> Matthew 6:1–4

When speaking of almsgiving, Jesus implies a condition for deserving a reward. You must have the right intention. If you make a sacrifice in order to receive an earthly reward, you deserve nothing more than an earthly reward. You may get the human praise you were seeking. But you will not receive any reward from God. If you give alms for the right intention—to help someone who really needs help—then God will reward you.

To receive a reward for your good deeds, right intention is not the only condition. You must also live in the state of grace. If you commit a mortal sin, you lose all merit. No matter how many sacrifices you made earlier, it counts for nothing unless you repent. If you repent, all the merit that was lost through sin is restored along with the grace received through the sacrament of penance.

Because the merit is real, the rewards the saints receive in heaven are equally real. It makes a big difference whether you give a lot instead of being satisfied with giving just a little. As Jesus said, "The measure you give will be the measure you get back" (Lk 6:38). When it comes time to judge, the Master rewards the servants differently. The one who did more is given a greater reward: the servant who earns ten talents of gold governs over ten cities whereas the servant who earns five talents of gold governs over five cities (cf. Lk 19:16–19).

Hope: Trusting God

Trust God. Being infinitely powerful, he can forgive all your sins. St. Paul urged the early Christians to hope for salvation:

> For in this hope we were saved. Now hope that is seen is not hope. For who hopes for what he sees? But if we hope for what we do not see, we wait for it with patience.
>
> Romans 8:24–25

One of the reasons for having such great hope is that God has given us the Holy Spirit as a pledge of future glory.

Some people have a mistaken idea of hope. They think Christians no longer have to worry about whether they are going to be saved. They use the following argument: "Christians are saved because they

Wisdom of the Saints

I have always desired to become a saint, but in comparing myself with the saints I have always felt I am as far removed from them as a grain of sand . . . compared to a mountain whose summit is lost in the clouds. Instead of feeling discouraged by such reflections, I concluded that God would not inspire a wish that could not be realized, and that in spite of my littleness I might aim at being a saint.

. . . We live in an age of inventions. We need no longer climb laboriously up flights of stairs; in well-to-do houses there are lifts. And I was determined to find a lift to carry me to Jesus, for I was far too small to climb the steep stairs of perfection. I came across these words from the Book of Proverbs: "Whoever is simple, let him turn in here!" (Pr 9:4) . . . Jesus, your arms, then, are the lift that will raise me up to heaven. To reach heaven I need not become great. On the contrary I must remain little. I must become even smaller than I am.

St. Thérèse of Lisieux, *Story of a Soul*, ch. 31

have accepted Jesus as their Lord and Savior. Being saved means, among other things, that Christians are sure they will go to heaven no matter what happens in the future. Because God forgave them when they accepted his grace, Christians will enter into his kingdom as long as they continue to believe they have been saved." According to this notion of salvation, God wants each Christian to believe—as if it were something Jesus had revealed—"Because I have been saved, it is impossible for me to lose God's grace."

One of the reasons why some Christians make this mistake comes from a false interpretation of a text written by St. Paul:

> Who shall bring any charge against God's elect? It is God who justifies. . . . Who shall separate us from the love of Christ? . . . For I am sure that neither death, nor life, nor angels, nor principalities, nor things present, nor things to come, nor powers, nor height, nor depth, nor anything else in all creation, will be able to separate us from the love of God in Christ Jesus our Lord.
>
> Romans 8:33, 35, 38–39

Nothing should ever trouble a Christian who *remains faithful* to Jesus. This is beyond all doubt. However, other biblical texts imply that any Christian—St. Paul included himself in this category—is capable of being *unfaithful*. What does it mean to be unfaithful?

One interpretation of St. Paul's words says that not even sins committed after "getting saved" can take away God's grace. This interpretation was condemned by the Church at the Council of Trent. By following the mistaken interpretation, people fail to understand the true horror of sin. When Christians sin in some serious matter, they lose the gift of God's grace. Their sin is worse than the sin of a pagan because they commit their sin while living in friendship with God:

> If it were an enemy who taunts me, then I could bear it. If it were an adversary who deals insolently with me, then I could hide from him. But it is you, my equal, my companion, my familiar friend. We used to hold sweet conversation together. Within God's house we walked in fellowship.
>
> Psalm 55:12–14

Once you sin, you lose the grace God gave you. Once you lose his grace, you have been cut off from God. If you do not repent, you will go to hell. You must learn to be horrified by the thought of committing a mortal sin. If you commit a mortal sin, you can only go to heaven if you repent and seek forgiveness.

Christians should never be afraid of God. Even if they have the misfortune of falling into serious sin, God will forgive them, as long as they repent. God is our Father in heaven. He is ready to forgive as often as necessary. That is why Jesus instituted the sacrament of penance. He knew his disciples would need forgiveness for sins committed after baptism.

Jesus wants you to cling to the hope that you will go to heaven in spite of being a sinner. He also wants you to be humble. Do not trust your own strength. No matter how fervent your faith is now, you are capable of betraying Jesus and losing God's grace. You are capable of losing it not just for a few days or few years but truly forever, ending up condemned in hell.

Every Christian is capable of falling away and being damned forever. This is the only conclusion one can draw from the chilling words written in the Letter to the Hebrews:

> For it is impossible to restore again to repentance those who have once been enlightened, who have tasted the heavenly gift, and have become partakers of the Holy Spirit, and have tasted the goodness of the word of God and the powers of the age to come, if they then commit apostasy, since they crucify the Son of God on their own account and hold him up to contempt.
>
> Hebrews 6:4–6

Is it really possible for anyone to enjoy knowing God intimately and yet fall from grace? The text just quoted certainly says so and says it quite clearly.

Great intelligence and great willpower do not guarantee perseverance to the end in either men or angels. After coming to know God—after "tasting the heavenly gifts"—we are free to rebel and turn our backs on the Creator, either for a time or forever. "Therefore let any one who thinks that he stands take heed lest he fall," St. Paul warns (1 Cor 10:12).

Based on God's revelation as recorded in the Scriptures, the Church teaches that no one should believe with absolutely certainty that he or she will enter into heaven. Instead, each Christian should acknowledge that everybody, no matter how holy, is capable of falling. Everyone is capable of committing sin at any time in the future and then capable of refusing to repent.

The Church goes one step further and reminds us that, even if we think we have been truly sorry for our sins, we cannot be *absolutely* certain. The Church insists that every Christian should be humble and reserved when talking about his or her own holiness:

> No pious person should doubt the mercy of God, the merit of Christ, and the virtue and efficacy of the sacraments. But when considering our lives, our weaknesses, and lack of generosity, all of us may entertain fear and apprehension as to our own grace, since no one can know with the certainty of faith—which cannot be subject to error—that he or she has obtained the grace of God.
>
> Council of Trent, *Decree on Justification,* ch. 9

When it comes to looking at the state of your soul, you can deceive yourself, like the hypocrites in the times of Jesus. They thought they were holy. Jesus tried to tell them that they were "blind" to their sins and that their "guilt remained" (Jn 9:41). They paid no attention to him.

If anyone ever asks you whether or not you are sure you are going to enter into the kingdom of God, you can truthfully answer, "No." If anyone asks you whether or not, even at this very moment, you are living in the state of grace, you can use the wonderful answer that St. Joan of Arc gave when someone asked her: "If I am not, may it please God to put me in it; if I am, may it please God to keep me there" (*CCC*, n. 2005).

REVIEW QUESTIONS

1. What does the Bible mean when it uses the terms "righteousness" and "justification"?
2. If only God can make us holy, then why do we have to struggle to be saints?
3. Describe the three different kinds of grace.
4. Explain what the Church teaches about the possibility of losing sanctifying grace.

22.

Conscience

You should follow your conscience. Before you understand what it means to follow your conscience, you need to know what we mean by conscience. Then you need to learn how to form your conscience.

God's voice

Every man, woman and child has a conscience. Conscience is like a voice coming from God. The Church teaches:

> Deep within his conscience man discovers a law which he has not laid upon himself but which he must obey. Its voice, ever calling him to love and to do what is good and to avoid evil, sounds in his heart at the right moment.
>
> Vatican II, *The Church in the Modern World*, n. 16

This voice is inside of you. It is not a voice you can hear. It is a voice that does not use words. It tells you whether something is good or evil.

If you ignore that voice, you will ruin your life. St. Paul hints at this when recalling what happened to some friends who used to be fervent Christians: "By rejecting conscience, certain persons have made shipwreck of their faith, among them Hymenaeus and Alexander . . ." (1 Tim 1:19–20). He does not say these men never had faith. On the contrary, they had faith but "wrecked" it because of failing to follow their conscience.

When you listen to the voice of conscience, you are facing God. You are looking at the truth of your actions. You are asking yourself, "Have I done good? Or have I done what is evil in the eyes of God?"

We compare conscience to a voice, but in reality it is something more subtle than a voice. Conscience is a judgment—in other words, an act of your intellect looking at certain facts and judging them. This act of judgment takes place in your mind. Using the power of human reason, you judge whether your act is good or evil.

For instance, if you spend some time in prayer, your conscience will probably tell you that this was good. If you steal some money, your conscience will probably tell you that this was evil. In both cases, you are judging your actions. This act of judging is your conscience.

Morality

How do you know when an act is good or evil? What makes an act *good*? What makes an act *evil*?

Morality is the good or evil of a desire, word, or action. For the sake of simplicity, let's talk about the *morality of an act*, covering all forms of human acting—thinking, desiring, speaking, gesturing, working, etc. These are all acts where a person makes some kind of decision.

The good or evil of a specific act depends on the three moral aspects of the act:

1. **OBJECT:** When I choose to do something, *what* am I choosing?
2. **INTENTION:** *Why* am I choosing it?
3. **CIRCUMSTANCES:** What else is happening that affects my decision?

Let's look at these three aspects separately.

The object of the act

To identify the object of the act, ask yourself: "When deciding to act, *what* did I do? *What* did I choose?" When you act, you choose whether or not you will do something. Think of the object of the act as the answer to the question "What?" You are not asking yourself *why*. You are asking *what*. Consider the following examples.

Sacred Scripture

See, I have set before you this day life and good, death and evil. If you obey the commandments of the LORD your God which I command you this day, by loving the LORD your God, by walking in his ways, and by keeping his commandments and his statutes and his ordinances, then you shall live and multiply, and the LORD your God will bless you in the land which you are entering to take possession of it. But if your heart turns away, and you will not hear, but are drawn away to worship other gods and serve them . . . I call heaven and earth to witness against you this day, that I have set before you life and death, blessing and curse; therefore choose life, that you and your descendants may live, loving the LORD your God, obeying his voice, and cleaving to him . . .

Deuteronomy 30:15–17, 19–20

A man named Max shoots a gun at another man standing close by. Max pulls the trigger, firing a bullet that kills the other man. How would you judge the morality of this act? Perhaps your first reaction is to assume it must be evil since someone just got killed. Certainly the death of the other man is an objective evil. It should have been avoided if possible. However, before we can judge the good or evil of Max's action (pulling the trigger), we have to know a lot more. So far, we know nothing about the *decision*. We do not know *what* Max was choosing to do. We do not know the *object* of the act. Max may not have decided anything; he may have pulled the trigger by accident. This is why the object of the act is always the first thing to consider when judging the morality of an act.

We need to know what Max was choosing. There are several possibilities. Was Max hallucinating under the influence of some drug, not even conscious of the fact that he was pointing a gun at another person? Was it an accident that happened while Max was showing his gun to a friend? Was Max trying to kill, knowing the other man was innocent? Was Max trying to defend himself because the other man was attacking him? Let's look at each of these four cases.

1. If Max was hallucinating, we cannot speak of the morality of the act. Because Max had no awareness, he was not making a decision of any kind. There was no object because there was no decision.

2. If it was an accident, this determines the nature of the act. Max knew he was holding a gun. He knew his friend was with him. He was making a decision, but it had nothing to do with killing his friend. In this case, the object of the act was to show the gun to a friend. Let's say the two men were recruits in the army. Max's friend wanted to see the new gun, and then the accident happened. Perhaps there was some negligence, since Max should have checked to make sure the gun was not loaded. However, whether or not there was negligence, the objective decision remains the same: Max was not trying to take another man's life. He was only trying to show his gun to a friend. In this case, the object of the act was Max's decision to show off his new gun.

3. If Max pulled the trigger in order to kill an innocent person, the object of the act would be murder. Let's say Max made a plan, got a gun, and then found the best moment to shoot the other man at close range to make sure he would kill him. Such an act is cold-blooded murder. We may not know *why* Max wanted to kill the other man; we may not know his intention. Maybe he did it because it was easier to rob the other man by killing him first, making greed the primary motive. Maybe he did it because the other man was a colleague who had blocked his promotion at the office, making revenge the primary motive. Whether the intention was greed or revenge, the object of the act remains the same. Max decided to kill an innocent person. The object of the act was murder.

4. Finally, let's suppose Max shot the gun to defend himself. He probably did not have much time to think. Still, he was making a decision with full awareness. However, look closely at exactly what he was—and was not—deciding. Max did not want to take the life of the other man. He would have let the other man live if the other man had agreed to leave him alone. Max wanted to save his own life and had the right to use to force in order to do so. It was not an act of murder. It was an act of self-defense. The object of the act was self-defense.

When looking at these four possibilities, remember that all of them can be described by the same physical act (a man shooting a gun, causing the death of another man); yet the object of the act is different in each case. Before you can judge intention or circumstances, you have to determine the object of the act. In other words, you have to determine what *decision* you were making when acting. If the object was evil, then your act was evil—even if your intentions were good.

The intention

After figuring out the decision or object of the act, look at the motive or reason for making that particular decision. Whenever you act—whenever you make a decision—you may have several motives that explain why you chose to act the way you did. The decision is the *objective* part of the act. The intention is the *subjective* part of the act. The object of the act (i.e., the decision) answers the question: *What* am I doing? The intention answers the question: *Why* am I doing it? The intention is all about motives.

Some motives are pure emotion—despair, rage, fear of disgrace, or craving for pleasure. The emotion leads you to make a decision. The emotion may be so strong that it blinds you to the consequences of the act. In such cases, your motive for acting—the intention of the act—is a response to an emotion that you feel here and now.

The intention of the act is not always based on emotion. Some motives are more subtle, based on calculations of possible effects. For instance, you might smile at someone hoping that this will attract his attention and get him to listen to you more carefully. You decide to smile, and you do it consciously. In this case, the *object of the act* is defined by your decision to be warm and friendly towards the other person. Your *intention* is to get the other person to pay attention to you.

When trying to judge the morality of an act, most people start with the intention.

FATHERS OF THE CHURCH

Examine your conscience with the greatest accuracy. . . . Do not cheat your conscience. It knows the hidden things of your heart. If you cheat it, it will become an obstacle to you during your time of prayer; it will accuse you at the time of your death.

St. Maximus the Confessor, *The Four Centuries on Charity*, IV, 33

The intention behind your decision is often more obvious to you than the decision itself. For instance, the love of shedding blood is rarely the intention behind an act of murder. Usually the murderer has some other intention—e.g., seeking revenge or stealing money. So when the murderer looks at his decision to kill, the first thing he usually sees is the intention that moved him to act. The intention is what comes first. The intention comes before the decision.

Our tendency to notice intention first can be confusing. Many people assume that the intention behind the act determines whether the act was good or evil. This is a mistake. For an act to be good, good intentions are not enough. A good intention cannot change an evil act and somehow make it good. If the object of the act is evil, then the act is evil no matter how good the intention is.

Take the following example of a good intention. Suppose I am a doctor and I think I have a good reason for killing a baby—for instance, hoping this will spare a pregnant student from having to cut short her studies at the university. Suppose this is the only reason that leads me to perform an abortion. The intention is excellent. I want to help someone get an education. If it leads me to go through with the abortion, I have made a deliberate decision to shed the blood of an innocent human being. I wanted the baby to die. There was some part of me that was hoping there would be another way of solving the young woman's problem. Because I could not find another way of doing it, I killed the baby. The intention was good, but the act was evil because the object of the act was evil. I deliberately killed an innocent human being.

We just looked at a situation where the objective decision was evil and the intention was good. Let's look at an example where the object of the act is good but the intention is evil. Remember that, if your intention is evil, the act is evil.

Suppose I decide to give food to some poor people who have nothing to eat. This is a good deed. Suppose I have to make a personal sacrifice to buy the food. I could use the money to buy some nice things for my house. Instead, I buy food and give it to the poor. This requires sacrifice, which makes the decision even more noble and worthy of praise. But suppose the motive for my generosity is pure vanity. I give food to the poor because I want my friends to praise me.

In this case, the object of the act is good. The intention, though, is evil. What could have been a very good act turns into an evil act. Instead of gaining merit for a good deed, I have offended God and committed a sin. This is why Jesus said, "When you give alms, do not let your left hand know what your right hand is doing" (Mt 6:3).

Circumstances

When you act, the circumstances include all those minor factors that surround the act: who is with you, where you are, time of day, etc. For an act to be morally good, the circumstances have to be good. For instance, if a person wants to watch a documentary on war, it would normally be a good act. However, if there are children present who will suffer harm because of the violence depicted in some scenes, watching the documentary would be evil.

To judge the morality of an act, we have to look at all three aspects of morality. If the object of the act, the intention motivating the act, and the circumstances are good, then the act is good. If only one of these three is evil, then the whole act is evil, regardless of how good the other two are.

Secondary effects

Sometimes additional factors influence the morality of your decision, especially unintended secondary effects. The fact that you do not want a particular side effect to occur does not mean you can ignore it. You should consider it when judging the morality of an act. The more likely the secondary effect, the more importance you must give it.

For instance, suppose I want to invite some friends over to my house to watch a game when my favorite team is playing. The decision is good, and the intention is good. For me and my friends, the circumstances are ideal. However, there is this one additional factor. I know from experience that every time I have done this in the past, my brother, who is an alcoholic, will use it as an excuse to join us and start drinking. He will drink a few beers with us and then go out to a bar afterwards and come home drunk. He may decide to start drinking no matter what I do, but it is all the more probable that he will start drinking if I go ahead with my plan.

This is a typical case of an unintended secondary effect. I do not want the secondary effect. I do not want my brother to get drunk. Am I doing anything wrong if I go ahead with my plan?

Determining morality for secondary effects can be difficult. In the example given, I would have to ask myself: How much does my brother need to avoid absolutely *all* occasions of drinking? How important is it for me to relax with my friends at my house, watching this particular game at this particular time?

Whenever you find it hard to calculate competing benefits in questions of secondary effect, a simple guide will help. It is called the "golden rule." Jesus said, "So whatever you wish that men would do to you, do so to them" (Mt 7:12). If you were the one who really needed help avoiding alcohol, what would you want your brother to do for you? St. Paul referred to this problem when discussing difficulties that some Christians had with food and drink:

> Do not, for the sake of food, destroy the work of God. Everything is indeed clean, but it is wrong for any one to make others fall by what he eats; it is right not to eat meat or drink wine or do anything that makes your brother stumble.
>
> Romans 14:20–21

There are moments when you will have to sacrifice something good in order to make sure your enjoyment does not become a stumbling block for someone else. Besides, there are usually other alternatives. With some modifications to the original plan, it is possible to do things so that everyone benefits.

When judging the morality of an act, you have to consider all these aspects: the decision (or object of the act), the intention, the circumstances, and any secondary effects. Pay special attention to the way your decisions affect others when going about your professional work. For instance, it is tempting for those operating a business to turn a blind eye to damage being done by products they sell. Some excuse themselves saying, "I'm just trying to earn a living!"

Consider the case of someone who sells arms used in military combat. Because these arms are extremely powerful and often deadly, they have limited usefulness. Making moral judgments in such an industry is notoriously difficult even when one is careful to judge all the factors. If the salesman is approached by a group that he suspects will use these weapons for some evil purpose, despite their stated intentions, he cannot excuse himself by saying, "I'm just doing a fair deal that is perfectly legal in the eyes of the government." Our moral obligations go beyond laws set by the government. Each person stands before God. It is not man's law but God's law that determines the good or evil of our decisions. When examining our conscience, this is the standard by which we must judge.

Just once

Everybody agrees they should avoid doing evil. Nevertheless, some people are convinced that there are times when they need to do something wrong *just once* to solve an immediate problem. The Church teaches that it is never right to do something evil hoping that good will come from it.

> There are some concrete acts—such as fornication—that it is always wrong to choose. . . . One may not do evil so that good may result from it.
>
> *CCC*, nn. 1755–1756

The idea is clear. Even so, some people wonder why.

Consider the case of a truck driver who accepts a deal to transport some drugs along with his other cargo. He may be thinking, "I just need to do this once. With the money I get from the drug dealers, I can buy my own truck. Then I can set up my own business. I know selling drugs is wrong. But all I have to do is deliver this package. It's not like I'm selling drugs. After it's over, I'll tell God I'm sorry and he'll forgive me."

Similar scenarios arise frequently. People contemplate all kinds of one-off schemes: stealing some money at the office to make a mortgage payment, having an abortion for a baby conceived in embarrassing circumstances, satisfying some frivolous craving just once, etc. The logic used to justify these schemes seems compelling: "It's the only way I can solve my problem. Once it's over, I'll never do it again. God knows how hard my life is. I'm sure he'll forgive me."

If you ever have to help someone in this situation, the first thing to do is plant the doubt: "How do you know you're going to be sorry? You're not sorry now." If a man or woman is not sorry while contemplating the evil they are about to do, what will make them change their minds and be sorry later?

Look at the case of the truck driver thinking about helping a drug dealer deliver a shipment of drugs. He assumes God will forgive him and everything will be fine. Will it? What if he gets caught? Even if he avoids that problem, won't he have to remember for the rest of his life that he helped some criminals do something that causes enormous harm to many other people?

God will forgive anything and everything—no matter how disgusting, no matter how selfish, no matter how diabolic. But our little cheating games are deadly. Any plan to do one bad thing now hoping for lots of good later does not bring peace or happiness. God will forgive all, but only if we are sorry. Never take sorrow for granted. It is not a light switch you can flick on and off at will. It is a mystery of grace.

Sin is never trivial. If you deliberately choose evil, you become evil. Never underestimate the power of God's grace, but remember that evil is also mysterious. There are many people who thought they would be sorry. The irony is that they were sorry. Seeing how evil they had become, they despaired. Then they plunged headlong into a world of sin they never knew existed, only to discover they could not escape—or worse, they began to revel in it.

"With the temptation," St. Paul wrote, "[God] will also provide the way of escape, that you may be able to endure it" (1 Cor 10:13). An evil deed often seems to be the only way to resolve a problem. But God has a better way.

Whenever you are tempted to think you have a problem that desperately needs to be solved and that evil is the only way to solve it, first pray. God can show you a different way of looking at your life. He can show you that the problem you have now is going to help you be a better person. Accept your situation instead of running away from it. It is the cross of Christ—the cross Jesus wants you to carry in order to follow him. When you face trials and temptations, remember St. Paul's words of encouragement:

> I consider that the sufferings of this present time are not worth comparing with the glory that is to be revealed to us.
>
> Romans 8:18

Whenever it seems that one evil deed will lead to lots of good, remember that this is a lie. The truth is just the opposite. Many good things you cannot imagine depend on refusing to yield to evil desires, no matter how much suffering you have to endure.

There is another reason why God wants you to resist evil even when evil seems like the only solution to your immediate problem.

> For this slight momentary affliction is preparing for us an eternal weight of glory beyond all comparison . . .
>
> 2 Corinthians 4:17

Learning to resist evil trains you. Until you learn that lesson, you are a selfish person, addicted to your own pleasure, your own gain, or your own comfort. You are prepared to make someone else suffer an injustice rather than suffer yourself. Reverse that logic. Learn to put up with something that makes you suffer so that others will not have to suffer. This is how you learn to love others.

Forming your conscience

God gave us the Ten Commandments so we would know how to make correct judgements about good and evil. Christ completed the Ten Commandments in the Sermon on the Mount. These revelations from God show us what God wants. We use them to judge between what is holy and what is sinful.

Besides *following* your conscience, you need to *form* your conscience. Everyone starts with one basic moral fact: Do good and avoid evil. Most people know a few more basics. They know it is wrong to lie, murder, and steal. But they are easily confused when it comes to other issues. Many people ask, "Why is sex before marriage always wrong? Why is

Magisterium

Conscience is not an infallible judge. It can make mistakes. . . . Jesus alludes to the danger of the conscience being deformed when he warns: "The eye is the lamp of the body. So if your eye is sound, your whole body will be full of light; but if your eye is not sound, your whole body will be full of darkness. If then the light in you is darkness, how great is the darkness!" (Mt 6:22–23).

The words of Jesus just quoted also represent a call to form our conscience. . . . Christians have a great help for the formation of conscience in the Church and her Magisterium. As the Council affirms: "In forming their consciences the Christian faithful must give careful attention to the sacred and certain teaching of the Church. For the Catholic Church is by the will of Christ the teacher of truth. Her charge is to announce and teach authentically that truth which is Christ, and at the same time with her authority to declare and confirm the principles of the moral order which derive from human nature itself."

It follows that the authority of the Church, when she pronounces on moral questions, in no way undermines the freedom of conscience of Christians. . . . [F]reedom of conscience is never freedom "from" the truth but always and only freedom "in" the truth. . . . [T]he Magisterium does not bring to the Christian conscience truths that are extraneous to it; rather it brings to light the truths which it ought to possess already, developing them from the starting point of the primordial act of faith. The Church puts herself always and only at the service of conscience, helping it to avoid being tossed to and fro by every wind of doctrine proposed by human deceit (cf. Eph 4:14), and helping it not to swerve from the truth about the good of man, but rather, especially in more difficult questions, to attain the truth with certainty and to abide in it.

St. John Paul II, *The Splendor of the Truth*, nn. 62, 63, 64

it wrong to get drunk? Why is it wrong to use contraceptives? Why is it wrong to lie?"

Forming your conscience means looking for answers. There are several reasons why you may hesitate. You are afraid you may have to change your life. You are too lazy to look for someone who can help you. You worry about what your friends will say.

All these reasons lead to the same consequence. Many people adopt the prevailing opinion among their friends. Perhaps you have noticed this. If most people think there is nothing wrong with casual sex, you can end up thinking the same way until you make an effort to find the truth.

One way of explaining how you form your conscience is to look at the different "types" of conscience. Conscience is a judgment that you make with your mind. You can correctly judge that the earth is round—or you can make a mistake and think the earth is flat. The same thing happens to your conscience. You can correctly judge whether your act is good or evil. Or you can make a mistake and conclude that an act is evil (even though it is good) or that an act is good (even though it is evil).

- **Correct conscience** Your conscience is correct when you judge your actions correctly. For instance, suppose you have to defend yourself against a lunatic randomly firing a machine gun at your family. Having no other option of stopping him, you shoot him and he dies. If you judge that this was the right thing to do, your conscience is correct. You may feel sad at having to shed blood. But you did the right thing even if you do not feel good about it. Take another example. If you steal your friend's money so you can buy some new clothes, and later you judge that this was an evil thing to do, your conscience is correct.
- **Erroneous conscience** Your conscience is erroneous when you make the wrong judgment. The problem is that you *think* you made a *correct* judgment. Suppose, for instance, that without realizing how evil it is, you developed a habit of watching pornography or reading steamy romance novels. Some of your friends do it. They seem to be normal. So you conclude that it's good. Your judgment is wrong. Without realizing it, you are doing something that harms you and others. Even if they don't realize it, your friends are also doing something wrong.
- **Doubtful conscience** Your conscience is doubtful when you are not sure whether a specific act is good or evil. For instance, suppose you are married and you have been using contraceptives for several years without thinking much about it. One day, a friend tells you that the Church says it's wrong for you to use contraceptives. This sounds strange to you. Other friends who go to church with you told you there is nothing wrong with it as long as you have really good reasons for it. But this new friend insists that it's always wrong, no matter what. You are left in doubt.

All men and women have an obligation to seek the truth—especially the truth about God and their eternal salvation. If you have a doubtful conscience, keep searching until you find the truth. If you continue to do evil deeds with a doubtful conscience while making no effort to find the truth, you are guilty of all that evil.

Vincible and invincible ignorance

If you have an erroneous conscience, you have an obligation to seek the truth. The problem is that you think you already have it. The Church distinguishes between "vincible" and "invincible" ignorance.

> Invincible ignorance . . . [is] an ignorance of which the subject is not aware and which he is unable to overcome by himself.
>
> St. John Paul II, *The Splendor of the Truth*, n. 62

Suppose you are a Muslim and you read a book explaining why you should believe that Jesus Christ is the Son of God. Relying on what your parents taught you, you assume the Christian book is wrong. You think it would be wrong to believe in Jesus. Your conscience is erroneous, because Jesus is the Son of God. It would be good for you to believe in him. But you do not know this and, even after reading a good book on the subject, remain convinced that you should continue to be a Muslim. In such cases of invincible ignorance, you should follow your conscience even though you are mistaken. If the day comes when God gives you the grace to see that Jesus is the Son of God, then you have an obligation to follow your conscience and believe in Jesus.

Vincible ignorance is ignorance *resulting from neglect*. You are ignorant *because* you have made little effort to discover the truth. The Church teaches:

> Conscience, as the ultimate concrete judgment, compromises its dignity when it is culpably erroneous, that is to say, when man shows little concern for seeking what is true and good, and conscience gradually becomes almost blind from being accustomed to sin.
>
> St. John Paul II, *The Splendor of the Truth*, n. 63

Vincible ignorance becomes worse if you deliberately foster ignorance. Suppose you have made no effort to learn the difference between good and evil. You habitually get drunk, thinking there is nothing wrong it. The deterioration of your health will be a sign that something is wrong. If, despite this warning sign, you continue to neglect the need to form your conscience, you become wilfully blind.

If you have made very little effort to study the teachings of the Church, you probably have an erroneous conscience. You live in a world where most people are confused on many moral issues without having the slightest clue of how wrong they are. It would be amazing if, making no effort to study the Church's teachings, you managed to avoid all the confusion by pure chance. Your notions of good and evil are probably just as mixed up as those of the people around you.

If you neglect to form your conscience, you will cause a lot of harm. You will think that you are doing the right thing when, in fact, you are causing harm. Form your conscience by seeking advice. Then you can have a correct conscience all the time. This goes beyond a friendly suggestion to study the Church's teachings. If you suspect that you may not know the truth, you cannot content yourself with saying, "I have to follow my conscience." You have an obligation to follow your conscience, but you also have an obligation to seek the truth. Only those who seek God's will can enter the kingdom of heaven.

Scruples

Though scruples affect few people, it is worth noting this defect of conscience. Scruples are exaggerations—mistakenly judging venial sins to be mortal sins. The scrupulous get carried away by a desire to be absolutely free not only from all possible faults but from temptations as well. They think a saint is someone who never makes any mistakes. With the exception of the Blessed Virgin Mary, even the greatest saints had their defects. Most saints had to struggle with temptation even after years of faithful service to the Church. Seeing their many defects, scrupulous believers become overly anxious. They need to humble themselves and, like anyone else, continue their efforts to discover the truth.

Freedom of conscience

There are two realities that some people have a hard time putting together. Each person is free. Each person has a conscience.

Freedom of conscience does not mean you are free to decide which acts are good and which acts are evil. It is a serious error to say: "I am free to decide whether murder is good or evil. I am free to choose whether adultery is good and evil." You are not free to decide this.

You are free to refrain from murder and adultery—and lying and stealing and any other sin. You are free to murder, to lie, to steal, and to commit adultery. You are free to choose between good and evil. However, if you choose evil, it will always be evil, no matter what your conscience tells you. If you choose good, it will always be good, no matter what your conscience tells you. Hopefully your conscience makes correct judgments. If it does not, then you need to form your conscience better.

To grasp the true meaning of freedom of conscience, remember the warning Jesus gave his disciples: "Judge not, and you will not be judged; condemn not, and you will not be condemned" (Lk 6:37). You have no right to judge another person. If another person does something that is objectively evil, like committing murder or adultery, do not hesitate to conclude that the deed is evil. Condemn the sin but not the sinner. No one has a right to say that the person who committed the crime is evil. Only God has the right to judge the conscience of another human being. The Church teaches:

> Conscience is man's most secret core, and his sanctuary. There he is alone with God whose voice echoes in his depths.
>
> Vatican II, *The Church in the Modern World*, n. 16

A sanctuary is any holy place where one enters to be alone with God. When you have done good, you hear the voice of approval. You know that God is pleased with you. When you realize that your deed was evil, you hear the voice of reproach. You know that you have offended God. Your conscience is the most secret core of your being because no one else can enter there except God himself.

This is why you must follow your conscience. If you think in the depth of your heart that God prohibits you from doing something and you do it, what creature can free you from guilt for having disobeyed God? If you think in the depth of your heart that God wants something and you do not give it to him, what excuse can you offer God for having listened to someone else instead of listening to him?

Each one of us must stand alone before God at the moment of judging the good or evil of our lives. Each one of us is personally responsible. Responsibility always implies freedom. The *Catechism* explains:

> Man has the right to act in conscience and in freedom so as personally to make moral decisions. He must not be forced to act contrary to his conscience. Nor must he be prevented from acting according to his conscience, especially in religious matters.
>
> *CCC*, n. 1782

Even when Christians are rightly convinced that God wants all men and women to follow Christ, they have no right to stand before non-Christians and condemn them for failing to accept the gospel.

Does this mean that all religions are equal? Does this mean it makes no difference whether a Christian goes to a Catholic church, an Orthodox church, or a Protestant church? Does this mean that is makes no difference what religion a particular person follows?

It *does* make a difference. Each person must seek the truth. God wants everyone to believe the Good News, to be baptized, and to follow Christ by accepting the fullness of the truth found in the Catholic Church.

Only God can judge whether a particular Christian was faithful to the gospel. Only God can judge Jews, Muslims, and those who follow other non-Christian religions. Only God knows when people have rejected the gospel despite seeing clearly that they should have accepted it.

The Church asks Christians to respect the conscience of each person. We should never try to force a person to accept the gospel. Catholics should never try to force non-Catholics to attend a Catholic church. The Church does not *impose*. Instead, the Church *proposes* the truth, hoping that everyone will see it as God's revelation and accept it.

Learning to examine your conscience

To examine your conscience, you look at yourself and all your decisions. This means sitting down for a few minutes every evening. You look at the good things you did. You look at the evil things you did. Thank God for all the good things. Ask him to continue helping you. Be sorry for the sins you committed. Ask God to forgive you.

If you are a Christian and you committed a mortal sin, you need to go to confession with a priest so God can forgive you. Ask God while you are examining your conscience to give you the strength to do that as soon as you can.

People who are spiritually lazy fail to examine their conscience. They drift away from God, committing lots of sins. Since they never bother to look at the good and evil in their lives, they become blind to what is happening. They get used to their evil deeds.

People who have a habit of examining their conscience are ready to meet God. They have defects just like everyone else. But they face their defects without fear. Instead of making excuses, they admit their faults. They turn to God and ask him to forgive their sins.

Examine your conscience every day before you go to bed. Then you will be able to improve a little bit every day.

God enlightens

Besides making our own effort to examine our conscience, we need a special grace from God to see ourselves as we really are. This is part of becoming as holy as God is holy. This action of enlightening our minds is the work of the Holy Spirit.

Saintly Wisdom

If you want to have peace in your soul and be perfectly united to God in blessed love, forget about the deeds you have seen in others and look only at yourself and your own deeds. If you see anything that needs to be corrected, correct it immediately.

Thomas à Kempis, *The Imitation of Christ*, ch. 5

On the night before he was crucified, Jesus said he would send the Holy Spirit. He said the Paraclete would have the power to "convince the world concerning sin" (Jn 16:8). The Holy Spirit does this because he is the "light of consciences," the one who shows us the whole truth:

> The Holy Spirit "convinces concerning sin," that is to say, he makes man realize his own evil and at the same time directs him toward what is good. . . . Thus the conversion of the human heart, which is an indispensable condition for the forgiveness of sins, is brought about by the influence of the Paraclete.
>
> St. John Paul II, *On the Holy Spirit*, n. 42

Some people live in a state of sin for many years, giving it little importance. They seem unaware of the harm they are causing. They remain insensitive to the pain and loneliness in their hearts. Then suddenly, one day, without being able to explain why, they suddenly wake up. A light shines within them. It is the Holy Spirit showing them how much they need to change and how to do it.

REVIEW QUESTIONS

1. What is conscience?
2. Why do you have an obligation to form your conscience?
3. What do we mean by correct, erroneous, and doubtful conscience?
4. Explain the connection between conscience and freedom.

23. Worshiping God

The first commandment

After coming down from the mountain, Moses gave the Israelites the Ten Commandments. He repeated for them what God had told him:

> And God spoke all these words, saying, "I am the LORD your God, who brought you out of the land of Egypt, out of the house of bondage. You shall have no other gods before me. You shall not make for yourself a graven image, or any likeness of anything that is in heaven above, or that is in the earth beneath, or that is in the water under the earth; you shall not bow down to them or serve them . . ."
>
> Exodus 20:1–5

In the first commandment, God commands us to adore him and no one else. God concludes the first commandment, saying, "I the LORD your God am a jealous God" (Ex 20:5). He wants us to love him above all things.

We can take Jesus' words as a summary of the first commandment when he said: "You shall worship the Lord your God and him only shall you serve" (Mt 4:10).

There are many false gods. Jesus warned us against making money our god:

> No one can serve two masters; for either he will hate the one and love the other, or he will be devoted to the one and despise the other. You cannot serve God and mammon.
>
> Matthew 6:24

You cannot serve both God and the riches of this world. God wants you to put your trust in him, not in riches. It is easy to feel safe when you have a lot of money in the bank. That is why money easily becomes a false god.

When Jesus warned his disciples of this danger, others failed to see the point. "The Pharisees, who were lovers of money, heard all this, and they scoffed at him" (Lk 16:14). These were the same ones who ended up condemning Jesus to death.

People today have as much a tendency to worship false gods as the ancient pagans. For instance, the world around us suggests that we should worship self, when it says: "Believe in yourself. Take care of number one." This advice is wrong. God invites us to believe in him. We are not supposed to believe in ourselves. We are not supposed to make ourselves "number one." Self can become a false god.

Sacred Scripture often speaks of the need to love your neighbor "as you love yourself." But Jesus also spoke of a need to "hate" ourselves if we want to be his disciples (cf. Lk 14:26). We cannot let anything come between God and us. We have a tendency to put self where God is supposed to be. Instead of devoting our lives to serving God and others, we tend to be devoted to self—doing only what pleases us, gratifying our every whim and caprice.

You can see this tendency in such a simple thing as entering a room. Without thinking, you may choose the most comfortable seat for yourself. Jesus asks us to "hate" self—that is, to overcome this tendency to selfishness.

Distinguishing good and evil

Most people tend to think of the Ten Commandments as prohibitions. This is natural since most of them begin with the words: "You shall not . . ." To understand what God wants, you need to see both the positive command and the negative prohibition.

To do God's will—and find happiness—there are certain good deeds you need to do and certain virtues you need to exercise. This is the positive side of each commandment. To escape the slavery of sin, there are certain evils you must avoid. This is the negative side. It means learning to say no to some things you like. Your salvation depends on learning to do it.

You can only be a good person if you avoid *all* evil. God wants you to fight against all your bad habits. It is not enough to struggle to overcome most of them and cling to one, like pride or greed or lust. You will never be happy until you make up your mind to overcome all your defects.

To make it easier for you to distinguish between good and evil, each chapter in this section includes two lists. One explains the virtues and other positive aspects of the commandment. The other explains the prohibitions and vices. After each explanation, a reference to the Bible illustrates the idea.

Good deeds to do

Faith To believe in God, make an act of faith. Tell him, "I believe in you. I believe that you created me. I believe that you listen to me." Even a child can say this. If you can say it, not just with your lips but also with your heart, you have faith. A Christian can go one step further and tell God, "I believe that you are my Father. I believe that I am your child." The next thing faith requires is to believe all that God has revealed. Faith means believing the truths taught by the Church not because they make sense but because God revealed them—and he can neither deceive nor be deceived.

The cure of the centurion's servant: Matthew 8:5–13

Sacred Scripture

Again, the devil took him to a very high mountain, and showed him all the kingdoms of the world and the glory of them; and he said to him, "All these I will give you, if you will fall down and worship me." Then Jesus said to him, "Begone, Satan! for it is written,

'You shall worship the Lord your God
and him only shall you serve.'"

Matthew 4:8–10

Hope When it seems you have no chance of making it to heaven, hope is the virtue that keeps you from giving up. To trust in God; make an act of hope. Tell God that you trust him. This takes no effort when your life is calm and peaceful. But a moment comes when things go wrong.

When that happens, you will be tempted to do something evil: steal money to pay a debt, abort an unborn child when pregnancy is difficult, tell a lie to cover up a mistake, engage in bad behavior to please your friends, etc. When these temptations come, God wants you to reject the temptation and place your trust in him. He wants you to trust in him even though your whole world falls apart. God will give you all the grace you need to do his will. He will reward you for trusting him. He will take to you to heaven.

Susanna puts her trust in God: Daniel 13:19–23

Love This is the greatest of all virtues. Sometimes the Bible calls it "charity." To love God, start by remembering that he loved you first. He gave you the gift of faith. He gave you grace to be sorry for your sins. Thank him for these gifts. Tell him that you love him. Choose whatever words you want. More important, show him *with deeds* that you love him. Show him by adoring him, by making sacrifices for him and by serving others. Besides being ready to do his will, remain open to the love he wants to show you.

Parable of the two sons: Matthew 22:28–32

Adoration To adore or worship God means calling him "Creator." You say, "I exist because you made me. If you cease to sustain me, I cease to exist." Certain exterior acts are signs of adoration: kneeling, bowing low, prostration, to using incense. Adoration must also be interior; otherwise, the external act is hypocrisy. True adoration implies total submission. You say, "God, I belong to you. I am ready to do anything you ask." Worshiping the one true God is the essence of religion.

The Virgin Mary adores God: Luke 1:46–49

Prayer Praying to God has many aspects: talking to him, listening to him, adoring him, thanking him, entering into communion with him, being sorry for sins, asking him for help, seeking light to know his will, and asking for strength to do it. Because the term "pray" originally comes from a word that means to ask, it is quite common to speak of praying to the saints. This does not mean that we adore the saints or ask them to forgive our sins. Instead, it means that they are our friends in heaven and that we turn to them the same way we ask our friends here on earth to help us.

Parable of the widow and the unjust judge: Luke 18:1–8

> **Fathers of the Church**
>
> If we do God's will, make his commandments our rule of life, and love what he loves, then "he who raised the Lord Jesus will raise us also" (2 Cor 4:14).
>
> St. Polycarp, *Second Letter, 2*

Sacrifice In the most literal sense, to sacrifice means to make something sacred, that is, to set it aside for God. The person offering a sacrifice takes something valuable and dedicates it completely to God by placing it on an altar. From that moment on, the item belongs to God and the person sacrificing cannot touch it. Even if no altar is involved, you sacrifice by dedicating something completely to God, allowing him to do whatever he wants with it. Jesus said, "I desire mercy, and not sacrifice" (Mt 9:13). God is not interested in your possessions. He wants *you.* He wants you to sacrifice your body and soul, your mind and will, your whole heart, your whole self. The first sacrifice God wants is for you to turn away from sin, so he can show mercy. Then he wants you to do his will, so he can make you happy. Jesus' sacrifice on the cross is the only sacrifice capable of washing away sin. For this reason, it is the sacrifice most pleasing to God. To have any merit before God, all other sacrifices must be united to his.

Saul's disobedience (*1 Samuel 15:10–23*)
Jesus' obedience (*Hebrews 10:4–10*)

Caring for others Loving God is linked with loving our neighbor. Any spirituality that gives great importance to loving God and little to loving others is a caricature of Christian charity: "For he who does not love his brother whom he has seen cannot love God whom he has not seen" (1 Jn 4:20). The gospel teaches us to measure how much we love Jesus by looking at the good deeds we do to serve others.

Parable of the sheep and goats: Matthew 25:31–46

Evils to avoid

Activism This means being too busy to pray, too busy to read the Bible, too busy to find the truth about God. Many people are too busy making money or pursuing a career. The things of this world can lead us to God. But they become an obstacle when we make work more important than prayer. Though rarely mentioned, activism is the main reason why people end up knowing nothing about God's love. It is the main reason why they fail to discover the joy and peace he has prepared for them. The sad thing is that some Christians fall into this defect when trying to spread the gospel. If you do lots of good for others but never stop to pray, your failure to pray will eventually cripple you. You may even lose the faith you are so eager to share with others.

Parable of the wedding feast: Luke 14:15–24

Heresy, apostasy, schism These three sins are different forms of rejecting God's revelation. Though claiming to be Christian, a heretic obstinately and publicly rejects some truth of revelation that, for whatever reason, he thinks is false. For instance, a heretic may believe Jesus is the Son of God and yet refuse to accept the fact that Jesus remained celibate during his life on earth, even though this is also one of the definitive teachings of the Church. An apostate is a Christian who abandons faith in Jesus after baptism. For instance, a Christian who leaves the Church to become a Muslim is an apostate. A schismatic is a Christian who divides the Church by drawing a group of Christians away from the authority of the Pope, asking them to submit to another authority instead. Even though the schismatic intends to uphold the Church's teaching and to enact the liturgy with great faithfulness, he does great harm to the Church by rejecting the Pope's authority.

Demas, one of the companions of St. Paul, abandons his faith: Philemon 23; 2 Timothy 4:10

Doubt In general, you doubt when you hesitate to accept a statement someone else claims to be true. Doubt can be good. You ought to doubt something that you once believed if you discover that God did not reveal it and that it contradicts the teachings of the Church. Doubt is wrong when you hesitate to accept a truth revealed by God even though it is obvious to you that God has revealed it and that the Church teaches it.

Jesus condemns the Pharisees for refusing to accept the cure of the man born blind: John 9:24–41

Hypocrisy A hypocrite is a person who pretends to be very religious, always engaged in acts of devotion and making great sacrifices, but only to impress others. It is all a show—useless in the eyes of God.

Jesus condemns the Pharisees for "lip-service": Matthew 15:1–9

Idolatry To worship anything or anyone other than God is to worship an idol. Since the devil has real power and can use it to entice us, Satanism is the most dangerous form of idolatry. In the broader sense, anything you dedicate all your time and energy to becomes an idol. The world is full of idols. Power, pleasure, beauty, fame, food, drink, entertainment, and money can easily become idols. Some people are also tempted to make a god out of things like their race, their tribe, their country, or even their football team.

Rebels refuse to stop devil worship after a third of the human race is destroyed: Revelation 9:18–21

Despair You despair if you give up hope thinking that God will refuse to forgive you even if you repent. Even if you cannot imagine how you will overcome your bad habits, God can save you as long as you turn to him and ask for forgiveness. The only sin God cannot forgive is your refusal to repent.

Judas despairs after betraying Jesus: Matthew 27:3–5

Presumption This means presuming that you do not need God's grace to be saved from sin or that you do not need to be sorry for your sins. It can also mean presuming you will enter the kingdom of heaven despite living an idle and useless life, making no effort to serve God.

Parable of the Pharisee and the publican: Luke 19:11

Parable of the servant who buried his talent: Matthew 25:24–30

Indifference This means having no interest in finding the truth. The religiously indifferent person does not care about God, about why he created us, or about what he has planned for us. Since we cannot find happiness without God, it is a great evil to ignore him. Indifference is often a mask for fear—fear of facing God and fear of facing the truth. Then come the excuses: "I don't get anything out of going to church. I'll worry about God when I'm ready to die. I'm not the kind of person who likes to pray. Church is for hypocrites and cowards." Anyone who makes such excuses will not escape God's judgment. The person who deliberately refuses to look for God cannot be saved.

Those indifferent to the gospel will be punished more severely than the inhabitants of Sodom and Gomorrah: Matthew 10:11–15

Lukewarmness Like indifference, this defect is a form of spiritual laziness. It usually follows discouragement. As the initial enthusiasm of conversion fades, most converts are dismayed to discover how hard it is to overcome their defects. Some continue to struggle. Some give up completely. Some are content with trying to avoid mortal sin. The lukewarm person seeks this latter compromise and looks at personal sanctity as an absurd ideal, reserved to a handful of extremists. The lukewarm person flees from the cross of Christ and reduces morality to being pleasant to others while seeking as much comfort as possible.

Jesus warns the Christians in Laodicea: Revelation 3:14–16

Hatred Some people react to God's revelation by cursing him. They resent God's revelation and see it as an intrusion. They do not want to know the truth because they do not want to change their lives. At times this hatred arises because of some injustice suffered in the past, leading the victim to blame God for allowing it to happen. You hear an echo of this pain every time people ask: "If God is good, then why is there so much evil in the world?" They usually forget that there were times when they committed sins and would have been very angry if God had tried to stop them.

Herodias hates St. John the Baptist and has him killed: Mark 6:17–29

Superstition A superstitious person imagines that a certain word has to be said, a certain item has to be worn, or a certain deed has to be done in order to chase away evil spirits and bring good luck. Such practices are superstitious since the words, items, and deeds have no power to have an effect on anything. Believing in horoscopes, astrologers, or

Magisterium

Since "without faith it is impossible to please him" (Heb 11:6) and attain to the fellowship of his sons, no one is justified without it. Nor will anyone attain eternal life except the one who "endures to the end" in faith (Mt 10:22).

Moreover, in order that we may satisfactorily perform the duty of embracing the true faith and of continuously persevering in it, God, through his only-begotten Son, has instituted the Church, and provided it with clear signs of his institution, so that it can be recognized by all as the guardian and teacher of the revealed word.

Vatican I, *Dogmatic Constitution on the Catholic Faith*, ch. 3

fortune-tellers is superstition. It is wrong to believe a prediction coming from a person who knows nothing about the future. Just because a person knows the past does not mean he or she knows the future.

Jewish soldiers try to protect themselves with pagan amulets: 2 Maccabees 12:40

Witchcraft Many superstitions arise from witchcraft. This involves asking a witchdoctor or a witch to curse your enemies so they will suffer. It can also involve wearing amulets to ward off curses from other witchdoctors and witches. Witchcraft is more harmful than superstition. It means calling upon Satan and other demons, knowing that these spirits have certain natural powers as fallen angels. If nothing else, the demons can tempt people to do evil things and thus cause real damage. Even if you consult a witchdoctor or witch for a good purpose—e.g., trying to cure a sick child—you do great evil because you are abandoning hope in the God who loves you and putting your trust in a spirit who wants to destroy you. Satan is the evil one. He will destroy you if you place yourself in his hands.

Saul consults the witch of Endor: 1 Samuel 28:3–25

Tempting God If you put yourself in a difficult situation with no real need, counting on God to save you from disaster, you are tempting God. For instance, if you present yourself—with no need to do so—before a group of extremists known for their hatred of Christian faith and declare that you are a Christian, you are tempting God. If you do such a thing to become a martyr, the Church will not declare you a martyr. You are asking God to use his power in some extraordinary way when there is no need for it. The fathers of the Church condemned the practice of deliberately provoking martyrdom, recalling how some Christians who tried it, thinking they were brave enough, ended up denying their faith once the torture began in earnest.

Satan asks Jesus to jump off the pinnacle of the temple: Luke 4:9–12

Sacrilege Anything or anyone consecrated to God must be treated with as much respect as we would treat God himself. Profaning holy objects, holy places, or holy persons is a form of sacrilege. This means showing disrespect towards a holy person, place, or object. For instance, using a chalice, reserved for the celebration of Mass, to drink beer during a birthday party is a sacrilege. Committing adultery with a nun or a priest—besides being an act of lust—is a sacrilege. Any display of contempt for the Church's liturgy, sacred objects, or sacred persons is a serious form of sacrilege. An attempt on the life of the Pope (because he is the Vicar of Christ) and contempt shown towards the Eucharist (because Jesus is present in the Eucharist) are the worst possible sacrileges. Receiving Holy Communion without being properly prepared (e.g., neglecting to go to confession after committing a mortal sin) is a sacrilege even if you receive with the intention of getting closer to God.

King Belshazzar uses sacred vessels for a party: Daniel 5:22–31

Simony Anyone who sells indulgences, blessings, holy water, or other spiritual things commits the sin of simony. This includes any attempt to offer money to a bishop in order to be ordained to the priesthood or to obtain some position within the Church. Church law states that no one is ever obliged to give money to a priest in order to receive the sacraments. The sacraments are not for sale. They are to be administered freely because they are gifts from God. (At the same time, Christians have an obligation to support the clergy precisely to make sure that priests are always available to administer the sacraments and not occupied doing business to earn a living.) The sin of simony is named after the magician who tried to buy the power of working miracles from St. Peter.

Simon offers St. Peter money: Acts 8:18–24

Special Topics

Catholic belief

Worship depends on faith. If you believe all that the Catholic Church teaches, those beliefs will determine the way you worship God. If you believe the teachings of some other Christian community (Lutheran, Baptist, Pentecostal, etc.), this will affect the way you worship God.

St. Paul wrote: "No one can say 'Jesus is Lord' except by the Holy Spirit" (1 Cor 12:3). Though many Christians are not in full communion with the Church, they have true faith in Jesus. Because of complicated historical circumstances, they reject the need for the Magisterium, the teaching authority of the Church exercised by the Bishop of Rome and bishops in communion with him.

Some of these Christians belong to communities inspired by the Protestant reformation of the sixteenth century. They are generally called "Protestants," though many prefer other terms. Some refer to themselves as Catholics, e.g., Anglican Catholics or Evangelical Catholics. They are not "catholic" in the true sense of the word until they return to full communion with the Church. However, because they have been baptized and seek salvation from Jesus Christ, they are Christians.

These non-Catholic Christians are called by God to seek the full truth of Christ's revelation. They have an obligation to seek the truth as much as Catholics. When they discover that only the Pope and bishops in communion with him have a special gift from God to transmit revelation faithfully and to interpret the Scriptures correctly, the only way to follow their conscience is to accept this truth. This will be hard because some of their friends and relatives will assume they are making a mistake. It means they will have to stop attending the services organized in the Christian community they grew up with and begin to attend Mass on Sundays in a Catholic church. When they are ready, the priest at a Catholic church can receive them into full communion with the Church and invite them to receive the sacrament of Holy Communion.

Non-Christian religions

The Church does not hesitate to say that God calls all people—including Jews and Muslims—to believe in Jesus Christ and to be baptized. However, this does not mean that the Church condemns people who belong to other religions. Christians should show respect to all people, no matter what religion they follow and no matter what they believe in their hearts. Far from condemning the acts of adoration and belief that Jews and Muslims offer the one, true God, the Church praises them.

Because Christians want others to know the truth, they do not hesitate to spread the gospel to Jews, Muslims, and those following other non-Christians religions. Christians help them by telling them clearly that the whole truth can be found only in the teachings of the one, holy, catholic, apostolic Church. We tell them that Jesus has given the Church the mission to spread the gospel until he returns in glory at the end of time.

While showing respect for other religions, we need to remember that we cannot find the whole truth of God's revelation outside the Church. We believe that we have the whole truth and do not need any revelation other than the revelation that comes to us from Jesus through the Church. This may sound arrogant to non-Christians. However, it is simply the truth.

A Christian has Jesus Christ, and Jesus Christ is God. If you have Christ, you have all wisdom, all power, all glory.

> . . . [Christ] in whom we have redemption, the forgiveness of sins. He is the image of the invisible God. . . . For in him all the fulness of God was pleased to dwell. . . . For in him the whole fulness of deity dwells bodily, and you have come to fulness of life in him . . .
>
> Colossians 1:14–15, 19; 2:9–10

It is useless to seek a revelation beyond Christian revelation. It is useless to look for some spiritual perfection that was not already communicated to us through Jesus Christ. It is useless because no such perfection exists. By sending Jesus to be our Savior, God has revealed everything that can be revealed.

It is a great mistake to believe any revelation—no matter how apparently convincing it is—that does not come to us from God through Jesus Christ. Seeing their confusion, St. Paul warned the Christians in Galatia about the danger of false revelations:

> I am astonished that you are so quickly deserting him who called you in the grace of Christ and turning to a different gospel—not that there is another gospel, but there are some who trouble you and want to pervert the gospel of Christ. But even if we, or an angel from heaven, should preach to you a gospel contrary to that which we preached to you, let him be accursed. As we have said before, so now I say again, If any one is preaching to you a gospel contrary to that which you received, let him be accursed.
>
> Galatians 1:6–9

The Church teaches that, until Christ returns, there will be no additions to the revelation made through the Apostles two thousand years ago.

Any message claiming to correct that revelation contradicts Jesus and therefore must be rejected as false.

Religious freedom

Jesus asked his disciples to spread the gospel. Christians do this with the greatest respect for the beliefs of other people. The Church teaches:

> Nobody may be forced to act against his convictions, nor is anyone to be restrained from acting in accordance with his conscience in religious matters in private or in public, alone or in association with others, within due limits.
>
> Vatican II, *Declaration on Religious Freedom*, n. 2 cf. *CCC*, nn. 2104–2109

The Church speaks of religious freedom "within due limits." What are those limits? Maintaining public order is the criterion stated by the Second Vatican Council:

> Society has the right to defend itself against possible abuses committed on the pretext of freedom of religion. It is the special duty of government to provide this protection. However, government is not to act in an arbitrary fashion or in an unfair spirit of partisanship.
>
> Vatican II, *Declaration on Religious Freedom*, n. 7

No one has a right to kill others or commit other crimes, claiming that God has asked him to do it. No one has a right to practice Satanism, as if it were one more religion among many. No one has the right to love what is evil, much less adore the evil one. The government has a duty to be on guard against any abuse of religious freedom.

Therefore, the right to religious freedom demands:

- **Freedom of worship**: Everyone has a right to practice his or her belief in God—both privately and publicly—without interference from the government or from those belonging to other religions.
- **Freedom of speech:** Everyone has a right to privately express his or her belief in God to friends, relatives, and colleagues and a right to use the media to publicly express those same beliefs.

- **Maintaining public order:** The government has a duty to outlaw attacks on religious belief, to protect citizens from being forced to join a particular religion, and to provide a legal framework that allows citizens to organize themselves, building churches, synagogues, mosques, or temples where they can worship publicly.

These rights are based on the very nature of the human person. Every man and woman has a right to seek the truth, especially the truth about the mysteries that determine our ultimate fate in eternity. All parents have a right to pass on their faith to their children.

Any attempt to force people into following a particular religion—no matter how convinced its adherents are—contradicts the very nature of faith. Either people believe because of their own personal conviction and freely practice their faith or their religious practice is empty and useless. Those who force the conversion of people to their own religion are offending God, even if they think they are doing something good and holy. This is true as much for Christians as for those of other religions.

Ideologies

An ideology is a structured collection of convictions aimed at establishing an entire system of economics, politics, and social order. There are many ideologies.

By spreading the gospel, Christians try to make the world a place where it is natural to believe, natural to pray, and natural to be a good person. Unfortunately, the world is a place where faith, devotion, and uncompromising virtue remain difficult and require heroic effort. Some people find it almost impossible to imagine the world as being anything other than pagan. There are many reasons why Christians have not yet succeeded in changing society. One of the reasons is the persuasive force of several ideologies that have controlled the culture of the Western world for the past two centuries.

Liberalism, Marxism, and secularism are the main reason why many Christians have experienced doubts about their faith. They constitute systematic denials of man's need for God. Using articulate assaults on religious faith, they have led people away from God. Each one of them deserves extensive analysis. Here, they are summarized in a few lines. This will give you some idea of how much damage they have done and continue to do. While not mentioned in the summaries provided here, each of these ideologies have relied on the support of scientific research, twisted in one way or another to suit a particular argument against Christian faith.

Liberalism The leading intellectuals of the Enlightenment laid the foundations for a new theory of government. Kings and queens eventually ceased to rule nations, being replaced by presidents, prime ministers, and parliaments. Although this gave rise to democratic rule—which is good—the Enlightenment defined liberty as man's freedom from all religious authority, portraying the Church and her clergy as the enemy of progress and prosperity. In practice, the liberal ideal translated into a license to indulge in greed, lust, and oppression of the poor. Many people began to disregard the mysteries of revelation, and some openly mocked religious ideals. The prestige of several philosophers promoting liberalism gave this way of life a veneer of nobility.

Marxism While European industry grew by leaps and bounds in the nineteenth century, workers in the factories and peasants on the farms suffered brutal poverty because of unjust business practices. Karl Marx devised a new economic system with the hope of resolving this social disorder. However, his theory was anti-Christian and atheistic. Marx claimed that belief in God was one of the causes of social disorder. To solve this "problem," he said it was necessary to destroy the Church. He also claimed that revolution and class struggle would eliminate social injustice. Freedom and prosperity for the "proletariat masses" could only be achieved by slaughtering those who owned land and factories. The poor had to kill the rich. The new government had to abolish all private property.

Secularism Though neither has disappeared completely, the influence of liberalism and Marxism have declined. The overt hatred for Christian revelation and the Church, shared by these two ideologies, has transformed itself and been reborn as secularism. Secularists claim not to hate anybody or anything. They claim to be open to all truth. What they really mean is that nobody knows the truth with any certainty and that faith is a matter of feeling good about God. A secularist is happy with those who believe in divine revelation as long as they refrain from believing they know the truth. For a secularist, dogma is the enemy of freedom. When a secularist says that all believers have a moral obligation to respect people's freedom, he means believers have to set aside their religious beliefs when making decisions that affect society. People who fail to limit their faith to private affairs are considered to be religious fanatics.

How ideologies influence society

Some people in positions of influence and power—in politics, business, journalism, academia, medicine, law, and other professions—cannot tolerate any mention of God. They are intent on shutting God out of the world. This determination to shut God out of the world is the essence of secularism. (*Seculum* is the Latin word for "world.")

It is good to be secular; it is good to love the world. The world comes from God, and he has commanded us to care for it. Secularists have a different view of the world. They believe in taking care of the world but do not believe it came from God. They think man has no need of God. They think God is the enemy of our freedom. They say man does not need God to reveal what is good and evil. For the secularist, man is the one who determines what is good and evil.

Secularists do not mind what you believe in private. But they will claim you are imposing your faith on them if they sense that your faith influences the way you think and act. They are blind to how

Wisdom of the Saints

Many things, whether they be material, technical, economic, social, political, or cultural, when left to themselves, or left in the hands of those who lack the light of the faith, become formidable obstacles to the supernatural life. They form a sort of closed shop which is hostile to the Church.

You, as a Christian and, perhaps, as a research worker, writer, scientist, politician, or laborer, have the duty to sanctify those things. Remember that the whole universe—as the Apostle says—is groaning as in the pangs of labor, awaiting the liberation of the children of God.

St. Josemaría, *Furrow*, n. 311

absurd it is hold this position. They expect you to respect their desire to legislate the laws they think are best while showing no respect for your right to legislate the laws that you think are best. They expect everyone to take an agnostic position in public debate. If you do not—if you insist that faith should influence the way you think and act—they may refuse to allow you to take part in the business of organizing society and in the affairs of your chosen profession. No matter how competent you are, they may avoid entrusting you with any serious responsibility.

There are other candidates missing from this list given above—other ideologies that have done great harm to the Church and Christian faith, such as the Nazi movement in the twentieth century and, more recently, the New Age movement. Though brief, the above summary may open your eyes to the existence of powerful movements within human history that have led to massive atheism and agnosticism. It is no exaggeration to say that these ideologies have led to the ruin of many people, putting them in danger of eternal damnation. It would be foolish to ignore the hand of Satan in fostering and spreading these errors.

The Church summarizes the problem, pointing out how much damage secularism continues to do:

> The attempt to set freedom in opposition to truth, and indeed to separate them radically, is the consequence, manifestation, and consummation of another more serious and destructive dichotomy, that which separates faith from morality.
>
> This separation represents one of the most acute pastoral concerns of the Church amid today's growing secularism, wherein many, indeed too many, people think and live "as if God did not exist." We are speaking of a mentality which affects, often in a profound, extensive, and all-embracing way, even the attitudes and behavior of Christians, whose faith is weakened and loses its character as a new and original criterion for thinking and acting in personal, family, and social life. In a widely dechristianized culture, the criteria employed by believers themselves in making judgments and decisions often appear extraneous or even contrary to those of the gospel.
>
> St. John Paul II, *The Splendor of the Truth*, n. 88

In many countries, the culture that dominates is "dechristianized." It appears to be Christian because many people still call themselves Christians, but their beliefs openly contradict the gospel.

To confront this culture, God needs men and women who are willing to live their faith in the middle of the world without being afraid of what other people will say.

It is urgent, then, that Christians should rediscover the newness of the faith and its power to judge a prevalent and all-intrusive culture. As the Apostle Paul admonishes us: "Once you were darkness, but now you are light in the Lord. Walk as children of the light (for the fruit of the light is found in all that is good and right and true), and try to learn what is pleasing to the Lord. Take no part in the unfruitful works of darkness, but instead expose them. . . . Look carefully then how you walk, not as unwise men but as wise, making the most of the time, because the days are evil."

St. John Paul II, *The Splendor of the Truth,* n. 88
(cf. Eph 5:8–11, 15–16; 1 Th 5:4–8)

No matter how powerful evil appears to be, God will be victorious in the end. No matter how successful evil appears to be, we should not fear it. However, we must not forget that God wants us to overcome evil through our faith, our hope, and our love.

Asking for faith, hope, and love

To live the first commandment, we need faith, hope, and love. These are not virtues you acquire by being a good person. These virtues are gifts from God. After God gives you these virtues at the moment of baptism, he can make them grow in your soul. Tell God, "Increase my faith. Strengthen my hope. Deepen my love."

Love is the greatest of these virtues. This gift from God goes far beyond warm feelings or fleeting attractions. It is the love that gives you courage to forget about your petty ambitions and dedicate yourself to God's plans. It is the love that makes you sacrifice your whole life in order to make others happy.

This kind of love takes faith. This kind of love takes hope. You have to put your trust in God. He will show you how to make others happy.

By yourself you can do nothing to make others happy. By yourself, you might make them miserable even when trying to make them happy. The secret is to rely on God and not on yourself.

REVIEW QUESTIONS

1. Even though most of the commandments in the Decalogue (the Ten Commandments) are written as prohibitions, Christians see this as positive, instead of something merely negative. Why?
2. What are the acts commanded by God in the first commandment?
3. What are the acts prohibited by God in the first commandment?
4. What are ideologies? How have some ideologies caused harm to the Church and to people's faith in God?

24. Respecting God's Name

The second commandment

God is holy. His name is holy. You expect others to use your name with respect. Whenever you utter God's name, he expects you to show even more respect. The second commandment of the Decalogue states:

> You shall not take the name of the LORD your God in vain; for the LORD will not hold him guiltless who takes his name in vain.
>
> Exodus 20:7

God has many names. Yahweh, Elohim, and El-Shaddai are the ones used most often in the Old Testament. The New Testament speaks of God the Father and his Son, our Lord Jesus, and the Holy Spirit. Whenever you use these names, use them with the utmost respect.

The mystery of names

A name is a collection of sounds and letters from the alphabet. As Shakespeare famously put it: "A rose, by any other name, would smell as sweet." And yet, words and names have great power to affect the way we think and act. Everyone knows that calling someone a "pig" or a "dog" is an insult. Jesus condemned the practice of calling someone a "fool" (cf. Mt 5:22). Names are a force that affects people for good or for evil. St. Josemaría described this power, saying:

> Speech . . . is one of the most precious talents ever bestowed on men by God, a most beautiful gift for the expression of deep thoughts of love and friendship towards the Lord and his creatures.
>
> St. Josemaría, *Friends of God*, n. 298

Words and names have the awesome power to inspire love and to communicate love. This explains why God inspired St. John to call his Son the "Word of God."

The easiest way to get someone's attention is to call out his or her name. Why are names so powerful? One of the simplest questions people ask is also the hardest to answer—and we ask it all the time: "Who are you?" If someone asks you, the only answer you can give is to tell them your name. So you say, "Louis" or "Louise"—or whatever name your parents gave you. That's the best you can do.

Suppose your name is Louis or Louise. Does that name explain *who* you are? Not really. Your parents gave you the name because they liked the sound of it or they wanted to name you after someone else. The name does not capture the essence of who you are. And yet, it is your name, and you want others to use it with respect.

The same holds true for the name "God." This is the name we use for the One who created us. The name is just a name. It says almost nothing about the One who created heaven and earth. But it is the name we use for our Creator. That makes it the holiest name in all of creation.

Among the many names used in the Bible to speak of our Creator, one is special because it is the name he gave himself. When Moses saw the burning bush on Mount Sinai, he asked God what his name was.

> Then Moses said to God, "If I come to the people of Israel and say to them, 'The God of your fathers has sent me to you,' and they ask me, 'What is his name?' what shall I say to them?" God said to Moses, "I AM WHO AM." And he said, "Say this to the people of Israel, 'I AM has sent me to you.'"
>
> Exodus 3:13–14

Sacred Scripture

Let no evil talk come out of your mouths, but only such as is good for edifying, as fits the occasion, that it may impart grace to those who hear. And do not grieve the Holy Spirit of God, in whom you were sealed for the day of redemption. Let all bitterness and wrath and anger and clamor and slander be put away from you, with all malice . . .

Ephesians 4:29–31

The Israelites revered the name "Yahweh," this being the Hebrew equivalent of "I AM."

The name Yahweh has one peculiar feature. Because God revealed it as his own proper name, Christians realized that it says something about God's very essence. By calling himself "I AM," God has told us that his very essence is *to be*. Whereas your essence is to be a man or a woman, and St. Michael's essence is to be an archangel, God's essence is simply to be. A human being is finite. Even angels are finite. But God has no limitations. He is the fullness of pure being.

For the people of the Old Testament, that simple phrase, I AM, was the most sacred name of the many names used for God. Remember this when you read the Gospel and hear the story of the Pharisees picking up stones to throw at Jesus. They thought he was blaspheming when he called himself: "I AM." The Church teaches:

> "In the beginning was the Word." St. John is speaking of the divine pre-existence of Jesus. It is because of this pre-existence that Jesus can use the divine name "I AM": "Amen, amen, I say to you, before Abraham was, I AM" (Jn 8:58). This name indicates the fullness of being, not subject to any kind of becoming. When Jesus uses the name "I AM," he is saying that eternity has entered time, and therefore his words and actions have a value that will never pass away.
>
> St. John Paul II, *Catechesis,* November 26, 1997

Value of your words

Showing respect for God's name requires attention to little details in all your conversations. Be on guard against bad habits you may have acquired unawares, imitating the way those with no faith speak about God. The fact that you say nothing outrageous against God does not mean that your speech is pleasing to him. Jesus warned us of loose talk and idle conversation:

> I tell you, on the day of judgment men will render account for every careless word they utter; for by your words you will be justified, and by your words you will be condemned.
>
> Matthew 12:36–37

Take great care in the way you speak. You will be judged for *every* word. How much more important are those words you use to speak about God!

To learn how to respect God's name with greater finesse, look at the good deeds commanded by the second commandment and the evil he wants you to avoid.

Good deeds to do

Praise the Lord at all times There are hundreds of texts in the Bible commanding us to praise God. It is easy to praise God when things go well. If you truly love God, you will praise him even when things go wrong.

Satan tempts Job to curse God: Job 1:6–12

Pray the Lord's Prayer When Jesus taught his disciples to pray, he taught them to ask God for all the things they needed. The very first request is the petition: "May your name be held holy." We ask God to give everyone the knowledge of the truth. Then they will know that he is holy and bless his name.

Jesus teaches his disciples to pray: Luke 11:2

Give thanks to God You feel hurt if you give someone a gift and the person takes your gift for granted, especially if that gift cost you a lot. God deserves at least as much gratitude as any human being. God has given us many good things: life, faith, family, friends, etc. We have an obligation to thank him for all these blessings. God's greatest gifts cost him dearly. Jesus had to die on the cross so he could forgive our sins and then send the Holy Spirit. We thank God for this grace by celebrating the Eucharist. The word "Eucharist" means thanksgiving.

Fathers of the Church

We should give thanks to Christ when we awake, and do all the deeds of the day in the presence of the Savior. . . . The name of Christ should preside over all our actions. We should refer all the activities of our life to him. . . . And when night falls, we ought to praise him and sing his glory . . .

St. Maximus of Turin, Sermon 73, 3

Jesus rewards the Samaritan leper for giving thanks to God: Luke 17:11–19

Speak the truth under oath If you take an oath, you are calling upon God as a witness. When you swear to tell the truth, you are telling others that God himself guarantees the truth of your words. This kind of oath is used when giving testimony in court and should not be used except when necessary. When you are under oath, people have more confidence in the truth of your statement because you are asking God to reward you for telling the truth—or to condemn you for lying. An oath is also used to make a solemn promise. For instance, by "being sworn in" when taking office, politicians recognize that their authority comes from God and promise him that they will fulfil their duty. A vow is another instance where people make a promise before God. For instance, the marriage vow consists in one man and one woman making a solemn promise in a public ceremony declaring they will remain faithful to each other. When taking a vow, you commit yourself before God to keep your promise.

God swears by his own name when making his promise to Abraham: Genesis 22:16, Hebrews 6:13

Evils to avoid

Blasphemy You blaspheme whenever you deliberately show disrespect for God. The worst form of blasphemy is to put yourself in God's place, as if you were God—as if you deserved to have other people adore you. Satan blasphemes when he seeks worship from creatures, pretending to be the lord of all creation. A tyrant does something similar when thinking of himself as the master of the universe, as a ruler who has the right over the life and death of other people.

King Herod is struck down for glorifying himself instead of God: Acts 12:20–23

Insulting God This is a form of blasphemy. It consists in speaking words of hatred, contempt, or defiance against God. Some people fall into this defect by blaming God for all the evil in the world. They end up cursing God as if he himself were evil. People are guilty of this form of blasphemy when they speak with disrespect about Jesus Christ, the Blessed Virgin, the angels, the saints, or the Church.

The Assyrian king insults God at the walls of Jerusalem: 2 Kings 18:35

Abusing God's name This means using God's name in a trivial way. You do this when using God's name as if it were a curse or a swear word to express anger or surprise. Perhaps you do it without thinking. Still, it causes harm by diminishing the love and honor due to God. You show disrespect towards God whenever you reduce his importance and make him cheap, speaking of him as if he were an afterthought. In general, you should avoid swear words of all kinds, even those that do not imply disrespect for God. Remember that God hears every word you ever say.

Jesus upbraids the Pharisees for making God seem worthless compared to the Temple gold: Matthew 23:16–22

False oaths Never make a promise if you do not intend to keep it. Never make a promise to do something evil. With all the more reason, never make such a promise under oath; if you do, it is a double sin—first for desiring evil and second for asking God to help you do it. Do not swear unless there is a serious need. Some people acquire the habit of saying, "I swear to God" every time they say something they want everybody to believe. It is precisely against such an abuse that Jesus said: "Let what you say be simply 'Yes' or 'No'; anything more than this comes from evil" (Mt 5:37).

Jephthah displeases God by making a rash oath: Judges 11:29–40

Special Topics

Remembering God throughout the day

"Good-bye" is the contraction of "God be with you." It was a Christian way of saying farewell. Many other phrases, like "thank goodness" and "good night," have also lost their original meaning. Without doing anything unusual, you can revive the Christian custom by remembering the real meaning of such phrases every time you use them.

Many people blurt out offensive phrases without thinking. You will be more conscious of God's presence in your life if, instead, you keep acts of praise and thanksgiving on the tip of your tongue. For instance, it is easy to say, "Thanks be to God," every time something good happens. You can say, "Have mercy on us, O Lord," whenever you see something that offends God and does harm to others.

Controlling your tongue

Be careful of the way you speak about others. Comparing your tongue to a fire raging in a forest, St. James describes how much harm you do when destroying a person's good name.

> So the tongue is a little member and boasts of great things. How great a forest is set ablaze by a small fire!
>
> And the tongue is a fire. The tongue is an unrighteous world among our members, staining the whole body, setting on fire the cycle of nature, and set on fire by hell. For every kind of beast and bird, of reptile and sea creature, can be tamed and has been tamed by humankind, but no human being can tame the tongue—a restless evil, full of deadly poison. With it we bless the Lord and Father, and with it we curse men, who are made in the likeness of God.
>
> James 3:5–9

It makes no sense to speak well about God and then turn around and speak ill of your neighbor. Just as God's name deserves respect, the names of those you live and work with also deserve respect. Everyone has a right to their good name.

Every name is a mystery. God's name is holy. The more clearly we understand what it means to be created in God's image and likeness,

MAGISTERIUM

Among all the words of revelation, there is one which is unique: the revealed name of God. God confides his name to those who believe in him; he reveals himself to them in his personal mystery. The gift of a name belongs to the order of trust and intimacy. "The Lord's name is holy." For this reason man must not abuse it. He must keep it in mind in silent, loving adoration. He will not introduce it into his own speech except to bless, praise, and glorify it.

Catechism of the Catholic Church, n. 2143

the more we respect the names we use for one another. Christian parents apply this logic when giving names to their children. God himself will use this name, given at baptism, to call that child later in life. The *Catechism* says:

> God calls each one by name. Everyone's name is sacred. The name is the icon of the person. It demands respect as a sign of the dignity of the one who bears it.
>
> *CCC*, n. 2158

God does not deal with us as a mass of nameless robots, as if we were slaves with no choice but to do whatever he commands. We are his image and likeness. We are his children, and he calls each one of us by our name personally. He asks us to serve him with a spirit of freedom and love.

Because God knows us better than anyone, the time will come for him to tell us our true name. Referring to this future act, the *Catechism* quotes the Book of Revelation:

> The name one receives is a name for eternity. In the kingdom, the mysterious and unique character of each person marked with God's name will shine forth in splendor. "To the one who proves victorious, I will give the hidden manna and a white stone—a stone with a new name written on it that no one knows except the one who receives it."
>
> CCC, n. 2159; Rev 2:17

If you "prove victorious," that is, if God allows you to enter the kingdom, he will give you a new name. This secret name will be a unique name that captures the essence of the person you truly are.

God links his name with man

When revealing himself to Moses, before calling himself "I AM," God first says, "I am the God of your father, the God of Abraham, the God of Isaac, and the God of Jacob" (Ex 3:6). God is mysterious. His name is also mysterious. In some sense, he changed it when he made a covenant with Abraham, Isaac, and Jacob. Having made the covenant, he began to call himself the "God of Israel." Yahweh spoke to Jeremiah, asking him to address the Israelites:

> You shall say to them, Thus says the LORD, the God of Israel: Cursed be the man who does not heed the words of this covenant . . . and do all that I command you. So shall you be my people, and I will be your God . . .
>
> Jeremiah 11:3, 4

By calling himself the "God of Israel," God made it clear that he belonged to Israel and that they belonged to him. To emphasize this sense of belonging to one another, God inspired the prophets to speak of him as the "husband of Israel" and to speak of Israel as his bride. The Church teaches:

> In choosing Israel, God is united with his people through love and grace. He is bound with a special bond, profoundly personal. Therefore Israel, even though a people, is presented in this prophetic vision of the covenant as a spouse or wife, and therefore, in a certain sense, as a person: "For your Maker is your husband . . ." (Is 54:5). Yahweh is the Lord of Israel, but he also becomes her Spouse.
>
> St. John Paul II, *Theology of the Body*, p. 358

This union of God with Israel foreshadows Christ's union with the Church. As God somehow changes his name—and therefore his identity—the Son of God changes his identity when he becomes the Bridegroom for the Church.

Wisdom of the Saints

God's name is holy. "At the name of Jesus every knee should bow, in heaven and on earth and under the earth" (Phil 2:10). *Those in heaven* refers to the angels and the saints. *Those on earth* refers to the people living in this world who do so for the love of heaven which they wish to enter. *Those in the underworld* refers to the damned who praise God out of fear.

St. Thomas Aquinas, *Commentary on the Lord's Prayer* (first petition)

REVIEW QUESTIONS

1. What does sacred Scripture say about God's name?
2. What are the acts commanded by God in the second commandment?
3. What are the acts prohibited by God in the second commandment?
4. Why is it important to control your tongue?

25.

Keeping the Lord's Day Holy

The third commandment

Sunday is the Lord's Day. It is a holy day, that is, a day set aside for God. Many people think of it merely as a holiday. They have forgotten that "holiday" comes from the phrase "holy day." Because Sunday is a holy day, we cannot treat it the same way we treat other days of the week. Therefore, in the third commandment, God says:

> Remember the sabbath day, to keep it holy. Six days you shall labor, and do all your work; but the seventh day is a sabbath to the Lord your God; in it you shall not do any work, you, or your son, or your daughter, your manservant, or your maidservant, or your cattle, or the sojourner who is within your gates; for in six days the Lord made heaven and earth, the sea, and all that is in them, and rested the seventh day; therefore the Lord blessed the sabbath day and hallowed it.
>
> Exodus 20:8–11

The Old Testament—the old covenant between God and Israel—was centered on the seventh day. It was the Lord's Day because God "rested" on the Sabbath after creating the world.

Jesus established a new covenant by dying on the cross and rising from the dead. In the New Testament, Sunday is the day dedicated to God. It is the day when the Son of God "rested" after completing his "work"—when he rose from the dead after offering sacrifice for our sins. It is the day of the "new creation." By resurrecting, Jesus made all things new (cf. 2 Cor 5:17). He made it possible for all men and women to be "born again" (cf. Jn 3:3–8).

The Lord's Day

The name "Sunday" comes from pagan worship of the sun. Jesus has changed that and turned Sunday into the Lord's Day. All Sundays of the year are holy days. St. Jerome, one of the Church Fathers, wrote:

> The Lord's Day—the day of resurrection, the day of Christians—is our day. It is called the Lord's Day because this was the day the Lord rose victorious to the Father. If pagans call it the "day of the sun," we willingly agree, for today the light of the world is raised, today is revealed the "Sun of Justice" with healing in his rays.
>
> St. Jerome, cf. *CCC*, n. 1166

Since Sunday is the Lord's Day, we need to do something special in order to dedicate this day to God.

Going to Sunday Mass

From the beginning, Christians have traditionally celebrated the Lord's Day by gathering together for the celebration of the Eucharist. We see the evidence for this in the Acts of the Apostles. There St. Luke explains how the Christians in Ephesus met for the breaking of the bread—for the celebration of the Eucharist—"on the first day of the week" (Acts 20:7). The most important obligation Christians have on Sunday is to attend Mass.

About a hundred years after Jesus rose from the dead, St. Justin wrote a lengthy description of Sunday Mass. He was writing a letter to Emperor Antoninus. He explained how Christians would come from all over—within the city and from the countryside—gathering in a place where they could celebrate the Eucharist.

The Eucharist is the greatest of the seven sacraments. The Church teaches:

> It is crucially important that all the faithful should be convinced that they cannot live their faith or share fully in the life of the Christian community unless they take part regularly in the Sunday Eucharistic assembly. The Eucharist is the full realization of the worship that humanity owes to God, and it cannot be compared to any other religious experience.
>
> St. John Paul II, *The Lord's Day*, n. 81

SACRED SCRIPTURE

Six days shall work be done; but on the seventh day is a sabbath of solemn rest, a holy convocation; you shall do no work; it is a sabbath to the LORD in all your dwellings.

Leviticus 23:3

In the other sacraments, we receive God's grace. In the Eucharist, we receive Christ himself. Therefore, the life of the Church revolves around the celebration of Mass.

The Mass is so important for Christians that the Church insists that we go to Mass on all Sundays of the year and all holy days of obligation, like Christmas. As soon as children are old enough to understand what is happening at Mass, they should go to Sunday Mass. God wants parents to pass on their faith to their children by bringing them to Mass with them.

Perhaps because they have yet to discover how important the Eucharist is, some Christians are not sure why they need to go to Mass every Sunday. There are many ways to explain why the Church has always insisted on going to Mass every Sunday. One is the presence of Jesus on the altar.

When the priest celebrates Mass, Jesus becomes present on the altar. His body is on the altar. His blood is in the chalice. He is there. You cannot see him. But it is Jesus—the same Jesus that was born in Bethlehem, the same Jesus that was nailed to the cross and then rose from the dead, the same Jesus with wounds in his hands and feet, the same Jesus who now sits at the right hand of his Father in heaven. That Jesus is on the altar, and he wants you to be there with him. If you are too busy or too lazy to go to church on Sunday—the day of his resurrection—don't expect him to be happy with you on the day of your resurrection. If you deliberately skip Mass and then insist that you really want to be with Jesus in his kingdom, your actions contradict your words. How can you tell Jesus you want to live with him *forever* if you can't spend a couple of hours with him on Sunday?

Going to Mass on Sunday is not optional for a person who loves God above all things. Unless they are seriously ill or taking care of a family member who is sick, people show up for work. And if it's a special day, when the boss is waiting for them to come, they would never think of skipping work just because they would rather stay home and relax.

If that is the attitude people have towards work and making money, shouldn't a Christian be even more willing to go to church on Sunday and be with Jesus?

The Letter to the Hebrews mentions the practice of going to Mass on Sunday:

> . . . not neglecting to meet together, as is the habit of some, but encouraging one another, and all the more as you see the Day drawing near.
>
> Hebrews 10:25

The "Day drawing near" refers to the day of our resurrection from the dead. This New Testament text was warning Christians not to fall into the habit of skipping Mass—a habit that some of them had developed.

Which comes first: God or the world? You offend God when deeds show that your business, your parties, your sports, and your comfort in bed are more important than going to church. If you cannot put God first in your plans for Sunday, how will you learn to put him first during the ordinary days of the week? Remember the words of Origen, an early Christian writer:

> The perfect Christian lives every day as the Lord's Day and is always celebrating Sunday.
>
> Origen, cf. *The Lord's Day*, n. 83

Sunday is a day of rest

In the Old Testament, the Sabbath rest was one of the most serious obligations. The Law of Moses stated that the Sabbath was a day "of solemn rest, a holy convocation; you shall do no work" (Lev 23:3). For other great feast days in the calendar, the Law stated: "You shall do no laborious work" (Lev 23:36). This was a stark contrast to the days of slavery in Egypt when the Israelites were never allowed to rest. The obligation to rest was a blessing from God.

By rising from the dead on the first day of the week, Jesus announces a totally new "sabbath rest." He has promised to raise the saints from the dead and take them into his kingdom where they will rest forever.

This new creation is often called the "eighth day" in early Christian writings. (The greatest feasts of the Old Testament concluded, after a week of celebrations, on the eighth day. Sunday is the *eighth day* since it comes after the seventh.) Every Sunday is a day to remember Jesus' resurrection and look forward to our own resurrection.

Christ entered into his Sabbath rest by rising from the dead. Our resurrection will be the moment when we enter into our Sabbath rest, that is, when we reach our final goal, our eternal perfection. God wants us to anticipate this event by resting every Sunday.

For centuries, until recent times, people worked for six days and rested only one day a week. Now many people work for five days and have the whole weekend free. The Church explains the gospel approach to this phenomenon:

> All of this responds not only to the need for rest, but also to the need for celebration. . . . Unfortunately, when Sunday loses its fundamental meaning and becomes merely part of a "weekend," it can happen that people stay locked within a horizon so limited that they can no longer see "the heavens." Hence, though ready to celebrate, they are really incapable of doing so.
>
> The disciples of Christ, however, are asked to avoid any confusion between the celebration of Sunday—which should truly be a way of keeping the Lord's Day holy—and the "weekend," understood as a time of simple rest and relaxation.
>
> Today I would strongly urge everyone to rediscover Sunday: Do not be afraid to give your time to Christ! Yes, let us open our time to Christ, that he may cast light upon it and give it direction. He is the One who knows the secret of time and the secret of eternity, and he gives us "his day" as an ever new gift of his love. Time given to Christ is never time lost, but is rather time gained.
>
> St. John Paul II, *The Lord's Day*, nn. 4, 7

You will not lose time by dedicating it to God. You will gain time. By being closer to God, you will know how to use your time better. You will work better during the week. Your hours of study will lead you to deeper understanding. Your time with your family and friends with be filled with greater joy. You will have peace in your soul and the desire to share it with others. These are the reasons why we need to dedicate one day of rest to God instead of just running around for the weekend.

Good deeds to do

Attend Mass on Sunday Christians in full communion with the Church must go to Mass every Sunday and attend the whole Mass, from the opening prayers until the final dismissal. (Being in full communion with the Church is what most people call being a Catholic, a Christian who accepts the authority of the Pope.) Catholics can attend Sunday Mass in any Catholic church. They can fulfill their obligation to attend Sunday Mass by attending Mass during the evening of the previous day (also called the "vigil Mass"). They do not fulfill this obligation by attending services in some other Christian community: Anglican, Lutheran, Presbyterian, Baptist, etc.

Christians gathered to celebrate the Eucharist: Acts 2:42–46

Keep the holy days of obligation Obligation here means that Christians are obliged to attend Mass. The holy days of obligation are those special days, like Christmas, when Christians should go to Mass and rest from work the same as they would on Sunday. The bishops in each country determine which days are holy days of obligation.

The Israelites celebrated special feasts in addition to the Sabbath day: Leviticus 23:5–36

Rest from work Sunday is not just another day for business as usual. You need to rest. Resting does not mean wasting the day lying in bed. (Unless you're sick, that is not rest; it's sheer laziness.) Rest means changing activity and doing something fun, something that helps you relax. There is no easy rule. The cooking, carpentry, or gardening that is relaxing to someone who works in an office all week would be tedious for the person who uses such activities to

Fathers of the Church

Those who lived according to the old order of things have come to a new hope, no longer keeping the sabbath, but the Lord's Day, in which our life is blessed by him and by his death.

St. Ignatius of Antioch, cf. *CCC*, n. 2175

earn a living. The idea is to rest in some way that gives each person a break from the routine of daily work. Employers have an obligation to make sure their employees rest at least one day a week.

God establishes the sabbath rest as a sign of the covenant between himself and Israel: Exodus 31:12–17

Make Sunday a family day As the rushing around to get jobs done makes it harder to spend time with your family, the need to stop and take better care of your parents, spouse, and children becomes more urgent. It is also the ideal time to visit the sick, the elderly, and the lonely.

Jesus declares the Sabbath as the day for works of mercy: Matthew 12:9–13

Evils to avoid

Missing Mass on Sunday If you deliberately skip Sunday Mass for no good reason, you commit a serious sin. You are excused from attending Mass if you have some serious difficulty that makes attendance impossible—if you are sick; if there is no Mass at your church and other churches are too difficult to reach; if you have to care for a sick person; if you have some public duty from which you cannot be excused. All of this applies equally to missing Mass on holy days of obligation.

Some Christians were reproached for failing to attend "the meetings": Hebrews 10:25

Work that hinders worship and leisure While those running businesses should avoid work on Sundays, some services, like transportation and restaurants, are necessary to help people rest. Even so, God wants us to reject the tendency to make Sunday one more day of business simply to make money. While it is impossible to go beyond generalities when defining how people should rest on Sundays, one idea applies to everyone: activities meant to help people rest are wrong if they make it impossible to go to Mass on Sunday. Going for an outing or a picnic becomes an obstacle to rest if it prevents you from being together with Jesus for the celebration of the Eucharist.

Nehemiah reprimands the Jewish leaders for doing business on the sabbath: Nehemiah 13:15–22

Special topics

Hunger for the Eucharist

In most countries Christians have all the leisure in the world to attend Mass on Sunday. The early Christians had to endure great hardships to gather together for the Eucharist on Sundays. This is the story of the catacombs and the early Roman martyrs. Some Roman emperors, like Diocletian, persecuted Christians for attending Sunday Mass.

> When, during the persecution of Diocletian, their assemblies were banned with the greatest severity, many were courageous enough to defy the imperial decree and accepted death rather than miss the Sunday Eucharist. This was the case of the martyrs of Abitina, in Proconsular Africa, who replied to their accusers: "Without fear of any kind we have celebrated the Lord's Supper, because it cannot be missed; that is our law"; "We cannot live without the Lord's Supper." As she confessed her faith, one of the martyrs said: "Yes, I went to the assembly and I celebrated the Lord's Supper with my brothers and sisters, because I am a Christian."
>
> St. John Paul II, *The Lord's Day*, n. 46

MAGISTERIUM

Sharing in the Eucharist should be the heart of Sunday for every baptized person.

St. John Paul II, *At the Beginning of the New Millennium*, n. 36

If you are ever faced with a situation making it difficult to attend Mass, remember the attitude of the early Christian martyrs. This can stir up the same kind of hunger they had to be with our Lord no matter what the cost.

The weekly Easter and the weekly Pentecost

Do you want to keep the Lord's Day holy? Every Sunday, remember that the end of the world is coming. Every Sunday, remember that the world as we know it will soon change. Ever since Jesus rose from the dead, we have been living in the last times.

The Church encourages us to think this way, warning us against the temptation to look at this world as our permanent home.

Wisdom of the Saints

"O taste and see that the LORD is good!" (Ps 34:8) . . . Just as the tired body needs rest, so does the soul. But the soul's proper rest is in God. . . . However, before the soul arrives at this rest, three other kinds of rest must come first.

The first is the rest from the turmoil of sin: "But the wicked are like the tossing sea; for it cannot rest" (Is 57:20). The second rest is from carnal passions: "For the desires of the flesh are against the Spirit, and the desires of the Spirit are against the flesh" (Gal 5:17). The third rest is from the occupations of the world: "Martha, Martha, you are anxious and troubled about many things; one thing is needful. Mary has chosen the good portion, which shall not be taken away from her" (Lk 10:41–42).

St. Thomas Aquinas, *Catechetical Instructions*
(Third Commandment)

> Since Sunday is the weekly Easter, recalling and making present the day when Christ rose from the dead, it is also the day that reveals the meaning of time. It cuts through human time—the months, the years, the centuries—like a directional arrow that points Christians toward their target: Christ's Second Coming . . . Everything that will happen until the end of the world will be no more than an extension and unfolding of what happened on the day when the battered body of the Crucified Lord was raised by the power of the Spirit and became in turn the wellspring of the Spirit for all humanity.
>
> St. John Paul II, *The Lord's Day,* n. 75

Jesus' resurrection was both spectacular and unexpected. Our resurrection will be the same. Everything that happens to you here on earth is nothing more—and nothing less—than a preparation for the day when you will rise from the dead. Jesus had his Easter two thousand years ago. You will have your Easter some day in the future. God wants you to take at least one day a week to remember it.

This does not mean locking ourselves up in church waiting for something that may not take place for another thousand years. Christians gather together for the Eucharist in order to be filled with God's grace. It is a peace and a love that urges us to shout from the rooftops.

> Sunday, the day of light, could also be called the "day of fire." . . . The outpouring of the Spirit was the great gift of the Risen Lord to his

> disciples on Easter Sunday. It was again Sunday when, fifty days after the Resurrection, the Spirit descended in power, as "a mighty wind" and "fire" upon the Apostles gathered with Mary. Pentecost is not only the founding event of the Church, but is also the mystery that forever gives life to the Church. . . . The "weekly Easter" thus becomes, in a sense, the "weekly Pentecost," when Christians relive the Apostles' joyful encounter with the Risen Lord and receive the life-giving breath of his Spirit.
>
> St. John Paul II, *The Lord's Day*, n. 28

After receiving the Spirit at Pentecost, Jesus' disciples went out to tell everyone else the Good News. At the end of Mass, the priest sends Christians away from the church to the places where they live and work. Sunday is the "weekly Pentecost" where God fills us with the Holy Spirit so that we may go out and talk to our friends about the joy of knowing Jesus.

How to attend Mass

Showing up for Mass on Sunday does not mean going to church and standing outside so you can chat with your friends. Even if some people call it "going to church," it is the same as missing Mass. You have to take part in the celebration. God does not need a warm body filling a bench to make the ceremony look like a success. As Jesus told the Samaritan woman at the well, God the Father wants believers who will worship him "in spirit and truth" (Jn 4:24).

When you attend Mass, pray the prayers. Don't mumble. Speak intelligibly. Say "Amen" with conviction. Sing the hymns. If you don't know the prayers and hymns, learn them.

Beware of the false notion that you go to church to be entertained. It does not matter if the singing and preaching are not up to your standards. Though they can help, sermons and music are not the reason why God wants you to go to Mass every Sunday. You go there to worship Jesus Christ. No matter who the priest is—worthy or unworthy—no matter what kind of Christians gather in church, Jesus makes himself present whenever the Eucharist is celebrated. His body and blood become present on the altar. It's him—Jesus—and he's there for you.

REVIEW QUESTIONS

1. Why do Christians call Sunday the Lord's Day?
2. What are the acts commanded by God in the third commandment?
3. What are the acts prohibited by God in the third commandment?
4. Why is Sunday called the "weekly Easter" and the "weekly Pentecost"?

26.

Honoring Your Parents

The fourth commandment

This is the one commandment in the Decalogue that includes a promise:

> Honor your father and your mother, that your days may be long in the land which the Lord your God gives you.
>
> Exodus 20:12

To honor your parents, you need to respect them and love them. "Children, obey your parents in the Lord, for this is right," writes St. Paul (Eph 6:1). As long as you remain under the authority of your parents, God expects you to obey them.

Why do you owe such a great debt to your parents? There are many reasons. The most obvious is the sacrifice they made to bring you into this world. They raised you to be a responsible young man or woman.

You probably cannot remember all the sleepless nights your mother spent taking care of you. You cannot imagine how crucial it was for your sense of peace and security to have a father giving you patient guidance day after day for years until you were mature enough to make your own decisions. These facts are already enough to explain the debt of gratitude you owe your parents. There is, though, a deeper mystery.

The mystery of being a parent

You are bound to honor your parents because they are the ones who cooperated with God to bring you into existence.

Your mother carried you in her womb and gave birth to you. The prophets often depicted God caring for his people using the image of a mother caring for her child (cf. Is 42:14; 46:3–4; 49:14–15; 66:13; Ps 131:2–3). To understand the sacrifices God has made for you, look at the way your mother pampered you when you were a baby. Because of his relationship with you, your father also led you to know God. Remember how Jesus taught us to use this name—Father—to speak to God?

There is a certain resemblance between God and your parents. Reflect on this mystery and you will understand why, in some sense, the fourth commandment comes first in practice. The image God wants you to have of him was meant to begin with the image you have of your father and mother. Even if your parents have their defects—they are only human, after all—they did give you life. This is an image of the eternal life God wants to give you.

Sacred Scripture

For the Lord honored the father above
the children,
and he confirmed the right of the
mother over her sons.
Whoever honors his father atones for sins,
and whoever glorifies his mother is
like one who lays up treasure.
Whoever honors his father will be
gladdened by his own children,
and when he prays he will be heard.
Whoever glorifies his father will have
long life,
and whoever obeys the Lord will
refresh his mother.
O son, help your father in his old age,
and do not grieve him as long as
he lives;
even if he is lacking in understanding,
show forbearance;
in all your strength do not despise him.
Whoever forsakes his father is like
a blasphemer,
and whoever angers his mother
is cursed by the Lord.

Sirach 3:2–6,12–13,16

Respecting authority

Just as every child has an obligation to honor his or her parents and obey them, all citizens have a similar obligation to honor and obey their religious and political leaders.

Questions arise when defining the need to obey ruling authorities. Further questions arise about the relationship between church authority and government authority (also called "ecclesiastical" and "civil" authority). To answer these questions, we have to ask where authority comes from.

Your first notion of authority begins with your parents. As you grow up, your respect for authority at home leads you to respect God's authority. This leads you to respect all human authority.

Your parents' authority comes from God. So does the authority of the Church. Even the government's authority comes from God. This teaching comes from the Apostles. They taught this truth at the very beginning of the history of the Church when Christians were beginning to wonder whether the government had any authority over them. The Roman emperor was persecuting them. Many Christians suffered martyrdom after enduring cruel torments. Even so, St. Peter insisted:

> Be subject for the Lord's sake to every human institution, whether it be to the emperor as supreme, or to governors as sent by him to punish those who do wrong and to praise those who do right. . . . Honor all men. Love the brotherhood. Fear God. Honor the emperor.
>
> 1 Peter 2:13–14, 17

To be good citizens, Christians obey the just laws of the country where they live. They also obey international laws as agreed upon among the nations of the world.

Note the term "just laws." A law is *just* when it commands some deed that fits with the demands of justice. An unjust law is a law that contradicts one of God's commandments. If a law goes against the demands of justice, you have no obligation to obey it—and in some cases, you may have a strict obligation to disobey it. The most common example of an unjust law is the one declaring that mothers have a right to take the life of their child by having the unborn baby aborted. If anyone ever tries to force you to cooperate in an abortion, you have an obligation to refuse, no matter what the law says. Act as the Apostles acted. When commanded to disregard God's law and obey the decision of the Sanhedrin, they stated, "We must obey God rather than men" (Acts 5:29).

Any government or institution that issues an unjust law or policy is abusing the authority it has received from God. This does not mean that the government has lost all authority. Citizens must continue to respect the authority that has issued the unjust law or policy. In the meantime, they defend their legitimate right to resist the unjust law and to organize means to change it.

Good deeds to do

Honor your parents This means showing them respect and obeying them. By leading a virtuous life, you honor your parents because all will assume you learned discipline from them. When convinced that it would be evil in God's eyes to obey a particular order from your parents or elders, you should refuse to comply. Otherwise, as long as a child lives at home, the fourth commandment demands obedience—even when your parents seem to make unreasonable demands. Once you leave home to start your own life, you acquire new responsibilities. God calls you to form your own family or to follow some other vocation to do his work. Though you are no longer bound to obey your parents in these new circumstances, you are still obliged to respect them. In their old age, you also have a duty to support them, especially when they are sick or lonely or distressed.

Jesus submits to his parents as a child in Nazareth: Luke 2:51

Respect ecclesiastical authority This means showing the same respect for the Pope and the bishops that you would show Jesus and the Apostles. It also means obeying the laws of the Church and supporting the Church as needed. Because revelation comes from God and cannot be changed, you have no right to criticize the Church's teaching. However, within the government of the Church, some matters are questions of opinion. For example, in all affairs concerning ways of using money or land to build and operate churches, schools, and hospitals, ordinary Christians work together with the hierarchy by giving timely advice and occupying positions of responsibility when appropriate.

St. Joseph and the Blessed Virgin Mary go to the Temple to fulfill the law of purification: Luke 2:22–24

St. Peter reminds Christians how they must obey the elders: 1 Peter 5:5

Respect civil authority This means showing respect for leaders of government. Because everyone has a right to suggest improvements in public policy, you have a right—sometimes a duty—to criticize laws, legislative proposals, and public projects, trying to win support for better ways of managing resources. However, this must be tempered by the need to respect the opinions of others, refraining from personal attacks.

St. Joseph goes to Bethlehem to register for the census: Luke 2:1–5

Fulfill your duties as a parent Besides cooperating with God to bring children into the world and to provide for their basic needs, this means educating them in faith and morals. Your children need lessons about prayer and the law of God. They also need to learn by imitating what you do. They need to see you pray, go to confession, receive Holy Communion, exercise self-control, care for the poor and the sick, etc. You need to choose a school for them where they can learn Christian virtues and live them. You need to respect their freedom when they choose their profession and state in life, while at the same time giving them advice and guiding them through difficulties.

St. Paul tells parents to strike a proper balance between severity and lenience: Ephesians 6:4

Fulfill your duties as a citizen Begin by obeying all just laws and paying taxes. You have a duty to cooperate with others to build up the common good, especially for the poor. You also have a duty to love and serve your country while also appreciating the nobility and achievements of other nations. This is patriotism. Demand your *rights* as a citizen because you need them in order to fulfill your *obligations* as a citizen.

St. Paul demands an apology from the magistrates: Acts 16:35–40

Fulfill your duties as a leader This means using your authority to promote the common good. This means setting policies that facilitate the creation of wealth for all citizens, as opposed to policies that favor only the rich. It also means protecting the fundamental rights of all individuals: right to life; to freedom of worship; to food, clothing, and shelter; to employment; to forming a family, to free expression of political opinion, to migration, etc.

St. John the Baptist reminds Herod that even kings have to obey God's law: Luke 3:19–20

Evils to avoid

Disobeying parents This means refusing to do what your parents ask.

God punishes the sons of Eli for refusing to obey their father: 1 Samuel 2:22–36; 4:11

Disrespecting parents This means speaking or acting against your parents, either privately contradicting them or publicly bringing shame upon them. Any evil you do tends to reflect on your family, and on your parents in particular.

Ham, one of the sons of Noah, makes fun of his father's mistake: Genesis 9:20–27

Ingratitude This is the failure to appreciate the sacrifices your parents have made for you. This also applies to any lack of patriotism—either because you despise your homeland or you refuse to make sacrifices for the common good of your compatriots.

Esau sells his birthright for a plate of beans: Genesis 25:29–34

Disobeying authorities This means refusing to follow the just laws established by the legitimately established government, either locally, nationally, or internationally. Treason is the extreme case; this means attempting to destabilize or overthrow the legitimate authority of your own country.

Korah leads a rebellion against Moses: Numbers 16:1–35

Disrespecting authorities This means insulting a leader of government. It includes any show of contempt for office by using words or gestures that imply defiance, that is, a total refusal to obey that arises when you do not want to have any authority over you. This is sometimes called a *disordered* desire for independence. While no one should be subjected to slavery, everyone is subject to some form of authority. If a slave wins freedom, such independence is noble and just. If a free citizen refuses to submit to the lawful authority of government, his desire for independence is out of order because he is doing harm to the common good. He is acting unjustly and deserves to be restrained and perhaps punished as well.

Aaron and Miriam speak against Moses claiming to have as much as authority as their brother had: Numbers 12:1–10

Abusing authority This means taking advantage of political power to make yourself rich, persecute your rivals, make yourself indispensable, seek personal glory, or exempt yourself from the rule of law.

God punishes Heliodorus for trying to steal funds meant to support widows and orphans: 2 Maccabees 3:1–34

Fathers of the Church

Why should they not be according to Joseph [the two genealogies of Jesus Christ in the Gospel (cf. Mt 1:16 and Lk 3:23)]? Was he not Mary's husband? . . . Scripture states, through the authority of an angel, that he was her husband. "Do not fear," says the angel, "to take Mary your wife, for that which is conceived in her is of the Holy Spirit." Joseph was told to name the child, although not born from his seed. "She will bear a son," the angel says, "and you will call him Jesus."

Scripture recognizes that Jesus is not born of Joseph's seed, since in his concern about the origin of Mary's pregnancy, Joseph is told that it is of the Holy Spirit. Nonetheless, he is not deprived of his fatherly authority from the moment that he is told to name the child. Finally, even the Virgin Mary, well aware that she has not conceived Christ as a result of conjugal relations with Joseph, still calls him Christ's "father" (Lk 2:48).

By reason of [Mary and Joseph's] faithful marriage, both of them deserve to be called Christ's parents, not only his mother, but also his father, who was a parent in the same way that he was the mother's spouse—in mind, not in the flesh.

St. Augustine, cf. St. John Paul II,
The Person and Mission of St. Joseph, n. 7

Nationalism This means showing disrespect for the good qualities of other nations. You think your country is better than others. You assume you have a right to treat other nations as inferior and their citizens as your servants. This vice, which is often confused with patriotism, also manifests itself as racism or tribalism. It usually leads to slavery, oppression, exploitation, hatred, and war.

St. James explains how pride in one's wealth leads to bloodshed: James 3:16–4:3

Special Topics

Priorities in a family

God wants us to love everyone. But this does not mean that we have to treat everyone the same. Justice requires priorities, especially when it comes to loving others and especially when it comes to organizing family activities.

The best thing a couple can do for their children is to love each other very much. Speaking to husbands, one of the Church fathers pointed out this need centuries ago:

MAGISTERIUM

The "civilization of love" is strictly bound up with the family. For many people, the civilization of love is still a pure utopia. Indeed, there are those who think that love cannot be demanded from anyone and that it cannot be imposed: Love should be a free choice which people can take or leave.

There is some truth in all this. And yet there is always the fact that Jesus Christ left us the commandment of love—just as God on Mount Sinai ordered, "Honor your father and your mother." Love then is not a utopia. It is given to mankind as a task to be carried out with the help of divine grace. It is entrusted to man and woman in the sacrament of matrimony, as the basic principle of their "duty," and it becomes the foundation of their mutual responsibility: first as spouses, then as father and mother. In the celebration of the sacrament, the spouses give and receive each other, declaring their willingness to welcome children and to educate them. On this hinges human civilization, which cannot be defined as anything other than a "civilization of love."

Yes, the civilization of love is possible; it is not a utopia. But it is only possible by a constant and ready reference to the "Father from whom all fatherhood (and motherhood) on earth is named" (cf. Eph. 3:14–15), from whom every human family comes.

St. John Paul II, *Letter to Families*, n. 15

> Show your wife you appreciate her a lot and that—because she is there—you prefer to be at home rather than outside. Show her preference among all your friends and even above the children she has given you. Love them because of her.
>
> St. John Chrysostom, *Commentary on Ephesians*, 20

To put this into practice, the husband and wife have to make time for each other. Instead of letting work become the priority, both husband and wife have to put the family first. This means getting home early instead of late, if they work outside the home. It also means overcoming any tendency to think that a career in the professional world is more "fulfilling" than being a good spouse and a good parent.

God gives the husband and wife a vocation to love each other. The husband must give priority to his wife and the wife must give priority to her husband. No matter how much attention parents give their children, the children only feel secure when they see that their father and mother love each other. Children feel confused, rebellious, and resentful when they sense that their father and mother do not get along. Some parents assume that they have to put the child first. This is a mistake. They should give priority to God first and then to each other. Paradoxically, parents who give first priority to the children do harm to their children in several ways.

For instance, some parents think they have to make their children as comfortable as possible. They become anxious about getting money to buy things for their children. They fail to see how this anxiety teaches their children to become materialistic instead of spiritually sensitive to the things of God.

Some parents think that having more children will be harmful to the children they already have. The reverse is true. The children will benefit more from having another brother or sister than they will from having their own room, their own toys, their own computer, etc.

Society and authority

All that was said above about respecting authority is the foundation for the Church's teaching on social issues—what we call the Church's "social doctrine." To understand it better, we have to explain what we mean by society.

The Church is a society. Every nation is a society. Any grouping of people for a common cause is a society. All societies need authority. An individual has authority within a society when he or she can expect others to obey after making a decision.

Man is social by nature. To develop his or her own personality, each person needs the companionship of other people. Our social nature requires living together for another reason. By coordinating efforts, ten people working together can accomplish more than ten people working on their own. This gives rise to the need for having an authority that can make decisions for the common good.

Citizens must respect and obey those in charge. But those in charge must be careful not to abuse their authority. They should command only those deeds that are truly necessary for the common good. This demand of good government can be divided into four specific needs:

1. Promote subsidiarity This means allowing people to do what they are capable of doing instead of trying to do things for them. Subsidiarity requires a balance. On one hand, the government has to foster the common good; for instance, getting everyone to work together to build roads, dams, schools, hospitals, etc. On the other hand, the government must promote private initiative and not allow people to become dependent on handouts. A government must collect some goods (usually in the form of taxes) and then distribute them wisely to promote the common good. However, the government does not exist to collect all goods and then distribute them. It exists to make laws and enforce them, setting policies that allow people to manage their own affairs in a way that benefits both themselves and everyone else.

2. Refuse personal benefit Leaders are not given authority so they can grab as much as they can from everybody else for their own benefit. Any leader who acts this way is a criminal. The most furious condemnations in sacred Scripture are directed against such men and women (cf. Am 6:1—9:10; Jm 5:1–6). Leaders have an obligation to serve the people under their authority.

3. Protect the weak and the poor The rich and the powerful can protect themselves. Widows, orphans, and other people in similar straits are often at the mercy of unscrupulous manipulators who manage to turn the law to their own advantage and leave the poor to suffer in misery. One of the main functions of government is to protect the poor and the weak by ensuring that their rights are respected. Since the unborn child and the elderly poor are the weakest members of society—at times having no one to protect them, not even their own relatives—the leaders of society have a special duty to defend them.

4. Respect the fundamental rights of all citizens All people have a right to life and a right to exercise their talents when doing their work to earn a living. They have a right to form a family and care for it. They have a right to free association and a right to express their opinions. The rights of any one citizen are limited by the equivalent rights of his or her neighbors. These rights are natural and inalienable—*natural* because they come from God, not from the government; *inalienable* because they do not depend on the mood of the majority and cannot be ignored when others find it profitable or convenient to do so.

Civil disobedience

There are times when the government enacts a law or establishes a policy that causes grave harm. Citizens have a right and a duty to raise their voice and unite in common cause to correct it. In recent times, some governments have abused their authority by enacting laws legalizing abortion-on-demand, laws making it easy for couples to divorce, laws permitting the cloning of human embryos, and laws prohibiting Christians from being able to gather for public worship.

When it is necessary to oppose such decisions, citizens have a right to engage in peaceful demonstration against the government and to resist its attempt to impose the unjust policy. If the government suspends the right of citizens to protest and the injustice requires urgent action, citizens can take the risk of engaging in civil disobedience. This means risking arrest by ignoring the government's refusal to allow citizens to protest.

Wisdom of the Saints

The parents are the first persons responsible for the education of their children, in human as well as in spiritual matters. They should be conscious of the extent of their responsibility. To fulfill it, they need prudence, understanding, a capacity to love, and a concern for giving good example. Imposing things by force, in an authoritarian manner, is not the right way to teach. The ideal attitude of parents lies more in becoming their children's friends—friends who will be willing to share their anxieties, who will listen to their problems, who will help them in an effective and agreeable way.

Parents should find time to spend with their children, to talk with them. They are the most important thing—more important than business or work or rest. In their conversations, parents should make an effort to listen, to pay attention, to understand, to recognize the fact that their children are sometimes partly right—or even completely right—in some of their rebellious attitudes. At the same time, they should help their children to direct their efforts and to carry out their projects properly, teaching them to consider things and to reason them out. It is not a matter of imposing a line of conduct, but rather of showing the human and supernatural motives for it. In a word, parents have to respect their children's freedom, because there is no real education without personal responsibility, and there is no responsibility without freedom.

St. Josemaría, *Christ Is Passing By*, n. 28

Military coups and revolutions cannot be compared to civil disobedience. These are violent actions that often cause great harm to nations, lasting for decades. It means overthrowing a legitimately established government. The *Catechism* teaches:

> Armed resistance to oppression by political authority is not legitimate, unless all the following conditions are met: 1) there is certain, grave, and prolonged violation of fundamental rights; 2) all other means of redress have been exhausted; 3) such resistance will not provoke worse disorders; 4) there is well-founded hope of success; and 5) it is impossible reasonably to foresee any better solution.
>
> *CCC*, n. 2243

Even if driven by desperate need to get rid of a corrupt government that has lost all authority, military coups and revolutions are rarely, if ever, a wise decision. They can easily leave no one in authority. Then the most ruthless people take control.

Familiar as she is with corrupt regimes that have ruined both the economy and the spiritual health of various nations, the Church urges citizens to persist patiently in finding ways of resolving disputes without using violence.

> It is a question of showing that the complex problems faced by those peoples can be resolved through dialogue and solidarity, rather than by a struggle to destroy the enemy through war.
>
> The Gospel parable of the weeds among the wheat teaches that it is for God alone to separate the subjects of the kingdom from the subjects of the Evil One, and that this judgment will take place at the end of time. By presuming to anticipate judgment here and now, man puts himself in the place of God and sets himself against the patience of God.
>
> St. John Paul II, *On the Human Person* (*Centesimus Annus*), nn. 22, 25 (cf. Mt 13:24–43)

No regime is perfect. Even the holiest leaders of government make mistakes when deciding what will be best for the common good. And even corrupt leaders may have some virtues and may feel some responsibility for helping their people.

Citizens have the right to establish the political regime they judge best for their needs and to appoint the rulers of their choice. However, the desire to improve everything at once causes more harm than good. Any decision to improve requires political experience, broad-based education, and time for people to assimilate new ways.

Helping your family come closer to God

Ask God to take care of your family. This is the best way of showing gratitude for all they have done for you. Pray for them. Your prayers will move God to help them in ways that you cannot imagine.

When visiting Nazareth, the village where he grew up, Jesus had to quote the proverb: "No prophet is acceptable in his own country" (Lk 4:24). If Jesus had a hard time with his relatives, you have to expect some opposition from yours, too. If you find that one of your relatives—father, mother, child, spouse, sibling—refuses to accept your faith in Christ, be patient and be humble. Do not judge. Do not argue. Arguments generate lots of heat and little light.

Though it is good to explain what you believe, do not rely on your ability to speak. Pray that God will give them the same grace he has given you. Then they will understand—or at least cease to oppose you. Perhaps the same words that used to make them angry will come from their own mouths—and with greater conviction and eloquence than you ever had yourself.

REVIEW QUESTIONS

1. Explain the distinction between the need to obey just laws and to oppose unjust laws.
2. What are the acts commanded by God in the fourth commandment?
3. What are the acts prohibited by God in the fourth commandment?
4. What is necessary for good government?

27.

Respecting Life

The fifth commandment

Look at any human being: man, woman, or child. The life of that person is sacred. Only God has the right to decide whether this person will live or die. Each and every human being is the image and likeness of God. Jesus Christ shed his blood for every single one of us. Respect all human life, no matter how weak or sick the person seems to you. There is no such thing as a useless human life.

To respect life, the first priority is to protect life. The fifth commandment of the Decalogue states this clearly:

> You shall not kill.
>
> Exodus 20:13

This commandment asks us to respect life. It also demands overcoming any tendency towards hatred and anger. The *Catechism* explains this by recalling the golden rule: Treat others the same way you want them to treat you.

> Scripture specifies the prohibition contained in the fifth commandment: "Do not slay the innocent and the righteous." The deliberate murder of an innocent person is gravely contrary to the dignity of the human being, to the golden rule and to the holiness of the Creator. The law forbidding it is universally valid: it obliges each and everyone, always and everywhere.
>
> In the Sermon on the Mount, the Lord recalls the commandment, "You shall not kill," and adds to it the proscription of anger, hatred, and vengeance. Going further, Christ asks his disciples to turn the other cheek, to love their enemies.
>
> CCC, nn. 2261–2262

Turning the other cheek does not mean you should be a pacifist, resigned to suffer in silence when others violate your rights.

You have a right to life. All other human beings have the same right. Because *they* have a right to life, you should not kill them or harm them. Because *you* have a right to life, you have a right to defend yourself when someone tries to kill you or harm you.

Abortion is murder

Abortion takes place when the mother of an unborn child—or anyone else—decides to end the pregnancy by doing something to kill the baby. There are many ways of doing this. The medical procedure may bear a technical name like "terminating pregnancy." Do not be fooled by euphemisms. To abort unborn babies, doctors butcher them or poison them. They extract the pieces and throw the dead baby in the garbage as if it were trash. Abortion is murder. It is a deliberate desire to get rid of an unborn baby by killing it—by making sure it dies.

Abortion is everywhere. It is the most common form of murder in today's world. Blessed Mother Teresa of Calcutta used to say that the womb of a mother has become the most dangerous place on earth. This is a fact. More human beings die in their mother's womb than anywhere else. For many decades abortion has been the number one cause of death.

The problem has become so serious that hundreds of millions of men and women have been directly involved in an abortion. Anyone who has will find it painful to face the reality of their guilt before God. Still, they need to know that abortion is murder. This is not meant to condemn anyone. On the contrary, the Church only wants to help those guilty of this sin to seek forgiveness. God always forgives as long as we repent.

God prohibits murder

Long before God gave Moses the Ten Commandments, he warned the people of ancient times to refrain from shedding blood.

There is nothing more at odds with Christian faith than the desire to kill another human being. St. John links the need to respect life with the commandment of love:

> For this is the message which you have heard from the beginning, that we should love one another, and not be like Cain who was of the evil one and murdered his brother. And why did he murder him? Because his own deeds were evil and his brother's righteous.
>
> 1 John 3:11–12

Jesus said that Satan was a murderer from the beginning. People who murder become evil—as evil as Satan. They "belong to the Evil One."

The Book of Genesis describes how Cain killed Abel. Abel was innocent. Cain tricked him into taking a walk in the fields and murdered him in cold blood. God was angry. He appeared to Cain and said:

> What have you done? The voice of your brother's blood is crying to me from the ground.
>
> Genesis 4:10

God condemns murder as one of the most serious sins a man or woman can ever commit. It is a crime that cries out to heaven for justice.

People did not learn from Cain's experience. They fell into habits of great wickedness. It was so bad that "the LORD was sorry that he had made man" (Gen 6:6) and decided to destroy the world with the Flood. He saved only Noah and his family. After floating on the floodwaters in the ark and once again settling on dry ground, Noah heard God tell him to refrain from shedding innocent blood:

SACRED SCRIPTURE

Cain said to the LORD, "My punishment is greater than I can bear. Behold, thou hast driven me this day away from the ground; and from thy face I shall be hidden; and I shall be a fugitive and a wanderer on the earth, and whoever finds me will slay me." Then the LORD said to him, "Not so! If any one slays Cain, vengeance shall be taken on him sevenfold." And the LORD put a mark on Cain, lest any who came upon him should kill him.

Genesis 4:13–15

> For your lifeblood I will surely require a reckoning . . . of man; of every man's brother I will require the life of man. Whoever sheds the blood of man, by man shall his blood be shed; for God made man in his own image. And you, be fruitful and multiply, bring forth abundantly on the earth and multiply in it.
>
> Genesis 9:5–7

These two commands go together: have lots of children and never kill anybody. God loves life and hates death. He wants a universe full of life. He wants many children—more than we can imagine. He prohibits murder and will punish anyone who commits it.

Murder takes place all the time, tens of millions of times every year. It is your problem, and it is my problem. If there is one great moral danger that you face, this is it. We have all become used to murder. We hardly pay attention when it happens. Don't let yourself be seduced by the frequency of this crime. The fact that it takes place day in, day out, year after year, does not mean that God ignores it. Do not think that the Scriptures are exaggerating when they speak of God's justice:

> For we know him who said, "Vengeance is mine, I will repay." And again, "The Lord will judge his people." It is a fearful thing to fall into the hands of the living God.
>
> Hebrews 10:30–31

God is just. He will not allow murderers to keep killing for all eternity. One day he will put an end to all bloodshed. The Book of Revelation describes that moment with eerie finality: "Thy wrath came, and the time . . . for destroying the destroyers of the earth" (Rev 11:18).

God is just. He is also merciful. He loves life so much that even when punishing, he wants the murderer to change and become a good person who will no longer shed innocent blood.

> But if a wicked man turns away from all his sins which he has committed and keeps all my statutes and does what is lawful and right, he shall surely live; he shall not die. None of the transgressions which he has committed shall be remembered against him; for the righteousness which he has done he shall live. Have I any pleasure in the death of the

> wicked, says the Lord God, and not rather that he should turn from his way and live?
>
> Ezekiel 18:21–23

All your sins will be forgiven if you repent. However, don't make the mistake of thinking God will look the other way if you defy him by shedding innocent blood and refusing to be sorry.

Good deeds to do

Recognize the sanctity of all human life This means cultivating an interior disposition—a spiritual reflex—that leads you to look at other human beings as your brothers and sisters. Never think of someone as a rival or an enemy. Love all people, no matter what their race, their color, their tribe, their social standing, their health, or their habits. Even criminals deserve your respect because they can repent and become holy. Their conversion may depend on having someone who can be compassionate and understanding with them.

Jesus commands us to love our enemies: Luke 6:27–35

Defend life You always have a right to defend yourself and your family against an unjust aggressor. Depending on your duties (for instance, if you belong to the police force), you may have an obligation to use force against an unjust aggressor. When repelling an unjust aggressor, use as much force as necessary but no more. While it would be legitimate self-defense to strike a lethal blow to someone trying to shoot you, it would wrong to kill a thief who has already started to run away or to kill a neighbor because you suspect he wants to kill you. An aggressor, e.g., someone threatening you with a weapon, is *unjust* when using

Fathers of the Church

God drove Cain out of his presence and sent him into exile far away from his native land, so that he passed from a life of human kindness to one which was more akin to the rude existence of a wild beast. Because he preferred the correction rather than the death of a sinner, God did not want a homicide to be punished by the exaction of another act of homicide.

St. Ambrose, cf. St. John Paul II, *The Gospel of Life*, n. 9

force against you without any right to do so. However, if you are the criminal and the police use force to arrest you, you are guilty of killing an innocent person if you kill someone while resisting arrest.

St. Paul explains the divine authority behind the "power of the sword": Romans 13:4

Comfort the dying This means showing a sick person warmth and affection. At the very least, you must provide food and water and other basic necessities. You may also want to provide special medical treatment, like having an operation. However, if medical treatment has ceased to offer any hope of healing the patient or it becomes burdensome to the patient, you can suspend it, even if this will hasten the moment of death. Likewise, you can use medicines to relieve pain, even if these shorten the patient's life or reduce consciousness, as long as you do so not to bring about death but to help the patient endure his or her suffering calmly. You are guilty of euthanasia whenever you *seek* the patient's death and then *cause* it. In the case of terminating medical procedures or using painkillers, it is not euthanasia because you do not intend the patient's death and, in fact, would like the patient to survive.

Parable of the Good Samaritan: Luke 10:29–37

Evils to avoid

Homicide This means taking the life of an innocent person. It is called murder when it is direct, i.e., when you kill the person yourself. It is still seriously wrong when indirect—i.e., when you place someone in danger hoping it will lead to death.

God punishes David for killing Uriah: 2 Samuel 12:9

Abortion This is a special case of homicide. It means killing a child while still in the mother's womb. If a doctor needs to carry out a medical procedure to save the life of a pregnant woman, knowing this could be harmful to the unborn child, no one is guilty of abortion if the child dies as long as every reasonable effort was made to save the child. However, it is murder if the doctor decides to kill the unborn child even if he does it only because he wants to save the mother's life. No one has the right to save another person's life by killing an innocent person. An unborn child is always innocent. An unborn child can never be considered as an unjust aggressor, as if the mother had a right to defend herself against her own child.

God gives life to the child in the womb: Psalm 139:13–15; Jeremiah 1:5
St. John the Baptist, still in his mother's womb, recognizes the presence of Jesus, the unborn baby in the Virgin's womb: Luke 1:39–44
God punishes the Israelites for killing their babies: Psalm 106:36–40

Euthanasia This is a special case of homicide. It means causing death to someone who is suffering—either by doing something or failing to do something—with the intention of causing death so that the person will cease to suffer. Even though the intention is good—alleviating the suffering of the sick and the elderly—the action (or omission) is evil. You do not have the right to dictate who should live and who should die. Nor do you have the right to say *when* someone should die. If you deliberately

Magisterium

Therefore, by the authority which Christ conferred upon Peter and his Successors, and in communion with the Bishops of the Catholic Church, I confirm that the direct and voluntary killing of an innocent human being is always gravely immoral.

Therefore, by the authority which Christ conferred upon Peter and his Successors, in communion with the Bishops—who on various occasions have condemned abortion and who in the aforementioned consultation, albeit dispersed throughout the world, have shown unanimous agreement concerning this doctrine—I declare that direct abortion, that is, abortion willed as an end or as a means, always constitutes a grave moral disorder, since it is the deliberate killing of an innocent human being.

Euthanasia in the strict sense is understood to be an action or omission which of itself and by intention causes death, with the purpose of eliminating all suffering. Euthanasia must be distinguished from the decision to forego so-called "aggressive medical treatment," in other words, medical procedures which no longer correspond to the real situation of the patient, either because they are by now disproportionate to any expected results or because they impose an excessive burden on the patient and his family. Taking into account these distinctions, in harmony with the Magisterium of my Predecessors and in communion with the Bishops of the Catholic Church, I confirm that euthanasia is a grave violation of the law of God, since it is the deliberate and morally unacceptable killing of a human person.

St. John Paul II, *The Gospel of Life*, nn. 57,62,65

withdraw food and water from a patient, this constitutes an omission that causes death and is therefore an act of euthanasia.

God alone is Lord of life and death: Deuteronomy 32:39; Job 12:10; 1 Samuel 2:6

Suicide This means taking your own life. You are not the master of your own life. God is. If you are in pain, if you are unhappy with your life, God wants you to endure your suffering patiently. When you suffer, look at Jesus dying on the cross. Thank him for giving you a chance to share his suffering. By sharing his suffering now in this world, you prepare yourself to share his glory in the next life. If you know of someone who has committed suicide, the Church asks you not to despair of that person's salvation, even though the person has done something seriously wrong. Faith teaches us to believe that God has ways, known only to him, by which he helps people repent even in the most tragic circumstances.

Sarah wants to commit suicide because she is miserable: Tobit 3:10

Scandal This means leading another person into sin. When you scandalize someone, you cause his or her spiritual death—a death that could lead to eternal condemnation. You cause scandal by asking another person to commit a sin together with you, for instance, engaging in acts of pre-marital sex or committing adultery. You also cause scandal any time you command someone to do something wrong or merely recommend the idea. Business leaders who set up businesses—or government officials who legislate laws—that encourage evil deeds (such as fraud, pornography, divorce, or abortion) are guilty of causing scandal. This includes those who prey on human weaknesses to make a profit, encouraging people to get drunk, use drugs, visit prostitutes, etc. It also includes those people that teach teenagers to use contraceptives.

Jesus speaks of tying a millstone around the neck of those causing scandal: Matthew 18:6

Violent assault This means causing physical or psychological harm to another person. It includes terrorism, torture, and kidnapping. It also includes provoking a fight or quarrel, desiring vengeance, and any kind of anger resulting from annoyance, bitterness, or hatred towards your neighbor. Not all anger is evil. Anger is sometimes necessary—and therefore justified—in order to restore public order or to protect the rights of the innocent.

Jesus says that anyone angry with his brother is liable to judgement: Matthew 5:21–26

Jesus cleanses the Temple: John 2:13–22

Seeking revenge This means getting back at someone for some evil you had to suffer unjustly. Those who quote the Old Testament phrase about "eye for an eye and tooth for a tooth" have forgotten Jesus' command to "love your enemies" (cf. Mt 5:38–48).

David refuses to curse King Saul even when being persecuted: 1 Samuel 24:1–16

Insulting others Jesus calls insults a sin against the fifth commandment: "If a man calls his brother 'Fool,' he will answer for it before the Sanhedrin; and if a man calls him '*Raca*,' he will answer for it in hell fire" (cf. Mt 5:22). (*Raca* seems to be the Greek version of an Aramaic word *reqah* meaning "empty-headed.") Insults destroy an atmosphere of peace and love and can ruin the lives of innocent people. Jokes that insult others are evil jokes.

All the insults used against Sarah lead her to despair: Tobit 3:7–10

Drug abuse The fact that a chemical substance produces a strong effect on your mind or body does not make it evil. Medicines can do great good by relieving pain or healing mind and body. Caffeine (e.g., in coffee and tea) can help a person be more alert. Alcohol produces a sedative effect and is not harmful when taken in small quantities. Drug abuse means using a chemical substance—even if it is a medicine—in any way that does harm to your mind or body. Drugs most abused include marijuana, cocaine, and heroin, plus synthetic drugs like amphetamines. Besides being affected by the drug and putting yourself at risk of a premature death, you do great harm to yourself if you become a drug addict. You lose control over your life. You become incapable of working and fulfilling your other obligations. While smoking a cigarette is not necessarily evil (since the smoke has no immediate harmful effect), tobacco is often abused, and the habit of smoking can lead to premature death.

References to dissipation and debauchery apply to drug abuse: Luke 21:34; Galatians 5:21

Alcohol abuse This means drinking so much alcohol that you get drunk. By losing your ability to reason, you do serious harm because, when intoxicated, you act without knowing what you are doing. You have deliberately put yourself in a situation where you can do great harm to others and not even realize it. Therefore, even if you do no harm while drunk, intentionally getting drunk is seriously wrong. You do great harm to your own body when you acquire a habit of heavy drinking, usually leading to premature death.

Drunkards cannot enter the kingdom of God: 1 Corinthians 6:10

Special Topics

War

War means two or more nations fighting with each other. The Church praises those who serve in the armed forces, risking their lives to defend their country. "If they carry out their duty honorably, they truly contribute to the common good of the nation and the maintenance of peace" (CCC, n. 2310). However, the obligation of political leaders is to avoid war. Using military force must always be the last resort when all attempts to keep peace have failed.

The *Catechism* lists conditions to be judged when deciding whether a nation is justified in declaring war or engaging in military conflict:

1. The damage inflicted by the aggressor on the nation or community of nations must be lasting, grave, and certain.
2. All other means of putting an end to it must have been shown to be impractical or ineffective.
3. There must be serious prospects of success.
4. The use of arms must not produce evils and disorders graver than the evil to be eliminated. The power of modern means of destruction weighs very heavily in evaluating this condition.

CCC, n. 2309

If *all* of these conditions exist, a nation has a right to use military force to defend itself, even though this leads to enormous loss of human life on both sides. Political leaders have the responsibility for declaring war and working towards peace once war begins. When rebels revolt against the government, the same criteria are used when judging the use of military force internally.

For those directly involved in a war, it can be difficult to judge which nation is the unjust aggressor and which is defending itself. When war breaks out, political leaders have an obligation to limit the number of casualties on both sides of the conflict. Being at war does not justify the use of weapons of mass destruction. The Church teaches:

> Every act of war directed to the indiscriminate destruction of whole cities or vast areas with their inhabitants is a crime against God and man, which merits firm and unequivocal condemnation.
>
> Vatican II, *The Church in the Modern World*, n. 80

The gospel says little on the topic of war. What little it says is a sober warning. Why do war and terrorism continue to threaten us?

> What causes wars, and what causes fightings among you? Is it not your passions that are at war in your members? You desire and do not have; so you kill. And you covet and cannot obtain; so you fight and wage war.
>
> James 4:1–2

Following the reasoning of St. James, the Church insists that greed of the rich against the poor continues to be the main reason for war. After witnessing the ravages of war in his own country and around the world, Pope John Paul II declared:

> "Never again war!" No, never again war, which destroys the lives of innocent people, teaches how to kill, throws into upheaval even the lives of those who do the killing and leaves behind a trail of resentment and hatred, thus making it all the more difficult to find a just solution to the very problems which provoked the war. . . . At the root of war there are usually real and serious grievances: injustices suffered, legitimate aspirations frustrated, poverty and the exploitation of multitudes of desperate people who see no real possibility of improving their lot by peaceful means.
>
> St. John Paul II, *On the Human Person* (*Centesimus Annus*), n. 52

Political leaders who tolerate corruption and thus fail to ensure economic development are guilty of sowing the seeds of war. Political leaders who initiate war, invading another nation, cause harm to the whole world and remain responsible for the devastation they have caused by ignoring possibilities for a peaceful settlement.

Political leaders should feel responsible for promoting the welfare and security of all peoples. Among other initiatives, they must do what is in their power to reduce the sale of arms and the development of weapons. The mere possession of costly weapons often incites nations to war. The sense of having wasted vast sums of money drives leaders to use the weapons before they become obsolete. Worse still, using limited financial resources to buy weapons, especially in undeveloped nations, aggravates poverty and greed, which are the root cause of all war.

Capital punishment

Political leaders, including judges and law enforcement officials, have an obligation to apprehend criminals and imprison them. However, the goal of punishment is not only to protect citizens from danger to life and property but also to correct criminals and reform them, teaching them how to serve the common good.

While deserving punishment when proven guilty, criminals still retain certain rights. For this reason, inflicting the death penalty should be used only as a last resort. The *Catechism* teaches:

> Assuming that the guilty party's identity and responsibility have been fully determined, the traditional teaching of the Church does not exclude recourse to the death penalty, if this is the only possible way of effectively defending human lives against the unjust aggressor. If, however, non-lethal means are sufficient to defend and protect people's safety from the aggressor, authority will limit itself to such means, as these are more in keeping with the concrete conditions of the common good and more in conformity with the dignity of the human person.
>
> CCC, n. 2267

In *The Gospel of Life*, St. John Paul II goes on to explain that cases where the death penalty remains the only way of protecting society from further harm are "very rare, if not practically nonexistent" (n. 56).

Non-lethal means of protecting society include the option of life imprisonment. This provides criminals with the possibility of repenting, finding salvation, and seeking holiness. While some remain hardened criminals, others have changed their lives completely in such circumstances. Besides, some prisoners condemned to death have eventually been proven innocent.

Special penalty for abortion

Because abortion is one of the greatest evils in the world today, the Church attaches a special penalty to this sin. It is called "excommunication." The *Catechism* explains:

> Formal cooperation in an abortion constitutes a grave offence. The Church attaches the canonical penalty of excommunication to this crime against human life. A person who procures a completed abortion incurs excommunication. . . . The Church does not thereby intend to restrict the scope of mercy. Rather, she makes clear the gravity of the crime committed, the irreparable harm done to the baby who is put to death, as well as to the parents and the whole of society.
>
> *CCC*, n. 2272

The penalty of excommunication falls on anyone who cooperates effectively in an act of abortion. The mother who asks for the abortion, the father who pays for it, anyone who encourages the woman to do it—besides being guilty of serious sin—are excommunicated by the very fact of deliberately and knowingly committing this sin. This also includes doctors and nurses who do the abortion, though in their case the crime is especially heinous because they are the ones who kill the baby.

Being excommunicated means that they have separated themselves from communion with the Church. They can no longer receive Holy Communion until they go to confession and the excommunication is lifted by the competent authority. If it is public knowledge that a Catholic performs abortions, or that a Catholic actively supports abortion either by campaigning politically in favor of it or by promoting access to abortion, then priests cannot allow this person to receive Holy Communion.

Call for help

At times a pregnant woman feels desperate because giving birth seems likely to ruin her future. It is often called a "crisis pregnancy." If you know a woman in this situation, try to encourage her to contact a pro-life organization or a crisis pregnancy center. There is usually one available if you take the trouble to look for it.

A crisis pregnancy center gives pregnant women guidance and practical help. The woman usually thinks that giving birth to the child will ruin her life, while an abortion will solve her problem. She doesn't know that an abortion will destroy her spiritually, psychologically, and perhaps even physically. By helping a woman give birth to the baby, you are saving her from disaster.

Connection between abortion and contraception

Abortion is everywhere. This is the sad fact of the world we live in. At times human life is treated like trash. Based on abortion rates published by those keeping official statistics, about 1 billion unborn babies have been murdered in the past century. It depends on how accurate the statistics are, of course. However, the history of the phenomenon is clear and well-documented. Since the 1960s, into the present millennium, abortion-on-demand has become routine almost everywhere in the world. But that is only half the story. The abortion statistics only count abortions performed when the doctor doing the abortion was sure that the mother was pregnant.

Judging the number of abortions counted in official statistics depicts a grim situation. There is more. First there is the massive problem of abortifacient contraceptives. This type of contraceptive produces many abortions never counted in statistics. Many methods used by women to avoid conception (pills, implants, coils) rely on chemical or mechanical devices that are designed not only to prevent fertilization but also to kill the child conceived, if for some reason conception takes place. These devices get rid of the baby before the woman discovers she is pregnant. Such contraceptives are called "abortifacient." The name literally translates as "abortion causing" contraceptives. The clearest case of the abortifacient contraceptive is the so-called "morning after pill," also known

Magisterium

What is urgently called for is a general mobilization of consciences and a united ethical effort to activate a great campaign in support of life. All together, we must build a new culture of life . . .

In particular, there is a need for education about the value of life from its very origins. It is an illusion to think that we can build a true culture of human life if we do not help the young to accept and experience sexuality and love and the whole of life according to their true meaning and in their close interconnection.

Sexuality, which enriches the whole person, manifests its inmost meaning in leading the person to the gift of self in love. The trivialization of sexuality is among the principal factors that have led to contempt for new life. Only a true love is able to protect life. There can be no avoiding the duty to offer, especially to adolescents and young adults, an authentic education in sexuality and in love, an education that involves training in chastity as a virtue that fosters personal maturity and makes one capable of respecting the "spousal" meaning of the body.

St. John Paul II, *The Gospel of Life*, nn. 95, 97

as "emergency contraception." It is designed to make sure the unborn child is expelled before getting a chance to attach to the mother's womb and develop naturally.

The number of women using abortifacient contraceptives is measured by the tens of millions. There is no way of knowing for one particular woman how often a new human life is killed by these contraceptives. The woman herself has no idea. It all takes place invisibly. In any case, the number of children dying in their mother's womb because of these contraceptives could be a very large number, one that dwarfs the usual statistics on abortion. It could be double or triple the number of clinical abortions.

The fact that nobody sees it does not make the problem any less serious. Any woman using abortifacient contraceptives is using a product that can kill an unborn child in her womb just as systematically as cutting the baby to pieces in a clinical abortion. Most people do not know this because companies do not stick a label on their products saying "abortifacient." They just call them "contraceptives." This leads most women to believe mistakenly that the products do nothing more than prevent fertilization.

Asking all men and women to take the matter seriously, the Church explains:

> Despite their differences of nature and moral gravity, contraception and abortion are often closely connected, as fruits of the same tree. It is true that in many cases contraception and even abortion are practised under the pressure of real-life difficulties, which nonetheless can never exonerate from striving to observe God's law fully. Still, in very many other instances such practices are rooted in a hedonistic mentality unwilling to accept responsibility in matters of sexuality, and they imply a self-centred concept of freedom, which regards procreation as an obstacle to personal fulfillment. The life which could result from a sexual encounter thus becomes an enemy to be avoided at all costs, and abortion becomes the only possible decisive response to failed contraception.
>
> The close connection which exists, in mentality, between the practice of contraception and that of abortion is becoming increasingly obvious. It is being demonstrated in an alarming way by the development of chemical products, intrauterine devices, and vaccines which, distributed with the same ease as contraceptives, really act as abortifacients in the very early stages of the development of the life of the new human being.
>
> St. John Paul II, *The Gospel of Life*, n. 13

A contraceptive mentality arises from the use of contraceptives. This leads to social acceptance of abortion. Once couples have made up their minds that they will do anything to avoid the conception of a child, abortion seems like a solution to their "problem" whenever contraceptives fail. When contraceptives began to be used by hundreds of millions of women in the twentieth century, it changed the way people understand sex. This changed the way people look at human life. Both became trivial. We created a culture of death.

Although it may strike you as being utterly impossible, society must reject the use of contraceptives. As long as people think contraceptives are good, they will find themselves thinking that abortion is necessary. As the Church teaches, the two cannot be separated. The only way to stop the widespread practice of abortion is to convince people that the contraceptive mentality is evil.

Special questions in biotechnology

All over the world, it has become routine for medical personnel in fertility clinics and biologists doing research in laboratories to take sperm from men and ova from women, store them, and then mix them. It happens millions of times every year. Every time biotechnicians do this, conception takes place the same way it takes place in the womb—a new human life comes into being. The mixing process in a clinic or laboratory is called *in vitro fertilization* ("vitro" meaning glass, referring to glass dish or tube where the fertilization occurs).

Some researchers act with no intention of creating new human life. They mistakenly think human life begins several weeks after fertilization. Whether or not the researchers know what they are doing, the practice constitutes a serious crime against humanity. As biotechnicians carry out these procedures, they destroy the vast majority of the new lives created. The procedure also leads to experimentation on innocent human beings, making human life trivial and numbing the consciences of all those involved.

To explain the evil involved in this procedure, the Church teaches:

> The various techniques of artificial reproduction, which would seem to be at the service of life and which are frequently used with this intention,

WISDOM OF THE SAINTS

[Abortion] is really a war against the child, and I hate the killing of innocent children, murder by the mother herself. And if we accept that the mother can kill even her own child, how can we tell other people not to kill one another?

How do we persuade a woman not have an abortion? As always we must persuade her with love. . . . The father of that child must also give until it hurts. . . . By abortion the father is taught that he does not have to take any responsibility at all for the child. . . . So that father is likely to put other women into the same trouble. So abortion just leads to more abortion.

Any country that accepts abortion is not teaching its people to love one another but to use any violence to get what they want. This is why the greatest destroyer of love and peace is abortion.

Blessed Mother Teresa of Calcutta, National Prayer Breakfast Speech,
Washington, D.C., February 3, 1994

> actually open the door to new threats against life. Apart from the fact that they are morally unacceptable, since they separate procreation from the fully human context of the conjugal act, these techniques have a high rate of failure: not just failure in relation to fertilization but with regard to the subsequent development of the embryo, which is exposed to the risk of death, generally within a very short space of time. Furthermore, the number of embryos produced is often greater than that needed for implantation in the woman's womb, and these so-called "spare embryos" are then destroyed or used for research which, under the pretext of scientific or medical progress, in fact reduces human life to the level of simple "biological material" to be freely disposed of.
>
> St. John Paul II, *The Gospel of Life*, n. 14

To respect the dignity of every child, fertilization should take place only in the mother's womb. Deliberately planning conception outside the mother's womb is seriously wrong, even when carried out for the noble purpose of helping childless couples conceive.

It is the procedure that the Church condemns. The Church teaches that all those men and women who have been conceived outside their mother's womb are precious to God and just as capable of salvation as any other human being.

Review Questions

1. What are the acts commanded by God in the fifth commandment?
2. What are the acts prohibited by God in the fifth commandment?
3. Describe the obligations of a political leader when confronted with the possibility of war.
4. Describe the tragic effects of abortion in the world today.

28. Respecting Marriage

The sixth commandment

The sixth commandment of the Decalogue summarizes God's plan for marriage. It states:

> You shall not commit adultery.
>
> Exodus 20:14

Besides forbidding adultery, the Law forbids all acts of promiscuity. These are mentioned in other sections of the Bible (cf. Leviticus 15, 18, and 20).

In his infinite wisdom God decided to make sexual union the way to create new human life. He also decided that he would join a man and woman—making the two become one—through their act of becoming "one flesh." He wants the man and woman to get married before engaging in acts of sexual intimacy.

Just as God is the Lord of life and death, he is the Lord of human sexuality. You do not decide what is good and what is evil when engaging in sexual acts. God alone decides this. In his covenant with Abraham, God made this visible by demanding that all men be circumcised. Because he had faith, Abraham obeyed. From then on, all boys born among the people of Israel were circumcised on the eighth day—including Jesus himself—as a sign of the covenant between God and his people. This shows that sexual intimacy between husband and wife is sacred. Acts contrary to God's plan for marriage are an abomination in his eyes.

We must show the same respect towards human sexuality that we show towards human life. To explain how God connects these two realities, St. Josemaría wrote:

> We have been created by God and endowed with an intelligence which is like a spark of the divine intellect. Together with our free will, another gift of God, it allows us to know and to love. And God has also placed in our body the power to generate, which is a participation in his own creative power. He has wanted to use love to bring new human beings into the world and to increase the body of the Church. Thus, sex is not a shameful thing; it is a divine gift, ordained to life, to love, to fruitfulness.
>
> This is the context in which we must see the Christian doctrine on sexuality. Our faith does not ignore anything on this earth that is beautiful, noble, and authentically human. It simply teaches us that the rule of our life should not be the selfish pursuit of pleasure, because only sacrifice and self-denial lead to true love.
>
> St. Josemaría, *Christ Is Passing By*, n. 22

According to the Church's teaching, sexual intimacy for a married couple is beautiful, noble, and authentically human as long as the man and woman respect God's plan for marriage.

Jesus defines purity

The Old Testament emphasized ritual purity. The many precepts for physically cleansing the body with water—not to mention dozens of household items like pots and pans—built up a culture that focused on external purity. Add to this more precepts regulating clean and unclean food. Anyone who failed to keep these precepts to the letter was "unclean" and therefore "impure." The ninth commandment emphasized the gravity of interior acts of impurity, but with the passing of time, people ceased to give much importance to what was in their heart. They paid attention only to external deeds.

Jesus changed that. When he commented on the sixth commandment, he redefined the virtue of purity and emphasized *spiritual* cleanliness. By talking to us about the human heart, he changed the focus from exterior cleansing to interior purity.

> You have heard that it was said, "You shall not commit adultery." But I say to you that every one who looks at a woman lustfully has already committed adultery with her in his heart.
>
> Matthew 5:27–28

Sacred Scripture

When the door was shut and the two were alone, Tobias got up from the bed and said, "Sister, get up, and let us pray that the Lord may have mercy upon us." And Tobias began to pray,

"Blessed art thou, O God of our
fathers,
and blessed by thy holy and glorious
name for ever.
Let the heavens and all thy
creatures bless thee.
Thou madest Adam and gavest him
Eve his wife
as a helper and support.
From them the race of mankind
has sprung.
Thou didst say, 'It is not good that the
man should be alone;
let us make a helper for him
like himself.'

And now, O Lord, I am not taking this sister of mine because of lust, but with sincerity. Grant that I may find mercy and may grow old together with her." And she said with him, "Amen." Then they both went to sleep for the night.

Tobit 8:4–9

Adultery is the act of a married man or woman having sexual relations with someone else besides their spouse. Jesus tells us that the external act is not the only way men and women fall into sins of lust. You become guilty of serious sin whenever you look lustfully at another person.

To explain how God wants us to live the virtue of holy purity, we must distinguish between love and lust. But before we can do this, we have to explain why God created us male and female.

God's plan

God's plan for relations between men and women combines both physical and spiritual elements. Those who emphasize only the physical element reduce human sexuality to mere animal sexuality. Sexual urges are only one aspect of human sexuality.

> Sex is something more than the mysterious power of human corporality, which acts almost by virtue of instinct. . . . It is bound up with choice.
>
> St. John Paul II, *Theology of the Body*, pp. 49–50

Animal sexuality works by instinct. Animals do not choose to act or to refrain from acting. Human beings are different because they choose.

God gives each person a free will. The human person engages in sexual activity by making a free and conscious decision. This freedom allows each person to choose between following God's plan or working against it.

To grasp the full mystery of human sexuality, you need freedom. You need an ability to act or to refrain from acting. Human freedom is perfected by God's grace. If you do not have much willpower—in this area of life or any other—it is a defect. You lack freedom because you lack self-control. With God's grace and your effort to seek good and avoid evil, you can achieve a greater sense of freedom. Having more self-control, you will appreciate the beauty of God's plan. Those who allow themselves to be swept away by sexual desire become blind to God's plan.

Besides having the ability to make free choices, each person needs to recognize truth. God wants us to know why he created us as male and female. God wants everyone to know his plan for sex. He wants each person to follow it.

The two purposes of marriage

God's plan for human sexuality can be summarized by saying that he wants one man and one woman to make a permanent commitment to each other in marriage.

God designed the sexual union of man and woman to achieve a purpose—actually two purposes that are complementary and inseparable.

- **Unitive purpose:** God joins the man and woman so completely that the two become one flesh. The husband and wife become one. This is meant to lead them to a sense of intimacy and communion with each other.
- **Procreative purpose:** The husband and wife cooperate with God in the act of creation. The spouses become parents of the child that is conceived through their sexual union.

Any act involving sexual intimacy before marriage or outside of marriage is a serious sin. Any deliberate attempt to seek sexual arousal before marriage or outside of marriage is a serious sin. Instead of leading you to peace and joy, such acts will leave you feeling frustrated and lonely.

Acts involving sexual intimacy should take place only between a man and woman who have who committed themselves to each other for life in marriage. Such acts must be used for both the procreative and unitive purposes. In other words, such acts must be used not merely to provoke feelings of pleasure. They must always remain open to new human life. They must always be an occasion for the husband to give himself completely to his wife and for the wife to give herself completely to her husband.

God gave the conjugal act these two different purposes or dimensions—union and procreation. The husband and wife cannot separate them. Any attempt to do so will cause the couple harm. If the couple wants a child, but the woman cannot conceive naturally, it is wrong to skip the conjugal act and ask a doctor to "solve the problem" in a laboratory, using procedures that produce a baby in a test tube. If the couple wants to express their love through the conjugal act but uses contraceptives to prevent their union from being fruitful, it will damage their love for each other. The Church teaches:

> The acts in marriage by which the intimate and chaste union of the spouses takes place are noble and honorable; the truly human performance of these acts fosters the self-giving they signify and enriches the spouses in joy and gratitude. Sexuality is a source of joy and pleasure.
>
> The Creator himself established that in the generative function, spouses should experience pleasure and enjoyment of body and spirit. Therefore, the spouses do nothing evil in seeking this pleasure and enjoyment. They accept what the Creator has intended for them. At the same time, spouses should know how to keep themselves within the limits of just moderation.
>
> The spouses' union achieves the twofold end of marriage: the good of the spouses themselves and the transmission of life. These two meanings or values of marriage cannot be separated without altering the couple's spiritual life and compromising the goods of marriage and the future of the family.
>
> *CCC*, nn. 2362–2363

The Church speaks here about "moderation." Moderation is like the peak of a mountain between two valleys. It is the peak of virtue between two defective extremes.

On one extreme, there is the defect of fear. A husband and wife ought to avoid any fear of showing affection to each other. On the other hand, a husband and wife have to avoid making sexual pleasure the priority. Pleasure is not the priority. Being one with each other and having children are the two purposes of marriage. Pleasure is not an end but a means—and even then, only one among several means for achieving union and procreation.

Good deeds to do

Learn self-control You were created to love. Self-control is crucial to finding love. This means learning to control your desire for sexual pleasure. It also applies to other aspects of life where you need control over feelings and emotions: control over appetite, control over emotions of love and hatred, control over sadness and despair, etc. Virtues are the key to self-control. Struggle to acquire the virtues of continence, chastity, and fortitude. By mastering self, you gain an inner freedom that allows you to love with greater passion.

Wisdom of the perfect husband: Proverbs 5:1–23
Poem on the perfect wife: Proverbs 31:10–31

Practice continence Continence is like a big iron bar that you must use to smash temptations against purity. When temptations come, show no mercy. It means rejecting any fantasies or any touching that leads to impure acts. It is easy to extinguish a tiny flame. It is almost impossible to extinguish a roaring blaze that you have fostered by dialoguing with temptation. Continence is a habit you acquire by always stamping out the first sparks of passion. It means fleeing from temptation and

Fathers of the Church

A young husband should say to his wife: "I have taken you in my arms, and I love you, and I prefer you to my life itself. For the present life is nothing, and my most ardent dream is to spend it with you in such a way that we may be assured of not being separated in the life reserved for us. . . . I place your love above all things, and nothing would be more bitter or painful to me than to be of a different mind than you."

St. John Chrysostom, cf. *CCC*, n. 2365

avoiding occasions of sin—for example, staying alone together. If you are not married, learn how to make friends with those of the opposite sex and how to distinguish between a show of affection and anything that causes sexual arousal. Because an act that is not sexually arousing for you can be arousing to the other person, be reserved even in your show of affection. In the strict sense, continence is only for those who are not married. However, married men and women must live continence with all persons other than their spouse. If you are married, you practice continence by fleeing from temptation and avoiding occasions of sin when you feel attracted to someone who is not your spouse.

Jesus explains the need to avoid occasions of sin: Mark 9:43–50

Cultivate chastity While continence focuses on the negative—learning how to say no—chastity focuses on the positive. It is expressed in different ways for different people. A married person lives chastity by fostering thoughts, words, and deeds that lead to deeper union with his or her spouse and greater desires to serve both spouse and children. Those who are engaged to be married live chastity by refraining from any kind of sexually arousing acts until they are actually married. This protects the freedom they need to decide whether they really want to get married. Those who are committed to celibacy live chastity not only as a renunciation of forming a family (being a "eunuch for the kingdom") but also as a joyful affirmation (looking forward to the "wedding feast of the Lamb"). They live chastity by longing for a greater gift from God—a greater love than married men and women experience in this world. Young men and women also live chastity by pondering in prayer what God wants them to do with their lives.

The bride longs for the coming of the bridegroom: Song of Songs 3:1

Practice fortitude There is a fortitude needed to overcome fear: it helps you say yes. You practice it by making commitments and keeping them. Cowards refuse to make commitments—or having made a commitment, invent excuses and try to slip away. There is a fortitude needed to overcome lust: it helps you say no. You practice it by running away from occasions of sin. Cowards think they're being brave by laughing at the people who flee from temptation, but they end up getting trapped themselves.

Tobias overcomes his reluctance to marry Sarah: Tobit 6:14–18

Joseph flees from the woman who tries to seduce him: Genesis 39:7–20

Cherish children This means looking at children as a gift from God. This used to be obvious in ages past. Today many people have developed an aversion to children—as if children were a burden. Therefore, it is necessary to insist: Children are not the enemy of a couple's happiness. Children are not the enemy of economic development. Greed, pride, and lust are the enemies. If you are married and God sends you many children, he is blessing you. Your reward will be great both in this life and in the next. It requires generosity and sacrifice, but no more than people put into other affairs like amassing wealth, acquiring prestige, and seeking adventure. All the money, fame, and thrills in the entire universe cannot match the worth of a single child. Wealth, prestige, and adventure all pass away. Heaven and earth will pass away. But every child is destined to exist forever.

Children are a blessing from God: Psalm 128

Evils to avoid

Adultery This means having sexual relations with the spouse of another person. If you are married, you also commit adultery if you engage in sexual relations with someone who is not married. Murder is an attack on God's image and likeness because it attacks the union of body and soul. Adultery is an attack on God's image and likeness because it attacks the union of husband and wife. God commanded the Israelites to stone both the man and woman caught committing adultery because he wanted to impress upon them how much harm this sin does to society. While we should not apply this same punishment today, the underlying logic still applies. Adultery harms not only the man and woman who commit the sin. It also does enormous harm to others.

After forgiving the woman caught in adultery, Jesus tells her: "Sin no more": John 8:11

Divorce and remarriage When asked if there are any circumstances that justify divorce, Jesus clearly stated that any man who divorces his wife and marries another woman commits adultery. He also said that any woman who divorces her husband and marries another man commits adultery (cf. Mk 10:11–12). There are no exceptions. Those who say that the unfaithfulness of a spouse is a special circumstance that permits a man or woman to divorce and remarry are wrong. When Jesus talked about separating in the case of fornication (cf. Mt 19:9), he was referring to couples who are living together *before getting married*: these can separate and both the man and woman can get married to someone else. In fact, they should either get married or separate since the man and woman are living in a state of fornication—that is, living in sin.

St. John the Baptist reproaches King Herod for living with Herodias after she left her husband: Mark 6:17–20

Fornication This means having sexual intercourse before marriage. The worst case is concabinage or trial marriage, a man and woman living together before getting married. If you are not married, you do serious harm to yourself and your partner if you engage in any kind of pre-marital sexual relations. This includes minor sexual contact

MAGISTERIUM

The two dimensions of conjugal union, the unitive and the procreative, cannot be artificially separated without damaging the deepest truth of the conjugal act itself.

Particularly conscious of the problem of man and his calling, the Second Vatican Council states that the conjugal union—the biblical "*una caro*" (one flesh)—can be understood and fully explained only by recourse to the values of the person and of gift. Every man and every woman fully realizes himself or herself through the sincere gift of self. For spouses, the moment of conjugal union constitutes a very particular expression of this. It is then that a man and woman, in the "truth" of their masculinity and femininity, become a mutual gift to each other. All married life is a gift; but this becomes most evident when the spouses, in giving themselves to each other in love, bring about that encounter which makes them "one flesh" (Gen 2:24).

The person can never be considered a means to an end; above all never a means of "pleasure." The person is and must be nothing other than the end of every act. Only then does the action correspond to the true dignity of the person.

St. John Paul II, *Letter to Families*, n. 12

like passionate kissing, petting, etc. Such acts are a serious sin even if you are engaged to be married. Such acts rob you of the freedom you need on the day of your wedding—the freedom to say yes or no when asked if you are ready to commit yourself to your spouse for life. Youth who have made mistakes in the past can prepare for a holy marriage. As with any other sin, God is ready to forgive once a person guilty of fornication repents. The purity that has been damaged by sin can be healed by acts of penance.

Jesus describes fornication and adultery as evils that begin in the heart before they manifest themselves exteriorly: Mark 7:21–23

Contraception According to God's plan, every act of sexual intimacy between husband and wife must remain open to life. Whether used by the man or the woman, a contraceptive is any chemical or mechanical device designed to prevent conception. If either spouse uses a contraceptive before, during, or after sexual intercourse with the deliberate intention of preventing conception, this action always constitutes a serious sin. If the husband or wife deliberately uses the act of withdrawal in order to prevent conception, this also constitutes a serious sin. Sterilizing either the man or the woman with the intention of preventing conception is more seriously evil since sterilization is often irreversible. If either husband or wife has to use a medicine with a side effect that prevents conception—and no other effective alternatives can be found to cure the disease or irregularity being treated by the doctor—there is nothing wrong with using the medicine.

Jesus speaks of his special love for little children and the need to "receive" them: Mark 9:36–37, 10:13–16

Polygamy A man is polygamous if he attempts to have two or more wives. A woman is polygamous if she attempts to have two or more husbands. Old Testament passages portray Israel's kings taking many wives. The New Testament ethic has changed the defective attitude of the Old Testament kings. Jesus insisted on following the plan that God established in the beginning when he joined one man with one woman. God unites the husband and wife with a bond. To explain how exclusive the bond is, St. Paul says that the husband's body belongs to his wife and that the wife's body belongs to her husband. This rules out polygamy. A husband cannot share his body with two women. A wife cannot share her body with two men.

St. Paul states that husband and wife have exclusive rights over each other's body: 1 Corinthians 7:3–4

Homosexual acts This means any kind of sexual activity between a man and another man or a woman and another woman. Even those who experience normal sexual attraction towards the opposite sex experience sexual disorders. They feel tempted to commit acts of adultery, fornication, etc. Temptations to adultery and fornication are not sins. Feeling is not the same as consent. Because of original sin, everyone has to struggle to master unhealthy sexual desires. However, in the case of those who feel same-sex attraction, the struggle presents an additional difficulty. If you experience sexual attraction to those of the same sex, remember that, even though the feeling is not in itself a sin, it is a disorder. It can be corrected, but it will take effort to live chastity—over and above the usual effort others have to make. People with disorders usually do not see their condition as a disorder. After experiencing strong feelings of same-sex attraction for years, the attraction can feel as if it were normal. If you have it, you will only be able to correct it by being humble enough to admit that feelings of same-sex attraction go against nature—even when they "feel natural" to you. The disorder is easier to correct if you speak to someone who can help you before the disorder gets worse by engaging in homosexual acts.

St. Paul calls homosexual acts "unnatural practices": Romans 1:26–27

Masturbation This means deliberately stimulating your own sexual organs to derive sexual pleasure. It is also called "self-abuse." Sexual acts are only good within marriage and only when each spouse makes a gift of self—whole and entire—to the other spouse. Any kind of sexual activity outside of marriage is evil. Any kind of sexual activity deliberately excluding procreation is also evil. Masturbation within marriage is wrong. Instead of directing the self to another person—instead of directing the "I" to a "you"—masturbation turns a person in on himself or herself. It leads the person to many interior complications, like indulging in self-pity and being preoccupied with self.

No one guilty of sexual indecency of any kind can enter God's kingdom: Ephesians 5:5–7

Prostitution This means buying and selling sexual pleasure. This includes not only the act of a prostitute in the usual sense but also any action that reduces sexual intimacy to a form of entertainment that people pay for. The one who offers this for sale, or who pays for it, is committing not only a sin against the virtue of purity but also a sin of scandal (the act of leading others into sin). Men who pay women for prostitution are often more guilty than the women because they use financial coercion to keep women enslaved.

Judah recognizes his guilt after he threatens to have a prostitute burned alive: Genesis 38:1–26

Rape This means forcing another person to engage in some form of sexual contact against his or her will. Because it involves violence, it is also a failure to respect the life and health of others.

Amnon, one of King David's sons, violates Tamar: 2 Samuel 13:1–22

Incest This means any kind of sexual contact with a close relative: between parents and their children; between siblings or cousins; and between uncles or aunts and their nephews and nieces.

St. Paul reproves a Christian guilty of incest: 1 Corinthians 5:1–5

Special Topics

Friendship between men and women

When striking up friendship with others, whether with those of the same or the opposite sex, be prudent. Distinguish between those you can trust and those you cannot trust. Try to be friends with everybody. But remember, there are some who ridicule anyone who wants to be pure. Knowing nothing about purity, they think they are doing you a favor when they lure you into sin. St. Jude wrote:

> And convince some, who doubt; save some, by snatching them out of the fire; on some have mercy with fear, hating even the garment spotted by the flesh.
>
> Jude 22–23

This advice applies to all friendships, especially when dealing with members of the opposite sex. Prudence demands recognizing two extremes. Being incapable of forming friendships with those of the opposite sex is one extreme. Being frivolous, giddy, or flirtatious is the other extreme.

Different cultures have developed various understandings about the nature of friendship between men and women. Jewish customs restricted conversation in public between men and women. For instance, they would never eat together. This is why the Apostles were surprised when they saw Jesus speaking to the woman at the well in Sychar (cf. Jn 4:27). Jesus made friends with all kinds of different people, both men and women. Those who strive to acquire virtue also know how to develop healthy friendships with the people they live and work with. The *Catechism* states:

> The virtue of chastity blossoms in friendship. It shows the disciple how to follow and imitate Jesus who has chosen us as his friends, who has given himself totally to us and allows us to participate in his divine estate. . . . Chastity is expressed notably in friendship with one's neighbor. Whether it develops between persons of the same or opposite sex, friendship represents a great good for all. It leads to spiritual communion.
>
> *CCC*, n. 2347

Besides being open to all, Jesus enjoyed close friendship with many. St. Francis de Sales noted:

> No one can deny that our dear Lord loved Sts. John, Lazarus, Martha, Magdalene with a special tender friendship, since we are told so in sacred Scripture. And we know that St. Paul dearly loved Sts. Mark, Petronilla, Timothy, and Thecla. . . . And St. Augustine says that St. Ambrose loved St. Monica by reason of her many virtues and that she in return loved him as an Angel of God.
>
> St. Francis de Sales, *Introduction to the Devout Life*, III, ch. 19

By imitating Jesus and the saints, Christians learn to value friendship with others.

This does not mean that you have to develop the same level of friendship or the same intensity of friendship with everyone. Again, Christ's way of dealing with others is the paradigm. Perhaps the most telling phrase of the Gospel in this regard is the one St. John mentions after telling the story of Jesus cleansing the Temple:

> Jesus did not trust himself to them, because he knew all men and needed no one to bear witness of man; for he himself knew what was in man.
>
> John 2:24–25

There were some people—both men and women—that Jesus spoke to with an open heart (cf. Jn 4:25–26). With others he was reserved, even though they were his own relatives (cf. Jn 7:8). On one occasion, he refused to say a single word to someone despite that person's desire to engage in conversation (cf. Lk 23:9).

Young people need to learn how to be friends with the opposite sex. It is part of the normal development of the human person. Feelings of sexual attraction can be confusing at first. Remember that you are not friends with someone just because both of you feel attracted to each other. Get to know the other person and treat that person with respect. Learning this kind of respect while you are young prepares you to have the same attitude towards friends of the opposite sex when you are married.

Wisdom of the Saints

There are four ways of overcoming concupiscence:

First, by fleeing occasions of sin, for instance, bad company, and whatever may be an occasion for this sin: "Gaze not upon a maiden lest her beauty be a stumbling block to you" (Sir 9:5).

The second way is not allowing thoughts which, of themselves, tend to provoke lustful desire. And this must be done by mortification of the flesh: "I chastise my body and bring it into subjection" (1 Cor 9:27).

The third way is perseverance in prayer: "Unless the Lord builds the house, they labor in vain who build it" (Ps 127:1).

The fourth way is to keep oneself busy with wholesome occupations: "Idleness teaches all sorts of mischief" (Sir 33:28) . . . St. Jerome says, "Be always busy in doing something good, so that the devil may find you occupied at all times."

St. Thomas Aquinas, *Catechetical Instructions*
(Tenth Commandment)

Contraception harms love between spouses

Contraceptives have changed the way most people look at God's decision to create man as male and female. The Church has always taught and will always teach that it is wrong for a married couple to use contraceptives even when they need to avoid childbirth.

Besides accepting the Church's teaching, you need to understand it so you can help others. What is at stake is nothing less than our understanding of God's plan for happiness within marriage.

The Church teaches that the widespread acceptance of contraception has caused enormous harm and will continue to do so until people stop using contraceptives. The *Catechism* states that using contraceptives is always "intrinsically evil" (*CCC*, n. 2370). Even if the couple has a good reason for avoiding childbirth, using contraceptives will do harm to their marriage. Couples who use them may feel threatened by this teaching, as if discontinuing their use would ruin their lives. The Church insists that, on the contrary, their lives will be better if they stop using contraceptives.

The Church does not argue that all couples trying to avoid childbirth are selfish. Some are, but many are not. A couple may need to do so for medical, financial, or other reasons. If a couple can have children and has the means to take care of them, God wants them to have children.

Natural regulation of fertility

When a couple needs to avoid childbirth, the Church tells them to use either total abstinence or the natural regulation of fertility. Natural regulation of fertility is also called "natural family planning." The couple engages in sexual intercourse only during the wife's infertile periods. Unlike the outdated "rhythm method" (based on calendar calculations), modern methods of natural family planning work. Gynecologists specializing in the field report that these methods are better than using contraceptives. These natural methods are effective. They have no side effects and pose no risk to a person's health.

The natural regulation of fertility differs radically from using contraceptives. The first respects God's plan. The second negates it so completely that, according to the Church, the conjugal act between husband

and wife using contraceptives "ceases to be an act of love" (St. John Paul II, *Theology of the Body*, p. 398).

In circumstances where a married couple needs to avoid childbirth, the *Catechism* explains:

> For just reasons, spouses may wish to space the births of their children. Periodic continence, that is, the methods of birth regulation based on self-observation and the use of infertile periods, is in conformity with the objective criteria of morality. These methods respect the bodies of the spouses, encourage tenderness between them, and favor the education of an authentic freedom.
>
> CCC, nn. 2368, 2370

The husband and wife can use their own experience. By doing so, they find out why natural family planning gives them a greater sense of freedom. They discover how this allows them to make a total gift of self and how this encourages tenderness.

The mere fact of husband and wife discovering this secret together is the first step towards being more intimate and more loving with each other—as God wants them to be. This is the main reason why many couples who need to avoid childbirth have switched from using contraceptives to natural family planning.

Why do contraceptives keep the spouses from giving themselves completely? The husband is holding back the potential he has within himself to be a father. The wife is holding back the potential she has within herself to be a mother. This may not seem like much, but consider the following.

The potential to be a father forms the very essence of being a man. If he holds it back, he is refusing to give himself—his true masculine self—to his wife and giving her less instead of giving everything. Likewise, the potential to be a mother forms the very essence of being a woman. If she holds it back, she is refusing to give herself—her true feminine self—to her husband and giving him less instead of giving everything. Contraception puts a barrier in the middle of the union. That barrier blocks the union. This is why the Church insists that the conjugal act ceases to be an act of love and, instead, becomes an act of selfishness.

How does natural family planning avoid this problem? By engaging in sexual intercourse only during those days when the couple knows the wife will most likely not conceive, they avoid conception while at the same time giving themselves to each other. They give themselves completely, without holding anything back and without putting any barrier in the way. Their act *remains open* to the *possibility* of conception.

When using the natural regulation of fertility to avoid childbirth, the couple remains open to childbirth in every act of sex. Despite their desire to avoid conception, a child may be conceived. However, in this case, the couple will be prepared to receive the child with as much love and affection as they show towards their other children. Couples using contraceptives have a different mentality. Despite using contraceptives, the woman may conceive a child. Because their acts of sexual intimacy are not open to life, the couple will look at their child as a "mistake" or even an "enemy." They may be tempted to put the child to death by abortion.

If a couple does not need to avoid childbirth and decides to avoid having another child for selfish reasons, they are not living their vocation as husband and wife. They are not living the way God wants them to live. This does not lead to true happiness. They are being irresponsible. Having children is one of the reasons why God calls a man and woman to marriage.

Once you grasp this truth, you understand the practical difference between the use of contraceptives and the use of the natural regulation of fertility. Couples using contraceptives hardly ever discuss whether they need to avoid childbirth. The husband and wife using natural family planning get around to pondering and discussing this issue frequently.

Sterility

When the wife fails to conceive, both spouses will often feel frustrated and suffer for many years. However, this does not mean there is anything wrong with their marriage or with their love for each other. They can use their talents to serve God and others in a different way—for instance, dedicating themselves to social services, adopting children, caring for the elderly, etc.

The term "procreation" denotes the parent's role in creation. The man and woman are not the ones who create. Only God can create the human soul. We believe that God creates the child's soul at the moment of fertilization. Because the man and woman are responsible for this moment, they "procreate," that is, they "cause" the event that in turn "provokes" God to create.

Today many people fail to see God's role in conjugal union. They no longer realize that God unites husband and wife. They have no idea that God intervenes to create when fertilization takes place. This has led some people to think of children as a product that can be manufactured in a laboratory.

The infertile couple can use those medical procedures that may give them a better chance of having a child through the normal act of marital union. However, the Church condemns the use of any means where the child is conceived outside the womb. Speaking of techniques used to produce so-called "test tube babies," the *Catechism* states that those techniques are wrong because they separate the sexual act from the procreative act.

> The act which brings the child into existence is no longer an act by which two persons give themselves to one another, but one that entrusts the life and identity of the embryo into the power of doctors and biologists and establishes the domination of technology over the origin and destiny of the human person.
>
> A child is not something owed to one, but is a gift. The "supreme gift of marriage" is a human person. A child may not be considered a piece of property, an idea to which an alleged "right to a child" would lead.
>
> CCC, nn. 2377–2378

The couple does not have a *right* to have a child. Each child is a *gift* from God.

Dealing with peer pressure

Having friends is more important to your happiness than health and success, wealth, and pleasure. In the midst of disaster, people often remain calm as long as they have friends to support them. For most people, companionship constitutes one of their deepest emotional cravings. This is why peer pressure affects us.

Peer pressure can be positive. When your peers encourage you to be good, it is easier for you to be good. Peer pressure turns negative when your friends urge you to do something evil.

Peer pressure affects all areas of life. It is particularly forceful when it comes to living the virtue of holy purity.

Promiscuity blinds. Anyone engaging in adultery or fornication or any other form of impurity—including a married person using contraception—becomes blind to the truth. Everything becomes confusing. Even those struggling to be pure find it hard, at times, to see why there is anything wrong with pornography, polygamy, masturbation, pre-marital sexual relations, etc. Once people fall into any of these vices, they may feel liberated initially. They think they have found a source of unlimited pleasure that will bring nothing but joy and contentment. They fail to realize how false and fleeting this sense of freedom is.

Because of blindness, they will think there is something wrong with you if you refuse to join them. They may call you names. Perhaps you seek their approval and friendship. This makes it hard to say no when they invite you to join them in their pursuit of pleasure. This is why you must get used to saying no. It is the only way to remain pure.

Remember the positive side of peer pressure. You can influence your friends and help them appreciate the beauty of being pure. Perhaps some of your friends have been too weak to resist temptation and are waiting for someone to help them. They will not change immediately. Some may pretend not to care. Pray for them and you will see how Jesus repeats the miracles of the Gospel: "The blind receive their sight and the lame walk, lepers are cleansed and the deaf hear, and the dead are raised up." (Mt 11:5).

Learning self-control

Sexual relations within marriage are all about making a gift of self. If you want to give someone a gift, it has to be yours before you can give it. You have to have control over it. The same applies to giving yourself in marriage. You need control over your heart, your emotions, your imagination, your feelings, and your body. Here are some tips on how to learn self-control:

- Get out of bed on time. Self-control starts from the first minute of the day. Don't let your body control you. Learn to control your body.
- Keep order in your desk, your locker, your closet, your workshop, your office, your room. Control over self starts with control over the things you own.
- Eat less of the food you like. Accept discomfort when it's hot or cold. Do this in little things like food and comfort. Then you can do it in big ones like controlling sexual urges.
- Sit up straight. Only lie down at night when going to bed. Controlling posture is key to controlling your body.

REVIEW QUESTIONS

1. What are the acts commanded by God in the sixth commandment?
2. What are the acts prohibited by God in the sixth commandment?
3. Why is it always wrong for either husband or wife to get a divorce and marry again?
4. Is it wrong for a couple to avoid childbirth? Why is it wrong to use contraceptives? What is the difference between using contraceptives and the natural regulation of fertility?

29.

Respecting Property

The seventh commandment

Because you need things to live—food, clothing, and shelter, for starters—you have a right to own things. So does everyone else. No one has a right to take your things away from you unjustly. How do you feel when someone steals your property? You feel offended because your right to private property has been violated. Someone has done harm to you. The more necessary those possessions were for your survival and well-being, the greater the harm. For the same reason, you do harm to others if you steal their property. This is why the seventh commandment of the Decalogue states:

> You shall not steal.
>
> Exodus 20:15

Included in the concept of stealing are all acts of taking someone's property unjustly.

Note the word *unjustly*. The definition of stealing is more complicated than most people imagine. The right to private property is not absolute. There are situations in which others can take something you possess and do it justly because they have a right to that property.

For instance, imagine a man who is starving to death. He is acting justly if he takes food from you—assuming you have more than enough for yourself and your family. If he desperately needs it to feed himself and his family, he is not stealing. He is not violating the principles of justice. On the contrary, he has a right to take the food he needs even though you are convinced that the food belongs to you. After all, if you knew how desperate his situation was, you would give him what he

Sacred Scripture

You shall not oppress a hired servant who is poor and needy, whether he is one of your brethren or one of the sojourners who are in your land within your towns; you shall give him his hire on the day he earns it, before the sun goes down (for he is poor, and sets his heart upon it); lest he cry against you to the LORD, and it be sin in you.

You shall not have in your bag two kinds of weights, a large and a small. You shall not have in your house two kinds of measures, a large and a small. A full and just weight you shall have, a full and just measure you shall have; that your days may be prolonged in the land which the LORD your God gives you.

Deuteronomy 24:14–15; 25:13–15

needs and give generously, wouldn't you? But even if you were so selfish that you would send the man away empty-handed, he has the same right that you have to the basic necessities of life.

The example of the poor man taking food illustrates the complex nature of justice. It is not always easy to determine when a person has a right to possess a particular good here and now. We can only determine it by first remembering that everyone has a right to possess the basic goods needed to live.

By teaching people that the right to own goods is not absolute but relative, the Church reminds us that the goods of this world are destined for the whole human race. The *Catechism* says:

> The right to private property acquired or received in a just way, does not do away with the original gift of the earth to the whole of mankind. The universal destination of goods remains primordial, even if the promotion of the common good requires respect for the right to private property and its exercise.
>
> In his use of things man should regard the external goods he legitimately owns not merely as exclusive to himself but common to others also, in the sense that they can benefit others as well as himself.
>
> *CCC*, n. 2403

God will ask you to account for the way you have used your possessions: money, land, cars, houses, food, clothes—everything. If you use these things selfishly, obsessed with your own pleasure and comfort, your possessions will choke you. Instead of making you a better person, they will become chains of slavery. When you use your possessions to help others, making life more pleasant for them, you become a better person. This is what the Church means by saying that our goal is not to "have" more but to "be" more.

Two principles for judging property rights

Two principles must be balanced, one against the other, when determining the just distribution of property:

1. **The right to private property:** Each person has a right to own private property.
2. **The universal destination of goods:** God provides the goods of this earth for the whole of mankind.

These two principles complement each other. Neither one is absolute. As we saw when looking at the case of the man starving to death, he had a right to food. This right is guaranteed by the principle of the universal destination of goods.

The Church teaches that both of these principles are primordial. In other words, they are not determined by civil law. They are determined by human nature. They are fixed by the way God created man in the beginning.

Your right to own private property is a basic human right. The right of all people to enjoy the goods of this world is also a basic human right. Any system of government that denies either of one of these two rights will cause grave harm to the whole of society.

Justice

To be a just person, you must give to others what belongs to them. This act of giving is the essence of justice.

An act of justice always involves one person who gives and another who receives. Besides this giving and receiving, justice requires a judgment. To act justly, both the person giving and the person receiving make a judgment. They judge how much the person giving has an obligation to give. This is based on how much the person receiving has a right to receive.

Besides being just, God expects us to be merciful. "Blessed are the merciful, for they shall obtain mercy" (Mt 5:7). If a person has no right to a particular good and you give anyway, you are showing mercy. This is sometimes called "charity" because it shows how much you love that person. If a person deserves punishment and you do not enforce it, this can be an act of mercy—but only if this does not violate the rights of a third party.

Jesus described mercy as an act requiring the person offended to overlook the offense:

> To him who strikes you on the cheek, offer the other also; and from him who takes away your coat do not withhold even your shirt. Give to every one who begs from you; and of him who takes away your goods do not ask them again.
>
> Luke 6:29–30

Does this mean that justice is no longer necessary? No, because our Lord was the first to demand that anyone who steals must undo the damage done by giving back what was stolen (cf. Lk 19:1ff).

Mercy and justice do not contradict each other. They work together. If failure to punish results in harm to others—if a judge lets a thief keep stolen goods—this is not mercy because it is a lack of justice. Because judges have a strict obligation to restore justice, any judge that deliberately refuses to demand that a thief return stolen goods becomes an accomplice to the crime.

God himself is both infinitely just and infinitely merciful. This is the reason why he will forgive all sins as long as the sinner repents and yet refuses to forgive the sinner who will not repent. God allows a repentant sinner to enter heaven because that person no longer desires to cause harm. God cannot allow anyone to enter heaven who wants to continue doing harm. This person would destroy the happiness of the saints. To fulfill his promises, God has to prevent that from happening.

Because the Pharisees "devour widows' houses and for a pretense make long prayers" (Mk 12:40), Jesus called them "whitewashed tombs . . . full of dead men's bones and all uncleanness" (Mt 23:27–28). Referring to the way he would judge them on the Day of Judgment, he concluded: "They will receive the greater condemnation" (Mk 12:40). He did not mean that God refuses to forgive thieves. On the contrary, he showed mercy to the "good thief," one of the two men crucified with him (cf. Lk 23:43). He condemned the Pharisees for stealing while pretending to administer justice and defend the Law.

Good deeds to do

Respect the goods of others Treat property that belongs to others the same way you expect others to treat your own possessions.

Jesus summarizes the "meaning of the Law and the Prophets" in the golden rule: Matthew 7:12

Honor contracts Entering into a contract means making a commitment for land use, for labor, for lease or sale of goods, etc. Both parties agree to honor the terms of the contract. Your obligation to fulfill the contract ceases if you were forced to enter into it or if you discover that the other party acted in bad faith, deceiving you on some matter directly related to the contract. For instance, if the other person deceived you and demands rent on property that he does not own, you have no obligation to pay him. When a dispute arises over a contract, the ruling of a court is assumed to be fair and just unless proven otherwise.

When some tax collectors ask for advice on justice, St. John the Baptist tells them: "Exact no more than your rate.": Luke 3:13

Relieve human misery This means doing whatever is necessary to solve problems of hunger, pain, poverty, loneliness, and any other cause of suffering troubling those around you. This means doing works of mercy—going out of your way to do more than you have a strict obligation to do. You cannot call yourself a just person if you do nothing to help others in a moment of need.

Jesus promises great rewards to all who are generous: Luke 6:38

Fathers of the Church

Not to enable the poor to share in our goods is to steal from them and deprive them of life. The goods we possess are not ours, but theirs.

St. John Chrysostom, cf. *CCC*, n. 2446

When we attend to the needs of those in want, we give them what is theirs, not ours. More than performing works of mercy, we are paying a debt of justice.

St. Gregory the Great, cf. *CCC*, n. 2446

Practice solidarity This means looking at all people as your brothers and sisters, seeing their problems as your problem, especially in caring for the poor. While relieving misery refers to works of mercy, solidarity refers to social justice and social action. A modern proverb contrasts two approaches: "Give a man a fish and you feed him for a day. Teach a man to fish and you feed him for life." Both approaches are necessary, depending on a person's immediate needs. To help the poor, both works of mercy and social action are necessary. Many people remain trapped in poverty even after acquiring skills. Some of the problems of the poor are the direct result of corruption and abuse of power. Some problems arise because of the indifference of those who have accumulated great quantities of wealth. The poor suffer because no one helps them secure their rights. Christians can often use their ordinary work to find ways of resolving these problems.

St. Paul equates "fulfilling the Law of Christ" with "bearing one another's burdens": Galatians 6:2

Restitution In general, this means undoing any harm done. Related to the seventh commandment, it means giving back money or goods you have stolen and fixing damage you caused by acts of vandalism. Restitution also applies to paying debts or taxes that you should have paid but neglected to pay. Restitution follows the general principle of justice. Give others whatever belongs to them, that is, whatever they have a right to receive from you. Restitution does not demand that you admit to others that you did something wrong. For instance, if a thief confesses to a priest that he stole money, the priest will explain the obligation of restitution but normally will not require the person to reveal the crime. However, there may be circumstances that make such a revelation necessary (e.g., when an innocent person has been put in prison after being accused of stealing the money).

After his conversion, Zacchaeus the tax collector promises Jesus he will return money to those he has cheated: Luke 19:8

Evils to avoid

Theft This means taking someone's property without that person's permission. Robbery is a special case of theft. It means stealing by using force. A person who robs violates justice twice: by stealing and by causing physical harm (or threatening to do so).

Judas Iscariot stole money from the common fund: John 12:6

Fraud This means using some form of deceit to convince a person that you deserve something and then accepting it as if you truly deserved it. A person who defrauds is guilty of both stealing and lying. The typical examples of fraud include: confidence schemes, forging checks and invoices, using inaccurate weights and measures to cheat customers, or collecting payment for goods you have no intention of delivering.

The prophet Amos condemns the leaders of Israel for using false measures to sell grain: Amos 8:4–6

Exploitation If you take advantage of the hardships of the poor to force them into some form of servitude, you are exploiting the poor. Employers have an obligation to pay a just wage and not simply a wage that workers are willing to accept because they have no other choice. It is impossible to define an exact figure when determining a just wage. It is not a question of calculating the money as much as looking at the real needs of the employee. An employer who lives in luxury while his workers do not earn the minimum necessary to take care of their families is guilty of exploitation. Some of the greediest people sincerely believe that they are not guilty of greed. They are so obsessed with increasing their profits that they don't care—or simply don't notice—the suffering of the workers who make those profits possible. Like murder in cold blood, withholding wages is one of the crimes that "cry out to heaven."

God condemns the leaders of Israel for "devouring the flesh of my people," that is, for oppressing the poor: Micah 2:8–10, 3:1–4; also Amos 6:1–7
St. James describes the pains of hell reserved for those who live in luxury while their workers die of starvation: James 5:1–6

Usury Usury is a form of exploitation. A money lender charging exorbitant interest to poor people caught in a desperate fix is guilty of this form of exploitation. The Church does not condemn the practice of charging interest on loans but does condemn usury, understood as any form of money lending aimed at keeping the poor perpetually in debt and therefore at the mercy of the money lender.

Moses forbids usury: Exodus 22:24.

Manipulation of the market This is a special form of exploitation. It causes great harm to the poor. If you hoard goods to create a false shortage in the marketplace, knowing this will drive up prices and make your profit much greater when selling, you are manipulating the market. This crime is punishable by law in most countries because it is a form of stealing.

The prophet Amos also refers to this practice when condemning the leaders of Israel for oppressing the poor: Amos 8:4–6

Works of Mercy

Because justice alone is not enough, you must look for ways of alleviating the suffering of those around you. The corporal and spiritual works of mercy are ways of doing this.

SPIRITUAL WORKS OF MERCY

Besides the general practice of going out to all nations to spread the Gospel, spiritual works of mercy include instructing the ignorant (especially by teaching the mysteries of faith to those who seek God), admonishing the sinner (showing those who go astray how to come back to God), comforting the afflicted, forgiving offenses, bearing wrongs patiently, and praying for the living and the dead (praying especially for the sinners most in need of God's mercy and for the holy souls in purgatory).

CORPORAL WORKS OF MERCY

Besides the general practice of giving alms to the poor, corporal works of mercy include feeding the hungry, giving the thirsty something to drink, clothing the naked (i.e., replacing the rags worn by the poor with good clothes), sheltering the homeless, visiting the sick, visiting those in prison, and burying the dead.

Political corruption This includes any abuse of public office where politicians, judges, police, or other government officials use their authority to extort money from citizens or take possession of land and other goods. It also includes the private use of public property wherever the law specifically forbids it. The theft of public funds is worse than merely stealing for two reasons. First, because the politician or official has taken an oath of office, making a solemn promise before God to protect and foster the common good. Second, because it is hard to stop a thief from stealing if the thief is the one responsible for punishing theft.

Elijah condemns King Ahab and his wife Jezebel for grabbing Nabaoth's land: 1 Kings 21:8–26

Bribery You are guilty of bribery if you offer money (or other goods) to politicians, judges, police officers, or other government officials in order to obtain some benefit you do not deserve (e.g., a job or a contract), to excuse yourself from paying taxes, or to escape punishment you deserve for breaking the law. You are also guilty of bribery if you accept such an offer. Bribery can occur in the private sector—for instance, when someone bribes an employee to obtain favors that the company would otherwise refuse to offer.

Moses contrasts bribery vs justice, blindness vs vision: Deuteronomy 16:18–20

Extortion Extortion is not the same as bribery. Extortion takes place when a government official demands that you pay a fee—to be personally pocketed by the official—before you will be allowed to secure goods and services that in normal circumstances you deserve to receive. The official demanding the payment of the fee is the one guilty of injustice. Racketeering is a special form of extortion. It means demanding money from someone while offering protection from harm—harm to be inflicted when the one making the demand does not receive money. Blackmail is another form of extortion. It means threatening to reveal damaging information while offering to refrain from doing so if the one being threatened will pay some form of compensation—cash, favors, etc.

When soldiers ask for advice on justice, St. John the Baptist tells them: "No intimidation! No extortion!": Luke 3:14

Magisterium

In our own time, the successes of science and technology make it possible to attain material well-being to a degree hitherto unknown. While this favors some, it pushes others to the edges of society. In this way, unilateral progress can also lead to a gradual loss of sensitivity for man, that is, for what is essentially human. In this sense, our time in particular awaits the manifestation of that "genius" which belongs to women, and which can ensure sensitivity for human beings in every circumstance: because these beings are human!—and because [God's] greatest gift "is love" (cf. 1 Cor 13:13).

St. John Paul II, *On the Dignity of Women*, n. 30

Tax evasion You are guilty of this sin if, motivated by greed, you refuse to pay taxes owed to the government. Citizens have a strict obligation to pay taxes because paying taxes is essential to supporting the common good—building roads, schools, hospitals, etc. The amount of tax to be paid is usually determined by law.

St. Paul urges Christians to pay taxes to the Roman government: Romans 13:6–7

Vandalism This means willfully damaging private or public property for no good reason. If you do it out of revenge, then you are twice guilty: for a sin against justice and a sin against charity.

The Babylonians are declared guilty for destroying the city of Jerusalem: Jeremiah 51:24

Retaining lost or stolen property If you know that something you possess was stolen from another person, you have an obligation to return the stolen goods. If you retain possession of these goods, then you are guilty of injustice because you are refusing to give to others what belongs to them. If you knew the goods were stolen when you bought them, you have an obligation to find out who the goods belong to so that you can return the goods to that person. If you found out after the sale, you still have an obligation to return the stolen property, even if this means losing the money you paid for the goods. In both cases, you have a right to seek compensation from the person who sold you the stolen property. The same logic applies to lost property. If you take possession of lost property, you acquire an obligation to give it back to its rightful owner, if possible. Lost property can be rightfully acquired if no owner can be found.

Moses commands the Israelites to return lost property: Deuteronomy 22:1–3

Special Topics

Love for the poor

Because God created the goods of this earth for everyone, justice demands that they benefit everyone and are available for everyone. You live in a world where many people suffer from hunger and never receive an education. If you turn your back on them, you cannot call yourself a good Christian.

> If a brother or sister is ill-clad and in lack of daily food, and one of you says to them, "Go in peace, be warmed and filled," without giving them the things needed for the body, what does it profit?
>
> James 2:15–16

After asking this question, St. James concludes that our faith is "dead" unless it moves us to do good deeds—especially good deeds aimed at helping the poor. St. John wrote:

> But if any one has the world's goods and sees his brother in need, yet closes his heart against him, how does God's love abide in him? Little children, let us not love in word or speech but in deed and in truth.
>
> 1 John 3:17–18

Helping the poor is neither your only obligation nor your most important obligation. But it is an obligation. The Church encourages you to think of ways to help them. Doing your work well can some times be the best way.

Professionals in medicine, law, science, academia, business, and the arts can use their talents and find ways to help. This kind of assistance often proves more useful to the poor than merely giving them money, and it enriches the lives of those who provide these services. Many rich people have discovered that they benefit more than the poor they were trying to assist.

The Church reminds us that poverty is defined by spiritual as well as material misery. At times, the greatest suffering takes place among people surrounded by luxuries of every kind. Their loneliness, depression, or bitterness can make them feel as neglected as a hungry orphan.

Promoting social justice

The world needs rich people who are poor in spirit—hardworking men and women who use their money and talents to improve the lives of the poor. Giving to the poor will always be necessary. But social action is just as important. Many of the world's poor could escape from poverty if only they had the same opportunities for education and employment that others enjoy.

In the social doctrine of the Church, you will find many ideas on how to promote the well-being of the poor.

> In certain developing countries, millions of people are forced to cultivate land belonging to others and are exploited by the big landowners, without any hope of ever being able to gain possession of even a small piece of land of their own. There is a lack of forms of legal protection for the agricultural workers themselves and for their families in case of old age, sickness, or unemployment. Long days of hard physical work are paid miserably. Land which could be cultivated is left abandoned by the owners. Legal titles to possession of a small portion of land that someone has personally cultivated for years are disregarded or left defenseless against the "land hunger" of more powerful individuals or groups.
>
> St. John Paul II, *On Human Work,* n. 21

WISDOM OF THE SAINTS

If you love the poor, seek them out and take special pleasure in bringing them to your home and in going to theirs. . . . How touchingly St. Louis, one of the greatest kings, fulfilled this duty, serving the poor in their own houses, while having three poor people eat at his table every day—often being so humble that his own food consisted in the leftovers from their meal.

St. Francis de Sales, *Introduction to the Devout Life,* III, ch. 15

The rich have an obligation to change the political, financial, and institutional structures that prevent the poor from prospering. In this way, rich people become poor in spirit. They overcome any obsession with seeking their own comfort and worry instead about how to make life more pleasant for others. With ingenuity, they can use their work to find solutions to the immediate social problems of the community where they live.

Being poor in spirit also demands taking care of material goods so that they will last as long as possible. In this way, material goods will serve both your immediate needs and the needs of others in the future.

Be on guard against consumerism—the tendency to buy things you do not need, either to satisfy the whim of a moment or to look good in front of your friends by showing them how rich you are. If you live this way, you waste the resources God has given you. Jesus never wasted anything. After working a miracle by multiplying the loaves of bread, he told his disciples: "Gather up the fragments left over, that nothing may be lost" (Jn 6:12).

Besides taking good care of your personal possessions, you have an obligation to care for the environment. The *Catechism* teaches:

> The seventh commandment enjoins respect for the integrity of creation. Like plants and inanimate beings, animals are by nature destined for the common good of past, present, and future humanity. Use of the mineral, vegetable, and animal resources of the universe cannot be divorced from respect for moral imperatives. Granted by the Creator, our dominion over inanimate and living beings is not absolute; it is limited by concern for the quality of life of our neighbor, including generations to come; it requires a religious respect for the integrity of creation.
>
> Animals are God's creatures. He surrounds them with his providential care. By their mere existence they bless him and give him glory. Thus we owe them kindness. We should recall the gentleness with which saints like St. Francis of Assisi or St. Philip Neri treated animals. . . . It is contrary to human dignity to cause animals to suffer or die needlessly.
>
> *CCC*, nn. 2415, 2416, 2418

Justice requires us to use all the goods of creation wisely.

Economic activity and social justice

Social justice depends mainly on three factors: 1) policies set by the government; 2) attitudes of employers towards their employees; and 3) solidarity among nations.

Government has an obligation to choose policies that make it possible for everyone to find work—not just a job but employment that allows them to provide for their families. The Church teaches:

> Economic activity, especially the activity of a market economy, cannot be conducted in an institutional, juridical, or political vacuum. On the contrary, it presupposes sure guarantees of individual freedom and private property, as well as a stable currency and efficient public services. Hence the principal task of the State is to guarantee this security, so that those who work and produce can enjoy the fruits of their labors and thus feel encouraged to work efficiently and honestly. The absence of stability, together with the corruption of public officials and the spread of improper sources of growing rich and of easy profits deriving from illegal or purely speculative activities, constitutes one of the chief obstacles to development and to the economic order.
>
> St. John Paul II, *On the Human Person* (*Centesimus Annus*), n. 48

The government does well to respect the rights of people in business to make a profit. But the marketplace alone will never ensure just remuneration to all workers, nor will it take care of the needs of the destitute poor. Protective policies and collective action will always be necessary.

While business owners have a right to make a profit, they have obligations towards their employees:

> Those responsible for business enterprises are responsible to society for the economic and ecological effects of their operations. They have an obligation to consider the good of persons and not only the increase of profits. Profits are necessary, however. They make possible the investments that ensure the future of a business and they guarantee employment.
>
> CCC, nn. 2432–2433

Government policies and business practices must ensure open access to employment to all without unjust discrimination: men and women, healthy and disabled, natives and immigrants.

Finally, there is the reality of globalization. No one country rises or falls alone.

> Rich nations have a grave moral responsibility toward those which are unable to ensure the means of their development by themselves or have been prevented from doing so by tragic historical events. . . . The efforts of poor countries working for growth and liberation must be supported. This doctrine must be applied especially in the area of agricultural labor. Peasants . . . form the overwhelming majority of the poor.
>
> *CCC*, nn. 2439–2440

The development of many rich nations was made possible by the hard work of many poor people in less developed nations. Justice demands economic support to help them develop their resources instead of merely exporting them.

REVIEW QUESTIONS

1. What are the acts commanded by God in the seventh commandment?
2. What are the acts prohibited by God in the seventh commandment?
3. Explain the obligation a person has to make restitution.
4. What obligation do you have to care for the poor?

30.

Respecting Truth

The eighth commandment

When you ask a question, you want people to tell you the truth. For the same reason that you want others to tell you the truth, you also have an obligation to tell the truth. This obligation is all the more serious when you are speaking under oath. The eighth commandment of the Decalogue states:

> You shall not bear false witness against your neighbor.
>
> Exodus 20:16

The commandment condemns lying, especially while "giving witness," that is, after you have taken an oath swearing to tell the truth.

Jesus took the idea one step further and told his disciples they should never swear at all:

> Do not swear at all. . . . Let what you say be simply "Yes" or "No"; anything more than this comes from evil.
>
> Matthew 5:34, 37

How are we supposed to understand this command? Is it wrong to take an oath and swear to tell the truth?

Jesus said these words during the Sermon on the Mount. He was explaining how he wants us to go beyond the Ten Commandments. We need to be as perfect as our heavenly Father (cf. Mt 5:48). The New Testament presents God swearing an oath: "The Lord has sworn and will not change his mind." (cf. Heb 7:20–25). Rather than condemning the practice of taking an oath in court, Jesus was demanding simplicity in everyday speech.

Jesus wants us to be straightforward and direct. He wants us to tell the truth all the time. When a whole society becomes addicted to lying, nobody trusts anybody. Cynicism sets in and hardens. Everyone is convinced that everyone else is always cheating. That is when people resort to the silly expedient of swearing to tell the truth any time an argument begins. It is silly because even then nobody really believes that the person is telling the truth.

People need truth

The *Catechism* says that "lying consists in saying what is false with the intention of deceiving one's neighbor" (*CCC*, n. 2508).

Perhaps someone refuses to answer a question and deliberately hides the truth from you. You may be irritated, but at least you know the person is being honest. Besides, you do not have a right to know everything about others. And there are certain things that others have no right to know about you. You, too, have a right to remain silent. All this changes when you ask someone a question and the person deliberately makes a false statement in order to deceive you. When people lie to you, you are being cheated.

When you look at it from this point of view—the way you feel when people cheat you—it is easy to see why lying causes harm. But do you feel the same way when you tell a lie? Do you think you are allowed to lie and then excuse yourself by saying, "I had to do it to get out of trouble"?

You may have a tendency to think that you need to lie in order to cope with the messy affairs of this world. Because many people think this way, you may assume you have to "make exceptions" in order to "get things done." You may think that lying is a necessary part of life. Like so many others, you may think lying is necessary for running a business, for keeping up good appearances with strangers, and even for getting along with friends and relatives—especially one's spouse and children. "Only a nun living in a convent can afford to be honest," some people say. They think Christians living in the middle of the world need to lie from time to time or they will end up being outwitted by the people who think nothing of lying all day long. This attitude is wrong.

Sacred Scripture

Let not many of you become teachers, my brethren, for you know that we who teach shall be judged with greater strictness. For we all make many mistakes, and if any one makes no mistakes in what he says he is a perfect man, able to bridle the whole body also. If we put bits into the mouths of horses that they may obey us, we guide their whole bodies. Look at the ships also; though they are so great and are driven by strong winds, they are guided by a very small rudder wherever the will of the pilot directs. So the tongue is a little member and boasts of great things. How great a forest is set ablaze by a small fire!

James 3:1–5

Many people lie and do so habitually. There is no denying this fact. It is equally true that some people will try to take advantage of you. This is why Jesus warned his disciples "Be wise as serpents . . ." (Mt 10:16). You would be foolish to believe that everyone is honest.

Jesus once talked about the Pharisees being sons of the devil (cf. Jn 8:44). He told them that Satan was their father because they were hypocrites, always lying to cover up their sins. But Jesus was not cynical. If you become cynical, it is a lack of faith in God's plans for love and peace. A cynical person assumes that the smart people learn how to lie with an outward show of poise and charm—learning how to be very good liars—and then use this skill to their advantage whenever they think they can get away with it. A cynical person assumes that anyone who tries to tell the truth is a simpleton. Christians flee from cynicism, knowing that the day is coming when God will reveal the thoughts of all men and women who have ever lived. "For there is nothing hid, except to be made manifest; nor is anything secret, except to come to light" (Mk 4:22).

Besides telling his disciples to be as cunning as serpents, he also told them to be "innocent as doves" (Mt 10:16). You should never use the truth to harm others. There are times when you have to keep silent. Avoid humiliating someone in public when you have other ways of correcting a fault. At other times you will remain silent, refusing to tell others about your good deeds, focusing attention on others instead of yourself.

Jesus loved the truth. But more than loving the truth, he *is* the truth:

> Jesus said to him, "I am the way, and the truth, and the life; no one comes to the Father, but by me.
>
> John 14:6

If you want to love Jesus Christ and get to know God, you must love the truth. The first step towards loving the truth is to learn how to tell the truth. If you lie, you cause harm, first to yourself and then to others.

How does a person damage his or her own interests by lying? Everyone needs truth in order to have friends and keep them. I demand to know the truth when people speak to me—and all the more so if the person speaking is my relative, friend, or colleague. But I cannot expect others to tell me the truth unless I am willing to tell them the truth.

If I lie, others will not trust me. It is useless to think I will somehow never get caught. If my friend sees me lying to get out of a tight corner—while witnessing a conversation at work or at home or at school—I may "get away with it." The person I lied to may not find out for years to come, if ever. But my friend—the one who saw me lie—will not trust me the next time the two of us talk. My friend will think: "That guy lied. I saw him do it. He probably does that with everybody, including me. I don't trust him anymore." Perhaps this conclusion is never explicitly formulated in the mind of the friend who saw me lie. It may remain implicit. Still, I have lost trust because I lied.

The Book of Revelation says that liars will share the same fate as those who fornicate, murder, and worship idols (cf. Rev 21:8). Jesus called Satan a "liar and the father of lies" (Jn 8:44). From the beginning the devil was described as the wiliest of all creatures because he was intent on deceiving Adam and Eve. He lied to Eve when he told her they would not die if they ate the fruit. His words blatantly contradicted God's warning about the death they would experience if they disobeyed. It is no mere coincidence that Jesus also calls the evil one a "murderer from the beginning." Satan lied because wanted to see Adam and Eve suffer and die. By lying to Eve, he got what he wanted. He brought death into the world.

Lying is evil. It leads to loneliness. It leads to death. People who do not trust each other cannot be friends. The anger people feel after being cheated often breeds hatred. This hatred leads to violence and bloodshed.

As more people are tempted to think that lying is necessary for survival, world events become ever more entangled in cover-ups and intrigue. This is why peace eludes us. Peace depends on knowing how to be honest. Personal peace starts when I learn to be honest with everyone around me. This means telling the truth, not only when it is convenient but even when it hurts. We cannot claim to love the One who *is* Truth unless we love telling the truth.

Good deeds to do

Be honest More than simply speaking the truth, honesty is an interior attitude. It means clinging to the truth even when it causes misunderstanding, suffering, or embarrassment. Jesus explains the worth of making this effort when he told his disciples: "The truth will make you free" (Jn 8:32). Being honest may be your most difficult challenge in life. Truth requires you to face realities about yourself that imply a need to change the way you live or the way you think. To face reality, first examine your desire to know God. If you are not interested in knowing the ultimate truth—the meaning of your own existence—you are unlikely to understand the daily realities meant to lead you to God. To face reality, learn how to tell the truth in little things. If you cannot be honest in little things, how will you tell the truth when the whole world is watching, waiting for your answer? When dealing with people bent on rebelling against God, you have to be humble enough to love the truth—and daring enough to speak the truth. You may sense that they will ruin or even kill anyone who tries. But if you lie, you betray God.

King Saul slaughters the High Priest and his family for speaking the truth about David, the future king of Israel: 1 Samuel 22:12–19

Respect a person's good name The same way that everyone has a right to life, people have a right to their good name. Just as you expect others to respect your reputation, you ought to respect theirs. All people, especially those working in the media, have a serious obligation to avoid complicity in rumormongering and the manipulation of facts aimed at discrediting either public figures or private individuals. Besides avoiding sins that damage a person's reputation, you have a positive obligation to promote the reputation of those doing the most to build up the common good. Fostering respect for the good name of those in positions of authority is crucial for economic and spiritual prosperity. Stirring up distrust against those in authority makes it impossible for people to work together effectively.

Even though the emperor was persecuting the Christians in Rome, St. Peter told them to "honor the emperor": 1 Peter 2:17

Hold your tongue This is part of learning self-control. "If you cannot speak kindly of someone, say nothing." There are times when you will have to warn others of danger. An obligation of justice may require you to speak boldly, knowing it will make a handful of "opinion makers" furious. You may even anticipate the ways they will vent their anger once they realize how effectively you have exposed something they were trying to hide. However, even in these situations, avoid personal attacks. A Christian never seeks the downfall of anyone, but only the greater good for everybody, even those in error. Never confront another person as an enemy you need to destroy. Treat the one who has made a mistake as a child of God who deserves your respect. Since you do not know the intentions of the heart, assume ignorance and human weakness instead of malice and bad faith. Even in the worst of circumstances, make excuses for those who do evil, remembering that you might have acted the same way if you had suffered the same kind of temptations.

> **Fathers of the Church**
>
> A person is lying when he states what is false for the purpose of deceiving. Therefore, it is plain that a false statement spoken with the intent to deceive is a lie.
>
> St. Augustine, *On Lying*, 4

Because God alone is the judge, even angels refrain from accusing sinners before the Lord: 2 Peter 2:10–11

Keep secrets Even if someone has a right to know the information you have, you must not reveal it if you promised to keep it a secret—unless it is clear that the person you promised would want you to reveal it. The obligation applies even to information that reflects positively on the person concerned. If someone demands that you reveal the information, you have a right to remain silent or, if it seems more prudent, to use evasive answers. If you work in a profession that requires you to maintain confidence for clients, the normal obligation to respect the privacy of others is all the more serious. No matter how necessary or urgent it may seem, no priest is ever allowed to reveal a sin someone has confessed to him.

Jesus asks Peter, James, and John not to tell anyone about his transfiguration until after his resurrection: Matthew 17:9; Luke 9:36

Promote transparency This means creating a culture where people have a natural inclination to speak the truth, plus a natural distaste for intrigue (circulating rumors) and innuendo (giving the impression of wrongdoing to deeds that were either harmless or virtuous). When leaders with authority and prestige demonstrate to the public that they are open to the truth—sometimes it takes only one such person—this counters the prejudice of all who say no public figure can afford to be honest. Just as solidarity fosters social justice, transparency fosters social honesty. Just as social justice means making it easy for individuals and institutions to obtain their rights, social honesty means giving persons and institutions the power to prosper while remaining honest. If only those who lie manage to profit and succeed, it is usually because ordinary people no longer appreciate the value of telling the truth. Promoting transparency in such a society is difficult. But anything less will fail. A society built on lies will fall into ruin under the weight of its own rot and corruption.

Jesus compares the house built on sand (lies) with the house built on rock (truth): Matthew 5:24–27

Evils to avoid

Lying This means saying something false with the intention of deceiving. A statement is a lie only if you know in your own mind and heart that you are saying something false. (If you say something that turns out to be false, you are not guilty of lying as long as you were convinced at the time that you were speaking the truth.) A statement is a lie only if you want to deceive the person listening to you. Exaggerating a story when telling a joke is not a lie since others know you have no intention of getting anyone to believe the story. Cheating on an exam or job interview is a form of lying. By pretending to know something you don't know, you may also be doing an injustice, unfairly appearing to be better than other candidates.

St. Paul urges everyone to "put away lying and speak the truth": Ephesians 4:25

Dissimulation This kind of lie is a concealment of one's thoughts, feelings, or character.

Eleazar refuses to dissimulate in order to escape death: 2 Maccabees 6:24

Perjury This means lying after you have taken an oath to tell the truth. When you take an oath, you ask God to be your witness. You solemnly declare that God himself knows you are telling the truth. If you lie under oath—no matter how important you may think it is to lie at that moment, for instance, to protect yourself or your family—you seriously offend God. You are asking him to support the truth of your statement even though you know that your statement is not true. Calling upon God as a witness is always a serious act. Therefore, you must also avoid taking an oath for trivial matters. For example, it is wrong to swear that you are telling the truth while telling a story at a party.

Daniel condemns two men for giving false witness against Susanna: Daniel 13:49

Flattery This is any attempt to gain someone's favor by falsifying or exaggerating that person's qualities or deeds. It is a special case of lying. Avoid the use of flattery for your advantage in business, politics or other endeavours. Have the humility to recognize flattery when others try to boost your ego, especially when they do it to entice you into committing a sin.

An unworthy man becomes High Priest by using flattery to win the favor of the king: 2 Maccabees 4:23–24

The prophet describes how God's enemies corrupt people by using flattery: Daniel 11:31–32

Slander This means saying something false that damages a person's reputation. It is also called "calumny." If you deliberately tell a lie about someone and you have some idea how much damage you are doing, then your guilt is determined by the damage you have done. If you did not lie—if you mistakenly thought you were speaking the truth—you still have an obligation to make up for the damage you caused.

The Pharisees accuse Jesus of being a glutton and drunkard: Matthew 11:19

Detraction This means revealing a person's fault to someone who has no right to know about it. It is always evil—even if you do it carelessly by talking too much. It becomes malicious when you do it with the intention of ruining that person's reputation. Detraction causes harm for yet another reason. As a Christian you should be trying to help the person who did something wrong to repent and come back to God. If the person has already repented, love for your neighbor compels you to show that person how to overcome problems created by past mistakes. How can you help people if you are busy publicizing their mistakes? Instead of providing bread when they need bread, you are handing them scorpions.

Jesus corrects the Pharisees for exposing a woman caught in adultery: John 8:3–11

Gossip Also called "loose talk," this means spreading rumors that could be damaging to someone's reputation. It also refers to the habit of exaggerating someone's public faults or harping on them. This usually makes the guilty party look worse. It is wrong to enjoy listening to gossip: "One who rejoices in wickedness will be condemned, and for one who hates gossip evil is lessened" (Sir 19:5–6). Faultfinding is a form of

Magisterium

Truth as uprightness in human action and speech is called truthfulness, sincerity, or candor. Truth or truthfulness is the virtue that consists in showing oneself true in deeds and truthful in words, and in guarding against duplicity, dissimulation, and hypocrisy.

People could not live with one another if there were not mutual confidence that they were being truthful to one another. The virtue of truth gives another his just due. Truthfulness keeps to the just mean between what ought to be expressed and what ought to be kept secret: it entails honesty and discretion. In justice, as a matter of honor, one person owes it to another to manifest the truth.

Catechism of the Catholic Church, nn. 2468–2469

gossip that occurs whenever you criticize someone publicly for a petty mistake. Backbiting occurs whenever you criticize someone for a mistake, speaking behind that person's back instead of having the courage to speak face-to-face in order to help the guilty party correct his or her behavior. The obligation to make reparation when guilty of these sins depends on the seriousness of the harm done to the good name of the person concerned.

Jesus explains how Christians are supposed to make fraternal correction to help someone who has made a mistake: Matthew 18:15–17

Judging rashly This happens whenever you believe that a person is guilty of a crime—or simply inferior in some way—while being aware that you know little or nothing about that person. Rash judgement also includes suspecting someone of evil intent when you have no grounds for being suspicious; for instance, thinking someone wants to cause harm because the person has an ugly scar or some other physical defect. Discrimination (because of a person's race, creed, gender or nationality) also amounts to rash judgment. Discriminating in the pejorative sense means victimizing someone unjustly. However, there is nothing wrong with using your good judgement to decide whether someone is capable of performing a service you would like the person to do.

Jesus reprimands John for prohibiting a person from doing good deeds just because he was not one of the disciples: Mark 9:38–41

Adulation This is misplaced hero worship, leading you to praise people for a virtue they do not have or for success they never achieved. Adulation is the opposite of rash judgment. Instead of thinking evil where no evil exists, you think well of someone where no good exists. Unlike flattery, where you are deliberately twisting the truth for your own ends, adulation arises from ignorance. You praise without having taken the trouble to determine prudently whether or not the praise is justly deserved. Though rarely ever mentioned, this sin can do great harm to private individuals and public institutions. It puts incompetent people in positions of authority. It encourages those obsessed with vanity. It misleads those who have to decide how to allocate public funds or give awards to those who deserve it.

Speaking to King Herod, the crowds shout, "It is a god speaking, not a man": Acts 12:20–23

Cursing others You curse someone when you ask God to make that person suffer. Though sometimes understood as the use of foul language, the sin of cursing also consists in wishing harm to another person for no reason other than your own jealousy or envy. There are some cases when a holy person has to curse, that is, ask God to punish someone who is doing great evil. However, the need to do this is so rare that you want to avoid it, if you can, for as long as you live. Like casting out devils, cursing evil is better left to those who have been chosen by divine authority to do it.

Jesus will tell the damned to go to hell with their curse upon them: Matthew 7:23 and 25:41

Special topics

Reparation

If you steal someone's property, you have to give it back. If you ruin someone's reputation, it is like stealing—you have taken away that person's good name. Whenever you are guilty of the sins of slander, detraction, or gossip, reparation is due. In other words, you have an obligation to repair the damage you caused.

If someone loses income because you ruined that person's good name, you have an obligation to restore his or her good name and also make up for the loss of income. This is more difficult to do after a sin of detraction. Because the information you revealed is true, the damage caused can be much worse than that caused by slander. A lie can be corrected by telling the truth. Once revealed, the truth cannot be hidden again. Even so, after harming someone's good name by revealing hidden faults without good reason, try to make reparation as best you can.

Always tell the truth

Jesus is the model for what it means to tell the truth—even in those difficult moments when doing so leads to death. When the High Priest asked him if he was the Son of God, Jesus said, "I am" (Mk 14:62). Jesus expects his disciples to follow this example by openly demonstrating their faith whenever someone asks them to deny it. Many Christians have died for doing so, and the Church calls these men and women "martyrs," that is, witnesses for Jesus Christ. Martyrdom is the heroic extreme that Christians must be prepared to embrace in order to love truth.

Jesus always told the truth. One incident, though, leaves some Christians perplexed. St. John narrates the scene:

> Now the Jews' feast of Tabernacles was at hand. So his brothers said to him, "Leave here and go to Judea, that your disciples may see the works you are doing. For no man works in secret if he seeks to be known openly. If you do these things, show yourself to the world." For even his brothers did not believe in him. Jesus said to them, "My time has not yet come, but your time is always here. The world cannot hate you, but it hates me because I testify of it that its works are evil. Go to the feast yourselves; I am not going up to this feast, for my time has not yet fully come." So saying, he remained in Galilee.
>
> But after his brothers had gone up to the feast, then he also went up, not publicly but in private.
>
> John 7:2–10

Jesus did go to the festival. But he was not lying when he said, "I am not going to this festival." His phrase has a particular meaning in the context of the conversation.

Take the following analogy. If you tell your brother, "I'm going to bed now," and you putter around for another hour (locking the door, grabbing a last minute snack, brushing your teeth, taking a shower, and saying your prayers), your brother is not going to feel cheated by the statement you made even though, strictly speaking, you did not go directly to your room and put your head on the pillow.

Jesus' words about not going to the festival were understood by his relatives in a similar way. There was no deception. On the contrary, Jesus' words made a deep impression on them. When they told him he should go to the festival, they were talking about making a public appearance so he could declare himself king. They did not believe he was the Messiah, the King promised by the prophets. They were making fun of him, taunting him, telling him the time had come to reveal himself. Jesus would eventually do that, a few days before he was crucified. But on this occasion he tells them that "the right time has not come yet." By telling his relatives, in this particular context, that he was not going to the festival, Jesus was not making a statement meant to deceive them into thinking he would stay in Galilee. He was making a statement about their disbelief. He was saying he needed to wait before he was ready to make a triumphal entry into Jerusalem. Having tried to make fun of him, his relatives were probably amazed that Jesus was taking them seriously and that he was, indeed, planning to "reveal" himself later—that is, to show the whole world that he was sent to be the King of kings and Lord of lords.

Being evasive

Using discreet language or hiding the truth is not the same as telling a lie. We have ways of speaking that others come to respect and understand. Suppose someone comes to your house, asking to speak to your sister, and she happens to be there. She wants to avoid seeing the visitor and tells you to make up an excuse. There is nothing wrong with telling the caller, "Sorry, she's busy." This has nothing to do with lying. It is a polite answer that says nothing. Similarly, there is nothing wrong with excusing yourself from an inconvenient situation—for instance, suddenly foreseeing an encounter with someone you need to avoid—and saying to a friend, "Sorry, I have to go now. I just remembered something I have to do."

The demands of justice and charity make it necessary at times to refrain from telling someone what they want to know. The *Catechism* states:

> This requires us in concrete situations to judge whether or not it is appropriate to reveal the truth to someone who asks for it. . . . The good and safety of others, respect for privacy, and the common good are sufficient reasons for being silent about what ought not be known or for making use of a discreet language. The duty to avoid scandal often commands strict discretion. No one is bound to reveal the truth to someone who does not have the right to know it.
>
> CCC, nn. 2488–2489

Using discreet language does not mean lying. It means using some turn of phrase that hides the truth without denying the truth.

Difficult cases

Situations arise when it is impossible to use discreet language to hide the truth. Some of these seem to justify an outright lie. For instance, a tax collector may ask a businessman to state if the accounts for the company are correct, and the accounts have been falsified to protect the company from being excessively taxed. Then there is the classic case, more hypothetic than real, of the enemy soldiers who invade a convent looking for fugitives suspected of being protected by the nuns, and the Mother Superior knows the fugitives will be killed if discovered.

Is it good for the businessman to tell the taxman his accounts are true when he knows they are false? Is it good for the Mother Superior to tell the army officer there are no fugitives hiding in the convent even though there are lots of them?

In these cases, there is no room for being evasive. The person seems to have only two choices—either tell the truth and suffer the consequences or lie to avoid serious harm.

> **WISDOM OF THE SAINTS**
>
> It is wrong for anyone to lie in order to rescue another, no matter what the peril. One may, however, prudently hide the truth.
>
> St. Thomas Aquinas, *Summa Theologiae*, II–II,110, 3, 4

Some argue that you can say something false deliberately—knowing that your false statement will deceive the person listening—as long as this person has lost his or her right to know the truth in that particular situation. They compare it to being attacked by an unjust aggressor. Just as you have a right to use force against a person trying to kill you, you have a right, according to this argument, to use deceit against people acting unjustly by demanding to know something they intend to use against you.

There is an element of truth in this argument. When someone threatens to harm you—and has no good reason for doing so—you do well to resist. Two questions remain, though. Does an "unjust aggressor" forfeit the right to know the truth? Assuming he does forfeit the right to know the truth, does that mean you can use false statements with the intention of deceiving?

This is a complicated problem. Christians have argued over it for centuries. For the same reason a man convicted of murder loses the right to move freely in public and is justly locked up in prison, it seems obvious that people lose the right to know the truth when they threaten to use it in order to harm others. Far from solving the dilemma, this fact makes it harder to come up with a satisfactory answer to the second question. Are you *lying* if you deliberately deceive someone who has no right to know the truth? Are you doing that person any harm by lying? If so, do you still have a right to protect yourself or someone else by lying?

You can refuse to tell someone the truth by remaining silent. That is obvious. It is not obvious that it would be good to deceive someone simply because that deceit will save someone's reputation or someone's freedom or even someone's life. With this in mind, go back to the two cases mentioned above.

Even if he knows his company will suffer unjustly by telling the truth, the businessman has an obligation to tell the truth to the tax collector. This becomes all the more serious when the businessman has to swear that the accounts are genuine. There are two related issues. First, that the end does not justify the means. It is good for the businessman to prevent his business from going bankrupt. However, if he lies, he does something evil. No matter how much good this achieves materially in profits for the company, the lie is a mortal sin that destroys his friendship with God. It is a serious sin because it involves a serious matter, namely, the oath taken to tell the truth. Secondly, there is a social issue. This example assumes that the rate of taxation is inherently unjust, as indeed it is in some countries. Until someone—it could be this businessman—confronts the unjust collection of taxes, the whole of society remains inherently corrupt. It is not just one businessman telling one lie to one tax collector once. The whole nation has become a society of liars. This is a serious evil that someone has to have the courage and the patience to tackle.

As serious as the first case is, the problem of the second case is more difficult because innocent people are about to be slaughtered in cold blood. Examples of genocide abound in times of war. If enemy soldiers show up at the convent door asking Mother Superior to hand over some fugitives that they intend to execute, the nun clearly has both a right and an obligation to resist. Because of their genocidal intent, the soldiers have no right to know whether the fugitives are in the convent. Even so, this is a difficult case. If Mother Superior tries to deceive the commanding officer making the inquiry by making statements she knows are false, will she be guilty of lying?

Some argue that Mother Superior does nothing to displease God if she manages to prevent a massacre by outwitting the officer with a few cleverly chosen false statements. After all, she (or anyone else) could use lethal force if the soldiers stormed the convent in an attempt to kill the fugitives and anybody that got in their way. Others say it is wrong to deceive people intentionally *even if they have no right to know the truth.*

The second opinion best represents the teaching of the Catholic Church. The *Catechism* does not make any exceptions when it states that lying means "speaking or acting against the truth in order to lead someone into error" (*CCC*, n. 2483). The *Catechism* could have specified that you are lying only when the person you lead into error is someone "who has a right to know the truth." The Church deliberately rejected this additional phrase when publishing the final version of the *Catechism*.

This applies to the case of the Mother Superior facing an army officer ready to give orders to his soldiers. Because of his genocidal intentions, the officer has no right to know whether fugitives are hiding in the convent. However, this man and his soldiers are souls who need salvation. If instead of asking questions the soldiers had stormed the convent straight away, Mother Superior would have been spared the ordeal of answering a difficult question. And this is precisely the point. He could use force and carry out a search. Instead, he is considerate enough to ask. He is open to the truth. Rather than focusing on the nun's moral obligation to give an honest answer to a threatening question, the problem is resolved by looking at her obligation to tell this army officer that God condemns genocide. Precisely because the man has enough respect to expect an honest answer from a nun, God can use her words to move his hardened heart. Perhaps the man will repent some day because one woman had the courage to stand up to him. This is the logic that follows from our Lord's words when he asked his disciples to preach the coming of God's kingdom: "And do not fear those who kill the body but cannot kill the soul; rather fear him who can destroy both soul and body in hell" (Mt 10:28). Telling the truth is more important than survival. Saving someone's soul for eternity is more important than saving someone's earthly life.

If you are caught in a situation where telling the truth seems both useless and dangerous, use your wits to escape, if you can. But never worry if the world falls apart because God's enemies give you no other choice than to tell the truth. There are times when truth is the only weapon Christians have against the great evils that threaten them.

Truth and art

All art is meant to achieve beauty. The *Catechism* explains the relationship between truth and beauty:

> Created "in the image of God," man also expresses the truth of his relationship with God the Creator by the beauty of his artistic works. . . . Like any other human activity, art is not an absolute end in itself, but is ordered to and ennobled by the ultimate end of man.
>
> CCC, n. 2501

For a work of art to be beautiful, it must lead people to the truth. All artistic productions—literature, painting, sculpture, film, dance—should be an attempt to capture the truth about God and his creation.

Some novelists and film directors produce art that portrays people committing serious sins. This is not necessarily wrong. As the old saying goes, life is a mixture of shadows and light. To portray life realistically, an artist will often want to capture the struggle between good and evil. However, portraying this struggle can itself be evil, either because the artistic production inspires despair instead of hope or, worse yet, because the artistic production is an occasion of sin for anyone who reads it or sees it.

How can you judge which novels, paintings, magazines, and movies are good and which are bad? Common sense is usually sufficient to recognize pornography. Once you are aware that something is pornographic, stay away from it.

Some works of art can harm your faith. Because threats against your faith are usually subtle and affect some people more than others, it is more difficult to define what to look for. Keep in mind two general criteria.

- Avoid anything that openly attacks Jesus Christ, the Catholic Church, the Bible, the sacraments (especially matrimony), or the saints (especially the Virgin Mary). No matter how many experts praise the "artistic" qualities of such a work of art, it is not good art. It is evil because it leads people away from the truth. It could easily lead you away from the truth.
- If you have doubts, ask for advice from someone you can trust. Just as you would never swallow a pill unless you were sure it was good for you, you should be careful what you pour into your mind and heart when setting out to read a book or watch a movie.

The Spirit of truth

You come to love the truth perfectly when you come to know the "Spirit of truth" (Jn 16:13).

Jesus once sent his disciples to the nearby towns and villages. He said, "And preach as you go, saying, 'The kingdom of heaven is at hand'" (Mt 10:7). After his resurrection, he commanded these same disciples to go out to the whole world and tell everyone the Good News. God expects Christians to do the same today.

You can talk to others about Jesus Christ. Talk to your friends and relatives. Repeat the simple message that the kingdom of God is close at hand. In other words, tell them God will give his grace to *anyone* who repents and believes in the gospel. As you speak, the same thing that happened to the first disciples will happen to you. Jesus described it this way: "It is not you who speak, but the Spirit of your Father speaking through you" (Mt 10:20).

Even if you tell your friend something simple—such as Jesus is Lord!—it will not be you speaking but the "Spirit of truth" speaking within you. In other words, your attempt to talk to someone about God will resonate powerfully in that person's soul. No matter how awkward your effort is, God uses it. He moves the person from deep inside in a way that you cannot see. This is the Holy Spirit "speaking."

There are many ways of getting to know the Holy Spirit. It is amazing to discover, through your own personal experience, that he speaks whenever you speak to others about believing in God.

REVIEW QUESTIONS

1. What are the acts commanded by God in the eighth commandment?
2. What are the acts prohibited by God in the eighth commandment?
3. In what ways does lying harm the person who lies? How does it harm others?
4. What obligation do you have to repair damage caused by sins of slander and detraction?

31. Keeping Your Mind and Heart Pure

The ninth and tenth commandments

The last two commandments go together. The ninth commandment tells us how to have a pure heart. The tenth commandment tells us how to have a generous heart. All the other commandments focus mainly on externals, that is, actions or omissions in the world around us. The ninth and tenth commandments focus on "coveting," that is, *internal* sins. Internal sins include all the fantasies we deliberately entertain, desiring to do something wrong without actually doing it. The original phrasing of the ninth and tenth commandments specifies the obligations of a man towards his neighbors. Since women have the same obligations, the commandments can be phrased to apply to both:

> You shall not covet your neighbor's wife.
> You shall not covet your neighbor's goods.
>
> Exodus 20:17

Coveting your neighbor's spouse means entertaining a desire to engage in any kind of sexual activity with that person. You covet someone's goods when you entertain a desire to take something away from your neighbor and make it your own.

Coveting does not refer to some passing fancy or sensation, which comes and goes as a mere temptation. It refers only to deliberate acts of the will. The traditional distinction between these two realities—temptation and sin—is summed up in the saying: "Feeling is not the same as consent."

Greed versus noble ambition

Coveting generally starts with a *disordered* desire to have things. A desire is disordered if it goes against God's plan for us and leads us away from happiness. The *Catechism* explains:

> The sensitive appetite leads us to desire pleasant things we do not have, e.g., the desire to eat when we are hungry or to warm ourselves when we are cold. These desires are good in themselves; but often they exceed the limits of reason and drive us to covet unjustly what is not ours and belongs to another or is owed to him.
>
> CCC, n. 2535

Does this mean that you are always wrong when you want something that your neighbor has?

It is a noble desire to seek goods that you need. You are a human being, not an angel. Your needs go beyond basic necessities like food, shelter, and clothing. You cannot acquire knowledge and culture, nor can you develop your talents and personality, without the means to do so. Consequently, there is nothing wrong with hoping that you, too, may one day come to possess goods similar to those your richer neighbors already enjoy. The *Catechism* teaches:

> It is not a violation of the [tenth] commandment to desire to obtain things that belong to one's neighbor, provided this is done by just means.
>
> CCC, n. 2537

There is nothing wrong with wanting some good or service your neighbor has. After all, you could offer to buy it at a fair price or buy it from someone else.

Sacred Scripture

As for the rich in this world, charge them not to be haughty, nor to set their hopes on uncertain riches but on God who richly furnishes us with everything to enjoy. They are to do good, to be rich in good deeds, liberal and generous, thus laying up for themselves a good foundation for the future, so that they may take hold of the life which is life indeed.

1 Timothy 6:17–19

How can you distinguish between the *noble ambition* to possess goods you need and the *sin* of "coveting your neighbor's goods"? Having no immediate plan to steal, you begin to covet when you *entertain the desire to steal* something from your neighbor. Coveting is an internal desire fueled by greed.

In a broader sense, you also covet when you want goods you don't need—usually because you are motivated by jealousy. You suffer mainly because your neighbor has something you don't have. You suffer not because you need something, but because your neighbor has something. Being unable to acquire it makes you feel inferior or ashamed.

Coveting sometimes goes beyond wanting physical possessions. This happens when coveting results from envy. A farmer covets when he dreams of some disaster that will wipe out a neighbor's harvest so he can sell his grain at higher prices. A woman covets when she fantasizes about her beautiful friend being disfigured in an accident so people will shun her friend and pay more attention to her. A businessman covets when he hopes someone's business will fail so he can make a profit on the other man's loss. A doctor covets when he looks forward to the spread of a disease that only he can cure. A scientist covets when he wishes a colleague's experiment would fail, giving him a chance to make an important discovery first. These are a few examples of the subtle ways people can be guilty of coveting.

Good deeds to do

Seek first the kingdom of God The greatest desire you can ever have is the desire to see God, to know him and to live with him forever. God's love and only God's love can satisfy your deepest longings. Most problems of lust, greed, or envy arise because of the emptiness in your heart. If you do not discover God's love, you end up pursuing other goals—some noble and generous, others frivolous and depraved—but always goals that, when achieved, leave you disappointed. Seeking God's kingdom first means, in practice, doing his will instead of yours. This requires nothing less than dying to yourself and living for God. Pursue the noble goals of life—vocation, career, adventure—but in a way that leads to God.

Jesus prays in the Garden of Gethsemane: "Father . . . not my will, but thine, be done": Luke 22:42

Purify your heart This means correcting your tendency towards evil. Overcome idleness and laziness. Acts of penance—self-denial in your choice of food, drink, posture, comfort, and entertainment—are also essential. But prayer comes first. This means asking God to make you pure. Only his grace has the power to cleanse your heart from all the impurities accumulated over the years. Go to confession often—once every two weeks will do wonders. Receive Holy Communion frequently—daily, if possible. Pray to the Blessed Virgin Mary, especially in moments of temptation. Do not worry if temptations are both strong and frequent. It happens to everybody. Never give up after a moment of weakness, but start over and trust God to help you.

The Gospel gives us the example of Mary's Immaculate Heart: she had a habit of "pondering" God's word "in her heart": Luke 2:19 and 2:51

Practice modesty This means choosing ways of speaking, behaving, and dressing that make it easy for you and everyone else to remain pure of heart. Purity is impossible without modesty. Just as you must learn to be modest about exposing your body, learn to be modest with your emotions. It is good to be spontaneous, but spontaneity without prudence can do as much harm as remaining inhibited and unapproachable. A husband and wife live modesty by reserving the intimate expressions of marital love to a time and place when they can be alone. Those preparing for marriage live modesty by being reserved in their expressions of affection, avoiding situations where they would be alone together.

God gives Adam and Eve their first set of clothing: Genesis 3:21

Detach yourself from things This means being satisfied with few possessions, getting rid of things you never use, and refusing to buy things you do not need. It also means trusting in God in moments of need, even in the midst of famine or war or any other crisis. The worst that could possibly happen to you is that you die and, for a Christian, death is never a tragedy; it is the gateway to eternal life.

Jesus encourages us to be like the birds of the air and the lilies of the field: Luke 12:22–32

Evils to avoid

Lust of the flesh, lust of the eyes, and the pride of life These are the three forms of coveting listed by St. John the Apostle in his first letter (1 Jn 2:16). Lust of the flesh is simple lust—the vice of desiring any form of sexual pleasure that goes against the purpose for which God created it. Lust of the eyes is greed—the lust for money and the desire for limitless possessions. The pride of life is the lust for power. It is sinful to crave power so you can reduce those in your command to slaves dedicated to satisfying your whims. It is also sinful pride to think you are better than others simply because you have authority over them. This form of pride is also called "vainglory"—empty glory—seeking glory in the eyes of the world instead of giving glory to God.

Jesus warns his disciples that no one can serve two masters: "You cannot serve God and mammon": Matthew 6:24

Consumerism This is a subtle form of greed that arises whenever you desire material possessions that exceed your real needs. Ancient peoples were just as prone to this sin as anyone else. However, mass production of consumer goods has made it possible for billions of people to indulge in this vice. Because of the superabundance of goods available at low prices, everyone, even relatively poor people, have to guard against the temptation of buying things they do not need or buying a better version of some gadget they already have simply because it is for sale.

Based on his own sad experience, King Solomon equates chasing after wealth with chasing after the wind: Ecclesiastes 2:8–11

Indecency God made us beautiful, but sin has made us weak. Sexually provocative clothing does not make you look good, even though it attracts a lot of attention. It makes others look at you as an object instead of a person. If your style of dress provokes bad intentions in others, you are guilty of scandal. You are leading them into sin by stirring up lustful desires in their hearts. You can only be elegant if you dress with modesty. If your words provoke bad intentions in others, you are also guilty of scandal. You lead others into sin if your conversation stirs up lustful desires.

Jesus speaks of a millstone wrapped around the neck of anyone who deliberately leads others into sin: Mark 9:42

Flaunting wealth Sometimes called extravagance, this includes any calculated attempt to make others think you are rich by showing off your possessions in public or by spending money lavishly in order to impress others. Even if you rightfully own your possessions or have some other reason for spending a lot of money, flaunting wealth is always wrong. You are provoking jealousy in the hearts of both friends and strangers. It is the same as scandal because it may lead them into the sin of coveting. You are humiliating the poor and, for this injustice, you will one day be humiliated.

"And behold, some are last who will be first, and some are first who will be last.": Luke 13:30

Envy This means becoming sad because someone else succeeds, acquires possessions, or seems satisfied with life. Sadness is the key to detecting envy. If you are envious, you will feel sad no matter how much success you already enjoy, no matter how many possessions you already have, no matter how well your own life is progressing. You want your success, your possessions, and your life to look more spectacular. You are not sad because you lack something. It is your neighbor's happiness that makes you sad. Envy becomes worse when you take delight in someone's misfortune or suffering. Envy is a great sin and often leads to many other sins.

Because Satan was envious of Adam and Eve, he tempted them to rebel against God: Wisdom 2:24

Jealousy Similar to envy, jealousy refers to the resentment someone feels towards a rival, and more specifically to rivalries for romantic affection. When it comes time for giving out awards and promotions, jealousy towards classmates at school, colleagues at work, or fellow athletes in competition is understandable but still wrong—usually a venial sin. When jealousy motivates a person to long for someone else's failure, it becomes a serious sin. As with envy, jealousy often leads to sins of hatred, slander, and violence. When touching on the desire of a husband or wife towards their spouse, jealousy is not evil—on the contrary, it is very good. The Old Testament often speaks of God being jealous for his people. Like a husband, Yahweh demands faithfulness from Israel, his bride. He was eager to see Israel remain faithful to him and angry whenever the Israelites chased after false gods. Romantic jealousy is evil if a single man gets furious with a woman who decides to marry someone else—he is not respecting her freedom—and, vice versa, when an unmarried woman becomes jealous when her rival wins the affection of the man she was hoping to marry.

In a fit of jealousy, King Saul tries to kill David: 1 Samuel 18:6–11

Special Topics

Desire for God

The New Testament speaks about being "led by the Spirit" and "walking by the Spirit." Perhaps you have read such phrases and wonder what they mean. It is all about having a desire for God. The Holy Spirit will show you how much freedom you can enjoy if you allow him to act. It is a freedom of love that comes from desiring God above all things. But he cannot show you unless you agree. God never forces us to accept his will. You have to love him because you want to.

> **Fathers of the Church**
>
> Seek what suffices. Seek what is enough, and don't desire more. Whatever goes beyond that produces anxiety instead of relief. Instead of lifting you up, it will weigh you down.
>
> St. Augustine, *Sermon* 85, 6

Don't think you have to spend the whole day in church on your knees. God wants the vast majority of men and women to find him through their ordinary daily activities. By learning to do your work well, you will find God. Gradually, you will learn to turn everything you do into an encounter with Jesus Christ.

You may hear someone say that hard work is the best remedy for any serious problem of concupiscence. Without a doubt, laziness is the single biggest reason why many people end up having problems of envy, jealousy, lust, etc. If you want to have a pure and generous heart, learn to work. Use your time well. But this helps only if you work for the right reason.

Many people have acquired a habit of working intensely for long hours and have never learned how to master sexual urges and their craving for wealth or power. They work long hours only to get lots of money to satisfy a long list of whims and caprices. It is necessary not only to work but to work with the intention of discovering God through your work.

Fleeing from temptation

Purity is the virtue that helps you control sexual desire. Men feel sexually attracted to women. Women feel sexually attracted to men. God made us that way. It is normal to feel this attraction. It is abnormal not to feel it. Men and women who fail to feel attracted towards the opposite sex—and feel same-sex attraction instead—have a serious emotional or physical dysfunction. They usually require professional counseling to overcome some difficulty experienced during childhood before they feel normal attraction.

Feeling sexual attraction is positive. However, we also experience something negative called "concupiscence." You feel it within yourself when you discover that it is difficult to *master* your feelings and emotions. Like everyone else, you have probably experienced this difficulty.

Though the ninth commandment speaks only of the case of a man desiring to commit adultery with another man's wife, coveting applies to all situations where a man or a woman deliberately entertains *any kind* of lustful desire.

A person is guilty of serious sin whenever he or she desires sexual pleasure in a way that goes against God's plan for marriage. Jesus spoke strong words to warn his disciples against this danger. Following the wording of the Ten Commandments, he phrased his warning in terms of the sin a man would commit. Women can commit this sin too. Speaking at the Sermon on the Mount, he stated:

> You have heard that it was said, "You shall not commit adultery." But I say to you that every one who looks at a woman lustfully has already committed adultery with her in his heart. If your right eye causes you to sin, pluck it out and throw it away; it is better that you lose one of your members than that your whole body be thrown into hell. And if your right hand causes you to sin, cut it off and throw it away; it is better that you lose one of your members than that your whole body go into hell.
>
> Matthew 5:27–30

Though Jesus talked about dozens of virtues, he treated the virtue of purity with exceptional rigor. Nowhere else does Jesus use such severe language—plucking out eyes, amputating limbs.

It would be a mistake to think that Jesus wants us to start cutting off body parts every time we have a temptation. The Church condemns mutilation of the body performed with the intention of trying to preserve purity. Jesus uses hyperbole—a rhetorical device based on exaggeration—to convey the absolute necessity of purity. When temptation comes, you must be ready to use all the energies of your heart and soul to flee from evil.

Fleeing from temptation is the secret to being pure. The example comes from Joseph, one of the twelve sons of Jacob in the Old Testament. He literally ran away (cf. Gen 39:12). This is the only thing that works. It is both pointless and stupid to try to control sexual desire by needlessly standing up to it. The saints have always advised one simple course of action: When temptation comes, flee. This advice is just common sense. If someone looks like he's getting ready to dump a bucket of sewage over your head, you don't start a discussion on the evils of sewage. You run.

Fleeing from temptation will solve most of your problems. As simple as this advice sounds, it can feel like you are plucking out an eye or cutting off a hand, because it may not come naturally. You must "force" yourself to do it.

Distinguishing between love and lust

Any desire for sexual relations before marriage or outside of marriage constitutes an interior act of lust and is always seriously wrong. Even so, lust cannot be reduced to a simple rule, as if anything that happens between husband and wife is good.

The virtue of chastity is necessary within marriage. When it is lacking, the love uniting husband and wife grows cold. The Church teaches:

> Man can commit this adultery "in the heart" also with regards to his own wife, if he treats her only as an object to satisfy instinct.
>
> St. John Paul II, *Theology of the Body*, p. 157

This statement refers to Jesus' remark: "I say to you that every one who looks at a woman lustfully has already committed adultery with her in his heart" (Mt 5:28). A husband can look at his wife with sexual desire and be moved by nothing but love. Or a husband can look at his wife with sexual desire and be guilty of lust.

This is, perhaps, one of the most difficult aspects of Church teaching to understand. However, it is crucial for married couples and for those preparing for marriage. What exactly has to take place in the man's heart for him to treat his wife "as an object"? How can a husband tell if he is guilty of lust towards his wife? How can he overcome it and love her as she deserves?

It is not the intensity of the desire that constitutes lust, nor is it the experience of sexual pleasure. Sexual pleasure can be noble and holy in the eyes of God—and will be as long as the husband and wife truly love each other. If the husband's interior desire is motivated by love, then his desire is good. If instead his desire is motivated by lust, it is an evil desire.

Purity of Heart—Modesty in Action

Living the virtues of modesty and holy purity means knowing what to do and what to avoid. Here are some examples:

- Pray. Be humble. Ask God to show you how to be pure so you can learn how to love.
- Guard your sight. Remember King David (cf. 2 Sam 11:2).
- Avoid impure conversations. When people start talking that way, tell them to stop. If they refuse and the conversation gets worse, walk away.
- Use styles of dress that help others be pure. If you want to be truly elegant, start with being modest.
- Reject any kind of pornography immediately. Even if you think it doesn't affect you, flee from it. It is a poison that does enormous harm once it gets inside.
- Learn to control your feelings, your emotions, and your imagination.
- Protect the purity of others. If your friend has a problem, do not judge. But don't remain passive. Help with your example. Encourage with your words.
- Be sincere in spiritual direction. Speak clearly about any difficulties to someone who can guide you. You can't do it alone. You need support and advice from others.
- Turn to the Blessed Virgin Mary and St. Joseph. This devotion has helped countless Christians to discover the beauty of living chastity.

Because both good desire and evil desire are interior—because both are desires of a husband for his own wife—it is hard to tell the difference between love and lust. Note that the same logic applies to a wife's desire for her husband. Once people realize this, they naturally ask: "What is the difference between love and lust?"

Love gives. Lust takes. Love seeks to satisfy the needs of the other person. Lust is only interested in satisfying its own needs. Love makes whatever sacrifices are necessary to make the other person happy. Lust doesn't care how much the other person has to suffer as long as it gets what it wants.

When a husband or wife reduces the marital act to lustful desire, the human heart is left dissatisfied. When a man and woman express true love for one another, the human heart rejoices.

Relying on God's grace

God our Father knows our weaknesses. He is full of mercy. He will forgive anyone who repents as often as necessary. At the same time, he wants us to believe that purity is possible. It is difficult and yet possible. He expects us to learn how to resist temptation.

Concupiscence affects everybody. A person can have great desires to be close to God and serve others but still be subject to concupiscence. St. Paul described this vividly:

> So I find it to be a law that when I want to do right, evil lies close at hand. For I delight in the law of God, in my inmost self, but I see in my members another law at war with the law of my mind and making me captive to the law of sin which dwells in my members. Wretched man that I am! Who will deliver me from this body of death? Thanks be to God through Jesus Christ our Lord! So then, I of myself serve the law of God with my mind, but with my flesh I serve the law of sin.
>
> Romans 7:21–25

St. Paul does not mean there is something wrong with the human body. Instead, he is describing how difficult it is to control our feelings and emotions. He is describing our lack of control due to original sin. We call this lack of self-mastery "concupiscence." St. Paul is essentially saying that through God's grace, Christians learn to master their inclination towards evil.

Other saints also spoke of their struggle to be pure. Everyone who wants to be close to God has to fight this battle. Concupiscence is a wound left deep in our heart by Adam and Eve's sin. With the exception of the Blessed Virgin Mary, conceived without sin, all men and women are born into the world with this wound. Our physical and emotional reactions will never be completely perfect until the resurrection of the dead. We have to struggle for as long as we live. This means being humble and never being surprised when we see our defects.

You have the same struggle everyone else has. With God's grace, you can win the battle. You learn to master your body, your heart, and your imagination. It's worth it. Those who are pure of heart "shall see God" (Mt 5:8). But to be pure of heart, you need God's grace. If you want to see God, ask him to make you pure.

At the same time that St. Paul complained about "this body of death," he thanked God for giving him the strength to overcome temptation. "I can do all things in him who strengthens me" (Phil 4:13). If you dedicate time to prayer every day, God will give you the grace you need to be pure.

Being poor in spirit

Jesus spoke about condemning souls because they were so wrapped up in the selfish pursuit of comfort that they never noticed the suffering of the poor. To go through life and not notice how much others suffer would be a sign that you are headed for eternal damnation. You must repent and change.

God expects you to do something more than simply respect the property of others. Jesus spoke frequently about being poor in spirit. It goes hand in hand with "hungering for righteousness" and being as merciful as our heavenly Father is merciful (cf. Mt 5:3–9).

Jesus asked—and still asks—some of his disciples: "Go, sell what you have, and give to the poor . . . [then] come, follow me" (Mk 10:21). These disciples renounced the right to possess anything, no matter how trivial. Jesus did not ask everybody to do this. Joseph of Arimathaea and

Magisterium

Side-by-side with the miseries of underdevelopment, themselves unacceptable, we find ourselves up against a form of super-development, equally inadmissible, because like the former it is contrary to what is good and to true happiness. This super-development, which consists in an excessive availability of every kind of material good for the benefit of certain social groups, easily makes people slaves of "possessions" and of immediate gratification, with no other horizon than the multiplication or continual replacement of the things already owned with others still better. This is the so-called civilization of "consumption" or "consumerism," which involves so much "throwing away" and "waste." An object already owned but now superseded by something better is discarded, with no thought of its possible lasting value in itself, nor of some other human being who is poorer.

All of us experience firsthand the sad effects of this blind submission to pure consumerism: in the first place a crass materialism, and at the same time a radical dissatisfaction, because one quickly learns—unless one is shielded from the flood of publicity and the ceaseless and tempting offers of products—that the more one possesses the more one wants, while deeper aspirations remain unsatisfied and perhaps even stifled.

[There is a] difference between "having" and "being." . . . To "have" objects and goods does not in itself perfect the human subject, unless it contributes to the maturing and enrichment of that subject's "being," that is to say unless it contributes to the realization of the human vocation as such.

Of course, the difference between "being" and "having," the danger inherent in a mere multiplication or replacement of things possessed compared to the value of "being," need not turn into a contradiction. One of the greatest injustices in the contemporary world consists precisely in this: that the ones who possess much are relatively few and those who possess almost nothing are many. It is the injustice of the poor distribution of the goods and services originally intended for all.

St. John Paul II, *Social Concern*, n. 28

Nicodemus continued to be very wealthy men while being his disciples. They provided Jesus with a tomb and a proper burial on the day he was crucified. Even so, Jesus demanded total detachment: "Whoever of you does not renounce all that he has cannot be my disciple" (Lk 14:33).

To be poor in spirit, be detached from your possessions. This is what Jesus had in mind when talking about the carefree life of the birds of the air and the lilies of the field. They never worry about food and drink and clothing. You also need to be free from anxiety. Trust God to care for your needs:

> And do not seek what you are to eat and what you are to drink, nor be of anxious mind. For all the nations of the world seek these things; and your Father knows that you need them. Instead, seek his kingdom, and these things shall be yours as well. Fear not, little flock, for it is your Father's good pleasure to give you the kingdom.
>
> Luke 12:29–32

Many Christians suppose that poverty is a virtue reserved for priests and nuns. This is a great mistake. Ordinary Christians, living in the middle of the world, should also be detached from the things of this world.

One of the saints explained it this way. Poverty of spirit cannot be equated with possessing nothing. The poverty Jesus wants us to live is not achieved by being dirty and walking around in rags. After explaining this, St. Josemaría went on to say:

> John the Baptist, who had a special vocation, wore a garment of camel's hair and ate locusts and wild honey. Our Savior wore a seamless tunic. He ate and drank as the others did, rejoiced at their happiness, was moved by the sorrows of his neighbors, and did not refuse the rest and shelter that his friends offered him. He made no secret of the fact that he had earned his living for many years working alongside Joseph the craftsman. This is the way we should behave in this world: as our Lord did. I could sum up my advice very briefly as follows: We ought to go about in clean clothes, with a clean appearance and, most important of all, with a clean soul.
>
> St. Josemaría, *Friends of God*, n. 121

Ordinary Christians are poor in spirit when they use the goods of this world to serve others. They live poverty by doing their work well. By working as a carpenter for thirty years, isn't that what Jesus showed us? The Son of God was "poor in spirit" when he died without any worldly possessions, nailed to a cross. He was also "poor in spirit" during his years in Nazareth, while using his tools to do his daily work and earn a living.

Wisdom of the Saints

After the name of Jesus, there is no other in which we find such powerful assistance and salvation as in the great name of Mary. . . . Therefore St. Peter Chrysologus says "that the name of Mary is an indication of chastity"; meaning, that when we doubt whether or not we have consented to thoughts against this virtue, if we remember having invoked the name of Mary, we have certain proof that we have not sinned.

St. Alphonsus Liguori, *The Glories of Mary*, ch. 10

Freedom of heart

Jesus once told a parable about the sower going out to sow seed in a field. The seed represents the gospel. The soil represents the heart of each person who hears the gospel. Each person either accepts it or rejects it. The story has a happy ending. Many hearts are "rich soil" where the gospel yields a harvest (cf. Mt 13:23). The fruits of the harvest are the same as what St. Paul calls the "fruits of the Spirit": love, joy, peace, patience, kindness, goodness, faithfulness, gentleness, self-control (cf. Gal 5:22–23). Spiritual life depends on having a heart where the gospel can produce these fruits.

Besides comparing it to rich soil, the parable compares the human heart to three other kinds of soil, that is, three other interior attitudes. Unlike the "rich soil," these three make faith impossible. They prevent men and women from opening their hearts to the action of the Holy Spirit. One is a path (where Satan makes faith impossible), the second is rocky soil (where fear of public opinion makes faith impossible), and the third is a patch of brambles (where concupiscence and greed make faith impossible).

A path is a place where nothing can grow because many people are constantly walking back and forth, trampling the ground and making it hard. Your heart becomes hardened—totally insensitive to the breath of the Paraclete—if you allow anything and everything to pass through. If you want to experience the awesome power and the tender gentleness of God's love, you must learn to guard your heart against the many perversions typical of worldly life. This means learning to guard your senses. Do not look at anything that stirs up lust or greed. Do not listen to evil talk. If you do not guard your heart—if you leave it open to every experience the world has to offer—you will soon find yourself enslaved to those experiences. In such a heart as that, Satan is master; he does whatever he wants.

Rocky soil is a place where a seed sprouts but does not take root. Many souls who would love to be close to God but fear what others might say. Friends, neighbors, and colleagues turn them away from committing themselves completely to God. This is why Jesus warned his disciples that they had to be ready to "hate" or "leave behind" father and mother, brothers and sisters, and anybody else or anything else that got in the way of their dedication to the gospel (cf. Mt 19:16–29 and Lk 14:26).

The patch of brambles is a patch of ground where thorns grow freely and choke all the good plants. Do not pamper yourself with luxury. Do not allow yourself to become fussy about food and drink. Austerity gives you the freedom to fly, to soar like an eagle above the cares of this world.

This freedom of heart is the whole point of the ninth and tenth commandments. St. Paul expressed it as a battle between the flesh and the spirit, where "flesh" represents our tendency to indulge in selfish behavior and "spirit" represents generosity inspired by the Holy Spirit:

> Walk by the Spirit, and do not gratify the desires of the flesh. For the desires of the flesh are against the Spirit, and the desires of the Spirit are against the flesh; for these are opposed to each other, to prevent you from doing what you would. But if you are led by the Spirit you are not under the law.
>
> Galatians 5:16–18

St. Paul says that being led by the Spirit frees you from the Law. This means having mastery over lust and greed. It means being able to brush off temptations without giving them any importance. This is true freedom.

REVIEW QUESTIONS

1. What are the acts commanded by God in the ninth and tenth commandments?
2. What are the acts prohibited by God in the ninth and tenth commandments?
3. Give some examples of the ways people covet their neighbor's goods.
4. Why does your heart have to be free if you want to follow Jesus?

Part Four

The Way Christians Worship

32.

Liturgy and Sacraments

The angels and saints worship God: "Day and night they never cease to sing . . ." (Rev 4:8). The liturgy of the Catholic Church reflects the worship that angels and saints give God in heaven. Jesus is now seated at the right hand of his Father. Before ascending into heaven, he established the Church's pattern of worship by teaching us how to pray and by instituting the seven sacraments. All the sacraments—especially the Eucharist—make him present among us. The *Catechism* explains:

> In Christian tradition, "liturgy" means the participation of the People of God in "the work of God." Through the liturgy, Christ, our redeemer and high priest, continues the work of our redemption in, with, and through his Church.
>
> *CCC*, n. 1023

"Do this in memory of me." Jesus said these words to his Apostles at the Last Supper. He was giving them a mission—and the power to fulfil that mission. He wanted them to make him present to all people after he ascended into heaven. He wanted them to do this by celebrating the Eucharist and by administering the other sacraments.

The Seven Sacraments

The liturgy consists of specific signs and rites. The most important are the sacraments because these were instituted by Jesus himself. They are meant for the good of all men and women of all times.

There are seven sacraments. They all give grace. They give grace by being signs of the grace they give. Each gives grace in a different way.

- **Baptism** gives sanctifying grace. This grace frees men and women from their sins and makes them children of God.
- **Confirmation** gives the gift of the Holy Spirit that the first disciples received at Pentecost.
- **The Eucharist** gives Christ's Body and Blood to those seeking union with him and the Church.
- **Penance and reconciliation** restores sanctifying grace to those who lost it by committing sins after baptism.
- **Anointing of the sick** gives a special grace to Christians in danger of death because of sickness or old age.
- **Holy orders** changes a man to make him a deacon, priest, or bishop.
- **Matrimony** unites a man and woman to each other, making them husband and wife.

Jesus wants all men and women to benefit from the graces given by these sacraments.

Three sacraments—baptism, confirmation, and the Eucharist—are called "sacraments of initiation." Christian life begins with baptism. It is strengthened by confirmation. It reaches its fullness in the Eucharist.

Two sacraments—penance and anointing—are called "sacraments of healing" because they have the power to heal our weaknesses and spiritually restore us.

Two sacraments—holy orders and matrimony—are meant for building up the Church.

The Church and the Holy Spirit

Jesus wants the Church to make us holy by administering the sacraments. Each sacrament has its own special minister. For instance, the bishop is usually the one who is the minister for confirmation. However, it is not simply the minister acting. The whole Church acts in each sacrament. And the Holy Spirit acts whenever the Church administers a sacrament.

> This happens because, by the will of her Lord, through the individual sacraments, the Church fulfils her salvific ministry to man. This sacramental

> ministry, every time it is accomplished, brings with it the mystery of the "departure" of Christ through the Cross and the Resurrection, by virtue of which the Holy Spirit comes. He comes and works: "He gives life." For the sacraments signify grace and confer grace: *they signify life and give life.*
>
> The Church is the *visible dispenser* of the sacred signs, while the Holy Spirit acts in them as the *invisible dispenser* of the life which they signify. Together with the Spirit, Christ Jesus is present and acting.
>
> St. John Paul II, *On the Holy Spirit,* n. 63

The Church is the visible dispenser of the sacraments. You can see the minister acting. The Holy Spirit is the invisible dispenser of God's grace. You do not see him acting, but he is present, giving us God's grace. The sacraments have the power to make us holy because the Holy Spirit is acting inside us whenever the Church administers a sacrament.

Liturgy and mystery

Christian worship relies on signs. The signs are words, objects, and gestures that point to realities we cannot see—realities from a world beyond us. The laying on of hands used during the liturgy of ordination is a sacramental sign. The bishop who is ordaining a priest places his hands on the head of the candidate during the rite of ordination. This symbol was used in the Old Testament to symbolize the conferring of power. This sign has assumed greater significance in the New Testament. Now it bears all the power of Christ himself. The bishop passes on his priestly power to the man he is ordaining. You cannot see the power passing from the bishop to the man becoming a priest. You can only see the laying on of hands.

Sacred Scripture

I heard around the throne and the living creatures and the elders the voice of many angels, numbering myriads of myriads and thousands of thousands, saying with a loud voice, "Worthy is the Lamb who was slain, to receive power and wealth and wisdom and might and honor and glory and blessing!" And the four living creatures said, "Amen!" and the elders fell down and worshiped.

Revelation 5:11–12, 14

The sacraments are not only signs. They are *efficacious*

signs. They are signs that *really work the effect* they signify. Each sacrament works its effect because God has given each sign a special power. For example, at baptism, it is the pouring of water while the minister says the baptismal formula that washes away sins. God is the one who has given power to the water to wash away sins when the minister baptizes. God is the one who has given power to the priest to forgive your sins when you go to confession.

The liturgy draws us into the mystery of God revealing himself to us. It follows the logic of the Incarnation—the logic of the divine Word becoming human flesh, the invisible becoming visible. Therefore, the liturgy is both natural and supernatural. Like Christ, it is both human and divine.

The liturgy reinforces the mystery of God dwelling with us. Just as the Son of God dwells with us in human flesh, God's saving power comes to us through signs. God chose natural symbols like water to represent supernatural realities like the cleansing from sin. We are lifted up by this liturgy. We glimpse God's infinite love contained within ordinary realities. When we celebrate the Eucharist, we see the appearances of bread and wine, but we hear the priest tells us, as only Jesus can tell us, "Take this and eat it; this is my body. Take this and drink it; this is the cup of my blood."

In every sacrament, the sign is twofold. The sign is matter and form. The sign is some action combined with some word. The one being baptized must have water poured over the head and the minister must call out his or her name while saying, "I baptize you in the name of the Father and of the Son and of the Holy Spirit." The words and actions combine to form a single sign. The sign points to an invisible reality. When the minister says the words of the baptismal formula and pours the water, a mystery takes place that no one can see or feel. The person baptized is radically changed. Not only are all sins forgiven, but that person truly becomes a child of God and a member of the Mystical Body of Christ.

Every liturgical ceremony includes a reading from the Word of God. Sacred Scripture narrates for us the history of God's work of creation and redemption. By reading an appropriate text, we come to understand better what God seeks to accomplish through the sacrament being celebrated.

Sacred images and music also form an indispensable part of liturgical celebration. The *Catechism* explains:

> The contemplation of sacred icons, united with meditation on the Word of God and the singing of liturgical hymns, enters into the harmony of the signs of celebration so that the mystery celebrated is imprinted in the heart's memory and is then expressed in the new life of the faithful.
>
> *CCC*, n. 1162

Icons are the representations of Jesus Christ, his Blessed Mother, and the angels and saints. These sacred images facilitate our worship. They remind us that God's Son truly became a man with flesh like ours. The images remind us that Jesus will forever be one of us and that the saints are destined to rise from the dead.

The Celebration of the Eucharist

The celebration of the Eucharist is the central focus of all liturgical celebrations. The Eucharist is a sacrament with several names. It is called the celebration of "Mass." We also call it "Holy Communion," referring to the act of receiving the Body and Blood of Jesus Christ. The Eucharist is also called the "Lord's Supper," indicating the way Jesus commanded, "Do this in memory of me" at the Last Supper. Sometimes we call it the "breaking of the bread" because Jesus broke the bread and consecrated it at the Last Supper and the Apostles imitated this gesture when celebrating the Eucharist.

At Mass the priest changes bread and wine into the Body and Blood of Christ. This ceremony usually takes place on an altar inside a church. You cannot see Jesus, but he is present. He is there, and it is crucial to your own salvation that you remember this simple fact. Jesus makes himself present for you. This is why you need to attend Mass. He wants you to be with him. He is on the altar waiting for you.

Liturgical rites

All sacraments are usually administered within a rite. A liturgical rite is a sacred ceremony that provides the proper context for administering the sacrament. For instance, a priest administering baptism performs the rite that includes, among other prayers, a blessing of the water. During the rite, the priest leads the faithful and, most especially the ones to be baptized, in making their baptismal promises. After the candidates have made this profession of faith, then the priest baptizes them.

In case of an emergency, the priest can dispense with the rite of baptism and administer baptism directly, pouring water over the person's head and using the words commanded by Christ for baptism. Similar logic applies to the administration of the other sacraments, with the exception of holy orders and the Eucharist, which must always be celebrated with the full rite prescribed by the Church.

> **Fathers of the Church**
>
> I wept at the beauty of your hymns and canticles. I was powerfully moved by the sweet sound of your Church's singing. These sounds flowed into my ears, and the truth streamed into my heart. My feeling of devotion overflowed and the tears ran from my eyes and I was happy in them.
>
> St. Augustine, *Confessions*, IX, 6

Since the Eucharist is the greatest of all the sacraments, the Mass is the Church's most important rite. There are several different ways of celebrating Mass, depending on the rite. The Pope in Rome follows the Latin rite, as do most local churches throughout the world. Some local churches follow other rites, usually referred to under the general title of the Eastern rites.

The Eastern rites originated in the East, that is, around Jerusalem, Antioch, Alexandria, Constantinople, and other cities east of Rome. In these cities, during ancient times, each local church developed its own liturgical prayers and practices. Even though the Eastern rites are different from the Latin rites, the seven sacraments of the Catholic Church are the same no matter which rite is used to celebrate them. Receiving the Eucharist in the Eastern rite is exactly the same as receiving the Eucharist in the Latin rite.

MAGISTERIUM

In the earthly liturgy we take part in a foretaste of that heavenly liturgy which is celebrated in the Holy City of Jerusalem toward which we journey as pilgrims, where Christ is sitting at the right hand of God, Minister of the holies and of the true tabernacle. With all the warriors of the heavenly army, we sing a hymn of glory to the Lord. Venerating the memory of the saints, we hope for some part and fellowship with them. We eagerly await the Savior, our Lord Jesus Christ, until he—our life—appears and we, too, appear with him in glory.

Vatican II, *Constitution on the Sacred Liturgy*, n. 8

The local churches of the Eastern rites are totally united to the Bishop of Rome. These churches recognize and accept the Pope's supreme authority as the Vicar of Christ. These local churches of the Eastern rites must be distinguished from the Orthodox Churches. The Orthodox Churches also administer the seven sacraments instituted by Christ, but, at least for the time being, they are not in full communion with the Pope. In practice, this means that the Pope readily invites the bishops of the Eastern rites to concelebrate the Eucharist with him, whereas the Pope and the bishops of the Orthodox Churches are still in the process of overcoming past misunderstandings before they can agree to concelebrate the Eucharist.

The liturgy in some Christian communities has been reduced to the celebration of baptism, either because they expressly reject the need for other sacraments or because they lack validly ordained bishops and priests capable of celebrating the sacraments. The Catholic Church recognizes the validity of the sacrament of baptism when it is properly celebrated in these communities—for example, among the Anglicans, Lutherans, Presbyterians, etc. Anyone baptized within these communities is truly Christian and receives the gift of sanctifying grace. Catholics should not receive Communion during the services held by these communities, if, for instance, they are attending funerals or weddings. Because these communities generally do not have validly ordained priests, it is impossible for them to have the Eucharist. Either their Communion service is only symbolic—they do not believe that bread and wine can be changed into the body and blood of Christ—or their celebration of the Lord's Supper is not a true celebration of the Eucharist because the minister is not a validly ordained priest. Catholics who actively participate in their liturgy and attempt to receive Communion cause confusion and perhaps even scandal, while endangering their own faith.

This does not mean that Catholics consider themselves better than these Christians. On the contrary, it is obvious that many of these Christians live the beatitudes with heroic perseverance. Catholics must keep in mind St. Paul's words: "No one can say 'Jesus is Lord' except by the Holy Spirit" (1 Cor 12:3). While recognizing God's grace working in these men and women who are, for now, not in full communion with the Bishop of Rome, Catholics pray that all Christians may come to believe everything taught by the Church's Magisterium and profess the Catholic faith in its entirety.

Sacramentals

Jesus instituted the seven sacraments. To help Christians understand their faith better and practice it with more devotion, the Catholic Church instituted sacramentals. For instance, within the official liturgy of the Church, Christians are invited every year to approach the altar on Good Friday and kiss a crucifix. A crucifix is an image of Jesus shedding his blood for us on the cross. Kissing the crucifix is a sign of the way each Christian is meant to love Jesus.

Like the sacraments, sacramentals are visible signs for spiritual effects. The difference is that sacramentals do not achieve their effect in the same way. The sign of a sacrament works because God gives power to the sign itself. The sign of a sacramental works because of the way it helps us desire greater union with God. The Church teaches:

> Sacramentals do not confer the grace of the Holy Spirit in the way that the sacraments do; but by the Church's prayer, they prepare us to receive grace and dispose us to cooperate with it.
>
> *CCC*, n. 1670

For instance, making the sign of the cross is a sacramental. It reminds us of the Trinity, as we say, "In the name of the Father, and of the Son, and of the Holy Spirit." It reminds us of the power of the cross to forgive our sins and make us children of God. Sprinkling of holy water is another sacramental. It reminds us of baptism.

> *Wisdom of the Saints*
>
> According to St. Peter, Noah's ark is a symbol for the Church. There is no entering into salvation outside the Church, just as no one outside of the ark was saved in the time of the deluge.
>
> St. Thomas Aquinas, *Summa Theologiae*, III, 73, 3, cf. 1 Pt 3:20–21

Exorcism is a sacramental. Acting publicly in the name of Jesus Christ, the exorcist demands that Satan cease to possess or influence some person or object. A solemn exorcism can only be carried out by a priest and with the permission of the bishop. The priest must proceed with prudence, strictly observing the rules established by the Church. "Before an exorcism is performed, it is important to ascertain that one is dealing with the presence of the Evil One, and not an illness" (*CCC*, n. 1673).

The liturgical year

The Church follows a cycle of celebrations every year, the three most important feasts being Christmas, Easter, and Pentecost. This annual cycle follows the life of Christ and the history of salvation.

The list on the next page shows the various seasons and the solemn feasts. Not included, but also important to the daily celebration of the liturgy, are the feasts of the saints. The entrance of a saint into heaven is usually celebrated on his or her *dies natalis*, (literally the "day of birth"), that is, the day that the saint ended life on earth and entered in heaven. For instance, the feast of St. Josemaría, the founder of Opus Dei, falls on June 26th because he died on that day in 1975.

Seasons of the Liturgical Year

SEASON OF ADVENT

From the First Sunday of Advent until Christmas Eve. It always includes the Four Sundays of Advent.

We prepare to celebrate Jesus' birth in Bethlehem. We anticipate our Lord's Second Coming at the end of the world. This is a time of penance.

CHRISTMAS SEASON

From Christmas Day until the feast of the Baptism of our Lord.

We celebrate our Lord's birth, his Epiphany (when the Magi came to adore him), and his baptism in the Jordan River. We also celebrate the feast of the Holy Family during this season.

ORDINARY TIME

From the day after the feast of our Lord's baptism until the Tuesday before Ash Wednesday.

SEASON OF LENT

From Ash Wednesday until the Easter Triduum.

Like the time of our Lord's fasting in the desert, Lent lasts for forty days (not counting the Sundays, which even during Lent remain a day dedicated to celebrating our Lord's resurrection). It is a time of penance. We prepare for Easter: the celebration of our Lord's passion, death, and resurrection. We stir up sorrow for our sins and do works of penance, especially acts of self-denial like fasting and almsgiving. The Easter Triduum comprises the holiest of all days. During these three days we celebrate the Mass of the Lord's Supper (Holy Thursday), commemorate our Lord's crucifixion (Good Friday) and burial in the tomb (Holy Saturday), finally celebrating his glorious resurrection on the third day (Easter Sunday).

HOLY WEEK

From Palm Sunday until Holy Saturday.

Holy Week forms part of Lent. It begins with a procession on Palm Sunday, commemorating our Lord's triumphal entry into Jerusalem. Palm Sunday is also called "Passion Sunday," since we read the account of our Lord's passion and death at Mass on that day. Holy Week culminates with the celebrations held on Holy Thursday and Good Friday.

continued

Seasons of the Liturgical Year *continued*

EASTER SEASON

From Easter Sunday until Pentecost Sunday.

This period marks the forty days Jesus spent with his disciples, appearing to them in Jerusalem and Galilee, leading up to Ascension Thursday. It also includes the ten days from Ascension Thursday to Pentecost, commemorating the days when the disciples gathered around the Virgin Mary in the Upper Room to prepare for the descent of the Holy Spirit. Pentecost marks the fiftieth (and last) day of the Easter Season. The Easter season is a period of rejoicing. It is especially appropriate to baptize converts to the faith during the Easter Vigil, as was customary in the early Church.

ORDINARY TIME

Ordinary time resumes beginning on the Monday after Pentecost and lasts until the end of the year.

During ordinary time, the Church celebrates the feasts of the Assumption of the Virgin Mary (August 15th) and All Saints Day (November 1st). The liturgical year closes with the celebration of the Feast of Christ the King on the last Sunday of the year—last according to the Church's calendar. The calendar begins again on the First Sunday of Advent.

REVIEW QUESTIONS

1. Explain each of the seven sacraments.
2. What do the sacraments do for us?
3. What is a liturgical rite?
4. Name the different liturgical seasons.

33.

Baptism

In the Old Testament, circumcision was the rite necessary for any man who wanted to become a member of God's chosen people. St. Paul describes the way God saves us now:

> In him also you were circumcised with a circumcision made without hands, by putting off the body of flesh in the circumcision of Christ; and you were buried with him in baptism, in which you were also raised with him through faith in the working of God, who raised him from the dead. And you, who were dead in trespasses and the uncircumcision of your flesh, God made alive together with him, having forgiven us all our trespasses . . .
>
> Colossians 2:11–13

Circumcision was the sign of the Old Covenant. Baptism is the sign of the New Covenant.

Jesus chose a specific sign for each sacrament. The one he chose for baptism was water. It has to be poured over the head of the person being baptized. Every sacrament requires words to complete the sign. Jesus commanded the Apostles: "Go therefore and make disciples of all nations, baptizing them in the name of the Father and of the Son and of the Holy Spirit" (Mt 28:19).

During a baptism you see water washing someone clean. You do not see the reality symbolized by that sign. God wants you to believe what you cannot see. He wants you to believe that, as a person is baptized, God is cleansing the soul from all sins and making that person holy. The Church teaches:

> Through baptism we are formed in the likeness of Christ: "For by one Spirit we were all baptized into one body" (1 Cor 12:13).
>
> Vatican II, *Dogmatic Constitution on the Church*, n. 7

Baptism produces a radical change. The Holy Spirit transforms the one being baptized and makes that man, that woman, a likeness of the Word made flesh. Having become somehow equal to the Son of God, a Christian is truly a child of God.

Entering the kingdom

One night a Pharisee named Nicodemus came to see Jesus. He said, "Rabbi, we know that you are a teacher who comes from God; for no one could perform the signs you do unless God were with him." Jesus answered:

> Truly, truly, I say to you, unless one is born anew, he cannot see the kingdom of God.
>
> John 3:3

Nicodemus did not understand. Did Jesus expect his disciples to be born a second time? Nicodemus asked: "How can a grown man be born? Can he go back into his mother's womb and be born again?" He wanted to know what Jesus meant. The Master answered:

> Truly, truly, I say to you, unless one is born of water and the Spirit, he cannot enter the kingdom of God. That which is born of the flesh is flesh,

Sacred Scripture

Now when they heard this they were cut to the heart, and said to Peter and the rest of the apostles, "Brethren, what shall we do?" And Peter said to them, "Repent, and be baptized every one of you in the name of Jesus Christ for the forgiveness of your sins; and you shall receive the gift of the Holy Spirit. So those who received his word were baptized, and there were added that day about three thousand souls.

Acts 2:37–38, 41

> and that which is born of the Spirit is spirit. Do not marvel that I said to you, "You must be born anew."
>
> John 3:5–7

Jesus wants us to be "born through water and Spirit." Pouring of water over the person to be "born again" causes spiritual birth. This is the essence of Christian baptism.

When Jesus was baptized, God the Father spoke from heaven, saying, "Thou art my beloved Son" (Lk 3:22). When you are baptized, God looks upon you the same way he looked upon Jesus two thousand years ago. Though you do not hear a voice from heaven as Jesus did, you become a child of God at the moment of baptism. You are "born of the Spirit." God truly becomes your Father in heaven. You become a brother, a sister, to the only Son of God. You are born again. You receive new life—the life of God.

Watching St. John the Baptist baptize them, the Jews connected the practice of pouring water with spiritual cleansing. John's baptism was an invitation to repent. Jesus elevated this ritual to a higher plane. When he asked St. John to baptize him in the Jordan, the Holy Spirit appeared visibly. This showed how the Father wanted to send the Spirit to us through baptism. At baptism, the Holy Spirit makes each person another Christ—an "anointed one" who has been *anointed with the Spirit*. Because of baptism, we are all "sons in the Son" (Vatican II, *The Church in the Modern World*, n. 22). Each Christian is *alter Christus, ipse Christus*: another Christ, Christ himself.

Being washed clean by Christ

When Jesus announced the mystery of being "born from above," Nicodemus was slow to believe. He said, "How can this be?" Jesus told Nicodemus he was wrong to hesitate: "Are you a teacher of Israel, and yet you do not understand this?" (John 3:9–10).

Jesus was reminding the Pharisee that expertise in the Law of Moses is not enough. He said to him:

> Truly, truly, I say to you, we speak of what we know. . . . No one has ascended into heaven but he who descended from heaven, the Son of

> man. And as Moses lifted up the serpent in the wilderness, so must the Son of man be lifted up, that whoever believes in him may have eternal life.
>
> John 3:11, 13–15

Jesus was "lifted up" when he was crucified. He had to shed his blood as a sacrifice for our sins. The power of this sacrifice reaches each person through baptism. Jesus told his disciples to baptize all those who want to enter God's kingdom.

St. Paul explained that each person who is baptized enters into Christ's death. The Christian dies to the old life of sin and is reborn to new life in the Holy Spirit.

> Do you not know that all of us who have been baptized into Christ Jesus were baptized into his death? We were buried therefore with him by baptism into death, so that as Christ was raised from the dead by the glory of the Father, we too might walk in newness of life.
>
> Romans 6:3–4

Having the water poured over your head—being covered with water—is a symbol of burial. This "burial" is your death to sin. Your old self dies and a "new you" is born. Just as Jesus broke loose from the tomb where he was buried and ascended into heaven, you emerge from the water and begin to live a new life. The old self dies because baptism washes away all your sins. The "new you" lives because the Holy Spirit makes you a child of God.

Baptism depends on Jesus' sacrifice. The Holy Spirit says that Christians are washed clean by Jesus' blood. "How much more shall the blood of Christ . . . purify your conscience from dead works to serve the living God" (Heb 9:14). St. Peter tells us that we have been "sprinkled" with Christ's blood (cf. 1 Pt 1:2). It is a metaphor describing the way Jesus takes away our sins. St. Peter then says:

> You know that you were ransomed from the futile ways inherited from your fathers, not with perishable things such as silver or gold, but with the precious blood of Christ, like that of a lamb without blemish or spot.
>
> 1 Peter 1:18–19

Baptism is a gift from God. Jesus had to pay a price to make it possible. You pay nothing.

Next time you are tempted to throw away God's grace by falling into sin, remember how precious the gift is. It would be the height of foolishness to think grace is worth little just because it cost you nothing. If you have been baptized, treasure the grace God gave you. It is worth more than all the riches of the world.

Administering baptism

When Christian parents want their newborn child to be baptized, they go to their local church. Adults seeking salvation in Christ enter the catechumenate before being admitted for baptism. This is a period of formation in the faith. Men and women going through the catechumenate are called "catechumens."

Anyone in danger of death can be baptized immediately as long as the person requests it. Normally only deacons and priests baptize. If someone is about to die and wants to be baptized, anyone—even a person who has yet to be baptized—can perform the rite of baptism.

To baptize someone, pour water over the head, while calling out the person's name and saying, "I baptize you in the name of the Father, and of the Son, and of the Holy Spirit." We use these words because our Lord told the Apostles:

> All authority in heaven and on earth has been given to me. Go therefore and make disciples of all nations, baptizing them in the name of the Father and of the Son and of the Holy Spirit, teaching them to observe all that I have commanded you.
>
> Matthew 28:18–20

The person being baptized takes a Christian name. The *Catechism* states:

> This can be the name of a saint, that is, of a disciple who has lived a life of exemplary fidelity to the Lord. The patron saint provides a model of charity; we are assured of his intercession. The baptismal name can also express a Christian mystery or Christian virtue. Parents, sponsors,

> and the pastor are to see that a name is not given which is foreign to Christian sentiment.
>
> *CCC*, n. 2156

"Intercession" means that your patron saint will intercede for you. In other words, the saint will stand before God and present your needs to him.

Everyone needs to be baptized

God wants all people to be saved. He wants all people to be baptized. Even babies need baptism. When a baby is born, the baby has many smears and stains all over the body. So the mother and her friends (or the doctor and the nurse) wash the baby. Something similar is needed for the soul. The baby needs baptism as soon as possible. Baptism means washing away all stain of sin from the soul.

Fathers of the Church

Do you want to know the power of baptism? As the one being baptized emerges from the water, the gates of the kingdom of heaven are thrown open.

The Venerable Bede, *Commentary on Luke*, I, 3, 21

A baby cannot commit sins. A baby is too little to know the difference between right and wrong. A baby is too young to choose between good and evil. Even so, babies need baptism. They do not have any personal sins. But they inherit the sin of Adam and Eve. That sin is called "original sin." It stains our souls from the very first moment of our existence and prevents us from being pleasing to God. When the Church teaches that babies are born with original sin, she is saying that they are spiritually dead. This is why babies need to be baptized as soon as possible. The *Catechism* says:

> The sheer gratuitousness of the grace of salvation is particularly manifest in infant baptism. The Church and the parents would deny a child the priceless grace of becoming a child of God were they not to confer baptism shortly after birth.
>
> *CCC*, n. 1250

By having a baby baptized, Christian parents are giving their child the best gift they could possibly give. It is the gift of God's grace.

Adults need baptism first to cleanse them of original sin and then to wash away their own personal sins. As Jesus told Nicodemus, "I tell you most solemnly, unless a man is born from above, he cannot see the kingdom of God" (Jn 3:3). Jesus used even stronger words when he spoke to his disciples after the resurrection:

> Go into all the world and preach the gospel to the whole creation. He who believes and is baptized will be saved; but he who does not believe will be condemned.
>
> Mark 16:15–16

If you want Christ to save you from your sins and you have not been baptized yet, you must get baptized.

Becoming a Christian goes far beyond joining an organization of people you admire. Before you can be baptized, you need to commit your whole life to Jesus once and for all. You are essentially doing what the first disciples did when Jesus told them "Follow me," and they left everything behind to follow him (cf. Mk 1:18 and Lk 5:11). This takes faith. You have to believe that God will care for you first in this world and later in the next world. Contrition is also necessary. Be sorry for all your sins. Ask God to forgive you. Begin to go to Mass on Sundays at a Catholic church. Learn the teachings of the Catholic Church. Clarify any doubts you have.

Baptism by blood, baptism of desire

Is anyone ever saved without being baptized? One of the Church Fathers answered the question by quoting another Father of the Church:

> Since the words "This day you shall be with me in paradise" were addressed to a thief who was not baptized, St. Cyprian presents a strong case for claiming that suffering can sometimes take the place of baptism. I have carefully thought this matter over myself many times and concluded that, besides suffering for the sake of Christ, faith and conversion of heart can also make up for the lack of baptism whenever difficult

> circumstances make it impossible for the person to receive the sacrament of baptism.
>
> St. Augustine, *On Baptism*, IV, 22

From the earliest times, the Church has taught that there are some men and women who are saved even though they were never baptized with water. They are like the repentant thief (cf. Lk 23:43).

The Church teaches that martyrs and catechumens can be saved if they die before they have a chance to be baptized. Those who do not know the gospel but seek God and strive to do his will can also be saved even though they have not received the sacrament of baptism. The *Catechism* says:

> Since Christ died for all, and since all are in fact called to one and the same destiny, which is divine, we must hold that the Holy Spirit offers to all the possibility of being made partakers of the Paschal mystery, in a way known to God. All those who are ignorant of the gospel of Christ and of his Church, but seek the truth and do the will of God in accordance with their understanding of it, can be saved. It may be supposed that such persons would have desired baptism explicitly if they had known its necessity.
>
> *CCC*, n. 1260

We use the phrase "baptism of blood" to describe the way God saves those who shed their blood for Christ. We use the phrase "baptism of desire" when speaking of those who, through no fault of their own, do not know Christ and yet will be saved by trying, as best they know how, to do God's will.

A question arises when speaking about babies who die before being able to receive baptism. Baptism is necessary. Even those ignorant of the gospel must have at least an implicit desire for baptism—*implicit* because they desire to do God's will without any reservations and would be baptized if they knew it was God's will. What happens to those who are too young to desire? The *Catechism* teaches:

> As regards children who have died without baptism, the Church can only entrust them to the mercy of God, as she does in her funeral rites

> for them. Indeed, the great mercy of God, who desires that all should be saved, and Jesus' tenderness toward children which caused him to say: "Let the children come to me, do not hinder them," allow us to hope that there is a way of salvation for children who have died without baptism. All the more urgent is the Church's call not to prevent little children coming to Christ through the gift of holy baptism.
>
> CCC, n. 1261

Because baptism is necessary for salvation, it would be seriously wrong for parents to delay the moment of their baby's baptism. This does not imply that God condemns unbaptized babies, least of all a baby the parents wanted to baptize but who died before baptism was possible. This is why the Church allows a funeral rite for an unbaptized baby of Christian parents, similar to the way the Church holds a funeral rite for a catechumen who died before baptism was possible.

Effects of baptism

Baptism changes you radically. It does many things for you.

- It cleanses you from the stain of original sin.
- It takes away all your personal sins.
- It cancels all punishment due to sin—all eternal punishment and all temporal punishment.
- It gives you sanctifying grace.
- It leaves a spiritual mark or seal on your soul.
- It makes you a child of God.
- It fills you with faith, hope, and love.
- It gives you the gifts of the Holy Spirit.
- It makes you a member of Christ's Church and an heir to God's kingdom.
- It gives you a share in the priesthood of Christ so that you can offer spiritual sacrifices pleasing to God.

The Church teaches that baptism and the other sacraments work their effects *ex opere operato*—from the working of the work—that is, by the very fact of receiving the sacrament. In other words, the effects that baptism is supposed to work in your soul do not depend on what kind of person baptizes you or how holy he is. The effects depend instead on the sacrament itself. It is the very act of baptizing that makes you holy.

Baptism leaves a spiritual mark or seal on your soul. It is called "sacramental character." It cannot be removed. No sin can erase it. Once baptized, you can never be baptized again. When Christians who were validly baptized in another Christian community (e.g., with the Anglicans, Lutherans, etc.) decide to become Catholics, they do not get "baptized again." They are already Christians. They *cannot* be baptized again. When they decide to become Catholics, they are received into full communion with the Catholic Church in a special ceremony totally distinct from the rite of baptism.

> **MAGISTERIUM**
>
> By his power, Jesus is present in the sacraments so that when anybody baptizes it is really Christ himself who baptizes.
>
> Vatican II, *Constitution on the Sacred Liturgy*, n. 7

Even though baptism forgives all sins and cancels all punishment for sin, it does not remedy human weakness. A person who dies immediately after being baptized will go straight to heaven. But as long as Christians live in this world, they have to struggle. The *Catechism* explains:

> Certain temporal consequences of sin remain in the baptized, such as suffering, illness, death, and such frailties inherent in life as weaknesses of character, and so on, as well as an inclination to sin that sacred Tradition calls "concupiscence," or metaphorically, the *fomes peccati*, "the tinder for sin."
>
> CCC, n. 1264

Even after being baptized, a yearning for evil things drags us down. This is concupiscence and is compared to tinder (chips of bark and scraps of paper used to start a fire).

Wisdom of the Saints

We have to become saints . . . the kind that could be canonized. If not, we shall have failed as disciples of the one and only Master. . . . Some of you might think I am referring only to a select few. Don't let the promptings of cowardice or easygoing ways deceive you so easily. Feel, instead, God urging each one of you on, to become another Christ, *ipse Christus*, Christ himself.

. . . Certainly our goal is both lofty and difficult to attain. But please do not forget that people are not born holy. Holiness is forged through a constant interplay of God's grace and the correspondence of man. As one of the early Christian writers says, referring to union with God, "Everything that grows begins small. It is by constant and progressive feeding that it gradually grows big." So I say to you, if you want to become a thorough-going Christian . . . then you will have to be very attentive to the minutest of details, for the holiness that Our Lord demands of you is to be achieved by carrying out with love of God your work and your daily duties, and these will almost always consist of small realities.

St. Josemaría, *Friends of God*, nn. 5, 6, 7

Every Christian has to fight against this inclination to evil. St. Paul mentioned his own experience. After years of faithful service, he had to struggle to live a holy life:

> Brethren, I do not consider that I have made it my own; but one thing I do, forgetting what lies behind and straining forward to what lies ahead, I press on toward the goal for the prize of the upward call of God in Christ Jesus.
>
> Philippians 3:13–14

Christian life is spiritual combat—a marathon from birth to death. Jesus provided us with seven sacraments to get through life. Baptism is the first. We receive the others only after we are baptized.

To serve God in this world and reach your heavenly home, you need grace. Though baptism does not cure you of concupiscence, it gives you the grace you need to overcome it. Though baptism does not free you from suffering, it gives new meaning to your suffering. Baptism enables you to confront all difficulties with joy. St. Paul says:

> Who shall separate us from the love of Christ? Shall tribulation, or distress, or persecution, or famine, or nakedness, or peril, or sword? As

> it is written, "For thy sake we are being killed all the day long; we are regarded as sheep to be slaughtered." No, in all these things we are more than conquerors through him who loved us.
>
> Romans 8:35–37

If you have been baptized, you have a serious responsibility to live a holy life. Jesus will not be content with an idle existence. It is not enough to avoid mortal sin.

Jesus shed his blood to make you a child of God. He has given you the free gift of grace. He wants you to be a saint. If you aim for anything less, you are betraying him. It is useless to argue that he should have chosen someone else. He wants everybody—literally every child ever born into this world—to be holy. God will not tolerate mediocrity or lukewarmness.

To drive this truth deep into our souls, the Church asks us to renew our baptismal promises once a year at Easter. During this ceremony, the priest asks us to reject Satan and all his works and all his empty promises. Then he invites us to profess our faith in God the Father, God the Son, and God the Holy Spirit.

REVIEW QUESTIONS

1. How is baptism administered?
2. Why do babies need to be baptized?
3. What does baptism do for us?
4. What do Christians have to do after being baptized?

34.

Confirmation

When building a house, the first thing you do is lay the foundations. Baptism, confirmation, and the Eucharist lay the foundations of your life as a Christian.

Perfecting baptism

Confirmation perfects the grace of baptism. It binds us more perfectly to the Church. It makes us more daring in spreading and defending the faith. It sharpens our spiritual vision so we can see how much we need union with Christ in the Eucharist. The term "confirmation" is used for this sacrament because it con-*firms*. It makes something firm. It makes your commitment to Christ stronger. It gives your spiritual life a solid foundation.

Our Lord often compared Christian life to a plant growing in good soil and bearing fruit. Because you are called to bear fruit, you need deep roots. Confirmation sinks the roots of your soul more deeply into the Church so you can receive God's grace more abundantly.

Christians bear fruit by drawing others to Jesus. God calls you to bear fruit, that is, to help your friends and relatives discover God. There, where you live, you will find many people who need to hear the news about God's mercy. They need your help. If you don't help them, they may drift away from God, becoming blind to God's mercy. If you help your colleagues, friends and relatives, you are helping Jesus spread the gospel.

The rite of baptism is modeled on Jesus' baptism, with water being poured over your head. When you receive confirmation, it is similar to the day of Pentecost. At Pentecost God gave his disciples courage to go out to the whole world and tell everyone the Good News. The Acts of the Apostles describes this event. Ten days after Christ's ascension, his disciples were gathered together with the Virgin Mary in the Upper Room. Suddenly, the Holy Spirit appeared. Wind filled the house and fire came down from heaven. A tongue of fire rested over the head of each disciple.

The wind and fire at Pentecost are symbols of the Holy Spirit. Through these visible, external signs, each disciple received the invisible, interior gift of the Holy Spirit. The Acts of the Apostles describes how the disciples astounded the people visiting in Jerusalem: "We hear them telling in our own tongues the mighty works of God" (Acts 2:11). The Holy Spirit gave Jesus' disciples deep conviction. This compelled them to speak to everyone about Jesus.

When you receive the sacrament of confirmation, you receive the same interior gift that the first disciples received at Pentecost. The external signs are different. You cannot see tongues of fire. No wind fills the church. But deep within your soul, Jesus gives you the same gift he gave his first disciples—the gift of the Holy Spirit.

The Holy Spirit led the first disciples go out and speak to others about Jesus. Confirmation gives you the courage to speak to others about your faith. As happened at Pentecost, people will be amazed to hear you speak with conviction. This conviction comes from the Holy Spirit. As Jesus once told his disciples, "It is not you who speak, but the Spirit of your Father speaking through you" (Mt 10:20).

The first disciples received the gift of the Holy Spirit through wind and fire. Those who came later received this gift by the laying on of hands—the same way we do today. The Acts of the Apostles tells us how newly baptized Christians received the Holy Spirit when they were confirmed after baptism.

> Now when the apostles at Jerusalem heard that [some people in] Samaria had received the word of God, they sent to them Peter and John, who came down and prayed for them that they might receive the Holy Spirit; for it had not yet fallen on any of them, but they had only been baptized

> in the name of the Lord Jesus. Then they laid their hands on them and they received the Holy Spirit.
>
> Acts 8:14–17

Baptism does not give you the gift of the Holy Spirit. That is why you need confirmation. Sts. Peter and John made the Holy Spirit come down on the baptized Christians by laying hands on their heads. Before they died, the Apostles gave their successors this power of passing on the gift of the Holy Spirit. A bishop is a successor of the Apostles. He has the power to give the gift of the Holy Spirit to other Christians.

The confirmation rite

The confirmation ceremony usually takes place within the celebration of Mass. It begins by having the candidates renew their baptismal promises. This emphasizes the way confirmation builds on the graces received at baptism.

Following apostolic Tradition, the bishop does three things when confirming you:

- He makes the sign of the laying on of hands.
- He anoints your forehead with sacred chrism.
- He calls you by your confirmation name and says, "Be sealed with the gift of the Holy Spirit."

The bishop calls each candidate one by one. Your sponsor stands next to you, with a hand on your shoulder, and tells the bishop your

SACRED SCRIPTURE

When the day of Pentecost had come, they were all together in one place. And suddenly a sound came from heaven like the rush of a mighty wind, and it filled all the house where they were sitting. And there appeared to them tongues as of fire, distributed and resting on each one of them. And they were all filled with the Holy Spirit and began to speak in other tongues, as the Spirit gave them utterance.

Acts 2:1–4

confirmation name. After hearing your confirmation name, the bishop dips his thumb into the chrism. He anoints your forehead with the sacred chrism, making the sign of the cross. While anointing you, the bishop calls you by your confirmation name. He says, "Be sealed with the gift of the Holy Spirit." You respond, "Amen." Then he says, "Peace be with you." You answer, "And also with you." This exchange of peace demonstrates your communion with the bishop and all the faithful in Christ's Church.

Sacred chrism is a special oil mixed with balsam. Balsam is a perfume. At a solemn Mass celebrated once a year during Holy Week—called the "Chrism Mass"—the bishop blesses the chrism in preparation for all the confirmations that will take place in the diocese during the coming year.

Anointing means having oil poured over your head. In this case, the chrism on your forehead symbolizes the Holy Spirit being poured over you. When describing the anointing with chrism that takes place during confirmation, the *Catechism* says:

> This anointing highlights the name "Christian," which means *anointed* and derives from the name of Christ himself whom God "anointed with the Holy Spirit" (Acts 10:38).
>
> CCC, n. 1289

"Messiah" is the Hebrew word for the Anointed One. "Christ" is the Greek term meaning someone who is anointed. Jesus is the Christ because he was anointed with the Holy Spirit. The Church Fathers called Christians *alter Christus, ipse Christus*—another Christ, Christ himself—because we are also anointed with the Holy Spirit.

> Having predestined us to be adopted as his sons, God has conformed us to the glorious Body of Christ. So then you, who have become sharers in Christ, are appropriately called "Christs."
>
> St. Cyril of Jerusalem, cf. *CCC*, n. 2782

When anointing you, the bishop says that he "seals" you. The anointing imprints a spiritual seal, the seal of the Holy Spirit. The *Catechism* explains:

> A seal is a symbol of a person, a sign of personal authority, or ownership of an object. Hence soldiers were marked with their leader's seal and slaves with their master's. A seal authenticates a juridical act or document and occasionally makes it secret.
>
> Christ himself declared that he was marked with his Father's seal. Christians are also marked with a seal: "It is God who establishes us with you in Christ, and has commissioned us; he has put his seal upon us and given us his Spirit in our hearts as a guarantee" (2 Cor 1:21–22). This seal of the Holy Spirit marks our total belonging to Christ, our enrolment in his service forever, as well as the promise of divine protection in the great eschatological trial.
>
> *CCC*, nn. 1295–1296

The "great trial" is the battle between Christ and Satan. It is called "eschatological" because it becomes increasingly intense as we approach the *eschaton*, that is, the end of the world.

St. Paul once told St. Timothy to learn how to endure hardship "as a good soldier of Christ Jesus" (2 Tim 2:3). Because we have entered Christ's side in the battle between God and Satan, the Church speaks of those being confirmed as "soldiers of Christ."

God does not want us to use violence. The weapons we use in this battle are faith, hope, and love. Ours is a battle of peace. Those who use violence to spread the gospel make themselves God's enemies and contradict the divine message they claim to spread. Even so, we must fight—and fight for real. Those pursuing a comfortable life, constantly shunning hardships, are not following Jesus. We have to fight against our evil inclinations. If we don't, we will end up being slaves of our emotions and slaves of Satan. Confirmation gives us the strength to fight. Confirmation gives us the courage to keep fighting even when we see others abandon their faith.

During the ceremony, the sponsor is the person who accompanies you at the moment of confirmation, standing beside you. The sponsor must be a practicing Catholic and has the duty of giving you good example together with spiritual assistance whenever you need it. The *Catechism* suggests that "one of the baptismal godparents" act as the confirmation sponsor "to emphasize the unity of the two sacraments" (cf. *CCC*, n. 1311).

Why you need confirmation

On the day of Pentecost, the first Christians went out to tell everyone about Jesus' resurrection and the forgiveness of sins. That was two thousand years ago. Today there are still many people who do not know Jesus Christ. There are many people who don't know about the forgiveness of sins. Christ wants to send you the same way he sent his first disciples. He wants to send you to all those people who do not know him. He wants you to be an apostle.

In today's world, being an apostle means being one of those daring men and women who try to convince others to commit themselves to Christ. Before you can convince others to do it, you have to be committed yourself. That's why you need confirmation.

Confirmation gives you courage to believe in Jesus without being afraid of what people will say. Confirmation gives you the power of the Holy Spirit. With that power in your soul, you will know how to talk about Christ. With the power of the Holy Spirit inside, you will never be ashamed of being a Christian.

Effects of confirmation

Confirmation does many things for you.

- It gives you the same outpouring of the Holy Spirit granted on the day of Pentecost.
- It increases and deepens baptismal grace.
- It roots you more deeply in divine filiation, which makes you cry, "Abba! Father!"
- It unites you more firmly to Christ.
- It increases the gifts of the Holy Spirit in your soul.
- It imprints a spiritual mark or indelible character on the Christian's soul.

Fathers of the Church

Beware of thinking that the chrism [used for the sacrament of confirmation] is simply ordinary oil and nothing else. Just as the bread of the Eucharist after the invocation of the Holy Spirit is no longer just bread, but the body of Christ, so when the Holy Spirit has been invoked on the sacred chrism, it is no longer mere ointment. It is the gift of Christ. By the presence of his divinity, this oil becomes the instrument through which we receive the Holy Spirit. While symbolically, on our foreheads and senses, we see our bodies being anointed with the oil, our souls are being sanctified by the holy and life-giving Spirit.

St. Cyril of Jerusalem, *Mystagogica*, III, 3

You can receive this sacrament only once.

Confirming means making something stronger. Because of confirmation, your love for God grows stronger. Your bond with other Christians grows stronger. Your faith grows stronger. This impels you to look for ways of winning souls for Christ. You feel the need to show others how they too can discover God's love. You speak the name of Christ boldly. You never feel ashamed of being a Christian.

Obviously this means a big change. You probably don't notice it immediately. It's like a baby changing from feeding from his mother's breast to eating adult food. It's a big change, though it takes time before you begin to see how much it affects everything you do.

Christian life has often been compared to climbing a mountain. At first the climb is easy. As we get closer to the summit—closer to union with God—the path gets steeper. You need to make more effort to persevere. One of the hardest parts is to fight against the triple concupiscence that St. John describes as "the lust of the flesh and the lust of the eyes and the pride of life" (1 Jn 2:16). Because of original sin, we feel attracted towards evil. This attraction makes evil things appear to be good in a moment of temptation.

Besides giving us the strength to fight against the triple concupiscence, confirmation gives us the spiritual wisdom needed to detect evil inclinations in our soul. The greatest problem is not that people have a sensual body, lustful eye, and pride in possessions. The greatest problem is that many think that it is very good to indulge in as much sensual pleasure as possible and amass as much wealth as possible—regardless of how much evil they do in order to satisfy their cravings. Worst of all, they take special delight in making sure others admire them for living such useless lives.

Unfortunately, most people are so confused that they do not see this problem. Confirmation gives the grace to see it.

Preparing for confirmation

To prepare to receive confirmation, the *Catechism* says:

> Preparation for confirmation should aim at leading the Christian toward a more intimate union with Christ and a more lively familiarity with the Holy Spirit, his actions, his gifts, and his biddings, in order to be more capable of assuming the apostolic responsibilities of Christian life. To this end catechesis for confirmation should strive to awaken a sense of belonging to the Church of Jesus Christ, the universal Church as well as the parish community. The latter bears special responsibility for the preparation of confirmands.
>
> To receive confirmation one must be in a state of grace. One should receive the sacrament of penance in order to be cleansed for the gift of the Holy Spirit. More intense prayer should prepare one to receive the strength and graces of the Holy Spirit with docility and readiness to act.
>
> *CCC*, nn. 1309–1310

Preparing for confirmation requires several things. Besides having a sponsor and choosing a confirmation name, you need to look at your

Magisterium

The Christian faithful . . . must profess before others the faith they have received from God through the Church. By the sacrament of confirmation they are more perfectly bound to the Church and are endowed with the special strength of the Holy Spirit. Hence they are, as true witnesses of Christ, more strictly obliged to spread the faith by word and deed.

Vatican II, Dogmatic *Constitution on the Church*, n. 11

soul. Confirmation perfects the grace of baptism, the gift of sanctifying grace that God gives anyone who is baptized. Confirmation does not restore God's gift of grace to your soul if you have lost it. If you are not living like a Christian, confirmation will not give you strength to defend your faith. Before you can defend your faith and spread it to others, you have to live it yourself first.

Christians lose the grace of baptism—they lose sanctifying grace—if they commit a mortal sin. So if you deliberately skip Mass on Sunday, you lose sanctifying grace. If you steal a lot of money, you lose sanctifying grace. If you read pornography or engage in any kind of sexual activity before marriage, you lose sanctifying grace. If you get drunk or use drugs, you lose sanctifying grace. If you help somebody get an abortion, you lose sanctifying grace.

These deeds are seriously wrong. If you do them with full knowledge and full consent, you commit a mortal sin. Once you commit a mortal sin, you lose the sanctifying grace given to you at baptism. From that moment on, you have broken your communion with God and you are living in the state of sin. It doesn't mean you can't pray anymore. Nor does it necessarily mean you have lost faith in God. It means that you no longer have God's life within you.

If you repent of your sins and go to confession, then God forgives you and gives back the grace you lost. Your soul is once again filled with sanctifying grace and you live in communion with God.

If you are guilty of mortal sin, go to confession. This is necessary if you want confirmation to work. Receiving confirmation in the state of mortal sin is an offence against God.

Even if you are free from mortal sin, it is good to go to confession before confirmation. You can confess your venial sins. This will prepare you in the best possible way for receiving the gift of the Holy Spirit. The Church strongly recommends confession of venial sins because it helps you form your conscience, fight against evil tendencies, and progress in the life of the Spirit.

One of the best resolutions you can make on the day of your confirmation is to promise our Lord that you will go to confession frequently. Frequent confession will purify your soul and make you sensitive to the motions of the Holy Spirit within you. The saints often speak of feeling the breath of the Paraclete as a whisper, a gentle nudge from God to show them the way. To be more aware of these subtle motions—to "feel" the Holy Spirit within you—fight against the selfish habits that make you insensitive to him, especially laziness at the moment of prayer.

The confirmation name

If you were baptized as a child, you were given a Christian name. It has become traditional for young adults receiving confirmation to choose a confirmation name. The bishop will call you by this name when he confirms you. For their confirmation name, some like to use the Christian name already received at baptism. Some like to have a new name, which will be added to their baptism name.

When choosing a name, you must choose the name of a saint or a Christian virtue. Choose a name that attracts you because of something in the life of that saint (or in the practice of that virtue). The saint can help you imitate that aspect of Christ's life that he or she lived while here on earth. For instance, a young man may want to imitate St. Francis Xavier's daring to spread the gospel. So he chooses the name Xavier for confirmation. A young woman may specially admire St. Cecilia's joyful prayer in the midst of persecution. So she chooses the name Cecilia.

When you choose your confirmation name, you are asking that saint to be your patron for the rest of your life. A patron is someone who looks after you. Having a patron saint in heaven means that you are asking that saint to help you be a good Christian. You ask that saint for intercession. Remember how, after Pentecost, St. Peter worked many miracles in the name of Jesus Christ? Well, now that St. Peter sees God face-to-face in heaven, he—and all the other saints—can help people even more.

Apostles for Christ

When you think of spreading the gospel, perhaps you think of someone like St. Paul crossing continents to reach people in far away lands.

If you think God is calling you to carry out such missionary work, find a way to do it. But the vast majority of Christians stay where they are, working in ordinary jobs and living with their families. If you find yourself in that position, remember that God wants you to spread the gospel as much as any of the great missionaries of past centuries. Even if you do not call yourself a missionary, God has given you a mission.

How do ordinary Christians spread the gospel? There is no particular formula for it. You must find your own way. Or rather, you must allow yourself to be guided by the Holy Spirit. As Jesus promised, "I will give you a mouth and wisdom, which none of your adversaries will be able to withstand or contradict" (Lk 21:15). This ability to speak about your faith with conviction comes from the Holy Spirit. He will inspire you.

REVIEW QUESTIONS

1. How is confirmation related to Pentecost?
2. Why do Christians need confirmation?
3. How does someone prepare to receive confirmation?
4. How does confirmation lead you to be an apostle?

35.

The Eucharist

Bread and wine are the material signs Jesus chose for the Eucharist. His words spoken at the Last Supper are the words used for this sacrament. The priest pronounces them when he celebrates Mass.

At Mass you see bread and wine. They are signs of spiritual food and spiritual drink. You do not see the reality symbolized by these signs. God wants you to believe what you cannot see. He wants you to believe that, as you receive Holy Communion, you are eating and drinking the body and blood of Christ. This eating and drinking makes you one with Jesus.

The night before he was crucified, Jesus ate the Passover with the Apostles. This was the traditional meal established by Moses to commemorate the night when God freed Israel from slavery. Gathered together in the Upper Room, Jesus and the Apostles ate the Passover lamb, the bitter herbs, and unleavened bread, following the ritual prescribed in the Law. After the Passover meal was finished, Jesus instituted the Eucharist. To understand what Christ was doing when he instituted the Eucharist, look at the connection between the Jewish Passover and Christ's Passover.

The paschal sacrifice

"Paschal" refers to anything connected with the Passover. Every year, the Israelites celebrated Passover to remember the night before the Exodus from Egypt. Every family had to slaughter a male sheep or goat the same way their ancestors did it in Egypt (cf. Ex 12:5). They ate it at the Passover meal.

At the Last Supper, while eating the Passover meal with the Apostles, Jesus instituted a new kind of *paschal* sacrifice. He is the new "Lamb of God" for a new kind of Passover. When Jesus died and rose from the dead, he was "passing over" to his Father, leaving this world to enter into glory. Jesus anticipated this new Passover—his "exodus" from the world—by instituting the Eucharist in the Upper Room the night before he was crucified. At the Last Supper, Jesus introduced his Apostles into this new Passover by giving them his flesh to eat and his blood to drink.

Whenever Christians celebrate the Eucharist, they renew Christ's Passover. The Eucharist is the celebration of Jesus' paschal sacrifice. The Passover was the central ceremony of the Old Testament. It commemorated the covenant between God and Israel. The Eucharist is the central sacrament of the New Testament. It established a new and everlasting covenant between God and the Church.

New food for a new covenant

In the times of Moses, God gave the Israelites manna in the desert. This was the bread they needed to reach the Promised Land. Jesus promised a completely new kind of food. It is the "bread of life" that we need to reach heaven. He called it the "food which endures to eternal life" (Jn 6:27). He gave it to us by instituting the Eucharist at the Last Supper.

> Jesus took bread, and blessed, and broke it and gave it to them, saying, "This is my body which is given for you. Do this in remembrance of me." And he took a cup . . . saying, "Drink of it, all of you; for this is my blood of the new covenant, which is poured out for many for the forgiveness of sins."
>
> Cf. Mt 26:26–28; Mk 14:22–24; Lk 22:19–20

First Jesus changed bread into his body. Then he changed wine into his blood. His body looked like bread. His blood looked like wine. When Jesus gave it to them, the Apostles ate his body, hidden under the appearances of bread. Though it looked like bread and tasted like bread, it was not bread. It was Jesus' body. That is why Jesus said, "Eat this. *This* is my body." When Jesus gave them the cup, they drank his blood

Sacred Scripture

I am the bread of life. Your fathers ate the manna in the wilderness, and they died. This is the bread which comes down from heaven, that a man may eat of it and not die. I am the living bread which came down from heaven; if any one eats of this bread, he will live for ever; and the bread which I shall give for the life of the world is my flesh.

John 6:48–51

hidden under the appearances of wine. Though it looked like wine and tasted like wine, it was not wine. It was Jesus' blood. This is why Jesus said, "Drink this. *This* is my blood."

Jesus is truly present in the Eucharist. His body is hidden under the appearances of bread. His blood is hidden under the appearances of wine. The Church calls the Eucharist the "sacrament of sacraments." All other sacraments lead us to Jesus. The Eucharist *is* Jesus.

Jesus told the Apostles twice: "Do this in remembrance of me" (1 Cor 11:25, 26). He wanted them to do for other Christians what he did when instituting the Eucharist at the Last Supper. Ever since then, the Apostles and their successors have been celebrating the Eucharist. They have been repeating the words and gestures that Jesus used to institute the Eucharist. They use bread and wine. They change it into Christ's Body and Blood. Then they give it to other Christians so that everyone can eat his flesh and drink his blood the same way the Apostles did at the Last Supper.

When a bishop or priest celebrates the Eucharist, we call it the "Mass" or the "Lord's Supper" or the "breaking of the bread." Every time Mass is celebrated, Jesus gives us his body to eat and his blood to drink.

Mystery of faith

The Eucharist is a mystery. When you see a priest celebrate Mass, you cannot see the bread change into the body of Christ. You cannot see the wine change into the blood of Christ. You need faith to believe that Jesus is truly present, hidden under the appearances of bread and wine. Only those who have faith know that Jesus is present in the Eucharist. This faith is a gift from God.

How does the priest change bread and wine into Jesus' body and blood? Strictly speaking, it is not the priest who does it. Jesus is the one who does it. The mystery of the Eucharist is linked to the mystery of Christian priesthood. Somehow Jesus is present within the priest—*the priest is Jesus*—at the moment when the priest repeats our Lord's words, saying, "Take this and eat it, this is my body. Take this and drink it, this is my blood."

The priest is saying the words that only Jesus can say. By saying, "This is *my* body," the priest changes bread into Jesus' body. By saying, "This is *my* blood," the priest changes wine into Jesus' blood. The priest does not say, "This is *his* body, *his* blood." The priest speaks in the first person. He talks about "my body" and "my blood" because Jesus is the one speaking. At that moment, the priest speaks not "in the name" of Jesus but *in persona Christi*—"in the person" of our Lord Jesus Christ.

We call this moment the "consecration." The priest is consecrating bread and wine, that is, making them holy by changing them into Jesus' body and blood. After consecration, the priest invites Christians to "proclaim the mystery of faith." At that point, we join together to make a collective act of faith. We say that we believe Jesus has become present among us on the altar.

Transubstantiation

What is the best way to describe this change of bread and wine into the body and blood of Christ? The Church teaches that the change takes place by *transubstantiation*. This means that the whole *substance* of the bread changes into the whole *substance* of Jesus' body. Only the *appearances* of bread remain behind, and these appearances hide the presence of Jesus' body on the altar. The appearances are the color, taste, weight, size, etc. The substance is the thing itself. Likewise, the whole substance of the wine is changed into the whole substance of Jesus' blood. Only the appearances of wine remain behind, and these appearances hide the presence of Jesus' blood in the cup.

Transubstantiation is different from a mere transformation. A cup of water can be transformed into its elements. During transformation, one substance (water) is changed into two other substances (hydrogen and oxygen). This transformation gives a new *form* to the hydrogen and oxygen that were in some way already present in the water. When the priest changes bread into Jesus' body, we cannot say that he is transforming the bread, because Jesus' body is not in any way present as an element within the bread before the change takes place. The oxygen and hydrogen come from the water. Jesus' body and blood do not come from the bread and wine. Rather, the old substance (bread and wine) is *totally* changed so that a new substance (body and blood) becomes present.

Even though you cannot see him, Jesus is present on the altar during Mass and present within every Christian who receives Holy Communion. It is not just a spiritual presence. The *Catechism* says:

> In the most blessed sacrament of the Eucharist, the body and blood, together with the soul and divinity of our Lord Jesus Christ—and, therefore, the whole Christ—is truly, really, and substantially contained.
>
> CCC, n. 1374

Because Jesus is alive and because he is God, the whole Christ must be present wherever his body becomes present. Likewise, the whole Christ must be present wherever his blood is present. The whole Christ means his humanity—body, blood, and soul—united to his divinity. Therefore, his *body, blood, soul, and divinity* are hidden together under the appearances of bread or wine. The *whole Christ* is hidden under the appearances of bread. And the *whole Christ* is hidden under the appearances of wine. To receive the whole Christ in Holy Communion, a Christian only needs to eat the sacred host or drink from the chalice. By receiving either one, Christians have Jesus present within them.

Two species

Normally Christians receive Communion under only one species—they receive Jesus only under the appearances of bread. To receive "under both species" means to eat the sacred host and also drink from the chalice. The priest celebrating Mass always receives under both species. On certain special occasions, ordinary Christians can also receive the Eucharist under both species. The *Catechism* says:

> Since Christ is sacramentally present under each of the species, communion under the species of bread alone makes it possible to receive all the fruit of Eucharistic grace. For pastoral reasons this manner of receiving Communion has been legitimately established as the most common form in the Latin rite. But the sign of Communion is more complete when given under both kinds, since in that form the sign of the Eucharistic meal appears more clearly. This is the usual form of receiving Communion in the Eastern rites.
>
> *CCC*, n. 1390

The Latin rite refers to the way Mass is celebrated in most dioceses throughout the world. The rite that developed in Rome is called "Latin" because that was the language of the Romans and is the official language of the Church. The Eastern rite refers to the special norms used for celebrating Mass among Catholics in the East, where for centuries the dominant language was Greek, the original language of the New Testament.

In the Latin rite, the local bishop determines which occasions are best for priests to offer Holy Communion under both species.

Jesus explains the Eucharist

Jesus once multiplied five loaves of bread and two fish to feed thousands of people. The crowd ate as much as they wanted. After working the miracle, Jesus went to the top of a mountain to be alone. He wanted to spend the night in prayer. A few hours before dawn, he saw his disciples rowing their boat out on the lake. A heavy wind was blowing against them. He walked on top of the water and went out to meet them. When they saw Jesus, they thought it was a ghost. Jesus said, "Take heart, it is I; have no fear" (Mt 14:27).

Peter stood up in the boat. He said, "If it is you, Lord, tell me to come to you on top of the water." Jesus said, "Come!"

Fathers of the Church

It is not man that causes the things offered to become the body and blood of Christ, but he who was crucified for us—Christ himself.

St. John Chrysostom, cf. *CCC*, n. 1375

Peter got out of the boat and walked towards Jesus. But he was afraid. He started sinking in the water. He cried out, “Lord! Save me!” Jesus took him by the hand and pulled him out of the water. They walked to the boat and got in.

The next day was the Sabbath. Jesus went to the synagogue. Many of the disciples who had seen him multiply the loaves were there. They said to Jesus, “Then what sign do you do, that we may see, and believe you? . . . Our fathers ate the manna in the wilderness” (Jn 6:30–31). They wanted more bread.

Jesus said, “It wasn’t Moses who gave you that bread from heaven. It was my Father. For the bread of God is the one who comes down from heaven and gives life to the world.” They answered, “Lord, give us this bread always.”

Jesus told his disciples, “I am the bread of life. Your fathers ate manna in the desert, but they are dead. If you eat the bread that comes down from heaven, you will never die. I am the living bread that came down from heaven. If any man eats this bread, he will live forever. The bread I will give is my flesh—which I will give for the life of the world.”

Some of Jesus’ disciples were troubled by these words. They started arguing among themselves, saying, “How can this man give us his flesh to eat?” Jesus replied:

> Truly, truly, I say to you, unless you eat the flesh of the Son of man and drink his blood, you have no life in you; he who eats my flesh and drinks my blood has eternal life, and I will raise him up at the last day. For my flesh is food indeed, and my blood is drink indeed.
>
> John 6:53–55

It was obvious to everyone listening to Jesus that he wanted them to eat his flesh and drink his blood. Many of the disciples thought this was absurd. They said they could not accept what he was saying.

Jesus was disappointed with their lack of faith. He said, “It is the Spirit that gives life. The flesh has nothing to offer. The words that I have spoken to you are spirit and they are life.” He wanted his disciples to eat his flesh and drink his blood not because it was food for their bodies but because it was food for their souls. He insisted once again on the need for faith: "But there are some of you that do not believe. . . . This is why I told you that no one can come to me unless it is granted him by the Father" (Jn 6:64, 65)

You need grace to understand

Being good is not enough to make you believe in eating Christ's body and drinking his blood. You believe only if you receive grace from the Father. It is a supernatural power that enlightens your mind and moves your heart. It makes you aware of Jesus' presence hidden under the appearances of bread and wine. It makes you desire to have Jesus living within you. It makes you hunger for the Eucharist.

The description given above is a summary of the Gospel texts on the Eucharist (cf. Mt 14:22–33; Jn 6:1–71). The story reminds us that many people were ready to believe that Jesus could multiply loaves of bread and work other miracles. Why were these same people slow to accept a gift infinitely more precious than a loaf of bread? It is difficult to say. One thing is clear. Jesus wants to give us not only good things but the best he can possibly give. He wants to give us his very self—everything he has, everything he is. If he is willing to give us his flesh to eat and his blood to drink, he must love us more than we can imagine.

Jesus told his disciples: "As the living Father sent me, and I live because of the Father, so he who eats me will live because of me" (Jn 6:57). The Father gives his Son life—divine life. When we receive the Eucharist, the Son gives us the same life the Father has given him. He gives us the same infinite love the Father gives him. It is a life that knows no boredom and no pain. It is a love that knows no betrayal and no weariness.

Accepting Jesus' teaching

After listening to Jesus explain the Eucharist, many of his disciples walked away. They ceased to be his disciples. Do you feel sad when you read this in St. John's Gospel? Let it remind you that following Jesus is not a matter of picking and choosing what you like. It is not a matter of believing only the parts that make sense.

> ***Magisterium***
>
> By the Eucharistic celebration we already unite ourselves with the heavenly liturgy and anticipate eternal life, when God will be all in all.
>
> *Catechism of the Catholic Church*, n. 1326 (cf. 1 Cor 15:28)

It was hard to listen to Jesus speak of eating his flesh two thousand years ago. Who is in his right mind wants to eat the body of another man? It was even harder for the Jews to listen to Jesus talk about drinking his blood. The Old Testament strictly prohibited drinking blood of any kind. Even so, Jesus expected his disciples to accept his teaching.

On that occasion, he said nothing about the Last Supper. He said nothing about the way priests would celebrate the Eucharist. He said nothing about how easy it would be to eat his flesh since it would be hidden under the appearances of bread. He said nothing about his blood being hidden under the appearances of wine. The first time he announced the Eucharist, Jesus simply repeated that he wanted them to eat his flesh and drink his blood.

When many of his disciples walked away, Jesus did not chase after them. He did not plead with them to come back. He did not make any compromise. Anyone who wanted to be his disciple had to believe in the Eucharist. The same is true today. Far from compromising, Jesus said to the Apostles, "Do you also want to go away?" Belief in the Eucharist was so crucial to faith in him that Jesus would rather see the Apostles leave if they were not ready to accept this mystery. He was challenging their faith. Simon Peter answered, "Lord, to whom shall we go? You have the words of eternal life" (Jn 6:68).

When St. Peter answered Jesus, maybe his clothes were still damp. A few hours earlier, he got out of his boat and walked on the water towards Jesus. As he got further away from the boat, he began to doubt. As he began to doubt, he began to sink. After crying for help, Peter found himself being pulled up out of the water. Jesus said, "O man of little faith, why did you doubt?" (Mt 14:31)

Jesus asked the Apostles to choose between believing his words and walking away like the others. St. Peter did not hesitate. Maybe he had no idea how they were going to eat Jesus' flesh and drink his blood. It probably sounded just as crazy to Peter as it did to those who walked away. But this did not prevent him from believing. If Jesus insisted on having them eat his flesh and drink his blood, then Peter was convinced it had to be done—somehow, someway. Watching many disciples leave the synagogue and turn their backs on Jesus, he probably sensed that this was a moment for him to speak not only for himself but also for the other Apostles—to encourage them in their faith. So he spoke in the plural: "We have believed, and have come to know, that you are the Holy One of God" (Jn 6:69).

Belief of the early Christians

The early Christians took our Lord's words on the Eucharist in their most literal sense. From the very beginning of the Church, everyone believed that they were eating the body of Christ and drinking his blood whenever they received the Eucharist.

St. Paul was not present at the Last Supper. He did not become a Christian until after Pentecost. Before his conversion he used to persecute Christians. Nevertheless, Jesus chose him to be an Apostle—a disciple chosen to announce the full revelation of the gospel. There are two events from our Lord's life that St. Paul described in his letters. One was the resurrection. The other was the Last Supper. Writing to those in Corinth, he warned them that to be worthy of receiving Holy Communion, a Christian must believe that Jesus is truly present in the Eucharist.

> For I received from the Lord what I also delivered to you, that the Lord Jesus on the night when he was betrayed took bread, and when he had given thanks, he broke it, and said, "This is my body which is for you. Do this in remembrance of me." In the same way also the cup, after supper, saying, "This cup is the new covenant in my blood. Do this, as often as you drink it, in remembrance of me." For as often as you eat this bread and drink the cup, you proclaim the Lord's death until he comes.
>
> Whoever, therefore, eats the bread or drinks the cup of the Lord in an unworthy manner will be guilty of profaning the body and blood of the Lord. Let a man examine himself, and so eat of the bread and drink

> of the cup. For any one who eats and drinks without discerning the body eats and drinks judgment upon himself.
>
> 1 Corinthians 11:23–29

With these words, St. Paul teaches us that the Eucharist is really and truly the body and blood of Jesus. The Eucharistic bread looks like bread, but it is not bread. It is the body of Jesus Christ. The Eucharistic cup looks like a cup of wine, but it is not wine. It is the blood of Jesus Christ.

Anyone who says that the Eucharistic bread and wine are nothing more than symbols of Jesus' body and blood is contradicting the words of sacred Scripture. The only ones worthy of receiving the Eucharist are those who "recognize" the Lord's body and blood hidden under the appearances of bread and wine. If the Eucharist were merely a symbol, there would be no body and blood to recognize.

Preparing for Communion

Anyone who wants to receive Holy Communion must be baptized first. Only Christians are allowed to eat the flesh and drink the blood of Jesus Christ. Holy Communion is meant to draw us into union with Jesus and union with the Church. That is impossible until we are first healed of the stain of original sin and cleansed of all personal sin through the waters of baptism. Baptism opens the door to receiving all the other sacraments. At baptism, we are filled with God's grace—sanctifying grace. We need this grace to receive Holy Communion. Just as healthy eyes are necessary for seeing light, sanctifying grace is indispensable for receiving Holy Communion fruitfully. For the same reason, those who have lost the state of grace cannot receive Holy Communion until their sins are forgiven.

Catholics who do not accept the Church's teachings should not receive Holy Communion—even if they are convinced of having very good reasons for rejecting a particular Church teaching and even if they feel certain of being in the state of grace. If a Christian is publicly known for contradicting the dogmas of the Church or known for living a life contrary to Christian morals, the priest has an obligation to inform the person that he or she needs to change before being admitted to Communion. If that person refuses to change, the priest must refuse to give Communion.

There are many faithful Christians who have been baptized in communities not in communion with the Church and who would like to receive Holy Communion. Even if they are not yet in full communion with the Church through no fault of their own, they cannot receive Holy Communion in the Catholic Church. This is true even for Christians who lead a morally upright life and firmly believe that Jesus is present in the Eucharist. They must first be admitted into full communion with the Church by making a public declaration of faith. This means recognizing the authority of the Bishop of Rome as Supreme Pastor of all the faithful and accepting all the teachings of the one, holy, catholic, and apostolic Church. Once these Christians have been received into full communion with the Church, the Church confirms them with the sacrament of confirmation (unless they were already confirmed) and offers them the Eucharist. This makes them full members of the Church.

All Christians intending to receive Holy Communion have a serious obligation to prepare themselves properly. To help them do this, the priest begins Mass with a ceremony called the penitential rite. After making the Sign of the Cross and calling down the Holy Spirit upon the congregation, the priest asks everyone to make a brief examination of conscience. He says, "Let us call to mind our sins," or similar words.

If you are aware of having committed a mortal sin, you need to go to confession before going to Holy Communion. If you have only venial sins, you do not need to go to confession; tell Jesus you are sorry and ask him to prepare you to receive him. Anyone who knowingly receives Holy Communion in the state of mortal sin commits another mortal sin—the sin of sacrilege. If you are guilty of mortal sin, it is not enough to tell Jesus you are sorry. First go to confession and then you can receive Holy Communion.

Besides being in the state of grace, every Christians needs to fast for an hour before receiving Communion. The Church asks us to fast for an hour as a way of reminding us how precious the Eucharist is. When you go to Mass, you do not have to receive Communion; but, if you want to receive, you have an obligation to fast. This is a serious matter. If you have not fasted for an hour, then you should not receive Communion. Fasting for an hour is the minimum sacrifice needed to prepare for God's greatest gift. Just because we can receive Communion frequently does not make this event any less awesome.

Taking medicines or water before Communion does not break the fast. Those who are sick or responsible for caring for the sick are not obliged to fast at all before receiving Communion.

Is there anything else necessary to prepare for Communion? Many things, but to summarize, remember to pray. Put your mind into what you are doing. Ask the Virgin Mary and St. Joseph to help you fill your imagination with the scenes of Jesus' birth in Bethlehem, his work in Nazareth, his transfiguration on Mount Tabor, his crucifixion on Calvary, his resurrection in the garden. This will make you more conscious of the fact that Jesus is now standing in front of you, telling you, "Eat my body. Drink my blood." The body he wants you to eat is the same one that rose from the dead—the same Jesus who is now seated at the right hand of the Father in heaven.

Cultivate silence

We can only see the signs of bread and wine—and not Jesus himself. Many Christians ask why he remains hidden. This is an excellent question. Jesus has his reasons for not letting us see him or hear him. He is trying to teach us another way of communicating. This is the secret of spiritual life.

To prepare yourself to receive Jesus in Communion, you need to cultivate interior silence. This is called "recollection." You "collect" your senses one by one—sight, hearing, touch—and rein them in. You recollect not only your senses but also your mind, heart, and imagination. These can be just as wild as your senses, refusing to focus on Jesus and occupying themselves instead with idle thoughts and desires.

Have you noticed your tendency to focus on noisy things—the things that please your senses? In the Eucharist Jesus comes to place his body and blood inside of you. He is teaching you to focus on his presence within. Church art, liturgical ceremony, and sacred music are meant to help you do this. This is why the Church strictly regulates the liturgy.

She wants to promote only the kind of art, music, and ceremonies that help people recollect.

To describe why recollection is crucial to discovering the secret of the Eucharist, one of the great mystics wrote:

> It is odd, the way of lovers. They like to enjoy one another's companionship alone, far away from any interference, far from anyone else's presence. If some stranger is present, they do not enjoy each other freely. This is true even if they are together and can speak to one another openly . . . even if the stranger remains silent. The reason they desire to commune with each other alone is that love is a union between two alone.
>
> St. John of the Cross, *The Spiritual Canticle*, Stanza 36

While the celebration of the Eucharist is always an act of the Church gathered together, Holy Communion reminds us that Jesus seeks intimacy with each person.

The sacrifice of the Mass

The Eucharist is a sacrament. The Eucharist is also a sacrifice. When offering his body and blood as food and drink, Jesus offered the Eucharist as a sacrifice. At the Last Supper, he told the Apostles that his body was being "handed over" and that his blood was being "poured out for many for the forgiveness of sins" (cf. Mt 26:28; Lk 22:19).

Jesus surrendered himself as a victim when he died on the cross. When instituting the Eucharist at the Last Supper, he was *anticipating* that sacrifice. Whenever a priest celebrates Mass, he offers the Eucharist as a *memorial* of that sacrifice. At every Mass, Jesus renews the sacrifice he offered on the cross. The *Catechism* says:

> Because it is the memorial of Christ's Passover, the Eucharist is also a sacrifice. The sacrificial character of the Eucharist is manifested in the very words of institution: "This is my body which is given for you" and "This cup which is poured out for you is the new covenant in my blood." In the Eucharist Christ gives us the very body that he gave up for us on

> the cross, the very blood that he "poured out for many for the forgiveness of sins." The Eucharist is thus a sacrifice because it re-presents (makes present) the sacrifice of the cross . . .
>
> *CCC*, nn. 1365–1366

Jesus wanted to give us a way to be present at the cross. To do this, he instituted the Eucharist. Every time you are present before the altar during Mass, you are standing in the presence of Jesus offering his body and blood to his Father for the forgiveness of your sins.

We call the Mass a "renewal" of the sacrifice as opposed to a repetition. Jesus offered his body and blood to God once and only once. That happened when he died on the cross. Each Mass makes Jesus' sacrifice present on the altar. We call Mass a *sacramental* renewal because the sacrifice takes place by means of a sign. We cannot see Jesus' body and blood, nor can we see him offer it.

"The sacrifice of Christ and the sacrifice of the Eucharist are *one single sacrifice*" (*CCC*, n. 1367). They are not two different sacrifices. They are one single sacrifice because the priest is the same and the victim is the same. On the cross, Jesus was the priest offering the blood and Jesus was the victim shedding blood. At every Mass Jesus is the priest. At every Mass Jesus is the victim. Whenever a priest celebrates Mass, he uses Jesus' words, speaking as only Jesus himself can speak, offering the sacrifice that only Jesus can offer.

The sacrifice of the Mass is the same as the sacrifice of the cross. But the *manner* of offering sacrifice is different. At Mass Jesus does not shed his blood. At Mass Jesus does not die. Without shedding blood and without dying, Jesus offers his sacrifice by giving a priest the power to make his body and blood present *under separate signs*. Because Jesus' body becomes present under the appearances of bread, whereas his blood becomes present under the appearances of wine, the separating and reuniting of these two signs symbolizes Christ's death and resurrection. The sign goes beyond mere symbolism, though. Jesus' sacrifice becomes really and truly present because of the separate signs.

The Eucharist is a true sacrifice that has the power to forgive our sins. The Church teaches:

> Because the same Christ who offered himself once in a bloody manner on the altar of the cross is contained and offered in an unbloody manner in that divine sacrifice which is carried out during the Mass, that sacrifice is truly propitiatory.
>
> Council of Trent, *Doctrine on the Sacrifice of the Mass*, ch. 2

A sacrifice is *propitiatory* when God is so pleased with the offering that he forgives our sins. In this case, Jesus unites us to himself, so that in some mysterious manner, we are present with him on the altar. Because the Father sees Jesus present on the altar, he is pleased with the sacrifice. Jesus unites us to himself so completely that he takes the guilt of our sins upon himself. Therefore, God forgives our sins.

When you attend Mass, make a conscious decision to unite yourself to Jesus. If you go to Mass and make no effort to unite yourself to Christ, you have failed to take part in the Mass. You cannot limit yourself to going to Mass merely to listen to some preaching, say some prayers, and sing some hymns. God wants you to take part in Jesus' sacrifice. You are there to *offer yourself* together with Christ. The *Catechism* says:

> The Eucharist is also the sacrifice of the Church. The Church, which is the Body of Christ, participates in the offering of her Head. With him, she herself is offered whole and entire. She unites herself to his intercession with the Father for all mankind. In the Eucharist the sacrifice of Christ becomes also the sacrifice of the members of his Body. The lives of the faithful, their praise, sufferings, prayer, and work are united with those of Christ and with his total offering, and so acquire a new value. Christ's sacrifice present on the altar makes it possible for all generations of Christians to be united with his offering.
>
> *CCC*, n. 1368

To unite yourself to Jesus on the altar, tell him that you offer your work, your rest, your joys, your sorrows.

If something great just happened to you, like seeing someone you love after being separated for a long time, tell him, "I'm so happy, Jesus. Make it yours and offer it to the Father so that this joy becomes holy." If something horrible just happened to you, like the death of a friend, tell him, "I'm so sad, Jesus. Make it yours and offer it to the Father so that this grief becomes holy."

The Church teaches Christians to attend Mass with the intention of uniting themselves to the words and actions of the priest.

> Taking part in the Eucharistic sacrifice, which is the source and summit of the whole Christian life, they offer the divine victim to God, and offer themselves along with it.
>
> Vatican II, *Dogmatic Constitution on the Church*, n. 11

When you see the priest lift up the paten and the chalice at the offertory, place all your joys and sorrows—place your whole self—on that paten and in that cup. Offer yourself to the Father together with Jesus.

When you do this, Jesus draws you to himself. He unites all your actions, thoughts, and desires to his sacrifice. That way, all your actions, thoughts, and desires become holy. They belong to God. You belong to God.

Jesus promised: ". . . And I, when I am lifted up from the earth, will draw all men to myself" (Jn 12:32). At Mass, Jesus draws all men and women to himself. He draws the whole of creation to himself.

One body, one spirit

Jesus promised that the Eucharist would make us one with him: "He who eats my flesh and drinks my blood abides in me, and I in him" (Jn 6:56). He promised a resurrection of glory to anyone who receives the Eucharist: "I will raise him up at the last day" (Jn 6:54). The Bible also says that the Eucharist makes us one with each other in Christ. St. Paul wrote:

> The cup of blessing which we bless, is it not a participation in the blood of Christ? The bread which we break, is it not a participation in the body of Christ? Because there is one bread, we who are many are one body, for we all partake of the one bread.
>
> 1 Corinthians 10:16–17

Eating the same body and drinking the same blood makes us one with each other.

The power of the Eucharist to unite Christians is mysterious. We do not see Jesus become present on the altar. Nor do we see how the Eucharist unites us with one another. The Holy Spirit makes it happen, acting through our Lord's body and blood: "Grant that we, who are nourished by his body and blood, may be filled with his Holy Spirit, and become one body, one spirit in Christ" (Third Eucharistic Prayer).

The Church calls this union with one another in Christ the unity of his Mystical Body. This unity happens because we receive the Eucharist.

> The Eucharist makes the Church. Those who receive the Eucharist are united more closely to Christ. Through it Christ unites them to all the faithful in one body—the Church. Communion renews, strengthens, and deepens this incorporation into the Church, already achieved by baptism. In baptism we have been called to form but one body. The Eucharist fulfils this call.
>
> *CCC*, n. 1396

Union with Christ and with one another is the goal of our life on earth. This union is why we were baptized. This union is our ultimate vocation. The Church teaches:

> Those who feed on Christ in the Eucharist need not wait until the hereafter to receive eternal life: *they already possess it on earth.*
>
> St. John Paul II, *The Eucharist: Life of the Church*, n. 19

The Eucharist makes our union with Christ and with one another a reality here and now. ". . . We who are many are one body, for we all partake of the one bread" (1 Cor 10:17). We cannot see it, but it happens.

Think of it this way. Imagine that a friend gave you a gift all wrapped up and told you what the gift is. Even though you know what it is, you want to unwrap it. But imagine that he says, "No, you have to wait. The gift is yours. But you can't unwrap it till Christmas." This is just an analogy. When you receive the Eucharist, something similar happens. You possess eternal life now. You become one with Christ now. But you can't see Christ. You cannot enjoy this union *completely* until you rise from the dead.

Frequent Communion

The Church teaches that "the Eucharist is the source and summit of Christian life." We should receive Communion at least once during the Easter Season. If possible, we should receive the Eucharist as viaticum at the hour of our death. The *Catechism* adds that we ought to hunger to receive Jesus in Communion as frequently as possible:

> It is in keeping with the very meaning of the Eucharist that the faithful, if they have the required dispositions, receive Communion when they participate in the Mass. . . . The Church strongly encourages the faithful to receive the holy Eucharist on Sundays and feast days, or more often still, even daily.
>
> *CCC*, nn. 1388–1389

Some Christians go to Mass and receive Communion every day. This is the ideal. Frequent Communion cleanses us from habits of sin. It preserves us from committing serious sin in the future—or at least gives us an urgent desire to be free from guilt any time we fall into sin.

Jesus promises that you will grow in love for him if you receive the Eucharist. Jesus will give you the life the Father gives him. Your heart will often overflow with joy. Some men and women, like St. Thérèse of Lisieux, were so pure that they experienced this joy the very first time they received Communion. It was probably something similar to the ecstasy that the Virgin Mary experienced as Jesus became present within her and she cried out, "My spirit rejoices in God my Savior . . . for he who is mighty has done great things for me, and holy is his name" (Lk 1:47, 49).

All those who have experienced this joy understand why Jesus once exclaimed, "I came to cast fire upon the earth . . ." (Lk 12:49). The saints often use the analogy of an iron bar being thrust into fire. Though it is hard and ugly when cold, it glows hot and red—as if transformed into the very fire that heats it. Like the iron bar absorbing heat, you are meant to absorb God's love whenever you receive the Eucharist. Quoting one of the Fathers, the Church teaches:

> Through our communion in his body and blood, Christ also grants us his Spirit. St. Ephrem writes: "He called the bread his living body and he filled it with himself and with his Spirit. He who eats it with faith, eats Fire and Spirit. . . . Take and eat this, all of you, and eat with it the Holy Spirit. For it is truly my body and whoever eats it will have eternal life."
>
> St. John Paul II, *The Eucharist: Life of the Church*, n. 17

Being the union of Father and Son, the Holy Spirit is the cause of all union. By eating the body of Christ, we also consume the divine union that makes us one with Jesus. Being a fire of love, the Holy Spirit is the cause of all love. By eating the body of Christ, we consume the divine fire that sets our hearts ablaze with love for Jesus.

If you do not experience this joy—or used to but no longer experience it—do not be surprised. You need to be purified before Jesus can completely unite himself to you. You need to be more conscious of his presence before he can fill you with peace and joy. Receiving Communion frequently is not enough. Do penance. Strive to be humble. Immerse yourself in an attitude of constant dialogue with Jesus throughout the day.

In the same way that an athlete gets ready to run the marathon, in the same way that a student prepares for his final exams, in the same way that a man and woman get ready for their wedding day, focus your whole being on that one moment when you will receive Jesus in Communion. St. Josemaría wrote:

> That Christ you see is not Jesus. At best it is only the pitiful image that your blurred eyes are able to form. Purify yourself. Make your sight cleaner with humility and penance. Then the pure light of love will not fail you. And you will have perfect vision. The image you see will really be his: Him!
>
> St. Josemaría, *The Way*, n. 212

Jesus wants to reveal himself to you during Holy Communion. One of the great mystics said it depends on your desire to see him:

> When you have received the Lord, and you are in his very presence, try to shut the bodily eyes and open the eyes of your soul and look

> into your own heart. I tell you . . . that if you practice this habit of *staying with him*, not just once or twice, but whenever you receive Communion . . . he will not come so much disguised. . . . [He will] make his presence known to you by various means, according to the desire you have of seeing him. Your longing for him may be so great that he will reveal himself to you completely.
>
> St. Teresa of Avila, *The Way of Perfection*, ch. 35

To take this advice seriously, begin to go to Mass frequently—every day, if possible. Learn to cultivate silence. When you receive Communion, concentrate on Jesus. Block out everything else. Tell him you want to know who he is. Then you will begin to understand why Jesus told the Apostles: ". . . He who loves me will be loved by my Father, and I will love him and manifest myself to him" (Jn 14:21).

Pledge of future glory

The Eucharist offers you a foretaste of heaven. It gives you a glimpse of the joy that you will experience at the "marriage supper of the Lamb" in the heavenly Jerusalem (cf. Rev 19:9). The *Catechism* says:

> If the Eucharist is the memorial of the Passover of the Lord Jesus, if by our communion at the altar we are filled "with every heavenly blessing and grace," then the Eucharist is also an anticipation of heavenly glory.
>
> *CCC*, n. 1402

You will only understand the Eucharist completely when you get to heaven. Still, God wants you to glimpse the beauty of it. More than any other sacrament, the Eucharist demands meditation since it is a pledge of future glory.

The Eucharist suggests just how powerful Jesus is. He can change bread and wine into his flesh and blood. This is a pledge of the way he can change your earthly body into a "spiritual body." St. Paul wrote:

> But our commonwealth is in heaven, and from it we await a Savior, the Lord Jesus Christ, who will change our lowly body to be like his

> glorious body, by the power which enables him even to subject all things to himself.
>
> Philippians 3:20–21

Jesus wants us to believe that the Eucharist can change our bodies into copies of his body.

This sacrament is so powerful that it can change us into him. It *is* already changing us, preparing us for the resurrection. In heaven we will be so completely identified with Jesus that we will speak as only he can speak and act as only he can act. By letting us eat his flesh and drink his blood now, he is preparing us to do that. Even in this world, despite the miseries that weigh us down, he wants us to begin to think of ourselves as "other Christs"—Christ himself.

Those reading chapter six of St. John's Gospel—the one we looked at earlier—may notice a striking detail. Jesus insists on two actions: eating and resurrecting. The original Greek has Jesus telling us to *eat his flesh*: "Truly, truly, I say to you, unless you eat the flesh of the Son of man . . . you have no life in you." (Jn 6:53). It also has Jesus promising four times that he will raise us from the dead if we do it.

To explain what he has in mind, Jesus contrasts the manna in the desert and the living bread of the Eucharist. The Israelites who ate the manna are all dead. Those who receive the Eucharist will never die. Jesus says several times, "If any one eats of this bread, he will live for ever" (Jn 6:51). This is a strange promise to make while also promising to raise us from the dead. What is the idea?

It is good to immerse ourselves in prayer. But true spiritual life does not consist in escaping from our bodies. Our ultimate goal is not to reach

Wisdom of the Saints

Eternal happiness begins now for the Christian who is comforted with the definitive manna of the Eucharist. . . . This is the Good News. *News,* because it speaks to us of a deep love which we never could have dreamed of. *Good*, because there is nothing better than uniting ourselves to God, the greatest Good of all. It is *Good News,* because in some inexplicable way it gives us a foretaste of heaven.

St. Josemaría, *Christ Is Passing By*, n. 152

ecstasy in prayer. Before we will be truly happy, we have to rise from the dead. Our Lord tells us that we need to eat his body and drink his blood in order to do that. For reasons we do not understand, this eating and drinking prepares us for what we are supposed to do after the resurrection.

Once our bodies are freed from the corruption of sin and death, we can enjoy the beatific vision perfectly. Once we resurrect, God wants us to do something *in our bodies* that will give him glory and make us happy. No matter how intense our spiritual experience is in this life, something greater awaits us in the next life. It is the "freedom and glory of the children of God" that Christians can only experience once "our *bodies* have been set free" (cf. Rom 8:21, 23).

Because it is the *risen* Jesus who becomes present on the altar, the Eucharist gives us an idea of the great things God is preparing for us. The Church teaches:

> This pledge of the future resurrection comes from the fact that the flesh of the Son of Man, given as food, is his body in its glorious state after the resurrection. With the Eucharist we digest, as it were, the "secret" of the resurrection.
>
> St. John Paul II, *The Eucharist: Life of the Church*, n. 18

The Eucharist makes the risen Jesus present inside you. You become a living tabernacle. Jesus does this every day as a sign of what eternity will be like. If your lowly, impure body is already capable of containing the flesh and blood, the soul and divinity of God's only Son, what will happen in heaven once your body has been freed from corruption?

At Mass the altar is surrounded by the Virgin Mary and St. Joseph, by the angels, the Apostles, the holy women, the martyrs, the virgins, and all the saints. They are present in some way we cannot describe. They worship the Son of God. The Eucharist gives us a glimpse of the liturgy that takes place before God's throne in heaven. The Church calls this our communion with the Church in heaven:

> The Eucharist is truly a glimpse of heaven appearing on earth. It is a glorious ray of the heavenly Jerusalem that pierces the clouds of our history and lights up our journey.
>
> St. John Paul II, *The Eucharist: Life of the Church*, n. 19

By letting us eat his body and drink his blood, Jesus unites us to each other here on earth. This prepares us for the communion that we will experience once we have risen from the dead—the communion of all the saints and angels in their final glory. The Eucharist prepares us for that moment when Christ's prayer at the Last Supper will come to perfect fulfillment: ". . . May all be one; even as thou, Father, art in me, and I in thee" (Jn 17:21).

REVIEW QUESTIONS

1. Explain transubstantiation.
2. Why should you examine your conscience before receiving Holy Communion?
3. What makes the Eucharist a sacrifice?
4. Why does the Church recommend that we receive Communion frequently?

36.

Adoring the Eucharist

We worship the Eucharist because the Eucharist is Jesus. We go down on our knees or bow down in profound adoration. Understanding this gesture is crucial to understanding the Mass. The custom is rooted in a practice of the early Church that comes straight out of the Bible.

The Greek word for prostration is used more than fifty times in the New Testament. It is used to describe people going down on their knees in front of Jesus. It is often translated simply as they "worshipped him." It literally means that they fell face down on the ground or got down on their knees.

St. Matthew uses the word several times. Once, after the Apostles saw Jesus walk on the water, "those in the boat worshipped him, saying, 'Truly you are the Son of God'" (Mt 14:33).

A similar episode took place after Jesus cured the man born blind. The Pharisees harassed the man for believing in Jesus and expelled him from the Temple. Jesus found him and asked him if he believed. "The man said, 'Lord, I believe'; and he worshipped him" (Jn 9:38). Translated literally, the text says the man got down on his knees.

In ancient times, kneeling was the best way to convince someone that you wanted to worship him. It meant that you considered him equal to God. Nothing illustrates this better than St. John's experience with an angel:

> Then I fell down at his feet to worship him, but he said to me, "You must not do that! I am a fellow servant with you. . . . Worship God."
>
> Revelation 19:10

From the beginning Christians equated the act of kneeling with worship. For the same reason, they refused to bend their knees to pagan idols, and many died a martyr's death for it.

Describing the way all people will one day acknowledge the divinity of Jesus, St. Paul speaks in the same terms:

> Therefore God has highly exalted him and bestowed on him the name which is above every name, that at the name of Jesus every knee should bow, in heaven and on earth and under the earth, and every tongue confess that Jesus Christ is Lord, to the glory of God the Father.
>
> Philippians 2:9–11

The next time you attend Mass and see people kneeling, you will understand what is going on. Christians kneel for the same reason that the first disciples did it two thousand years ago. Once the priest has changed the bread and wine into Christ's Body and Blood, we adore Jesus. We kneel because we believe Jesus is present on the altar and we believe that he is God.

Eucharistic worship

There are three rites of Eucharistic worship: the celebration of the Lord's Supper (Mass); exposition and benediction of the Blessed Sacrament; and solemn procession. Benediction and procession both depend entirely on the Mass.

The Mass consists of five parts, all woven together to form a single act of worship: 1) Introductory Rite, 2) Liturgy of the Word, 3) Liturgy of the Eucharist, 4) Communion Rite, and 5) Concluding Rite. The following is a detailed description of each part. As you read this description, you will discover how the Mass is one prolonged acclamation of texts from sacred Scripture.

Introductory Rite

As the priest enters, the congregation stands. We welcome him with the belief that this man represents Jesus and will act "in the person of Christ." In other words, we believe that only Jesus himself can celebrate the Eucharist, changing bread and wine into his Body and Blood. The *Catechism* states:

> Christ himself is the principal agent of the Eucharist. He is high priest of the New Covenant; it is he himself who presides invisibly over every Eucharistic celebration.
>
> *CCC*, n. 1348

We stand to greet Jesus because he comes to offer a sacrifice to his Father in heaven.

The celebrant approaches the altar. He bows before it and kisses it. The altar is a symbol of Christ, the "supernatural rock" in the desert from which the waters of salvation flow (cf. 1 Cor 10:1–4). Everyone makes the Sign of the Cross, remembering that the liturgy is an act of Father, Son, and Holy Spirit in their divine unity, blessing us with every spiritual blessing (cf. Eph 1:3). The celebrant once again invokes the Trinity: "The grace of the Lord Jesus Christ and the love of God and the fellowship of the Holy Spirit be with you all" (2 Cor 13:14)—sometimes abbreviated as "The Lord be with you"—asking God to fill us with the Holy Spirit.

Sacred Scripture

I saw a Lamb standing, as though it had been slain . . . and he went and took the scroll from the right hand of him who was seated on the throne. And when he had taken the scroll, the four living creatures and the twenty-four elders fell down before the Lamb . . .

Revelation 5:6, 7, 8

The celebrant invites us to stir up sorrow for our sins. He pauses so that all may look into their souls. We ask God to forgive any venial sins we have committed. If we have committed any mortal sins since our last good confession, we ask him for the grace necessary for conversion and the determination to go to confession as soon as possible.

We strike our breast when we admit our faults, as a sign of contrition. (A *contrite* heart literally means a heart shattered to pieces, undone by sorrow for our guilt.) We are imitating King David, who wrote: "The sacrifice acceptable to God is a broken spirit; a broken and contrite heart, O God, thou wilt not despise" (Ps 51:17). We ask for mercy, either in vernacular or using the ancient Greek formula: *Kyrie, eleison. Christe, eleison. Kyrie, eleison.* Like all the suffering and sick who begged Jesus for a miracle with these words, we also plead with humility and expectation: "Have mercy on me, O Lord, Son of David" (Mt 15:22).

On feast days we recite or sing the Gloria. This hymn recalls God's majesty, repeating the song of praise the angels sang for the birth of Jesus: "Glory to God in the highest, and on earth peace among men with whom he is pleased!" (Lk 2:14).

The celebrant then recites the opening prayer, with hands outstretched like Moses on the mountain interceding for the people (cf. Ex 17:8–13). He calls upon God, once again invoking him as Father, Son, and Holy Spirit. This prepares us to open our minds and hearts to listen to the Word of God.

Liturgy of the Word

A lector comes to the lectern to read, while the celebrant takes his seat in the chair reserved for him. All sit to listen to the first reading, which is taken either from the Old Testament or from one of the New Testament letters or the Acts of the Apostles or the Book of Revelation. The congregation joins the lector or choir for the responsorial psalm. On Sundays and solemn celebrations, there is a second reading. Then everyone stands to chant the Gospel acclamation.

For solemn celebrations, incense is used to honor God's holy Word. Incensing is another ancient symbol of worship. In this case it reminds us that the words we hear from the Gospel speak to us of the Word made flesh and that these words—like the Son of God incarnate—are divine even though they appear to be merely human. If a deacon is assisting the celebrant, he reads the Gospel. Otherwise, the celebrant reads it and then gives a homily.

Only an ordained minister can preach—bishop, priest, or deacon. The preacher represents Christ and must be given the power to do so through the sacrament of holy orders. When preaching, the first duty of the minister is to exhort everyone to accept the words just read as "the Word of God, which is at work in you believers" (1 Thes 2:13).

After the homily, all rise. On Sundays and solemnities, we pray the Creed. The celebrant then leads the people in the Prayer of the

Faithful. We present our needs before God and ask him with humility to hear our prayer. The *Catechism* says:

> After the homily . . . come the intercessions, according to the Apostle's words: "I urge that supplications, prayers, intercessions, and thanksgivings be made for all men, for kings and all who are in high positions" (1 Tim 2:1–2).
>
> *CCC*, n. 1349

We pray for the Church, for civil authorities, for all men and women, especially those in need.

Liturgy of the Eucharist

This is the main part of the Mass. It begins with the Offertory. This is an act of offering the bread and wine that will become Christ's body and blood. On special occasions, some people from the congregation form a procession. They bring the bread and wine to the altar, along with other gifts. This offering takes us back to the mysterious action of Melchizedek, the first king of Jerusalem mentioned in the Bible. By offering bread and wine for Abraham, this "priest of God Most High" foreshadowed the perfect priesthood of Jesus Christ (cf. Gen 14:18; Heb 5:9).

Abraham felt obliged to tithe to Melchizedek, that is, to give him a tenth of everything. Likewise, Christians give generously during the collection taken up during the Offertory. Quoting one of the Church Fathers, the *Catechism* says:

> From the very beginning, Christians have brought, along with the bread and wine for the Eucharist, gifts to share with those in need. This custom

Fathers of the Church

For what is the bread? It is the body of Christ. And what do those who receive it become? The Body of Christ—not many bodies but one body. For as bread is completely one, though made of up many grains of wheat . . . so too are we mutually joined to one another and together united with Christ.

St. John Chrysostom, *Commentary on Corinthians*, 24, 2

> of the collection, ever appropriate, is inspired by the example of Christ who became poor to make us rich. As St. Justin wrote: "Those who are well off, and who are also willing, give as each chooses. What is gathered is given to him who presides to assist orphans and widows, those whom illness or any other cause has deprived of resources, prisoners, immigrants and, in a word, all who are in need."
>
> *CCC*, n. 1351

When giving something for the collection, Christians recall our Lord's advice: "Do not let your left hand know what your right hand is doing, so that your alms may be in secret" (Mt 6:3–4). Give without letting others know. The gift God treasures most is not the biggest gift, but the gift of the poor widow, who "out of her poverty put in all the living that she had" (Lk 21:4). We become pleasing to God only when we give him our whole life. Therefore, as the priest raises up the paten, we place our lives there and offer ourselves to God.

Before offering the wine, the priest adds a few drops of water to the chalice. The water symbolizes our work. Like the water added to the wine, all our earthly activities are added to Christ's offering and become a sacrifice of infinite value. As the celebrant adds these drops of water, he says

> By the mystery of this water and wine, may we come to share in the divinity of Christ, who humbled himself to share in our humanity.

This prayer echoes St. Peter's words: You will be able to "become partakers of the divine nature" (2 Pt 1:4). God desires to raise our human nature to the heights of divine glory. Eating Christ's body and drinking his blood will make this a reality.

The celebrant calls on the congregation: "Pray, brothers and sisters, that my sacrifice and yours may be acceptable . . ." They respond, "May the Lord accept the sacrifice . . ." Then the priest prays the prayer over the gifts.

After the Offertory comes the Eucharistic Prayer. It begins with a preface. There are dozens of different prefaces: some for Sunday Mass, some for weekday Mass, some for feast days, some that are used only once a year. The preface always ends by asking everyone to join the angels and saints in their hymn of praise. We join the "choirs of heaven." We begin with the ancient prayer revealed to the prophet Isaiah when he saw God in the Temple (cf. Is 6:3). We conclude with the triumphant acclaim used to praise Jesus when he entered Jerusalem in triumph a few days before his crucifixion:

> Hosanna! Blessed is he who comes in the name of the Lord! Blessed is the kingdom of our father David that is coming! Hosanna in the highest!
>
> (Mk 11:9)

In the Eucharist, Jesus comes to us with greater humility than he did when seated on a donkey. By hiding under the appearances of bread and wine, Jesus does not impose his majesty upon us. He insists on being meek and gentle because he thirsts for our love: "Those who are well have no need of a physician, but those who are sick. Go and learn what this means, 'I desire mercy, and not sacrifice'" (Mt 9:12–13).

There are several different Eucharistic Prayers. The priest uses the one most appropriate for the occasion.

Eucharistic Prayer I may be used on any day. It is also called the "Roman Canon" because it was fixed in Rome sometime in the fifth century. It is best for the solemnities of Christmas, Epiphany, Easter, Ascension, and Pentecost, since it contains special prayers to commemorate these events. It is also good for feasts of the Apostles and other saints mentioned in this prayer.

Eucharistic Prayer II is particularly suitable for weekdays; **Eucharistic Prayer III**, for Sundays. Both have a special addition to be used during a funeral Mass. **Eucharistic Prayer IV** provides a summary of the history of salvation.

Besides, these four, there are Eucharistic Prayers for special occasions, for example, when celebrating Mass for children. All Eucharistic Prayers have several elements in common:

- **Preface:** We express thanksgiving. The priest thanks God the Father for the work of salvation.
- **Acclamation:** By singing or reciting the "Holy, holy, holy," we remember the action of the Trinity. The Father sends his Son so that by sacrificing his body and blood, we can be filled with the Holy Spirit.

- **Epiclesis:** This Greek word means "calling down upon." Holding his hands over the chalice, the celebrant calls the Holy Spirit to come down upon the bread and wine. The *Catechism* says:

> In the epiclesis, the Church asks the Father to send his Holy Spirit (or the power of his blessing) on the bread and wine, so that by his power they may become the body and blood of Jesus Christ and so that those who take part in the Eucharist may be one body and one spirit. The priest also makes the sign of the cross over the offering to bless the bread and wine.
>
> *CCC*, n. 1353

- **Consecration:** The consecration is twofold. The words used are the same ones Jesus used at the Last Supper. The words of consecration are identical for all Eucharistic Prayers. First the celebrant takes bread and changes it into the body of Christ, saying, "Take this all of you and eat it: This is my body which will be given up for you." He raises the sacred host in silence for all to adore. Placing the host on the altar, he genuflects to adore Jesus. Then he takes wine and changes it into the blood of Christ, saying, "Take this all of you and drink from it: This is the cup of my blood, the blood of the new and everlasting covenant. It will be shed for you and for all so that sins may be forgiven. Do this in memory of me." The celebrant raises the chalice in silence for all to adore. Then he genuflects to adore Jesus. He invites everyone to proclaim the "Mystery of Faith."
- **Anamnesis:** This Greek word means "recalling a memory." The celebrant recalls Christ's passion, resurrection, and ascension.
- **Offering:** The celebrant offers Jesus—the victim now present on the altar—to the Father in the Holy Spirit. By offering this victim, we learn to surrender ourselves, through Christ the Mediator, to an ever more complete union with the Father and with each other, so that at last God may be all in all.
- **Intercessions:** Having offered Christ's sacrifice, the celebrant asks God to care for the Church and all its members, living and dead. The celebrant prays for the Pope and the bishop; every celebration of the Eucharist is meant to join the priest and all the faithful into

closer union with the successor of Peter in Rome and the successor of the Apostles in the local church.

- **Final doxology:** The celebrant holds the sacred host and the chalice with our Lord's blood. He raises them for all to see, and prays: "Through him, with him, in him, in the unity of the Holy Spirit, all glory and honor is yours, almighty Father, forever and ever." The people make an act of faith, responding in unison, "Amen." On special feasts, this can be prolonged as a triple "Amen." A doxology is a prayer praising the Trinity, reminding us that God is the unity of three divine persons: Father, Son, and Holy Spirit. The doxology concluding the Eucharistic Prayer is called the "Great Amen." It is *great* because it is an answer to the great mystery—Jesus offering his sacrifice to the Father and then offering us his body and blood as food and drink. It is an *amen* because the congregation uses this word to express their faith. They are essentially saying: "Yes, I believe that everything you have said is true."

Communion Rite

The celebrant invites everyone to pray the Lord's Prayer. After asking God to "deliver us from evil," the celebrant pleads with God again and says, "Deliver us, Lord, from *all* evil." We want to be totally purified of sin and free from anxiety: "There is no fear in love," (1 Jn 4:18). The people answer this prayer with another doxology: "For the kingdom, the power, and the glory are yours now and forever."

Magisterium

The Most Blessed Eucharist contains the entire spiritual good of the Church, that is, Christ himself, our Pasch and Living Bread. . . . Therefore the celebration of the Eucharistic, over which the priest presides, is the very heart of the faithful as they gather together. For this reason, priests will teach the people to offer the Divine Victim to God the Father during the sacrifice of the Mass, and then how to offer their own lives together with that Victim.

Vatican II, *Decree on the Ministry and Life of Priests*, n. 5

Because one of the purposes of the Eucharist is to unite all believers and make them one, we prepare for Communion by asking God to give peace and unity to the Church. The celebrant repeats our Lord's promise at the Last Supper: "Peace I leave with you; my peace I give to you" (Jn 14:27). The Roman Missal suggests that at this point in the celebration, "we offer some sign of our love for one another." The bishops' conference determines which sign is most appropriate in accordance with the culture and customs of the people.

The celebrant breaks the sacred host. This "breaking of the bread" reminds us of the way Jesus "took bread, and blessed, and broke it" (Mt 26:26). Christ's gesture was so unforgettable to the Apostles that it became the name for the Eucharistic (cf. Acts 2:42). Like the two disciples going to Emmaus on the day of our Lord's resurrection, we also want to "recognize him" when he breaks the bread (cf. Lk 24:31). This is a sign that we are sharing in the one loaf, which is Christ, and becoming one body even though there are many of us (cf. 1 Cor 10:17). The celebrant drops a piece of the host into the chalice, saying, "May the mingling of the body and blood of our Lord Jesus Christ bring eternal life to us who receive it." During the breaking of the bread and the commingling, the congregation recites or sings the hymn "Lamb of God," asking Jesus for mercy and peace.

As the priest prepares to eat the body and drink the blood of Christ, the faithful do the same in silence. He then lifts up the sacred host and says, "This is the Lamb of God, who takes away the sins of the world. Happy are those who are called to his supper." This recalls God's promise in the Book of Revelation: "Blessed are those who are invited to the marriage supper of the Lamb" (Rev 19:9). The faithful respond, using words similar to those uttered by the Roman centurion (Lk 7:1–10): "Lord, I am not worthy to receive you, but only say the word and I shall be healed."

At this part of the Mass, Catholics who are prepared to receive Holy Communion go to receive Jesus. The priest holds the body of Jesus before each person and says, "The body of Christ." Each person answers, "Amen." This shows that the one receiving believes that Jesus is truly present in the Eucharist. After receiving Communion, the Christian eats the sacred host and swallows it, in expectation of our Lord's promise: "As the living Father sent me, and I live because of the Father, so he who eats me will live because of me" (Jn 6:57). During Communion, it is good for the congregation to sing a song expressing joy and love for Jesus.

Everyone spends some time in silent prayer. Then the celebrant asks all to stand for the closing prayer.

Concluding Rite

The priest gives the final blessing over the people. He sends them out into the world so that they can spread Christ's message of peace and joy to others. On special occasions, the celebrant can pray a solemn blessing over the people.

Liturgical music

The angels and saints sing praises before God's throne day and night (cf. Rev 4:8). Music makes our acts of worship similar to the heavenly liturgy. St. Paul instructed the early Christians that liturgical song would help them pray while gathered together for the Eucharist and throughout the rest of the day:

> Be filled with the Spirit, addressing one another in psalms and hymns and spiritual songs, singing and making melody to the Lord with all your heart, always and for everything giving thanks in the name of our Lord Jesus Christ to God the Father.
>
> Ephesians 5:18–20

Jesus himself sang psalms with his disciples at the Last Supper (cf. Mt 26:30).

The Church uses many forms of art to communicate God's revelation and inspire us to love the Word made flesh with our whole heart and soul. Sacred music is the most important of all. The *Catechism* says:

> The musical tradition of the universal Church is a treasure of inestimable value, greater even than that of any other art. The main reason for

> this preeminence is that, as a combination of sacred music and words, it forms a necessary or integral part of solemn liturgy.
>
> *CCC*, n. 1156

Art can help us pray. Singing is prayer. We sing to lift up our minds and hearts to God. "The one who sings prays twice."

The music used for the liturgy should have a sacred character. It can be enchanting, somber, or triumphant, as the moment requires. But it cannot be reduced to entertainment or accompaniment. Rather than focusing us on externals, sacred music seeks to evoke the spirit of recollection needed for contemplation.

Experiencing emotion when attending Mass is not the essence of adoration. If you lack enthusiasm, God is still pleased with your prayer. When you feel empty, remember when Jesus "prayed more earnestly," pleading with his Father in the garden of Gethsemane (Lk 22:44). Nevertheless, it is good when the liturgy moves us to experience peace and joy.

We are not pure spirits. We love with acts of the will, but we also love with hearts of flesh. We love when moved by the dictates of reason. We also love when moved by our hearts.

We love according to the dictates of reason when we love the good our mind sees as good. We love moved by our hearts when we do not know how to live without the one we love. We should love God with our whole mind and also with our whole heart. The liturgy is meant to move us both ways—intellectually and sentimentally. The liturgy is meant to be a light that enlightens our minds. The liturgy is also meant to be a fire that sets our hearts aflame with the love of God: "My heart and flesh sing for joy to the living God" (Ps 84:2).

The Church has centuries of experience in composing and selecting the music most appropriate for Eucharistic worship. The *Catechism* states:

> Song and music fulfil their function as signs in a manner all the more significant when they are more closely connected with the liturgical action, according to three principal criteria: beauty expressive of prayer, the unanimous participation of the assembly at the designated moments, and the solemn character of the celebration.
>
> *CCC*, n. 1157

Jesus gives us his body and blood in the Eucharist in order to make us one with him and with one another. Sacred music is best when it makes it easier to enjoy this union, setting aside any other desire or ambition.

Reserving the Eucharist

The Blessed Sacrament is the name used to speak of the Eucharist when the priest sets aside some of the sacred hosts consecrated during Mass and keep them for Eucharistic Adoration and for taking Holy Communion to the sick.

During Mass, the celebrant can reserve the Blessed Sacrament in the tabernacle. To do so, the priest takes some of the sacred hosts and puts them in a ciborium, which is a container used for distributing Communion. He takes the ciborium from the altar and places it inside the tabernacle. Then he locks the door of the tabernacle.

The tabernacle in each church or chapel looks different, so it is hard to describe it. Some are small and look like a very ornate box covered with jewels and precious metals. Others are very big and covered with a veil, the color of the veil changing from time to time depending on the liturgical season.

In general terms, the tabernacle is a sacred place where the Eucharist is kept—always locked with a special key and used exclusively for storing the Eucharist. You can usually recognize it because there is a candle or lamp burning beside it twenty-four hours a day throughout the year. This light reminds us that Jesus, the Light of the World, is present in the tabernacle. If you have any doubt about where the tabernacle is in the church you attend, ask someone who knows. For security reasons—if there is great risk of thieves stealing the Eucharist—some churches and chapels do not have a tabernacle.

Wherever there is a tabernacle, remember that Jesus is waiting there for you. Go and spend time with Jesus in prayer. This devotion is so powerful that the Church grants a plenary indulgence, under the usual conditions, to those who spend a half hour in prayer before the tabernacle.

Christians genuflect every time they pass in front of a tabernacle. The genuflection is an act of faith. It shows they believe that Jesus is truly present in the tabernacle. The genuflection is also act of adoration. We adore Jesus because we believe he is the Son of God.

Processions and benediction

Mass can be celebrated at any time of the day throughout the year except for three days: Holy Thursday, Good Friday, and Holy Saturday. No Mass is celebrated on Good Friday, or Holy Saturday. The celebration of the Lord's Supper on the evening of Holy Thursday is one of the most ancient liturgical ceremonies of the Church and marks the beginning of these holy days. This Holy Thursday celebration includes a solemn procession and exposition of the Blessed Sacrament.

On Holy Thursday, the celebrant begins the procession by intoning the Eucharistic hymn *Pange lingua gloriosi* ("Sing my tongue the Savior's glory"). He takes the ciborium containing the Blessed Sacrament from the altar where he has just celebrated the Mass of the Lord's Supper. The congregation continues singing until the celebrant arrives at another altar prepared for this occasion, called the "altar of repose." He places the Blessed Sacrament there and kneels to adore Jesus. While he incenses the Eucharist, all sing the hymn *Tantum ergo Sacramentum* ("Down in adoration falling"). Then the Blessed Sacrament is left on the altar of repose for the night so that everyone can come to adore Jesus and spend time in prayer.

> **Wisdom of the Saints**
>
> "This is my body which is given for you. Do this in remembrance of me." Jesus could not have commanded anything more lovable, for this sacrament produces love and union.
>
> St. Albert the Great, *Commentary on Luke*, 22:19

With the passing of time, the Church decided to have other ceremonies outside of Mass—processions and times of exposition of the Blessed Sacrament followed by benediction. This was done to allow the faithful to express their desire to adore Jesus with great solemnity. A special feast was instituted, called *Corpus Christi* (The Body and Blood of Christ). On this day the Church organizes a solemn procession of the Blessed Sacrament.

Following ancient tradition, exposition and benediction of the Blessed Sacrament is frequently celebrated throughout the year. The Church explains the reason for these liturgical acts:

> [Let us] encourage . . . the practice of Eucharistic adoration, and exposition of the Blessed Sacrament in particular, as well as prayer of adoration before Christ present under the Eucharistic species. It is pleasant to spend time with him, to lie close to his breast like the Beloved Disciple (cf. Jn 13:25), and to feel the infinite love present in his heart. . . . This practice . . . is supported by the example of many saints. Particularly outstanding in this regard was St. Alphonsus Liguori, who wrote: "Of all devotions, that of adoring Jesus in the Blessed Sacrament is the greatest after the sacraments, the one dearest to God, and the one most helpful to us."
>
> St. John Paul II, *The Eucharist: Life of the Church*, n. 25

Exposition and benediction of the Blessed Sacrament begins when the priest takes the sacred host from the tabernacle to the altar. We sing hymns to our Lord and spend time in prayer. This is followed by benediction. Benediction means blessing. The priest or deacon takes the Blessed Sacrament in both hands and makes the Sign of the Cross. With this act, Jesus is blessing us. It reminds us that all graces come to us because of his sacrifice on the cross.

REVIEW QUESTIONS

1. Explain the significance of kneeling before the Eucharist.
2. Explain the five parts of the Mass.
3. Why do we genuflect before the tabernacle?
4. What is the difference between the Mass and benediction of the Blessed Sacrament?

37.

Penance and Reconciliation

Penance and reconciliation is the sacrament that forgives sins committed after baptism. To receive this sacrament, you confess your sins to a priest. The sacrament is also called "confession." Like all the other sacraments, the sacrament of penance was instituted by Christ and entrusted to the Church.

To explain how sins after baptism affect us, St. Paul wrote to the early Christians:

> Now the works of the flesh are plain: fornication, impurity, licentiousness, idolatry, sorcery, enmity, strife, jealousy, anger, selfishness, dissension, party spirit, envy, drunkenness, carousing, and the like. I warn you, as I warned you before, that those who do such things shall not inherit the kingdom of God.
>
> Galatians 5:19–21

Any Christian who commits a serious sin after baptism cannot enter God's kingdom without repenting. Repentance requires seeking God's forgiveness in the sacrament of penance.

When you are baptized, God gives you sanctifying grace. This grace makes you holy. You lose this grace when you commit a mortal sin. One mortal sin destroys the sanctifying grace you received at baptism. God wants you to live in the state of grace all the time. When you go to confession, God restores the grace you lost through sin. The *Catechism* says:

> Christ instituted the sacrament of penance for all sinful members of his Church: above all for those who, since baptism, have fallen into grave

> sin, and have thus lost their baptismal grace and wounded ecclesial communion. It is to them that the sacrament of penance offers a new possibility to convert and to recover the grace of justification.
>
> CCC, n. 1446

The grace of justification is another name for the grace you receive at baptism. Serious or grave sin is another name for mortal sin. Mortal sin kills God's life in your soul.

The Church fathers compare the moment of committing a mortal sin to a shipwreck. They compare confession to a lifesaver to keep you from drowning, that is, to keep you from being damned to hell forever. Confession offers you salvation a second time—or third or fourth or whatever. The one who told us to forgive others "seventy times seven" (cf. Mt 18:22) is also ready to forgive us as many times as he has to in order to prepare us for heaven.

Acts of the penitent

Receiving the sacrament of penance requires three acts. The three acts are called the acts of the penitent. You are the penitent, that is, the one doing penance for sins. The three acts of the penitent are:

- **Contrition:** Be sorry for your sins.
- **Confession:** Tell your sins to a priest.
- **Satisfaction:** Fulfill the penance the priest gives you.

If you want God to forgive sins committed after baptism, you must perform all three acts.

Contrition

To prepare for confession, examine your conscience. Look at your past and recall your sins. Ask the Holy Spirit to give you light to see and courage to admit your sins. Contrition means being sorry for yours sins. Being sorry does not mean shedding tears or feeling deep emotion. Tears can be a sign of sorrow, but true sorrow can exist without tears. Besides, tears can also be a sign of self-pity and wounded pride—neither of which have anything to do with true sorrow.

Sacred Scripture

And behold, they brought to him a paralytic, lying on his bed; and when Jesus saw their faith he said to the paralytic, "Take heart, my son; your sins are forgiven." And behold, some of the scribes said to themselves, "This man is blaspheming." But Jesus, knowing their thoughts, said, "Why do you think evil in your hearts? For which is easier, to say, 'Your sins are forgiven,' or to say, 'Rise and walk? But that you may know that the Son of man has authority on earth to forgive sins"—he then said to the paralytic—"Rise, take up your bed and go home." And he rose and went home. When the crowds saw it, they were afraid, and they glorified God, who had given such authority to men.

Matthew 9:2–8

Besides sorrow of soul, contrition requires hatred for your sins. Pray to God and tell him, "I wish I had acted differently. I wish I had never committed that sin." If you cursed the people you hate and were glad to see them suffer, God cannot forgive you until you have a change of heart. You must hate the sin. You do not hate it as long as you take delight in it.

If instead of repenting, you are glad that you committed sin, ask God to pierce your heart with sorrow. Never look upon sin as trivial. Sin is what nailed Jesus Christ to the cross. Ask God to give you a sense of horror towards mortal sin and deliberate venial sin.

If you are sorry, God will forgive you. The effort it takes to go to confession, is usually a good sign that you are sorry. Even so, when you go to confession stir up sorrow by making acts of contrition. The Jesus Prayer is one of the best ways of telling God that you are sorry: "Lord Jesus, Son of God, have mercy on me a sinner" (cf. *CCC*, n. 2616). To express contrition, many Christians like to use this prayer during confession. It is adapted from the cry of the blind man Bartimaeus when he asked Jesus to give him back his sight: "Jesus, Son of David, have mercy on me!" (Mk 10:47).

Contrition demands that you resolve not to sin again. This does not mean you have to swear before God that you are sure you will never sin again. You may feel so weak that you have no idea how you will avoid falling. Even so, you must stand before God and tell him, "I do not want to commit this sin again. Help me." If you can say this, your contrition is good enough for God to forgive you.

The *Catechism* distinguishes between two kinds of contrition:

- **Perfect contrition**

  When it arises from a love by which God is loved above all else, contrition is called "perfect" (contrition of charity). Such contrition remits venial sins; it also obtains forgiveness of mortal sins if it includes the firm resolution to have recourse to sacramental confession as soon as possible.

- **Imperfect contrition**

  The contrition called "imperfect" (contrition of fear or "attrition") is also a gift of God, a prompting of the Holy Spirit. It is born of the consideration of sin's ugliness or the fear of eternal damnation and the other penalties threatening the sinner. Such a stirring of conscience can initiate an interior process which, under the prompting of grace, will be brought to completion by sacramental absolution. By itself, however, imperfect contrition cannot obtain the forgiveness of grave sins, but it disposes one to obtain forgiveness in the sacrament of penance.

CCC, nn. 1452–1453

Because we are moved by love, perfect contrition is enough for God to forgive all our sins. It assumes we are eager to go to confession. When we are moved by fear, our contrition remains imperfect; we still are not truly sorry for our sins. However, the sacrament of penance has the power to change our motivation from fear to love. Even if the fear of suffering in hell is the only reason you go to confession, go. You will discover how God's mercy is infinitely more powerful than all your worst sins put together.

Finally, contrition demands forgiving others. Jesus made this a condition:

> For if you forgive men their trespasses, your heavenly Father also will forgive you; but if you do not forgive men their trespasses, neither will your Father forgive your trespasses.
>
> Matthew 6:14–15

Confession

When you go to confession, you need to tell the priest all the mortal sins you have committed, specifying the number of times for each mortal sin.

Be concrete and specific when you go to confession. You cannot limit yourself to saying, "I was a very bad person. I did many bad things." If you skipped Mass three Sundays, then you must tell the priest, "I missed Mass on Sunday three times." If you got into a fight on two different occasions, you must tell the priest, "I used violence against my neighbor twice."

The Church teaches:

> Since all mortal sins—even internal desires—make us "children of wrath" (Eph 2:3) and enemies of God, it is necessary to ask pardon for all of them from God by an open and humble confession. When Christ's faithful strive to confess all the sins that they can remember, there is no doubt that they have placed all of them before the divine mercy to be forgiven. But those who fail to do so, and knowingly conceal certain sins, place nothing before the divine goodness for forgiveness through the priest. "For if the sick person is too ashamed to show his wound to the doctor, the medicine cannot heal what it does not know."
>
> Council of Trent, *Doctrine on the Sacrament of Penance*, ch. 5 (quoting St. Jerome)

Why does the penitent have to tell the priest the number of times for each mortal sin? The main reason is that each sin has to be forgiven.

Ecclesiastical Writers

Penance must not be performed solely within one's conscience but must be shown forth in some external act. . . . By humbling a man, it exalts him. By covering him with guilt, it cleanses him. By accusing, it excuses. By condemning, it absolves. . . . Most men, however, shun this duty because it involves a public exposure of themselves. Or they put it off from day to day because, it seems to me, they care more about their shame than about their salvation. They are like those men who have contracted some disease in the more private parts of the body and try to conceal it from their doctor. They preserve their modesty but lose their lives.

Tertullian, *On Penance*, 9–10

Besides, it is the only way the priest can determine what kind of reparation is necessary.

If you forget a mortal sin in confession, all your sins are forgiven. You have made a good confession, but in the next confession, you need to confess the mortal sin you forgot to mention previously.

If you feel ashamed and deliberately hide a mortal sin from the priest in confession, none of your sins are forgiven. Deliberately refusing to confess a mortal sin when making your confession means you are not truly sorry. This lack of contrition makes it impossible for God to forgive you at that moment. Instead of making a good confession, you have offended our Lord by thinking you can hide your guilt from him. You need to go to confession again, explain what happened, and then confess all the sins you have committed since your last good confession.

If you cannot remember the exact number of times for one of your sins, tell the priest how often you committed the sin (e.g., "I committed the sin roughly once a week") or approximate as best you can (e.g., "I committed the sin about a dozen times.")

Explain any circumstances that might affect the nature of the sin. For instance, if your children were watching when you yelled at your spouse, you should mention this detail. If you not only skipped Mass on Sunday but also gave bad example to your friends by doing so, this is another example of a circumstance that makes a sin more grievous. You should never tell the priest the names of other people. Avoid narrating the whole story behind every sin. All the priest needs to know is the nature of each mortal sin and how many times you committed it.

There are some cases where the priest may ask you questions. For instance, if you say, "I committed an act of impurity," he will ask you whether you did this alone or with someone else. He asks not out of curiosity, but only to verify exactly which sin you are confessing. This also helps him give you advice on how to avoid occasions of sin.

Satisfaction

After you have confessed all your sins, the priest imposes a penance. The *Catechism* explains:

> Absolution takes away sin, but it does not remedy all the disorders sin has caused. Raised up from sin, the sinner must still recover his full spiritual health by doing something more to make amends for the sin: he must "make satisfaction for" or "expiate" his sins. This satisfaction is also called "penance."
>
> *CCC*, n. 1459

For your penance, the priest may ask you to pray a prayer, give alms, perform a work of mercy, or make an act of self-denial. By performing the penance, you are making satisfaction for your sins. You are making up for the temporary punishment due to sin. You show Jesus that you want to be completely purified. You want to be as ready to enter God's kingdom as you were on the day you were baptized.

Jesus Christ's sacrifice on the cross is the only true satisfaction for sin. The penance imposed by the priest is nothing compared to what you deserve. God shows great mercy when he accepts your act of penance as satisfaction for your sins. Always perform your penance in a spirit of humility, being grateful to our Lord. The *Catechism* explains:

> The penance the confessor imposes . . . can consist of prayer, an offering, works of mercy, service of neighbor, voluntary self-denial, sacrifices, and above all the patient acceptance of the cross we must bear. Such penances help configure us to Christ, who alone expiated our sins once for all. They allow us to become co-heirs with the risen Christ, "provided we suffer with him" (Rom 8:17).
>
> *CCC*, n. 1460

The worth of your penance is not determined by how much it costs you; it is determined by how much it unites you to Christ.

When giving you advice, the priest will explain occasions of sin that you must avoid—e.g., to get rid of a book, magazine, or video that is doing you harm, to stop seeing someone who leads you into sin, to stay away from a place where you usually fall into bad habits, etc. He will also explain the need for reparation. The *Catechism* teaches:

> Many sins wrong our neighbor. One must do what is possible in order to repair the harm (e.g., return stolen goods, restore the reputation

> of someone slandered, pay compensation for injuries). Simple justice requires as much.
>
> CCC, n. 1459

After you have confessed your sins, the priest will specify what deeds of reparation are necessary. If you stole money, for instance, the priest will ask if you can return it. If you slandered someone, the priest will ask you to find some way of undoing the harm done to that person's reputation.

You should fulfill the obligation of making reparation as soon as you can. If you foresee any difficulty, inform the priest during confession, or come back to see him again if necessary. Deliberately neglecting to make reparation is a sin. Making satisfaction for our sins is just as important as being sorry for them.

How to go to confession

Even if you have been to confession many times, review the following steps for making a good confession to be sure that you are doing all that God wants.

- **Make an examination of conscience.** Try to remember your sins. Tell Jesus you are sorry. If it has been a long time since you last went to confession, you can ask the priest for some help to remember your sins once you are in the confessional. To examine your conscience, it may help to review the Ten Commandments, the beatitudes from the Sermon on the Mount, and your social and family duties. If you are not sure whether something was a sin, ask the priest during confession.
- **Enter the confessional.** The confessional is the place where the priest listens to your confession. Once you enter, close the door behind you so that your confession remains private. The priest does not have to know who you are. You can tell the priest who you are or you can remain anonymous. The confessional has a screen between you and the priest so that he cannot see you. You kneel down and make the Sign of the Cross.

- **Pray the prayer at the beginning of confession.** If you do not know how to do this, the priest will tell you. Traditionally, many people begin by saying, "Bless me, Father, for I have sinned. My last good confession was . . ." (here you indicate when you made your last good confession, e.g., a month ago, a year ago, five years ago, or whatever). Then you express your desire for God's mercy by reciting some phrase from sacred Scripture, for example, "Lord, you know everything; you know that I love you" (Jn 21:17).
- **Confess your sins to the priest.** Tell the priest all the mortal sins you remember. (For example, mortal sins include skipping Sunday Mass, getting drunk, using drugs, murder, stealing, fornication, adultery, using contraceptives, abortion, violent assault, and perjury; whereas telling lies, being lazy, being moody, using bad language, and gossiping are usually venial sins.) If you have a sin to confess but do not know what name to give it, tell the priest. You must specify the number of times for each mortal sin. Be brief, concise, and complete. You can also tell him any venial sins you wish to confess. If you are not sure whether a sin is mortal or venial, ask the priest.
- **Listen to what the priest tells you.** The priest will give you a penance. He will also indicate what you have to do to make up for damage caused by your sins. You do your penance *after you finish confession*. You repair damage done as soon as you can. If you are not sure whether you can repair the damage done (e.g., you stole a lot of money but no longer have it), inform the priest of this difficulty so he can advise you.
- **Make an act of contrition.** Tell Jesus that you are sorry for your sins.
- **Receive absolution.** The priest absolves your sins, using the formula established by the Church. Absolution is the act that God uses to forgive your sins. He says: "I absolve you from your sins in the name of the Father and of the Son and of the Holy Spirit." You answer, "Amen."
- **Leave the confessional and do your penance.** Do the penance that the priest gave you during confession. Thank Jesus for taking away your sins.

If you have never been to confession, tell the priest. If you are not Catholic but you would like to go to confession, speak to the priest first, explaining the situation so he can prepare you properly. Under normal circumstances, only Catholics can go to confession.

Reconciliation

During Jesus' public life, he forgave many sinners. Besides forgiving their sins, he dined with them. The Pharisees were scandalized as much by the dining as by the forgiving. Others were delighted at the way Jesus connected these two acts—acts we could call forgiving the sin and re-establishing communion. The Church looks at our Lord's way of acting and imitates it. After forgiving sins, she welcomes the sinner back to communion with the Church.

Sin cuts us off from God. It also cuts us off from the Church. The sacrament of penance and reconciliation restores our friendship with God and restores our communion with the Church. The *Catechism* says:

Confessing your sins

Be clear. An accusation like "I sinned against the Ten Commandments" is not clear. You have to say exactly what the sins are; and for mortal sins, you also have to say how many times you committed each sin.

Be concise. Some people start narrating events: "This guy came to our house, and we talked for a while and then I turned on the TV, and watched a few shows and then my mother came in and told me turn off the TV, and then . . ." Confession is not a time for telling stories. Confess your sins and skip the rest.

Be complete. If you make a "bad confession," God does not forgive any of your sins. This happens any time when, because of fear or shame, you hide a mortal sin from the priest while confessing. When you confess a mortal sin, confess the kind of sin and also tell the priest how many times you committed that particular sin. For instance, if you say, "I watched bad movies," tell the priest how many bad movies you watched. If you stole money, tell the priest how much money you stole. Never go to confession trying to hide a mortal sin. If you deliberately hide a mortal sin out of shame, none of your sins will be forgiven—not even the ones you confessed.

Be contrite. Say your sins without making excuses. You are telling your sins to Jesus so that he can forgive you.

> Sin is before all else an offense against God, a rupture of communion with him. At the same time it damages communion with the Church. For this reason conversion entails both God's forgiveness and reconciliation with the Church, which are expressed and accomplished liturgically by the sacrament of penance and reconciliation.
>
> *CCC*, n. 1440

To understand reconciliation, go back to the Church's teaching on the communion of saints. Any evil you do harms other members of the Church, even if nobody sees you commit the sin. This is hard for some people to understand. What if you watch pornography while you're alone? How does that hurt other people?

Because we are dealing with a mystery we cannot see or touch, this is difficult to explain. Think of the analogy St. Paul uses comparing the Church to the human body. If your hand gets crushed under the wheel of car, it may be only one small part of your body, but it will cause so much pain that all of you suffers. The same thing happens to the Church when you commit a sin: "If one member suffers, all suffer together" (1 Cor 12:26). The good news is that the whole Church rejoices when you go to confession: "I tell you, there is joy before the angels of God over one sinner who repents" (Lk 15:10).

> **MAGISTERIUM**
>
> [T]he sin that breaks our friendship with God and deprives us of eternal life . . . is called "mortal sin." Recourse to the sacrament of penance is necessary even when only one mortal sin has been committed.
>
> St. John Paul II, *Catechesis on the Creed*, Vol IV, p. 162

Jesus linked forgiveness and reconciliation together when he said first to St. Peter and then to the rest of the Apostles: "Truly, I say to you, whatever you bind on earth shall be bound in heaven, and whatever you loose on earth shall be loosed in heaven" (Mt 18:18). The *Catechism* says:

> The words "bind and loose" mean: whomever you exclude from your communion, will be excluded from communion with God; whomever you receive anew into your communion, God will welcome back into

> his. Reconciliation with the Church is inseparable from reconciliation with God.
>
> CCC, n. 1445

Even though we confess our sins privately in a confessional, confession is never a merely private affair. The priest is not acting on his own authority. Nor is he limited to forgiving you and offering advice on how to avoid sin in the future. He is doing something more mysterious. By demanding that you do penance and that you repair the damage done by sin, he is healing a wound that you inflicted on the Church.

Confession is necessary

People often ask, "Why do I have to confess my sins to a priest? Why can't I just tell my sins to God? Is he going to refuse to forgive me if I don't go to confession?" There is one simple answer: Jesus wants all Christians to confess their sins to a priest. We go to confession *because he asks us to.*

It would make no sense to stand before God and tell him, "I want you to forgive me," and then turn around and say, "I refuse to confess my sins to a priest, even though I know you want me to do it." A man guilty of a crime does not tell the judge how to conduct the trial. *We* do not tell God how he has to forgive our sins. *He* tells us. And he has told us very clearly that he has given men the power to forgive sins. To read the gospel and come to any other conclusion would be dishonest. God gave men the power to forgive sins.

Just as God is the only one who can work miracles, he is the only one that has the power to forgive sins. Perhaps the greatest miracle is that he shares both powers with men. Jesus could have reserved all power to work miracles for himself. He could have reserved all power to forgive sins for himself. Instead, Jesus told the Apostles on the day of his resurrection:

> Receive the Holy Spirit. If you forgive the sins of any, they are forgiven; if you retain the sins of any, they are retained.
>
> John 20:22–23

Jesus foresaw the need of forgiving sins committed after baptism. He gave the Apostles and their successors the power to forgive these sins; but he also gave them power to retain sins. Having both power to forgive and power to retain, the priest has to make a decision—whether to forgive a sin or to retain it. The decision depends on making a judgement. Priests can only make a prudent judgment if Christians confess their sins.

For instance, a priest hearing confessions may find a penitent who stole a great sum of money. He will explain to the penitent the serious obligation of restitution, that is, giving the money back to the rightful owner. Normally the penitent is ready to do this, so the priest pronounces the words of absolution. The penitent is forgiven and gives back the money. However, it may happen that the penitent refuses to return the money—thinking confession is a "short cut" to God's mercy while being able to keep the money. The priest has to advise the penitent to come back another day. God does not forgive sins until the penitent is truly sorry. Therefore, the priest judges, among other things, sorrow for sin; but before he can do this, he has to know the sins committed. This is possible only if the penitent makes a sincere confession.

If you have been baptized already and you want God to forgive sins committed after baptism, you need to go to confession. Just as water is the only ordinary way for people to be baptized, confessing sins to a priest is the only ordinary way for Christians to obtain forgiveness for sins committed after baptism. The Church teaches:

> This sacrament of penance is just as necessary for the salvation of those who have fallen after baptism as baptism is for those who have not yet been regenerated.
>
> Council of Trent, *Doctrine on the Sacrament of Penance,* ch. 2

By baptism, a man or woman or child is regenerated, that is, "born of water and the Spirit" (Jn 3:5). We need baptism to enter the kingdom of God. Similarly, anyone who has sinned after being baptized needs to go to confession in order to enter God's kingdom.

Jesus instituted the sacrament of penance when he gave the Apostles the power to forgive sins. The Apostles passed on that power to their successors, that is, to the bishops who came after them. In other words, the bishops of the Church today have the power to forgive sins because the Apostles gave it to them. The Apostles had it because Jesus gave it to them. Priests get the power to forgive sins through their bishop.

When you go to confession, the priest acts "in the person of Christ." In other words, it is Jesus himself who forgives your sins when the priest says, "I absolve you from your sins."

There is another way of explaining why confession is necessary. No matter how sorry Christians are for their sins, they need someone who can tell them, "You have an obligation to do such-and-such a deed in order to make up for the harm you caused by stealing, insulting, murdering, slandering, scandalizing, etc." The priest can do this—*he has a strict obligation to do this*—when you go to confession. If people did not confess their sins, who would instruct them on their obligation to make reparation? This argument is not as important as the fact that God himself instituted the sacrament of penance. Still, it might help you understand *why* God wants you to go to confession.

Fear of confession

You may find it difficult to tell your sins to a priest. Remember that God is a loving Father who waits day after day for the prodigal son to come home. When the sinner finally comes back to God, like the father in Jesus' parable, God runs out to meet the one who repents. He embraces the sinner and arranges for a feast. He says, "Bring quickly the best robe, and put it on him; and put a ring on his hand, and shoes on his feet" (Lk 15:22). God will not only forgive you if you are sorry. He will give you back all the dignity you lost. He will take away your shame. No matter how bad the sin was—even if you have killed somebody—God will forgive you if you go to confession. Confession offers nothing but consolation. There is nothing to be afraid of.

Those living in the state of sin must remember that Satan has dominion over them. The Letter to the Hebrews explains that Satan's power consists in using fear to keep men and women enslaved—first fear of death but also fear of pain, fear of embarrassment, and so on (cf.

Heb 2:15). Satan takes away our shame when tempting us to sin and then gives it back in a double dose to make sure we remain his slaves. Because he knows that confession frees us from sin, he will do anything to keep us away from it.

If they have not been to confession for many years, some people experience intense fear when faced with the need to confess their sins to a priest. They usually need to be encouraged by others who have already been through it—others who can tell them, "Don't worry, the priest won't get angry with you. God just wants to forgive your sins and take away your guilt. You won't believe how happy you'll feel once you do it!"

Despair is another reason why some people stay away from confession. For those afflicted with the temptation of doubting God's desire to forgive them, the following words, taken from the diary of a saint, may help. Her words describe how God shows mercy to all who seek forgiveness through the sacraments:

> Were a soul like a decaying corpse so that, from a human point of view, everything was already lost and there was no hope of coming back to life, God sees it differently. The miracle of Divine Mercy restores that soul completely. Oh, how miserable are those who do not take advantage of the miracle of Divine Mercy! You will call out in vain, but it will be too late.
>
> St. Maria Faustina Kowalska, *Divine Mercy in My Soul,* Notebook V

This message reminds us that it's never too late as long as we are still alive. God will forgive us no matter how many sins we have. But these words also remind us that we cannot wait forever, or otherwise it will be too late.

Frequent confession

At the very least, Christians need to go to confession once a year. The precept of the Church says:

> After having attained the age of discretion, each of the faithful is bound by an obligation faithfully to confess serious sins at least once a year.
>
> CCC, n. 1457

It is good to go to confession often—once every two weeks or once a month. Frequent confession benefits us in many ways:

- You acquire a habit of being sorry for your sins. It's similar to physical exercise. If you exercise only once a year, the experience may be invigorating, but you will spend most of the year being flabby and weak. Spiritual life works the same way. If you only go to confession once a year, you will probably spend most of the year ignoring your sins. The easiest way to stir up sorrow for your sins is to acquire a habit of being sorry for them. This habit also makes it is easier to avoid sin. Frequent confession and daily examination of conscience is the best way to acquire the habit.
- You get advice on how to live a holy life. If you go to confession only once a year, you will probably have many sins to confess. All the priest can do is encourage you to start over and trust the mercy of God. Frequent confession gives the priest a chance to explain practical ways of overcoming sinful habits. Besides, you then have a chance to ask questions.
- Frequent confession makes you more sensitive to the difference between good and evil. By examining your conscience often, you see how much damage sin does both to yourself and to others.
- You obtain grace to overcome sinful habits. Never get tired of confessing your sins. God never gets tired of forgiving as long as you make the effort to be sorry.
- You become humble. You learn to rely less on your strength and more on God's. You are more understanding with the defects you see in others.
- You are better prepared to receive Holy Communion. Confession has divine power to cleanse your soul from the least trace of evil. It prepares you for more intense union with Jesus. In the same way that a guest feels more at home when everything is brightly polished, Jesus takes delight in the soul that is totally pure. By going to confession frequently, you allow him to purify you so that you can receive him "in splendor, without spot or wrinkle . . . without blemish" (cf. Eph 5:27).

Some people think they are abusing confession by going too frequently. While you do need to avoid scruples, you should feel free to go to confession whenever you need it. You are not the bothering the priest. The whole reason he became a priest is to forgive sins.

A person becomes scrupulous by imagining that something is sinful when it is not. Like a hypochondriac who thinks that every ache and pain is a sign of cancer, a person may begin to feel that every mistake is a mortal sin. This tends to be a passing phase in one's spiritual life. Though it is always painful to the person who suffers it, scrupulous souls must learn to laugh at themselves and not take themselves so seriously. Even then, they should not give up the habit of going to confession frequently, following the advice of their confessor. They should remember that many scrupulous people, by abandoning the habit of being sorry for their sins, have passed to the opposite extreme, feeling no remorse at all for sins that cry out to heaven.

Other people think frequent confession is a waste of time since they have no mortal sins to confess. They fail to realize that one of the greatest benefits of frequent confession lies here. Precisely by learning to be deeply sorry for venial sins—and even minor faults—we grow in holiness. The *Catechism* says:

> Without being strictly necessary, confession of everyday faults (venial sins) is nevertheless strongly recommended by the Church. Indeed, the regular confession of our venial sins helps us form our conscience, fight against evil tendencies, let ourselves be healed by Christ, and progress in the life of the Spirit. By receiving more frequently through this sacrament the gift of the Father's mercy, we are spurred to be merciful as he is merciful.
>
> *CCC*, n. 1458

Confessing venial sins helps you distinguish the difference between good and evil. It helps you overcome temptations to serious sin. It also leads you to a deeper love for Jesus.

The Church reaches its greatest holiness and the world achieves its most exalted beauty when priests make themselves available in the confessional. Praising these priests, who number in their thousands throughout the world, Pope John Paul II wrote:

> I wish to pay homage to the innumerable host of holy and almost always anonymous confessors to whom is owed the salvation of so many souls who have been helped by them in conversion, in the struggle against sin and temptation, in spiritual progress and, in a word, in achieving holiness. I do not hesitate to say that even the great canonized saints are generally the fruit of those confessionals, and not only the saints but also the spiritual patrimony of the Church and the flowering of a civilization permeated with the Christian spirit! Praise then to this silent army of our brothers who have served well and serve each day the cause of reconciliation through the ministry of sacramental penance!
>
> St. John Paul II, *Reconciliation and Penance*, n. 29

The Church asks priests to develop their own personal habit of going to confession frequently. She also asks them to be available so that other Christians can acquire the habit of frequent confession. Many great blessings from God depend on it.

Practices of penance

The sacrament of baptism and the sacrament of penance both forgive sins. But they are different sacraments and have different effects.

The sacrament of penance takes away all sins committed after baptism. Unlike baptism it does not leave us totally purified. The Church teaches:

> The fruit of baptism is one thing; that of penance is another. For by "putting on Christ" by baptism (cf. Gal 3:27), we are made an entirely new creature in him, obtaining a full and complete remission of all sins. We cannot arrive to this newness and integrity by the sacrament of penance without many tears and labors on our part. Divine justice demands this. Thus, the Fathers of the Church have justly called this sacrament "a laborious kind of baptism."
>
> Council of Trent, *Doctrine on the Sacrament of Penance*, ch. 2

To cleanse your soul of habits of sin, do penance. The principal acts of penance are prayer, fasting, giving alms, works of mercy, and acts of self-denial.

Wisdom of the Saints

In this adventure of love, we should not be depressed by our falls, not even by serious falls, if we go to God in the sacrament of penance contrite and resolved to improve. A Christian is not a neurotic collector of good behavior reports. Jesus Christ our Lord was moved as much by Peter's repentance after his fall as by John's innocence and faithfulness. Jesus understands our weakness and draws us to himself on an inclined plane. He wants us to make an effort to climb a little each day. He seeks us out, just as he did the disciples of Emmaus, whom he went out to meet. He sought Thomas, showed himself to him and made him touch with his fingers the open wounds in his hands and side. Jesus Christ is always waiting for us to return to him; he knows our weakness.

St. Josemaría, *Christ Is Passing By*, n. 75

If you shun penance, you are in great danger of becoming lukewarm. To those who are "neither cold nor hot," God says, "I will spew you out of my mouth" (Rev 3:16).

To show us the importance of penance, the Church asks Christians to do penance on Fridays and organizes two seasons of penance: Advent, when we prepare for Christmas; and Lent, when we prepare for Easter. The normal practice for penitential days is fasting and abstinence or simply abstinence, depending on the general precept established by the Church and additional norms established by local bishops.

A normal fast in the tradition of the Catholic Church means eating only one full meal. Water, black tea, and black coffee (no milk, no sugar) are taken at any time. Fasting means that you eat no snacks during the entire twenty-four hours. Abstinence means abstaining from meat. This requires eliminating any kind of beef, pork, chicken, goat, or lamb from the meal, and also any meat products like stew and soup. Instead, fish, milk, and eggs are allowed on days of abstinence.

Like the precept of going to confession once a year, the Church's precepts on fasting and abstinence represent the *minimum* penance Christians undertake to purify their minds and hearts.

The best way to develop a spirit of penance is to make sacrifices that enable you to do your work better and serve others with a smile. Go to bed on time and wake up on time. Show up on time for work and start right away without wasting your time and everyone else's in idle conversation. Be patient with people that bother you. Be cheerful when things go wrong. Never complain when others treat you badly.

Then there is the problem of the rebellious flesh that craves for pleasure and comfort. If you have a habit of wasting time on useless or harmful entertainment, overindulging in food and drink, or succumbing to sexual temptations, it is not enough to resolve to never commit these sins again. You need serious penance. Otherwise, you will never acquire the habit of self-control.

St. Paul wrote "always carrying in the body the death of Jesus, so that the life of Jesus may also be manifested in our bodies" (2 Cor 4:10). We feel the "death of Jesus" in our flesh whenever we have to suffer. At times it comes when we least expect it. St. Paul also had in mind the practices of penance, like fasting, that we voluntarily seek. Referring to the prize—a wreath of branches from an olive tree—given to the winner of the Olympics in ancient times, St. Paul encouraged the early Christians to practice mortification and penance:

> Do you not know that in a race all the runners compete, but only one receives the prize? So run that you may obtain it. Every athlete exercises self-control in all things. They do it to receive a perishable wreath, but we an imperishable. Well, I do not run aimlessly, I do not box as one beating the air; but I pommel my body and subdue it, lest after preaching to others I myself should be disqualified.
>
> 1 Corinthians 9:24–27

Athletes exhaust themselves, after enduring countless deprivations, just to win a gold medal. What should you do to prepare for union with God?

REVIEW QUESTIONS

1. Describe the three acts of the penitent.
2. How does a Christian go to confession?
3. Why do we confess our sins to a priest?
4. Why is it good to go to confession frequently even if we have no mortal sins to confess?

38.

Anointing of the Sick

Like the sacrament of penance, anointing of the sick is a sacrament of healing.

One day, when Jesus was preaching about the kingdom of God, some men brought a paralytic on a stretcher. The house was too crowded, so they lowered him through a hole they made in the roof. Jesus worked two miracles for the paralytic. First he forgave the man's sins. Then he also healed his body, telling him: "I say to you, rise, take up your pallet and go home" (Mk 2:11). Though Jesus did not carry out anointing with oil, he did something that established the sacrament of anointing. He forgave the man's sins and restored him to bodily health.

Even when anointing of the sick does not restore bodily health, it prepares the sick person for death by announcing hope in the resurrection. It shows that, in the next world, Jesus will not only restore health. He will change us physically so that our bodies will be set free from concupiscence, from disease and death, from tiredness and pain, from all deformity and any other defect.

Purpose of anointing

Like the other sacraments, anointing of the sick is a sign instituted by Christ to give us grace. Each sacrament gives us a particular grace. God uses the sign of anointing to strengthen the sick person. St. James, one of the Twelve Apostles, explained the purpose of anointing of the sick:

> Is any among you sick? Let him call for the elders of the church, and let them pray over him, anointing him with oil in the name of the Lord;

> and the prayer of faith will save the sick man, and the Lord will raise him up; and if he has committed sins, he will be forgiven.
>
> James 5:14–15

The Apostle connects this sacrament with preparing Christians for the day when the Lord will raise them up. Anointing of the sick prepares a dying person for heaven and the final resurrection.

Sickness, old age, and death can cause fear, suffering, and pain. Anointing of the sick brings peace in the midst of suffering. It gives strength to endure pain. It helps Christians face death with a spirit of hope. People who are dying need that hope. They need to be reminded that death is not the end but the beginning.

Sometimes anointing of the sick can even restore health and help a dying Christian live longer here on earth.

This sacrament also forgives sins. Some Christians get confused on this point and think that anointing of the sick is a substitute for confession. ("Oh, good," they say. "That way I don't have to tell my sins to the priest!") This is a great mistake. Sorrow for any sins committed after baptism must always include the *desire to confess* these sins in the sacrament of penance. Anointing of the sick forgives sins, as St. James says, but only if the person was sorry for his or her sins and is unable to receive the sacrament of penance—for instance, if the sick person is already unconscious.

The primary purpose of this sacrament is to prepare for death. When are Christians best prepared to die? When are they ready to go straight to heaven? When they are totally purified from their sins. Therefore, Catholic theologians have reasoned that the "forgiving" power of this sacrament reaches its climax when it cleanses the soul from every last vestige of sin—what we call the remains of sin or the temporal punishment due to sin.

Like all the sacraments, anointing of the sick works best when the person receives it with the proper dispositions. Those dispositions are best when the sick person has acquired the habit of frequent confession. Then, when the sick person is anointed, God gives a sacramental grace that purifies the soul completely. The soul is inflamed with a love so spiritual and so passionate that the dying Christian will leap into heaven without any need to be purified after death.

Celebration of the sacrament

When a Christian is dying, call a priest as soon as possible so he can anoint the sick person. It is better not to wait until the last minute. It is better for the sick person to be anointed while still fully conscious.

Those who are elderly or sick can experience strong temptations against faith. They need all the spiritual comfort this sacrament offers. Call a priest to administer the sacrament as soon as there is any danger of death because of sickness or old age.

> **Sacred Scripture**
>
> And he called to him the twelve, and began to send them out two by two, and gave them authority over the unclean spirits. . . . And he said to them, "Where you enter a house, stay there until you leave the place. . . . And they cast out many demons, and anointed with oil many that were sick and healed them.
>
> Mark 6:7, 10, 13

The main elements of anointing of the sick are:

- The laying on of hands, done in silence.
- Prayer over the sick person.
- Anointing with the oil of the sick.

The oil of the sick is one of the sacred oils blessed by the bishop on Holy Thursday. In an emergency, the priest can bless the oil himself. The *Catechism* says:

> The sacrament of anointing of the sick is given to those who are seriously ill by anointing them on the forehead and hands with duly blessed oil—pressed from olives or from other plants—saying, only once: "Through this holy anointing may the Lord in his love and mercy help you with the grace of the Holy Spirit. May the Lord who frees you from sin save you and raise you up."
>
> CCC, n. 1513

Only a bishop or a priest can administer this sacrament.

The dying need strength and consolation

Mary, the sister of Martha and Lazarus, anointed Jesus before he died. The Master praised her for having done this and said, "In pouring this ointment on my body she has done it to prepare me for burial" (Mt 26:12). This anointing was a great consolation to Jesus. In a similar way, the sacrament of anointing gives consolation to the sick and prepares them for death. The oil symbolizes the Holy Spirit, the Consoler. By anointing the sick, the Church offers a comfort that only the Holy Spirit can give us.

When people are in danger of death, they can feel anguish, fear, and pain. Jesus, being the Son of God, experienced great distress (cf. Mt 26:37) the night before he died. We should not be surprised that his disciples have to endure intense suffering when death approaches. This is not a *lack* of faith. It is a *test* of faith.

In his mercy, God has provided a sacrament to give Christians the strength they need to overcome their fear of death, to endure their pain together with Jesus, and to leave this world peacefully—joyfully—knowing that they are going to see God face-to-face.

Death is the crucial moment. It is the last battle. It decides our eternal fate. No matter how much we have sacrificed ourselves in life to serve God, we must never take for granted that we will persevere to the end. St. Peter warned the early Christians:

> Be sober, be watchful. Your adversary the devil prowls around like a roaring lion, seeking some one to devour. Resist him, firm in your faith . . .
>
> 1 Peter 5:8–9

Satan can attack at the last moment with the same kind of fury we see in our Lord's crucifixion. Nothing else than diabolic force can explain the hatred unleashed on a man who spent years doing nothing but working miracles and telling everyone about God's love. Satan does not cease to tempt people when he sees them dying. On the contrary, he redoubles his efforts.

God thinks thoughts of peace, not affliction. His power is infinite. He uses it for his children, to protect them against evil. St. Paul wrote:

> Blessed be the God and Father of our Lord Jesus Christ, the Father of mercies and God of all comfort, who comforts us in all our affliction, so that we may be able to comfort those who are in any affliction, with the comfort with which we ourselves are comforted by God.
>
> 2 Corinthians 1:3–4

Those of us who are full of life and health forget how much a person needs this consolation at the hour of death. We may forget that the sick person needs not only the consolation we can provide, but, more importantly, the spiritual comfort that only God can give. By instituting the sacrament of anointing, Jesus has shown us how much the sick need a sign of God's tenderness and love when death approaches.

Death can be a moment of confusion and darkness. Even Jesus had to endure it when hanging on the cross. He had to listen to the Pharisees ridicule him.

> And when the sixth hour had come, there was darkness over the whole land until the ninth hour. And at the ninth hour Jesus cried with a loud voice, "Elo-i, Elo-i, lama sabach-thani?" which means, "My God, my God, why hast thou forsaken me?"
>
> Mark 15:33–34

Jesus was the Son of God. His holy Mother Mary and several disciples were there to accompany him in his hour of sorrow. And yet, he felt alone. It seemed as if his Father was far away. If this could happen to Jesus, it can happen to those who fall sick. To help them in their moment of need, God gives them strength to overcome fear and temptation through the power of sacramental anointing.

Final perseverance

The disciple who perseveres "to the end" will be saved (cf. Mt 10:22). But no one can merit the grace of final perseverance. This is perhaps the most important reason for making sure that those who are dying receive anointing of the sick. Like the first grace that leads us to conversion, the last grace is a free gift from God. The Church teaches:

> Even those who have been reborn and healed [by baptism] must always implore the help of God that they may arrive at a good end and may persevere in good works.
>
> Second Council of Orange, c. 10

No one can say, "I have lived such a good life that I am sure I am going to be saved." We must "always implore."

To reaffirm this teaching, the Council of Trent quotes St. Paul's warning against trusting in our own good deeds: "Therefore let any one who thinks that he stands take heed lest he fall" (1 Cor 10:12). Because we can never be absolutely sure that we are free from all serious sin, we must approach death with humility. We cannot stand before God and demand a reward. That would make us like the Pharisee who was convinced he was perfect. Like the publican, we beat our breast and ask God for mercy (cf. Lk 18:9–14). St. Paul wrote:

> . . . work out your own salvation with fear and trembling; for God is at work in you, both to will and to work for his good pleasure.
>
> Philippians 2:12–13

Paradoxically, this is the best way to overcome fear. Do not trust in your own ability and your own achievements. Trust in God like a little child.

The value of suffering

Anointing of the sick also teaches Christians the value of their pain and suffering. It reminds them that Jesus suffered, that Jesus felt pain, and that Jesus died. It leads the dying to unite their pain to the pain of Jesus suffering on the cross. When Christians are dying, it is very good to give them a crucifix so they can hold it and kiss it.

Many people look at pain as a curse. God asks us to look at it as a blessing. The Church teaches:

> Those who share in the sufferings of Christ are also called, through their own sufferings, to share in glory. Paul expresses this in various places. To

Fathers of the Church

Jesus Christ "deliver[ed] all those who through fear of death were subject to lifelong bondage" (Heb 2:15). By sacrificing his own body, he did two things. He put an end to the law of death, which barred our way to heaven; and giving us the hope of resurrection, he made it possible for us to start a new life. By one man death gained its power over all men; by the Word made Man, death has been destroyed and life has been raised to life. This is what Paul says: "For as by a man came death, by a man has come also the resurrection of the dead. For as in Adam all die, so also in Christ shall all be made alive" (1 Cor 15:21–22). Therefore, when we die, we no longer die as men condemned to death. Instead, we have already begun the process of rising from the dead while we await the general resurrection of all men and women . . .

St. Athanasius, *On the Incarnation*, II, 10

> the Romans he writes: "[We are] fellow heirs with Christ, provided we suffer with him in order that we may also be glorified with him. I consider that the sufferings of this present time are not worth comparing with the glory that is to be revealed in us" (Rom 8:17–18). In the Second Letter to the Corinthians we read: "This slight momentary affliction is preparing for us an eternal weight of glory beyond all comparison, because we look not to the things that are seen but to things that are unseen" (2 Cor 4:17–18). The Apostle Peter will express this truth in the following words of his first letter: "Rejoice in so far as you share Christ's sufferings, that you may also rejoice and be glad when his glory is revealed" (1 Pt 4:13).
>
> St. John Paul II, *On the Christian Meaning of Human Suffering*, n. 22

Suffering has the power to unite us to Jesus and prepare us to share his glory. It tempers our spirit. It teaches us the way of virtue.

More mysteriously, suffering is also "creative."

> The Apostle's experiences as a sharer in the sufferings of Christ go even further. In the Letter to the Colossians we read the words which constitute as it were the final stage of the spiritual journey in relation to suffering: "Now I rejoice in my sufferings for your sake, and in my flesh I complete what is lacking in Christ's afflictions for the sake of his body, that is, the Church" (Col 1:24). And in another letter he

> asks his readers: "Do you not know that your bodies are members of Christ?" (1 Cor 6:15).
>
> St. John Paul II, *On the Christian Meaning of Human Suffering*, n. 24

This does not mean that God the Father found anything missing in Christ's suffering on the cross. That sacrifice had infinite value. The Son of God himself offered a perfect sacrifice by shedding his blood. How then does a Christian "complete" what is "lacking" in Christ's suffering?

The idea is that redemption is not closed but open. In his great mercy, God has made it possible for all men and women to share in Christ's suffering. Although this does not make sense at first, there is a secret here. God allows pain, tears, loneliness, and anxiety to make us so completely one with Jesus that God can look at us and say, "This is my Son offering his suffering to me." Our suffering, our pain, and our loneliness unite us to Jesus.

St. Paul captured this mystery perfectly when he said, "I have been crucified with Christ; it is no longer I who live, but Christ who lives in me" (Gal 2:20).

> And for this reason suffering also has a special value in the eyes of the Church. It is something good, before which the Church bows down in reverence with all the depth of her faith in the Redemption. She likewise bows down with all the depth of that faith with which she embraces within herself the inexpressible mystery of the Body of Christ.
>
> St. John Paul II, *On the Christian Meaning of Human Suffering*, n. 24

What is this "mystery of the Body of Christ"? St. Paul learned it from Jesus himself. Jesus appeared to Saul, the man who would one day be St. Paul. The Risen Lord asked, "Saul, Saul, why do you persecute me?" (Acts 9:4). Saul thought he was persecuting *Christians*. But, in God's eyes, that was the same as persecuting *Jesus*. Saul learned from these words that when a Christian suffers, it is Jesus who is suffering.

Some people think that wealth is a sign from God that they have been blessed. Jesus' hour on the cross reveals something different. Suffering is a sign that God has blessed us.

Euthanasia

Some do not know this mystery. Others know about it but do not believe it. They think is better to kill a friend or relative who is suffering in the last stages of life. They call it "mercy killing" or "euthanasia." This is a rebellion against God's plan for suffering. The Church teaches:

> Euthanasia must be called a false mercy, and indeed a disturbing "perversion" of mercy. True "compassion" leads to sharing another's pain; it does not kill the person whose suffering we cannot bear. Moreover, the act of euthanasia appears all the more perverse if it is carried out by those, like relatives, who are supposed to treat a family member with patience and love, or by those, such as doctors, who by virtue of their specific profession are supposed to care for the sick person even in the most painful terminal stages.
>
> St. John Paul II, *The Gospel of Life*, n. 66

If a person in pain begs us to "end it all" in order to avoid suffering—to end his or her life prematurely—we must refuse. Instead, we turn to God and ask him to give us more faith. When those who are dying see our faith, they have greater courage to face their own ordeal. We can also recall the Church's practice of administering the sacrament of anointing of the sick. It should be repeated whenever the patient's health deteriorates and the suffering becomes worse.

The Last Rites

Priests anoint Christians who are in danger of death because of sickness or old age. It is administered only to those who have reached the age of reason.

The first sacrament you receive is baptism. Anointing of the sick is "a preparation for the final journey":

> If the sacrament of anointing of the sick is given to all who suffer from serious illness and infirmity, even more rightly is it given to those at the point of departing this life; so it is also called *sacramentum exeuntium* (the sacrament of those departing).
>
> CCC, n. 1523

When Christians are dying, the Church offers them the last rites. The last rites include three sacraments: confession, anointing of the sick, and the Eucharist. The three sacraments of initiation—baptism, confirmation, and the Eucharist—prepare us for life in this world. The last rites are a kind of initiation for life in the next world.

When the time comes for you to die, you may have received the sacraments of penance and Eucharist many times. However, even if you are free from mortal sin, it is good to make a final confession. If you are in the state of mortal sin, you *need* to go to confession. In either case, you go to confession so you can be totally free from sin. Your time has come to face God and render an account of the good and evil in your life. After confession and anointing, then you receive Holy Communion to express your desire to be raised from the dead on the last day and enter into God's kingdom.

When Christians receive the Eucharist as a preparation for their death and resurrection, the Church calls it "Viaticum"—which literally means something needed for a long journey. The Church is giving you Jesus hidden in the Blessed Sacrament. If you have Jesus, you have all you need. The *Catechism* says:

> In addition to the anointing of the sick, the Church offers those who are about to leave this life the Eucharist as Viaticum. Communion in the body and blood of Christ, received at this moment of "passing over" to the Father, has a particular significance and importance. It is the seed of eternal life and the power of resurrection, according to the words of the Lord: "He who eats my flesh and drinks my blood has eternal life, and I will raise him up at the last day" (Jn 6:54). The sacrament of Christ once dead and now risen, the Eucharist is here the sacrament of passing over from death to life, from this world to the Father.
>
> CCC, n. 1524

Because of the connection between anointing of the sick and the Eucharist, it is best, if possible, to do the anointing during the celebration of Mass. However, given the weak state of those who are in danger of death, priests often administer the last rites at home or in a hospital.

Mystery of death

If your grandfather or grandmother dies at the age of 105, you will not ask why. If anything, you may want to know how they managed to live so long. But if someone dies in the prime of life, you wonder why.

Some people are shocked when they see friends or relatives dying "before their time." They may even experience a crisis of faith. They can be prey to the empty promises of false prophets who claim to have a special power of healing. They can be cheated into paying money to receive such a favor. When no healing takes place, they give up on God, as if it were his fault that they have been cheated.

Christians have often been deceived into putting too much emphasis on physical healing. They think Jesus promised all his disciples a long and prosperous life. The sacrament of anointing can give physical as well as spiritual strength. But Jesus did not institute this sacrament to eliminate death. Jesus instituted this sacrament to give sick people the strength they need to face death. The Church never promises to work miracles, like curing cancer.

The Church teaches that anointing of the sick heals the soul "and, moreover, in so far as it is *expedient*, the body too" (Council of Florence). The measure of expediency is eternal salvation. If recovery is not *expedient*—not good for the person dying—God will not grant recovery. This, of course, is something that only God can judge. Maybe the sick person is already holy. Maybe the sick person would suffer some setback in the spiritual life if granted a longer life. If it is spiritually good for the sick person to recover, then God will use this sacrament to make it happen. However, even in this case, people should not expect a complete and sudden recovery, as if the sick person were going to jump out of bed and resume normal life.

God is less interested in external activity and more interested in how much we grow in love for him and for others. The recovery may only be minimal—barely enough to maintain consciousness for a few more days. A time comes for every man and woman when God knows, in his infinite wisdom, that this is the best time to leave this world and appear before him.

REVIEW QUESTIONS

1. When should Christians receive anointing of the sick?
2. How does the priest administer anointing of the sick?
3. How can you explain the meaning of suffering so that the sick person sees it as a blessing instead of a curse?
4. Describe the last rites.

39.

Holy Orders

Holy orders is the sacrament that makes a man a deacon, a priest, or a bishop. These three orders correspond to the three degrees of the sacrament: the diaconate, the presbyterate, and the episcopacy. Only men can receive this sacrament.

Jesus Christ is the eternal high priest. The Father sent him to preach the Good News and to offer a sacrifice to purify the people of God. From the beginning of the Church, certain men were chosen to be "as servants of Christ and stewards of the mysteries of God" (1 Cor 4:1). Jesus shares his priesthood with all Christians. But he shares it with these "stewards" in a way that other Christians do not share. These stewards or ministers are the deacons, priests, and bishops. They preach the gospel and administer the sacraments to others.

After years of preparation, the man to be ordained kneels in front of a bishop. The bishop lays his hands on the man's head in silence and then, immediately afterwards, prays a prayer that consecrates him—that is, makes him a deacon or priest. When a priest is chosen to become a bishop, he kneels before three (or more) bishops to receive the full powers of holy orders. The laying on of hands is the essential sign of the sacrament for all three degrees. A different prayer is used in each case: one for deacons, one for priests, and one for bishops.

Together with matrimony, we call holy orders a "sacrament at the service of communion." Holy orders gives men the power to make others holy. By celebrating the Eucharist, priests draw all people together into the unity of the Mystical Body of Christ. This is a service of communion, because it builds up the Church, following God's plan.

New and eternal priesthood

God appointed Aaron, the brother of Moses, to be the first priest of the covenant with Israel. Aaron was from the tribe of Levi. Aaron's priesthood was the *levitical* priesthood. Only Aaron and his descendents could offer sacrifice on the altar, because they were the only ones chosen to be priests. The high priest of the Old Testament was the most important of all the priests. He was the only one who could enter the Holy of Holies in the Temple of Jerusalem—where the ark of the covenant was kept. He entered only once a year.

Jesus established a new and eternal priesthood. He was not from the tribe of Levi. He was from the tribe of Judah. His priesthood was not levitical—a priesthood that depended on birth and ended with death. Jesus is the "new Adam"—the new beginning of the human race (cf. 1 Cor 15:45). He is also the "new Melchizedek," that is, the beginning of a new priesthood that will last forever (cf. Heb 7:15).

The priests of the Old Testament were constantly offering the blood of animals in a man-made sanctuary on an altar of stone. Jesus offered his own blood once and for all, entering into heaven, "now to appear in the presence of God on our behalf" (Heb 9:24). Jesus' sacrifice was perfect. It can never be repeated. "He has appeared once for all at the end of the age to put away sin by the sacrifice of himself. . . . Christ, having been offered once to bear the sins of many" (Heb 9:26, 28).

Sacred Scripture

For this Melchizedek, king of Salem, priest of the Most High God, met Abraham returning from the slaughter of the kings and blessed him; and to him Abraham apportioned a tenth part of everything. He is first, by translation of his name, king of righteousness, and then he is also king of Salem, that is, king of peace. He is without father or mother or genealogy, and has neither beginning of days nor end of life, but resembling the Son of God he continues a priest for ever.

. . . This [the need for a new priesthood] becomes even more evident when another priest arises in the likeness of Melchizedek, who has become a priest, not according to a legal requirement concerning bodily descent but by the power of an indestructible life. For it is witnessed of him [Jesus Christ], "Thou art a priest for ever, after the order of Melchizedek."

Hebrews 7:1–3, 15–17

Just as there is only one sacrifice, there is only one priest. Jesus is the only priest of the Church. He is the perfect high priest:

> For it was fitting that we should have such a high priest, holy, blameless, unstained, separated from sinners, exalted above the heavens. He has no need, like those high priests, to offer sacrifices daily, first for his own sins and then for those of the people; he did this once for all when he offered up himself.
>
> Hebrews 7:26–27

Jesus is the only priest and the only victim. He was the perfect high priest because he is the Son of God. His sacrifice was perfect because he offered his own blood.

Priests in the Church today are priests only because they have the power to "be Christ" when "re-presenting"—making present again—the one and only sacrifice Jesus offered on the cross. The *Catechism* teaches:

> Everything that the priesthood of the Old Covenant prefigured finds its fulfilment in Christ Jesus, the "one mediator between God and men" (1 Tim 2:5). The Christian tradition considers Melchizedek, "priest of God Most High," as one prefiguring the priesthood of Christ, the unique "high priest after the order of Melchizedek"; "holy, blameless, unstained," "by a single offering he has perfected for all time those who are sanctified," that is, by the unique sacrifice of the cross.
>
> The redemptive sacrifice of Christ is unique, accomplished once for all; yet it is made present in the Eucharistic sacrifice of the Church. The same is true of the one priesthood of Christ; it is made present through the ministerial priesthood without diminishing the uniqueness of Christ's priesthood: Only Christ is the true priest, the others being only his ministers.
>
> *CCC*, nn. 1544–1545 (cf. Heb 5:10; 7:26; 10:14)

The Church describes the action of priests by saying that they act "in the person of Christ the Head." We call Christ the "Head of the Church." Using St. Paul's analogy: Christ "nourishes and cherishes . . . the church, because we are members of his body" (Eph 5:30). The priests have a special function within the body of Christ. It is a function that other members cannot perform. Priests can perform these functions because they have sacred power.

Sacred power

A man becomes a priest when he receives the sacred power of Christ's new and eternal priesthood. No one has this sacred power unless he is ordained by a bishop that is a true successor of the Apostles. The essence of this sacred power consists in being able to act and speak as only Jesus himself can act and speak. Like Jesus, every priest is called to be a "priest forever, after the order of Melchizedek" (Heb 7:17).

When a priest celebrates the Eucharist, he speaks in the first person: "This is my body. This is the cup of my blood." When a priest forgives sins, he also speaks in the first person, "I absolve you from your sins." Priests use the first person knowing that Jesus is the one changing bread and wine into his body and blood; that Jesus is the one forgiving sins.

When a man receives the sacrament of holy orders, he receives the power of Christ to carry out the Church's sacred rites and ceremonies. These are the main powers:

- **Deacons** baptize, proclaim the gospel, preach, assist the priest at the altar, and distribute Holy Communion. They can conduct weddings. They can preside over prayers for burial. They also dedicate themselves to caring for the poor.
- **Priests** celebrate Mass, hear confessions, and administer the anointing of the sick. They also have the power to do everything deacons do.
- **Bishops** have the full powers of the priesthood. They rule the local church entrusted to them. They administer confirmation. They administer holy orders to the men they have chosen to be deacons and priests. Any bishop has the power to make a priest a bishop, but only the Pope has the authority to decide which priests will be ordained bishops.

Bishop: successor of the apostles

A bishop is a successor of the Apostles. The Church teaches that bishops "take the place of Christ himself—teacher, shepherd, and priest—and act as his representative" (*CCC*, n. 1558). They represent Christ for the faithful of that part of the Church entrusted to them. Most bishops are the head of a diocese, which is a territory designated as a local church. They can also be the head of some other grouping of Christians not based on a territory.

The bishop's main church is called a "cathedral." This is the most important church in the diocese because it contains the *cathedra* (Latin for "chair"). From this chair, the bishop teaches and rules as Good Shepherd to the flock entrusted to him.

Bishops do not operate on their own. They form a College of Bishops. The episcopacy is *collegial*. In other words, the bishops of the entire world are united together under the authority of the Bishop of Rome. They pray, teach, and work in communion with the Pope. Being Bishop of Rome, the Pope is the successor of St. Peter, the first Bishop of Rome. To make it obvious to people that the bishops work together as a College of Bishops, many bishops gather together when ordaining a priest to be a bishop. At least three bishops are supposed to lay their hands on the head of the priest who is being consecrated a bishop.

The episcopacy is also collegial because each bishop feels responsible for all Christians all over the world—indeed, for all men and women everywhere. The *Catechism* says:

> As Christ's vicar, each bishop has the pastoral care of the particular Church entrusted to him, but at the same time he bears collegially with all his brothers in the episcopacy the solicitude for all the Churches. Though each bishop is the lawful pastor only of the portion of the flock entrusted to his care, as a legitimate successor of the Apostles he is, by divine institution and precept, responsible with the other bishops for the apostolic mission of the Church.
>
> *CCC*, n. 1560

St. Paul expressed this universal outlook. He talked of feeling the needs of other Christians like a weight on his soul:

> And, apart from other things, there is the daily pressure upon me of my anxiety for all the churches. Who is weak, and I am not weak? Who is made to fall, and I am not indignant?
>
> 2 Corinthians 11:28–29

Priest: co-worker

> **Fathers of the Church**
>
> If you want God to pay attention to you, pay attention to the bishop. I offer myself up for those who obey the bishop, priests, and deacons.
>
> St. Ignatius of Antioch, *Letter to Polycarp*, 6

Priests are co-workers of the bishops. In the Church, every priest works under the authority of a bishop. They have the sacred power to consecrate the bread and wine at Mass. They also have the power to forgive sins when hearing confessions. However, rather than going off on their own wherever they feel most useful, they look to their bishop. They go wherever he sends them. The *Catechism* says:

> Priests can exercise their ministry only in dependence on the bishop and in communion with him. The promise of obedience they make to the bishop at the moment of ordination and the kiss of peace from him at the end of the ordination liturgy mean that the bishop considers them his co-workers, his sons, his brothers, and his friends, and that they in return owe him love and obedience.
>
> CCC, n. 1567

To show union with their bishop, all priests of the diocese concelebrate the Chrism Mass with him on Holy Thursday. During this Mass, they renew their promise to obey the bishop and be faithful to their priestly vocation.

Deacon: one who serves

The Act of the Apostles narrates the story of the first deacons (cf. Acts 6:1–6). These seven men were ordained to serve. "Deacon" means one who serves. They are called to imitate Jesus, who described himself as one who came "not to be served but to serve" (Mk 10:45). Some men are ordained deacons who will later become priests. Others are ordained as "permanent deacons"; if not married, these can also be ordained priests later.

Apostolic succession depends on holy orders

From the beginning, the celebration of the Eucharist depended on the Apostles. They were the only ones who had the sacred power to change the bread and wine into the Body and Blood of Christ. They received this power directly from Jesus Christ. The Apostles passed on this power to other men by the laying on of hands. The New Testament calls the successors of the Apostles *episkopoi* (Greek for the "elders"), from which we get the words "episcopal" and "bishop."

The first bishops passed this power on to other men. These new bishops eventually did the same for the next generation, ordaining new bishops. This is how the episcopal power has been passed on from one generation to the next. It will be this way until the end of time. The Church calls this "apostolic succession." It defines the way that a bishop today can trace his sacred power to the bishops who came before him and they can trace it to the bishops who came before them—on and on, all the way back to the Apostles.

A bishop does not become a bishop by being elected by the people or by declaring himself to be a bishop. The only true bishops are those who have received sacred power through this unbroken chain of the laying on of hands by the bishops before them.

The Church depends on this unbroken chain. This is what we mean when we say that the Church is built on the Apostles. If that chain of succession from one bishop to the next is broken—as it has been broken in some Christian communities—that particular community

MAGISTERIUM

In carrying out their work of sanctification, parish priests should ensure that the celebration of the Eucharistic Sacrifice is the center and culmination of the entire life of the Christian community. It should also be their aim to ensure that the faithful receive spiritual nourishment from a frequent and devout reception of the sacraments and from an attentive and fervent participation in the liturgy.

Parish priests must bear it constantly in mind how much the sacrament of penance contributes to the development of the Christian life and should therefore be readily available for the hearing of the confessions of the faithful.

Vatican II, *Decree on the Pastoral Office of Bishops*, n. 30

has no bishop. That community can no longer celebrate the Eucharist because no one in that community has the power to change the bread and wine into the Body and Blood of Christ. That community no longer has anyone with the power to hear confessions and therefore no one who can forgive sins committed after baptism.

Bishops have the mission of preserving unity by using their authority to govern the Church. They also have the mission of passing on the sacred power they have received. They pass it on from one generation to the next by the laying on of hands, that is, by the sacrament of holy orders.

Holy orders requires a vocation

Not everyone can receive holy orders. A man must be chosen by God. He needs a special calling from God and the approval of his bishop. The *Catechism* states:

> No one has a right to receive the sacrament of holy orders. Indeed no one claims this office for himself; he is called to it by God. Anyone who thinks he recognizes the signs of God's call to the ordained ministry must humbly submit his desire to the authority of the Church, who has the responsibility and right to call someone to receive orders. Like every grace this sacrament can be received only as an unmerited gift.
>
> *CCC*, n. 1578

For a man to become a deacon, priest, or bishop, he should have a vocation—a calling from God to receive the sacrament of holy orders. Every vocation follows the "logic of gift." God gives; the man receives. Even our Lord Jesus submitted to this logic: "So also Christ did not exalt himself to be made a high priest, but was appointed by him who said to him, 'Thou art my Son, today I have begotten thee'" (Heb 5:5; Ps 2:7).

Only men can receive holy orders

The Church does not allow any bishop to ordain a woman to be either a deacon or a priest. Some say this contradicts the radical equality of men and women in the Church. To explain why this argument is mistaken, it is first necessary to state that men and women are equal. Then we have to explain why the Church does not ordain women, even though they are equal to men.

The equality of men and women is radical, real, and eternal. Every Christian—man or woman—is "clothed" with Christ. If there is any "inequality" in heaven—where some are "greater" and others are "less"—it has nothing to do with being male and female. Who is greatest in the kingdom of God? It is not the minister but the saint—the one closest to Jesus. St. Paul wrote:

> . . . in Christ Jesus you are all sons of God, through faith. For as many of you as were baptized into Christ have put on Christ. There is neither Jew nor Greek, there is neither slave nor free, there is neither male nor female; for you are all one in Christ Jesus. And if you are Christs, then you are Abraham's offspring, heirs according to promise.
>
> Galatians 3:26–29

God sent the Holy Spirit into the hearts of women just as powerfully as he has sent the Spirit into the hearts of men. As much as any man, a woman can cry out "Abba! Father" with the same consciousness of being God's "son"—the consciousness of being another Christ. This crying out is proof that you are "sons" (cf. Gal 4:6)—proof that you share in God's divine nature.

Having explained why men and women are equal, it is necessary to explain why the Church does not ordain women. To understand the argument, remember two facts of revelation. First, men and women have exactly the same rights, but no one has a *right* to be ordained—not even a man. Second, the Church relies on revelation—not social convention—when deciding how to administer the sacraments.

Holy orders is a mystery. We get some glimpse of this at Mass. When offering the sacrifice of Christ's body and blood, the priest prays to the Father, saying: "Almighty God, we pray that your angel may take this sacrifice to your altar in heaven" (Roman Canon). The sacrifice on our altar reflects the eternal sacrifice taking place on heaven's altar. We have little idea of what happens in heaven for "now we see in a mirror dimly" (1 Cor 13:12). Not being able to see what happens on the heavenly altar, who are we to say what is supposed to happen in our churches?

As Korah's rebellion against Moses reminds us (cf. Num 16:1–11), the most important law of liturgy is to do what God has commanded, and not what we think is best. For the liturgy of the Old Testament, God said to Moses: "You must follow exactly all that I show you concerning the pattern" (Ex 25:9). In the liturgy of the New Testament, we handle not the blood of goats and bulls but the blood of God's only Son. It is infinitely more important to do things exactly as God wants them done.

When administering the sacraments, the Church can only do what Jesus established. The Church has no authority to invent new sacraments and no authority to change them. The Church has no authority to ordain women because Jesus never chose a woman to be an Apostle. It is remarkable that Jesus never chose any women to be priests. Refusing to follow the customs of his times, he treated *all* women with exceptional dignity. For instance, he did not hesitate to embarrass the Pharisees when they wanted to stone a woman caught in adultery. At the moment of the crucifixion, the holy women were more faithful and courageous than the Apostles. On the day of the resurrection, the women were the first ones to go to the tomb. Jesus appeared to them before appearing to the Apostles. The Blessed Virgin Mary is the holiest of all creatures—closer to God than any of the angels. Despite all this, Jesus never chose women for the priesthood. None of the Apostles ever chose a woman to be his successor. From the very beginning, the Church has ordained only men to be priests.

The Church teaches:

> Although the teaching that priestly ordination is to be reserved to men alone has been preserved by the constant and universal Tradition of the Church and firmly taught by the Magisterium in its more recent documents, at the present time in some places it is nonetheless considered still open to debate, or the Church's judgment that women are not to be admitted to ordination is considered to have a merely disciplinary force.
>
> Wherefore, in order that all doubt may be removed regarding a matter of great importance, a matter which pertains to the Church's divine constitution itself, in virtue of my ministry of confirming the brethren

> (cf. Lk 22:32) I declare that the Church has no authority whatsoever to confer priestly ordination on women and that this judgment is to be definitively held by all the Church's faithful.
>
> St. John Paul II, *Ordinatio Sacerdotalis*, n. 4

The Church has never ordained women, and the Church never will ordain women. Not even the Pope can change what Jesus established when choosing only men for this sacrament.

We could end the argument here and conclude, "That is the way God wants it. That is the way it has to be. So there's nothing more to discuss." In a sense that is true, as should be obvious from the facts just presented. However, it is also good to try to understand why God does not want women to be ordained. This requires trying to understand the difference between male and female and why the one who celebrates the Eucharist should be male.

Why the Church cannot change the sign chosen by Christ

It is not up to the Church to determine the exact nature of each sacrament. God alone decides that. The Church can change minor aspects of the sacraments. For instance, in the rite of baptism, the Church can decide to ask each candidate to wear a white garment or she can dispense with it; but the Church cannot decide that from now on baptism will be done with milk instead of water. Having a white garment—or blue or pink—does not change the substance of the sign established by Jesus Christ when he instituted the sacrament of baptism. But changing from water to milk would change the very essence of the sign established by Christ. The Church has no authority to change the essence of any of the sacraments. The Church teaches that only men can receive holy orders because being male constitutes an essential aspect of the sacramental sign.

In the eyes of God, equality is not measured by access to positions of authority. God defines equality by *inheritance*. Men and women are equal in the Church because both can be sons. St. Paul concludes,

"Through God you are . . . a son, and if a son then an heir" (Gal 4:7). Every Christian, man or woman, will receive the inheritance due to the Son. Women can be just as holy—just as Christ-like and just as close to God—as men. Every Christian, man or woman, can be "another Christ, Christ himself." Therefore, it is a deep mystery that women cannot be priests. How can we explain this?

Being equal does not make men and women the same. Even after being glorified in the resurrection, male and female will remain different from each other. Women cannot be given priestly authority because they cannot celebrate the Eucharist. We have to assume that they cannot do it because Christ was male and being male is essential to having the power to change bread and wine into his Body and Blood. To understand this, we have to look once again at the nature of authority.

Being under someone's authority does not make you inferior to the person in authority. The Trinity of Father, Son, and Holy Spirit is the clearest example. The Father has authority over the Son. He "sends" his Son, and his Son "goes." But this does not make the Son inferior to the Father. They are equal. When the Father and Son send the Holy Spirit, this does not make the Spirit inferior.

All three persons of the Trinity are equal to each other. They all have the same infinite power. Even so, there is a hierarchy—a sacred order. The Father gives life to the Son. The Son receives it. The Holy Spirit is the love expressing the union of Father and Son.

God established a similar order when he created us. Created as male and female, "man" is the image of the Trinity because the husband has authority over his wife—analogous to the Father's authority over the Son. "I want you to understand that the head of every man is Christ, the head of a woman is her husband, and the head of Christ is God" (1 Cor 11:3). Being "head" means, among other things, having authority—but not authority in the worldly sense of ordering people around. The husband is not the "boss" of his wife. The wife is not reduced to being his servant. On the contrary, having authority means that the husband has to be ready to serve his wife and sacrifice himself for her needs (cf. Eph 5:25).

The nature of authority depends on the concept of "author." An author is the *source* of something, like the author of a book. The Father has authority over the Son because the Son *comes from* the Father. The Father gives life, whereas the Son receives life. The woman *comes from* the man because the husband loves while the wife, being loved, returns love. The relationship of Father and Son is fixed. They cannot change places. The relationship bridegroom and bride is also fixed. The bride cannot change places with the bridegroom.

Father, Son, and Holy Spirit are one being. The essence of marriage demands that bridegroom and bride be one body. Being bridegroom or bride is not merely a role or job like being a lawyer or doctor. Women can be lawyers and doctors but they cannot be the bridegroom—that is, they cannot have authority over the man when the two are bound together as one body. This reality was fixed by God from the beginning and cannot be changed.

Christ the Bridegroom

The Church draws on this mystery to explain why she does not ordain women as priests. Priests have to celebrate the Eucharist. Jesus chose men to be Apostles because a priest has to be a sign of the Bridegroom sacrificing himself for the Bride.

Christ is the Bridegroom. The Church is the Bride. In the Eucharistic sacrifice, the Bridegroom gives himself to the Bride. This happens so that the two can be united as "one body":

> As the Redeemer of the world, Christ is the Bridegroom of the Church. The Eucharist is the Sacrament of our Redemption. It is the Sacrament of the Bridegroom and of the Bride. The Eucharist makes present and realizes anew in a sacramental manner the redemptive act of Christ, who "creates" the Church, his body. Christ is united with this "body" as the bridegroom with the bride.
>
> St. John Paul II, *The Dignity of Women*, n. 26

God created the Church for Christ. The blood and water flowing from Christ's wounded side on the cross signaled God's action of creating a bride for the Bridegroom. The Eucharist was instituted to *re-present* that moment. It makes present once again the moment when the Father used the Son's sacrifice to create a bride for him.

To re-present this moment, that is, *to make it really and truly present,* God wants the person offering the sacrifice to be male.

> Since Christ, in instituting the Eucharist, linked it in such an explicit way to the priestly service of the Apostles, it is legitimate to conclude that he thereby wished to express the relationship between man and woman, between what is "feminine" and what is "masculine." It is a relationship willed by God both in the mystery of creation and in the mystery of Redemption. It is the Eucharist above all that expresses the redemptive act of Christ the Bridegroom towards the Church the Bride. This is clear and unambiguous when the sacramental ministry of the Eucharist, in which the priest acts *in persona Christi,* is performed by a man.
>
> St. John Paul II, *The Dignity of Women,* n. 26

At the altar, more than *symbolizing* the Bridegroom, a priest has to *be* the Bridegroom. Therefore, the priest has to be male.

The typical masculine act is to *give* the gift of self. The typical feminine act is to *receive* that gift and reciprocate by also giving a gift of self. The priest has to say, "Take this Body and eat it. Take this Blood and drink it." This a masculine invitation to accept a gift. God wants this invitation to be so clearly masculine that a male priest must invite other Christians to accept the gift of our Lord's Body and Blood.

Besides being an invitation to communion, the words of consecration are words of sacrifice. The Body is being "given up"; the Blood is "being shed for the forgiveness of sins." The act of giving—whether it be in the Eucharist or in matrimony—does not begin as communion. It begins with sacrifice. Using words from the *Book of Genesis*, St. Paul states that this sacrifice begins with the "man leaving father and mother" (cf. Gen 2:24).

Christ on the cross is the Bridegroom. He makes his sacrifice in order to become one body with his bride. The Eucharist re-presents the Bridegroom's sacrifice—the man's sacrifice of "leaving father and mother" for the bride. Masculine giving starts when the man sacrifices what is most precious to him for the sake of the woman he chooses to be his wife. The woman also has to sacrifice herself to be the bride, but she can only make her sacrifice if the man makes his first by choosing her.

God established the masculine and feminine elements of sacrifice even in the Old Testament. The Passover lamb had to be male (cf. Ex 12:5). It was a symbol of the victim to be offered in the new covenant. This new covenant is sealed with a sacrifice where the "lamb" is the Son of God. In this new covenant, the Church is the "bride, the wife of the Lamb" (Rev 21:9). The Passover lamb had to be male in order to prefigure Christ as Bridegroom. The Passover lamb was just a symbol. The priest really is Christ and not merely a symbol. The priest must be male because, at the altar, he is not only Christ; he makes Christ present as the Bridegroom sacrificing himself for the bride.

Common priesthood of the faithful

God has promised that one day he would make his people a "kingdom of priests" (Ex 19:6). The Book of Revelation repeats this promise. The text implies that the fulfilment of the promise begins in this life and will be completely fulfilled in the next world once Christ's kingdom is fully established:

> Blessed and holy is he who shares in the first resurrection! Over such the second death has no power, but they shall be priests of God and of Christ, and they shall reign with him a thousand years.
>
> Revelation 20:6

Jesus wants all Christians to share in his resurrection and in his priesthood.

St. Peter told all the early Christians to think of themselves as priests of the New Covenant, sharing in the new priesthood of Christ:

> Come to him, to that living stone, rejected by men but in God's sight chosen and precious; and like living stones be yourselves built into a spiritual house, to be a holy priesthood, to offer spiritual sacrifices acceptable to God through Jesus Christ. . . . But you are a chosen race, a royal

> priesthood, a holy nation, God's own people, that you may declare the wonderful deeds of him who called you out of darkness into his marvelous light. Once you were no people but now you are God's people; once you had not received mercy but now you have received mercy.
>
> 1 Peter 2:4–5, 9–10

To offer "spiritual sacrifices," you do not need to be ordained a priest. All Christians can offer spiritual sacrifices to God, each in his or her own way.

By being baptized and confirmed, all Christians share in Christ's priesthood. This does not mean that all Christians are ordained priests. It means that through the common priesthood of the faithful, all Christians can unite their sacrifices to Christ's sacrifice.

For instance, if you make a sacrifice by giving money to the poor, you can tell Jesus, "Lord, I am giving away this money to show my love for you." Then your sacrifice helps not only that poor person; it helps the whole Church. You can tell Jesus, "Lord, I am doing my work now. It's difficult to finish because I'm tired. I do it to show how much I love you." You have united your little sacrifice to the sacrifice of Jesus on the cross. Your little sacrifice becomes part of his infinite sacrifice. God accepts your offering. He makes it his. Because it is no longer yours but his, it takes on a value far beyond anything we can measure.

The ministerial priesthood is different from the common priesthood of the faithful. These are the main differences:

- The ministerial priesthood is only for those who receive holy orders. The common priesthood of the faithful is for all Christians.
- Priests dedicate their lives to preaching, baptizing, hearing confessions, and celebrating Mass, relying on others to take care of their material needs. Ordinary Christians get jobs working in the world to support their family and to support the Church.
- Only the priest has the power to change bread and wine into the Body and Blood of Christ. Ordinary Christians must unite themselves to the priest when he offers the sacrifice of the Mass.
- Jesus uses the ministerial priesthood to lead his Church. Ordinary Christians cannot hold the highest positions of government within

Wisdom of the Saints

An apostle—that is what a Christian is, when he knows that he has been grafted onto Christ, made one with Christ, in baptism. He has been given the capacity to carry on the battle in Christ's name, through confirmation. He has been called to serve God by his activity in the world, because of the common priesthood of the faithful, which makes him share in some way in the priesthood of Christ . . .

Each of us is to be *ipse Christus*: Christ himself. He is the one mediator between God and man. And we make ourselves one with him in order to offer all things, with him, to the Father. Our calling to be children of God, in the midst of the world, requires us . . . to go out onto all the ways of the earth, to convert them into roads that will carry souls over all obstacles and lead them to the Lord.

St. Josemaría, *Christ Is Passing By*, n. 117

the Church. They do not have the power to "bind and loose" (Mt 18:18). They do not form part of the hierarchy of the Church.

To describe the common priesthood of the faithful, the *Catechism* says:

> Christ, high priest, and unique mediator, has made of the Church "a line of kings, priests to serve his God and Father" (cf. Rev 1:6). The whole community of believers is, as such, priestly. The faithful exercise their baptismal priesthood through their participation, each according to his own vocation, in Christ's mission as priest, prophet, and king. Through the sacraments of baptism and confirmation, the faithful are consecrated to be a holy priesthood. . . . The common priesthood of the faithful is exercised by the unfolding of baptismal grace . . .
>
> CCC, nn. 1546–1547

When you offer God your work or relaxation, you share in Christ's priesthood. Just as God was pleased with his Son's sacrifice, he is pleased with yours. Why? Because baptism has made you a child of God. Being his child, your offering is pleasing to him. God is pleased—like a father who smiles when his child gives him a gift, even if others think the gift is worth very little.

Priestly celibacy

The reason for priestly celibacy is simple and obvious: Jesus Christ, the eternal high priest, lived his entire life this way. Embracing celibacy is especially fitting for all those called to act and speak *in persona Christi*—in the person of Christ. Priests and bishops not only imitate the Master by striving to live holy lives; they speak using the first person singular when celebrating the Eucharist and when administering the other sacraments. A priest not only represents Christ at that moment; he is Christ himself.

Priestly celibacy is a gift from God. God grants each priest all the graces needed to be faithful to this vocation.

Christ did not establish priestly celibacy as a necessity for ordination. The Church established this law. The Church law allows married men to be ordained in the Eastern Rites of the Catholic Church. Married men are also allowed to be priests in the Latin Rite if they have been pastors in an Anglican or Lutheran community and now want to be received into full communion with the Catholic Church while also wishing to exercise priestly ministry.

Besides being a gift, priestly celibacy is generally necessary because of the nature of the priesthood. This is why priests cannot get married after ordination and also why only celibate priests can become bishops. The Church teaches:

> The Church, as the spouse of Jesus Christ, wishes to be loved by the priest in the total and exclusive manner in which Jesus Christ her head and spouse loved her. Priestly celibacy, then, is the gift of self *in and with Christ* to his Church and expresses the priest's service to the Church *in and with the Lord*. . . . Celibacy, then, is to be welcomed . . . as a witness to the world of the eschatological kingdom.
>
> St. John Paul II, *Apostolic Exhortation on the Formation of Priests*, n. 29

The Church needs priestly celibacy. It is a visible sign. It reminds all people that Christ gave himself—and continues to give himself—to the Church by "emptying himself out," by sacrificing his whole existence for her. It reminds people about the kingdom that God will establish once and for all at the end of the world, where men and women no longer marry.

REVIEW QUESTIONS

1. Explain the difference between deacons, priest and bishops.
2. How does apostolic succession depend on holy orders?
3. Why is the sacrament of holy orders administered only to men?
4. How does the common priesthood of the faithful differ from ministerial priesthood?

40.

Matrimony

A Christian man and woman receive the sacrament of matrimony when they go to church to get married. This sacrament makes them husband and wife. When they receive this sacrament, God unites them. St. Paul calls marriage a "profound mystery" (Eph 5:32). When the bridegroom and bride become one body, their union symbolizes the union of Christ with his Church. Their union is a great mystery because God himself creates the union. After God unites the man and woman, they remain united until one of them dies.

The bond of marriage is an unbreakable bond. This teaching comes from Jesus. When the Pharisees asked him whether a husband could divorce his wife, he answered:

> Have you not read that he who made them from the beginning made them male and female, and said, "For this reason a man shall leave his father and mother and be joined to his wife, and the two shall become one"? So they are no longer two but one. What therefore God has joined together, let not man put asunder.
>
> Matthew 19:4–6; cf. Genesis 1:28; 2:24

Becoming one body is sometimes translated as becoming "one flesh." The idea is the same in either case. It means that God has united the man and woman and bound them together in their very bodies. Once they are married, the two are one. They are one body, not only when they engage in acts of marital intimacy, but all the time, every day. Nothing except the death of one of the spouses can undo the

Sacred Scripture

Wives, be subject to your husbands, as to the Lord. . . . Husbands, love your wives, as Christ loved the church and gave himself up for her . . .

Ephesians 5:22, 25

bond uniting husband and wife. No judge can break the bond. Neither of the spouses can break the bond.

God unites the man and woman as husband and wife when they get married, that is, when they make a commitment to be faithful to each other. A man and woman are married if and only if they make a public commitment for life.

Marriage existed before Jesus

The sacrament of matrimony is different from the other sacraments. When instituting the sacrament of matrimony, Jesus took something that already existed—marriage—and made it a sacrament. For the reason, the Church calls matrimony the "most ancient sacrament."

Marriage existed from the very beginning of creation. The first man and woman were married to each other. Adam and Eve were husband and wife. God joined them together when he created them. The marriage bond uniting Adam and Eve was exactly the same kind of marriage bond as the one that unites a Christian couple today.

God gave so much importance to marriage in the Old Testament that he used it as a metaphor to describe his relationship with Israel. He often referred to himself as a husband devoted to his wife. Several prophets portrayed Israel as the bride of Yahweh.

Marriage exists for all people everywhere and in every age of history. If a man and woman living in ancient times got married, then, in the eyes of God, they were truly married.

No matter what religion the husband and wife follow, God unites them and makes them "one body" as long as they make a true commitment to marriage. Even a marriage between two atheists is a true marriage, as long as one man and one woman have the intention of committing themselves to each other *exclusively* as husband and wife for as long as they live. Exclusive love implies that they rule out the possibility of polygamy. Their marriage is not just a contract or an agreement, ruled by the laws of the country where they live. God has joined them together. Their union is a sacred union, blessed by God.

Marriage was a holy reality before Christ. When Jesus came to reveal the new and eternal covenant, he made marriage one of the seven sacraments.

Marriage is a vocation

Marriage is a vocation. A husband has a calling from God to be the spouse of his wife, while God also calls the wife to be spouse to her husband.

> A Christian marriage is not just a social institution, much less a remedy for human weakness. It is a real supernatural calling. . . . But when we talk about marriage and married life, we must begin by speaking clearly about the mutual love of husband and wife. Their pure and noble love is a sacred thing. . . . No Christian, whether or not he is called to the married state, has a right to underestimate the value of marriage.
>
> St. Josemaría, *Christ Is Passing By*, nn. 23–24

A few are called by God to imitate Christ by dedicating themselves to celibacy. But God wants most men and women to find their way to him through marriage. He gives them a vocation to marriage. He calls them to receive the sacrament of matrimony and persevere in this vocation.

If you can be faithful to your spouse within marriage and learn to make your spouse and your children happy, you will be ready to spend eternity being happy with God. By learning how to love your spouse in this world, you are ready to enjoy God's infinite love in the next world. If you want to be happy in heaven, learn how to be happy here on earth. Marriage is one way to do it. Marriage is a road to heaven.

Making spouse and children happy is relative. You cannot be completely happy in this world. They cannot be completely happy in this world. First, because of our own sins and defects. Second, because of suffering and death and all the other consequences of original sin. Finally, because we were created for something greater. We achieve perfect happiness only when we reach heaven and see God face-to-face. Nevertheless, the Church insists that marriage is a vocation precisely because it prepares both husband and wife to see God and to enjoy his infinite love.

Marriage is holy

Matrimony is holy because God himself intervenes to create the bond that makes the spouse "one flesh." Placing an offering on the altar makes it holy in the eyes of God. The marriage bed is like an altar. The conjugal act is holy in God's eyes. St. Paul wrote:

> Shun immorality. Every other sin which a man commits is outside the body; but the immoral man sins against his own body. Do you not know that your body is a temple of the Holy Spirit within you, which you have from God? You are not your own; you were bought with a price. So glorify God in your body.
>
> 1 Corinthians 6:18–20

Your body belongs to God. Because your body is holy, the conjugal act can be holy. When engaging in this act of giving your whole self, you give your spouse something holy, namely, your body. The act is also holy because God is the One joining husband and wife, making them one body.

The sacramental sign for matrimony

Jesus worked his first miracle at a wedding feast. He changed water into wine. This shows that marriage is an essential part of God's plan for salvation. This is how matrimony became one of the seven sacraments, that is, one of the means of giving us God's grace.

Like all other sacraments, matrimony consists of a sign. In all the sacraments, God uses a sign to give us a share in his divine life. In baptism, the sign consists in the pouring of water, as the minister says the baptismal formula. In the Eucharist, the sign consists of bread and wine, which the priest changes to Christ's body and blood. In matrimony, the sign consists of the bodies of the man and woman, together with their exchange of mutual consent. Consent must be manifested by a public statement from both the bridegroom and bride. They must declare that they intend to be husband and wife for as long as they live.

Consent is an act of the will. You consent to something when you decide interiorly that you want it to happen. The public declaration made by the couple during the wedding is called "consent" to emphasize the personal desire of the bridegroom and the personal desire of the bride.

First the man declares his intention. Then the woman declares her intention. If either one decides not to make this declaration—no matter what the reason—then there is no marriage. If either one makes the declaration without having the intention of getting married—no matter what the reason—then there is no marriage. The *Catechism* says:

> The Church holds the exchange of consent between the spouses to be the indispensable element that "makes the marriage." If consent is lacking there is no marriage.
>
> The consent consists in a human act by which the partners mutually give themselves to each other: "I take you to be my wife." / "I take you to be my husband." This consent that binds the spouses to each other finds its fulfilment in the two "becoming one flesh."
>
> The consent must be an act of the will of each of the contracting parties, free of coercion or grave external fear. No human power can substitute for this consent. If this freedom is lacking, the marriage is invalid.
>
> *CCC*, nn. 1626–1628

If either the man or the woman did not want to get married and went through the wedding ceremony because of fear or some other reason, the marriage is invalid. In others words, what looked like a marriage *was not a marriage*. God did not join the man and woman together. They are not husband and wife.

No one can see a person's intention. During a wedding, no one can see consent. However, the declaration is public, made before several witnesses. Therefore, the Church assumes that the man and woman are speaking the truth and always maintains that assumption unless it can be proven otherwise.

When husband and wife make a complete and sexual gift of self to each other after the wedding, we say they have "consummated their marriage." In other words, by becoming "one flesh," they have engaged in the act proper to a married couple. This act seals their union as husband and wife.

For Catholics, any man or woman who wants to get married must receive the sacrament of matrimony. This remains true even if the Catholic is getting married to a non-Catholic. If a Catholic does not speak to a priest to arrange for a proper wedding in the Church, no marriage has taken place even if the couple has a religious ceremony somewhere else.

The characteristics of marriage

If husband and wife are to love each other as fixed in God's plan for marriage, their marriage must be based on two indispensable characteristics: unity and indissolubility. Unity means that the union must be one man and one woman committing themselves completely to each other. Indissolubility means that the bond that unites them cannot be broken.

Polygamy contradicts the kind of *exclusive unity* God wants for a man and woman in marriage. Divorce and remarriage contradicts the nature of the *unbreakable bond* that God uses to join the man and woman when making them one body. The Church teaches:

> Polygamy . . . directly negates the plan of God which was revealed from the beginning, because it is contrary to the equal personal dignity of men and women who in matrimony give themselves with a love that is total and therefore unique and exclusive.
>
> Conjugal communion is characterized not only by its unity but also by its indissolubility. . . . It is a fundamental duty of the Church to reaffirm strongly . . . the doctrine of the indissolubility of marriage. To all those who, in our times, consider it too difficult, or indeed impossible, to be bound to one person for the whole of life, and to those caught up in a culture that rejects the indissolubility of marriage and openly mocks the commitment of spouses to fidelity, it is necessary to reconfirm the good

Ecclesiastical Writers

How can I ever express the happiness of a marriage joined by the Church, strengthened by an offering, sealed by a blessing, announced by angels, and ratified by the Father? . . . How beautiful the bond that unites two Christians, now one in hope, one in desire, one in discipline, one in the same service! They are as brother and sister, servants of the same Master. Nothing divides them, either in flesh or in spirit. They really are "two in one flesh." Where the flesh is one, the spirit is also one.

They pray together. They worship together. They fast together. They instruct one another, encourage one another, and strengthen one another. . . . They have no secrets from one another. They never shun each other's company. They never bring sorrow to each other's hearts. . . . They give alms without anxiety. They attend the sacrifice [of the Mass] without difficulty. They engage in their daily times of prayer without hindrance. . . . Hearing and seeing this, Christ rejoices. He gives his peace to such as these. "Where two are together," he is there, also present (cf. Mt 18:20).

Tertullian, *To His Wife*, II, 8

news of the definitive nature of that conjugal love that has in Christ its foundation and strength.

St. John Paul II, *Family in the Modern World*, n. 19–20
(cf. *CCC*, nn. 1643–1645, 2387)

The union of husband and wife does not end when they feel as if they no longer love each other. God is the One who joined them together. God is also the One who can give them the wisdom and the strength to begin again. Many couples discover that a deeper experience of mutual love awaits them, unexpectedly, by learning to overcome obstacles together.

The effects of matrimony

The sacrament of matrimony gives a Christian husband and wife a special grace to do three things:

- **Be one with each other.** This means learning how to love; how to express affection in a way that is pleasing to the other spouse; and how to be patient and kind. It also means that polygamy is wrong. If a man goes out and gets a second wife, he is doing something evil. It is wrong for Christians, and it is wrong for Jews, Muslims, Hindus, or anyone else. Polygamy goes against God's plan for marriage. According to God's plan—from the very beginning—a man can have only one wife, and a woman can have only one husband. Some think it is hard for people to live this way. By raising marriage to the dignity of a sacrament, Jesus has given men and women the grace they need to do it.

- **Be faithful to each other.** This means first of all that a man and woman preparing for marriage should refrain from acts involving sexual intimacy before getting married—with each other or with anyone else. Once married, they should engage in these acts only with each other and never with anyone else. If they have problems in their marriage—every couple does sooner or later—they have to work things out. Even if the government declares a divorce, neither the husband nor the wife can marry someone else. Jesus stated this clearly: "Whoever divorces his wife and marries another, commits adultery against her; and if she divorces her husband and marries another, she commits adultery" (Mk 10:11–12). Some think it is hard to live this way. Even the Apostles thought it was impossible. They said, "If such is the case of a man with his wife, it is not expedient to marry" (Mt 19:10). Grace gives a couple strength to be faithful to each other for their whole lives.
- **Be open to having children.** This means accepting children as a blessing from God. The conjugal act leads to having babies. This is the way God created us. God wants married couples to work together

MAGISTERIUM

Love for the kingdom of heaven can lead a person to choose not to marry. Marriage, however, remains the usual human vocation, which is embraced by the great majority of the people of God.

We need to pray that married couples will love their vocation, even when the road becomes difficult, or paths become narrow, uphill, and seemingly insuperable. We need to pray that, even then, they will be faithful to their covenant with God.

St. John Paul II, *Letter to Families*, nn. 14, 18

with him to create new life. Having children involves risks. Caring for children takes work. By having children, couples learn how to trust God and work together with him. It is wrong to get married with a preconceived plan to limit the size of your family. Being open to children seems difficult to many young couples planning to marry. That is why they need the grace of matrimony. This sacrament helps them to be generous. It helps them put God's plans in first place and their ambitions for career, wealth, and free time in second place.

Divorce and annulment

There is one and only one reason why you cannot get married again if for some reason you got divorced from your spouse. You cannot get re-married because, even after the divorce, you are still married to your spouse. No matter what others say, no matter what the laws of the country say, once you and your spouse are married, you will be husband and wife in the eyes of God until one of you dies.

Divorce is an attempt to break the bond uniting husband and wife. But that bond is unbreakable. Jesus said, "What therefore God has joined together, let not man put asunder" (Mt 19:6).

In the Church, there is a procedure called the "declaration of nullity," sometimes also called an "annulment." An annulment is not the same as divorce. Declaring the nullity of a marriage is radically different from divorce. The declaration of nullity is not an attempt to break the unbreakable bond of marriage. Instead, it is a declaration from the Church that a particular couple was never married even though they had a wedding ceremony in a church. This declaration can only be made after a thorough investigation by a panel of judges appointed by the local bishop. The *Catechism* explains:

> After an examination of the situation by the competent ecclesiastical tribunal, the Church can declare the nullity of a marriage, i.e., that the marriage never existed. In this case the contracting parties are free to marry, provided the natural obligations of a previous union are discharged.
>
> CCC, n. 1629

The "contracting parties" are the man and woman who mistakenly assumed they were married. Not having been married, they are free to marry. However, they may have obligations to fulfill: for example, caring for children born while they were living together.

There are several reasons why the Church declares that a marriage never took place even though a wedding ceremony was held. Impotence is one example; this is the total inability of one of the spouses to engage in the conjugal act. Force is another example. If someone used force on either of the spouses to convince the couple to get married, then no marriage exists. These are some of the reasons why the Church makes a declaration of nullity.

Working with God

God told Adam and Eve: "Be fruitful and multiply, and fill the earth" (Gen 1:28). A man and woman work together with God in the most sacred of all the acts of creation—the birth of new human life. God uses their love and makes it fruitful.

The Church teaches:

> These acts, by which husband and wife are united in chaste intimacy, and by means of which human life is transmitted, are, as the [Second Vatican] Council recalled, "noble and worthy," and they do not cease to be lawful if, for causes independent of the will of husband and wife, they are foreseen to be infecund, since they always remain ordained towards expressing and consolidating their union. In fact, as experience bears witness, not every conjugal act is followed by a new life. God has wisely disposed natural laws and rhythms of fertility which, of themselves, cause a separation in the succession of births. Nonetheless the Church, calling men back to the observance of the norms of the natural law, as interpreted by its constant doctrine teaches that each and every marriage act must remain open to the transmission of life.
>
> Paul VI, *On Human Life*, n. 11

A man and woman give glory to God if their conjugal act is open to conception. They offend God if they deliberately make their conjugal act sterile (using contraceptives) or they try to "manufacture" a child outside of the intimacy of their mutual love (asking doctors to produce a so-called "test-tube" baby).

If a couple has some difficulty like poor health or financial distress and needs to avoid childbirth, they may use the natural regulation of fertility. This is sometimes called "natural family planning." In this way, the couple respects God's plan for marriage, engaging in the conjugal act only during those days in the month when the woman is infertile. As long as the couple remains open to the possibility of conception—even though they are deliberately taking measures to avoid conception—the conjugal act during the infertile period continues to be an act of total self-giving and, therefore, holy in God's eyes. Their decision to abstain from sex during those days when they need to avoid the conception is also holy and pleasing to God.

Each child is a precious new life—as precious as your own life—and needs to be cared for with love. Each child needs to see how much his father and mother love each other. By seeing their love, the child comes to understand God's love.

Family size

Many people enter into marriage and spend the whole of their married lives thinking their happiness depends on limiting the size of their family. For instance, the husband or the wife or both will say, "We only want two children." Some will even say, "We don't want any children."

The Bible says that God created man to work. When God calls "man" to work, we understand this in the collective sense. God created the male and female to work. Part of their work is to cooperate with the Creator. They bring new human life into the world. They care for these children. They teach them about God.

Limiting work to the production of consumer goods is one of the worst mistakes of present-day society. Our first priority is not to produce goods. The first priority is to: "Be fruitful and multiply, and fill the earth and subdue it" (Gen 1:28). This is the command God gave Adam and Eve. Since we need goods to fulfil this command, we should produce goods, but goods are secondary.

If we make children the priority, we are doing what God created us to do. When we increase the production of goods and decrease the number of children, we have abandoned the mission God gave us. We are producing coal instead of diamonds. The diamonds—the children—take much more effort and sacrifice but they last forever. The goods we produce will all eventually turn to dust and blow away with the wind. One human being is worth more than all the galaxies in the universe. If you have any doubt about that, then you know nothing about *how precious you are* in the eyes of God—and how precious every child is in the eyes of God.

Having children is part of the very essence of getting married. God asks the man and woman to get married so they can help him create. We call it "procreation." It takes work. But that is precisely the kind of work that God wants from us. A couple does the work God wants them to do if they sacrifice themselves generously to bring children into the world and take care of them. The Church teaches:

> Marriage and conjugal love are by their nature ordained toward the begetting and educating of children. Children are really the supreme gift of marriage and contribute very substantially to the welfare of their parents. . . . Parents should regard as their proper mission the task of transmitting human life and educating those to whom it has been transmitted. They should realize that they are thereby cooperators with the love of God the Creator . . .
>
> Vatican II, *Church in the Modern World*, n. 50

God blesses parents with all the grace they need in order to fulfil his desire to create. In the end, though, he counts on the generosity of the parents themselves.

When speaking about a couple's decision to have another child, the Church teaches:

> The parents themselves and no one else should ultimately make this judgment in the sight of God. But in their manner of acting, spouses should be aware that they cannot proceed arbitrarily. . . . Trusting in divine Providence and refining their spirit of sacrifice, married Christians glorify the Creator and strive toward fulfilment in Christ when with a

> generous human and Christian sense of responsibility they fulfil the obligation they have to work together with God to bring new human life into the world.
>
> Vatican II, *Church in the Modern World*, n. 50

The couple makes their decision "in the sight of God." Therefore, besides speaking to each other, the husband and wife turn to God and speak to him as children speaking to a father, asking him to guide them.

The Church teaches:

> Decisions about the number of children and the sacrifices to be made for them must not be taken only with a view to adding to comfort and preserving a peaceful existence. Reflecting on this matter before God . . . parents will remind themselves that it is certainly less serious to deny their children certain comforts or material advantages than to deprive them of the presence of brothers and sisters, who could help them grow in humanity and to realize the beauty of life at all its ages and in all its variety.
>
> St. John Paul II, *Homily at National Mall*,
> Washington, D.C., October 7, 1979

The child is always the first one to prefer more brothers and sisters to more material possessions.

The wedding ceremony

The sacrament of matrimony takes place during a wedding ceremony. The key moment of the wedding ceremony comes when the priest asks the couple to express their consent. Before expressing consent, the priest presiding over the ceremony asks three questions to both the man and the woman. Each answers separately.

First, the priest asks them whether they are acting freely, without reservation, willing to give themselves to each other in marriage. If either the man or woman says, "No, I am not ready," then the priest calls off the wedding and everybody goes home. Second, the priest asks them whether they will love each other as husband and wife for the rest of their lives. Thirdly, the priest asks:

> Will you accept children lovingly from God, and bring them up according to the law of Christ and his Church?

Both bridegroom and bride have to say yes for the ceremony to proceed. The last question can be omitted if the bride is elderly.

Then comes the exchange of consent. To express his consent, the bridegroom states that he takes the woman to be his wife. To express her consent, the bride states that she takes the man to be her husband. The following is one of the typical formulas the bridegroom uses to do this, (after which, the bride uses the same formula to express her consent, changing the wording appropriately):

> I ____ take you ____ to be my wife. I promise to be true to you in good times and in bad, in sickness and in health. I will love you and honor you all the days of my life.

These are the classic words of commitment. "In good times and in bad, in sickness and in health" rules out the possibility of divorce from the very beginning of married life. Each spouse promises to remain faithful—no matter what happens—until one of them dies. (During the ceremony, the blank spaces are filled in with the names of the couple.)

After expressing consent, the spouses exchange rings as a sign of their love and fidelity. However, this part of the ceremony can be omitted. Such an omission might surprise some people. But the Church does not insist on having rings. The rings are not the essential sign of this sacrament. To explain the sanctity of marriage, St. Josemaría describes how the human body constitutes part of the essence of this sacrament:

> Marriage is a sacrament that makes one flesh of two bodies. Theology expresses this fact in a striking way when it teaches us that the matter of the sacrament is the bodies of husband and wife. Our Lord sanctifies and blesses the mutual love of husband and wife. He foresees, not only a union of souls, but a union of bodies as well.
>
> St. Josemaría, *Christ Is Passing By*, n. 24

The priest is not the minister of the sacrament. The husband and wife together act as a single minister when they exchange their consent. The priest receives the consent of the spouses in the name of the Church and gives them the Church's blessing (cf. *CCC*, n. 1630).

The nuptial Mass

When Catholics get married, they usually have the wedding during the celebration of the Eucharist. This is called a "nuptial Mass." There are many reasons for this. The *Catechism* says:

> It is therefore fitting that the spouses should seal their consent to give themselves to each other through the offering of their own lives by uniting it to the offering of Christ for his Church made present in the Eucharistic sacrifice, and by receiving the Eucharist so that, communicating in the same Body and the same Blood of Christ, they may form but "one body" in Christ.
>
> *CCC*, n. 1621

The Eucharist is the act of Christ uniting himself with his Church. It is the model for the union of the bridegroom and bride.

When planning their wedding, a Catholic couple should prepare to receive the Eucharist. It gives them a special grace. Every bridegroom and bride tends to forget how easy it is to "run out of wine" (cf. Jn 2:3) and how much they need God if they want to love each other. By giving due importance to preparing to receive Holy Communion, they more readily understand the secret of spousal communion. "In the joys of their love and family life," Jesus is the one who "gives them here on earth a foretaste of the wedding feast of the Lamb" (cf. *CCC*, n. 1642).

True love waits

In God's plan, all men and women are supposed to wait until marriage before engaging in any kind of sexual activity. Even if a man and woman are madly in love and about to get married, God wants them to wait until their wedding day.

By giving your body to your spouse, you are giving your very self. The gift is meant to be total. You give your whole self to one person and one person only. The gift is meant to be permanent. You can never take back the gift. Marriage requires giving not just your time or your friendship but your whole self. That is why virginity is the best preparation for marriage. Giving your spouse your virginity on your wedding day is the most precious gift you can give.

If a married person is getting married a second time after the death of his or her spouse, then the obligation to enter into marriage as virgin obviously no longer applies. However, when preparing for marriage in this case, the engaged couple still has the same obligation to refrain from all sexual contact before the wedding.

Due to prejudice, a man may go into marriage assuming virginity is only for the woman he marries. This attitude is perverse. It will do enormous harm to his marriage. He will look upon all women—his wife included—as a convenience for his sexual pleasure. He has no intention of giving himself to his wife. He will merely use her to satisfy his desire for sexual pleasure. When he gets tired of her, he will look for excitement somewhere else.

Giving your very self to your spouse is first and foremost a decision of the will. For a man to give himself completely to his wife, he must consciously decide to engage in acts of sexual intimacy only with her and never with any other woman. Then, *and only then*, can he say that he is giving *his whole self* to his wife. Until he makes this decision, he is not giving himself to her. Until he makes that decision and lives by it, he will never find true love. He is ready to make this decision on his wedding day only if he has made the sacrifice of refraining from sexual acts until that day.

The same logic applies to the woman getting married.

If a young man or woman has made a mistake by engaging in sex before marriage, he or she should make a commitment to live "secondary virginity." The emphasis remains the same. Each person needs to prepare for marriage by saving sex for marriage.

Those who look at marriage as a license to enjoy pleasure have completely misunderstood marriage. Those who see marriage as an act of giving one's whole self—even if they made mistakes earlier on in life—can find true love in marriage. Only those who remain virgins, or at least make a commitment to secondary virginity, are ready for marriage.

Trial marriage

You will hear some people talk about "trial marriage." A couple may think they should "try sex" before marriage to see if they like each other. They quickly discover that they like sex. But they do not find out if they are capable of loving each other. They can't. A man and woman living together in a trial marriage are lying to each other. They act if they were husband and wife. But they are not married, and they know they are not married.

Whenever your words say one thing and your deeds say another, it is a lie. A trial marriage is always a lie. Lying is the worst way to prepare for marriage.

There are some experiences you can try before committing yourself for your whole life—like studying for a career, finding a hobby or joining a club. Other activities begin with risk because you must make the commitment first and find out what it's like afterwards.

You cannot try out birth and then decide which couple you would like to have as your mother and father. You cannot try out death and then decide how you would like to die. You cannot try out marriage and then decide who your spouse is going to be. You do not have a spouse until you get married. Once you get married, the one you have married will be your spouse until death takes one of you away.

This is the mystery of human life. There is no trial birth. There is no trial death. There is no trial marriage. Each one of these realities is final. Each one immerses you into a world of incredible risk.

God is an infinite being who loves risk. He is constantly taking risks. He wants us to be like him. He created us in his own image and likeness. He demands that we take risks too. Marriage is one of them.

Being in love

In the beginning of a marriage, being in love tends to be easy for both husband and wife. But difficulties eventually multiply. Comparing married love with the union of Christ and his Church reminds us that, in this world, love means making sacrifices.

The spouses begin to notice each other's defects and find them annoying. Financial and social pressures may fill them with anxiety and leave them exhausted. Both need to make an effort to overcome these hardships, learning to be patient with each other. The couple experiences love not only in moments of passion, which are necessarily infrequent, but above all in moments when they learn to be understanding with each other.

God wants the husband and wife to be in love with each other from beginning to end—even as they grow old. In his letter to the Ephesians, St. Paul stresses the role of the husband, comparing the way he must love his wife with the way Jesus loves the Church. To do this, the husband has to see himself in her. The wife makes the same effort to see herself in her husband. The Church teaches:

> "He who loves his wife loves himself" (Eph 5:28) . . . Love makes the "I" of the other person his own "I." The "I" of the wife . . . becomes, through love, the "I" of the husband. The body is the expression of that "I" and the foundation of its identity. The union of husband and wife in love is expressed also by means of the body.

Wisdom of the Saints

God's invisible hand binds you together in the sacred bonds of marriage. . . . He gives you to each other. Therefore, cherish one another with a holy, sacred, heavenly love. The first effect of this love is the indissoluble union of your hearts.

If you glue together two pieces of wood, then, as long as the glue is strong, their union will be so tight that the wood will break more easily in any other part than where the glue holds. Now God unites husband and wife so tightly *in himself* that it would be easier to tear soul from body than husband from wife. Nor is this union to be considered as mainly a union of bodies; but even more so, it is a union of hearts, with all their love and affection.

St. Francis de Sales, *Introduction to the Devout Life*, III, 38

> The husband is, above all, he who loves and the wife is, on the other hand, she who is loved. One could even hazard the idea that the wife's submission to her husband . . . signifies above all the "experiencing of love." This is all the more so since the submission is related to the image of the submission of the Church to Christ.
>
> The Church, as bride, being the object of the redemptive love of Christ the Bridegroom, becomes his Body. Being the object of the spousal love of the husband, the wife becomes "one flesh" with him, in a certain sense, his own flesh.
>
> St. John Paul II, *Theology of the Body*, pp. 319–320

Instead of seeing "submission" to her husband as something negative, the wife will naturally respect the authority of her husband as long as he understands the notion of *mutual* submission. Since this is a new concept for many men, it is worth explaining.

The experience of love is an experience of union—an awareness of God making two become one. The wife experiences a sense of union when the husband sacrifices himself. He must put her needs first. The wife on her part ought to be ready to respect his authority.

> Likewise you wives, be submissive to your husbands. . . . So once the holy women who hoped in God and were submissive to their husbands, as Sarah obeyed Abraham, calling him lord. . . . Likewise you husbands, live considerately with your wives . . .
>
> 1 Peter 3:1, 5, 6, 7

St. Paul combined the wife's obedience with the husband's sacrifice by telling them both: "Be subject to one another out of reverence for Christ" (Eph 5:21).

Vocation to marriage

If God has given you a vocation to marriage, he wants you to learn how to love your spouse—or prepare for it if you're not yet married.

> The great danger for family life in the midst of any society whose idols are pleasure, comfort, and independence lies in the fact that people close their hearts and become selfish. The fear of making permanent

> commitments can change the mutual love of husband and wife into two loves of self—two loves existing side by side until they end in separation.
>
> St. John Paul II, Homily, Washington, D.C., October 7, 1979

Far from being negative about romantic love, the Church wants every husband and wife to be madly in love with each other. That is why she warns couples to flee from anything that leads towards separation.

Besides the husband's willingness to sacrifice himself and the wife's willingness to obey, being in love depends on the virtue of holy purity. A pure person knows how to love. A pure person is easy to love in return. Discovering the worth of this virtue means nothing less than discovering love. Jesus promised: "Blessed are the pure in heart, for they shall see God" (Mt 5:8).

The dignity of celibacy

Celibacy was not the invention of the Church. It was Jesus' idea from the beginning and has survived against all odds for two thousand years. Sometimes he asks a person to remain celibate. Celibacy is for some, not for all. When he asks someone to do this, he knows that he is asking for an extraordinary sacrifice. However, no one can outdo God in generosity. The one who embraces a vocation to celibacy does not find less love, but more love.

Celibacy is not a vocation to renounce love. It is calling from God to a greater love. It is God's way of giving us a glimpse of what life will be like in the next world. The *Catechism* says:

> From the very beginning of the Church there have been men and women who have renounced the great good of marriage to follow the Lamb wherever he goes, to be intent on the things of the Lord, to seek to please him, and to go out to meet the Bridegroom who is coming. Christ himself has invited certain persons to follow him in this way of life, of which he remains the model. He said: "For there are eunuchs who have been so from birth, and there are eunuchs who have been made eunuchs by men, and there are eunuchs who have made

> themselves eunuchs for the sake of the kingdom of heaven. He who is able to receive this, let him receive it."
>
> *CCC*, n. 1618 (Mt 19:12)

There are many examples of men and women who remained celibate for the sake of God's kingdom. They are imitating Jesus. In some way they are also imitating the example of the Virgin Mary and St. Joseph. It is a dogma of the Church that Jesus' mother was virgin before she gave birth to Jesus and that she remained virgin always, while continuing to be Joseph's wife after Jesus was born.

Celibacy is a mystery. What could possibly motivate any normal human being to give up the one thing that many people treasure as their greatest hope of joy and happiness? Some people say men and women incapable of entering into an intimate marital relationship try to hide their problem by choosing celibacy.

There is one obvious inconsistency with this attempt to discredit the value of celibacy. It was Jesus himself who chose not to marry. Much to the surprise of his disciples, he invited some of them to imitate him: "He who is able to receive this, let him receive it" (Mt 19:12). Millions of men and women, after accepting Jesus' challenge, have remained faithful to a lifetime of celibacy.

Celibate men and women experience the same sexual urges and emotional attractions as their friends. No matter how normal a person is most of the time, even those who are married or intending to get married experience temptations to adultery or fornication. Everyone feels these tendencies, whether they are celibate or married.

St. Paul gives his testimony in the First Letter to the Corinthians. After explaining how God wants Christians to deal with their natural inclinations, he concludes that marriage is good and celibacy is better (cf. 1 Cor 7:32). Note the way St. Paul connects celibacy with marriage. First he exalts marriage defining it as "a great sacrament." It is great because it reflects the greatness of God. It is great because it is a sign of the "marriage" of Christ and his Church. The Church fathers explain this connection between celibacy and marriage:

> Whoever denigrates marriage also diminishes the glory of virginity. Whoever praises it makes virginity more admirable and resplendent. What appears good only in comparison with evil would not be truly good. The most excellent good is something even better than what is admitted to be good.
>
> St. John Chrysostom, cf. *CCC*, n. 1620

When a man and woman achieve communion, becoming one with each other in marriage, their nuptial union reflects the divine union of Father, Son, and Holy Spirit. Marriage is a visible sign of God's invisible perfection. God intervenes in the life of a celibate person to work an even greater miracle of love.

What would this miracle of love be? Here one must rely on prayer more than books. Even so, *The Living Flame of Love* by St. John of the Cross and *The Interior Castle* by St. Teresa of Avila give some idea of what it means to enter into the "bridal chamber" where Christ takes possession of his bride, the Church. The main reason for celibacy is the call from God to experience this "nuptial union" with Christ that we faintly glimpse in the writings of these mystics.

REVIEW QUESTIONS

1. What is the sacramental sign for matrimony? What is the most important part of the wedding ceremony?
2. What are the two characteristics of marriage? What is wrong with polygamy? Why is it impossible for a married person to divorce and marry someone else?
3. What does the Church teach about family size?
4. Even though marriage is a sacrament and virginity is not, why is celibacy for the kingdom of heaven better than marriage?

Part Five

The Human Person

41.

You Are a Person

You are not a thing. You are a person. If something breaks, you can throw it away. A person is different. You are not a thing people can throw away if you get sick or grow old. This is not an exact definition of the human person, but it gives you a rough idea of where to begin.

God has revealed many great truths about man. The Incarnation and redemption are the greatest. What could be greater than having God reveal this:

> I will welcome you, and I will be a father to you, and you shall be my sons and daughters, says the Lord Almighty.
>
> 2 Corinthians 6:17–18

What could be greater than having the Son of God become one of us? What could be greater than becoming sons and daughters of God?

This mystery implies many truths about man. Among them is the truth about the human person. This section is meant to study it. This is merely an introduction. You may want to study the topic in greater depth later. For now, the idea is to review the basics by focusing on what the Catholic Church teaches about the human person.

Why study this topic? The most common errors that prevent people from understanding the gospel are errors about the human person.

Compared to the way people lived hundreds of years ago, we have improved the quality of life enormously. We continue to make progress in all fields. This is wonderful. However, the culture that dominates society makes it hard for people to have faith. At times, Christians suffer persecution as open and as brutal as anything the first martyrs suffered under the Roman Empire. More often, though, the persecution is subtle. Many people look at Christian faith and conclude that it is a threat to the progress we have achieved. The sad part is that some Christians whose faith has been "infected" by this culture think this way without noticing it. Wherever this culture dominates, anyone eager to live Christian virtue is treated like an alien whose presence is merely tolerated.

To understand why these things happen, you need to study the truth about the human person. Then maybe you, together with others, can change the culture.

In the early twentieth century, when the world was burdened by war—what historians call the "world wars"—St. Josemaría wrote:

> A secret, an open secret: these world crises are crises of saints. God wants a handful of men [and women] "of his own" in every human activity. And then . . . *pax Christi in regno Christi*—the "peace of Christ in the kingdom of Christ."
>
> St. Josemaría, *The Way*, n. 301

The crises are all around us. Bloodshed and poverty are the obvious ones; but many who enjoy peace and wealth feel miserable and unhappy. There is only one solution. God needs men and women willing to live a holy life. God needs men and women whose greatest desire is to live as sons and daughters of God.

To study the human person, we'll look at mind, will, and body. Finally, we will examine the relationship between the human person and society. Before getting into the details, it may help to get an overview of common errors about the human person. There are many.

Multiple errors

One error misjudges the nature of the human mind. There are two extremes: rationalism and relativism. Rationalists think nothing exceeds our ability to know and comprehend. They assume that all mysteries ultimately reduce to questions of science. They think there will be no more mysteries once we understand all about the material world. Relativists think no one is capable of knowing the truth with certainty.

They claim that no one knows the truth with certainty because they deny the existence of any absolute truth beyond what we can see with our own eyes. If willing to admit that absolute truth does exist, they deny the power of human reason to grasp it.

Another error misjudges the nature of the human will. Again, there are two extremes: determinism and nihilism. The determinist denies the existence of human freedom, saying everyone is a slave to animal instincts and social conditioning. Nihilists talk about the "will to power"; they claim that human freedom is "beyond good and evil." Nihilism denies the very existence of human nature. Each individual is free to choose how good and evil should be defined. All are free to become the man or woman—or whatever else—they want to be.

> **SACRED SCRIPTURE**
>
> . . . that they may all be one; even as thou, Father, art in me, and I in thee, that they also may be in us, so that the world may believe that thou hast sent me.
>
> John 17:21

Another error misjudges the nature of the human body. There are several positions: naturalism, paganism, and dualism. According to naturalism, there is nothing sacred about the human body; we are no different from animals; men and women are as much an accident of evolution as fruit flies and bacteria. Paganism takes on many forms, most of them based on pantheism. Pantheists think that the human body is somehow divine because all matter taken together is God. The gnostic heresy and the heresy of the Manicheans are forms of dualism. Those influenced by dualism think the human body, like all matter, is something evil. Sexual purity—and more particularly, sexual self-control—is impossible because the human body is incapable of purification and will always be a burden that prevents men and women from being truly spiritual.

The consequences of these errors

Errors about human nature have led many people to accept promiscuity, contraception, abortion, divorce and unbridled greed as a normal way of life. As these vices become socially acceptable, people then begin to accept homosexuality, eugenics, and euthanasia.

As these aberrations become routine, people can become radically materialistic. They absorb a strange way of looking at life, thinking it is normal simply because many think this way. They begin to presume they have a right to manipulate their bodies into whatever they want. They reduce the distinction between male and female to a social construct. Genders are merely social roles that we can alter in whatever way we want to. The materialistic culture portrays the heterosexual male and heterosexual female as two gender roles favored among a wide variety of other possibilities, including homosexual male, homosexual female, bisexual male, bisexual female, etc.

If you accept—or simply end up with—this mentality, your faith reduced to picking and choosing teachings from different religions. You try to mold yourself into the kind of person you want to be. Once that happens, you look at the fixed dogmas of the Catholic Church as relics of the past.

The result of this trend is to depersonalize the human being. If you allow yourself to be influenced by these errors, you end up thinking of others as mere things, and eventually, you look at yourself as a mere thing. It becomes pointless to talk about God and pointless to talk about life after death.

This trend has led some people to view abortion-on-demand as a basic human right. It also leads them to condone all kinds of bizarre sexual relationships. It leads them to support research for cloning. They end up favoring euthanasia in order to end their lives painlessly, once they get tired of living. They want cloning because they say it will cure diseases. A few are so far from the truth about the human person that they think they can "recreate" themselves once some scientific genius finds a way to reassemble their DNA as it was when they were born.

These errors are the ideological justification for hidden crimes being committed all over the world in unprecedented numbers. The Church calls it the "culture of death." This section is meant to open your eyes to this threat by helping you understand human nature and the human person.

Human nature and the human person

God created man. The Father's only-begotten Son became man. Jesus is perfect God and perfect man. He is not two persons—a divine person called "Son of God" and a human person called "Jesus of Nazareth." No, Jesus is one person in two natures—one person who is both divine and human. These statements make sense only if we can define "nature" and "person."

The Church has always given great importance to defining man and defining human nature. You cannot understand yourself and you cannot understand Jesus unless you have clear definitions. To speak of the mystery of Jesus and the mystery of our own existence we need to answer the perennial question: What is man?

> **FATHERS OF THE CHURCH**
>
> God made us in such a way that, by our very nature, we consist of two elements, thus joining the spiritual with the earthly.
>
> St. Gregory of Nyssa, *The Creation of Man*, 3

St. Thomas Aquinas gave the classic definition: "Man is a rational animal." The term "animal" means that we are physically similar to animals. The term "rational" means that we have intelligence and free will, similar though not identical to that of angels. In the end, though, man is not an animal and man is not an angel. How, then, can we define human nature? What is this physical element that makes us similar to animals? What is this spiritual element that makes us similar to angels?

Before looking at this—before examining the notion of being both body and soul—remember that we also need to define the human person. Besides asking "What is man," we need to ask more subtle questions: Who are we? Where did we come from? Defining the human person begins by defining human nature, but goes beyond it.

When asking "What is man," we are trying to define human nature. *Nature* answers the question: What? *Person* answers the question: Who? When someone asks Who are you, you tell them your name. You would be hard-pressed to give a better answer. In your heart of hearts, you know that you are much more than a name. Some other concept beyond a name is needed to define the human person.

The chapters in this section are an introduction to both questions: What is man? What is the human person? Or if you want to be more personal, the questions would be: What are you? Who are you? Let's start by looking at what it means to be a human person.

The concept of person

Ask any man or woman "Are you a person or a thing?" and they will immediately respond: "I am a person." Despite the depersonalizing effect of modern culture, nobody really thinks he or she is a thing. But what is the difference between *thing* and *person*?

Most creatures are either pure matter (rocks, plants, animals) or pure spirit (cherubim, seraphim). You are more complex because you are both matter and spirit. You are body and soul. You are capable of physical feelings and interior emotions. Being a "little less than God" (Ps 8:5), you also have a mind capable of infinite knowledge and a will capable of infinite love. This complexity is made more mysterious because you are either male or female and will always be male or female.

All these complexities—mind, will, body, gender—are straightforward compared to a greater mystery. There is a further complexity within you that defies exact definition. Even though you will never be able to define it, it is, oddly enough, easy to recognize and identify. It is not your mind. It is not your will. It is not your body. It is not your gender. It is simply *you*. In fact, this is the essence of the human person—you being *you* and me being *me*. It is the mystery of the human *self*—the self I have to give, the self you have to give, if we are ever to discover the reason why God created us.

Do you remember the moment when you were first able to recognize your own existence—when you became aware of yourself? It happened before you knew anything about the existence of mind and will.

The mystery of each person comes down to this. There is a *me* who has written this book and there is a *you* reading it. Billions of other people have the same experience of looking inside and seeing *someone* there. Each one sees a *self*. This *self* is the very definition of a human person.

What do I see when I look inside? What do you see when you look inside? A human person, yes. But not just a person *in general*. You see the unique, unrepeatable man or woman God created years ago—that one and only *you* that will ever exist, the one and only *you* that can never be repeated anywhere in all creation. Therefore, besides asking "*What* do you see when you look inside?" you have to ask: "*Who* do you see when you look inside?"

Discovering who you are

To answer what it means to be a human person review this text from the Second Vatican Council. It speaks of a "certain likeness" between human nature and divine nature. The text states:

Magisterium

When the sense of God is lost, the sense of man is also threatened and poisoned, as the Second Vatican Council concisely states: "Without the Creator the creature would disappear. . . . But when God is forgotten the creature itself grows unintelligible." Man is no longer able to see himself as "mysteriously different" from other earthly creatures; he regards himself merely as one more living being, as an organism which, at most, has reached a very high stage of perfection. Enclosed in the narrow horizon of his physical nature, he is somehow reduced to being "a thing," and no longer grasps the "transcendent" character of his "existence as man." He no longer considers life as a splendid gift of God, something "sacred" entrusted to his responsibility and thus also to his loving care and "veneration." Life itself becomes a mere "thing," which man claims as his exclusive property, completely subject to his control and manipulation.

Thus, in relation to life at birth or at death, man is no longer capable of posing the question of the truest meaning of his own existence, nor can he assimilate with genuine freedom these crucial moments of his own history. He is concerned only with "doing," and, using all kinds of technology, he busies himself with programming, controlling, and dominating birth and death. Birth and death, instead of being primary experiences demanding to be "lived," become things to be merely "possessed" or "rejected."

By living "as if God did not exist," man not only loses sight of the mystery of God, but also of the mystery of the world and the mystery of his own being.

St. John Paul II, *The Gospel of Life*, n. 22

> The Lord Jesus, when he prayed to the Father "that all may be one . . . even as we are one," opened up new horizons closed to human reason. For he implied a certain likeness between the union of the divine persons and the union of God's children in truth and love. This likeness reveals that man, who is the only creature on earth God willed for its own sake, cannot fully find himself except through a sincere gift of self.
>
> Vatican II, *The Church in the Modern World*, n. 24

This teaching identifies a *person* as "the self"—the "I" and the "you." It also speaks of "discovering self"—me discovering *who* I am and you discovering *who* you are. It concludes by pointing towards a goal. The goal is the "union of God's children in truth and love." We are called to form a communion of persons. We are called to form a union of love similar to Trinitarian union. There is only one way for you to reach this goal. You have to make a "sincere gift of self."

The words of the Vatican Council state how crucial it is for a man or woman to give "self." To explain the concept of person more exactly, the Church teaches:

> A human being, whether male or female, is a person, and therefore, "the only creature on earth that God willed for its own sake"; and at the same time this unique and unrepeatable creature "cannot fully find himself / herself except through a sincere gift of self."
>
> St. John Paul II, *The Dignity of Women*, n. 10

By giving *self*—by giving your *you* to someone else—what do you discover? You discover that you are unique and unrepeatable. You discover that God created you not because you are a means to some other end. You discover that God created you "for your own sake."

To be created for your own sake is a way of saying that, in some sense, *you* are the goal. You are not a means towards an end. You are not a stepping-stone. Somehow, you are an end in yourself. Understand this carefully, though. You are not your own end.

You are not an end for yourself. You cannot make yourself happy. You are an end *for someone else*. You can make someone else happy. This is why your happiness depends on giving yourself completely. As we saw before, and will review again later, you can do this either through a vocation to marriage or a vocation to celibacy. Before looking at this, first let's examine what the Church means by saying that you are "unique and unrepeatable."

Being unique, being unrepeatable

The human person is unique. However, we all know the joke: "You're unique, just like everybody else." Besides being unique, you are "unrepeatable." You are unique not because God—or some technician in a lab making clones—has yet to make a copy of you. No one can make another person the same as God made you. There will never be another you.

To discover the meaning of your existence, the Church does not talk about giving your work, your money, your time, or your talents. She talks about you giving your very *self.* Because the gift of self must be reciprocal, you have to do this either in marriage or celibacy. In other words, you need to make this gift of self to another person who will be grateful for your gift—so grateful that he or she is willing to reciprocate.

Here are five key notions needed to understand what it means for you to be a human person:

1. Being a person means you can make a sincere gift of yourself.
2. Being a person means you can accept someone else's gift of self.
3. Being a person means that, to be happy, you have to make a sincere gift of self to some other person who will accept the gift and reciprocate.*
4. This reciprocal giving means entering into a "communion of persons" similar to the union of Father, Son, and Holy Spirit.
5. You are unique and unrepeatable. Therefore, your gift of self is unique and unrepeatable. No other person—no matter who he is, no matter who she is—can make that same gift. As you discover this fact about yourself, you discover who you are.

---

* Those called to dedicate themselves completely to God in celibate life make this gift of self to Christ.

SAINTLY WISDOM

The times in which we are living provide particularly strong confirmation of the truth of what Simeon said: Jesus is both the light that shines for mankind and at the same time a sign of contradiction. If now . . . Jesus Christ is once again revealing himself to us as the light of the world, has he not also become, at one and the same time, that sign which, more than ever, people are determined to oppose?

St. John Paul II (Karol Wojtyla), *Sign of Contradiction*, ch. 22

The mystery of being human

You are a human person. This makes you a great mystery. You are a human being. Though it seems to say the same thing, this is a different mystery. To discover who you are, you also need to understand *what* you are.

An angel does not have a body. Therefore, it takes little effort to figure out why we are not angels and why we cannot be angels, even though we can be like them.

Is being human different from being an animal? Is man just one more step up the ladder of evolution? Is being aware of self just a mechanical ability achieved by having a complex brain? Or is there is a true *self*—a person? Is your awareness of self due to something in your brain or is there a real *someone*—a living soul called "you"? Do you have a mind or just a brain? When you reflect on yourself, are you looking interiorly at the person you are? Or is this self-awareness just a biologically useful fantasy—nerve-cell pulsations that merely create the *sensation* of being a unique person? Is your awareness of self real or just an illusion?

In the same way you ask about your mind by focusing on awareness of self, ask about your will by focusing on freedom. Are you truly free? Or is your sense of choosing just an illusion? Are you the one who decides what you want? Or are your decisions determined by hidden physical forces that control you?

These questions are crucial. You cannot give your very *self* if there is no *you*. You cannot give your very self unless you are capable of making a *free* decision to give. You cannot give your very self if you are a slave programmed by your genes to follow your fate.

Order of Being

God – The Supreme Being

God is perfect. God is infinite. Divine being is the source of all other being. Divine life is the source of all other life. With all-powerful intellect, God knows and judges all things perfectly—past, present, and future. With one immutable act of his divine will, God decides his plan for creation.

Angelic beings

Angels are pure spirits. They have intellect and free will. They have no body. They are not composed of any material element. Their acts of intellect and will do not depend on matter. They know without relying on information from the senses. They know without needing to reason. They grasp the whole intuitively—without proceeding as human intellect often has to, moving one logical step at a time. They make their decisions without experiencing feelings or emotions.

Human beings

Each human being is body and soul. Each person is gifted with intellect and free will, and this makes us like angels. Because of our body, we bear some semblance to animals. Our true similarity, however, is to God—not angels or animals. Man, created male and female, was made in the image and likeness of God. Our most spiritual acts depend on our bodies in many ways, while our physical acts depend, in part, on mind and will; this dependence is obvious when we want to read a novel, cook dinner, engage a friend in conversation, etc. Some acts are external, like walking or eating. Some acts are merely internal, like believing what someone says or rejecting it because we suspect the person is not worthy of trust. Our spiritual acts of mind and will are influenced by the way we feel—the way we feel physically and the way we feel emotionally. The whole world of emotions is the most complex aspect of the human person. This is the world of the human heart, where mind and will, sensations and passions come together.

Animal life

Elephants and mice, dogs and cats possess an interior force that allows them to feel the world around them and manipulate it to get food and water comfort, and pleasure, etc. Animals show only a limited "intelligence" and "power of choice." They operate by instinct. They can only respond to what they feel through the senses.

continued

Order of Being *continued*

Plant life

The vegetable life of flowers and trees—or any other organism lacking a nervous system—is a world without feelings. Lacking the ability to sense other objects, their control over the world is limited to absorbing what is available in their immediate surroundings.

Other beings

Galaxies and stars, rocks and sand, though generally called "non-living" beings, exhibit beauty, dynamism, and structure. Even these beings reflect God's infinite power and majesty.

If you are just an animal, then you cease to exist when you die. If there is no self to be aware of, you have no rights because there is no *you*. If self-awareness is merely a nervous condition made possible by the complexity of your brain, it doesn't matter whether you live or die. It matters even less whether you give your very self to someone else. If you are just an animal, Jesus Christ wasted his life sacrificing himself to save you.

Before looking at the details of your mind, your will, and your body, look at the big picture. Animals do not take up a chisel to leave records in stone for future generations. Animals do not gather together to listen to a concert, act out a play, write a constitution, or celebrate Christmas. Animals have no sense of comedy or tragedy. Animals do not bury the dead or preserve sacred writings containing revelations about eternity. Animals do not build cathedrals where they worship their Creator. We do all these things and more because we are more than animals. We are human persons created in the image and likeness of God.

REVIEW QUESTIONS

1. What do we mean by the term “nature”?
2. What do we mean by the term “person”?
3. Explain the notion: “human person.”
4. What makes man different from angels and animals?

42.

Your Mind

Your mind and will are spiritual powers of the soul. With your mind, you know truth. You can make mistakes when attempting to know the truth. You can be deceived into thinking that something is true even though it is false. When that happens, you can search for the truth and correct the mistakes.

Your mind was made for truth. This is why you feel stress when you tell a lie. The greater the lie, the greater the stress—so much stress that others can sometimes detect it. You feel anger or anxiety when you realize that someone has lied to you. The more intimate you are with the person lying, the greater your anger or anxiety.

If you sense that you have yet to find the truth, you feel a need to search for it. If truth eludes you, you feel frustrated. There is no peace without truth. This is deeply ingrained. God created you for truth. Jesus said, "The truth will make you free" (Jn 8:32).

The most important truth your mind hungers to know is the truth about God. God made human reason capable of intuiting his existence from the beauty and order of creation. Speaking of people from all nations, St. Paul wrote:

> For what can be known about God is plain to them, because God has shown it to them. Ever since the creation of the world his invisible nature, namely, his eternal power and deity, has been clearly perceived in the things that have been made.
>
> Romans 1:19–20

By using human reason, even those who do not have the benefit of revelation can know something about God.

God wants us to know everything about him. Therefore, he has revealed himself to us through Jesus. Your heart is restless until it rests in God; your mind is also restless until you discover the whole truth about Jesus Christ. An honest person eventually wants to know: Was Jesus the Son of God? Why did the Son of God become man?

God expects you to use your mind

Abraham's decision to sacrifice his son Isaac was a heroic act of faith. For Christians, Abraham is "our father in faith" (cf. Rom 4:16). When we look at his decision to put Isaac on an altar and raise a knife to slit his throat, we usually focus on the will-power he needed to obey God. We tend to overlook the way this act of faith depended on using human reason.

It would have been reasonable for Abraham to assume: "God would never ask me to spill the blood of my own child on an altar. Satan might ask me to do that—but not God." Faced with the flat contradiction of this basic assumption, Abraham had to use his mind to understand. He concluded that, after sacrificing his son, God would fulfil the promise he had made about Isaac's future.

How many people bother to think about God? How many use human reason to discover what God wants them to do? How many

Sacred Scripture

The Lord appeared to Solomon in a dream by night; and God said, "Ask what I shall give you." And Solomon said: "Give your servant an understanding mind to govern your people, that I may discern between good and evil . . ."

It pleased the Lord that Solomon had asked this. And God said to him: "Because you have asked this, and have not asked for yourself long life or riches . . . but have asked for yourself understanding to discern what is right, behold I now do according to your word. Behold I give you a wise and discerning mind, so that none like you has been before you and none like you shall arise after you."

1 Kings 3:5, 9, 10–12

. . . That the God of our Lord Jesus Christ, the Father of glory, may give you a spirit of wisdom and of revelation in the knowledge of him . . .

Ephesians 1:17

manage to overcome prejudice, even when they have irrefutable proof? How many draw a conclusion that contradicts their basic assumptions? Abraham had to think. He had to draw such a conclusion. His act of faith required a strong will. It also required a courageous mind. Besides accepting God's command to sacrifice, Abraham had to discern truth when truth was difficult to discern.

God told Abraham he was going to be the "father of a great nation" through his son Isaac (cf. Gen 21:12). God told Abraham he had to sacrifice Isaac (cf. Gen 22:2). As far as we can tell from the Book of Genesis, God never stated that he would raise Isaac from the dead. But to have children, the 12-year-old boy had to live at least a few more years. The Letter to the Hebrews implies that Abraham drew his own conclusion from these facts.

> By faith Abraham, when he was tested, offered up Isaac, and he who had received the promises was ready to offer up his only son, of whom it was said, "Through Isaac shall your descendants be named." He considered that God was able to raise men even from the dead; hence, figuratively speaking, he did receive him back.
>
> Hebrews 11:17–19

Abraham believed that Isaac would resurrect after being sacrificed.

God expected Abraham to put two and two together, come to a conclusion—and then *believe* that conclusion. He expected Abraham to believe something that was not explicitly revealed. Why would he expect so much from Abraham's ability to reason? There is only one logical answer: God trusts the power of human reason. He trusts it so much that he expects us to believe something when it can be deduced from truths that have been revealed.

Knowing truth with certainty

We do not know the exact limits of animal intelligence. Animals have some ability to communicate with each other and with us. Even so, stories about talking animals are just stories.

Fathers of the Church

Now our very eyes and the law of nature teach us that God exists and that he is the efficient and maintaining cause of all things.

Our eyes teach us this because they fall on visible objects, and see them in beautiful stability and progress. If I may say so, these objects are immovably moving and revolving.

Natural law teaches us this because, through these visible things and their order, we reason back to their author.

For how could this universe have come into being or have been put together, unless God had called it into existence, and held it together? Everyone who sees a beautifully made lute, and considers the skill with which it has been fitted together and arranged, or who hears its melody, would think of none but the lute-maker . . . though he might not know him by sight.

. . . Thus reason leads us up to God through visible things.

St. Gregory Nazianzen, *Orations*, XXVIII, 6, 16

Animals never show a sense of choosing between good and evil. They show no inclination to question why they exist or to wonder what will happen to them after they die. They show no ability to reason with abstract concepts about God and creation or justice and peace. We conclude that they have no sense of self-awareness and no spiritual soul. This leads us to appreciate how different we are from animals. Our ability to reason and to choose between good and evil sets us apart from the rest of the visible world.

Your mind starts off blank, knowing nothing at all. But it has the power to grasp truth. By observing reality, you acquire knowledge. As you listen and talk to others, you learn more. You progress from basic needs to basic facts. This means learning to distinguish between true and false, reality and fantasy, good and evil. As you continue to grow, you come to know that God has revealed himself to man. If you are a Christian, you know the mysteries God has revealed through Jesus Christ. You also know that God wants you to believe these mysteries. For instance, you know he wants you to believe that Jesus is the Son of God.

Some people claim that science is the only thing we can be sure of. They are willing to admit that God may exist, that he may have revealed mysteries and that it would be wonderful if he did. But they doubt they are capable of knowing whether any of it is true. They say we cannot define spiritual realities with precision because we cannot see them. The best we can hope for is a vague knowledge that a Supreme Being exists. This knowledge is so vague that we have no means of establishing, among all the world's religions, where to find the truth. Since God's revelation remains beyond the reach of our senses, they claim we will never be sure what we are supposed to believe.

The same people may use this logic to ridicule your faith. They argue you have no grounds for being certain that your beliefs are true. Without being defensive or getting angry, try to explain why they are wrong. The human mind is capable of knowing truth with certainty. It is pointless for them to state that human reason cannot know truth with certainty. If there is no certainty, how can they say they are certain there is no certainty? Anyone who denies the possibility of being certain ends up contradicting himself.

Faith is one of several ways in which we know truth. Faith provides certainty. We can be sure that anything revealed by God is true because God can neither deceive nor be deceived.

Faith is one way of knowing truth

We know the difference between food and poison. We know what is *physically* good for us and what is *physically* bad for us. Similar logic applies to spiritual life. We know the difference between virtue and vice. We can determine what is *spiritually* good for us and what is *spiritually* bad for us. We know the difference between true and false. Human reason gives us the ability to recognize when someone has made an error.

Making an act of faith depends on your ability to reason correctly. If you were incapable of understanding words, all the revelations handed down through Tradition and Scripture would be unintelligible. If you were incapable of knowing truth with certainty, it would be impossible to believe God's revelation. Therefore, it is important to understand the human mind and the various kinds of knowledge.

There are several different kinds of human knowledge: simple observation, scientific knowledge, philosophical knowledge, human faith, and supernatural faith. Whether human or supernatural, faith is one of the main ways you come to know the truth.

- Human faith is knowledge you acquire by believing what other people tell you.
- Supernatural faith is knowledge you acquire by believing what God has revealed.

The way you acquire knowledge through observation, science, philosophy, or human faith is much different from the way you acquire knowledge through God's revelation. You do not need God's grace to recognize a tree when you see one (simple observation). You do not need grace to figure out the law of gravity (science). You do not need grace to perceive that truth cannot contradict truth (philosophy). You do not need grace to know the South Pole exists even though you have never seen it. All you need is someone to tell you his own experience after having seen it (human faith).

Believing God's revelation is different from these other kinds of knowledge. You cannot believe that Jesus is the Son of God unless God gives you the grace to believe it. This grace is a supernatural light given to the human mind, making it capable of accepting all that God has revealed. This grace is a motion of the will that leads you to accept a mystery your mind cannot comprehend. Faith is a gift. Because it is a gift, Christians should never judge those who do not believe in Jesus.

The debate about the origin of man

Understanding God's plan requires knowing where we came from and where we are going. Faith tells us what God has planned for us after death. Knowing where we came from depends on three branches of human knowledge: science, philosophy, and faith.

We know something about the origin of man because God has revealed it. The Bible states that God created Adam and Eve in his own image and likeness. It also states that God formed man out of the "dust from the ground" (Gen 2:7) and then breathed life into him. All men and women living today are descendants of this first couple. Because of Adam and Eve's sin, we now live an existence where evil abounds and virtue is difficult. We know these facts because God revealed them.

Some questions about the origin of man remain open to debate. By scientific investigation, we may get a clearer picture of the past. For instance, we may establish how long ago the first man and woman lived. Such knowledge would complement the mysteries of faith and help us understand more accurately what God has revealed.

Some scientists say that living organisms evolve. They say that, through a natural process, one species can become the common ancestor to several other species. Some scientists apply this logic to man. They claim that man evolved like all other organisms. According to this theory, a species that existed several million years ago is the common ancestor of chimpanzees and humans. Scientific journals and biology textbooks insist that this is a fact. Though they debate the details of how it happened, they say man evolved from a more primitive species.

Some scientists claim *Homo sapiens* is the end result of an evolutionary process. Revelation declares that God created man for a special purpose. Christians have to answer a crucial question. Is it logical to state that man evolved from a lower species while also stating that man is God's image and likeness? It can only be logical if God intervened at some point in the evolutionary process to create the human soul. Is that what happened?

This question is difficult even for those who believe in God. It has become more difficult to answer because some scientists reject belief in God and insist that evolution proves the Bible wrong. In their opinion man evolved from apes *without any intervention* of an intelligent Creator. They say man does not have a soul endowed with intelligence and free will any more than a monkey does. Man's intelligence and free will represent nothing more than a mechanical, biochemical advance in evolutionary development. This argument often concludes with the statement: "We do not need God to explain the origin of man. Science explains *everything* there is to know about *Homo sapiens*. The Book of Genesis is a myth. Evolution is a fact."

In centuries past, this claim caused confusion among believers. Some Christians still argue that the theory of evolution is completely false. Some say it doesn't matter whether scientific facts are true or not. Some say faith and science are "free to contradict each other," thinking that one deals with matter while the other deals with spirit. The Catholic Church accepts none of these positions. She teaches that it is necessary to resolve the conflict. We need to know the truth, especially the truth about man. To find the truth we must begin with the conviction that faith and science cannot contradict each other.

The debate on evolution is only one example among many issues where we depend on faith, philosophy, and science to know the whole truth about man. Conflicts similar to the one about man's origin arise when studying astrophysics, cosmology, neurology, and other fields. Most of these conflicts relate to the key questions posed by theories of evolution: Is man God's special creation? Does man have a spiritual soul? Or are we just a complicated mix of molecules, generated by chance, with the *mere appearance* of spiritual intelligence? Assuming each person does have a soul, how does it interact with the body?

Catholic teaching on evolution

Matter and spirit are different from each other. After forming a human body, God had to create Adam's spiritual soul. Otherwise, Adam would not have been an intelligent being but just an animal with a big brain. Our ability to reason depends on having a brain; but it also depends on having a spiritual soul. Being matter, the big brain of *Homo sapiens* may have been the result of an evolutionary process. But a spiritual soul cannot come from matter.

The Church has explained her teaching about evolution on several occasions. One of the most extensive commentaries came from Pope John Paul II, when addressing an assembly of scientists:

> New knowledge has led to the recognition of the theory of evolution as more than a hypothesis. It is indeed remarkable that this theory has been progressively accepted by researchers, following a series of discoveries in various fields of knowledge. The convergence, neither sought nor

Magisterium

Without philosophy's contribution, it would in fact be impossible to discuss theological issues such as, for example . . . God's creative activity in the world, the relationship between God and man, or Christ's identity as true God and true man. This is no less true of the different themes of moral theology, which employ concepts such as the moral law, conscience, freedom, personal responsibility and guilt, which are in part defined by philosophical ethics.

It is necessary therefore that the mind of the believer acquire a natural, consistent and true knowledge of created realities—the world and man himself—which are also the object of divine Revelation. Still more, reason must be able to articulate this knowledge in concept and argument. . . . [T]heology thus presupposes and implies a philosophy of the human being, the world and, more radically, of being, which has objective truth as its foundation.

. . . Recalling the teaching of St. Paul (cf. Rom 1:19–20), the First Vatican Council pointed to the existence of truths which are naturally, and thus philosophically, knowable; and an acceptance of God's revelation necessarily presupposes knowledge of these truths. . . . Although faith, a gift of God, is not based on reason, it can certainly not dispense with it. At the same time, it becomes apparent that reason needs to be reinforced by faith, in order to discover horizons it cannot reach on its own.

St. John Paul II, *Faith and Reason*, nn. 66–67

fabricated, of the results of work that was conducted independently is, in itself, a significant argument in favor of this theory.

It is possible that the human body, following the order impressed by the Creator on the energies of life, could have been gradually prepared in the forms of antecedent living beings.

St. John Paul II, *Address to the Pontifical Academy of Sciences*, October 22, 1996

Because scientists have yet to agree on one coherent explanation, St. John Paul II went on to state that "rather than *the theory* of evolution, we should speak of *several theories* of evolution."

From the beginning of the debate on evolution, the Catholic Church has held that evolution might explain the way God prepared Adam's body. But the Church adds that God *had to intervene* to create Adam's soul. No evolutionary process will ever explain Adam's intellect and free will. A theory of evolution may provide a glimpse of where we came from. It cannot explain the whole story. In the address quoted above,

St. John Paul II also stated: "If the human body takes its origin from preexistent living matter, the spiritual soul is immediately created by God."

Any theory of evolution claiming to prove that man has no spiritual soul or that this soul evolved from matter is necessarily mistaken when making this claim. The physical and biological sciences study matter. Such a theory of evolution would not be scientific. It would be the same as a scientific theory claiming to prove that angels do not exist.

Our mind depends on receiving information from the senses. Some kind of "processing" of information takes place physically in the brain and, among many other factors, depends on being awake or asleep. Therefore, science has much to say about certain physical aspects of human knowledge and consciousness. However, science can say nothing about *where* the spiritual soul came from. The human soul has *no matter* to detect or measure. For a spiritual soul to come into existence, an act of creation is necessary—and only God can create.

The Church teaches that God created Adam and Eve, because only he could create the human souls of the first man and woman. Therefore, the question about human evolution focuses only on the body. Can an evolutionary process explain how the body of the first man came from an animal species? The Church teaches that this is a question open to scientific investigation. The Bible states that God used preexisting matter to create Adam's body. It does not say *how* God did it. If science can prove that man's body evolved from some prehuman species, then it is a scientific truth that we should accept. But that is as far as science can go; it has nothing to say about the origin of man's soul.

The human soul is spiritual. It lies beyond the ability of science to investigate. This point is crucial when trying to understand human reason. Your intellect is one of the spiritual faculties of your soul. We cannot fully understand our intellect if we reduce it to the biological functions of the human brain.

Different ways of knowing truth

To appreciate the full wonder of human intelligence, we need to define science, philosophy, and faith. We want to understand how these different ways of knowing truth are related to each other.

Some people fall into fundamentalism. They fail to distinguish clearly between faith and science; they fail to recognize these as two different ways of knowing truth. Other people fall into scientism. They assume that science is the only reliable source of knowledge—as if science were the only rational way of judging reality and the only reliable way of knowing the truth. This assumption distorts their understanding of the human mind and human reason. They fail to grasp how all human beings—even scientists—rely on philosophy and faith to know truth.

Philosophy is not "scientific" in the usual sense of the word, but it is entirely *rational*. It is true knowledge acquired by using human reason.

Faith relies not on human reason but on revelation. Even so, faith is true knowledge. The human mind knows truth—and knows it with certainty—when accepting what God has revealed.

To know the whole truth about man, we need to draw on all three areas of human knowledge.

- **Science** is knowledge that comes from observing matter and deducing the laws that govern it.
- **Philosophy** is knowledge that comes from understanding being and nature.
- **Faith** is knowledge that comes from accepting God's revelation.

Each one of these constitutes true knowledge. Each uses a different method for arriving at its conclusions. The conclusions from each method must be properly demonstrated. If they are, we acquire true knowledge in each case. In some cases, the knowledge we gain from science may be confirmed by philosophy or revelation, and vice versa.*

Science

Science is knowledge about the way matter is organized. Science investigates objects perceived by the senses and tries to understand how

* Note that the following discussion is limited. It does not account for some distinctions: For instance, it does not explain the role of common sense (our ability to make judgments through simple observation); it does not explain the role of mathematics in science, etc.

they work. Science relies on empirical data or measurement. We gather empirical data by observing events that the senses are capable of perceiving. We observe the events either directly with our senses or indirectly using instruments. A scientific instrument, like a telescope, is an extension of our senses.

Scientific method relies on mathematics. We abstract quantities from the things our senses perceive and use mathematics to deduce conclusions about those quantities.

Science deals only with evidence about matter. Science can neither prove nor disprove the existence of spiritual realities. Because it measures matter and only matter, science can say nothing about man's spirit and nothing about God.

Faith is different from science. It is not based on experiment and proof. It is based on revelation. When God tells us that something is true, we believe it because he revealed it.

God can reveal things about the material world as well as things about the spiritual world. God has told us very few things about the material world. He has told us nothing about the forty-six chromosomes that biologically define *Homo sapiens*. We can only determine the existence of these chromosomes by scientific study. But God has revealed that he created Adam and Eve and that they rebelled against him in the beginning. Man's rebellion was a spiritual event that lies beyond anything science can prove or disprove.

Philosophy

Philosophy and science both rely on observation. Science is knowledge about the way things happen. Philosophy is knowledge about why things exist. Science measures quantities and works out the laws that control matter. Philosophy establishes the logic needed to distinguish between true and false, good and evil, being and nothing. Scientific knowledge is taken from empirical data—from measurements of size, mass, time, force, etc. Philosophical knowledge also begins with the observation of empirical realities. From these realities, human reason deduces facts that we could call "intellectual data." Intellectual data consists of the principles that are self-evident to our intelligence; for instance, the principle of non-contradiction and the principle of proportionate cause.

It is impossible for a thing to be and not be at the same time. If you exist, no one can correctly state that you do not exist. This is the principle of non-contradiction.

Every effect has a proportionate cause. If a wad of paper flies towards the teacher from the back of the classroom, he won't believe the students if they all claim innocence. There has to be a reason *why*. This is the principle of proportionate cause.

To find truth philosophically, we start with self-evident principles. Relying on further insights gained from observation, we use these principles to deduce more elaborate conclusions. For instance, we use philosophy to explain how our intellect and free will function; this enables us to understand our need for truth and love. Because human reason depends on the senses, philosophy requires the insights of science to give a full picture of our spiritual faculties.

Philosophy is crucial to our understanding of God's revelation. For instance, understanding the difference between matter and spirit requires philosophical reasoning. Think of an analogy with the colors red and blue. A color-blind person cannot tell the difference between red and blue. A normal person sees the difference immediately. Though it is difficult to *define* red and blue, it is easy to *see* the difference. In fact, it is impossible to explain the difference to a person who cannot see it for himself. Something similar happens with matter and spirit. It is hard to define matter and spirit. Just as most people can only say that red and blue are different colors, most can only say that matter and spirit are different realities. Note that it is just as hard to define matter as it is to define spirit. Science works with matter, but it cannot define matter. The Bible talks about the difference between the body and the soul, but it does not define either matter or spirit. Matter and spirit are philosophical concepts.

Science depends on philosophy

Human intelligence judges whether a statement is true or false. I can only formulate the law of gravity if I can judge whether my formulation of the law is true or false. Truth and error cannot be reduced to a material reality. The capacity to judge the truth or error of a statement is a spiritual capacity. If all reality were matter, there would be no such thing as science. Science cannot investigate spiritual realities, and yet, without the existence of spiritual realities—without human intelligence—there would be no science.

Science relies on philosophical principles—for example, the principle of proportionate cause. This principle states that every effect must have a proportionate cause. When observing a falling object and calculating gravitational force, scientists assumes the logic of cause and effect. They assume something must explain why the object falls. Nobody looks for a cause to explain an effect, unless one thinks an explanation is needed. You won't look for the cause of an effect unless you're convinced that all effects have a proportionate cause.

Scientists also need philosophy to make certain that scientific method provides valid conclusions. We have to judge our capacity to know truth. This judgment is a spiritual act. We conclude that scientific investigation, when properly conducted, provides true knowledge. If we were incapable of stating this philosophical principle, scientific investigation would be worthless. Science relies on philosophy *both before and after* doing its calculations.

Faith

Science and philosophy provide knowledge based on reason. Faith is knowledge based on revelation. When God reveals something, we accept this knowledge because of God's authority. If by using reason we can verify a particular truth revealed by God, then we know this truth both by faith and by use of reason. However, most of the truths God has revealed are mysteries in the strict sense of the word. What God has revealed about forgiving our sins goes beyond the capacity of reason to deduce or confirm. No scientific investigation or philosophical inquiry will ever determine whether Jesus was the Son of God, whether heaven and hell exist, whether or not we will rise from the dead at the end of the world, etc.

Faith goes beyond reason. Even so, faith depends on having the ability to reason. God cannot reveal himself to rocks, trees, or monkeys.

For God to reveal himself to a creature, the creature needs spiritual intelligence. The creature needs an ability to distinguish between true and false, an ability to connect truth with goodness and lies with evil and, most importantly, an ability to know truths about a world that lies completely beyond our senses.

Because you are capable of knowing truths about the spiritual world, God can reveal mysteries to you through the Church. When you accept these revelations, you possess true knowledge even though you have never seen the spiritual world described by these mysteries. For instance, you cannot see your sins being forgiven at the moment of baptism. You cannot see grace entering your soul. But through faith you can be absolutely sure that baptism forgives your sins and gives you grace.

Putting science, philosophy, and faith together

These three kinds of knowledge cannot contradict each other. Scientific truth cannot contradict philosophical truth. Scientific truth cannot contradict God's revelation. Science tells us truths about the universe. Because God created the universe, he cannot contradict himself by revealing as true something that is not scientifically true. All that we learn by using reason must be compatible with the mysteries God has revealed. The Church teaches:

> Even if faith is superior to reason, there can never be a true divergence between faith and reason, since the same God who reveals the mysteries and bestows the gift of faith has also placed in the human spirit the light of reason. This God could not deny himself, nor could the truth ever contradict the truth.
>
> Vatican I, *Dogmatic Constitution on the Catholic Faith,* ch. 4

The truths God has revealed cannot contradict the truths we know from science or philosophy. When there appears to be some contradiction between a scientific claim and our understanding of God's revelation, the contradiction is only a contradiction in appearance. Either the scientific investigation is not yet complete and is therefore inconclusive or our understanding of God's revelation is not yet complete and needs to be refined. God cannot use one truth to contradict another truth.

> ### *Wisdom of the Saints*
>
> Knowledge is one thing, virtue is another. . . . Philosophy, however enlightened, however profound, gives no command over the passions, no influential motives, no vivifying principles. . . . Quarry the granite rock with razors, or moor a vessel with a thread of silk, then may you hope with such keen and delicate instruments as human knowledge and human reason to contend against those giants, the pride and passion of man.
>
> Bl. John Henry Newman, *The Idea of a University*, V, 9

Science, philosophy, and theology all provide true knowledge about man. Each branch of knowledge offers insights into man's nature that lie outside the scope of other branches of knowledge. Science tells us things revelation and philosophy cannot. Philosophy tells us things science and revelation cannot. Revelation tells us many things—even about man's body—that neither science nor philosophy can tell us.

Jesus Christ will return in glory to judge the living and the dead. All people will rise from the dead with the same body they had in this life. All people will go to heaven or hell, where even in their flesh they will enjoy eternal pleasure or suffer eternal pain. If God had not revealed these mysteries, we would never know them. Because God has revealed them, he expects us to believe them.

Faith is knowledge. But it would be wrong to put the truths of revelation on the same level with the truths of science. Faith tells us about a world that will last forever. Science tells us about a world that is passing away. Faith shows us how to become God's children and enter into his kingdom. Science cannot tell us what heaven is like or where it is, much less how to get there. Faith leads us to experience God's love and joy. Science can only bow in reverence before God's plans for our eternal happiness. Nevertheless, it would be a mistake to despise the truth we learn from scientific investigation.

Relativism and subjectivism

Few Christians lose their faith thinking that science has proven the Bible wrong. Science leads to the truth about this world. And the truth about this world can lead us to God. The greatest source of confusion today comes not from science but from false philosophies.

Some people say there is no absolute truth. They insist it is impossible to say anything with certainty. The only certainty for them is that there are no certainties. This is self-contradictory. Even so, some people think this way.

If there is no absolute truth, everything is relative. If there is no absolute truth, how can God reveal mysteries? God may have appeared to Abraham and Moses. Jesus Christ may have preached the gospel. His revelation may apply to us. Then again, maybe it doesn't. In the world of relativism, God's revelation is just one more reality that is constantly changing.

Relativism implies subjectivism. If there is no absolute truth, there is no objective truth. All knowledge is merely subjective: I have my truth and you have yours. What is true for me today may not be true for me tomorrow. Each person believes whatever he or she wants to believe. Having many religions is an advantage. It allows for options. Each person can pick and choose to find the kind of God that suits his or her spiritual needs. Those accustomed to thinking this way claim that abortion may be evil for some people but not for others. They say it's good for some people to believe in God because it makes them happy, while for others it's a waste of time because they don't need it.

Relativism says we are all essentially good persons as long as we don't hurt anybody. Subjectivism says we're good as long as we're sincere. Our own inner comfort becomes the measure of whether or not we are being sincere. Using these criteria, a doctor performing an abortion is not hurting anybody as long as the woman feels comfortable with her decision; a serial killer is not guilty of murder as long as he remains convinced that killing others makes him happy.

A person who accepts the philosophy of relativism cannot have faith. Jesus called himself "the truth" (Jn 14:6). He said, "Heaven and earth will pass away, but my words will not pass away" (Mt 24:35). His parable about the storm descending on the house fits perfectly. Those who embrace objective truth build their house on rock. The storm of public opinion does not shake their faith, since their faith depends on God—not on fads, fashions, or the mood of the moment. Those who live by the philosophy of relativism build their house on sand. They cannot resist criticism. When the storm of public opinion crashes down on them—when the majority thinks it's absurd to accept the Church's teaching—they give up their faith and agree with the majority.

Those influenced by relativism and subjectivism may not notice their lack of faith. While insisting that they believe, they may not realize they have made the word *belief* meaningless. However, it's easy to explain how absurd it is for these people to live by the code of relativism. When a suicide bomber kills thousands of their friends and relatives, it makes no sense for them to keep saying: "There is no absolute truth. Morality is subjective." The bomber's act is always wrong, no matter what he thinks and no matter why he does it.

Truth is not a deal we negotiate, looking for the cheapest price. Truth is fixed by the very nature of the way God created us. The Church defends the power of man's reason to grasp the truth—and to hold on to it. We are capable of distinguishing between what is momentarily true and false—for example, whether the sun is shining. We are also capable of distinguishing between what is always true and always false—for example, that God is the Creator of heaven and earth.

Keeping your faith strong

God has a plan for creation. He has revealed it. He wants you to keep it clear in your mind. To keep a strong faith, you need to pray, receive the sacraments, reject evil habits, live a virtuous life, and do God's will. You also need to exercise your mind. Read the Bible every day. Study the Church's teachings. When faced with doubt, seek advice from someone who can explain the truth to you.

It is not enough to reject the arguments of those who promote error. Besides learning how to recognize the difference between what is true and false, learn how to explain your faith to others. Remember St. Peter's words:

> Always be prepared to make a defense to any one who calls you to account for the hope that is in you, yet do it with gentleness and reverence . . .
>
> 1 Peter 3:15

If you cannot explain your faith to others, your faith is weak. To have a strong faith, you have to study. "Faith seeks understanding," St. Anselm said.

Influencing others

To be faithful to Jesus Christ, you have to defend your faith against attacks from people who have no faith. One of the most serious challenges comes from those who tell you it is foolish to believe since faith contradicts the facts of science. The truth of faith and the truth of science come from the same God. These two orders of knowledge must be compatible. They cannot contradict each other. But no matter how clearly you explain this, some people will accuse you of rejecting the conclusions of science.

Many people will be open to your religious convictions. However, with some people, do not be surprised that you run up against a wall. Jesus said, "You will be hated by all for my name's sake. But he who endures to the end will be saved" (Mt 10:22). This is not an invitation to pessimism. We have to put our Lord's warning together with the other command he gave when telling us to expect opposition: "The harvest is plentiful, but the laborers are few; pray therefore the Lord of the harvest to send out laborers into his harvest" (Mt 9:37–38).

Some of those who oppose faith may be willfully blind. Most people are just confused. Perhaps until now, those who hold a prejudice against Christian faith or the Catholic Church have never met anyone smart enough and bold enough to shake their prejudices. Perhaps God has not given them as much grace as he has given you. Speak to them. Try to help them.

What matters is that you be faithful. St. Paul says: "Be watchful, stand firm in your faith, be courageous, be strong. Let all that you do be done in love" (1 Cor 16:13–14). Wherever you are, you can be sure of this: There are a few, maybe many, who will be amazed at your refusal to compromise in matters of faith and morals. Your determination and your wisdom will force them to think twice.

REVIEW QUESTIONS

1. Are faith and science compatible? Explain.
2. What do we know about the origin of man?
3. Why do we need philosophy?
4. How do relativism and subjectivism prevent people from believing what God has revealed?

43.

Your Will

Mind and will are the two spiritual faculties of a human person. With your mind, you know truth. With your will, you desire what is good or you desire something that, being good only in appearance, will do harm. With your will you make decisions. The most important decision you ever make is the decision to love—and to be loved.

Created for love

You were created for love. If you live without love, you feel lonely. Some times people talk about "finding fulfilment." They feel empty and look for something to fill that emptiness. The sense of having no meaning in life, the sense of being lost, the sense of being empty—these are not entirely negative. There are reminders that God created you not for just any love but for infinite love. This is the love you experience when God unites you to himself.

You face many choices in life. Your most radical choice is to choose between life and death. You can choose eternal life, which is union with God. Or you can choose eternal death, which is separation from God forever.

The culture of death portrays God as the enemy of freedom. The worst consequence of the culture of death is to lock God out of the world and treat him as a stranger. The Church calls it an "anti-culture" (Benedict XVI, *God Is Love*, n. 30).

The Church proclaims the "gospel of Life." She has a mission to open the minds and hearts of all people to their most basic needs—their need for life, their need for love, their need for God.

> We need to bring the *Gospel of Life* to the heart of every man and woman and to make it penetrate every part of society. This involves above all proclaiming the core of this Gospel. . . . It is the proclamation that Jesus has a unique relationship with every person, which enables us to see in every human face the face of Christ. It is the call for a "sincere gift of self" as the fullest way to realize our personal freedom. . . . The meaning of life is found in giving and receiving love . . .
>
> St. John Paul II, *The Gospel of Life,* nn. 80–81

You must find love if you want to be happy. That's obvious. What may be less obvious is that, to be happy, you have to be "in love" with somebody. In other words you have to enter into a personal relationship with some other person where you give love and receive love.

God is no stranger to romance. He wants us all to fall in love. To understand your place in this revelation, you may have to ask God who it is you're supposed to fall in love with. It might take time and effort to find the answer. Don't get discouraged. Before getting bogged down in the details, fix a simple conviction in your heart. Whether you're like Moses, called to reach the top of the holy mountain so you can spend your life face-to-face with the Almighty, or you're the kind of person who hesitates to venture further than your own home, you need to fall in love. No matter who you are, that is why you are alive.

God's freedom

God created you with a free will. You are free. Before examining human freedom, let's look at God's freedom. He was free to create or not create. He was free to create in one way rather than another. Just as human intelligence dimly reflects God's infinite knowledge, our limited freedom dimly reflects his infinite freedom.*

Some people wonder why God decided to allow evil to exist—why, for instance, totally innocent babies suffer. The *Catechism* asks:

> Why didn't God create a world so perfect that no evil could exist in it? With infinite power God could always create something better. But

* This chapter's analysis of freedom adds to the ideas given on freedom and law in chapter 19.

> with infinite wisdom and goodness God freely willed to create a world in a state of journeying towards its ultimate perfection. In God's plan this process of becoming involves the appearance of certain beings and the disappearance of others, the existence of the more perfect alongside the less perfect, both constructive and destructive forces of nature. With physical good there exists also physical evil as long as creation has not reached perfection.
>
> *CCC*, n. 310

God allows for physical good (beauty, wealth, pleasure) and physical evil (deformity, poverty, pain). He also allows for moral good (obedience, love, holiness) and moral evil (rebellion, hatred, sin). People sometimes ask why God allows any evil at all.

One day God will make the world perfect. In the meantime, God has given us the freedom to choose between good and evil. When we choose evil, we are the ones responsible for the "imperfections" that irritate us. Being free means we can do evil. It also means we can love others. If God had created a world where we had no choice, would we be better off? There would be no evil. But would there be any love?

Freedom allows us to cling to God or reject him. Our decisions are real decisions. Since choice is personal, perhaps it is best to use personal terms. My freedom is so radical that *my decision* in this life determines where I will end up in the next life—heaven or hell.

Sacred Scripture

Do not say, "Because of the Lord
I left the right way";
for he will not do what he hates.
Do not say, "It was he who led me astray";
for he had no need of a sinful man.
The Lord hates all abominations,
and they are not loved by those
who fear him.
It was he who created man
in the beginning,
and he left him in the power
of his own inclination.
If you will, you can keep the
commandments,
and to act faithfully is a matter
of your own choice.
He has placed before you fire and water:
stretch out your hand for whichever
you wish.
Before a man are life and death,
and whichever he chooses will be
given to him.

Sirach 15:11–17

God does not impose salvation on me. To be saved, I have to be open to his mercy. If I choose to reject it, I will be lost forever. The point is that I am free. I choose.

Our freedom reflects the perfect freedom of the One who created us. If God did not have a free will, he could not create us with a free will. He could not give us a perfection that he himself was lacking. The key to understanding free will is to remember that it is a perfection. It makes us more like God. God's freedom is perfect. He can desire no evil. Our freedom is limited because our intelligence is limited. Our freedom means we are capable of evil—capable of thinking that something is good when it is not, and wanting it because we think it is good. Because God cannot make that mistake, he cannot choose evil.

You can choose what is truly good. You can also fill your soul with the most wicked desires imaginable—thinking it is good for you. Your intellect can become so distorted by errors, lies, prejudices, and misunderstandings that you can end up wanting something evil, thinking it will make you happy.

Our freedom is mysterious. It is one of the greatest mysteries of God's creation. The *Catechism* explains:

> Angels and men, as intelligent and free creatures, have to journey toward their ultimate destinies by their free choice and preferential love. They can therefore go astray. Indeed, they have sinned. Thus has *moral evil,* incommensurably more harmful than physical evil, entered the world. God is in no way, directly or indirectly, the cause of moral evil. He permits it, however, because he respects the freedom of his creatures and, mysteriously, knows how to derive good from it. As St. Augustine says, "Almighty God, because he is supremely good, would never allow any evil whatsoever to exist in his works if he were not so all-powerful and good as to cause good to emerge from evil itself."
>
> *CCC,* n. 311

Our freedom explains why there is evil in the world. Evil exists not because God made some creatures evil. All that God created—everyone that God created—was good in the beginning. Evil exists only because at times we choose evil.

God will solve the problem of evil once and for all at the end of the world. He will separate good and evil definitively. For now, he reveals what is good; he forgives sins, and he asks us to look forward to the coming of his kingdom, where "he will wipe away every tear" (Rev 21:4).

Looking at God's freedom and his infinite wisdom raises questions about human freedom. Some people wonder how we can be truly free if God knows with infallible knowledge whether we will be saved or condemned even before we are born. This is one of the most difficult questions about human freedom. We will come back to it at the end of the chapter. Before tackling the question of predestination, we need to look at the nature of man's will and understand what we mean when stating that we are free. We say we have a free will. We discussed the nature of human freedom earlier. Now we need to ask a further question: Just how free are we?

Our evil inclinations do not negate freedom

Some people get addicted and then make a thousand excuses rather than face the need to overcome their addiction. What is true for drugs applies to other addictions: alcohol, pornography, violence, etc. Why do human beings embrace evil and cling to it even to the point where they destroy themselves in the process? We can say that they see it as a good. But how can they continue to think something is good when their choices cause them to suffer? Why do evil habits tend to obscure the intellect so much that addicts often refuse to recognize the connection between choice and consequence?

This blindness is perhaps the most mysterious aspect of free will. The will converts the mind into a kind of trial lawyer. The will has "made up its mind" to cling to evil and "hires" the mind as a "trial lawyer" to come up with whatever argument it can to justify the will's deliberate choice of evil.

Some say that people are not free. They argue that people acquire evil habits because they are genetically disposed and conditioned by family and social environments to desire these evil habits. This view is usually called "determinism." There is some truth to the idea that everyone has an inclination to at least one bad habit and that this happens both because of the way we were born (genetic code) and the way we were raised (nurturing). According to Christian revelation, all men and women, stained with original sin, are born with evil tendencies. Satan also pushes us towards evil. There is yet another factor—the *structures of sin* in society and the world around us. These "structures" are the "disastrous conditions and intolerable situations" like poverty and ignorance that make it extremely difficult for men and women to choose good. Such structures are the "result of the accumulation and concentration of many personal sins" (St. John Paul II, *Reconciliation and Penance*, n. 16).

> **Fathers of the Church**
>
> If someone brings us to Christ by force, we "believe" without wanting to. This is violence, not freedom. We can be forced to enter a church. We can be forced to approach the altar. We can be forced to receive the sacrament. But we can only believe if we want to.
>
> St. Augustine, *Treatise on John*, 26, 2

If we were not free, we would have no conscience. Conscience reproaches us for evil deeds and approves us for good deeds. This is a sign of freedom. If we were not free, we would not even be aware of the distinction between good and evil. If we were not free, we could never reject an evil habit and desire to change. Nor would we be responsible for our actions.

Generally, the ones who deny the existence of free will end up denying the existence of moral law. They usually conclude that abortion, drug abuse, fornication, pornography, and homosexual acts are good for those who are inclined towards these habits.

Christian revelation states that we fall into sin by our own free choice and that, with God's grace, we can overcome sinful habits. St. James says:

> Let no one say when he is tempted, "I am tempted by God"; for God cannot be tempted with evil and he himself tempts no one; but each person is tempted when he is lured and enticed by his own desire.
>
> James 1:13–14

If we sin, it is not because God created us that way or because the devil forced us. Sin happens because we deliberately choose evil.

We do not sin because we are forced into it. Everyone has temptations. By enduring temptations, Jesus showed us that they are an ordinary part of life. St. Paul encourages Christians not to exaggerate their difficulties:

> No temptation has overtaken you that is not common to man. God is faithful, and he will not let you be tempted beyond your strength, but with the temptation will also provide the way of escape, that you may be able to endure it.
>
> 1 Corinthians 10:13

God will give you the grace you need to overcome temptation. Many times the easiest way to overcome a strong temptation is to run away from it. It requires a quick and simple act of the will—running away the same way you would run if you saw an angry mob coming to attack you.

If we are fixed—not merely inclined but truly fixed—by genes or environment or some combination of the two, we are not free. If we are not free, then we are not responsible. If we are not free, then God's revelation is reduced to the mere announcement that some will be condemned (because they were born with evil inclinations they cannot control) and some will be saved (because God decided to have mercy on them). But if we are neither free nor capable of freedom, why did Jesus say, "You will know the truth, and the truth will make you free" (Jn 8:32)?

No one can accept God's revelation until he recognizes the fact that we are free. However, human freedom has been damaged by the sin of Adam and Eve. And this does make it difficult to be good. We are all born with the *fomes peccati*—an inclination towards sin. Jesus says:

> Enter by the narrow gate; for the gate is wide and the way is easy, that leads to destruction, and those who enter by it are many. For the gate is narrow and the way is hard, that leads to life, and those who find it are few.
>
> Matthew 7:13–14

It is easier to follow our evil inclinations—and many do. But we are free. When Jesus said, "Enter by the narrow gate," he was affirming a fact that we know from experience. We can if we want to. And the beauty of "taking the hard road" is this: we'll be happy if we do.

Freedom means more than being able to choose

The freedom you are meant to enjoy in the beatific vision poses the most interesting question about the human will. In heaven no one ever chooses evil. Will you still be free? Obviously, you have to be free, or heaven would be more like hell. And yet the question is difficult to answer. How can you be free if you are not free to choose?

God gives you freedom to choose. But being able to choose is not the essence of freedom. If it were, you would cease to be free once you made any choice that required you to give yourself completely. Choice is not the essence of freedom. The essence of freedom is making a decision to commit yourself *because you want to.*

No one pretends that this fact is obvious. Far from being obvious, it is one of the great paradoxes of human nature. Like any paradox, it puts together two statements that seem to contradict each other. For instance, take the classic paradox about building a skyscraper. The building towers over the city skyline. And yet, as every builder knows, "If you want to go up, first you have to go down." The taller the building you want to build, the deeper the foundations have to be.

Human freedom is a paradox. God made you free so that you could find love. But to find love, you have to do something that, at first, seems foreign to freedom. You are free to choose and yet, you will never be truly free until you decide to give your very self to someone else by locking yourself into a commitment that no one can ever break—a commitment that not even you can break.

Freedom to believe what God reveals

Focusing on what it takes to believe in Jesus Christ is another way of understanding human freedom. Imagine that you grew up in a Jewish family. Your father and mother both come from Jewish families. Being devout Jews, they go to the synagogue every Saturday. Following ancient traditions, you learn Hebrew so that on the day of your Bar

Mitzvah, you can read aloud from the Torah. You call yourself a son of Abraham with great pride. Because of the peculiarity of present circumstances, the best school in the city is run by Christians. Since your parents want to make sure you get a good career in a good university, they send you to that school. While you are there, you learn all about Jesus and even have a chance to attend Mass in the chapel. Learning about the Christian faith, you are struck by some phrases of sacred Scripture that you also hear in the synagogue.

After several years of attending these classes and reading the New Testament, you feel a subtle spiritual tension that robs you of your peace. You once heard your parents talk about the Messiah. You begin to think that maybe the Church is right. Maybe Jesus is the Messiah. Maybe you should believe in him. All the teachings of the Church ring true. The lives of the saints impress you. And for the first time in your life you wonder if maybe God wants you to get baptized and become a Christian.

More time passes. You study, you talk, you seek advice, and you ask a thousand questions. What started out as a search for the truth has hardened into a conviction. You have found the truth, but there is an obstacle. If you convert and become a Christian, your father will disown you. His reaction will be so radical that he will never allow you to set foot in his home again. He will cut you off completely—as if you were a traitor and a criminal. He will look at you as one condemned by God for abandoning the faith of Israel.

You know that you are not abandoning your faith. On the contrary, you know that the faith of your childhood has led you to Jesus. You know that Jesus is the Messiah that your own parents taught to look forward to seeing some day. Far from committing any crime that would offend God, you know that all your sins will be forgiven when you profess your faith in Jesus Christ and get baptized. But becoming an outcast before your own father troubles you.

If you were in that situation, what would you decide?

This case defines the nature of freedom at its deepest level—there inside your conscience, where you are alone with God.

Following God's will can be difficult. Even some Catholics have experienced this as they discovered God's plans for their future. They know their parents will get upset with any mention of dedicating themselves completely to God. Whether it is a Jew contemplating baptism or the lost sheep who wants to start over again or a devout Catholic contemplating vocation, changing your life to do God's will means leaving everything behind.

On one hand, you feel as if you are the luckiest person in the world. What God has shown you seems too good to be true—and yet it is true. On the other hand, you have to endure reproach from all the people who love you most. Without them and their love for you, you would never have discovered the true meaning of your existence. And yet, paradoxically, your family can be the greatest obstacle to making your dream come true.

Jesus knows that making a decision to accept God's will causes great upheavals in your life. He equated it with being crucified on a cross.

> Do not think that I have come to bring peace on earth; I have not come to bring peace, but a sword. For I have come to set a man against his father, and a daughter against her mother, and a daughter-in-law against her mother-in-law; and a man's foes will be those of his own household. He who loves father or mother more than me is not worthy of me; and he who loves son or daughter more than me is not worthy of me; and he who does not take his cross and follow me is not worthy of me. He who finds his life will lose it, and he who loses his life for my sake will find it.
>
> Matthew 10:34–39

Jesus does not want you to hate anybody. He wants you to love everyone, even your worst enemy. But put God first. You only begin to love others when you do what God wants. If you disobey God, your love for others is false. If others claim to love you but get in the way of doing what God wants, he expects you to ignore them—no matter how dear to you they are, no matter how much you depend on them. If it means being an outcast for the rest of your life, do it anyway.

The price is high. So is the reward. You find life. You discover an eternity of love with the One who is love. Never worry that people do not understand. If they really love you, they will come to understand your choice eventually. When they do, they will be proud of what you did. And if anyone ever accuses you of not being free, you can smile. Jesus takes human freedom so seriously that he demands heroic decisions.

Freedom to love

To understand freedom, you need to understand love. You need to know what it means to give love and receive love. Amazingly enough, many people go through life with no idea of what this means—or worse, they have the wrong idea of what it means to give love and receive love.

Perhaps the greatest error about human freedom was summarized in the phrase of the atheist who stated that: "Love can last or love can burn, but it cannot do both." When Jesus came to reveal the God who is love, he gave us a glimpse of how intense—and how eternal—love can be. He said he would baptize us with fire and the Spirit. Like the bush Moses saw on the mountain, God's fire burns without consuming. Lust is also a fire, but a fire that destroys everything in its path and only wanes when there is nothing left to destroy.

St. Paul said that Jesus' love for the Church is the model of all spousal love. By sacrificing himself for his bride, Jesus showed us how much a man and woman can love each other. He also showed us how much God loves us. He revealed to man what God wants man to be. He showed us how this everyday family love can prepare us for infinite divine love. Before he could do that, though, he had to show us that love and lust are not the same thing.

To understand love, there is no better text than St. Paul's "hymn to love":

> Love is patient and kind; love is not jealous or boastful; it is not arrogant or rude. Love does not insist on its own way; it is not irritable or resentful; it does not rejoice at wrong, but rejoices in the right. Love bears all things, believes all things, hopes all things, endures all things.
>
> 1 Corinthians 13:4–7

These words describe all relationships of love. First and foremost, they describe God's love for us.

> We love, because he first loved us.
>
> 1 John 4:19

We can love one another—even when we don't "feel like it"—because God loved us first. We can be patient and kind with other—even when we don't "feel like it"—as long as we open our hearts to God's gift. "So faith, hope, love abide, these three; but the greatest of these is love." (1 Cor 13:13).

Finding true love depends on finding God

Of all the many human relationships we could choose when defining the various aspects of love, it is best to choose spousal love because this is the image and likeness of God's Trinitarian love. The great saints talked about "falling in love" with God. Some of them wrote commentaries on the Song of Songs—a selection of poems in the Old Testament exalting the love of the bridegroom and bride on their wedding day. They saw human love as the only possible way to express what happens when a Christian comes to "obtain the glorious liberty of the children of God" (Rom 8:21). The various aspects of spousal love apply, analogously, to the love Christians will experience more perfectly when they see God face-to-face.

Generosity, passion, intimacy, benevolence, commitment, communion: these are aspects of conjugal love. It's like looking at the many faces of a diamond. Any one face is beautiful, but no one description of love captures the whole reality. They all combine as a whole that nobody will ever perfectly describe. These various dimensions of spousal love apply as much to those who choose celibacy as those called to marriage.

Many make the mistake of thinking that celibacy means being cold and empty of emotion. They think that, being pure spirit, God is somehow "heartless" and that dedication to celibacy requires a Christian to give up any desire for that "intoxication" of mind and will, body and soul, that people associate with "being madly in love." They do not realize that the opposite is true. The whole reason for celibacy is to show the world that true love does not depend on the flesh but on the will. True love does not depend on sensual pleasure but on something greater. Sensual pleasure can be good, but it is fleeting and ever so limited. It cannot satisfy anyone who longs for a love that is infinite and eternal. But what is this "something greater"?

Ultimately, the only real love is the love that comes from God. While this seems to define celibacy, it also defines married love. When God joins a man and woman together, the husband and wife discover the reason why they were created. They discover that they exist *for each other*. They discover that they were created to be God's image and likeness by becoming one body and one spirit. They discover that "the meaning of life is found in giving and receiving love." They discover that this giving and receiving depends on God joining.

How is this related to freedom and the human will? The mind rests—the mind reaches the end of its quest for truth—when it can gaze upon the beauty of reality in a simple act of knowing all that it can possibly know. We call this contemplation. Since you were created to know God, your mind rests only when you see him as he truly is. Something similar is true of the will. The human will reaches the satisfaction of its longing for love only when it takes possession of the infinite good. We call this joy. Since you were created to love God, your will rests only when you possess God and he takes possession of you.

Some people assume that the Church is the institution in the world most directly responsible for frustrating the desires of men and women to experience love. Why is this prejudice so widespread? With bishops and priests dedicated to celibacy, people mistakenly assume that the Church is opposed to sexual pleasure and only tolerates it so that men and women will have lots of children.

The Church does teach that one of the purposes of marriage is to have children because God created it that way (cf. Gen 1:28). The Church does teach that celibacy for the kingdom of God is better than marriage because celibacy anticipates the glory of eternal life when we will be like angels (cf. Lk 20:36; 1 Cor 7:38). However, it is not true to say that the Church is opposed to sexual pleasure and only tolerates it. She is opposed to adultery, fornication, and all the other perversions of human nature. She is opposed to them precisely because these perversions frustrate any desire that men and women have to find love. The

Church wants all of us to discover love, to enjoy it, and treasure it. She points out these two ways of finding it: marriage and celibacy.

The connection between mind and will

Your will is for loving, and your mind is for knowing. That is accurate, as far as it goes, but something is missing. True enough, you can love only because you have a free will, but it is not your will that loves others. *You* are the one who loves them. Even when it comes to knowing, remember that knowing truth means a lot more than reading books. God created you to know him and to know others. Again, you can know only because you have a mind, but it is not your mind that knows people. *You* are the one who knows them.

"You shall love the Lord your God with all your heart." After saying this, Jesus added a phrase, saying that you must also love God "with all your mind" (Mt 22:37). He once again hints at the connection between knowing and loving when he told his disciples:

> I know my own and my own know me, as the Father knows me and I know the Father . . .
>
> John 10:14–15

The connection between mind and will is crucial to understanding friendship.

Friendship

If you want to discover what it means to fall in love with one person—and ultimately with Christ himself—you must first make friends with the people you live and work with. The love of friendship is the foundation of all other love. As you try to make friends, you quickly discover that making friends exposes the ultimate connection between mind and will. You can only be good friends with someone you trust, that is, with someone who tells you the truth.

Try to be friends with everybody. Never count another human being as your enemy. Or as Jesus phrased it: "Love your enemies, do good to those who hate you . . ." (Lk 6:27).

Magisterium

Love can be "commanded" because it has first been given. . . . [I]n God and with God, I love even the person whom I do not like or even know. This can only take place on the basis of an intimate encounter with God, an encounter which has become a communion of will, even affecting my feelings. Then I learn to look on this other person not simply with my eyes and my feelings, but from the perspective of Jesus Christ. His friend is my friend. Going beyond exterior appearances, I perceive in others an interior desire for a sign of love, of concern. This I can offer them not only through the organizations intended for such purposes, accepting it perhaps as a political necessity. Seeing with the eyes of Christ, I can give to others much more than their outward necessities; I can give them the look of love which they crave. Here we see the necessary interplay between love of God and love of neighbor which the First Letter of John speaks of with such insistence. If I have no contact whatsoever with God in my life, then I cannot see in the other anything more than the other, and I am incapable of seeing in him the image of God. But if in my life I fail completely to heed others, solely out of a desire to be "devout" and to perform my "religious duties," then my relationship with God will also grow arid. It becomes merely "proper," and loveless. Only my readiness to encounter my neighbor and to show him love makes me sensitive to God as well. Only if I serve my neighbor can my eyes be opened to what God does for me and how much he loves me.

Benedict XVI, *God Is Love*, nn. 17–18

Loving someone who hates you is hard. Loving someone who lies to you is also hard. Friendship depends on trust. If someone deliberately lies to you and does so habitually, you will never be very good friends. This works both ways. You also have to be an honest person; if you're not, you'll never be good friends with anybody.

The Bible speaks of friendship as one of the great treasures in life: "A faithful friend is a sturdy shelter. . . . A faithful friend is an elixir of life." The same text goes on to state an equally important fact about friendship: "Whoever fears the Lord directs his friendship aright." (cf. Sir 6:14–17). Your closest friends will be those who believe the same truths about God that you believe.

Friendship is defined above all by sharing. You cannot make friends with others if you are stingy. A person who will not share with you is not your friend. Sharing begins with simple things like food and drink, possessions, money, time. Friendship solidifies as you and your friend share the experience of working and relaxing together.

The depth of your friendship ultimately depends on sharing joys and sorrows. The deeper the joys and sorrows you share, the deeper your friendship. Two people who share only superficial joys and sorrows—because their team wins or loses a game—enjoy no more than a superficial friendship. Two people who share that richest joys and sorrows—communion with God—experience a level of friendship that words cannot describe.

It was the more intimate kind of friendship that Jesus had in mind when he told the Apostles at the Last Supper:

> No longer do I call you servants, for the servant does not know what his master is doing; but I have called you friends, for all that I have heard from my Father I have made known to you.
>
> John 15:15

To be their friends, Jesus shared with his disciples the most untouchable treasure he possessed—the knowledge he had of his Father. Before he could do this, he had to teach them many things. Finally, they reached the point where they trusted him and he trusted them.

Your best friend will be the one who knows the most about you. This assumes, of course, that he reciprocates. You have to be able to say that you know all the deepest secrets of his life. It is this intimate stage of knowing him as fully as you are known (cf. 1 Cor 13:12) which explains what Jesus means when he asks you to love God "with all your mind."

For a Christian, friendship is more than a treasure, that is, more than a source of joy and consolation. It leads to spreading the gospel. You make friends by sharing your experience of faith with others. Knowing how much peace your friends will enjoy by accepting the Good News, you want to tell them all about it. If they accept, you become better friends. Perhaps they won't accept and you have to be patient. Even then, you will be better friends for having shared the best you have with them.

Predestination

Having examined one of the mysteries of freedom—the freedom to love—we have to look at another mystery of freedom that is even more difficult to understand. It is the mystery of predestination.

God is infinitely merciful. He understands our weakness. He is willing to forgive the greatest sinners that ever lived. As long as they repent, they are counted among the saints. Scripture says they are "predestined" (cf. Rom 8:28–30). These are the ones "he chose . . . before the foundation of the world, that [they] should be holy and blameless before him" (Eph 1:4).

If you are one of those that God knows will be saved, your name has been "written in heaven" (Lk 10:20). God knows the future. He knows who will win the next lottery. He knows the winning number of the next lottery, even though it will be chosen at random. He knows when the world will end. He knows when you will die. He knows whether you are going to heaven or to hell.

God's plan is to save everyone. The Church teaches:

> Predestination concerns all human persons, men and women, each and every one without exception.
>
> St. John Paul II, *The Dignity of Women*, n. 9

Wisdom of the Saints

Not only is work the background of man's life, it is a means and path of holiness. It is something to be sanctified and something which sanctifies.

It is well to remember that the dignity of work is based on love. Man's great privilege is to be able to love and to transcend what is fleeting and ephemeral. He can love other creatures, pronounce an "I" and a "you" which are full of meaning. And he can love God, who opens heaven's gates to us, makes us members of his family and allows us also to talk to him in friendship, face-to-face.

This is why man ought not to limit himself to material production. Work is born of love; it is a manifestation of love and is directed toward love. We see the hand of God, not only in the wonders of nature, but also in our experience of work and effort. Work thus becomes prayer and thanksgiving . . .

St. Josemaría, *Christ Is Passing By*, nn. 47–48

God's plan is to save everyone—but only as long as each one *wants* to be saved. God respects our freedom so much that he will not force anyone to enter his kingdom.

After Jesus was crucified, Judas Iscariot hung himself. Many ponder the mysterious words Jesus spoke at the Last Supper: "The Son of man goes as it is written of him, but woe to that man by whom the Son of man is betrayed! It would have been better for that man if he had not been born" (Mt 26:24). They ask: Why was Judas born? Some answer quoting Jesus again when he insisted that the prophecies foretelling the crucifixion had to be fulfilled. Speaking to his Father about the Twelve Apostles, Jesus said, "I kept them in thy name, which thou hast given me; I have guarded them, and none of them is lost but the son of perdition, that the scripture might be fulfilled" (Jn 17:12). Judas is the "son of perdition," the one who would fulfil the scriptural prophecy saying that the Messiah would be sold for thirty pieces of silver—exactly the amount of money Judas took from the Pharisees to betray Jesus (cf. Mt 26:15–16, 27:9). If God knew ahead of time that Judas was going to betray Jesus and exactly how he was going to do it, was it really Judas' fault?

Scriptural prophecies were "fulfilled," i.e., they turned out to be true, because God knew what would happen long before it happened. In the same way, he knows who will be saved and who will be condemned. Some might ask: "Is that fair? Why would God create someone knowing the person will go to hell forever?"

We can focus on the positive. Many will be saved. But that only provokes more questions. If God knows that you are going to be saved—St. Paul talks about being chosen in Christ "before the foundation of the world" (Eph 1:4)—why bother struggling to live a Christian life? Some try to get around this conundrum by insisting that virtue is a sign of salvation. Even if that were true—and it is not—it does nothing to answer a vexing personal question: "Is my wayward friend, spouse, or child going to stay in hell forever because he or she was predestined to go there?"

Condemning the error of those who say some people are predestined to go to hell, the Church has always insisted that God never created anyone to do evil, to suffer evil or to be evil. St. Paul wrote: "[God] desires all men to be saved and to come to the knowledge of the truth" (1 Tim 2:4). No one goes to hell *because they were incapable* of accepting God's mercy. The only ones who go to hell are those who *deliberately refuse to be sorry* for their sins. This is the sin against the Holy Spirit that "will not be forgiven, either in this age or in the age to come" (Mt 12:32).

God is so merciful that he will save absolutely anyone as long as they are sorry for their sins and do what God asks them to do, which is to repent and receive his grace through the sacraments. Great spiritual miracles take place every day, like the one when the "Good Thief" who asked Jesus, "Remember me when you come into your kingdom." We get a glimpse at God's all-powerful mercy when we listen to Jesus' response: "Truly, I say to you, today you will be with me in Paradise" (Lk 23:42–43).

In the end, though, people want to know about those who die without repenting, without being reconciled with God as far as we can tell. Jesus spoke frightening words about people going to hell: "Depart from me, you cursed, into the eternal fire" (Mt 25:41). Is it really their fault? God knew they were going to end up in hell before they were born. Did they have any choice?

Many people find it hard to answer this question. It confuses them because they fail to distinguish between intellect and will.

With my will, I *decide* to go to church today. With my intellect, I *know* why I need to go. Some people know they need to go to church and yet refuse to go. Knowing something is not the same thing as wanting it. This distinction is the key to understanding predestination. We must distinguish between our intellect and our will. We must also distinguish between what it means for God to know something and what it means for God to decide something.

God knows the past, present, and future perfectly because he stands outside of time. He sees it all in one simple vision. God can see the future infallibly because the future is present to him.

Did God know, even before creating him, that Satan was going to go to hell forever? Yes. He knew Satan was going to do evil things. Does that mean God wanted Satan to do evil things? No. Satan was the one who decided to embrace evil and become the evil one. God did not want him to do it. Was Satan free to be a good angel and serve God? Yes. But Satan said, "I will not serve!" If he had chosen to be good, God would have known beforehand that Satan was going to choose good instead of evil. God is not the one who decided that Satan would do evil things. Satan decided that.

The same logic applies to Judas Iscariot or anyone else. God knew what Judas was going to choose. Therefore, centuries before the event, God could inspire the prophets to speak of a man receiving thirty pieces of silver to betray the Messiah (cf. Zech 11:12–13). God did not want Judas to betray Jesus. God did not plan for Judas to do it. Knowing the future is not the same as deciding what will happen.

The same logic describes the good or evil you do. You are free. God knows in advance what you are going to do. But this does not diminish your freedom. You do not know what choices you are going to make in the future. God knows, but you don't. Just because he knows does not mean that he chooses. God does not choose. You choose. God knows what you will choose, but *knowing* is the not the same thing as *choosing*. That is why everyone must struggle to do what God wants. Many great things depend on whether you choose good or evil.

REVIEW QUESTIONS

1. What is free will?
2. How do evil inclinations affect our will?
3. Explain why it is not necessary to have a choice in order to be free.
4. What do we mean by predestination?

44.

Your Body

After speaking of human reason and free will, you may get the mistaken idea that you are composed of parts—as if your mind, will, and body were pieced together the way a car is assembled from wheels, chassis, engine, etc. The Church does not call the body and soul "parts" of the human person. She prefers to speak of "elements." This explains the *integrity* of the human person.

Integrity means you are a whole—a unity, a single piece. Machines are different. You can replace a car's engine with a new one. If your mind, will, flesh, and emotions were just parts, they could be replaced with new ones and you would be the same person.

The integrity of the human person explains the Church's teaching on resurrection. You are happy in heaven when enjoying the beatific vision. But you can only be perfectly happy when God raises you from the dead in your own body.

> The truth about the resurrection clearly affirmed, in fact, that the eschatological perfection and happiness of man cannot be understood as a state of the soul alone, separated from the body. . . . It must be understood as the state of man definitively and perfectly "integrated" through such a union of the soul and the body . . .
>
> St. John Paul II, *Theology of the Body*, p. 240

You can fully enjoy life in God's kingdom only after you are whole again. This will happen when your body and your soul are united in the resurrection.

Death leads to the destruction of the body. Dust returns to dust. When you rise from the dead, it is *your* body that rises. God somehow reconstitutes the very same body that was destroyed by death. Resurrected bodies will be different from earthly bodies—either glorious (if saved) or corrupt (if damned). Still, the body you have in this life is the same one you will have in the next life.

There will be no marriage or procreation after the resurrection. We will be "like angels" (Mk 12:25). The risen body will be glorious: "It is sown a physical body, it is raised a spiritual body" (1 Cor 15:44). Even so, our bodies will retain their gender. On one hand, "the sense of being a male or a female in the body will be constituted and understood in that age in a different way from what it had been from the beginning." On the other hand, "human bodies, recovered and at the same time renewed in the resurrection, will keep their masculine or feminine peculiarity" (St. John Paul II, *Theology of the Body*, p. 239).

The human body

The human body—your body—is a great mystery for several reasons. The Son of God became a man with a body of flesh and blood. That body was nailed to a cross. That body rose from the dead after being buried in a tomb. That body is in heaven now. If you ever hear someone suggest that the Church is opposed to the human body, you can smile, knowing that this is not true.

When you get baptized, your body becomes a temple of the Holy Spirit. Why is your body so important to God that he wants to live there? Before looking at this mystery, remember that your body is mysterious for another reason. It is made out of matter. Matter is mysterious. We do not completely understand matter. Though we experience matter directly, it has always been hard to define it.

Matter is a mystery*

When examining anything, we ask: "Where did it come from?" For instance, we can ask, "Where did God come from?" The only answer we

* In physics, matter is distinct from light. In the present context, I refer to all physical realities as matter—mass, energy, forces, fields, particles, etc.

can give is to reply, "He has no beginning and no end. He did not come from anything. He has no cause and no creator. He simply *is*."

If you ask an atheist where matter comes from, he would probably say, "Matter has no explanation. It did not come from anything. It simply is. It is both eternal and infinite." Anything that began to exist must depend on something that came before it. But is being eternal and infinite the same as being divine?

We know from revelation that matter did not always exist. But for the sake of inquiry, let's suppose that matter has always existed. Even then, a question remains: Why does matter behave the way it does? Who designed it to behave that way? Being able to see matter and touch it does not make it less mysterious than a spirit. It only makes it more familiar. Being able to write mathematical equations that describe the behavior of matter does not explain it. It doesn't tell us where it came from. It only makes it easier to predict how it will behave.

Even if matter were, in a material sense, both eternal and infinite, and even if we had perfect equations defining every aspect of matter, questions arise. The equations themselves simply become part of the mystery. What makes the equations work? Have they always worked that way? Will they always work that way? Where did they come from? Who designed them?

Because we look for answers to such questions, human reason leads us to conclude that God created matter. But the point here is not to focus on proving that God exists. The point is to focus on the mystery of matter. Whether finite or infinite, whether it has always existed or it had a beginning, matter remains a mystery, even if you're an atheist.

Sacred Scripture

"Food is meant for the stomach and the stomach for food"—and God will destroy both one and the other. The body is not meant for immorality, but for the Lord, and the Lord for the body. And God raised the Lord and will also raise us up by his power. Do you not know that your bodies are members of Christ? . . . Do you not know that your body is a temple of the Holy Spirit within you, which you have from God? You are not your own; you were bought with a price. So glorify God in your body.

1 Corinthians 6:13–15,19–20

We cannot explain how God created matter any more than we can explain how he created spirits. God had to use infinite power to create an angel. He had to use infinite power to create matter. If the whole universe consisted of nothing but dust and its existence was without beginning or end, God still needed infinite power to make it exist. The gap between nothing and something is infinite—even the gap between nothing and a piece of dust.

Where did matter come from? Those who believe in God usually give one of the following two answers. Either they say it came from nothing or they say it came from God. Neither one of these answers is precise. It is true that God created matter *out of nothing*. But this does not mean that matter *came from* nothing. Although God created all matter, it is not entirely accurate to say that matter came from God. Matter comes from God only in the sense that he used infinite power to bring it into existence. But God is pure spirit. He is totally immaterial. Matter is, in some sense, the opposite of God. Matter did not come from God. God had to create it out of nothing.

Your body is matter. It is made out of the same stuff as rocks and stars. You can see your body. You can feel it. This makes it familiar to you. But like all matter, your body is a mystery.

Spiritual acts depend on the body

Man is not an animal. Man has a spiritual mind and a free will, making him different from animals. The human body is not an animal body. Human sexuality is not animal sexuality.

A monkey's ability to use a rock or a stick to get food gives us insights into the nature of *material* intelligence. Being both *material and spiritual*, human intelligence allows us to engage in activities that go far beyond matter: to wonder where we came from, design tools, tell stories, make theories about space and time, celebrate birthdays, make commitments to our friends, seek justice for the poor, long for a better world, look for the meaning of life, etc. The most exalted of all these abilities is our ability to communicate with God. This communication with God will be expanded in the next world when we can "see" God, interiorly, through the beatific vision.

Even our evil habits suggest an enormous difference between animals and humans. Animals do not torture others and enjoy watching them suffer. Animals do not go out and get drunk when feeling lonely. Animals do not herd their companions into concentration camps, use them as slave labor, and then send them to the gas chambers.

Some people have made the mistake of assuming that human intelligence is merely material, like that of the animals. They assume that given enough brain cells—arranged in the right order by "natural selection" or some other natural force—an animal would be capable of the whole range of spiritual activity we are capable of. They think humans are capable of spiritual activity *only because of the material complexity of the human brain.*

The human brain is more highly developed than the brain of any other creature. Without a highly developed brain, we would not be able to reason. The mistake is to assume that this material development explains why we are capable of reason. Nevertheless, even our most spiritual knowledge comes through our senses. St. Paul seems to acknowledge this fact when he says:

> But how are men to call upon him in whom they have not believed? And how are they to believe in him of whom they have never heard? And how are they to hear without a preacher? . . . So faith comes from what is heard, and what is heard comes by the preaching of Christ.
>
> Romans 10:14, 17

Even faith depends on certain physical acts—in particular, hearing the word of God. This interweaving of matter and spirit is the real mystery of man.

Similar logic applies to understanding the spiritual nature of the human will. Chimpanzees can choose between oranges and bananas. The freedom of the human will goes beyond choosing our favorite meal.

God has created within us a longing for infinite love. Each person is a huge, gaping hole that only God can fill. Paradoxically, this emptiness explains how great we are. No animal could ever experience this infinite void inside the way we do. They cannot wilfully acquire senseless addictions to narcotics and vanities. We do it to deaden our frustrated desires for eternal happiness.

Evolution will never explain our ability to know the truth and love one another. This is not a prejudice based on man's superiority. It is a conclusion based on what it means to know and to love. Since knowing and loving are spiritual acts, only someone with spiritual powers can perform them.

To love another person intimately, you have to know the other person and trust the other person. If I am ever to love, I must first be aware of self and then give myself to another person who is equally aware of self. The other person must be aware of receiving not just any gift but a gift of self—and then reciprocate the gift by giving self in return. Knowing self and knowing another person cannot reduce to matter because the very concept of "self" goes beyond matter.

The human soul cannot be reduced to matter. We cannot reduce either truth or love to matter. To know, one has to distinguish between what is true and what is false. These concepts do not reduce to matter. To love by making an irrevocable gift of self, one has to make a commitment. Such decisions do not reduce to time and space.

FATHERS OF THE CHURCH

Just as bread that comes from the earth, after God's blessing has been invoked upon it, is no longer ordinary bread, but Eucharist, formed of two things, the one earthly and the other heavenly: so too our bodies, which partake of the Eucharist, are no longer corruptible, but possess the hope of resurrection.

St. Irenaeus, cf. *CCC*, n. 1000

Knowing truth and loving others are spiritual acts. Having a spiritual soul makes us mysterious. But having a body does not somehow make us easier to understand. On the contrary, we are the most mysterious of all creatures because we are both matter and spirit.

Even though knowing truth is a spiritual act, you come to know things through your senses. Even though loving another person is a spiritual act, you cannot give your *whole self* to someone else without giving your body. You cannot give your very self without allowing the other person to take possession of you so completely that your body "belongs" to that person. Your whole body must belong to the other person so much that you say, "I belong to you"—whether in marriage because your body belongs to your spouse or in celibacy because your body belongs to God.

This brings us back to where we started. The human body is a mystery. Throughout the Scriptures, there is a hint that Satan is jealous of man: "Through the devil's envy death entered the world" (Wis 2:24). He could not be jealous of our intelligence and free will. His are far superior. Of all visible creatures, we are God's masterpiece. That much should be obvious. There is more. Because the Word became flesh—because God's Son became a man with a male body just like any other male body—the mystery of the human body has reached infinite proportions. Even among angels, we are God's masterpiece. One day, a man named Jesus will rule over all creation—even over the angels.

Being a body

Though we tend to speak of our body as something we have, this is inaccurate. Your body is not something you own, like a possession. Thinking of your body as a possession may lead to the mistake of thinking: "I can do whatever I want with my body. It's mine." This mistake is often disguised in an abstract statement—for instance, when people talk about men and women having "reproductive rights." This tends to be a roundabout way of saying, "Nobody tells me what to do with my body. It's mine."

God tells us what we should or should not do with our bodies. He has plans for our bodies. He will raise all men and women from the dead at the end of the world.

God did not create you and then put you in a body. Your body is yours, but your body is not a thing. Your body is not a cage for your soul. Your body is not a box for the real you somewhere inside. Your body is not a tool for accomplishing your goals in life. Your body is not a toy you can use to entertain yourself. When God created your body, he created you. You are a creature who is both body and soul.

Perhaps the best way to express this is by exaggerating and saying: "You are your body." This is an exaggeration, because you are body and soul. To express the truth about the body, the Church teaches:

> The body reveals man. This concise formula already contains everything that human science could ever say about the structure of the body . . .
>
> St. John Paul II, *Theology of the Body*, p. 47

The body reveals man. Your body reveals who you are.

Perhaps the easiest way to understand this idea is to look at gender. Your body *determines* whether you are male or female. Your body also *reveals* whether you are male or female. The *physical* quality of being male or female makes you *spiritually* male or female. If you are male, you use your intelligence and free will the way men use them. If you are female, your use of intelligence and free will displays feminine characteristics. It's not just your body that is male or female. The whole person—all that you are—is either male or female.

The body reveals God's image and likeness

Your body expresses the need to exist for someone. How does your body reveal this need? To answer this, we have to go back to the Book of Genesis. Man became God's image and likeness by being created male and female. The Church teaches:

> When God Yahweh says: "It is not good that the man should be alone" (Gen 2:18), he affirms that, "alone," man does not completely realize this essence [the very essence of the person]. He realizes it only by existing *"with someone"*—and even more deeply and completely: by existing *"for someone."*
>
> St. John Paul II, *Theology of the Body*, p. 60

Adam's masculine body reveals the true Adam because it reveals that he was created for Eve. Eve's feminine body reveals the true Eve because it reveals that she was created for Adam. This becomes clearer when we examine Adam's solitude—that moment in time when he was alone.

The Bible says that Adam was alone until God created Eve. Even though God was with Adam—and Adam could talk to him and hear him—Adam was alone. The Bible does not say that Adam *felt* lonely. His solitude was something that philosophers call "metaphysical." It wasn't just a feeling; it was a fact. More than feeling alone, Adam *knew* he was alone.

Adam could work. He could take care of the garden. He could give names to all the animals. He knew what each animal had been created to do. Because of their bodies, the animals bore a certain resemblance to the human body: arms and legs, eyes and ears, head and shoulders, etc. And yet it was obvious to Adam that he was alone. He knew he was different from all the animals.

God said, "It is not good that the man should be alone" (Gen 2:18). God decided to make a companion for Adam. By creating a companion for Adam, God was completing his plan. By creating both male and female, God made a creature that was his image and likeness.

Adam's solitude was more mysterious than simply feeling alone. He was alone because he could not figure out the meaning of his life. He suffered a profound experience of being alone because his life did not make sense. He was alone because God had created him for someone and that person did not yet exist.

The body reveals our longing for something greater

It is good to look at Adam's solitude because it explains something about each one of us—and about our bodies. The Church teaches that the experience of solitude applies to all men and women:

> [M]asculinity and femininity . . . are *two "incarnations"* of the same metaphysical solitude before God and the world. They are the two ways of "*being a body*" and [are] at the same time [two ways of being] man, which complete each other. They are two complementary dimensions of self-consciousness and self-determination and, at the same time, two complementary ways of being conscious of the meaning of the body.
>
> St. John Paul II, *Theology of the Body*, p. 48, emphasis added

Being male is one way of "being a body." Being female is the other way of "being a body." Being male is one "incarnation" of man's solitude. Being female is the other "incarnation" of man's solitude. This boils down to a simple fact. Whether you are man or woman, you life will only make sense when you discover why God has created you.

No matter how complete your comfort and pleasure, no matter how numerous your riches, no matter how spectacular your achievements, no matter how many friends and relatives you have, you can still be alone in this world. More than feeling lonely, you sense solitude when you realize that something crucial to your happiness is missing. You realize that your life is empty and meaningless.

Can someone be rich and successful and yet feel empty? Can someone be surrounded by nice people and yet feel lonely? Obviously. But some people still make the mistake of thinking the loneliness and the emptiness will go away if they can just get more pleasure, more comfort, more money, more things, more friends—or whatever. People trying to distract themselves this way never find relief. The emptiness doesn't go away. The loneliness doesn't go away. In fact, the emptiness and loneliness get worse the more they try to fill their lives with distractions.

You were not created for comfort and pleasure. You were not created to achieve spectacular deeds. You were not created to amass wealth. You were not even created to help lots of people live better lives. All these things are good, but they are not enough. You were created for something greater.

Both a man and a woman go through this experience, but in slightly different ways. Without getting into the differences here, remember that it is your body that reveals the mystery of human "solitude." To paraphrase the Church's teaching quoted above, we can say that you only understand the "meaning of the body" when you realize that you were created to "exist *with someone*—and even more deeply and completely by existing *for someone*." You will always be alone in this world until you find out what you were created for—*who* you were created for. Either you discover the vocation that God invites you to follow and then follow it, or you will never be happy.

"Body and soul" in the Bible

It would be good to clarify some biblical phrases about body and soul that often confuse people.

Sacred Scripture uses various terms when speaking of the composition of the human being: flesh, blood, body, breath, heart, soul, and spirit. The biblical texts use the terms flesh, body, and blood for both man and animals. Just as some texts use the word "breath" to refer to a man's *life*, other texts use the same word to refer to the life of animals (cf. Ps 104:29). Though people speak of the "animal soul" of a dog or a horse and how it dies when the animal dies, sacred Scripture always reserves the word "soul" to describe the life or spirit of a man or a woman.

Jesus spoke of man as flesh and spirit: "The spirit indeed is willing, but the flesh is weak" (Mk 14:38). He also used the terms "body" and "soul" to describe a human being:

> And do not fear those who kill the body but cannot kill the soul; rather fear him who can destroy both soul and body in hell.
>
> Matthew 10:28

Death comes when your body has been destroyed either by the ravages of disease and old age or some other disaster. Body and soul can both be "destroyed" by the "second death" in the "lake of fire."

> This is the second death, the lake of fire; and if any one's name was not found written in the book of life, he was thrown into the lake of fire.
>
> Revelation 20:14–15

Magisterium

Nowadays Christianity of the past is often criticized as having been opposed to the body; and it is quite true that tendencies of this sort have always existed. Yet the contemporary way of exalting the body is deceptive. Eros, reduced to pure "sex," has become a commodity, a mere "thing" to be bought and sold, or rather, man himself becomes a commodity. This is hardly man's great "yes" to the body. On the contrary, he now considers his body and his sexuality as the purely material part of himself, to be used and exploited at will. Nor does he see it as an arena for the exercise of his freedom, but as a mere object that he attempts, as he pleases, to make both enjoyable and harmless. Here we are actually dealing with a debasement of the human body: no longer is it integrated into our overall existential freedom; no longer is it a vital expression of our whole being, but it is more or less relegated to the purely biological sphere. The apparent exaltation of the body can quickly turn into a hatred of bodiliness.

Christian faith, on the other hand, has always considered man a unity in duality, a reality in which spirit and matter compenetrate, and in which each is brought to a new nobility. True, eros tends to rise "in ecstasy" towards the divine, to lead us beyond ourselves; yet for this very reason it calls for a path of ascent, renunciation, purification, and healing.

Benedict XVI, *God Is Love*, n. 5

The whole person, body and soul, is reduced to abject misery when condemned with Satan to eternal fire after the resurrection. This explains what Jesus meant when he talked about both body and soul being "destroyed."

The biblical passages just quoted say much about hell. Indirectly they also reveal the mystery of the human person. All men and women are a unity of body and soul here on earth. All the saints are destined to be a unity of body and soul in heaven. Perhaps we could say that the men and women condemned to hell will be a "disunity" of body and soul where the body and soul are "stuck" together but warring with each other: spirit against flesh and flesh against spirit (cf. Gal 5:16–17).

Special meanings of "soul" and "spirit"

Scripture often identifies the human person as a creature of body and soul. However, sometimes the word "spirit" is added. St. Paul wrote:

> May the God of peace himself sanctify you wholly; and may your spirit and soul and body be kept sound and blameless at the coming of our Lord Jesus Christ.
>
> 1 Thessalonians 5:23

This echoes the way the Virgin Mary speaks, when saying, "My soul magnifies . . . and my spirit rejoices . . ." (Lk 1:46–47).

These phrases refer to a soul *and a spirit*. However, this is not meant to imply that we have two different invisible elements inside of us any more than "flesh" and "body" refer to two different kinds of matter. Flesh and body are two ways of referring to the same physical reality. "Soul" and "spirit" can be used interchangeably to refer to the same immaterial element of the human person.

Still, St. Paul uses the words "soul" and "spirit" as two different ideas. Before we can understand what he means, we need to examine the reality of human emotions.

Sensations, emotions, and passions

Our physical senses allow us to see and touch; hear, smell, and taste. We feel cold, heat, pleasure, pain, etc. Because of the way our mind works, our physical sensations engage our mind. It's as if our senses push us to use reason in order to observe, to reflect, to know, and to make judgements. Although our senses make us similar to animals, our physical sensations differ from those of animals in one crucial respect.

An animal feels cold when the temperature drops at sunset; but it cannot reflect on its experience and conclude: "It's cold." Much less can the animal stir up hope for the future, encouraging itself or its companions with the promise: "It will get warm when the sun rises tomorrow." A human being draws these conclusions—"almost without thinking," we say—though in fact the conclusion is possible, and practically automatic, because humans naturally tend to think.

Whether you judge a simple thing like temperature change or a complex reality like seeing someone staring at you, your power of physical sensation is tightly bound up with spiritual activity—with thinking and desiring. This is so true that a conscious human being cannot restrict the experience of feeling sensations to a merely animal level. This is why you will always suffer pain or enjoy pleasure more intensely than an animal does.

This is where your emotions and passions come in. Passions refer to those emotions that are felt with intensity. The *Catechism* explains:

> The passions are natural components of the human psyche; they form the passageway and ensure the connection between the life of the senses and the life of the mind. Our Lord called man's heart the source from which the passions spring.
>
> There are many passions. The most fundamental passion is *love*, aroused by the attraction of the good. *Love* causes a *desire* for the absent

Wisdom of the Saints

St. Francis sought occasion to love God in everything. He delighted in all works coming from God's hands. From the vision of joy on earth, his mind soared aloft to the life-giving source and cause of all creation. In everything beautiful, he saw the one who is beauty itself. He followed his Beloved everywhere by following the likeness of God imprinted on creation. Using all things, he made a ladder so that he could climb up and embrace the one who is all-desirable.

St. Bonaventure, *Major Life of St. Francis*, 9, 1

> good and the *hope* of obtaining it; this movement finds completion in the *pleasure* and *joy* of the good possessed. The apprehension of evil causes *hatred, aversion,* and *fear* of the impending evil; this movement ends in *sadness* at some present evil, or in the *anger* that resists it.
>
> *CCC*, nn. 1764–1765 (names of the *passions* are in italics)

This description lists names for the *passions* that are also names for *acts of the will*; for instance, love and hatred. Emotional feelings and acts of the will are so tightly bound together that many people confuse the two. An emotion is not a decision. It doesn't matter how strong the emotion is, it is not a deliberate act of the will.

To distinguish passions and acts of the will, take the following example. Love *as a passion* means that some good attracts you very strongly; this passion is an urge within that makes you feel like taking possession of the good. Love *as an act of the will* means that you make a decision to take possession of the good. Note that you can feel attracted to some good, and yet walk away from it no matter how strong the attraction is. Your passions are not free. Your will is. For this reason, you must use willpower to train your passions. If you do, you will usually feel attracted only to those things that are truly good.

The human heart

The human heart is like a place within us where mind, will, and passion come together. To grasp this idea, let's go back to sacred Scripture where it speaks about soul and spirit, clearly distinguishing between the two:

> For the word of God is living and active, sharper than any two-edged sword, piercing to the division of soul and spirit, of joints and marrow, and discerning the thoughts and intentions of the heart.
>
> Hebrews 4:12

The word "soul" here refers to the human heart—not a heart in the physical sense but heart in the emotional sense of loving and feeling loved. The heart is the "space" inside where body and spirit can no longer be distinguished.

Simeon's prophecy to the Virgin Mary literally states that a sword will pierce her *soul*. We translate it to say that a sword pierces her *heart* (cf. Lk 2:35). When Mary sees Jesus dying on the cross, the sight of his suffering is the *sword* that pierces. It affects both body and soul, as if she were the one dying. Her pain is both spiritual and physical—not as two separate pains but as one single act of suffering that took place "in her heart."

When distinguishing soul from the spirit, the Letter to the Hebrews is using the word "soul" to speak of the human heart. I have taken the trouble to explain this in detail, because this passage implies a great mystery about the human body and the human soul.

Your body and your soul are not the same. They can be divided (and will be when you die). Even when they are united, your body and soul are not the same. And yet body and soul are so closely bound together in one person—in one you—that not even you can tell where one begins and the other ends. This is what makes you mysterious. This is what makes every man and woman a mystery.

"Heart" (or sometimes "soul") is the word the Scriptures use when revealing this mystery. The heart is the place where body and soul are fused into one. Your heart is the place where your physical feelings, your deepest emotions, and the decisions of your mind and will come together as one single experience.

God asks you to keep your heart pure and announces his greatest promise in this beatitude: "Blessed are the pure in heart, for they shall see God" (Mt 5:8).

The human heart expresses the mystery of being a body and soul united together. You are not a mixture of body and soul, like a mixture of oil and water. Rather than speaking of a mixture, we say "union." The union of body and soul is so complete that your soul depends on your body and your body depends on your soul.

Think of yourself as if *you* were *your favorite song*. Like lyrics composed of rhyming words, your body is a collection of parts that fit together in a precise pattern. Like a melody that gives life to the lyrics and yet can be recognized without lyrics, your soul gives life to the body and yet can exist, incompletely, without it. The song is both lyrics and melody together—not just a mixture of words and music, but a single reality. In a similar way, the union of your physical body and your spiritual soul is a single reality called "you."

Each one of us is the union of body and spirit. Rather than focus on either the body or the spirit, the Church emphasizes the *union* of these two elements to explain human nature:

> It is typical of rationalism to make a radical contrast in man between spirit and body, between body and spirit. But man is a person in the unity of his body and his spirit. The body can never be reduced to mere matter. It is a spiritualized body, just as man's spirit is so closely united to the body that he can be described as an embodied spirit.
>
> St. John Paul II, *Letter to Families*, n. 19

Nothing you do can be reduced to an activity that is purely physical or purely spiritual. Even when you get to heaven and experience the beatific vision—when you see God face-to-face—it will be an experience that is both physical and spiritual.

The Church teaches that God will communicate his divine nature "not only to your soul, but also to your whole psychosomatic subjectivity," i.e., to that whole mystery of body and soul integrated together as one single you (cf. St. John Paul II, *Theology of the Body*, p. 242).

In heaven, you will experience God in both body and soul. Your soul will become godlike. Your body will also become godlike. This is why Jesus wants you to eat his flesh and drink his blood. He said: "It is the spirit that gives life, the flesh is of no avail" (Jn 6:63). Even so, when the Spirit gives you life, he gives divine life to your flesh and does this through Christ's flesh. That is why you should hunger to receive the Eucharist. Eating his flesh and drinking his blood is the most important thing you will ever do in this world. Because the next world is also a life of flesh and blood, eating his flesh and drinking his blood is the best preparation for the most important thing you will ever do in the next life.

The piercing of the body

Perhaps you are beginning to grasp what we mean when we say that the human body is a mystery. You glimpse the deepest mystery of the human body when you "look on him whom they have pierced" (Zech 12:10). Nothing says more about love than the wounds in the body of Jesus Christ. The Church asks us to fix our gaze on Jesus as the blood flows from his sacred wounds.

> His death on the cross is the culmination of that turning of God against himself in which he gives himself in order to raise man up and save him. This is love in its most radical form. By contemplating the pierced side of Christ (cf. Jn 19:37), we can understand the starting point of this encyclical letter: "God is love" (1 Jn 4:8). It is there that this truth can be contemplated. It is from there that our definition of love must begin. In this contemplation the Christian discovers the path along which his life and love must move.
>
> Benedict XVI, *God Is Love*, n. 12

If you want to see love, look at the wounds in Christ's body. They reveal love; they reveal God; they reveal that God is love. Jesus died with wounds in his body. He rose from the dead with those wounds. The wounds will never heal because they reveal the love that will never end.

REVIEW QUESTIONS

1. Why do we say that the human body is a mystery?
2. What can we learn from Adam's solitude?
3. Explain the difference between passions and acts of the will.
4. What does the Bible mean when it talks about *heart*?

45.

Person and Society

Sooner or later you will ask yourself the burning question: How can I be happy? Perhaps you sense that no person finds happiness alone. You cannot make yourself happy.

Does this mean you should wait for someone else to make you happy? This is the paradox of human existence. Only someone else can make you happy. And yet that is not going to happen unless you do something.

This is what society is all about. This is what the human person is all about. You need others, and others need you. It implies a simple, practical conclusion. Dedicate your life to making others happy.

Only love explains person and society

Jesus said that his life and the life of his disciples consisted in serving others. This means finding a way to make others happy. But serving others is not the whole picture. It is always a mistake to reduce the gospel to social service. If you solved all the problems of all the people in the entire world—if you eliminated all disease, all ignorance, all poverty, all hunger, all unemployment, and loaded everybody's home with the best consumer goods that technology can produce—you would not be happy, and they would not be happy. The Church teaches:

> We are dealing with human beings, and human beings always need something more than technically proper care. They need humanity. They need heartfelt concern. . . . Often the deepest cause of suffering is the very absence of God.
>
> Benedict XVI, *God Is Love*, n. 31

What a shame it would be if you poured out your life to the point of exhaustion solving many technical problems, only to discover that the people you were serving are still miserable.

This is not just a theory. Today's middle class enjoys levels of wealth, comfort, and leisure that kings and queens of old never imagined. And yet many are unhappy—some because they have been abandoned by both spouse and children; some because they cannot bring themselves to forgive and forget past grievances; some because they are cynical; some because they have given up any hope of ever finding love.

You need love. Everyone needs love. Nothing else satisfies. St. Paul was saying all this and much more when he wrote:

> If I speak in the tongues of men and of angels, but have not love, I am a noisy gong or a clanging cymbal. And if I have prophetic powers, and understand all mysteries and all knowledge, and if I have all faith, so as to remove mountains, but have not love, I am nothing. If I give away all I have, and if I deliver my body to be burned, but have not love, I gain nothing.
>
> 1 Corinthians 13:1–3

Jesus wants you to dedicate your life, as he dedicated his, to serving others. You could do that and remain a very unhappy person. To love others you must serve them; but serving is not enough. The Church reminds of this when she states that "man . . . cannot fully find himself except through a sincere gift of self" (Vatican II, *The Church in the Modern World*, n. 24).

Society and family

When trying to explain the relation between person and society, this need to "give self" has one practical consequence. The family is key to understanding society. Families are the place where people learn to give themselves to others. The Church teaches:

> The Creator of all made the married state the beginning and foundation of human society.
>
> Vatican II, *Decree on the Apostolate of Lay People*, n. 11

To understand society, begin with the small picture. Begin with the family. Begin with the love of one man for one woman, committing themselves to each other for life in marriage and opening themselves to cooperating with God to create new human life. This is a family. This is the "beginning and foundation of human society."

In today's world, it is hard for many people to accept this idea. They look at the average family and remain sceptical. There are many wonderful families; but there are some where life is hell. Some look at their own experience and conclude that families have nothing to do with personal happiness.

> **Sacred Scripture**
>
> And now I beg you, lady, not as though I were writing you a new commandment, but the one we have had from the beginning, that we love one another. And this is love, that we follow his commandments; this is the commandment, as you have heard from the beginning, that you follow love.
>
> 2 John 5–6

The only way to deal with this objection is to go back to Christ's notion of serving others. Service to others is not the whole picture. Still, the health of a family depends on the willingness of husband, wife, and children to serve each other at home and then to serve others outside the home.

Spirit of service

You make others happy by serving them. You probably agree and yet remain suspicious. A doubt remains: "What if I make sacrifices to help others and nobody makes any sacrifice to help me? What if I don't find anyone who knows how to make me happy?"

There are several ways of answering this question, but they all depend on believing something that no one can prove to you. The answers all depend on believing something God revealed. Jesus came to serve, but he also came to reveal. Of all the many things he revealed, he revealed the answer to the doubt just mentioned.

God tells you that you have a choice. You can forget about yourself and spend your life serving others, trying to make them happy. Jesus called this a decision to "lose your life." Or you can forget about others and spend your life "pursuing happiness."

Most of what is wrong in the modern world can be attributed to all the evil generated by people who make the second choice. They call it the "pursuit of happiness." It sounds wonderful, but it is deadly. In practice, it means finding ways to make yourself happy by *using* others, half-conscious of the fact that *they*, of course, will try to use you. The fact that people talk about serving can be deceptive. Look at their underlying attitude. If they talk about serving but then arrange things to make sure others to serve them, what kind of service is that?

This second choice—this pursuit of happiness—is what Jesus called "saving your life." He said it leads to "losing your life." Then he explained the way that leads to being happy:

> For whoever would save his life will lose it, and whoever loses his life for my sake will find it.
>
> Matthew 16:25

No one can prove the truth of these words. But lack of proof is a minor difficulty. You may balk at our Lord's promise because it flatly contradicts everything your "natural" tendencies suggest—the ones left over from original sin.

If you are like most people, you are convinced you have to grab as much as you can before others grab it and leave you with nothing. Jesus tells you to give and to give and never stop giving. He tells you: "Lose your life and you will find it." Satan tells you, "That is a load of nonsense. Don't be stupid, or you *will* be left with nothing. And then what will you do?"

It takes faith to believe that you will be happy if you listen to Jesus. It takes faith to overcome worldly prejudice.

Serve others. This is not the whole gospel. You must also find someone to whom you can give your whole self. But giving your whole self in marriage or celibacy is impossible until you commit yourself to serving others in small ways. If you cannot walk, how will you run a marathon? Don't be afraid of serving others. Don't be afraid you will end up miserable. It will not ruin your life. On the contrary, it is the only way to find love. It is the only way to find God.

What is society?

The term "society" comes from the Latin *socius*, which originally meant "friend." Society defines the way people organize relationships with each other. Different nations have different ways of organizing themselves. To understand a society, first look at the dominant culture. Then look at the institutions. To do this, look at the various parts of, and functions within, that society: individuals and families, church and state, academia and education, business and industry, military and police, media and communication, art and entertainment, etc.

Most societies are described mainly by church and state—that is, the way they organize religion and the way they organize government. The type of government (democracy, dictatorship, theocracy, monarchy) determines the kind of society a nation has. Still, all the other institutions are important, especially the church. Governments make laws, but the foundation of those laws depends on the moral standards set by the religious leaders of the nation.

Add to all this the reality of globalization. No nation determines its own fate, its own successes and failures, or its own culture.

What is culture?

The term "culture" comes from the Latin *cultus*, which defines what people believe about God and the way they worship him. If the majority of the people living in a nation practice one particular religion and take their faith seriously, that religion determines the culture. Christian culture is different from Jewish culture; Jewish culture is different from Islamic culture, etc.

Even within Christian culture, great variations occur. Catholic and Orthodox cultures emphasize the Eucharist above all else and focus people's attention on the liturgy. Protestant cultures often emphasize the Bible above all else and focus people's attention on preaching. These generalizations provide only a minimal overview of Catholic, Orthodox, and Protestant cultures.

While culture is determined primarily by religious belief and practices, it is heavily influenced by philosophical convictions, that is, the attitude people develop towards reality and the world. Almost unconsciously, the whole of society picks one or two values—justice, work, freedom, health, truth, peace, beauty, harmony, leisure, wealth, comfort—and constantly exalts them above all others. These values define a people's culture almost as much as their religion. This does not mean people give little importance to other values. Rather, it means that, when a crisis has to be resolved, people will tend to view their needs by putting their cultural values first and work from there.

Within any nation and within any province of that nation, there is usually a great mix of competing cultures. However, even within a so-called "multicultural society," one culture is usually dominant within a nation.

Purifying culture

Because of the influence of original sin, our personal sins, and the structures of sin resulting from personal sin, every culture needs to be purified. The Son of God came to forgive sin. He also came to reveal the truth about God and the truth about man. Spreading the gospel tends to uplift the cultural values of the people who accept it. Jesus not only redeems individuals. In some analogous sense, the gospel can also redeem a nation's culture.

If religious beliefs are primitive—if they have yet to be influenced by revelation—the culture is generally pagan but open to receiving God's revelation. If the religious beliefs of the majority grow weak, especially in a Christian culture, culture tends to revert back to pagan habits—but with a vengeance, becoming atheistic for all practical purposes. Jesus gave a hint of this when he said:

> When the unclean spirit has gone out of a man, he passes through waterless places seeking rest; and finding none he says, "I will return to my house from which I came." And when he comes he finds it swept and put in order.
>
> Luke 11:24–25

Ecclesiastical Writers

Christians are no different from other people in nationality, speech, or customs. They do not inhabit cities of their own. . . . As citizens, they share in all things with others, and yet endure all things as if foreigners. . . . They marry, as do all others. They beget children, but they do not destroy their offspring. They have a common table, but not a common bed. They are in the flesh, but they do not live according to the flesh. They pass their days on earth, but they are citizens of heaven. . . . To sum it up in one word—what the soul is to the body, that is what Christians are to the world.

Letter to Diognetus, 5–6

What happens to a man can happen to a whole society.

The greatest clash of cultures is not between Christian and Muslim or Muslim and Hindu, etc. The real clash of cultures takes place between those who are trying to live a Christian life and the materialistic culture of those who reject the very possibility that God would want to reveal himself to us. Jews, Muslims, and those of other non-Christian religions build up cultures which are much different from that typical of Christians. Still, they hold fixed moral values in common with Christians.

Those who opt for a materialistic culture follow the moral standards of relativism—their only moral standard is to avoid any fixed standard. The diametric opposition between having no fixed moral standard and having one forces a clash of cultures.

This is why the Church talks about the clash between the culture of life and the anti-culture of death.

Culture and anti-culture

When judging what kind of culture dominates a society, it is tempting to look first at religious practice. After all, religion generally determines culture. However, the complexity of human nature requires a more subtle approach. Perhaps a glimpse at the extremes of religious practice will indicate why.

On one hand, there are individuals who claim to be atheists and yet they are ready to sacrifice themselves to serve others. They also seem

Magisterium

Catholics versed in politics and, as should be the case, firm in the faith and Christian teaching, should not decline to enter public life. . . . They can work for the common good and at the same time prepare the way for the gospel.

Catholics are to be keen on collaborating with all those of good will in the promotion of all that is true, just, holy, all that is worthy of love (cf. Phil 4:8). They are to enter into dialogue with them, approaching them with understanding and courtesy. They are to search for means of improving social and public institutions along the lines of the Gospel.

Vatican II, *Decree on the Apostolate of Lay People*, n. 14

ready to admit mistakes when they have done wrong. These "atheists" spend their whole lives asking questions about God.

On the other hand, there are individuals who go to church regularly and yet give no importance to God. They have no fixed moral standard. They make little or no effort to serve others. They use religion as a social convenience for doing business.

These are the two extremes, with a lot of variation in between. Because of this, any attempt to identify culture by looking at church attendance—or synagogue, mosque, or temple attendance—is necessarily incomplete. It can even be deceiving. Looking at the health of family life within society gives a better picture of the dominant culture.

God created man in his image and likeness by creating us male and female. This is the inescapable reality of *what we are* and *why we exist*. This defines the nature of society. The link between God and family is wired into our bodies and souls. If people treasure family values, their culture is centered on God. If people give little importance to protecting family values and tolerate promiscuity, their culture starts to drift away from God. As people drift away from God, they cease to worship him. When they cease to worship him, they have no "cult"—no worship of God. Their culture begins to disintegrate. If people continue down that road, they begin to organize society in ways that destroy family life. Far from merely tolerating promiscuity, leaders organize society in ways that promote promiscuity.

When the Church talks about the culture of life and the anti-culture of death, she is contrasting these two different ways of living.

One respects sex and promotes family values. The other reduces sex to entertainment and reduces family life to the mutual convenience of sexual partners.

Those who are open to God, respect his plan for sex. Because of the consequences of original sin they have to struggle to overcome tendencies towards lust. But their attitude is clearly pro-family and pro-life. Their attitude towards children is centered on God. *They see children as a blessing from God.* They are horrified by the mere thought of abortion. These are people who love life. They live in a culture of life.

Those who *consciously* reject God's revelation have, by definition, rejected his plan for sex. To be more accurate, it is usually their conscious rejection of God's plan for sex that defines their attitude towards revelation. Perhaps they do not openly reject God, but they treat him like a distant relative who cannot be bothered with the specifics of how we live. People promoting the anti-culture of death may talk about God and give the impression of being committed to faith in God, but this is mostly appearance. To understand their cultural values—to understand what they really think about God—look at their attitudes towards the family, towards sex, and towards children.

Those dominated by this mentality do not define the family as husband and wife united by an unbreakable bond in marriage. Instead, "family" is reduced to any arrangement of any two people who want to engage in sexual acts on a regular basis. They tend to see the child as a consumer product. If the "couple" does not want a child, the child conceived as the result of sexual relations becomes an obstacle to the happiness of that couple. If the couple wants a child, all means should be available to ensure that the couple gets one—and gets *a good one*—not just any baby but a baby that meets their expectations. Any baby in the womb judged to be "below standard" gets aborted.

Those following the culture of life organize society to protect the bond that unites a man and woman as husband and wife. They want to avoid divorce. They want to avoid, or at least minimize, the harm done to individuals and society when promiscuity is tolerated. They protect the life of the unborn child. They care for the sick and the elderly.

Those following the anti-culture of death organize society to make divorce routine and easy. They make abortion a fundamental human "right" that must be "guaranteed" by law. They condone any sexual relationship between consenting adults, as if it were the same as marriage. They view the lives of the incapacitated elderly and the terminally ill as useless and meaningless, concluding that they would be better off dead. They favor any form of manipulating human life that makes their goals possible.

In this anti-culture, it is natural for people to think, perhaps unconsciously: "As long as you don't hurt anybody, grab as much as you can for yourself. If you can avoid it, don't put others in a situation where they feel forced to make you suffer. But if you have to choose, look out for yourself first. It's every man for himself and every woman for herself." Each person walks through life thinking: "Take care of your own needs first. After all, there are so many people in the world—billions of them—that there's probably not enough for everybody. Therefore, if you have any brains at all, get as much as you can now before it's too late."

This attitude arises from a suspicion about God and creation. If summarized in a few sentences, it would state: "We don't know enough about God to say what he had in mind when he created the world, assuming he exists at all. But several things are obvious. If he did create us, he stuck us in the middle of an enormous mess where evil abounds and disaster can strike at any moment. All that business about commandments and fixed moral principles is a distraction at best. Since God does not seem to have much interest in solving our problems, we have to solve them ourselves, using whatever means we can. The main problem at the present time is that there are too many people populating our planet. The priority for the indefinite future is to reduce the number of children being born, especially among the poor in developing countries. If we fail to do that, we will all starve to death. Contraception and abortion, far from being evil, are the key to saving future generations from poverty and misery. Contraception and abortion will prevent the bloodshed likely to result when people are ready to kill each other for a loaf of bread and a cup of water."

The culture of life expresses the opposite conviction about God and creation. It can be summarized this way: "God created us. He loves us. He will provide. When he created the world, he knew exactly how many people would populate our planet today. He also knew how many will populate it thousands of years from now. He has provided the resources needed for all of us—in our billions or more—to satisfy our real needs. He has made us capable of the intelligence and social skills needed to organize society so that everyone in every nation has enough food and water, space and comfort, security and shelter. As long as we follow his plan, especially his plan for family life, people will prosper. They will not be impoverished by the increase in numbers. On the contrary, as the human family grows to proportions that, even a mere hundred years ago, we would have thought impossible, everyone will be enriched. We will reach goals that today are not only impossible to reach but impossible to imagine. God loves life. He revels in increasing the human family more and more. From the beginning, he planned things so that we would have everything we need to live in peace and love one another."

Society and the family

This chapter is meant to alert you to a basic fact about the world you live in. Today's world is a battlefield where first you witness the all-out war between God and Satan and then you chose which side of the war you want to be on.

The battle between good and evil has many facets. For the individual man or woman, the key is getting to know Jesus and all that he revealed. For society as a whole—at least in the present time—peace and prosperity depend mainly on improving family life. The future depends on presenting men and women with new horizons. They must discover the beauty and grandeur of the vocation to love. They need to know that bringing many children into the world is a good thing to do. The Church teaches:

> The family in the modern world, as much as and perhaps more than any other institution, has been beset by the many profound and rapid changes that have affected society and culture. . . . At a moment of history in which the family is the object of numerous forces that seek to destroy it or in some way to deform it, and aware that the well-being of society and her own good are intimately tied to the good of the family,

> the Church perceives, in a more urgent and compelling way, her mission of proclaiming to all people the plan of God for marriage and the family, ensuring their full vitality and human and Christian development, and thus contributing to the renewal of society and of the People of God.
>
> St. John Paul II, *On the Christian Family in the Modern World*, n. 3

Each nation has a particular need for men and women who understand the nature of sex, marriage, and family life. The future of society depends on developing a culture of life.

REVIEW QUESTIONS

1. Explain the concept of society.
2. Explain the concept of culture.
3. What do we mean by the culture of life and the culture of death?
4. Why is it urgent for Christians to develop a culture of life within society?

Part Six

The Way Christians Pray

46.
The Purpose of Prayer

Why do Christians pray? We pray because we need God. We pray because Jesus prayed. The gospel shows Jesus spending time in prayer. On several occasions, he spent the whole night in prayer. We pray because Jesus taught us to pray.

There are lots of books about prayer. The following two chapters are a summary of ideas on Christian prayer. Books can be helpful for prayer. Some books help because they contain prayers composed by the saints. Other books help because they contain homilies or points for meditation. Still others help because they explain the different ways you can talk to God. All these are good. Even so, you will never learn very much about prayer by reading books. You may learn something, but not enough.

This applies even to reading the Bible. Prayer is more than merely reading the Bible. Does that sound like a shocking thing to say? It's true. Reading is not the same as prayer. You need much more than a book, even the Holy Book containing God's revelation. If you want to learn to pray, start a dialogue with Jesus, where the two of you talk together.

Getting to know Jesus

Speaking to his disciples, Jesus explained the goal God has set for every man and woman ever born into this world:

> And this is eternal life, that they know thee the only true God, and Jesus Christ whom thou hast sent.
>
> John 17:3

Knowing the Father and the Son is the goal for everything you do. For this reason, you must make it the goal of your prayer. Get to know God. Allow God to get to know you.

In Jesus Christ, God reveals everything he wants to reveal about himself and about man. It is a mystery that God wanted to reveal everything in one person. All the teachings of the Church can be summed up by this fact. God reveals everything about himself and everything about creation in this one person named Jesus Christ.

There are many ways of praying. But all prayer, no matter how you choose to pray, consists of one thing; raising your mind and heart to God. Jesus is the path we follow to reach that goal. "I am the way, the truth and the life," Jesus told his Apostles. "No one comes to the Father, but by me" (Jn 14:6).

Perhaps this book has helped you. It explains the basic truths God wants you to believe. It explains the commandments God expects you to obey. It explains how God forgives you when you sin and how he rewards you when you sacrifice yourself for him. It explains how God makes you holy through the sacraments, through your prayer, and through your work. But in the end, knowing all this is not enough.

God wants to reveal *himself* to you. More than having you know all about commandments and mysteries and sacraments, he wants you to know all about *him*. You get to know something about him by studying his revelation and by practicing Christian holiness. But these are means to an end. Even the act of receiving Holy Communion is a means to an end. The goal is not to master facts from a book, be good, and receive lots of sacraments. The goal is to know God. God has decided to reveal himself not through a book but through his Son. More than getting to know a book, God wants you to get to know Jesus.

Prayer in the Spirit

Prayer is the way you get to know Jesus. But prayer does not mean mumbling words. It means talking to Jesus and listening to him.

Prayer is difficult. It is difficult for several reasons. The main reason most people have trouble praying is that they try to pray without asking for help.

Sacred Scripture

And I tell you, Ask, and it will be given you; seek, and you will find; knock, and it will be opened to you. For every one who asks receives, and he who seeks finds, and to him who knocks it will be opened. What father among you, if his son asks for a fish, will instead of a fish give him a serpent; or if he asks for an egg, will give him a scorpion? If you then, who are evil, know how to give good gifts to your children, how much more will the heavenly Father give the Holy Spirit to those who ask him!

Luke 11:9–13

Do you remember what happened on the day of Pentecost—not when the Holy Spirit descended on Jesus' disciples in the Upper Room, but afterward when the Twelve Apostles began talking to all the people outside? You may feel exactly what those people felt when they listened to St. Peter. They did not know Jesus. But they were moved by Peter's words. They wanted to know Jesus. That is why they asked, "What do we need to do?"

St. Peter said they had to do three things; First, to be sorry for their sins; second, to be baptized in the name of Jesus Christ; third, to receive the gift of the Holy Spirit. These three things are still necessary today. If you skip any of these three steps, you will find it hard to pray.

You must be sorry for your sins. You must become a child of God through baptism and live in the state of grace. You must rely on the power of the Holy Spirit and not on your own strength. Those who try to pray without doing these things never learn to *communicate with God.* They may pray for a while, but they eventually lose heart and give up.

The whole point of studying God's revelation is to prepare you to pray, that is, prepare you to be friends with Jesus. Even among those who have already been baptized, many do not know how to pray. They have heard many things *about* Jesus, but they do not know him *personally*. Perhaps you are one of those. Perhaps you are eager to learn how to pray. Hopefully this encouragement, like the preaching of St. Peter at Pentecost, will lead you to that moment in your life when you can receive God's gift of the Spirit.

St. Paul explains why the Holy Spirit is necessary if you want to learn to pray:

> Likewise the Spirit helps us in our weakness; for we do not know how to pray as we ought, but the Spirit himself intercedes for us with sighs too deep for words. And he who searches the hearts of men knows what is the mind of the Spirit, because the Spirit intercedes for the saints according to the will of God.
>
> Romans 8:26–27

You learn how to pray when you let the Holy Spirit guide you. He can teach you to pray in a way that goes beyond words. It is a way of talking to God where no words are necessary.

To pray some people think they need to learn some kind of technique. While it does help to know about the different kinds of prayer, techniques are secondary. Even if you know nothing about the various kinds of prayer, you will learn to pray if you habitually live in the state of grace, receive the sacraments, and allow the Holy Spirit to lead you wherever he wants.

Qualities of prayer

Perhaps the first thing to understand about prayer is that it is often hard. Sometimes it comes easy, but it usually takes a lot of effort. The *Catechism* says:

> Prayer is both a gift of grace and a determined response on our part. It always presupposes effort. The great figures of prayer of the Old Covenant before Christ, as well as the Mother of God, the saints, and he himself, all teach us this: prayer is a battle. Against whom? Against ourselves and against the wiles of the tempter who does all he can to turn man away from prayer, away from union with God.
>
> *CCC*, n. 2725

Prayer is a battle. Like all battles, good tactics are necessary for success. The tactics you must use for prayer are faith, humility, perseverance, and trust.

- **Have faith in God.** Jesus told his disciples they would receive whatever they asked for as long as they had faith and were ready to do

God's will. Jesus said, "Have faith in God. Truly, I say to you, whoever says to this mountain, 'Be taken up and cast into the sea,' and does not doubt in his heart, but believes that what he says will come to pass, it will be done for him" (Mk 11:22–24).

- **Be humble.** Some people complain, saying, "God never listens to my prayers." And yet how many of these same people ignored God for years before deciding to pray. When you pray, do not turn to God demanding justice. Turn to God begging for mercy. St. Peter said, "God opposes the proud, but gives grace to the humble" (1 Pt 5:5).
- **Persevere.** Some people stop praying because they fail to get what they want. The *Catechism* reminds us that our Lord wants us to continue praying, even for a long time, before he answers our prayer: "Do not be troubled if you do not immediately receive from God what you ask him; for he desires to do something even greater for you, while you cling to him in prayer" (*CCC*, n. 2737). Many times people discover that God did them a favor by *not* giving them what they wanted and by giving them something better instead. The goal of prayer is not to convince God to give us what we want. The goal of prayer is to discover what God wants.
- **Trust God.** Like Zechariah, the childless priest praying in Temple, some people fail to trust God. Zechariah prayed for years asking God to send him a son. When God was finally ready to answer his prayer, Zechariah refused to believe the angel's message (cf. Lk 1:13–20). In contrast, Elizabeth praises the Virgin Mary for believing what seemed too good to be true: "And blessed is she who believed that there would be a fulfilment of what was spoken to her from the Lord" (Lk 1:45). Mary believed she would become the mother of God's Son and yet remain a virgin.
- **Aim high.** It is good to ask for material needs. God wants you to ask for your daily bread. But he will be disappointed if that is all you want. Jesus said we should ask God to give us a share in divine life: "Ask, and it will be given you. . . . The heavenly Father gives the Holy Spirit to those who ask him!" (Lk 11:9, 13). When you pray, what do you ask for?

You need prayer

People who pray understand the things of God. People who do not pray end up being very confused. They are confused because they can no longer distinguish between good and evil. The *Catechism* explains this by quoting one of the saints:

> Those who pray are certainly saved; those who do not pray are certainly damned.
>
> St. Alphonsus Liguori, cf. *CCC*, n. 2744

Do not use these words to figure out whether someone else has been saved or will be saved. Apply them only to yourself.

You need to pray every day. If you pray every day, even if it is only for a few minutes, you will stay close to God. The more you pray, the closer you will be. Even if you have the misfortune to fall into temptation, you will realize that you have sinned. Almost immediately, you will feel the need to run back to God.

If you do not pray, you will drift away from God. Like being out in a boat, you might not notice you are drifting. At first you may even feel that everything is fine because when you look up, you see the shore. In other words, if some crisis occurs, you will pray and ask God to help you. But if you pray only when crisis overwhelms you and fail to develop a habit of prayer, you will drift away from God the way a boat drifts out to sea. You will lose sight of land. You will be spiritually lost. God will begin to seem like a stranger to you—a stranger who lives very far away.

Fathers of the Church

Our Father: at this name love is aroused in us . . . as is the confidence of obtaining what we are about to ask. . . . What would he not give to his children who ask, since he has already granted them the gift of being his children?

St. Augustine, cf. *CCC*, n. 2785

The longer you delay picking up a habit of daily prayer, the more you will lose touch with God. The truths of faith—that once made you wonder in awe—will start to look dull or simply false. The distinctions between good and evil—that used to be so clear to you as a child—will appear tangled and complicated. You will begin to ask if there is such a thing as truth. If you seriously offend God, you will hardly notice. You will no longer feel an urgent need to go to confession. In the same way a corpse neither notices nor cares what is happening to those who are alive, you will cease to care about heaven and life with God.

If you develop a life of prayer, everything changes. God no longer seems far away, but close to you. You begin to understand the truth of Jesus' words: "And lo, I am with you always, to the close of the age" (Mt 28:20). Even in the midst of severe trials, you will have the strength to remain calm.

You choose

You can look for God. Or you can ignore God. All other choices in life come down to this one. The secret of learning to pray lies in this choice. If you look for God, you will learn how to pray for the simple reason that you will pray. Learning to pray is like learning to walk. You learn to walk by walking. You learn to pray by praying.

So prayer comes down to a simple question: Are you going to look for God? Or are you going to ignore him?

There are many ways of praying. This is just another way of saying that there are many ways of finding God. Perhaps the best way to explain this is to go back the Bible and remember a few of those men and women who met Jesus and decided to follow him.

John the Apostle was a young man when he found Jesus near the Jordan River. The Baptist pointed to Jesus as he was walking by and said to John, "Look, there is the Lamb of God!" John followed Jesus and became one of his disciples.

St. Matthew's story was completely different. He was a mature man who had "made it" in life. He was not any where near the Jordan River when he met Jesus Christ. He was counting money. And he had lots of it. He had a nice house and lots of friends. He was a tax collector—not exactly what people would call a holy person in those days. He had a reputation for being a sinner.

One day Jesus walked into his office and said, "Follow me." Matthew was shocked. He was not looking for Jesus. Jesus came looking for him. Matthew had to make a radical choice: to accept God or to ignore him. He accepted God. He accepted God's mercy. He chose to leave everything behind. He gave up his sinful habits and became one of Jesus' closest disciples—one of the Twelve Apostles.

Maybe your life has been a lot like St. John's. Maybe you are still young. Maybe you have not committed any great sins. Maybe your parents taught you a lot about God. Maybe you obey the Ten Commandments. Maybe you go to church every Sunday. Maybe you go to confession often and receive Holy Communion frequently. Maybe you kneel every night before you go to bed and say a prayer before falling asleep.

Then again, maybe you are more like St. Matthew. Maybe you have committed lots of sins. Maybe you are used to getting drunk, stealing, reading bad books, skipping church, harboring thoughts of jealousy, hatred, and all kinds of other evil things better left unsaid. Maybe you are so used to doing these things that they seem perfectly normal to you. Maybe the only time you think of praying is to ask God to curse the people you don't like. Maybe you are so used to evil that your evil life feels nice and comfortable, like an old pair of shoes.

The Bible tells us a lot about the holy women who followed Jesus. Like the Apostles, they, too, came from different backgrounds. Joanna had a respectable reputation. She was a woman with culture and class. She was the wife of Chuza, the steward for King Herod. Mary Magdalene was different. Her life was a mess when she met Jesus. The Gospels hint at this when explaining how Jesus had to cast out seven demons. Her life was a lot like St. Matthew's. Everyone thought she was a great sinner. She probably was. The truth is that *all of us* are great sinners. Her sins were just more obvious, that's all. She repented, she changed, and she decided to make Jesus the master of her heart and soul.

Whether your past is like St. John's or more like St. Matthew's, like St. Joanna's or St. Mary Magdalene's, now you have to choose. You can accept God's mercy. He will forgive your sins. It doesn't matter if you are the greatest sinner in the whole world or just average. God wants to forgive all your sins and show you how to be holy.

The only other choice is to ignore God's mercy. Your sins will not be forgiven. By refusing to accept God, you will exclude yourself from entering his kingdom. You will be left outside in the dark, where you will suffer forever.

REVIEW QUESTIONS

1. What is prayer?
2. Why do we call prayer a "battle"?
3. What qualities are needed for good prayer?
4. Why do we need to pray?

47.

How Christians Pray

When the disciples asked Jesus to teach them how to pray, he told them:

> Pray then like this:
>
> Our Father who art in heaven,
> Hallowed be thy name.
> Thy kingdom come.
> Thy will be done,
> On earth as it is in heaven.
> Give us this day our daily bread;
> And forgive us our debts,
> As we also have forgiven our debtors;
> And lead us not into temptation,
> But deliver us from evil.
>
> Matthew 6:9–13

This is the Lord's Prayer. Jesus used it to teach his disciples to call God "our Father."

The seven petitions

The Lord's Prayer is composed of seven petitions to our Father in heaven.

1. The Our Father starts with the most important of all petitions. We ask God to make others aware of his holiness. This teaches us to put God's kingdom first, ahead of our own immediate needs.

2. Jesus tells us to ask God to send his kingdom. This teaches us that our happiness depends on something that only God can do for us.
3. Then we ask God to do whatever he wants, doing it the same way here on earth as he does it in heaven. This teaches us that to be happy we have to do things the way the angels and saints do them in heaven.
4. Jesus tells us to ask God for our daily bread. This teaches us to ask God for all our needs, even the ones we take for granted.
5. We ask God to forgive us as we forgive others. This teaches us that God will only listen to our prayers if we forgive others, even our enemies.
6. Jesus tells us to ask God not to put us to the test. This teaches us not to trust in our own power to resist temptation but to trust in God and his desire to save us.
7. Finally, we ask God to deliver us from the evil one. This teaches us to beware of Satan, since he is a master at deceiving us to lead us away from God. We need God to save us from the power this "ancient serpent."

The perfect prayer

The Lord's Prayer remains the model of the perfect prayer. Jesus used it to teach us how to pray. However, remember that when teaching the Apostles this prayer, Jesus also said:

> And in praying do not heap up empty phrases as the Gentiles do; for they think that they will be heard for their many words. Do not be like them, for your Father knows what you need before you ask him.
>
> Matthew 6:7–8

Holy men and women experienced in prayer have insisted that many people fail to pray even when they think they are praying. They fail to *connect with God* because they mumble words instead of speaking to God.

Speaking to God means speaking to him the way you expect others to speak to you. How would you feel if a man was sitting in front of you mumbling words, talking to himself instead of talking to you? How would you feel if you tried to say something to him, and he ignored you as if you weren't even there? This is what we do to God when we mumble words and deliberately allow ourselves to get distracted in prayer.

When you pray, remember that you are talking to someone who is listening to you. Remember that God listens more carefully than anyone else has ever listened to you. He listens to every word you say, attentively, as if you were the only person who ever spoke to him.

God does not listen because he is anxious to find out something he doesn't know. One of the psalms says that God knows every word we will say before it is on our tongue:

> O LORD, thou hast searched me and known me!
> Thou knowest when I sit down and when I rise up;
>   thou discernest my thoughts from afar.
> Thou searchest out my path and my lying down,
>   and art acquainted with all my ways.
>
> Psalm 139:1–3

God knows everything about you. He pays attention to you because he loves you. Even if you are distracted, God is paying attention to you.

Prayer is not just you talking to God. He has ways of "talking" to you. Besides learning how to speak to God, learn how to listen to him.

Types of prayer

Based on centuries of tradition, the *Catechism* mentions three expressions of prayer: vocal prayer, meditation, and contemplation. The following summary explains them. Each represents a different way people use to enter into dialogue with God. However, before looking at the specifics, keep one thing in mind. There are *many* ways of praying. You do not need to worry about what kind of prayer you use when you pray.

No matter how you do it, true prayer is inspired by the Holy Spirit. St. Paul goes further and tells us that the Spirit can fill our hearts with such spiritual force that we feel compelled to cry out to God, calling him "Father" (cf. Gal 4:6). At other times, the Spirit makes up for our fatigue and mental confusion:

Sacred Scripture

I will extol thee, O LORD, for thou hast drawn me up,
 and hast not let my foes rejoice over me.
O LORD my God, I cried to thee for help,
 and thou hast healed me.
As for me, I said in my prosperity,
 "I shall never be moved."
By thy favor, O LORD,
 thou hadst established me as a strong mountain;
thou didst hide thy face, I was dismayed.
Hear, O LORD, and be gracious to me!
 O LORD, be thou my helper!
Thou hast turned for me my mourning into dancing;
 thou hast loosed my sackcloth
 and girded me with gladness,
that my soul may praise thee and not be silent.
 O LORD my God, I will give thanks to thee for ever.

Psalm 30:1–2, 6–7, 10–12

> Likewise the Spirit helps us in our weakness; for we do not know how to pray as we ought, but the Spirit himself intercedes for us with sighs too deep for words.
>
> Romans 8:26

This is the moment for what many of the saints called "prayer of the heart."

Beware of a mistake many people make. They live in two different worlds—one in church, where they pray, and another in the world, where they work and relax. Quoting one of the Church Fathers, the *Catechism* reminds us that prayer and work go together:

> It is possible to offer fervent prayer even while walking in public or strolling alone, or seated in your shop . . . while buying or selling . . . or even while cooking.
>
> St. John Chrysostom, cf. *CCC*, n. 2743

God wants us to learn how to turn our whole life into prayer. It is up to each person to learn how to do it. For this reason, there are as many different kinds of prayer as there are people in the world.

The following descriptions of vocal prayer, meditation, and contemplation are meant to give only a rough outline of the many ways people speak to God and listen to him. These three "expressions of prayer" are general categories. All prayer reduces to one essential act: lifting up your mind and your heart to God.

Vocal Prayer

You engage in vocal prayer whenever you talk to God using a prayer written in fixed words or, regardless of the words, whenever you pray out loud. Vocal prayer can be done either alone or with others.

The *Catechism* says that vocal prayer consists not only in speaking words but also in lifting up your heart. Thus vocal prayer is both interior (praying in your heart) and exterior (praying aloud).

> Vocal prayer is an essential element of the Christian life. . . . The need to involve the senses in interior prayer corresponds to a requirement of our human nature. We are body and spirit, and we experience the need to translate our feelings externally.
>
> *CCC*, nn. 2701–2702

Both the Old Testament and the New Testament contain many prayers. Together with others composed by the saints, these constitute a treasury of prayers that people can use for vocal prayer.

Some people think using fixed words to pray denotes a lack of spontaneity, as if all prayers have to be invented on the spot. But Jesus himself prayed by using vocal prayers. The Scriptures often show Jesus going to the synagogue on the Sabbath. From the time he was a child, he would have prayed the customary psalms together with everyone else (cf. Lk 4:16 and Mt 26:30).

The Lord's Prayer is the most perfect of all vocal prayers. Other vocal prayers from the Scriptures include the psalms. The Book of Psalms is a collection of prayers used by the Israelites for both daily meditation and solemn liturgy. The Old Testament has many other prayers that can be used for vocal prayer. Three of the more popular examples are: the Song of the Angels (Is 6:1–3), the Song of Hannah (1 Sam 2:1–10), and the Hymn of the Three Young Men in the Fiery Furnace (Dan 3:51–90).

In their letters, the Apostles included several prayers that were probably used when the first Christians gathered together. St. Paul gives us the Hymn to Christ the Head of All Creation (Col 1:15–20). In the Book of Revelation, St. John gives a new version of the Hymn of Moses (Rev 15:3–4). These are a few examples among many prayers included in the New Testament. The Gospels contain several vocal prayers, in addition to the Lord's Prayer. The Virgin Mary's *Magnificat* and Zechariah's *Benedictus* are the most widely used (cf. Lk 1:46–55 and 1:68–79). The "Hail Mary" is essentially a prayer composed from the words St. Gabriel and St. Elizabeth used to praise Mary, calling her the "full of grace" and the "Mother of God" (cf. Lk 1:28 and 1:42–43).

Meditation

Meditation goes by many different names: personal prayer, private prayer, etc. It is part soul-searching and part imagination; part adventure and part confrontation; part study and part conversation. It can be monotonous because you feel dull. It can be fascinating because you happen upon some text that grips your attention. It can be inspiring because you finally see what God wants you to do. If can be delightful because you feel intimate with God. But it can also be frightening. Even Jesus experienced fear during his agony in the garden, the night before his crucifixion. The one common element in all these cases is that meditation requires focusing your mind on God—which is why some authors call it "mental prayer." Sometimes this comes easy. At other times you have to work at it.

Fathers of the Church

Pray, whether you are in a church, or in your home or in the countryside; whether you are tending to your flocks, constructing a building or attending a meeting. Whenever you can, get down on your knees; and when this is not possible, call on God mentally, in the afternoon, in the morning or at noon. When you get out of bed in the morning, direct your first thoughts to God. If you put prayer ahead of any other activity, then sin will have no power over you.

St. Ephrem the Syrian, *On Prayer*, I–II, 1

Besides using your mind to mediate, meditation demands that you use your heart. Use your mind to understand what God wants. Use your heart to accept God's will. Or at least ask him to help you to do it.

The first step is to set aside time every day. It could be ten minutes or it could be an hour, depending on your own personal needs. Stop all external activity and focus exclusively on God. Jesus described this vividly: "Go into your room and shut the door and pray to your Father who is in secret; and your Father who sees in secret will reward you" (Mt 6:6). To meditate you need to be alone with God.

There is no clear second step. You may want to talk to God about some words that struck you when speaking with a friend. You may want to talk instead about plans for the future. You may want to unburden your heart, talking about your problems. Having no idea what to talk about, you may choose to pick up the Bible or a collection of homilies and try to find something that will help you focus on the things of God. To summarize these possibilities, the *Catechism* defines this form of prayer as a search for God's will:

> Meditation is above all a quest. The mind seeks to understand the why and how of the Christian life, in order to adhere and respond to what the Lord is asking. The required attentiveness is difficult to sustain. We are usually helped by books . . .
>
> Meditating on what we read helps us to make it our own by confronting it with ourselves. Here, another book is opened: the book of life. We pass from thoughts to reality. To the extent that we are humble and faithful, we discover in meditation the movements that stir the heart and we are able to discern them. It is a question of acting truthfully in order to come into the light: "Lord, what do you want me to do?"
>
> *CCC*, nn. 2705–2706

Try to see what God wants. Then ask him from the depths of your heart to make your will conform to his.

Contemplation

This type of prayer is the most difficult to describe. You enter into contemplation only when God gives you a special grace that makes it possible. Though all prayer means lifting up the mind and heart to God, contemplation depends less on your effort and more on God's desire to lift you up.

As one of many ways of trying to define the mystery of contemplative prayer, the *Catechism* states:

> Contemplative prayer is silence, the "symbol of the world to come" or "silent love." Words in this kind of prayer are not speeches; they are like kindling that feeds the fire of love. In this silence, unbearable to the "outer" man, the Father speaks to us his incarnate Word, who suffered, died, and rose; in this silence the Spirit of adoption enables us to share in the prayer of Jesus.
>
> CCC, n. 2717

This silence is a glimpse—a foretaste—of the way you will see God face-to-face in heaven. Contemplation means looking at God but, paradoxically, it is a "darkness." Even when enjoying the gift of communicating directly with God in contemplation, "we walk by faith and not by sight" (2 Cor 5:7).

One day a simple man, who spent his life taking care of his farm, came to church to pray. He stationed himself in front of the tabernacle. (The tabernacle is an ornate box where the priest places the Eucharist so that, after Mass, people may come to adore Jesus present in the Blessed Sacrament.) This farmer gazed at the tabernacle for a long time. The priest of this church was a very holy man named St. John Vianney. St. John asked the farmer what he was saying to Jesus. The man had been absolutely silent for a long time. The priest was curious to know what was happening. The farmer was not saying anything to Jesus—at least not in words. He answered the priest, explaining: "I look at him and he looks at me." This silent gaze before Jesus is the best way to understand the nature of contemplation.

Prayer to the saints

Christians pray to the saints, that is, to those men and women who are already in heaven and see God face-to-face. This has caused

Magisterium

St. Benedict wrote in his Rule: "Pray and work." St. Ignatius of Loyola said: "Pray as if everything depended on God and work as if everything depended on you." Even when we have done our work, the food we receive is still a gift from our Father; it is good to ask him for it and to thank him, as Christian families do when saying grace at meals.

Catechism of the Catholic Church, n. 2834

misunderstanding. The misunderstanding arises because of the two different meanings associated with the word "prayer."

The principle meaning of "prayer" is the prayer people direct towards God. It includes four different aspects:

- **Adoration:** We call God our Creator and our Savior.
- **Contrition:** We ask God to forgive our sins.
- **Thanksgiving:** We thank God for all his blessings.
- **Supplication:** We ask God to give us everything we need.

Some try to remember this using the acronym: ACTS.

It is wrong to adore anyone except God. So in this sense, we should only pray to God. However, there is another meaning to the word "prayer," at least in English. Originally, "to pray" meant nothing more than asking someone to help you. This is what Christians mean by the word "pray" when praying to saints.

Just as you naturally turn to your friends to ask for help—to finish your work or solve a problem—you can turn to the saints. They are your friends in heaven. You can ask them to help you. When a Christian talks to the saints this way, we call it a "prayer of intercession." This is completely different from adoration. When you pray to the Blessed Virgin Mary, to St. Joseph, or to any other saint, you seek their intercession. You ask them to help you. You believe they have power to do so because they are close to God.

The idea of asking someone for help in spiritual affairs goes back to the practice of the early Christians. St. Paul writes:

> First of all, then, I urge that supplications, prayers, intercessions, and thanksgivings be made for all men, for kings and all who are in high positions . . .
>
> 1 Timothy 2:1–2

Even before they get to heaven, Christians can intercede for others. Having been glorified in heaven, the saints have more power to intercede. They have power to ask God to give grace to someone who needs to convert, to be healed, to persevere in faith, etc.

To understand the power of the saints, remember what Jesus said in the parable about the talents. "Well done, my good servant! Since you have proven yourself faithful in a very small thing," the Master said to the servant, "you shall have the government of ten cities" (Lk 19:17). The saints are not just spectators. God has given them power to help us.

The New Testament mentions some of the ways God gave the first Christians power to work miracles. St. Luke narrates one example:

> And God did extraordinary miracles by the hands of Paul so that handkerchiefs or aprons were carried away from his body to the sick, and diseases left them and the evil spirits came out of them.
>
> Acts 19:11–12

Saintly Wisdom

The Rosary of the Virgin Mary, which gradually took form in the second millennium under the guidance of the Spirit of God, is a prayer loved by countless saints. . . . [I]t has all the depth of the Gospel message in its entirety. . . . With the Rosary, the Christian people sits at the school of Mary and is led to contemplate the beauty on the face of Christ and to experience the depths of his love. Through the Rosary the faithful receive abundant grace, as though from the very hands of the Mother of the Redeemer.

The Rosary is my favorite prayer. . . . Against the background of the words Ave Maria [Hail Mary], the principal events of the life of Jesus Christ pass before the eyes of the soul. They . . . put us in living communion with Jesus through—we might say—the heart of his Mother. . . . To recite the Rosary is nothing other than to contemplate with Mary the face of Christ.

St. John Paul II, *On the Most Holy Rosary*, nn. 1, 2, 3

Praying to the saints is a matter of common sense. God chose to work miracles through the saints before they were taken to heaven. Now that he has glorified them, God is all the more eager to grant favors through these men and women.

The text of St. Luke just quoted also speaks of the ancient tradition of venerating the relics of the saints. The "handkerchiefs and aprons" that touched St. Paul are examples of relics. Relics are articles of clothing or other objects directly connected to a saint that, at times, God uses to work miracles.

Devotion to the Holy Family

Of all the saints, two hold a special place in the life of prayer for all Christians. These two are the Virgin Mary and St. Joseph. They are the two most perfect creatures God ever created. God entrusted his Son to this man and woman. God trusted them so much that he was ready to leave his Son in their care. God is pleased whenever his children seek the care of that same father and mother.

REVIEW QUESTIONS

1. What are we asking God to do when we prayer the Lord's Prayer.
2. Describe the three different kinds of prayer.
3. What is the essence of all prayer?
4. Why do Christians mean when they talk about "praying" to the saints?

Epilogue

This book provides an explanation of the faith in the same style and spirit as Leo Trese's classic, *The Faith Explained*, published in 1965. That was the year Pope Paul VI closed the Second Vatican Council. Since that time, many things have happened that require an update. The Church never changes her teachings. But she does develop them. For instance, it took more than nineteen hundred years before Christians heard the Church declare as official teaching that "all are called to sanctity"—even those who have a vocation to marriage (Vatican II, *Constitution on the Church*, nn. 11, 32). This is merely one example of other far-reaching developments in Church teaching during the last fifty years.

Everything moves faster now. Perhaps this book will need an update in a few years. In the meantime, this overview of Christian faith constitutes a traditional presentation. It is based on quotes from sacred Scripture, the Church Fathers, and other great saints, together with pronouncements of popes and councils throughout the centuries, with special emphasis on the documents of Vatican II, the writings of Pope John Paul II, and the *Catechism of the Catholic Church*.

I wanted to end with a special tribute to that saintly pope who watched over the Church for more than twenty-six years. It was a time when Christians were called to evangelize a world that was saying in both deeds and words: "God is dead." St. John Paul demonstrated to billions of men and women that God is alive, that the Church is alive.

Though it would be an exaggeration to say that the world is dying, it would be foolish to ignore St. John Paul's warning. The world is dominated by a culture of death. It is waiting for Christians to bring about a culture of life. The change is taking place because of the witness of this great man and those who worked together with him, especially

Cardinal Joseph Ratzinger, who was elected to succeed him in April 2005 and who took the name Benedict XVI.

Those who accompanied the Polish pope in his final moments say that his last word was simply "Amen." He whispered this response as Mass was drawing to a close in the papal apartments an hour before he died. It was the Mass for the Feast of Divine Mercy, the one major feast in the Church calendar that he instituted during his pontificate.

Amen is equivalent to saying *yes* in Aramaic, the language Jesus learned to speak from the Virgin Mary and St. Joseph. Because this book incorporates many ideas on the universal call to holiness, it would be fitting to conclude with advice from the priest who preached that all men and women are called to be saints. Speaking of the decision a person makes when accepting God's invitation to become "another Christ, Christ himself," the founder of Opus Dei wrote:

> Ever since you said "Yes," time has broadened your horizons, giving them new and brighter colors and making them more beautiful every day. But you have to continue saying "Yes."
>
> St. Josemaría, *Furrow*, n. 32

Index

A

B

C

D

E

F

G

H

I

J

K

L

M

N

R

S

U

V

W

Z